Behind

the

Burnt

Cork

Mask

*A list of books in the series
appears at the end of this book.*

THE ONLY CORRECT &
AUTHORIZED EDITION.

MUSIC OF THE

ETHIOPIAN SERENADERS

Pell   Harrington   White   Stanwood   Germon

NEW YORK Published by WILLIAM HALL & SON 239 Broadway Cor: of Park Place. &:
FIRTH POND & Co. 1 Franklin Sqr.

Behind the Burnt Cork Mask

EARLY BLACKFACE

MINSTRELSY AND

ANTEBELLUM

AMERICAN

POPULAR CULTURE

William J. Mahar

UNIVERSITY OF ILLINOIS PRESS

URBANA AND CHICAGO

Publication of this book was supported by grants from the
H. Earle Johnson Fund of the Sonneck Society for American Music
and from The Pennsylvania State University.

This book is printed on acid-free paper.

Frontispiece: *Music of the Ethiopian Serenaders* (New York: William Hall and Son/
Firth Pond and Co., 1847). Courtesy, American Antiquarian Society.

Library of Congress Cataloging-in-Publication Data

Mahar, William J. (William John), 1938–
Behind the burnt cork mask : early blackface minstrelsy and Antebellum
American popular culture / William J. Mahar.
p.   cm. — (Music in American Life)
Includes bibliographical references (p.   ) and index.
ISBN 0-252-02396-X
ISBN 0-252-06696-0 (pbk.)
1. Minstrel shows—United States.
2. Popular culture—United States—History—19th century.
I. Title.
II. Series.
ML1711.M34   1999
791'.12'0973—dc21   97-3351
CIP
MN

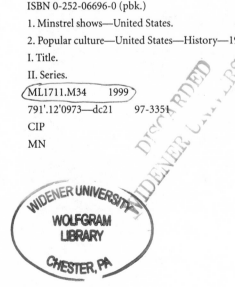

To my family, Connie, Andrew, and Jen,
for all the sacrifices and for all the understanding
during the seemingly endless years of research and
writing

To two distinguished scholars:
Hans Nathan, for seeing the potential significance
of minstrelsy in American popular culture, and
Bob Winans, for recognizing that music making
and archival research are complementary activities
for anyone trying to interpret American music

I cannot trust a man who never laughs, who is always sedate; that has no apparent outlet for those natural springs of sportiveness and gaiety that are perennial in the human soul.
—*Charley White's New Book of Black Wit and Darkey Conversations*

Contents

Musical Examples

Preface

This book is a study of antebellum blackface minstrelsy. It is not intended to be comprehensive because (1) too much of minstrelsy's history remains to be written; (2) the interactions between African American music and the other traditions of music making in the United States are rich sources for fresh investigations; and (3) my research was intended to be an interdisciplinary examination of archival evidence, performance practice, and theater history, territories that present a music historian plentiful opportunities for interpretive errors and outright mistakes.

The principal ideas and methods for this book are explained in the introduction, but I could not ask readers to begin there without first calling attention to all those who helped to make *Behind the Burnt Cork Mask* possible. My debt to my family is unrepayable; the time spent on an enterprise such as this spans years that unfortunately are simply lost. I will continue to owe that debt even as I embark on other projects.

I am grateful to my friend John Patterson for suggesting minstrelsy as a "great American studies topic" some ten years ago and to Judith McCulloh for encouraging my efforts after my first preliminary studies of minstrelsy began to appear in print in 1985. My colleagues in the School of Humanities at Penn State Harrisburg provided constant encouragement, invaluable insights, and sound critical reactions to my questions about the manner in which different disciplines consider the ideas I was investigating. Michael Barton, Simon Bronner, Irwin Richman, Alison Hirsch, and Allida Black helped in many ways. My (often feeble) attempts to deal with feminist theory and criticism of song were aided by Patricia Johnson, Theodora Graham, and Tace Hedrick, but none of these individuals is in any way responsible for the oversights I most surely have committed. The School of Humanities would never be so thoughtful toward students, so understanding of faculty, and so willing to help me with the efficient organization of my time without the services of the administrative and staff assistants Loretta Reigle, Sue Etter, and Cindy Leach. No adminis-trator or scholar has ever been served by such a dedicated group of thoughtful and cheerful persons.

I owe a special debt of gratitude to Penn State's Institute for the Arts and Hu-manistic Studies for supporting the archival research that I hope is one of this book's greatest strengths and to the Penn State Harrisburg Research Council for continu-ing to underwrite my numerous trips and research costs, as well as providing a partial subvention of the publication expenses. Howard G. Sachs, associate dean for Re-search and Graduate Studies, remained my greatest ally and strongest supporter through every phase of this study. Seldom is a research scholar blessed with such a graduate dean, for he not only helped to find the money to assist with the costs of this rather large project but also took the time to read the numerous manuscript versions and offer constructive criticisms that resulted in a virtually jargon-free text. Dr. Sachs's assistant, Sue Ellen Ramer, also helped immensely by handling the final printouts of the completed manuscript. My special thanks to Andrea Wilkinson for her creative and constructive help with the index.

Of all the librarians and curators who shared with me their expertise, generosity, and insights into nineteenth-century culture, those to whom I will remain grateful include Jeanne Newlin of the Harvard Theatre Collection, Georgia Barnhill and her colleagues at the American Antiquarian Society, and Rosemary Cullen of Brown University. Geraldine Duclow, the curator of the Theatre Collection at the Free Library of Philadelphia, and the music librarians at the Free Library always responded to my inquiries and offered invaluable assistance in locating minstrel show sheet music. My thanks also to Charles Mann and his staff of the Rare Book Room at Penn State's Pattee Library for providing a quiet refuge and access to its collection of Ethiopian sketches and to one of the few remaining copies of William Henry Fry's *Leonora*.

I owe a great debt of gratitude to Dale Cockrell, Bob Winans, Don B. Wilmeth, and the anonymous readers for all their suggestions on improving the manuscript. My special thanks also to Bruce Bethell of the press for his copyediting skills and his numerous suggestions about organization, documentation, and plain old com-monsense matters of style. A heartfelt thank-you to my surgeon, Dr. Ronald W. Lippe, as well as to the nursing staff at Harrisburg Hospital and HealthSouth-Rehab, without whose intervention and care I would never have been able to complete the final editorial work the book required.

In the end, the interpretations, theories, and flights of fancy in *Behind the Burnt Cork Mask* are entirely of my making, and I will take whatever praise or blame read-ers feel is justified. My earnest hope is that this study will make some small contri-bution to popular culture studies by emphasizing the importance of music and music making in the history of American entertainment.

Abbreviations

CNS1   *Christy's Negro Serenaders.* Containing all the choice songs as sung by that inimitable band of Melodists. New York: Elton and Vinten, 184[?].

CNS2   *Christy's Nigga Songster.* Containing Songs as are sung by Christy's, Pierce's, White's, Sable Brothers, and Dumbleton's Band of Minstrels. New York: T. W. Strong, n.d.

CPM1   *Christy's Plantation Melodies No. 1.* New York: Fisher and Brother, 1851.

CPM2   *Christy's Plantation Melodies No. 2.* New York: Huestis and Cozans (on first title page); New York: Turner and Fisher, 1853 (on second title page).

CPM3   *Christy's Plantation Melodies No. 3.* Philadelphia and New York: Fisher and Brother, 1853.

CPM4   *Christy's Plantation Melodies No. 4.* New York: Turner and Fisher, 1854.

CPM5   *Christy's Plantation Melodies No. 5.* New York: Fisher and Brother, 1856.

CPS1   *Christy's Panorama Songster.* Containing the songs as sung by Christy, Campbell, Pierce's Minstrels and Sable Brothers. New York: W. H. Murphy, 1857.

DJD1   *Dandy Jim and Dan Tucker's Jaw Bone; or, Cool White's Nigga Minstrel.* New York and Philadelphia: Turner and Fisher, 1844.

DSN1   *Deacon Snowball's Negro Melodies.* Philadelphia: Turner and Fisher, 1843.

EGB1   *The Ethiopian Glee Book.* Containing the songs sung by the Christy Minstrels; with many other popular Negro melodies in four parts arranged for quartett [*sic*] clubs by Gumbo Chaff. Boston: Elias Howe, 1848–49.

EGB2   *The Ethiopian Glee Book.* By Gumbo Chaff, A.M.A., first banjo player to the King of Congo. Boston: Oliver Ditson, 1850.

ESB1   *The Ethiopian Serenader's Own Book.* New York: Philip J. Cozans, n.d.

ESB2   *The Ethiopian Serenader's Own Book.* New York and Philadelphia: Fisher and Brother, 1857.

GEM1   *Gems of Song.* A selection of the most popular songs, glees, duetts [*sic*], and   choruses etc., also a great variety of Irish, Scotch, sentimental and com-
GEM2   ic songs and all the favorite Negro melodies. 2 vols. in one. New York: D. and J. Sadler [*sic*], 1847.

JJO1   *Julianna Johnston's Own Colored So-lo's.* New York: P. J. Cozans, 185[?].

LFM1   *The Lover's Forget-Me-Not, and Songs of Beauty.* A choice collection of sentimental, comic, and temperance songs, with all the latest Negro melodies. New York: N. C. Nafis, 1844; Philadelphia: John B. Perry, 1847.

MPB1   *Matt Peel's Banjo.* Being a selection of the most popular and laughable negro melodies, as sung by the renowned Peel's Campbell's Minstrels. New York: Robert M. De Witt [1858?].

MSON   *Minstrel Songs Old and New.* Boston: Oliver Ditson, 1882.

NFM1   *The Negro Forget-Me-Not Songster.* Philadelphia: Turner and Fisher, 1844.

NFM2   *The New Negro Forget-Me-Not Songster.* Containing All the New Negro Songs Ever Published with a Choice Collection of Ballad Songs, Now Sung in Concerts. Cincinnati: Stratton and Barnard, 1848.

NFM3   *The Negro Forget-Me-Not Songster.* Philadelphia: Turner and Fisher, 1855.

NNB1   *New Negro Band Songster.* Philadelphia: Fisher and Brother, ca. 1857.

NPS1   *The Non-Pareil Songster; or, Singer's Pocket Companion.* Being a Choice Collection of the Most Admired, Sentimental, Comic, Negro and Temperance Songs. Philadelphia: John B. Perry, 1847.

NSO1   *Negro Singer's Own Book, containing every Negro Song that has ever been printed.* Philadelphia: Turner and Fisher, ca. 1846.

RLS1   *My Dearest May and Rosa Lee's Song Book.* Philadelphia: Turner and Fisher, 184[?].

UNS1   *Uncle Ned's Songster.* New York: Fisher and Brother, 1857.

VFB1   *Vaughn and Fox's Banjo Songster; or, Minstrel Time Melodist.* Containing banjo solos, songs, duets, trios, quartettes, etc., etc., etc., as sung by those great banjoists, T[homas] and Harry Fox. New York: Frederic A. Brady, 1860.

VSS1   *The Virginia Serenader's Illustrated Songster.* Containing all the songs, as sung by the far-famed band of Original Virginia Serenaders for Upwards of 2000 Nights throughout the Principal Cities of the United States. Philadelphia: Turner and Fisher, 184[?].

WBA1   *Black Apollo Songster.* New York and Philadelphia: Turner and Turner, 1844.

WMS1   *Wood's Minstrel Songs.* New York: Garret and Co. [22 Ann Street], 1852. Also *Woods Minstrel Songs.* New York: Dick and Fitzgerald, 1855.

WNB1   *White's New Book of Plantation Melodies.* New York: H. Long and Brother, 1849.

WNE1   *White's New Ethiopian Song Book.* New York: H. Long and Brother, 1850.

WNI1   *White's New Illustrated Melodeon Songbook.* New York: H. Long and Brother, 1848.

WNN1   *The World of New Negro Songs.* Containing all the late and most popular songs of the day. Philadelphia: Fisher and Brother, 1854.

WNP1   *Wood's New Plantation Melodies.* New York: Garrett and Co., 1853 and 1855.

WSS1   *White's Serenaders' Song-Book.* New York: H. Long and Brother, 1854.

Behind
the
Burnt
Cork
Mask

Introduction

> The real history of minstrelsy in this country, were it to be honestly and com-
> prehensively written, would touch in one way or another every form of popular
> music we have and on some part of our composed tradition.[1]

The history of blackface minstrelsy does not just "touch" every form of popular *music;* it is linked to the very formation of antebellum popular *culture.* The power-ful effects and market dominance of the minstrel show were based on the variety of entertainment blackface minstrelsy offered at a relatively low cost and resulted from the frequent content adjustments managers and performers made to meet the expectations of antebellum audiences. Minstrelsy was a commodity, a collection of loosely related genres addressed to the lowest common denominator audience (but not always the lowest class) for the express purpose of providing at least a modest living for performers who seldom "crossed over" to other musical venues.

The primary convention that identified the minstrel show as entertainment was burnt cork makeup. The combination of burned, pulverized champagne corks and water (sometimes petroleum jelly or a similar substance) served as a *racial marker* announcing that a single actor or an ensemble offered what were selected aspects of (arguably) African American culture to audiences interested in how racial differences and enslavement reinforced distinctions between black and white Americans.

The makeup was also a *disguise* for white performers who chose parody and bur-lesque as techniques to satirize majority values while still reinforcing widely held and fairly conservative beliefs. Minstrel performers made blackface a *vehicle* for the creation of an "American" style of commercialized popular culture in what was es-sentially a postcolonialist entertainment environment. Finally, burnt cork was a *masking device* allowing professional and amateur entertainers to shield themselves from any direct personal and psychological identification with the material they were performing.

Behind the Burnt Cork Mask seeks to unmask minstrelsy's multiple meanings by arguing that blackface entertainers (1) borrowed from a variety of English,

French, and Italian musical, dramatic, and literary sources imported into the United States as part of a concerted effort to establish some sense of cultural parity with European society; (2) appropriated elements from African American and Anglo-American musical and cultural practices and re-presented them initially to primarily urban audiences; (3) toured extensively on three main circuits distributing the musical and theatrical contents of variety shows widely through the South, Midwest and West, and North (including lower Canada), following the same paths as the circuses, opera companies, and European virtuosi with whose repertories the minstrels were quite familiar; (4) contributed to the sometimes contradictory American beliefs and attitudes about race, gender, and class; (5) established themselves as the principal characters in a primarily masculine entertainment preserve that exalted competitiveness and helped to define acceptable standards for the expression of male sentimentality; (6) marginalized women in songs and sketches that restricted their sexual, domestic, and public roles in American society; and (7) demonstrated the possibilities for developing a popular, accessible, and profitable commercial product from the fusion of what often appear to be mutually exclusive stylistic ingredients.

Each of the preceding "arguments" assumes that burlesque was one of minstrelsy's essential traits and that, existing as they did in a postcolonialist society without a strong indigenous music style, blackface music and theater began with parodies or imitations of African American, English, Italian, and Anglo-American sources. Much of the Italian material entered the country in adaptations created for British audiences whose own distaste for imported opera led them to expect that complicated arias and choruses would be "dumbed down" or simplified to enhance their appeal. English burlesques and farces also provided sources for American playwrights and minstrel comedians because "well into the middle of the nineteenth century, American theaters continued to operate . . . as cultural outposts of London."[2]

The flow of musical and theatrical material went both ways, however. When Thomas Dartmouth Rice (1808–60) took his "Jim Crow" act to England in 1837, he bought a copy of Maurice Dowling's *Othello Travestie* (1813). Rice replaced many of the English songs with blackface material created in the United States, deleted obvious English references, and inserted some topical items into his adaptation, which was entitled *Otello* (1838). This burlesque was marketed as an "Ethiopian" opera, and Rice performed it throughout the eastern United States during the 1840s and 1850s. The piece was never part of any minstrel show, but its popularity showed other performers and stage managers how Americans could employ burnt cork makeup to construct nativist critiques of any foreign imports. This observation about minstrelsy's links with other aspects of popular culture introduces the first of the five major points that *Behind the Burnt Cork Mask* raises about antebellum minstrel shows.

The first point is that blackface comedians found specific subjects and musical styles in a limited number of Italian operas imported directly from Italy or diverted through English hands to arrive on the doorsteps of American theaters as adulterations. The first act of Vincenzo Bellini's (1801–35) immensely successful *La Sonnambula* (itself a sentimentalized, class-based, and improbably plotted piece of European "popular" culture) provided blackface entertainers with two very successful songs and dramatic scenes. The first song, entitled "See, Sir, See" (1853), was based on Rodolfo's aria "Vi ravviso, o luoghi ameni" (act 1, sc. 1) and the very popular "Lucy Neal" (1844). The second song was the famous "A fosco cielo," or "Phantom Chorus" (act 1, sc. 1), one of the most frequently performed part-songs in pre-1860 minstrel shows.

"Vi ravviso" was popularized by the famous English bass Arthur Edward Seguin (1809–52), who performed "As I View These Scenes So Charming" (one of the English translations of "Vi ravviso") frequently during the 1838–39 season of the Shireff-Wilson-Seguin Vocal Star Troupe in New York and during the Seguin Operatic Troupe's six-year sojourn (1841–47) in the United States.[3] The minstrel version was derived from this widely known and easily remembered operatic aria, whose Italian style became one of the primary ingredients in the creation of the sentimental American songs that appeared in sheet music editions and playbills from 1844 through 1860.

Michael William Balfe's (1808–70) opera *The Bohemian Girl* (London, 1843; New York, 1844) supplied several additional numbers for the minstrel stage, principally "I Dreamt I Dwelt in Marble Halls," which the minstrels transformed into "I Dreamt I Dwelled in Hotel Halls," and "In the Gipsy's Life You Read," which became "In the Darkies Life You Lead." Both were performed in at least three fairly lengthy burlesque versions of *The Bohemian Girl* by Buckley's Serenaders alone. Balfe's musical style was based on Italian musical models, and many of his hits were essentially melodic strophic songs, which made them even more suitable as interpolations into the minstrel repertory. The Italian and English influences on minstrelsy were as significant as anything borrowed from African American culture.

American opera was seldom chosen for parody because there was so little of it. Two choral sections of the first "Italian" opera composed by an American, *Leonora* (1845), by William Henry Fry (1813–64), became subjects in "De Colored Fancy Ball" (1848) and in one of early minstrelsy's greatest hits, "Dinah's Wedding Day" (1848). Those choruses and more than 100 others borrowed from Italian opera were staples in the over 200 playbills and newspaper advertisements considered for this study. Contemporary English stage materials were incorporated directly into the minstrel repertories regardless of whether a single note of African American music ever entered blackface minstrelsy. The issue, then, is to identify the role these and other burlesques played in the formation of minstrelsy and the forms of humor typical of antebellum popular culture.

The second major point deals with the relationship between minstrelsy and African American culture. Given the generally decreasing number of references to "southern plantation darkies" and "northern dandy Negroes" as the minstrel show developed, there is every reason to question minstrelsy's alleged connections with African American music and dancing. Nonetheless, the minstrel show was the first point of intersection between an African American culture with a rich musical heritage that included African retentions and a largely derivative English and Italian stylistic tradition mixed occasionally with Anglo-American folk materials. There is plenty of evidence that white and black Americans shared a good deal more music, humor, social rituals, and beliefs than has been acknowledged in most studies of minstrelsy. *Behind the Burnt Cork Mask* attempts to reassess the relationships among all the various traditions found in the blackface minstrel show.

Recent studies confirm the cultural interactions between the races in the plantation South and the urban North, interactions that were also occasions for cultural borrowings in both directions, as well as for cross-cultural satires that served as sources both for blackface entertainment and for African American comedy.[4] The racial element is certainly a complicating factor in any study of a form of entertainment that advertised its fidelity to portraits of African Americans. Blackface comedians have sometimes been unfairly diagnosed as sharing "a contaminated form of interracial desire" or an adult fixation on childhood fantasies in which the "smearing of soot or blacking over the body represents the height of polymorphous perversity, an infantile playing with excrement or dirt."[5] The evidence from minstrel songs, playbills, and analyses of the contents of typical shows does not support the notion that whites really wanted to be black or took great pleasure in imagining the effects of changing places with a race they generally sought to suppress.

The third point explored in *Behind the Burnt Cork Mask* deals with the issue of class, one of minstrelsy's most persistent subjects. Blackface comedy's irreverent treatment of authority figures and professionals resulted directly from the development of a class structure in what purported to be an egalitarian society. The American rite of passage from one class to another was often portrayed as a status change caused by the quick accumulation of wealth, usually by winning a lottery or some other stroke of fortune. Wealth brought with it the expectation for "respectability" and the presumed right of entrance into different social and cultural circles. One particularly telling example explored at length in the chapter on Ethiopian skits and sketches is the minstrel burlesque of Edward Bulwer-Lytton's (1803–73) *Lady of Lyons* (1837).

Bulwer-Lytton's play provides a colorful and apparently low-born gardener's son named "Claude Melnotte," played by Edwin Forrest (1806–72) in the 1838 American premiere. Claude, who is eventually revealed to be an upper-class gentleman, delivers a sentimental speech to his sweetheart, the upper-class Pauline Deschapelles, played most notably by the American actress and playwright Anna Cora Mowatt (1819–70) in 1845. The Claude character reappeared in a number of American burlesques of Bulwer-Lytton's play and in the popular Ethiopian sketch known as

The Hop of Fashion; or, The Bon-Ton Soiree (ca. 1856), where his most famous speech is used to mock male sentimentality and the pretentiousness of nouveau riche Americans.

The entertaining aspect of blackface interest in the class of newly wealthy Americans is found in minstrelsy's relationship to opera, a decidedly non-American commodity in the eyes of minstrel comedians, because opera attendance cost four to eight times as much as did attendance at the typical minstrel show and provided an opportunity for conspicuous display of class differences. Even though there was considerable class mixing at New York's Astor Place Opera House, access to the better houses was gradually restricted in the late 1840s and 1850s through "the slow but almost insidious expropriation of this musical-theatrical form by the wealthy and elite of American society, and the increasing exclusion from these performances of the other social classes that traditionally had been a normal part of the American theater audience."[6] This exclusion explains why Italian and English operas or operatic choruses performed on the New York stage became the subjects of burlesques within days of their premieres. Appearing first at New York's Olympic Theater between 1840 and 1858, many of these burlesques were cut significantly and transformed into Ethiopian sketches for performance by blackface comedians at Buckley's Chinese Hall, Christy's Mechanics Hall, and numerous other "opera" houses in eastern cities and towns.

Behind the Burnt Cork Mask explores gender issues in minstrelsy—the fourth issue—because male conceptions of the differences between men and women figured so prominently in blackface repertory. The songs about male-female relationships outnumber those about all other subjects combined.

Male dominance and sentimentality were two of minstrelsy's most common themes. Both subjects were approached via the burnt cork disguise and shaped into texts that presented the male body through the styles of dress and types of behaviors men commonly used when they appeared in public. These "display" songs flatter masculine egos, exalt manly behaviors, exploit male competitiveness, and project dominance over women through narratives about real or imagined sexual conquests.

Finally, as its fifth point, this book offers the first serious exploration of the social and cultural implications of minstrelsy's songs and sketches about women. Minstrel material assumes a double standard for the sexual behaviors of men and women. Male promiscuity is accepted and endorsed. Women are idealized as pure sweethearts before they are married and celibate shrews after the ceremony, sentimentalized kidnap victims worthy of rescue and street women suitable for exploitation.

Whatever else it was, minstrelsy was essentially a form of musical theater. There is scarcely a single antebellum minstrel playbill in which vocal and instrumental music does not occupy at least two-thirds of the program. *Behind the Burnt Cork Mask* is concerned with the role of minstrel show music (not all of which purported to have any connections with African American styles) in creating an "American" style. The question about such a style in American music is comparable to the serious concerns contemporary novelists and literary critics raised about a national literature. Minstrelsy's rise to public attention was related to the same concerns shared by optimistic Americans who agreed that "when it [American literature] does begin to be felt, it will be felt with a force, a directness, and a common sense in its application, that has never yet been known."[7]

As Richard Crawford pointed out, minstrelsy "helped to transform the world of American musical performance."[8] Minstrel music was the first popular American musical product exported to England and the Continent. The United States actually gave back a fairly familiar product, except that the performance practices helped non-Americans to recognize that some of the new musical elements they heard derived from African American culture. Nonetheless, however much minstrelsy borrowed, it was also new and different. As a genre of musical theater, minstrelsy was a populist product that commodified the art of excerpting, condensing, and recasting easily assimilated hits from all forms of American culture.

Throughout my investigation I have assumed that interactions between the races did occur, that cultural exchanges were not limited to a few casual musical encounters, and that "crossovers" have always been a part of America's musical history. Robert Cantwell argued that minstrelsy's popularity depended on the fact that the minstrels, "by taking on theatrically some form of the black image, whether rudely stereotyped or ethnographically scrupulous, had consciously or unconsciously entered upon a many-layered satire of Anglo-American life, a satire in which the minstrel himself was ultimately the object, and voluntarily so."[9] At their best, minstrel comedians were social satirists; at their worst—in regional amateur productions— the comics joined their neighbors in denigrating members of other ethnic groups in their own communities. Minstrel performers, even the rank amateurs, assumed, if only for an evening, that all races, classes, professions, and genders were fit subjects for comedy.

Behind the Burnt Cork Mask differs significantly from the standard works in minstrelsy studies: Hans Nathan's pioneering *Dan Emmett and the Rise of Early Negro Minstrelsy* (1962), Robert Toll's *Blacking Up* (1974), and Eric Lott's highly regarded *Love and Theft: Blackface Minstrelsy and the American Working Class* (1993). Lott's study, as one reviewer noted, reflects one of the "two distinct points of view [that] have structured modern histories of blackface minstrelsy in the United States." The first allows for connections and mutually beneficial exchanges between white and black forms of cultural production in antebellum popular culture, whereas the second, "building on Frederick Douglass's denunciation before the Civil War, emphasizes minstrelsy's debt to white fancy and its legitimation of racial domination."[10]

This study stands firmly with those authors who see connections between white and black cultures in minstrelsy because "cultural diffusion between whites and blacks was by no means a one-way street with blacks the invariable beneficiaries.

Afro-American impact on wide areas of American expressive culture has become increasingly obvious, though it has not yet been adequately assessed."[11] *Behind the Burnt Cork Mask* seeks to establish a middle ground by investigating and interpreting minstrelsy's primary evidence in new ways, and that task requires a reassessment of Douglass's often quoted phrase that blackface minstrels were "the filthy scum of white society."

The review reveals Douglass's opposition to the prosouthern and apparently pro-slavery views of Lewis Cass, the Democratic nominee for president in 1848, and Douglass's specific dislike for the "miserable old dough-face who edits the *Cass paper* in this city." That "self-elected umpire of taste" had dared to ridicule the Hutchinson Family Singers because he believed their abolitionist songs "would do well enough were there (to use his own diction) less of 'nigger' in them." This was the same man, Douglass went on, who did not object to "the Virginia Minstrels, the Christy Minstrels and the Ethiopian Serenaders" or any of the other "filthy scum of white society, who have stolen from us a complexion denied to them by nature, in which to make money, and pander to the corrupt taste of their white fellow-citizens." Douglass mentioned "Ole Zip Coon," "Jim Crow," "Old Dan Tucker," and "Jim Along Josey" as "specimens of America musical genius" before proceeding with his effusive praise of the Hutchinsons' performance of "Slave Mother's Lament," "Old Church Bell," "Bridge of Sighs," "Ship on Fire," and other items in the family's repertory.[12]

Douglass cited four minstrel songs as synecdoches for what was a quite varied repertory by 1848 and assumed that every company performed the same material. He rhetorically juxtaposed entertainers (minstrel ensembles) with barnstorming crusaders (the Hutchinsons) whose causes he endorsed, and he chose the moral high ground embodied in such Hutchinson standards as the "Slave Mother's Lament" and the emotional intensity of "Ship on Fire" instead of the low-class diversions found in the blackface forms of vernacular entertainment. The Hutchinsons were crusaders who, when they sang "the family song, brought into it the cause of temperance and anti-slavery, singing the latter with a spirit as well as the understanding." Douglass's judgment is concerned as much with class as it is with race, with Douglass proclaiming ideals all persons should live by and the minstrels ridiculing such pursuits with their nonsensical songs. This is very clear from Douglass's effusive praise of the Hutchinsons' performance: "Our hearts were touched and saddened by the 'Slave Mother's Lament'—cheered and delighted by the 'Good time coming'—wrapped in admiration of 'Exclesior'—filled with indefinable associations by the 'Old Church Bell'—softened to tears by the 'Bridge of Sighs'—inspired with dauntless courage by the 'Psalm of Life'—and terror-stricken at the 'Ship on Fire.'" Members of the audience paid twice the typical admission price to the Hutchinsons' concert, which must have been a special occasion arranged by Douglass because the black and white communities sat together, apparently something quite rare for Rochester in the 1840s. Douglass emphasized the importance of respectable and refined society as the standard for social behavior and observed that "the general expression of the audience, among white and black, confessed the truth of a common origin and a common brotherhood. We all looked and felt alike."[13]

Douglass believed that blackface entertainment compromised the search for racial harmony and treated differences in race and status as a subject for ridicule. His statement provides authority for anyone who sees burnt cork entertainment as a racist playground for whites wishing to define themselves by using a mirror that reflects only their sense of racial superiority. Douglass was at war with the idea of racial masquerade but not knowledgeable about what went on in a typical minstrel show during the late 1840s. The Virginia Minstrels had been out of business for five years, the Christy Minstrels had just purchased their own hall in New York and begun programs that emphasized "respectability," and the Ethiopian Serenaders were not one group but at least seven different ensembles, each with its own repertory. Douglass did not acknowledge the many meanings of blackface costuming and ignored the nonracial issues being played out in the burnt cork theater.

Sensitive to Douglass's assessment but cautious about what the evidence implies, *Behind the Burnt Cork Mask* is based on what I believe was a core repertory of blackface song, a repertory most likely to have been shared widely among various audiences throughout the eastern United States. The conclusions are based on songs whose performance histories have been confirmed as well as on the contexts that gave those texts their cultural resonance.[14] The same approach to the materials of minstrelsy explains why my deconstructions of sermons, lectures, sketches, and the other staples of the blackface repertory are juxtaposed with interpretations based as closely as possible on period performance practices. In the absence of vital information from audiences about how *they* interpreted minstrelsy, I resisted speaking on their behalf because I could not see "how the immediate enjoyment of a performance connects with memories derived from it to shape later action and belief," an objection Bruce McConachie made in his review of *Love and Theft.*[15]

Lott's generalizations and locations of meaning within the class differences of nineteenth-century society are provocative, insightful, and revealing. They will surely inspire a whole new generation of minstrelsy studies. Although I admire Lott's desire to complicate minstrelsy, I believe that complicating the study of the subject distances us from the contexts in which blackface comedy thrived. I thus seek to identify the materials of minstrelsy more carefully, clarify the role of the African and European American styles that entered mainstream pop culture, interrogate texts whose surface meanings are all too easily lost when their antebellum contexts are ignored, and, because I believe minstrelsy was essentially musical theater, bring a music historian's point of view to the subject. In the end, I hope that *Behind the Burnt Cork Mask* confirms that blackface minstrelsy touched every aspect of antebellum cultural development.

1 Revisiting Minstrelsy's History: The Playbill and Contextual Evidence

To help along a lonesome evening I went to Palmo's Opera House to see the "Ethiopian Serenaders" who sing and play on banjo, accordion, and bone casta-nets. Negro songs, glees, and other refinements of the same kind, helped along by worn out conundrums, form this refined amusement, which is very popular and fills the theater, in which so lately the scientific strains of Italian music float-ed over empty benches.[1]

1843–48

Blackface minstrelsy was "the national art of its moment . . . the soundtrack for the American 1848."[2] If a typical minstrel show of the 1845–55 decade had been cap-tured on videotape, modern audiences would see and hear blackface comedians singing and dancing to some of the tunes Joel Sweeney (1813–90) reputedly brought from Virginia; male mimics imitating Fanny Elssler's (1810–84) performances of the Spanish cachucha and the Polish *cracovienne;* opera arias performed by cross-dressed imitators of Jenny Lind (1820–87); American "fiddlers" glossing the musi-cal offerings served up by Ole Bournemann Bull (1810–80) and Henri Vieuxtemps (1820–81), two of the best-known violin virtuosos of the day; and motley attired characters discoursing on phrenology or describing in great detail the sounds of a steam locomotive.[3]

Minstrelsy was a commercial venture created for a mass market at a time when the United States lacked a definable *national* culture and when American perform-ers envied their European competitors, whose compensation for a single evening far exceeded what the average native entertainer could expect for blacking up five nights a week for several seasons.[4] The differences in compensation between Euro-pean performers and American entertainers were not lost on the minstrel compa-nies, and the subject became part of most early minstrel shows. Blackface comedi-ans complained that "Ole Bull come to town one day [and] got five hundred for to play"[5] when the typical pay for a Christy Minstrels ensemble member averaged $57.62 per evening. Three of minstrelsy's early fiddle players performed Ole Bull caricatures. Frederick ("Little Ole Bull") Buckley (1833–64), Harry ("Ole Bull") Mestayer, and J. Richard ("Ole Bull") Myers (1809–74) performed imaginary duels ("They played a match at Chestnut Street, All for to see which one could beat"), and their performances were designed to "beat Ole Bull from de Norway" and "take the shine off Paganini."

When the Buckleys appeared as the Boston Ethiopian Serenaders during their 1848 stay in New Orleans, the company of five collected $200 ($2,618 in 1992 dollars) per evening and brought in $1,100.00 ($14,399) at one benefit alone. Edwin Christy reported that the Christy Minstrels' gross income from 2,792 performances was $317,589.00 ($4,157,249 in 1992 dollars), or an average of $31,759.00 ($415,724.00) per year for ten years.[6] Christy's report may have been exaggerated, for New York newspapers, particularly the *Evening Mirror* (Aug. 9, 1854), estimated that the amount was closer to $160,873.60 ($711,061.31), or $57.62 ($254.68) per performance.[7] Based on a typical company roster of six to eight performers and on the assumption that the shares were distributed equally, the typical annual income of individual members of the most popular ensembles could have ranged from $2,700 ($25 per day, including matinees, at 180 days per season) to $5,293 ($29.50 times 180 days), amounts large enough to qualify each of Christy's colleagues for membership in "the most valuable class in any community . . . the middle class, the men of moderate means, living at a rate of a thousand dollars a year or thereabouts."[8]

Economic envy was only one of the factors underlying the blackface critique of America's admiration for European music and theater. So strong was the urge to burlesque European (particularly English) theater that many of the minstrel ensembles of the 1840s borrowed wholesale from William Mitchell's Olympic Theater (442–44 Broadway), where popular stage plays, Italian operas, English burlesques, and ballets performed by some of the most popular performers of the day were treated to skilled and hilarious rereadings. Mitchell's imported English burlesques and adaptations for American audiences provided the models that blackface performers used to generate their own comic parodies of Italian opera or popular stage works of the period.

Mitchell (1798–1856) retired in 1850, but his style of stage comedy was continued by William Burton (1804–60), who leased Palmo's Opera House (still called that even though Palmo went out of business in 1845) on Chambers Street in 1848 and refurbished it as Burton's Chambers Street Theater. Burton produced comedies there until 1856, when the theater became home to a number of minstrel ensembles.[9] Two of early minstrelsy's most famous burlesques were derived from works created by the Olympic's music director and playwright, George Loder (1816–68) and Dr. William Knight Northall, a dentist, journalist, and playwright. Loder and

Northall concocted the first American burlesque of *The Bohemian Girl* (1844), entitled *The Bohea-Man's Girl* (1845), and one of the most famous burlesques of Donizetti's *Lucia di Lammermoor* (1835), which was transformed into *Lucy-Did-Sham-Amour* (1848). The latter burlesque was set in contemporary New York, and two of its major hits were comedian Caroline Chapman's performance of the "Mad Scene" from Lucia (act 3, sc. 2) and her "hilarious mimicry of Madame [Anna Riviere] Bishops's trills and shakes in her famous rendition of 'On the Banks of Guadalquivir.'" This was the same Caroline Chapman who played Alcestis in the "Original Strong-Minded Woman" (May 18, 1851), which was called the "wittiest burlesque every written," and whose "work in low comedy" was "not only entirely unsurpassed, but nearly unrivaled."[10]

The number of connections between minstrelsy and New York theater history should not be underestimated. Minstrelsy's success owed as much to the burlesque creations produced by Mitchell and Burton as to depictions of plantation life or mimicry of African Americans living in northern urban centers. The minstrel show became a formidable rival to other forms of American popular theater because blackface comedy was more than a racist masquerade, more than a "carnivalization of race," and more than a form of entertainment designed solely to ridicule African Americans.

Blackface comedy presented another repertory—operatic choruses, mock versions of popular and folk songs, and comical concerts "signifying" on the performances of foreign visitors. These elements differed so much from the actual or imagined African American experience that the "nonplantation" elements of the minstrel show are often of greater consequence for understanding minstrelsy than is the exclusive investigation of its potential borrowings from African American culture. The minstrel show was the gathering place for a variety of entertainment forms, only some of which imitated aspects of African American culture. Many others exhibited mimetic features that depended on the minstrels' perceptions of the growing class divisions associated with New York performances of traveling opera and drama companies.

Burnt cork entertainment went well beyond the minstrel show proper and continued on the paths established by early nineteenth-century burnt cork performers. Solo blackface entertainers continued to perform on the stage and in circuses throughout the 1840s. Thomas Dartmouth Rice (1808–60) appeared during minstrelsy's early years in various New York and Philadelphia theaters with his repertory of burnt cork burlesques based on English models derived from Charles Mathews's "Trip to America" or "At Home" pieces, which featured a variety of caricatures of contemporary types.[11] Blackface comedians' interest in opera responded to the introduction of English and Italian opera to New York, especially Fernando Palmo's (1785–1869) attempts to stage Italian opera at Palmo's Opera House in what was known as the Chambers Street Theater, located between Broadway and Centre St., a house that William Burton eventually renamed Burton's Chambers

Street Theater in 1848. These blackface opera parodies were not minstrel shows, but they established opera as one of the primary sources for blackface burlesques.

Many of the most prominent early minstrels, Edwin Christy in particular, worked with Palmo's Ethiopian Opera Company in a performance of "the favorite burlesque, entitled *Som-am-bull-ole*," at New York's 1,500-seat Alhambra in 1845.[12] The same piece was presented by a mixed group of performers, including Mrs. Austin Phillips, Mrs. Sharpe, the versatile singer and arranger Nelson Kneass (1823–68), and three other individuals from yet another group calling itself the Ethiopian Serenaders, one of whom was Frank Lynch, famous during this period for his imitations of the legendary dancer John Diamond (1823–57). The Ethiopian Troupe of Burlesquers led by Kneass appeared at "Signor Palmo's Opera House" during the 1845–46 season (from February through March and once more from June through October), when they were advertised as "Palmo's Burlesque Opera Company" or "Palmo's Ethiopian Opera Company."

Nelson Kneass was one of minstrelsy's foremost performers. His formidable musical skills undoubtedly served him well as an arranger and vocalist in his own company's performance of the burlesque *Som-am-bull-ole* (note the Ole Bull reference) and *The Virginia Girl*.[13] Kneass's arrangements were used by a variety of other ensembles, and his development of the parody choruses established them as a prominent part of the minstrel show.[14]

None of the performances mentioned thus far was really a minstrel show, and none can truly be considered representative of the style of entertainment that typified "the national art of its moment." This point is easily demonstrated in period newspaper advertisements that identify opera burlesque as one of the key genres in which blackface makeup, not African American culture, played a prominent role:

ALHAMBRA, No. 550 Broadway. Positively the last week of Palmo's Ethiopian Opera Company. Monday evening, November 3, will be performed the favorite burlesque, entitled Som-am-bull-ole—taken from La Sonnambula. To conclude with the Virginian Girl, in which are introduced the gems of Balfe's celebrated opera of the Bohemian Girl. Also, a laughable Burlesque Polka. &c. On Thursday next will be produced a travestie on La Bayadere. Performances to commence at 7 1/2 o'clock. Admission 25 cts. (*New York Clipper,* Nov. 3, 1845)

NEW ORLEANS SERENADERS. At the Stuyvesant Institute, Broadway, a few doors above Bleecker St. **THIRD WEEK—EVERY NIGHT.** The entertainments of this Ethiopian Opera Company, embrace grand scenes from the Italian Opera with imitations of

Jenny Lind	Signor Lablache
Madame Grisi	" " Mario
" " Bishop	" " Gardionni

Admission 25 cts. Doors open at 7, concert at 8 O'clock. A Saturday afternoon concert at 3 O'clock. (*New York Clipper,* Dec. 14, 1848)

The only way to determine what was representative or typical of the different venues that employed blackface performers is to question what was performed by the various ensembles. That information is partially available from period playbills, newspaper advertisements and reviews, and myriad other sources describing entertainment venues in a number of American cities. These sources provide the information for the observations and conclusions throughout the rest of this study, beginning with one of the Virginia Minstrels' first playbills, which is most instructive for exploring the beginnings of the earliest shows.

The blackface quartet constituting the Virginia Minstrels presented a section of riddles and conundrums as a stand-up dialogue between two characters, a mock scientific lecture, and a so-called extravaganza created by acting out the textual implications of the "Lucy Long" song (1843) (see playbill 1; all playbills are located at the end of this chapter).[15] This early example shows the strong relationship between the stage action of the minstrel show and a limited number of real or imagined events in African American life, for example, slave weddings, harvest celebrations, coon hunts (a practice that was *not* restricted to African American bondsmen), and lovers' separations. Minstrelsy focused on relatively few occupations, the most typical being involved with the riverboat transportation and shipping characteristic of the prerail era in southern labor history. Two songs in particular illustrate the point, "De Boatman's Dance" (1843) and "'Twill Nebber Do To Gib It Up So" (1843), the former usually connected with boat traffic on the Ohio River and the latter associated with tobacco shipments on the James River in Virginia, the state mentioned most frequently in the texts and scripts of blackface songs and sketches.

The emphasis on Virginia as a locale in early minstrel songs has never been explained satisfactorily. Cecilia Conway established the preeminence of Virginia as a site for the largest number of documentary references to the banjo prior to 1840, but that does not explain why the state is mentioned so often in songs. She found that "despite popular influences, change, and extensive transmission, the twentieth-century folk music developments that depended upon the banjo arose in the same two geographic areas [the Upper South—particularly Virginia—and the Mississippi Valley] that were centers of the living tradition at the turn of the nineteenth century."[16] The reference confirms the persistent tradition that the earliest minstrels learned some of their material from Joel Sweeney (1813–60) or his brothers, who lived in Virginia and performed in Boston and New York during the late 1830s and early 1840s.

Several of the most characteristic early minstrel songs were attributed directly to Sweeney, who "traveled in a wagon throughout the South in the early 30s, and certainly as early as 1838 when he was with a circus that played in Lynchburg, Va." He continued to perform "chiefly through the South at intermittent periods up to within about a year or two of his death."[17] Sweeney's "Jenny Get Your Hoe Cake Done" (1840) describes a bread loaf prepared in an oven adjacent to the main cooking hearth in a typical Virginia cookhouse, the hoe being used to remove the cake from the oven.[18] Slaves often used the name "Jenny" as a code word in the expression "goin to set the floor wid Jenny tonight" to disguise the social plans African American women made and avoid tipping off the "missus."[19]

What is remarkable about this early playbill and its contents is that there is not a single sentimental song among the other musical numbers, all of which, judging from their titles and contents, were directed at a primarily male audience. Seven of the eleven song titles are for "full chorus," showing that early minstrel singing emphasized ensemble performance by a community of "characters" rather than several acts or caricatures presented by individual stars. Specialty solos were restricted to performances on the banjo by Emmett, Whitlock's burlesque lecture, and the presentation of riddles and conundrums[20] in the talk-around led by Pelham (see playbill 1).

The emphasis on a slave woman's social activities after work in "Jenny Get Your Hoe Cake Done" is also found in "Old Dan Tucker" (1843) and "Jonny Boker" (1840), two "character" songs designed to display specific behavioral traits characteristic of the various male stereotypes that dominated early minstrelsy.

"Old Dan Tucker" (Words by Daniel D. Emmett [Boston: Charles Keith, 1843])[21]

Verse 1
I come to town de udder night,
I hear de noise an saw de fight,
De watchman was a runnin roun,
Cryin Old Dan Tucker's come to town.

Chorus
So get out de way! Get out de way!
Get out de way! Old Dan Tucker.
Your to late to come to supper.

Verse 3
Here's my razor in good order,
Magnum bonum—jis had bought 'er,
Sheep shell oats, Tucker shell de corn,
I'll shabe you soon as de water get warm.

Chorus

Verse 4
Old Dan Tucker an I got drunk,
He fell in de fire an kick up a chunk,
De charcoal got inside he shoe,
Lor bless you honey how de ashes flew.

Chorus

This is a preeminent example of a blackface boasting song in which the lead character is both the subject and object, that is, the storyteller and the person about whom the story is told. "Tucker" refers to himself in the first person (verses 1, 3, 5 and 6) as well as the third person (verses 2, 4, and 7). The "shifting" persona observed here becomes one of the features of the early minstrel character song. The pronoun changes reveal how something that appears to be a solo song can involve other members of the group, each of whom contributes some of the information and frees the main character for other stage business, for example, dancing, pantomime, and conundrum or riddle performance.

"De Boatman's Dance" captures the playfulness of laborers loose on liberty and the camaraderie generated by an escape from the sometimes brutal life of the inland sailors working the boat traffic on American rivers. The verses constantly shift from references to the "boatmen" with the singular pronoun *he,* a characteristic marker of the nonredundant plural in Black English, to "boatmen" as a plural noun in the choruses. "They" is not required in the dialect because the pronoun is the gender marker and the noun is already a plural form.

"De Boatman's Dance" (Boston: Charles H. Keith, 1843)

Verse 1
De boatmen dance, de boatmen sing,
De boatmen up to eb'ry ting;
And when de boatman get on shore,
He spends his cash and works for more.
Den dance de boatmen dance,
O dance de boatmen dance,
O dance all night till broad daylight,
    an go home wid de gals in de morning.

Verse 3
I went on board de odder day,
To see what de boatmen had to say,
Dar I let my passion loose,
An dey cram me in the calaboose.
Den dance de boatmen dance,
O dance de boatmen dance,
O dance all night till broad daylight,
    an go home wid de gals in de morning.

Verse 5
When you go to de boatmen's ball,
Dance wid my wife, or don't dance at all,
Sky blue jacket an' tarpaulin hat,
Look out my boys for de nine tail cat.

Den dance de boatmen dance,
O dance de boatmen dance,
O dance all night till broad daylight,
   an go home wid de gals in de morning.

The texts use formulaic material and combine disjointed or unrelated phrases into the four-line verses. Those verses should not be considered meaningless or illogical just because the discontinuous and unrelated phrases do not seem to connect. They were part of a performance environment that involved dancing, some stage business, and probably some pantomime, and for practical reasons they might not have been intelligible to everyone in the audience. They should be viewed as "performance texts" that often refer to other minstrel songs or ensembles, borrow phrases from other well-known songs or tunes, and sometimes contain information created specifically to misdirect audiences.

The texts of "Uncle Gabriel" are particularly illustrative of a typical performance text. Although the original version of the Virginia Minstrels' performance is unknown, the two published sheet music editions show the variety characteristic of minstrel songs. The version quoted next was performed by the Ethiopian Serenaders (1847) and describes a coon hunt that culminates in the celebration of Uncle Gabriel's success as described in the following verse and chorus:

Verse 4
De niggers dey come all around, and kick up a debil of a splutter,
Dey eat de coon and clar de ground, to dance de chicken flutter,
Day dance all night till de broke of day, to a tune on de old banjo,
And den dey all did gwan away, before de chicken crow.

Chorus
O come along, O Sandy Boy, now come along O do;
O what will Uncle Gabriel say, ya eh eh eh ya eh eh eh;
What will Uncle Gabriel say, why Jinny can't you come along too?[22]

The text creates a neat transition into the dances mentioned in the song and shows how they were an integral part of the performance. It also illustrates how the events about which the comedians sang were related to activities occurring in slave communities in the South. The same is true of "Walk Along John," "Old Tare River" (also associated with a coon hunt), and "Goin Ober de Mountain" ("Ree, Ro My True Lub"), the most common text of which contains omnibus courtship verses with a comic description of the character's horse.

Song texts can be misleading, however, because there are often many different versions, and there is not enough information in the playbills to verify which one was performed. The two most common texts of "Goin Ober de Mountain" illustrate this point, as can be seen in the following excepts from each. A comic version is shown on the left, and a courtship text with the same chorus appears on the right.[23]

"Going Ober de Mountain"	"I'm Gwine Ober de Mountain"
(Boston: George P. Reed, 1843)	(Boston: Charles H. Keith, 1843)

Verse 2

O come my lub and go wid me,
I'm gwain to leave this country,
A horse shall tote you round,
Walk up hill and foot it down.

Chorus

Ree, Ro my true love,
Oh come along my darling,
Fare you well, Miss Dinah gal,
I'm gwain over de mountain.

Verse 4

Dis nigger went to feed de sheep,
He gib em green tobacco leaf,
He went some water for to get,
And carried it in a corn basket.

Chorus

Verse 2

Come my lub an go wid me,
I'm gwine away to Tennessee;
A hoss an cart shall put you roun,
Walk up hill an foot it down.

Chorus

Ree-ro my true lub,
O come along my darlin,
So fare you well, my Dinah gal,
I'm gwine over de mountains.

Verse 4

I fed my hoss in a poplar trough,
De old hoss catch de hoopin cough,
I lick him wid a hic'ry stick,
He paw de groun an begin to kick.

Chorus

Such textual variants run all through minstrel music and create difficulties with any general conclusions about the repertory on the basis of a single example. One version may come from a performing tradition of minstrelsy's earliest years, when blackface imitation called attention to comic behaviors that might have been considered racially dependent. The version on the left, for example, is a comic song in the form of a narrative about an incompetent farm hand. The other version, which begins with a courtship line and uses the same "getaway" chorus, deals with the character's misadventures with his mount. In the end, part of the song's comic meaning is that neither character actually gets "ober de mountain."

Although songs were an important part of the first minstrel program, spoken humor was also an integral part of the show. The sixth item on playbill 1 was Whitlock's "Locomotive Lecture," a standard minstrel item for the next fifteen years. The "lecture" was actually a recitation of an invented narrative somewhat similar to a "tall tale" accompanied by sound effects produced by bone castanets. Some playbills stated that the lecture featured Billy Whitlock, who "describes his visit to the Wild Animals, his scrape with this Sweetheart, and shows the white folks how the Niggers raise Steam."[24]

Other versions—for example, the "Railroad Overture"—entice the patron's interest by promising "imitations of the Locomotive, giving an exact imitation of the starting, the showing of steam at full speed, etc. for the first time, and last, never before done by any individual except W. Birch."[25] The steam locomotive was one of the great new inventions of the period, and percussion instruments were the ideal devices for encoding sonic impressions of contemporary life. Musical imitations of nature or of the "sounds of the streets" have always been a part of popular entertainment, and the appearance of castanets or tambourines would have been something new in the theater even if the sound effects "lectures" had not been introduced by "Ethiopian" characters.

The first show closed with the extravaganza of "Lucy Long," which Dan Emmett described as a "Lucy Long Walk Around." The performer playing the part of Lucy dressed in female attire, and the act established cross-dressing as "a usual feature in shows of this kind."[26] Period playbills usually indicate that "Lucy Long" was performed "in character," which means the act featured a cross-dressed character whose clothing and behavior mimicked women.

The contents of this early playbill establish some of the typical features of the minstrel show: (1) much of the material was borrowed (the Sweeney songs and other parodies) from other singers or composers, (2) the format of two parts plus a finale was sufficiently flexible to permit the insertion of different types of numbers, (3) the so-called lectures were already part of an established tradition of burlesque rhetoric, (4) instrumental and vocal music was the key element in what was essentially a compilation or variety style of entertainment, and (5) depictions of African American life based on observation and exaggeration were only one feature of minstrelsy's audience appeal.

The Virginia Minstrels performed together for less than six months, and their act, although widely imitated, did not establish all the conventions used in the typical minstrel show of the 1840s. The repertory and the structure of the show were left to other ensembles, many of which claimed preeminence for their contributions.[27] The subsequent development of the typical antebellum show falls into three distinct phases (1843–48, 1849–54, and 1855–60).[28]

The dates of the three phases are somewhat arbitrary because the various developments often depended on the location of the most innovative companies during the period, the frequency of their personnel changes, and their ability to respond quickly to events in the surrounding theatrical world. The division between the first two phases is clear, however, from the increase in the number of claims that the shows were entirely respectable and contained nothing likely to offend families.

The competition for audience attention and market share was fierce, and it was fought in the newspapers, in playbills, and on the stage by Edwin Christy (1815–62), James Buckley (1803–72), Sher (Sherwood Coan) Campbell (1829–74), and other managers who promoted their organizations. They did so with the same spirit of competitiveness that marked the onstage "challenge" dances Christy presented during his company's first New York appearance (Apr. 18, 1846). Christy claimed that because his group was "organized in 1842," he was "the *first* to harmonize Negro melodies, the originator of the present style of ETHIOPIAN ENTERTAIN-MENTS, the creator of the semicircular arrangement of five to six blackface entertainers at least as early as the 1846 season, and that he alone designed the first 'dandy' costumes."[29]

Christy's offerings included some of the same songs performed by the Virginia Minstrels in 1843 (see playbill 2). "Reel O'er the Mountain" was apparently a song-and-dance number designated as a walk-around in the manuscript copy attributed to Dan Emmett.[30] Three of the numbers were probably the same as those presented by Virginia Minstrels: "Old Tar River" is equivalent to "Old Tare River" (1840), "Dance of the Boatmen" is identical to "De Boatman's Dance," and "Uncle Gable" is probably the Christy's version of the two published texts of the "Uncle Gabriel" song. "Dandy Jim from Caroline" was by then the standard caricature of urban dandies found in most shows of the 1840s.

The playbill shows that Christy's "innovations" were restricted to the so-called trial dance, which had been a feature of novelty acts in New York from the late 1830s, and an increase in the number of songs and instrumental numbers. The trial, or challenge, dances emphasized individual virtuosity and were based on numbers introduced by three famous white jig dancers, Thomas Dartmouth Rice, Joseph Jefferson III (1829–1905), and Frank Lynch, "one of the great dancers of early minstrelsy"; the famous African American dancer, William Henry ("Master Juba") Lane (ca. 1825–53), whose accomplishments in England and the United States were legendary; and John Diamond (1823–57), the dance "instructor" to the original Virginia Minstrels referred to as "dingy" in a Chatham Theater playbill (Jan. 27, 1843).[31] These dances were typical examples of the male competitiveness theme symbolized as a mock duel beginning with a challenge, proceeding to a contest showing off the dancers' skills, and ending with the audiences' acclamations of the champion.

Christy's two-parts-plus-finale plan for the show was similar to that used in the early performances of the Virginia Minstrels. But there were other possibilities. Five months after Christy presented the program shown in playbill 2,[32] the Ethiopian Serenaders II devised a different plan by organizing their show into three parts of five numbers each, with the "Lucy Long" finale presented by the whole company (see playbill 3). The program contained at least three identifiable items from operas, namely, "The Colored Fancy Ball," from William Henry Fry's *Leonora*, and "I Dreamt I Dwelt in Marble Halls" (parodied as "I Dreamt I Dwelt in Kitchen Halls") and "When Other Lips and Other Hearts" (known as "Then You'll Remember Me"), from Michael William Balfe's *Bohemian Girl*.[33] At least one of the opera selections, "De Colored Fancy Ball," is a complex, four-part choral piece requiring some musical skill for a truly successful performance.

The program's two quicksteps were associated with the burgeoning tradition of brass band music in the United States during the 1840s. There is no indication that the Serenaders performed the quicksteps with only two banjos and an accordion, which could certainly work musically, but the two quicksteps provided an excellent opportunity for an instrumental music parody. Either number could have been played by a house brass band, a custom that became common during the early 1850s. In any event, this group reduced the number of obviously ensemble or part-music pieces to the *Leonora* and "Old Granite State" parodies. Finally, the other songs listed on the program, "The Old Jaw Bone" (a parody of "Young Bowshin's Bride"), "Picayune Butler," "Uncle Gabriel," "Miss Lucy Long," and "The Dandy Broadway Swell" (which ridiculed the Sunday promenades of young white males), were typical of the programs presented by Christy during the same period.[34]

The earliest minstrel comedians demonstrated real skill at ridiculing aspects of white culture, an obvious point revealed in one of the programs of the Congo Minstrels (actually James Buckley and his talented children, G. Swaine, Richard, and Frederick) on January 8, 1845 (see playbill 4).[35] The Buckley family was among the most significant groups in early minstrelsy because their programs differed from those of many other ensembles and their skills in their individual specialties distinguished them from other performers of the period. Another playbill from one of their first New York appearances contains relatively few identifiable "plantation" songs or numbers dealing with African American stereotypes. Two examples are "De Old Jaw Bone" and "Gaily the Nigger Boy," which is probably a parody. The Buckleys offered their own versions of "Lucy Long" and the "Firemen's Chaunt," another "sound effects" piece similar to the "Locomotive Lecture" and the "Railroad Overture."[36] The program featured a number of parodies, including one of the Hutchinson Family's "Old Granite State" (1843); "On Yonder Lovely Hill," from Auber's hit opera *Fra Diavolo; or, The Inn at Terracina* (Paris, 1830; New York, 1831); "Dinah's a Lady," based on "Lily's a Lady"; Dan Emmett's "Wild Goose Nation," a parody or adaptation of the 1844 version of "Gumbo Chaff" and the as yet unidentified "Dis Child's Tambourine."[37]

The Buckleys generally stressed solo work in their early performances and presented pieces without any identifiable African American instrumental styles, for example, the violin solo composed by Leopold Herwig (1815?-45), the "German Paganini," who was "unanimously acclaimed the best violinist ever to have been heard in New York."[38] The several instrumental solos by Frederick and G. Swayne Buckley are particularly good illustrations of the ensemble's trend toward featuring their stars' strengths.

Playbills 2–4 show that newer companies maintained some of the older numbers that were parts of the growing standard minstrel repertory but that, as the 1845 season developed, this material was often framed by an introductory overture and relatively standard closing number, usually some version of "Lucy Long." The repertory began to broaden that year, and playbill 5 illustrates the addition of newly composed material and a much more structured order of performance.

The group numbers in playbill 5 feature various soloists accompanied by a chorus composed of other members of the ensemble who perform the refrains, a performance pattern based on the structure of the songs. Each part of the show begins with an overture performed by the full band, although it is not clear whether the material was instrumental or choral. The program has a certain symmetry, with six items in the opening and closing sections and seven in the intervening one. The songs themselves are sometimes identified by short titles or by their first lines: "Going Along Down to Town" is the opening line of "Lynchburg Town," "Dandy Jim" is equivalent to the most common version of "Dandy Jim of Carolina," "Dinah's Hut" is most likely another parody of "I Dreamt I Dwelt in Marble Halls." "Dar He Goes, Oh Dat's Him" (1843), "Grey Goose" (probably "The Old Grey Goose"), and "Old Dad: A Fisherman's Luck" ("My Old Dad" or "Ole Dad") are songs originally published by Dan Emmett in 1843 and 1844. The bill also includes Frank Brower's "Old Joe" (1844), a song with short banjo breaks; introduces Thomas ("Pickaninny") Coleman (d. 1859), a famous early blackface performer, into the minstrel show; and features a song, "Bress Dat Lubly Yaller Gal," published by Charles White in 1845.[39]

The differences between innovative groups, such as the Christy Minstrels and Buckley's Serenaders, and the derivative or copycat groups, such as the Ole Bull Serenaders and Ethiopian Serenaders III, become clearer when playbills 1–4 are compared with playbills 5–6. These later ensembles presented little new or original material. Playbill 5 illustrates the tripartite organization of the show, the increased program length (twenty numbers instead of the eleven found in playbill 4), the use of "overtures" to open the parts, the continued emphasis on parody as part of minstrelsy's humor, and the tendency to feature a "front man" accompanied by the rest of the ensemble.

Playbill 4 shows that some songs and instrumental numbers achieved the status of standards ("Lucy Long" and "Old Jaw Bone"). The parody of Henry Russell's "Life on the Ocean Wave" ("A Life by the Galley Fire") confirms that his song was such a hit and so representative of class differences that it inspired the burlesques shown in playbills 5 and 6. Playbill 5 also shows the eclectic mix of musical sources in early minstrelsy, with Joel Sweeney's "Lynchburg Town" appearing under the title of its chorus ("Going Along Down to Town"), Emmett's "The Old Grey Goose" ("Grey Goose" in this playbill) concluding the third part of the show, and one of the versions of "Dandy Jim of Caroline" combined with the parodies of the Balfe and Russell songs.

Playbill 6 from August of the same year confirms the potpourri of stylistic sources created by the minstrel composers and arrangers. The Balfe and Russell songs reappear, with Russell now represented by the takeoff on his song "The Ivy

Green" ("Sugar Cane Green"); the parody of the Hutchinson's "Old Granite State" ("The Old Virginnny State") shows that the singing family was still being ridiculed by blackface performers; and the mock duels exemplified in "Ole Bull and Dan Tucker" were still popular.[40] The repertory of secondhand songs, which is what the parodies really were, is framed by quicksteps, marches, and overtures, whose incorporation into the minstrel show illustrates their popularity in the popular musical culture of the period. Those items also established more exciting openings for the various parts by allowing the performers to march onto the stage. Finally, the constant reappearance of "Lucy Neal," "Lucy Long," and "Fine Old Colored Gemman" (a parody of Henry Russell's "Fine Old English Gentleman") demonstrates just how groups imitated or covered one another and how much of the minstrel show material was shared.

There were, however, still opportunities for groups to introduce new material and greater variety into the minstrel repertories because the better-known (and most innovative) ensembles traveled often during minstrelsy's early years. The Buckley Serenaders toured England for nearly two years (1846–48). The core members of the Ethiopian Serenaders III (Francis Germon, Richard Pelham, and George Harrington) made the same trip during the 1848–49 season. The Sable Harmonists and similar bands (marked only by the name "Sable" in their bills) managed by Nelson Kneass were frequently absent from New York for tours of the South and the British Isles. The other Sable groups (Sable Harmonizers, Sable Brothers, and Southern Opera Troupe of Sable Harmonists) toured the Midwest, appearing in Pittsburgh, Cincinnati, St. Louis, and other towns along the Ohio and Mississippi Rivers.[41] Finally, the number of Ethiopian sketches increased after 1853, even though many of the examples performed were Charles White's arrangements and adaptations of the skits and "operas" Thomas Dartmouth Rice had presented repeatedly in his own performances during the late 1840s and early 1850s.

When the Buckleys embarked from New York in 1846, they left an opening for Edwin Christy to shape minstrelsy's development and establish a permanent resident company at Mechanics Hall, which he purchased in 1847. For all his public relations successes, Christy restricted the publication and distribution of playbills, preferring to limit the amount of publicity as a way of enticing the curious into his theater. Some of the extant Christy playbills state that the first part of the show represented the "Dandyisms of the Free Blacks of the North." The claim seems patently false because the show still included the now standard overture, a parody of the Hutchinson Family's "Old Granite State," and two opera burlesques including "The Darkey Gal's Dream of Home," which was another parody of "I Dreamt I Dwelt in Marble Halls," and "Whose [Who's] That Knocking at the Door," a version of Anthony F. Winnemore's "Stop That Knocking" (1843) based on his parody of an Italian operatic scene originally written for his own Boston Minstrels. That number appeared in both parts, perhaps allowing Thomas Vaughn an opportunity for an encore.

The dominant references in the first part of the Christy playbill are to women, for example, "The Darkey Gal's Dream of Home," "Git Along Home Yaller Gals," "Oh, Julia Is a Handsome Gal," and the operatic parody "Stop That Knocking." The Christys' version of that number was sometimes known as "Suzy [or Susey] Brown" because it described Sam's courtship of Suzy, a reticent but coquettish young lady whose inquiries about "who's that knocking at my door" demonstrated her resistance to Sam's persistence.

The distinctions many writers on minstrelsy make between the various parts of the typical minstrel show have been based on programs similar to playbill 7, which purports to represent the "Free Blacks of the North" (part I) and the "Peculiarities of the Southern Plantation Negroes" (part II). The contents of those parts were not established conventions, and most ensembles mixed up their offerings so much that the songs and instrumental numbers could hardly be characteristic of the distinctions in African American behaviors Christy suggested with the geographical labels. A few examples will reinforce this point. Emmett's parody of "Fine Old Irish Gentleman" was played by other companies in the *first* part of their shows. The "Railroad [or Rail Road] Overture" often appeared as an opening number, sometimes as a closing piece, and occasionally as a novelty act for the bones or tambourine player. The number of so-called peculiarities was quite small, with "Towser's Coon Hunt" and the "Down in Carolina" corn-shucking dance being the most likely candidates. There is certainly no connection to the South and plantation music in the parody of the Swiss bell ringers or the mock "Tyrolese" choruses satirizing the European families and performing groups with whom the minstrels competed. The Swiss "campanalogians" parodied in the example were ridiculed when their "instruments" were replaced with cowbells and their "European" repertory was displaced by American songs.[42]

The geographical confusion already mentioned is matched by an equally confused treatment of history, as illustrated by Christy's version of another early blackface convention. The "Uncle Gabriel" song, at least in the version Christy published in 1848, refers to the Southampton slave insurrection led by Nat Turner in 1831, but Christy confuses it with an earlier rebellion led by Gabriel Prosser in 1800. This song is set as a narrative for a singing storyteller (tenor) with a repeated response, "Hard Times in Old Virginny," at the end of every verse. The result is a garbled form of mock ballad recounting a history of current events (Southampton becomes Northampton in playbill 7) known to at least some northern and many southern members of the audience.[43]

The 1847–48 playbills show some of the changes in the contents and organization of the programs presented by the original Virginia Serenaders in 1843. There were several alternative ways of organizing the shows, and the Campbell's Minstrels II (1848) announced that *their* show (playbill 8) would open with an overture for "full orchestra" and include such novelty numbers as the "Laughing Chorus" and a "whistling" solo because there were "whistling Paganini's" to be had in New York.[44] The "Jenny Lind Polka" burlesque replaced "Lucy Long" as the closing number, confirming that, even before her tour of the United States in 1850, the Swedish soprano, who retired from the European opera stage in 1849, was already a celebrity.[45]

The Campbells played freely on the eponymous Scottish folk song, "The Campbells Are Coming" (ca. 1745). Their so-called statue dance became a burnt cork convention following the introduction to New York City on September 23, 1847, of Dr. Collyer's "Model Artistes." The "artistes" were a "band of male and female living models" who appeared at New York's Apollo Rooms "in a state of strategically draped nudity (or pseudo-nudity) . . . [and] posed in 'living pictures' or 'living statuary' to represent patriotic subjects, biblical subjects (Adam and Eve just as they appeared in the Garden of Eden, for instance) and famous works of art (the Venus di Milo). These poses promised that 'the strictest accuracy will be observed in relation to drapery.' All this took place to the strains of 'descriptive music' by Dodworth's Band."[46]

The statue acts became instant hits, and Odell notes that they appeared in the circus "or between play and farce at the minor theatres."[47] After the single reference to the "Lucy Long and Statue Dance" on playbill 8, the living statues parodied by the Campbells soon showed up in other minstrel shows as well. Blackface comedians could not pass up the opportunity to parody such obviously titillating demonstrations of male and female anatomy. Minstrel ensembles (the Ethiopian Melodists, Ole Bull Serenaders, and Kunkel's Band of Nightingales) soon joined the Campbells in presenting burlesques of "Ethiopian statuary" (some of whom apparently danced) and "model artists,"[48] which included elements distilled from the more popular stage pieces of the period.

Playbill 8 shows how far minstrelsy had moved from the relatively short presentation by the Virginia Minstrels in 1843. The program contained the "Laughing Chorus" and "Whistling Solo," many more songs about women (sentimental and nonsentimental) than in any previous program, more specialty dances ("Highland Fling") that may have been ridiculed or exaggerated, and the usual operatic choruses. The appearance of a chorus from *Ernani* is particularly interesting because that opera received its New York premiere in April 1847 by the Havana Opera Company, whose chorus was "better than any other opera chorus yet heard in North America."[49]

The revival of Italian opera in New York began with the appearance of yet another ensemble calling itself the Havana Opera Company in the spring of 1847. New York's elite had already undertaken the construction of the Astor Place Opera House, which opened its doors on November 22, 1847, for the express purpose of establishing Italian opera in the city, according to the *New York Herald* (Nov. 20, 1847). After the Seguins had provided many wonderful sources for minstrel companies to parody—for example, *The Bohemian Girl* and *La Sonnambula*—along came even more material for the blackface choruses to introduce into their variety entertainments. There was obviously enough Italian or English-Italian opera to keep the average blackface company stocked with at least three or four good choral numbers every evening.[50]

The Campbells' playbill represents the culmination of minstrelsy's development during the 1843–48 period and provides a stopping point at which to draw some conclusions about the repertory and structure of the early minstrel shows during this period:

1. The structure of the early shows was not fixed.

2. There are no references to an "olio" as the second part of the few specifically tripartite shows.

3. There is no evidence of "end men" or the banter commonly expected from the performers as they made the transition from one number to another, making it difficult to reconstruct the links between the various sections of the typical show.

4. The rosters of various minstrel companies show that the number of performers increased from 1843 to 1848.

5. The new company members usually possessed specific performance skills that ensembles exploited to emphasize the differences between themselves and other groups.

6. There are very few sketches, skits, or afterpieces in any of these early examples.

7. The few lectures are focused almost exclusively on phrenology, which is unexpected given the range of topics available for parody during the period.

8. There are virtually no extended parodies of operas by the major minstrel ensembles but only briefer two-to-eight-minute segments usually based on choruses taken from Italian or English and some French operas.

9. There are few specific references to the character types or stereotypes described in most accounts of minstrelsy.

10. Parodies of popular songs and operatic "hits" dominate the early blackface repertory.

11. The distribution of some songs among a wide variety of groups and the repetition of a limited number of items suggest a core of representative "hits" on which to base an analysis of minstrelsy's main ideas.

12. The early minstrel show probably contained a greater variety of musical styles than those typically associated with the "Ethiopian" business.

Near the end of the first half-decade of minstrelsy, minstrel company managers realized that their audiences were changing, perhaps in response to the general economic recovery from the Panic of 1837 and the demographic changes in major cities. Minstrel companies gradually settled into their own halls and theaters, which were usually renovated to increase the seating and, through changes in the interior design, to allow women and families to attend. The concern about the audience was generated in part by a desire to increase its size and to appeal to a different kind of public. The number of references to "chaste" dancing, "respectability," and the "inoffensive" nature of blackface entertainment increased, and as it did so, the number of references to "Buffalo gals," "New York gals," and any other "gals" who would "come out tonight" generally disappeared.

Christy recognized that repeat audiences needed greater variety, and family entertainment could be promoted only if the material was respectable. He announced that there was "change of programme every evening," promised "the music *in part* of the most popular OPERAS OF THE DAY," and guaranteed that "their CHASTE and INIMITABLE CONCERTS . . . have been received with every mark of favor by the Elite and Fashion."[51] By 1847 minstrel ensembles offered these disclaimers to defuse criticism of minstrelsy as a primarily lower-class entertainment. The Virginia Minstrels boasted

> of the patronage which the ELITE OF BOTH SEXES IN EACH CITY, have so liberally bestowed on their exertions, in truly delineating in a masterly and chaste manner, the Sports and Pastimes of the Virginia Colored Race, through the medium of Songs, Refrains, and Ditties, as sung by the Southern Slaves, at all their Merry Meetings, such as the gathering in of the Cotton and Sugar Crops, Corn Huskings, Slave Weddings and Junketings. The performance will be entirely free from every objectionable feature, either in word, look, or action, that could offend the most sensitive or fastidious beholders.[52]

The better ensembles took pains to distinguish themselves from the amateur and semiprofessional companies appearing in taverns or oyster cellars. Christy informed readers of the *New York Sunday Dispatch* (Oct. 10, 1847) that "in the displays of *refined* Negro dandyism, in the representation of the broad humors of plantation life,—in the Ethiopic parodies of the *highest* graces of European accomplishments, this band is equally unique and *admirable*. There is a variety which prevents the slightest feeling of monotony, and an elegance and perfection of art which removes the least shade of vulgarity."

The *New York Tribune* (Mar. 12, 1847) reported in a characteristic puff piece that "Christy's Minstrels are drawing crowded houses at the Society Library. Many of the most fashionable families attend, as the performers are a pleasing relief to the high-toned excitement of the Italian opera—Negro melodies are the very democracy of music." On April 18, 1847, a Christy playbill claimed that "appropriate seats are reserved for the ladies, who may attend with propriety, as nothing will be introduced that can possibly offend the most sensitive mind."[53] The Campbell's Minstrels II advertised (Sept. 28, 1848) that their entertainments included a "variety of chaste dancing, including the celebrated Statue Dance and Highland Fling, by Mr. Luke West."[54]

The appeals to different classes should not be pressed too far, for audience studies are too sketchy to establish any convincing demographic picture, even though it is evident that large numbers were often the rule—for example, a Wood's playbill of September 19, 1859, mentions that "over 11,500 Persons visited the hall last week." Nevertheless, the distribution of sheet music in middle-class homes, the income figures for those companies reporting their gate receipts, and the puff pieces appearing in most New York newspapers show that the composition of the typical audience was quite varied, especially after the major minstrel ensembles acquired their own halls. The major companies were seeking a more varied audience by the 1848 season and, working as they were in a market-driven economy, recognized that popular art usually aspires to a quality of respectability as business managers explore new markets for their entertainment products. When blackface minstrelsy began to pursue those audiences and adapt itself to a recovering entertainment market, the contents of its programs changed.

1849–54

The Christy Minstrels announced a three-part program (Feb. 26, 1849; see playbill 9) for some ten performers that relegated the "plantation" elements to just two songs in the first part ("Witching Dinah Crow" and "Gal From the South"), and two additional numbers in the final section of the show ("Old Uncle Ned" and "Sweep, Oh!"). "Lucy Neal," a song generally identified by its reference to the female character's experiences as a plantation slave, appeared in part I in combination with "See, Sir, See" (1852), a parody of "Vi ravviso, o luoghi ameni" from *La Sonnambula*.[55] The other burlesque song was "The Virginia Rosebud" (sometimes referred to as "We Hear the Hoofs"), a sentimental number from Daniel Auber's *Le Cheval de bronze* dealing with the kidnapping of a young child.

The new items included a topical parody of one of England's most popular brass ensembles, the famous Distin Family Quartet, headed by John Distin (1793–1863) and featuring his son Henry (1819–1903), "the greatest trumpeter of his age," according to the *New York Mirror*. The ensemble performed on the Distin horns, a new family of rotary valve brasswinds known as "saxhorns" after their creator, Adolphe Sax (1814–94); the elder Distin manufactured the instruments under license from Sax. The quartet debuted on January 10, and by early February the Christys had already produced a parody based on the Distin group's singing and brasswind playing. The reference to "SIX HORNS" is a pun on "saxhorns." The "six" may have indicated the number of persons Christy used in the burlesque.[56] What is most interesting about the burlesque of the *English* Distin Family is that there was no corresponding treatment of the *American* Dodworth Family Band, the most prestigious group of brasswind players on the New York scene during the 1850s.[57] And there are no references at all to any of the African American bands that performed regularly at ceremonies and festivals in black neighborhoods in many eastern cities.

Part III of playbill 9 reflects a significant change because the plantation characteristics are restricted to those described in Stephen Foster's "Old Uncle Ned" (1848) and in "Sweep, Oh," both of which appear to have been solos for George Christy. "Uncle Ned" is one of those sentimental songs that Henry James described as "going directly to the heart," a song "like Ossian's music of memory, 'pleasant and mournful to the soul.'" According to Charles Hamm, the song exhibited "a new spirit" because Uncle Ned is portrayed "as a gentle, kindly human being" whose relationship with his owners seems to be based on mutual affection and respect.[58] What is even more significant is that the whole show ends with a sentimental song and an ensemble number other than "Lucy Long."

The innovations of the 1849–50 season introduced new material to the minstrel show, but the new products reveal that the various minstrel companies did not agree on what constituted the "Negro" element of blackface minstrelsy. All seemed to concur on the need for variety and new material, for keeping up the comic pressure on Italian opera, and for continuing their ridicule of foreign performers. When the Buckleys returned to the United States for the 1849–50 season, they must have realized that Americans of all classes enjoyed parodies or burlesques of operas when they were presented in blackface because the burnt cork disguise, being an obvious "American" marker, provided a license for exaggeration and a vehicle for identifying the ensemble's work as comedy. But the Buckleys now included new types of instruments in their shows (the double bass and the melophone) that had no connection to any plantation or minstrel show sound. Edwin Christy accused "them damned Englishmen" of ruining minstrelsy with their emphasis on operatic and musical performances—this from the same manager who prided himself on his burlesque of the Distin Family Quartet.[59]

Even when the performers indulged their own musical interests by performing Italian or English material seriously—that is, without makeup—audiences, however much they enjoyed the singing, recognized that the minstrels could perform the songs as well as the original artists could while managing to mock a class-based foreign cultural product. The New Orleans Serenaders invited such comparisons by programming the "imitations of various singers" shown in playbill 10 and naming the artists whose signature performances would be subjects for burlesque: Jenny Lind; Madame [Anna Riviere] Bishop (1814–84); [Teresa] Truffi; [Marietta] Alboni (1826–94); and Sigs. [Sesto] Benedetti, [Luigi] Lablache (1794–1858), [Giovanni Matteo] Mario (1810–83), and Gardioni.

The roster of victims in the "Grand Scene" includes sopranos, tenors, and basses popular in the United States during the late 1840s and 1850s, performers associated with various opera companies, including the Astor Place Opera Company, directed by Maximilian (Max) Maretzek (1821–97). Burlesques of specific singers formed part of the Christy repertory whenever Edwin Christy could engage vocal specialists to perform them. Christy hired the famous female impersonator Max Zorer to sing "the celebrated Rondo from the Opera of *Linda di Chamounix* as sung by Mme. Laborde and Jenny Lind."[60] Zorer had been a member of the original Moravian Singers ensemble from Germany and was now the troupe's blackface prima donna. He continued to perform as a cross-dressed soprano in the "Echo Song a la Lind burlesque" for Wood's Minstrels on September 12, 1851.

Playbill 10 also contains the usual two or three choral parodies, including a burlesque of the "Phantom Chorus"; a whole range of new or novelty instruments (something of a trend in the 1850s); a number of songs and ballads; instrumental numbers illustrating the Buckleys' skills; and the most popular violin piece in the playbills, namely, "Carnival of Venice." This expansion of the minstrel show contents continued with the programs of the Virginia Serenaders, whose Boston performance featured the usual choral parodies from *Leonora*, some of minstrelsy's acknowledged standards, and a sketch called *The Dutch Drill*. *The Dutch Drill* was apparently a sketch focused on an officer and an enlisted man involved in a superior-inferior relationship that comedians used to generate much comic interplay on the minstrel stage. The same type of male rivalry rhetoric underlies the frequent references to short scenes in which a banjo duet is claimed to show "the power of music on the Ethiopian race" or tutorial sessions in which a fiddler or banjo player instructs an inept student. The typical outcome of such unequal relationships is that the inferior figures usually turn the tables, reverse the roles, and emerge triumphant from the confrontation.

Playbill 11 offers two other apparent curiosities to the minstrel show audience. The first is a burlesque entitled "The Black Shakers," "done by no other company," and the second is a version of "Old Dan Tucker" with special verses expanding the character's ethnic contacts to three other groups. There are remnants of the 1843–48 repertory also, especially the "Railroad Overture," still apparently a good novelty number wherever it appeared, "The Old Jaw Bone," "Old King Crow," and "Oh Lud Gals Gib Me Chaw Tobacco."

The newest feature, though "new" only to the claims of this company, is the "Black Shakers" burlesque (part I of playbill 11 and part II of playbill 13), which usually included "Fi, Hi, Hi! or: The Black Shakers Song" (1851).[61] The song parodied the performances of the several troupes of apostate Shakers or Shaking Quakers, whose tours—they appeared at Barnum's Museum in 1846—revealed something of the doctrinal and ritual "peculiarities of the Society's practices," as attested in the following newspaper advertisement:[62] "THE MOST EXTRAORDINARY Exhibition ever known.—The celebrated FAMILY OF SHAKER BROTHERS AND SISTERS . . . will give their second GRAND CONCERT AND LECTURE . . . consisting of a complete illustration of the system, mode of life, manner of worship, peculiarities . . . of this singular, and hitherto unknown people; their origins, progress &c; and their Chaunts, Dances . . . with the utmost fidelity and truthfulness of originality."⁶³

Some of the apostate groups may have had a legitimate desire to explain the practices associated with the sect to a curious public. But the apostates then became the targets for blackface comedians who often focused on a woman's choice to leave home and embrace the religious solace of a different group that was distrusted precisely because of that difference ("Bress dat lubly yaller gal, / De white folks call Miss Dinah; / Oh! pity me ye Shakers all, / And tell me where I'll find her").⁶⁴ Minstrelsy continued its practice of treating "others" as objects to be ridiculed, although the song's deeper meaning is that Dinah left her own family and religion, was accepted into what some viewed as essentially a cult, and came to behave with an embarrassing fervor.

By the beginning of the 1851 season, several other features entered the programs of many of the more successful ensembles, and these elements can be found in the playbills accompanying the performances of Wood's Minstrels (see playbill 12). The size of the typical ensemble and the diversity of the offerings are remarkable for a genre less than a decade old. The number of examples drawn from now forgotten operas—another example of minstrelsy's topicality—is quite extraordinary, with selections from what are now relatively unknown works by Bellini, Donizetti, Meyerbeer, Auber, Mercadante, Rossini, and Verdi. Playbill 11 identifies almost all parody choruses by title along with the name of the opera or opera burlesque from which the selection was taken.

The practice of merging an opera chorus with a popular minstrel song is shown in the second number, which combines material by Auber with "De Boatman's Dance," and the seventh, which combines a plantation song with Tyrolean yodeling. The number of instrumental solos is expanded to include pieces for the concertina and the accordion. Noteworthy also is the mixture of sentimental and comic songs, as well as the combination of twenty-one musical or instrumental numbers with the appearance of *The Returned Volunteer,* an Ethiopian sketch associated later with Dan and Jerry Bryant. Finally, the playbill illustrates how Wood's ensemble and many of the other contemporary groups increased the variety of their material and created opportunities for soloists to demonstrate their own talents while making fun of foreign subjects and performers.

Wood and his fellow managers brought all the English- and Italian-style traits into a polyglot popular musical culture capable of absorbing such disparate elements. This is the model for popular American music of the minstrel era as well as for that of the present, namely, the eclectic compilation of relatively brief and immediately attractive ingredients designed to reach the broadest possible audience. The variety found in the Buckleys' and Christys' playbills during the early 1850s was reflected in a special feature of Samuel Sanford's New Orleans Opera Troupe, then billed as "the greatest combination of talent ever concentrated in the Ethiopian business in the world." Sanford, who was responsible for most of the plantation roles when he was with the Buckleys, broke with the New Orleans Serenaders in May 1851.[65] He declared his independence from his former friends and employers in the *Charleston Daily Courier* (Nov. 8, 1851) by giving his potential audiences a list of reasons explaining why his ensemble was demonstrably superior to the Buckleys. Sanford was remarkably skillful as an advertising copywriter for his enterprises.

> The Entertainments given by the New Orleans Opera Troupe differ entirely from other minstrels, as they introduce all the best Original Songs, Ballads, Glees, Choruses, including the best selection of English, Irish, and Scotch Ballads. With their Burlesque Operatic Scenes, with the Dancing of the Ballet Troupe in their Burlesque Pas de Deux, Cachuchas, Flings, Reels, Jigs, Hornpipes, which were introduced . . . by this troupe, in order to satisfy their audiences in every variety. . . . The entertainment, throughout, is enlivened with Bon Mots, Jokes, Readings of Shakespeare, and Local Items of the day, by that inimitable punster, S. S. Sanford, which were originally introduced in concert rooms by this troupe.[66]

Sanford was not the only manager who followed the Buckleys' interest in opera burlesques. The Ethiopian Serenaders VII (1851) featured an overture from François Adrien Boïeldieu (1775–1834) and Eugene Scribe's (1791–1861) *La Dame blanche,* which was based on Sir Walter Scott's novels *The Monastery* (1820) and *Guy Mannering* (1815) and was performed in New York's Park Theater in 1827 (see playbill 13). The choruses on the bill are from Giuseppe Verdi's *Ernani* (New York, 1847), *La Sonnambula,* and Michael William Balfe's *Enchantress* (New York, Oct. 2, 1849).

Five of the nine numbers in part I of playbill 13 are of European or English origin. The burlesque Shakers were back among the blackface comedians, *The Dutch Drill* returned to delight the antimilitary members of the audience, and the living statues reprised their marmoreal poses for audiences interested in such titillating delights. It is not clear from any of the playbills whether this particular act involved the use of drapery, tights, or any other special garments to help the scene achieve its comic potential. The number of items in the show is reduced from twenty to accommodate the sketches and extended song and dance routines. The concluding number revives the preminstrel song "Old Tare River" as the musical accompaniment to the now popular burlesques of "living statuary." The revival of older musical numbers and routines, for example, "Julius's Bride," "The Coon Hunt," and "Old Tare River," show that the conclusions of the shows were still not fixed formulas.

Foreign instrumentalists and impresarios were still targets for minstrel humor during the 1849–54 period. Various groups targeted Louis Antoine Jullien (1812–60), who brought his hundred-piece symphony orchestra to the United States for a concert on August 17, 1853, the first full-size modern orchestra ever heard in this country.

John Sullivan Dwight reported in *Dwight's Journal of Music* (Oct. 8, 1853) that Jullien and his orchestra presented their "*eleventh* concert at Metropolitan Hall, and *thirty-fifth* concert in New York," and that "the dollar price is really cheap for such an unparalleled combination of talent as Jullien has had the enterprise and tact to muster and train together to complete unity for our entertainment." The dollar-a-seat cost for the Jullien concert should be seen in the context of the blackface entertainment available for twelve and one-half cents at a minstrel show matinee. Jullien's solo players were "each the very best of his specialty afforded by all of Europe." It did not take the blackface comedians long to offer their own "Concert *a la* Jullien, with solo parts for Cornet and Double Bass" (Wood's Minstrels, Oct. 13 and 25, 1853), and a "Burlesque on Mons. Jullien's Orchestra with R. Bishop Buckley as 'Black Jew-Lion' featuring *La Prima Donna Walse,* the *Carnival de Venise* played on a Tin Whistle, and an American Quadrille" (Buckley's Serenaders, Mar. 22, 1854).[67]

The Jullien burlesques continued throughout the last phase of antebellum minstrelsy, usually appearing in the second part of a show but seldom including more than three or four numbers (see playbills 14a and b). Blackface comedians seem never to have created a complete burlesque of any lengthy concert program by any legitimate instrumental group. Minstrel shows were popular culture samplers of other more complex entertainment forms reduced to a few characteristic numbers. They displayed how "foreigners" made music and how easily that music could be absorbed into an increasingly syncretic "American" style. The Jullien burlesques continued to appear through the 1850s and traveled across the country with the Backus, George Christy, and Sanford minstrel troupes during their tours of the Middle and Far West.

The different acts were distributed in various ways during each of the five-year periods. First, the walk-arounds appeared at least as early as 1851 in the playbills and occasionally thereafter. Second, dance numbers or extravaganzas continued to end the shows for some groups between 1849 and 1854, and burlesque operas were programmed by relatively few ensembles, for example, Buckley's New Orleans Serenaders. Finally, the number of Ethiopian sketches increased after 1853, even though much of the material actually came from the sketches and "operas" Thomas Dartmouth Rice had presented repeatedly in his own performances through the early 1850s.[68]

The persistence of burlesques on foreign performers or entrepreneurs shows that the minstrels were primarily interested in ridiculing European rather than American groups, except when the ensemble chosen for parody was led by or associated with women, as with Buckley's "Grand Burlesque" of the Kate Hayes California Orchestra with the "conductor's" part played by R. Bishop Buckley.[69] The idea that women could be equal to men provoked and threatened male performers and audiences who considered "public" women to be objects of ridicule even though some groups included women in the regular minstrel show, as shown by an example from one of Charles White's frequent benefit nights featuring the popular Scottish singer Jeanie (sometimes Jeannie) Reynoldson (see playbill 15).[70] Such "crossovers" were common because individual blackface acts or teams often appeared outside the minstrel show, just as the shows themselves included increasingly less material associated with African Americans.

Opera burlesques became an even more popular part of the show, and afterpieces, or the so-called Ethiopian skits and sketches, appear much more often on playbills and in newspaper advertisements after 1850 than before. The reasons for these changes are not hard to find. As Katherine Preston has shown, "The wealthy and elite of New York had set out to exclude those people who were not aristocrats from opera audiences," and the establishment of more or less permanent theaters in the city created "home bases" that "obviously facilitated the formation of traveling companies." The reason for the "proliferation of Italian opera performance during the 1850s was an artistic one: the presence in this country after 1848 of operatic and concert impresarios, Bernard Ullman, Maurice Strakosch, and Max Maretzek, each of whom had a significant impact on the culture of opera in North America."[71]

The better minstrel companies—those with the most talented soloists and highly skilled managers—continued to emphasize selected burlesque choruses from Italian and English operas and gradually incorporated the melodic, harmonic, and structural vocabularies of Italian music into the evolving body of American song. This technique of cultural appropriation involved mimicry not only of style but also of the singers who performed opera in United States. Blackface comedy thus included both types of burlesque: (1) the critique and appropriation of the musical style and (2) the ridicule of imported performance practices. These observations can be verified easily by examining the contents of playbills 15 and 16, which also illustrate that companies such as Buckley's New Orleans Serenaders continued to recognize the need for variety as a primary feature of blackface minstrelsy.

The Buckleys' interest in variety is apparent from the Fanny Bloomer sketch performed "in character" during part III of the performance advertised for December 16, 1853 (see playbill 16). The part was played by a cross-dressed male actor who ridiculed "bloomers" (a short skirt worn over loose trousers gathered or tied at the ankle) and Mrs. Amelia Bloomer's (1818–94) advocacy of greater freedom in women's fashions. The same desire for variety and novelty can be found in the other numbers as well, but the Buckleys always reserved time for their musical burlesques, such as their famous "Carnival of Venice."[72]

The Buckleys featured the "Carnival" as a flute solo, even though it was the most popular violin piece in minstrel shows during the mid-1850s. The number was a staple in the company's repertory since 1849 and was played regularly by Frederick "Ole Bull" Buckley. "Carnival" was probably presented in the United States for the first time in Ole Bull's concert of June 6, 1844, and he continued to perform it during the next season (Jan. 8, 1845). Max Zorer played it on the cello (June 24, 1844) when he was a member of the Moravian Singers and before he joined the blackface fraternity. The great Austrian pianist Leopold de Meyer (1816–83), "the hundred-fingered demi-god of Erard's thunder-proof seven octaves," made this piece the "gem of the evening" during his concert of November 7, 1845. Camillo Sivori (1815–94) played the whole piece on one string (Oct. 12, 1845), and the double bassist of the Havana Opera Company, Giovanni Bottesini (1821–89), offered a double bass version on March 27 and 28, 1849. Edouard Remenyi (1828–98), the Hungarian violinist and associate of the young Johannes Brahms, presented a version that delighted American audiences on January 19, 1850.[73]

The programming of selected instrumental numbers did not diminish the various blackface ensembles' interest in opera burlesques. The length of the burlesques attempted by some of the major companies, especially by Buckley's Serenaders, increased significantly at least by the 1853–54 season. The performance time of the minstrel show must have been extended from somewhere around an hour, assuming five to eight minutes for each song; ten to twelve minutes for a dance; ten to twenty minutes for a sketch, lecture, or "extravaganza"; another ten to fifteen minutes for instrumental numbers or general stage business; and a few more minutes for the verbal exchanges of riddles, jokes, and conundrums. In some cases the opera was cut to fit into the typical length of a minstrel show, that is, about ninety minutes. Only the highlights of the opera (about 10–12 numbers) were performed, as shown in playbill 17 (Mar. 6, 1854). However, when larger sections of the opera were performed and portions of the stage business and dialogue retained, the extended show must have taken up as much time as an evening at the legitimate theater, that is, about three hours. This is clear in another of the Buckleys' burlesques of The Bohemian Girl shown in playbill 18 (Oct. 30, 1854). That burlesque included most of the characters and much of the music from the opera and several songs from the minstrel repertory itself. The whole opera burlesque section had thirty-one separate numbers, much more than the twelve on playbill 17 taken from every act of Balfe's opera, or about ninety minutes of music for the Balfe items alone based on the most recent recording times for the work.[74] This particular burlesque drew on a significantly larger amount of original music and added at least another fifteen to thirty minutes of minstrel material ("Hit Him in the Eye Ball, Bim" and "Sich a Getting Upstairs") for a section that was only one part of a much longer playbill.

The tendency to produce longer burlesques differed strikingly from the practice of limiting the number of opera excerpts to a few choruses or arias that was characteristic of the playbills from minstrelsy's earlier years. The playbill evidence suggests that the better companies had several different burlesques of the most popular operas, such as The Bohemian Girl, La Sonnambula, or Norma, and varied their presentations of those selections each season, as the Buckleys did during the 1853–54 and 1854–55 seasons. The more elaborate burlesques required the same level of sustained interest from the minstrel show audience as the original works did in more upscale venues. These burlesques also confirm the Buckleys' claims that the group could cover virtually any operatic work. The contents of playbill 18 suggest that the group did a virtual rewrite of the original, preserving the opera's most popular songs while allowing for the insertion of whatever material the company thought would increase the size of the audience. The minstrel practice of selecting only the hits and cutting the intervening dramatic or narrative material is analogous to the modern interest in performing highlights from musicals or operas, producing recordings that eliminate the connecting scenes—recitatives or spoken sections—and delete the many distracting plot complications often found in more extended theater pieces.

The Serenaders continued to present their proven formats through 1849 to 1855, even though the nonfamily personnel changed. Other groups were not so fortunate, however, a fact made clear by one of the most significant personnel changes that occurred early in the 1853–53 season, the breakup of the long association between Edwin and George Christy. The split was a great personal blow to the senior Christy, because it left him without his stepson and greatest star. The day after George Christy formally joined Henry Wood (Oct. 23, 1853), the name of Wood's group changed to reflect a union that would eventually ruin Edwin Christy's career. His company was disbanded on July 15, 1854, and he lost the ownership of Mechanics Hall.[75]

The actual date of George Christy's defection is uncertain because he is featured on an October 16, 1853, playbill that confirms once again the developments in minstrelsy since George began his career in New York (see playbill 19).[76] Wood's program shows a mixture of old and new material as the group adjusted to the presence of one of minstrelsy's greatest dancers and female impersonators. The tripartite program features Christy prominently (his name appears in capital letters throughout) in a variety of his specialities, including the "Stump Oratory," the "Nebraska Reel," and the leading role of Julius in *Black Blunders; or, Forty Winks*. The two operatic selections bring back the ever-popular "See, Sir, See" and what was probably a chorus from Verdi's *Ernani*, namely, "We Come." Also featured are two songs by Stephen Foster, "Old Kentucky Home" and "Angelina Baker," and three numbers highlighting the talents of Master Eugene (Eugene d'Ameli), who would become another one of the greatest female impersonators in minstrelsy. He is obviously mentored here by the distinguished George Christy, who earned his early fame for the same type of act. In contrast to the extended opera burlesques presented by the Buckleys, the songs, specialty numbers, burlesque oratory, and Ethiopian sketches programmed by Henry Wood maintained the high degree of variety that was characteristic of Edwin Christy's programs.

The gap caused by Edwin Christy's difficulties left room for other managers, and the ever-enterprising Charles White presented playbill 20 on December 6, 1853. The piano overture served as the opening number, followed by another that the company performed as they entered the stage. Despite the claim that part I deals with

"Darky Negroes of the North," at least one of the songs is associated with slavery and escapes from it, namely, the well-known "Run, Nigger, Run," which is found in many African American sources. The program did not have a plantation scene, however, although some of White's offerings from 1852 do mention that the Serenaders would appear as "Plantation Darkies of the South."[77]

The Buckleys (without Sanford, who was racking up successes in Philadelphia) returned from their trip to the West with yet a different kind of minstrel program that ended with a lengthy opera burlesque and contained a significant amount of variety material. The company had been performing burlesque scenes from *La Sonnambula*, *Cinderella*, and *The Bohemian Girl*. They also presented Bellini's *Norma* (1831), Donizetti's *Lucia di Lammermoor* (1835), and some instrumental numbers from Herold's *Zampa* (1831). The group deemphasized one of its strengths, quartet singing, in favor of solos by Bishop and Swaine Buckley or Percival. The group's own "Sleigh [Sleighing] Song" was also very popular and seems to have been related to nineteenth-century sleigh rides. The Jullien burlesque was now a standard for the second part, which consisted primarily of instrumental numbers with a few variety elements, for example, the master-pupil or dominant-subservient character sketch found in other shows during this period.

1855–60

During the last five years of antebellum minstrelsy, minstrel shows went in at least two different directions. Some companies recognized the commercial power of nostalgia, and by the mid-1850s blackface minstrelsy became one of the first popular culture phenomena to double back on their own repertories as audiences recalled their first experiences with burnt cork comedy. Nostalgia was as marketable in the 1850s as it had been in the log cabin and hard cider days of the 1840 and 1844 political campaigns. Apparently a nation undergoing significant change or increased threats from the unstable social order of the day required a representation of its useful past. Henry Wood recognized the value of nostalgia when he announced, in the *New York Daily Times*, his intention to devote part of his program to old minstrel material: "The proprietor, by request, has set part of Thursday of each week, to be called the 'Old Nights,' when he will give a choice selection of old songs for the accommodation of his patrons" (see playbill 21).[78]

One curious feature of the playbill is that the songs featured in the first part were not that old. "Uncle Ned" was published in 1848, "Virginia Rosebud" appeared in 1849, and the earliest known copy of "Angelina Baker" was copyrighted on February 19, 1850, along with "Gwine to Run All Night," the original title of "Camptown Races."[79] The oldest songs were "Old Jaw Bone" (1844) and "Lucy Long" (1843). Neither item differed all that much from the others, except that the women characters in "Virginia Rosebud" and "Angelina Baker" were of the "pathetic" type associated with the departed-beloved conventions of the sentimental song.[80]

The nostalgia craze appears to be a constant in popular culture; each particular wave begins when the first generation to experience and enjoy an apparently new cultural phenomenon starts to age and see the delights of their youthful years replaced by some new form of entertainment. Within minstrelsy, older performers were invited back for guest appearances with famous companies. Frank Brower joined Sanford's Philadelphia company for a two-week engagement in January 1859, when he performed his "'original Uncle Tom Dance and Reel,' and appeared as Von Humbug in the burlesque of Van Amburgh's Circus and Animal Menagerie." Brower was back in October for "two weeks and appeared in a number of his better sketches."[81] Daniel Emmett returned to the stage for occasional solos and wrote walkarounds for various ensembles. His creation of "Dixie" for an April 4, 1859, performance by Bryant's Minstrels began the song's rise to fame that occurred after the tune was introduced into an April 9, 1860, performance in New Orleans of John Brougham's (1810–80) burlesque of *Po-ca-hon-tas; or, The Gentle Savage* (1855). Emmett also wrote *Hard Times,* an important Ethiopian sketch, or "Negro Extravaganza," for Charles White's Serenaders, who first performed the piece on October 12, 1855, at White's Opera House. Even Edwin P. Christy appeared occasionally, most notably for a two-week date with Sanford's Opera Troupe, "during which time he appeared as Joshua Scoreup in the 'original Christy burlesque' entitled *The Old Clock* . . . with Sanford in *The Double Bedded Room* [a *Box and Cox* derivative], and with Dixey in *The Rival Comedians* and *The Great Phantom Room,* and played Ginger Blue in *The Virginia Mummy.*"[82]

The nostalgia for early minstrelsy reflected how much minstrelsy had changed since 1843. Charley White's program for August 11, 1855 (playbill 22), confirms those changes because it contains two overtures, one by the house pianist and another by the band itself. The "miscellaneous varieties" in part II were part of an "olio" offering various kinds of ethnic material and musical parodies. The conclusion was an Ethiopian sketch; White used such sketches quite often during the late 1850s, after he apparently secured the rights or at least the scripts from a number of sketch writers, including Thomas D. Rice.

By the end of the decade, the typical minstrel bill presented something for almost everyone; it had become variety entertainment with little left of the satirical edge found in the early 1840s. An entertainment that started with "delineations" of African Americans now included Arabs or the more exotic "Bedouin Arabs" and female impersonators. *The Dutch Drill* and Chinese dances occurred occasionally, the plantation sketches became even more unrealistic depictions of southern life, and the topical burlesque scenes continued with material derived from Shakespeare and contemporary musical life (see playbill 25).

Pantomime violinists, imitations of bird calls, nostalgic sketches, sentimental songs, and acts having nothing to do with race or the plantation moved minstrelsy away from the acts created by the original Virginia Minstrels in 1843. In playbill 23 "The Bluebells of Scotland" replaces the "Carnival of Venice" as the subject of virtuosic thematic variations, and the finale is a topical opera burlesque based on an actual locale and incorporating musical materials from Boston's popular culture.

The emphasis on specialty acts rather than ensemble presentations is also revealed in the programs created by the Bryant (really O'Neill) family in the late 1850s. The Bryant brothers pooled their resources in 1857 to establish their own ensemble and revive some of the acts each one had developed earlier for other minstrel companies, for example, Dan Bryant's performance of "The Essence of Old Virginia," a popular dance act derived from the challenge dances of the late 1840s (see playbill 24). The *New York Clipper* correspondent who puffed the new company argued that "it is gratifying to find that we have yet among us those who will not suffer the original type of negro eccentricity to die out altogether. The connecting link . . . are [*sic*] the Bryant's Minstrels . . . and it is therefore to be hoped for that they will continue as they have begun, and stick to the 'old style' entertainment."[83]

Much of the material in the Bryant's 1857 program is derivative. The Christys' "See, Sir, See" makes yet another appearance, along with Foster's "Gentle Annie." The group revived "Down in Alabama" (known also as "Get Out de Wilderness"), the great closing number introduced by the original Christy Minstrels. These revivals confirm that the nostalgia for successful programs and the desire for proven crowd pleasers offset concerns about how the growing antagonism over slavery made new plantation elements risky commercial ventures in a form of entertainment greatly dependent on popular commercial support.

The Shakespearian "readings" sketch in this program is also noteworthy because of the nearly universal admiration for Shakespeare in American culture and literary life. But the emphasis on short scenes rather than extended burlesques, on "highlights" rather than any real involvement with the originals, reflects also the same tendency exhibited by other ensembles that used comedy to critique the "foreign" elements in American popular culture.

The bill of fare becomes even more diverse as the decade closes. The Wood and Bryant groups reintroduced circus elements into the minstrel show with "animal" acts featuring basket horses (a costume worn by one or two persons) and elephants presented by trainers with German names. It is not clear whether these acts were done in blackface or whether only those portions dealing with "darkey" characters—for example, the "Patriotic Darkey" or "Laughing Darkey" acts—were burnt cork pieces. There might have been something humorous in having Charles White play "Drizzleback Vondelsmith" in blackface, but the act might have been just as effective without the makeup.

Significant also is the increase in the so-called women's rights lectures, which exemplify one form of men's opposition to women's attempts to define their roles in American society (see playbill 25). Phrenology, hypnotism, and other esoteric subjects seem to have receded as the minstrels focused on what appeared to them and their audiences as a threat to male dominance. But no matter how often subjects of interest were ridiculed in the burlesque lecture genre, minstrelsy maintained its repertory of characters in elephant costumes, basket horses, novelty numbers, nostalgic songs, topical lectures, and burlesques of acrobatic acts. These are the various other elements that were part of the standard repertory of the late 1850s and have little or no connection with African Americans or their culture. This point was probably obvious earlier, because the songs that seem most characteristic of "northern dandies" or "southern plantation slaves" could occur anywhere in the typical minstrel show. Songs such as "Lucy Long," "Dinah's Wedding Day," and "Lucy Neal" were just as likely to be found in part I as in part III. The "Locomotive Lecture" or the "Railroad Overture" was performed in all parts of the shows, depending on the ensembles' particular performance interests. Stephen Foster's "Old Folks at Home" never appeared in the third part of the minstrel show, where such an expression of nostalgia for the old plantation might be expected; it usually appeared as a pathetic ballad in part I, which was sometimes subtitled as representing the "Dandy Darkies of the North."[84]

Even the titles of the so-called plantation scenes varied from "Representing the Peculiarities of the Southern or Plantation Negroes" to "Saturday Afternoon in Old Virginia" or "DOWN IN CAROLINA: Introducing the Cornshucking or Festival DANCE." It appears that local or regional specificity is not really applicable to minstrel material regardless of where the song is set. If "authenticity" had ever been a real goal, the minstrels could have chosen something more concrete than the mythical setting of "Old Virginia." Some songs were so infrequently programmed that they cannot be considered representative even though they appear in many songsters. For example, "Happy Are We Darkies So Gay" (1844), from *La Bayadere*, was performed only twice by the groups represented in over hundred playbills. Yet the same title appears in *CPM2, ESB2, NNB1,* and *WBA1* and, under the title "Happy Are We Niggars [Niggers] So Gay," is indexed in *GEM2, CNS1, CNS2, NFM1,* and *NSO1*. The conclusion should be apparent: a song that should be typical of the plantation section of the show was seldom performed there, and even the old plantation scene was not typical of most shows. As the playbills indicate, the conclusion of the show varied considerably from the models described in the literature ever since Wittke first wrote about minstrelsy in 1930.

As the last performance events in many of the shows demonstrate, the evening could conclude with a burlesque dance, an Ethiopian opera or sketch, a mock concert, a novelty act, or other type of stage business. The evidence confirms the differences between the earlier and later programs, showing that whereas songs and dances frequently concluded shows during the 1840s, sketches or burlesque operas often provided effective endings after 1853. Looking at the entire minstrel show as a rhetorical structure and assuming that a strong closing act might make for a more satisfying evening, it is somewhat surprising that no contemporary authors noticed the variety of closing acts or commented on the audience's reactions to them.

The partial list of closing acts in appendix B illustrates the change of emphasis in the minstrel show and demonstrates that (1) sketches became more common after 1853; (2) the opera burlesques still continued among some groups; (3) the so-called walk-arounds appeared as early as 1851; (4) some sketches appeared under other titles but were the same items performed for over a decade, for example, *The Black Statue, Oh Hush!* and *Love and Jewilrums;* (5) dancing continued to be an important and characteristic part of minstrel entertainment from the early 1840s through the end of the 1850s; and (6) some of Rice's material retained its interest even when Rice himself was no longer capable of playing the works.[85] The minstrel show format could accommodate considerable variety without apparently losing its unique qualities as a form of *American* theater. According to several 1840s sources, however, newer blackface groups risked failure unless they emphasized the "delineations of Negro *eccentricities*" or based their routines on the conventions or successes of the Christy Minstrels, who in the eyes of most critics accomplished "what is the legitimate object of their costumes and colored faces, namely the personation of the *witty* negro," who presumably lived on the idyllic southern plantation.[86] Judging from the songs and playbills, however, it appears that blackface minstrelsy never focused on the plantation or even on the mythical South as the source for most of its comedy. Throughout the history of minstrelsy, the interactions between the English tradition of comedy and the blackface American minstrels' pieces were more important than the plantation because burlesque was the foundation on which all minstrel entertainment rested.

The idea that minstrelsy dwelt principally on racial materials is widely held, but "nonracial jokelore constituted the largest part of the burnt-cork comedians' repertory."[87] Minstrelsy used cultural and physical differences as vehicles for humor. The burnt cork disguise became a complex symbolic device through which a variety of humorous, dramatic, and burlesque activities could occur. It is virtually impossible to determine what individual blackface entertainers actually intended by their mimicry—most seemed interested in entertaining audiences—but it is clear that racial disparagement, however prominently it figured as a humorous device and as a means of social control, was *not* the only function of the minstrel show, because blackface groups often "turned from racist humor to mocking the arrogance, imitativeness, and dim-wittedness of the upper classes . . . inserting, where appropriate, allusions to public figures and controversies that set the democratic mass against the elite purveyors of high culture and salvation."[88]

David Roediger has described minstrelsy's attempts to include a greater variety of music as a kind of "cultural pluralism" that led to a "liquidation of ethnic and regional cultures into blackface and, ultimately, into a largely empty whiteness." The outcome of "mixing" all the diverse elements of minstrelsy was that "blackfaced whites derived their consciousness by measuring themselves against a group they defined as largely worthless and ineffectual."[89] There is no doubt that African Americans were largely despised by whites, but the minstrels, whose personal thoughts and feelings are unknown to us, were "measuring" themselves against nonblacks as well, and they were "comparing" American music—their own music—against the products of non-American composers and performers.

Blackface comedians continued to use the burnt cork disguise as a way of critiquing "white" culture itself and also as a means of absorbing elements they enjoyed in European-based cultures. The blackface mask in those circumstances did *not* reflect white perceptions of black culture but served as a vehicle to express the disappointments and doubts of those "others" (including whites themselves) who dwelt on the margins of political power, economic comfort, and relative security in jobs, homes, and private life. The mixture of genders and classes in some of the minstrel halls suggests that the genre appealed to more than just working-class audiences and confirms that minstrelsy was the first commercially successful synthesis of the disparate cultural elements in the history of "American" popular culture. That is why I believe that (1) "the *real* essence of minstrelsy was burlesque . . . in every aspect of the show" and that (2) "the blackface minstrel, by taking on theatrically some form of the black image, whether rudely stereotyped or ethnographically scrupulous, had consciously or unconsciously entered into a many layered satire of Anglo-American life."[90]

PLAYBILL 1: VIRGINIA MINSTRELS, March 20–21, 1843

Part I

Old Dan Tucker, A Virginia refrain, in which is described the ups and downs of
Negro Life . . . . Full Chorus
Goin' Ober de Mountain, or the difficulties between Old Jake and his
sweetheart . . . . Full Chorus
Where Did You Come From . . . . Whitlock
Old Tar River, or the Incidents attending a Coon Hunt . . . . Full Chorus
Never Do To Give It Up So, or Mr. Brown's disasterious [sic] voyage down the
James River . . . . Emmett
LOCOMOTIVE LECTURE by Mr. WHITLOCK, in which he describes his visit to the Wild Animals,
his scrape with his Sweetheart, and shows the white folks how the Niggers raise Steam.

Part II

Uncle Gabriel, or a chapter on Tails [sic] . . . . Full Chorus
Boatman Dance, a much admired song, in imitation of the Ohio
Boatman . . . . Full Chorus
Jenny Get Your Hoe Cake Done . . . . Whitlock on the Banjo
Walk Along John, a celebrated Congo refrain as sung at Slave
Weddings . . . . Full Chorus
Fine Old Colored Gemman, a Parody written by Old Dan Emmett, who will on this occasion, ac-
company himself on the Banjo in a manner that will make all guitar players pale with delight.
Conundrums in any quantity, by R. W. Pelham and the other Minstrels

[Conclusion]

The Concert will conclude with the Boston Favorite Extravaganza of LUCY LONG

. . . .

PLAYBILL 2: CHRISTY MINSTRELS, New York, April 18, 1844

Part I

What's Going On . . . . Banjo Melody
The Raging Canal . . . . A comic song
Alligator Reel . . . . Banjo Accompaniment
The Broken Yoke [Jonny Boker?] . . . . First and Second Banjo
Old Tar River . . . . Dance and Banjo Accompaniment
Grey Goose and Gander . . . . Banjo, Violin, and Tambourine
Way Down in Old Virginia . . . . Banjo and Violin Accompaniments

Part II

The following Melodies will be sung to Banjo, Violin, Jawbone, Tambourine, and Bone Castinett
[sic] Accompaniment.
I Wonder Where He Went
Oh! Mr. Coon
Git Along Home, My Yaller Gals
Uncle Gable [Gabriel?], the Nigger General
Dance of the Boatmen [De Boatman's Dance]
Way Down South in the Alabama
Reel O'er the Mountain
Dandy Jim from Caroline
After which a trial dance between Masters Christy and Pierce which is universally acknowledged
to be the best specimen of Negro dancing ever exhibited.
Master Pierce will introduce his Railroad and Locomotive Imitation

[Finale]

To conclude with the Extravaganza of Miss Lucy Long

. . . .

PLAYBILL 3: ETHIOPIAN SERENADERS II, New York, September 15, 1844

Part I

Cazneau's Quickstep .... Full Band
Opening Chorus .... Company
Alabama's Sunny Shore .... G. W. White
Quartette—When de Moon Is on de Lake .... Company
The Old Jaw Bone .... G. A. Harrington
Chorus—The Colored Fancy Ball from *Leonora* .... Company
Picayune Butler .... F. C. Germon

Part II

Quickstep .... Full Band
Chorus .... Company
The Dandy Broadway Swell .... G. A. Harrington
I Dreamt I Dwelt in Kitchen Halls [*The Bohemian Girl*] .... F. C. Germon
You'll Remember Me [*The Bohemian Girl*] .... G. W. White
Glee—The Old Virginny State .... Company
Quartette—Let's Be Gay .... Company

Part III

Dandy Jim of Carolina .... F. C. Germon
Cynthia Sue .... G. W. White
Uncle Gabriel .... G. A. Harrington
The Banks of the Mississippi .... F. C. Germon
Duet (Accordion and Bones) .... M. G. Stanwood and R. Pelham

Finale

Miss Lucy Long .... Company

. . . .

PLAYBILL 4: BUCKLEY'S CONGO MINSTRELS, New York, January 8, 1845

Part I

Glee: Congo Fox Hunt .... J. L. Buckley
Parody of Tyrolese War Song .... J. Law Buckley and Chorus
Song: Gayly the Nigger Boy .... J. L. Buckley
Song: Violin Solo composed by himself .... Little Ole Bull
Song: Lucy Long, new style .... Sweeney Buckley
Sailor's Hornpipe (in character) .... Mr. King

Part II

Quartet (Italian) "Foxtonixtimor Foxteson" .... Sweeney and Chorus
Solo: Violin (composed by Herwig) .... Little Ole Bull
Solo: Old Jawbone .... Sweeney Buckley
Solo: Banjo .... Sweeney Buckley

[Finale]

FIREMAN'S CHANT: In imitation of the New York Firemen at an alarm of fire, composed and dedicated to the Fireman of New York by Pompey Nagel.

. . . .

PLAYBILL 5: OLE BULL BAND OF SERENADERS, New York, February 18, 1845

Part I

Grand Medley Overture . . . . Full Band
Dandy Jim—A Negro's Courtship . . . . S. Johnson and Chorus
Dinah's Hut—(Parody) composed and sung by . . . . W. B. Donaldson
Old Joe—A Plantation Refrain . . . . G. H. Morgan and Chorus
Bress Dat Lubly Yaller Gal . . . . H. Mestayer
Gib Us Chaw Tobacco . . . . T. Coleman and Chorus

Part II

Overture—Wrecker's Daughter . . . . Full Band
Life by the Galley Fire (Fine Parody on A Life on the
    Ocean Wave) . . . . S. Johnson
Old Dad—Or a Fisherman's Luck . . . . Donaldson
Going Along Down to Town . . . . Morgan
Ole Bull and Old Dan Tucker . . . . Mestayer
Susey Brown . . . . Coleman
Dance—Grape Vine Twist . . . . Pickaninny Coleman

Part III

Rail Road Overture . . . . Full Band
Jolly Raftsman (Parody on Love's Tell Tale) words by . . . . Donaldson
Boatman Dance . . . . Morgan and Chorus
Lucy Neale . . . . Johnson and Chorus
Dare He Goes, Dat's Him . . . . Donaldson and Chorus
Grey Goose . . . . Coleman and Chorus

[Finale]

To conclude with Lucy Long and Statue Dance by the . . . . Company

. . . .

PLAYBILL 6: ETHIOPIAN SERENADERS III, New York, August 16, 1845

Part I

QUICK STEP . . . . Full Band
Glee—A Life by the Galley Fire . . . . Germon and Chorus
Song—Fine Old Colored Gemman . . . . Harrington
Glee—The Wild Raccoon Track . . . . Company
Chorus—The Darkies Bride from *The Bohemian Girl* . . . . Company
Song—Picayune Butler . . . . Germon

Part II

Lawrence Quick Step . . . . Full Band
Glee—Merrily the Banjo Sounding . . . . Company
Song—Lucy Neal . . . . Harrington
Song—I Dreamt I Dwelt in Kitchen Halls . . . . Germon
Glee—The Old Virginny State . . . . Company
Song—Sugar Cane Green . . . . Harrington
Glee—Dis Young Nigger of Ohio . . . . Company

Part III

RAIL ROAD OVERTURE . . . . Full Band
Song—Buffalo Girls . . . . Company
Song—Ole Bull and Old Dan Tucker . . . . White
Song—Dis Nigger's Journey to New York . . . . Germon
Duett—Accordion and Bones . . . . Stanwood and Pelham
Finale—Lucy Long . . . . Harrington

. . . .

PLAYBILL 7: CHRISTY MINSTRELS, New York, March 3, 1847

Part I: Representing the Free Blacks of the North

Introductory OVERTURE . . . . Full Band
Glee: The Old Virginia State . . . . Company
Git Along Home Yaller Gals (original melody) . . . . E. P. Christy
Darkey Gal's Dream of Home: Parody from the Opera of the
    The Bohemian Girl . . . . E. P. Christy
Duet: Bones and Violin . . . . G. N. Christy and Hooley
Stop That Knocking: Original Operatic Burlesque . . . . T. Vaughn
Quick Step . . . . Full Band
Oh, Julia is a Handsome Gal . . . . T. Vaughn
Merrily the Banjo Sounding . . . . E. P. Christy
Uncle Gabriel, the Negro General, an original Refrain
    descriptive of the Northampton Insurrection . . . . E. P. Christy

Part II: Portraying the Peculiarities of the Southern Plantation Negroes

Virginia Juba, Banjo Melody with Solo . . . . E. Pierce
Towser's Coon Hunt . . . . Wells, Pierce and G. N. Christy
Locomotive Imitation and Characteristic Dance . . . . E. Pierce
Railroad Overture . . . . Full Band
Jim Crack Corn . . . . E. P. Christy
Work, Darkies, Work . . . . G. N. Christy
Fine Old Colored Gentleman Parody . . . . S. A. Wells
Gone to Alabama . . . . E. P. Christy
Sugar Cane Green, [parody of "The Ivy Green"] . . . . S. A. Wells
Whose That Knocking at the Door? . . . . T. Vaughn
DOWN IN CAROLINA, Introducing the Cornshucking or
Festival DANCE . . . . G. N. Christy and E. Pierce
After which, an Original and highly amusing Burlesque on the Popular SWISS
BELL RINGERS entitled the COWBELLOGIANS or VIRGINIA BELL RINGERS.
Violin Solo . . . . R. Hooley
Burlesque Cachucha . . . . G. N. Christy

Finale

Burlesque on the popular and fashionable POLKA . . . . G. N. Christy and T. Vaughn

. . . .

PLAYBILL 8: CAMPBELL'S MINSTRELS II, New York, October 17, 1848

Part I

Overture, Instrumental . . . . Full Orchestra
Campbell's Opening Chorus
    The Campbells are Coming, first time . . . . Company
Emma Snow, New . . . . Herman
Darkies, Our Master Has Gone to Town, New . . . . Company
Susan Dear, Original . . . . White
Operatic Chorus, Burlesque [unidentified] from *Ernani* . . . . Company
Miss Julia Tanner . . . . Herman
Duet: Bones and Violin . . . . Upson and Peel
Operatic Chorus from *Semiramide*, New and Original, first time . . . . Company
Burlesque Lecture on Phrenology . . . . White

Part II

Banjo Solo . . . . West
Old Nelly in the Morning, original . . . . R. White
Black Eyed Susianna . . . . West
Laughing Chorus . . . . West
Whistling Solo . . . . West
Statue Dance . . . . West and Peel
Ride on Darkies . . . . Bishop and Campbell
Belle of Baltimore . . . . Herman
Army and Navy Dance . . . . West
Plantation Dance . . . . Peel
Highland Fling . . . . West
The Days of Seventy Six . . . . White
Oh, Susanna . . . . Herman

Finale

Jenny Lind Polka . . . . West and Peel

. . . .

PLAYBILL 9: CHRISTY MINSTRELS, New York, February 26, 1849

Part I

Witching Dinah Crow . . . . Edwin P. Christy
The Virginia Rosebud (from *The Bronze Horse*) . . . . E. P. Christy
Burlesque Scene: See, Sir, See (from *La Sonnambula*) . . . . E. P. Christy
Lucy Neal . . . . E. P. Christy
The Gal from the South . . . . George Christy
Tyrolean Solo, with echo and double bass . . . . T. Christian

Part II

Voyage Musical, commencing somewhere and ending nowhere, comprising a variety of Airs . . .
selected from the most "unauthentic sources." To give effect to this MOST STUPENDOUS WORK,
which has "not" created such an extraordinary Sensation, the celebrated and DIS-TINguished
performers on the SIX HORNS will "Execute" the popular ARIA, *I Thought I Liv'd in Hotel Halls, etc.*

Part III

Representing the peculiar Characteristics of the Southern or Plantation Negroes
Old Uncle Ned . . . . George Christy
Sweep, Oh! . . . . George Christy

. . . .

PLAYBILL 10: NEW ORLEANS SERENADERS, Philadelphia, September 11, 1849

Part I

Grand Overture "Der Fried sheep" Introducing the Melophone and Banjella,
two new instruments, original with this company, which for compass and
sweetness of sound are unsurpassed . . . . Full Band
Opening Chorus "Hither We Come" from the Opera of *The Enchantress* . . . . Company
Song: Go Away Black Man . . . . G. Swaine
Song: Wake Up in the Morning . . . . N. Kneass
Ballad: Sally in our Alley . . . . J. H. Collins
Song: Laugh and Be Gay . . . . J. C. Rainer
Phantom Chorus, or The Darkey's Apparition from the opera
   of *La Sonnambula* . . . . Company

Part II

Violin Solo: Carnival de Venice . . . . Master Ole Bull
Banjo Solo: Hard Times, with Machine Poetry . . . . G. Swaine
Dance Ethiopian Pas de Deux a la Monplaisir . . . . Samuels and Lewis
Grand Scene from Italian Opera . . . . Imitations of various singers:
   Jenny Lind, Madame [Anna Riviere] Bishop, [Teresa] Truffi, Laborde, [Marietta] Alboni, and
   Sigs. [Sesto] Benedetti, [Luigi] Lablache, [Giovanni Matteo] Mario, and Gardioni.

Part III

We Hear the Hoofs; or, The Lost Child from
   The Bronze Horse . . . . N. Kneass and Co.
Song: The Sleigh Ride . . . . G. Swaine
Ballad: Dinah Crow . . . . J. H. Collins
Duet: Bone Castinets [*sic*] and Violin . . . . G. Swaine and Mast. Ole Bull
Song: Old Uncle Ned . . . . S. Samuels
Song: The Sweeps Refrain [Sweep Oh!] . . . . N. Kneass

Conclusion

Grand Musical Pa-Nor-A-Ma!
An original burlesque on Jullien's Grand Promenade Concerts,
introducing the MELOPHONE, BANJELLA, DOUBLE BASSO and a Solo
on a Pair of Kitchen Bellows . . . . G. Swaine
Solo on the Melophone . . . . Mast. Ole Bull
Guitar Accompaniments by . . . . N. Kneass
Finale: We Dreamt We Dwelt in Kitchen Halls and GRAND MARCH by the Wonderful
DIS-TIN-guished PERFORMERS, on their SIX RUSH-ING HORNS.

. . . .

PLAYBILL 11: VIRGINIA SERENADERS, Boston, March 2, 1850

Part I

Grand Overture .... Myers and Co.
Opening Chorus "Dinah's Wedding Day" .... Company
Cudjo's Wild Hunt .... Winnemore and Co.
The Nigger's Lament .... Harrington
By and By We Hope to Meet You .... Sanford and Co.
Song: Old Pine Tree .... Deaves and Co.
Don't Go Away Joe .... E. Horn

Grand Interlude

MISS LUCY LONG .... F. Solomon
OLD KING CROW .... Winnemore and Horn
THE BLACK SHAKERS For this night only .... and done by no other Company

Intermission of Five Minutes

Part II

THE DUTCH DRILL
RailRoad Overture .... Myers and Co.
We Are All Here .... Harrington and Co.
Uncle Ned .... Winnemore and Co.
Piece Tobacco Boys ["Gib Me Chaw"?] .... Sanford and Co.
Old Jaw Bone .... Deaves and Co.
The whole to conclude with the Laughable Song of Old Dan Tucker with Irish, Dutch and French Verses
CONCLUSION
Il Rago Africano
    Stufforo, the Chief .... Winnemore
    Broomdorni, a ruffian .... E. Horn
    Montoriari, a spy .... J. Sanford
    Clamo, a villain .... E. Deaves
    Angorina .... F. Solomon
    Bondo .... Harrington

. . . .

PLAYBILL 12: WOOD'S MINSTRELS I, New York, September 12, 1851

Part I

Introductory Overture, Crown Diamonds [from Auber's
  Les Diamants de la Couronne] . . . . Full Band
Opening Chorus, *Postillion of Longjumeau* [Auber] introducing
  the Boatman's Dance . . . . Company
Dear Native Home arranged for Wood's Minstrels . . . . M. Campbell
Lovely Rosa, the Belle of Broadway . . . . E. Horn
Poor Uncle Tom, written and composed expressly for
  Wood's Minstrels . . . . J. A. Herman
Nancy Till . . . . Winchell
Sweep, Oh, with Tyrolean solo and Chorus . . . . Campbell, Zorer and Co.
The Fireman's Death . . . . J. A. Herman
Pirate Chorus from the opera of *The Enchantress* . . . . Company
Grand Storm March Quickstep, new feature . . . . Full Band

Part II

Violin Solo, Irish airs, original varia . . . . L. De Meyer
Echo Song a la Lind burlesque . . . . Max Zorer
Banjo Solo De Yaller Gal wid de Green Corn . . . . T. F. Briggs
Fancy Hornpipe . . . . H. M. Williams
Concertina Solo, original and variations . . . . A. Sedgwick
Banjo Duet . . . . E. Horn and T. F. Briggs
Showing the power of Music on the Ethiopian race. Horn will here portray the influence of music
upon a respectable, aged colored individual from away down souf.
Double Polka . . . . Winchell and Williams
Accordeon [*sic*] Solo, by the infant prodigy . . . . Master Malatrat

Part III

Portraying the peculiarities of the darkies of the south
Plantation Song and Chorus, The Fish Question . . . . Company
THE RETURNED VOLUNTEER
George Frederick Fitzroy . . . . Campbell
Alphonso Fletcher D'Orsay Squibbs, his long lost brother . . . . E. Horn

Conclusion

Arkansas Walk-Around . . . . Horn, Winchell and Co.

. . . .

PLAYBILL 13: ETHIOPIAN SERENADERS VII, Boston, June 17, 1851

Part I

Grand Introductory Overture—*La Dame Blanche* . . . . Full Band
Opening Chorus—We'll Hunt the Coon (from *Ernani*) . . . . Serenaders
Song—Would I Were a Boy Again . . . . Campbell
Operatic Burlesque—See, Sir See (From *La Sonnambula*,
 introducing Lucy Neal) . . . . S. A. Wells
Tyrolean Solo Displaying a compass and flexibility of voice
 hitherto unknown . . . . Christian Galsianno
Song—Camptown Races (with bone imitations of horse racing) . . . . Birch
Refrain—Sweep, Ho! (with imitations) . . . . Campbell
Celebrated Pirate Chorus—Hither We Come—
 (from *The Enchantress*) . . . . Serenaders
Masquerade Waltz (With Automaton and Street Organ Imitations) . . . . Full Band

Part II

Violin solo, with Variations . . . . J. B. Farrell
Tyrolean Burlesque . . . . Company
Banjo Solo . . . . T. B. Briggs
Black Shakers—As originally performed by . . . . E. Horn and Company
Plantation Jig . . . . Briggs
Banjo Trio . . . . S. A. Wells, Horn, and T. F. Briggs
An Intermission of Five Minutes

Part III

The Dutch Drill Captain Wells and Lieut. Horn . . . . Wells and Horn
Song and Chorus—Away Down in Cairo . . . . Campbell
Song and Chorus—Julius's Bride . . . . Horn
Song and Chorus—The Coon Hunt . . . . S. A. Wells

FINALE

Song and Dance—Old Tar River. Introducing Specimens of Ancient and Modern Statuary

. . . .

PLAYBILL 14a: BACKUS'S MINSTRELS, Chicago, June 20, 1855

Part II: Grand Burlesque on Julien's Monster Concerts

Conductor: Jew Lion . . . . Monserio Fox
Prima Donna Waltz . . . . Orchestra
Trumpet Solo—Carnival of Venice, with Orchestral Accom . . . . Signor Wamboldi
Grand Finale: Yankee Doodle with Variations . . . . Full Orchestra

. . . .

PLAYBILL 14b: GEORGE CHRISTY'S MINSTRELS, Philadelphia, August 19, 1859

Grand Soiree Musicale: A Burlesque of Mons. Jullien's Monster Concert Arranged expressly for this company, by Mr. C. Koppitz—introducing a Quartet from the Opera of *Semiramide* arranged for Four French Horns—executed by Count Hermani, Count Perrini, Baron Campbellini, and No-Account Griffini.

. . . .

PLAYBILL 15: WHITE'S SERENADERS, New York, September 23, 1852

Part I

Grand Overture—Piano	Mr. Oldfield
Comic Song	R. J. McDonald
Ballad—Would I Were a Child Again	Jeannie Reynoldson
Ballad—I'm Afloat, I'm Afloat	By a Young Gentleman
Ballad—My Mother Dear	E. Lebars
Irish Song—Widow Machree	H. King
Favorite Ballad	By a Young Gentleman
Irish Song—The Low-Back'd Car	Jeannie Reynoldson

Intermission of Five Minutes

Part II

Instrumental Duett	Amateurs
Ballad—Highland Minstrel Boy	Jeannie Reynoldson
Comic Song	R. J. Macdonald
Accordeon Solo	Mr. Pike
Ballad—Sally in our Alley	E. Lebars
Favorite Ballad—Old Arm Chair	By a Young Gentleman
Song—John Anderson, My Jo	Jeannie Reynoldson

Part III

Whites's Serenaders will appear in the following pieces

Grand Overture—Linda Quick Step	Full Band
Dinah's Wedding (from the opera of *Leonora*)	Company
Nelly Bly	H. Neil
Sweep's Refrain	T. Waddee and Company
Colored Fancy Ball (from the opera of *Leonora*)	
Julianna Phoebiana Concertinia Brown	C. White
See, Sir, See (from the opera of *La Sonnambula*)	Company
Virginia Breakdown	Master Marks

. . . .

PLAYBILL 16: BUCKLEY'S SERENADERS, New York, December 16, 1853

Part I

Overture . . . Original .... Buckley's Serenaders
Operatic Chorus . . . Original . . . *Crowned with*
    the Tempest .... Buckley's Serenaders
Darkies Wedding . . . Original .... R. B. Buckley
Rosa May . . . Original .... W. Percival
Watkins' Evening Party ....G. S. Buckley
Buckley's Sleigh Song . . . Original .... R. Bishop Buckley
Bone Duet, from the Opera of *Zampa*, never attempted by any
    other performer ....G. S. Buckley
A Niggers Life for Me .... J. A. Basquin
Juliana Snow .... H. Wilson
Operatic Chorus, "Hark Again the Thrilling Horn"
    from *Cinderella* .... Buckley's Serenaders
Laughing Chorus, sung for 1,000 Nights ....G. S. Buckley

Part II

CONCERT A-LA-JULLIEN
    PRIME DONNA WALTZ
    BALLAD TROT, TROT, TROT .... MME. ANNA SEE-HER
    SOLO FLUTE: CARNIVAL DE VENISE
    AMERICAN QUADRILLE CONDUCTOR .... MONS. BISHOP JEW-LION
Violin Solo .... F. Buckley
Ballad [Unidentified] .... W. Percival
Concertina Solo .... H. S. Stevens
Burlesque Hornpipe .... J. J. Mullen
Chinese Fiddle Solo, never attempted by any
    other performer .... R. Bishop Buckley

Part III

Banjo Solo, Original ....G. S. Buckley
Banjo Duet "Waltz" with Variations .... Brothers Buckley
Banjo Duet—Pompey takes a Musical Lesson, on which occasion
    he will portray his capabilities of learning music .... R. B. Buckley
SHAKESPEARIAN READINGS .... [Performers not identified]
Solo on a Comb ....G. S. Buckley
Solo on Wood and Straw Instrument, introducing several
    favorite airs ....H. S. Stevens
Fanny Bloomer in character Song and Dance .... J. J. Mullen and Company
Melophone Solo, played by only .... F. Buckley

Conclusion

A New Grand Burlesque on the Opera of Norma .... Company

. . . .

PLAYBILL 17: BUCKLEY'S SERENADERS, New York, March 6, 1854

Part III

Grand Operatic Burlesque of the BOHEMIAN GIRL with the following Powerful cast

Thaddeus, fugitive Polish officer and aristocrat *replaced by* Lemuel, a banished Dukie

Arline, daughter of Count Arnheim *replaced by* Lucy, Supposed to be Contralto, searching for her Papa

Count Arnheim, Governor of Presburg *replaced by* Count CornCob, an elderly gent, looking for his daughter

Devilshoof, Chief of the Gipsies *replaced by* Possumheel

Queen of the Gipsies *replaced by* Aunt Debby, a fortune teller

Other characters in burlesque: Clara Snowdrop probably *replaces* Buda, Arline's nurse; Heeltoe, friend to Lemuel; Gumbo Twolips

Programme of Music*

1. Thaddeus/Lemuel: Silence the Lady Moon [sung by chorus in original]
[From act 2, sc. 1, of *The Bohemian Girl*]
2. Arline/Lucy: I dreamt I dwelt in marble halls*
[From act 3, sc. 1, of *The Bohemian Girl*]
3. Thaddeus/Lemuel: You'll Remember Me = When other lips and other hearts . . . then you'll remember me*
[From act 2, sc. 1, of *The Bohemian Girl*]
4. Thaddeus/Lemuel and Arline/Lucy Duet: That wound upon thine arm*
[Trio from act 3, sc. 1, of *The Bohemian Girl*]
5. Arline/Lucy, Thaddeus/Lemuel, Devilshoof/Possumheel: Through the world wilt thou fly love*
[From act 2, sc. 4, of *The Bohemian Girl*]
6. Chorus/Company: Happy and light of heart are those [not in currently published or recorded versions]
7. Count Arnheim/Corn Cob: The Heart bow'd down*
[From act 2, sc. 1, of *The Bohemian Girl*]
8. Chorus/Company: In the Darkie's life you lead = In the gipsies' life you read
[From act 2, sc. 4, of *The Bohemian Girl*]
9. Count/Corn Cob and Chorus/Company: They stole my child Away
[Probable interpolation of "The Virginia Rosebud" (1850) from Daniel François Auber's *Le Cheval de Bronze* (Paris, 1835; New York, 1837)]
10. Count/Corn Cob and Arline/Lucy: What visions round me rise*
[From act 3, sc. 1, of *The Bohemian Girl*]
11. Thaddeus/Lemuel: When the Niggars in Virginia = When the fair land of Poland
12. Arline/Lucy and Chorus: What full delight*

. . . .

[*Note:* Items marked with an asterisk were probably the same as or at least closely related to those in the following playbill. The burlesque examples do not always agree with the titles of the original because the playbills sometimes list songs by their titles, first line of first verse, first line of chorus, or first line shown in the libretto or piano-vocal score.]

Part III: New Burlesque on the Opera of Bohemian Girl
Arline (Lucy, daughter of Corn Cob)
Count (Corn Cob, a Darkie Overseer)
Thaddeus (Lemuel, A Runaway Slave)
Florestein (Billy Bean, newphew to the Count)
Devilshoof (Possum Heel, Chief of the Gipsies)
Queen of the Gipsies (Aunt Debby)
Buda (Nurse to Lucy)

Program of Music
Act 1, sc. 1: Corn Cob's Plantation: Celebration of Lucy's third birthday
    1. Chorus: Up with the banner
    2. Corn Cob: A Darkies life
    3. Lemuel: 'Tis sad to leave one's fatherland
    4. Lemuel and Possum Heel: Comrade your hand
Rescue of Lucy from the Wild Coon
    5. Lemuel: I left my home some time ago
    6. Lemuel: Stranger accept my galvanic thanks
Life on the Old Plantation
    7. Lemuel: The toast disdained
    8. Chorus: Rise old Corn Cob . . . Hit Him in the Eye Ball Bim
    9. [Character Unidentified]: Oh golly, I am a gonner
    10. [Character Unidentified]: Carry me to my palet [sic]
    11. [Character Unidentified]: Sich a Getting Up Stairs
    12. Chorus: Follow, follow.
End of act 1

Act 2, sc. 1: A Plantation by Moonlight
    13. Chorus (Company): Silence lady moon
    14. Lucy: I dreamt I dwelt in Chinese hall
    15. Lemuel: That wound upon thy arm
    16. Lemuel and Lucy: The secrét of her birth
    17. Lucy: Lemuel my lark
    18. Chorus: Happy and light
Sc. 2: A Wood
    19. Chorus: In the darkies life you lead
Sc. 3: The Fair Scene
    20. Lemuel: I can whip any darkie on the ground
Lucy arrested for the thief.
Sc. 4: Interior of Corn Cob's House
    21. Corn Cob: The heart bow'd down
    22. Corn Cob: Hold, hold
    23. Corn Cob: How came that mark
    24. Corn Cob: 'Tis thy Daddy stands before thee
    25. Chorus: Praised be heaven

Act 3, sc. 1: Corn Cob's Chamber. Lucy discovered meditating. Appearance of Possum Heel and Lemuel.
    26. Lemuel: Then you'll remember me
    27. Trio: Lemuel, Possum Heel and Lucy: Through the world wilt thou fly love
Entrance of Corn Cob and household. Lemuel concealed in the Chimney—discovered by Aunt Debby.
    28. Quintette: Tho' every hope
    29. Lucy: See at thy feet a suppliant one
    30. Lemuel: The fair land of Virginia
    31. Chorus: What full delight

Grande Finale [Unidentified]

· · · · · · · · · ·

PLAYBILL 19: GEO. CHRISTY AND WOOD'S MINSTRELS, October 16, 1853

Part I

Grand Overture .... Company
Opening Chorus, We Come .... Company
Old Kentucky Home ....M. Campbell
Angelina Baker .... GEORGE CHRISTY
Fare Thee Well, Kitty Dear ....J. A. Herman
Old Black Oak ....S. A. Wells
Lilly Dale ....J. A. Herman
Hush a Bye, Baby .... GEORGE CHRISTY
See, Sir, See from *Sonnambula* ....S. A. Wells

Part II

Banjo Song, Kemo Kimo .... G. H. Keenan
African Fling .... Master Eugene
Pas de Deux, Master and Pupil .... Master Eugene and GEO. CHRISTY
Violin Solo .... L. Meyer
Banjo Song "On the under side of Hobuck" in Dutch .... P. H. Keenan
First Music Lesson .... Keenan and GEORGE CHRISTY
Comic Trio .... Wells, Keenan, GEO. CHRISTY
Nebraska Reel .... GEORGE CHRISTY
Declamations, with specimens of Stump Oratory .... S. A. Wells and G. CHRISTY
Flute Solo ....E. Haslan

Conclusion

To conclude with a New Burlesque entitled Black Blunders; or, Forty Winks

Julius Crow, a Blacking Man .... GEORGE CHRISTY
Jocelyn Highflyer, a Dandy Barber .... Unidentified
Pompey Ducklegs, a Boarding House Keeper .... J. Herman
Major Raccoon, a Military Guardian ....M. Campbell
Sam Cesar, in love with Cynthia .... J. E. Mead
Joe Squashall, de right hand darkey at Mr. Ducklegs .... P. Keenan
Miss Cynthia Racoon, a runaway Evening Star .... Master Eugene
Mrs. P[ompey] Ducklegs .... F. Scott
Philissy Ann, de Kitchen Gal .... A. Edwards
Gum, Sam, and Jake. Visitors to the Convention ....A. Jones, W. Ellis, C. James

NOTICE: The new Song Books of George Christy and Wood's Minstrels, containing all their new Songs, are now ready and for sale at the Box Office, also at the publishers Long and Brother, 21 Nassau Street. In rehearsal, and will shortly be produced an entirely New Version of the celebrated Farce of *The Mummy*.

. . . .

PLAYBILL 20: WHITE'S SERENADERS, New York, December 6, 1853

Overture: Piano . . . . Charles Hiffert

Part I

White's Serenaders as Darky Negroes of the North

Overture Instrumental . . . . Full Band
Joy, Joy, Freedom to Day . . . . Company
A Little More Cider . . . . Budworth
Maggy by My Side . . . . George
Locust [illegible] . . . . Carroll
Spirit Bride . . . . Budworth
Wait for the Wagon . . . . C. White
Run, Nigger, Run or the M.P. will Catch you . . . . George
Quick Step . . . . Full Band

Part II: Miscellaneous Varieties

Thema with Variations . . . . Mast. Witters
Lovely Fanny; or, The Elssler Serenade . . . . Dan Gardner and C. White
Original Banjo Solo and Song . . . . Dan Emmitt

Part III [Ethiopian Sketch]

The Black Statue; or, The Marble Man . . . . Company

. . . .

PLAYBILL 21: WOODS MINSTRELS, New York, October 6, 1853

Part I

Introductory Chorus, "La Dame Blanche" . . . . Full Band
Opening Chorus, "Dinah's Wedding" . . . . Company
Rosa Lee . . . . J. A. Herman
Angelina Baker . . . . Jerry Bryant
Uncle Ned . . . . G. W. H. Griffin
Oh, Susannah . . . . Dan Bryant
Virginia Rosebud . . . . M. Campbell
Camptown Races . . . . Jerry Bryant
Old Jaw Bone . . . . S. A. Wells
Whar is de Spot . . . . Company
Bohemian Quickstep . . . . Full Band

Part II

Pas Seul, "La Favorita" . . . . J. T. Huntley
Concert *a la* Jullien, with solo parts for Cornet and Double Bass
Banjo Solo, Airs and Varia (original) . . . . T. J. Briggs
Pas D'Instruction . . . . J. Bryant and Huntley
Happy Uncle Tom . . . . Frank Brower
Tambourine Duet . . . . Jerry and Dan Bryant
Ballad . . . . J. A. Herman
Rabble Family . . . . Messrs F. Brower, S. H. Wells, Dan and Jerry Bryant
Fling (original) . . . . J. T. Huntley
Banjo Trio . . . . Briggs, J. Bryant, and Wells
Lecture on Woman's Rights . . . . J. T. Huntley

Part III

Good Bye Sally . . . . M. Campbell
To conclude with MISS LUCY LONG

. . . .

PLAYBILL 22: WHITE'S SERENADERS, New York, August 11, 1855

Overture: Piano . . . . J. Kohler

Part I
Overture: Instrumental . . . . White's Serenaders
Operatic Chorus . . . . Company
Night Trampers, or Hip, Hurrah! . . . . Carroll
Hold Your Horses . . . . Budworth
Star of Love . . . . Wood
POP GOES THE WEASEL . . . . C. White
Quick Step . . . . White's Serenaders

Part II
Miscellaneous Varieties
Violin Solo . . . . P. B. Isaacs
Comic Pas de Deux . . . . Budworth and Norton
Ethiopian Fling . . . . W. Vincent
Ballad [unidentified] . . . . G. Wood
NEGRO ECCENTRICITIES . . . . C. White, Budworth and Norton
Burlesque Medley Dance . . . . W. Vincent
Irish Jig . . . . T. Norton

Part III
The Black Shoemaker . . . . Company

. . . .

PLAYBILL 23: PERHAM'S OPERA TROUPE, Boston, July 31, 1856

Part I: By a Troupe of Twelve Darkies of the East
Overture . . . . Full Orchestra
Chorus—"Away, Away" from *Massaniello* . . . . Company
The May Queen, Solo and Chorus . . . . Snow
Aunt Dinah's Quilting Party (new) . . . . Edwards
Boston by Gaslight . . . . Jones
Old Tom Asher (Parody) . . . . Montgomery
Dearest Dine . . . . Duley
Shells of the Ocean . . . . Edwards
Closing Chorus
    "Awake, the Night is Beaming" . . . . Solos by Snow, Jones and Edwards

Part II: Varieties
Violin Solo, Thema and Variations "The Bluebells of Scotland" . . . . Edmonds
Laughable Burlesque of the Ocean Birds . . . . Company
Banjo Solo and Comic Song . . . . Jones
The Act of the Pantomime Violinist . . . . Duley
Old Bob Ridley (New version) . . . . Hunter

Conclusion
Burlesque Opera of the Barber of Seville Plot Laid in Boston with Local Hits

. . . .

PLAYBILL 24: BRYANT'S MINSTRELS, New York, May 27, 1857

Part I

Instrumental Overture . . . . Bryant's Minstrels
Opening Chorus: Operatic [unidentified] . . . . Company
Jennie with the Light Brown Hair . . . . T. B. Prendergast
The Aristocratic Darkey . . . original . . . . Jerry Bryant
Star of the Evening . . . . S. E. Clark
Gay is the Life . . . . Dan Bryant
Gentle Annie . . . new . . . . T. B. Prendergast
The Old Town Crier . . . . S. E. Clark
Mississippi Boat Song . . . . W. P. Lehr
Finale, "See, Sir, See" from *La Sonnambula*
  introducing Lucy Neal . . . . Bryant's Minstrels

Part II

Pas d'Fascination . . . . M. Lewis
Violin Solo, air et Varie . . . . P. B. Isaacs
Polka a la Militaire . . . . Lewis, Mallory, Jerry and Dan Bryant
Flutina Fantasia . . . . Neil Bryant
Favorite Ballad . . . . T. B. Prendergast
The Essence of Old Virginia . . . . Dan Bryant

Part III

Phantom Banjo Solo . . . . C. H. Fox
The House Servant and the Cotton Field Darkey . . . . Lehr and Dan Bryant
Summerset Jig ["Somerset" in other sources] . . . . B. Mallory
Shakespearean Readings with Lucimicus, a stage struck youth
  and Giscippus, the Tragedy, with Imitations . . . . Dan and Jerry Bryant

[Conclusion]

Plantation Song and Dance or Southern
Life Down in Alabama ["Old Gray Mare" or "Get Out de Wilderness"] . . . . Company

. . . .

PLAYBILL 25: WOOD'S MINSTRELS, New York, September 19, 1859

Part I

Grand Opening Overture . . . . Troupe
Opening Chorus . . . . Company
Row, Row the Boat . . . . J. Lynch
The Laughing Darkey . . . . Eph Horn
Near the Banks of that Lone River . . . . D. S. Wambold
Viva L'America, "Home of the Free" new,
  composed by H. Millard Esq . . . . R. Abecco
I'll Throw Myself Away . . . . Ned Davis
Lady Love, the Flowers Are Sleeping Serenade (new) . . . . J. H. Collins
Grand Finale [unidentified]

Part II

Dance . . . . Master M. Lewis
Ballad . . . . D. S. Wambold
THE PERFORMING ELEPHANT
Proprietor . . . . J. Lynch
Herr Drizzleback Vondelsmith, the Elephant Tamer . . . . Chas. White
Introducing the celebrated Elephant BOLIVAR, half brother to Round Heart
WOMAN'S RIGHTS LECTURE . . . . Eph Horn
Mob of Mischief-Making Musicians . . . . White, Davis, and Vaughn
Patriotic Darkey . . . . Ned Davis

Conclusion

The Bedouin Arabs, introducing the mysterious disappearance of Mr. Eph Horn in a flour barrel
and La Perch Equipose.

. . . .

2   Blackface Parodies of American Speech and Rhetoric: Burlesque Lectures and Sermons, Political Orations, Comic Dialogues, and Stories

BELOBED BRACK BRODREN,—Me tend to dress my scorce to you dis nite on de all imported subject of Language, an de various tongues ob difern nations and niggars, libbin and dead, known and unknown: an in so doing me shant stan shilly shally bout preface to de subject, but run bang at him at once like mad bull at "dam haystack."[1]

The first minstrel show in 1843 included the "Locomotive Lecture" delivered in dialect and recalling a young man's fanciful history of his social escapades. Within the year the Ethiopian Serenaders were offering burlesque lectures on phrenology, and by 1846 other companies regularly scheduled similar comic presentations dealing with the new popular "sciences" of biology, mesmerism, and psychology.[2] Minstrelsy did not invent the burlesque lecture or sermon. Both burlesque types were conventions of English stage comedy, recorded from orally transmitted folk parodies in England and the United States and re-created by professional and amateur writers for newspapers and magazines.[3] There were at least three established preminstrel sources that provided models for blackface comedians to develop: the burlesque sermon, the lecture parody, and the mock political oration. Each of those types had several variants that could be adapted to a variety of purposes. By the early 1850s, for example, blackface comedians donned female attire to lecture on women's rights and ridicule the changes in gender roles suggested by the major reform groups of the period.

Lectures or sermons were not included in every antebellum minstrel show but appeared often enough to have been important ingredients in the repertory. Table 1 reveals that the most popular subjects parodied in the minstrel shows were lectures on magnetism, phrenology, women's rights, and the typical commemorative addresses delivered on social and historical occasions. These rhetorical types are

Table 1. Representative Sample of Burlesque Lectures, 1843–60

Lecture Title	Performer/Company	Date
Locomotive Lecture	William Whitlock/Virginia Minstrels	Mar. 20, 1843
Burlesque Lecture on Magnetism	W. W. Newcomb/Virginia Serenaders	Apr. 29, 1844
Burlesque Lecture on Magnetism	Unidentified/Christy's Minstrels	Unknown [1845]
Skientifik Lecture on Phrenological Bumps	John Brown/Sable Brothers and Sisters	Mar. 13, 1845
Locomotive Lecture	R. Edwards/Ethiopian Melodists	Unknown [1848]
Burlesque Lecture on Phrenology	Cool White/Ethiopian Melodists	Sept. 5, 1848
Burlesque Lecture on Phrenology	R. White/Campbell's Minstrels	Oct. 10, 1848
Burlesque Lecture on Phrenology	R. White/Campbell's Minstrels	Oct. 17, 1848
Burlesque Lecture on Phrenology	S. A. Wells/Ethiopian Serenaders	Nov. 30, 1849
Lecture . . . on the Locomotive	Unidentifed/Virginia Serenaders	Sept. 22, 1849
Burlesque Lecture on Magnetism	S. A. Wells/Virginia Serenaders	Dec. 26, 1849
Burlesque Lecture on Phrenology	Wells and White/Pierce's Minstrels	Aug. 1, 1850
Burlesque Lecture on Psychology and Biology	Unidentified/Parker's Ethiopian Opera Troupe	Aug. 12, 1850
Lecture on Phrenology	Unidentified/Thorpe's Band of Minstrels	Dec. 12, 1850
Lecture on Biology	Francis Lynch/Harmoneons	Jan. 21, 1851
Brudder Bones' 4th of July Oration	Unidentified/Buckley's Serenaders	May 7, 1852
Burlesque Lecture on Phrenology	S. H. Denman/White's Serenaders	Nov. 7, 1852
Short Lecture on Woman's Rights	W. W. Newcomb/Wood's Minstrels	July 13, 1852
Burlesque Lecture on Phrenology	S. H. Denman/White's Serenaders	Nov. 7, 1852
Lecture on Woman's Rights	Unidentified/Campbell's Minstrels	Sept. 1, 1853
Lecture on Women's Rights	J. T. Huntley/Wood's Minstrels	Oct. 6, 1853
Burlesque Lecture on Woman's Rights	J. T. Huntley/Wood's Minstrels	Oct. 13, 1853
Burlesque Lecture on Women's Rights	Unidentified/Christy and Wood's Minstrels	Dec. 22, 1853 (?)
Lecture on Phrenology	Cool White/Sanford Opera Troupe	Oct. 19, 1857
Women's Rights Lecture	Eph Horn/Wood's Minstrels	Sept. 19, 1859
Seven Ages of Women	Dan Gardner/Sanford Opera Troupe	Oct. 3, 1859

related to other parodies performed by nonminstrel comedians and performers in a variety of entertainment contexts and are based on sermons, stump speeches, sales pitches, educational lectures, and other types of popular public discourse. Each general type contains its own special collection of attributes that comic writers could parody easily by exaggerating idiosyncrasies in speech, gesture, vocabulary, or rhetorical style into comical surrogates for listeners living in a primarily oral culture still dependent on legitimate forms of public rhetoric for much of its information.

Language and dialect differences were key elements in the earliest *published* blackface burlesque sermons written (some would now say "collected" in New York and Philadelphia) by Charles Mathews Sr. (1776–1835) during his first visit (1822–23) to the United States. Mathews presented the results of his discoveries in a series entitled *A Trip to America* (London, 1824), offering lectures, sermons, and other "impressions" similar to Charles Didbin's highly popular *Table Entertainments*.[4]

What Mathews brought to his English audiences was a series of scenes depicting the oddities of the American "colonials." Mathew's performances were apparently quite well known in the United States, a discovery he made during his second visit in 1834. This time he occasionally met near-riotous audiences of nativist Americans, one of whom suggested, "The scoundrel ought to be pelted from the American stage, after his writing that book which he did about six years ago, called 'Mathews Caricatures of America.' This insult upon Americans ought to be met with the contempt it deserves. After using the most vile language against the 'too easily duped Yankees,' he thinks thus to repay us for our kindness toward him. But we hope they will show him that we are not so easily duped as we were then, and drive the ungrateful slanderer from our stage forever."[5]

That criticism was representative of the range of opinions sometimes swirling around Mathews's caricatures. The financial news is even more telling evidence of Mathews's impact on American audiences. When he made his first tour, Mathews regularly reported home to his wife that he took in $1,200 to $1,800 (in 1820s dollars) nightly and was "congratulated on my $1000 benefit."[6] Mathews's popularity depended on his ability to make audiences believe that "the leer of the eye, the motion of the lip, the crook of the finger, the turn of the toe, the ringlet of a lock, intonation of voice, [and] every demonstration of emotions or passion" fit the caricature he was presenting.[7]

One of his most influential caricatures was that of a fund-raising preacher in a type of "preacher jest." This piece was a mock fund-raising sermon that questioned the sincerity of all preachers who depended on miscellaneous contributions for their livelihoods. Mathews provided models for satirists who ridiculed the sincerity of white *and* black revivalist preachers, the first type being what I have labeled the "fraudulent ask."

The Fraudulent Ask: "Letter to James Smith."

My wordy bredren, it a no use to come to de meetum-house to ear de most helly-gunt orasions if a no put a de *cent* into de plate; de spiritable man cannot get a on widout de temporarilities; twelve 'postles must hab de candle to burn. You dress a self up in de fine blue a cot and a bandalore breechum, and tink a look like a gemman but not more like a gemman dan put a finger in de fire, and take him out again, widout you put a de money in a de plate.[8]

Mathews focused his attention on preachers' compensation and class distinction. The request for money was a feature that remained constant in the genre, although it was not so prominent in examples performed and published during the 1850s. By that time the "passing of the plate" was relegated to the concluding section, where it appeared as a framing device reaffirming the "church" atmosphere after the preachers' sometimes ridiculous digressions.[9] The salutation ("my wordy bredren") served a similar structural function, for in most examples the preacher began with a clear statement of purpose, some reference to a "text," and a brief description of himself or of the general preacher "type" to which he belonged (the persona is always a *he*), all in a dialect appropriate to the social or economic class of a real or imaginary audience. The audience, which would have been both "worthy" and conscious of the pun on *wordy,* played an important part in these orations, and the behavior of the temporary "congregation" was consistent with the generally high level of interaction characteristic of the nineteenth-century theater in general and the religious revival or camp meeting in particular.

The Mathews and minstrel examples both emphasize a special lexicon reflected in portmanteau words chosen for their vague relationships to everyday vocabularies. *Spiritable* and *temporarilities* might be considered errors if the audience misunderstood the respective suffixes (*-able* and *-ality*), but both suffixes yield plausible portmanteau words for listeners able to determine quickly that the root words are *spiritual* and *temporal.* The word *hellygunt* suggests a pretentious pronunciation of *elegant,* something that a comic performer would have to display. The sound (*helly* + *gunt*) also suggests a regional pronunciation easily exaggerated. The deletion of the /h/ in *hear* and the substitution of /s/ for /t/ in *orasions* are not merely eye dialect (spelling differences having no effect on pronunciation) but probably reflect Mathews's English background, with the dropped voiced /h/ producing the homologue *ear* of some English dialects and the latter word given a spelling more suitable for Church of England prayers than for the invocations used in the humble evangelical American *meetum houses*—a term used in the Ethiopian songsters several decades later, where it usually characterizes differences between black and white religious practices.[10]

The /a/ served as a prefix, an enclitic, and apparently as a filler or coasting syllable, something a preacher could "ride" on until the next word came to mind or use as a rhythmic marker accompanying a breathy exhalation as the sermon intensified. In more conventional transliterations of creole dialects, the enclitic is linked to its parent word by a dash, as in *put-a* and *tink-a.* Presented in that manner, both words more closely approximate the enclitic forms, notably /a/ and /ee/, associated with the creolized variants of West African Pidgin English (WAPE).[11] In other places, such as the phrase *de fine blue a cot* (ascot?), the appearance of the *a* suggests a missing consonant /s/ that was not indicated by an apostrophe. The same phrase is part of the discussion of appropriate dress and includes what might have been intended as a pun, *bandalore* for *banderole* (a long narrow streamer or ribbon with an inscription) or *bandolier.*

The dialect in the example cannot be dismissed as marginal just because it appears to have some ungrammatical features, does not match the common patterns of Standard English, or is inconsistent with other transcriptions of black dialect. The question is whether it is similar to other dialect attestations from the same period. Does it belong to a family of dialects, or is it merely an idiosyncratic sample taken from one unrepresentative subject?[12] Mathews undoubtedly recognized one of the many American dialects in current use and unwittingly preserved a useful example that shows how preachers could use ethnicity or class distinction to motivate reluctant donors.[13]

Mathews's efforts found fertile ground in American comedy because burlesque backwoods sermons were published in sporting newspapers during the preminstrel period and in special collections available for purchase. Impromptu performances undoubtedly occurred in the oral tradition, especially in the frontier humor of the preminstrel period. The following sample appeared in *Spirit of the Times* (Sept. 7, 1834) and illustrates one of the mock eulogy types of American humor found in the minstrel show.

Mock Eulogy: "Parson Stovall's Hair-Suit Sarmon"

I am gonter take this 'casion, howsomeyer, to use Brother Bodymount as an object lesson to hole up afore all ove yew: see hum layin' thar, they monst'ous bushy growth fum his face acoverin' right near all ove him, includin' them new undertakin' clase [clothes]. . . . And rightcher I turns to what I has tex fer this soum [solemn] occasion. It am in the holy scripters, sumwhar atween the leds of the book known as the Book of Regurgitations, and when you finds it you'll find that it says: "Let them that hath beards hear what the *spirrit* seth unto the bushes: Shame unto them that cultivates hair: fer they hath not strength nor length elsewhere; woe unto them that flees from a razor, fer they shall be cut off in the latter day." . . . Sampson had a beard— whar *he now*? Abe Linkhorn hed a beard—whar *he now*? Sez I, what about *'im*? Linkhorn hed a beard, used it cover leetle bumps on his cheek—fer he is hidden in the business! Deekin Bodymount had a beard—whar *he now*? Ah! Let them thet hes beards hear what the *spirrit* seth unto the bushes: SHAME ontu them thet cultivates hair, fer they hath not strength nor length else where; WOE untu them thet flees from a razor, fer they shall be cut off in the latter day—Ah![14]

The essential stylistic ingredients of the burlesque sermon or lecture genre are present in this example. First, the humor often depends on an elaborate pun or pun chain. The controlling metaphorical basis for the quoted piece is the pun on *hirsute* and the extended play on attributes associated with hairy creatures in American folklore. Second, the biblical allusions are connected both to the style of the language (archaic prepositions characteristic of the King James Bible) and to the prescriptions of shame and woe (typical of prophetic literature). Third, the application of the burlesque to topical events is also obvious in the references to Lincoln, who was first elected to the Illinois legislature the same year the sermon was published, and to the popular belief, expressed in American advertising, that linked facial and body hair to male virility.

The mock political oration and its variants that ridiculed the language of lawyers, doctors, or other professionals were usually associated with public celebrations or occasions set up specifically to demonstrate the particular actor's skills. Court-room scenes could occur in comic skits, and political speeches could appear as part of the "musters" of local militia units whose annual drills provided occasions for "high ceremony and mockery." With the repeal of the militia laws in most states before the Civil War, the transformation of the militia into the National Guard, and the loss of interest in patriotic military displays since the 1960s, militia activities have largely become lost traditions for most Americans, although recent concerns about paramilitary groups have raised some questions about the history of such units.[15]

Militia muster day and other public holidays, particularly the Fourth of July, offered suitable subjects for literary comedy during the nineteenth century. The tradition dates back at least to Charles Mathews, who introduced a "Militia Muster" skit into his *Trip to America* that served as the inspiration for George "Yankee" Hill's "Joe Bunker" character in *Down East; or, The Militia Muster* (1830), a piece one English critic described as "an extravagant caricature of his fellow-countrymen's peculiarities."[16] Among the better-known examples of the burlesque militia muster from the antebellum period, as well as an outstanding model for other satirists of the era, was Oliver Hillhouse Prince's "Militia Drill," first published in 1834 and included in Augustus Baldwin Longstreet's *Georgia Scenes* (1835). Less well known but equally compelling as an account of actual practice was Emily Burke's description of the "manner in which military parades are conducted all over the South."

> In the first place all their musicians are colored men, for the white gentlemen would consider it quite beneath their dignity to perform such a piece of drudgery as to play for a company while doing their military duty. These colored musicians are dressed in the full uniform of the company to which they belong, and on the morning of the day in which the several companies are to be called out, each band in uniform, one at a time marches through all the streets to summon all the soldiers to the parade ground. . . . In Savannah there are five of that kind of companies that exist in all the states and are called by all names, composed of all such persons as only perform military duties because they are obliged. . . . Scarcely any two were dressed alike or took the same step, . . . some with shoes on one foot and a boot on the other, some with their guns wrong end up and others with them on their shoulders, wearing their knapsacks bottom up and wrong side out.[17]

The militia muster was more than a subject for the humor writers, however. Muster day was a time for active civic involvement in creative comedy and satirical social criticism of one's fellow citizens. The muster, which was regarded as a civic obligation for the men of the new republic, involved a parade that was subject to a considerable amount of good-hearted joking, because the troops often *were* a rag-tag bunch. One of the most common scenes of holiday fun featured a mocking of the mustered troops, with the jokers wearing motley costumes, carrying sticks or other such found objects as guns, and marching in less than orderly fashion.[18]

The persistence of the militia movement through the Jacksonian era and the development of "target groups" or "target excursion" clubs (these names were given to fraternal organizations devoted to public display in parades and marksmanship at local shooting ranges or fields) created opportunities for male socialization and display in America's growing cities during the antebellum era.[19] The militia, however, may also have been singled out as a special target for humorists because membership and leadership were often associated with class and wealth.

Prince's humorous story satirized an important social tradition of the 1830s and reinforced male fraternal beliefs and social attitudes. The muster provided opportunities for proud display of patriotism, class differentiation (most militia groups were organized along class lines), and sometimes benevolent but often raucous competition. In the 1840s and 1850s, minstrel companies found in militia drills a source for their own style of blackface comedy, the most popular pieces being something called *The Dutch Drill* and "Brudder Bones Fourth of July Oration." The search for further examples is imperative, for these preminstrel pieces are significant not only as ingredients in minstrelsy's contribution to American popular humor but also as clues for reconstructing the contexts in which blackface entertainment operated. This introduction to the various types of spoken humor sets the stage for a consideration of representative examples of the burlesque lecture, the mock sermon, and other materials of the typical antebellum minstrel show.

The most popular lecture in antebellum minstrelsy was probably the set piece (and its variants) entitled the "A Negro Lecture on Locomotion," the item already mentioned as one of the chief attractions of the first minstrel show in 1843. The lecture is actually a mock autobiographical boast similar to the roarer types encountered in Crockett and Fink tales.

A Negro Lecture on Locomotion: As Recited by Great Western and R. Edwards

I is what you call a skientific loco-smokive bulgine niggar. I is a gwine to gib you de multiblycation ob de variation. I had been radder an unfortunate niggar in my day— dar was five of us in the family, an I was de smartest ob 'am all 'up 'um. I used to tell de udder niggars whedder dey knowed nottin or nottin. I didn't know no more dan dey did all de time. De old woman, she took a great likin to me kaze she sed I dissembled my fadder: an so I did, he was darkcomplected an so did I. So you see, dey gib dis niggar his edjumfication, an I studied de pumbsologus; but all de bumps dat I could find, was de bumbs ob de bullgine. Well, I tho't I'de go a trabblin, an I starts off for de norph; while I was dar I gits in a good many 'sieties: one 'siety in 'ticklar, an dat was de mixation 'siety. I remained in dat 'siety until I got perfecly disgwasted, an den I leff' um. I said something one day in one ob dar boya-lition meetins, an dey tern'd de niggar out. Dar was a question came up 'fore de house: "Whedder de sun stood still while Julycum Cezar fought his battles." I rose up to consplain to be members de 'surdity ob de fack. I told 'um dat if de sun stood still on its own axletrees it would come in contract wid de sheanry ob de globe, bust de bulgine an turn de cars off de track. Berry soon arter dat, I receabed a perlite note, statin: dat I was compeled from de 'siety for an asswassination ob de meetin; so I bowed berry disgraceful to de president an retired in disguss. Eber since den, I'be joyed de company ob de white folks; but since I'be got use'd to um, I don't mind it much; besides dat, a white man is jis as good as a niggar if he only behabes himself. While I was dar, I gits quainted wid a white gal: she wanted me to marry her, but her mudder would not stan dat, kaze she sed if de people seen us walk down de street togedder' dey'd say she had lost some ob her relation, to see her hab *mournin'* hangin on her arm. Well, I did'nt marry her but I gits 'quainted wid a brack gall, dat was dar; an she was so brack in de face dat she couldn't tell when it was daylight; de wool curl'd so tight on de top ob her head dat she couldn't shut her eyes; an her nose—by golly! dat was so flat, dat whenever she went to blow it, she had to put tar on her fingers to keeb a good hold ob it; at last the poor critter died, an de reason of her deff' was: dat her legs was so crooked de blood couldn't circumlate freely frougout dem; she died ob de delirium triangles. Den I paid my distresses to annudder colored lady, an she had eyes his like de mudturkle dove, she shot a harrow right slam bang frough de niggars gizzard. Dar was a gwine to be a caravan come to town one day, so she ax't me to take her down to see it; so I took 'er down to de show, an we see'd all de wild beasteses—dar was de hippockopatamus, de rynossemhoss, de gygragge, de rangumerus, an de rangumsnou-routang wid all de udder animals; an she called de bullyphant de emigrant. I didn't say nottin I knowed it was be bullyphant all de time. But wha[t] tickled dis nigger most, was to see de ladies rid[e] on de bullyphant in such an elephant manner; it throwed de old niggar right up in de higest of his emigrant. Den I took her into de show to see de big animaconder sarbint. De showman sed it was 'bout 40 feet from de head to de tail, an 45 feet from de tail to de head; it eats a whole hog, tail and all, an sometimes, niggars when he sed dat, Dinar would'nt stay dar any longer case she sed de snake might eat her as it eat mudder Ebe. Besides dat, it was berry warm in dar dat arternoon, berry warm indeed! I ax'd her how de flemometar stood, an she set it was flirty tree degrees 'blow freze. I had to take her out, an as we were gwine throo de caravan, she got animal magumtized de guygraffe kicked at 'er. When we got home' I heard dar was a gwine to be a ball in town dat night among de niggars; but I did'nt get an invitation, so I thot I'de write one myself, an go down widout any. Arter I gits in de ball, I gets up in one corner; I did'nt say nobody to nottin, nottin did'nt say nobody to me. None ob de niggars did'nt see me, but it struck me berry forcibly dat I was dar all de time! I kept dark. Byme-bye de brack galls dey see me, an dey 'gin to come 'roun me, an try to coax me to dance. Well, I told 'um dat if dey'd coax me a good while, I couldn't desist 'em. I gets de steam up, an when I gin to dance, dey seed I was double jointed, but de gall sed my legs were hung on swibbles. Den I went ahead like de baggage car 'fore de bullgine; I danced so long dat de ole musician niggar bust his claminet all to pieces—one niggar jumped into a barrel ob oyster shells an scraped himseff to deff. Anudder niggar got so exited, dat he run his head through a board fence an, gin to holler *fire!* But to cap all de ole fiddle niggar, he begin to cutup some o' dem carleykues ob his'n an fell ober one ob de benches an run a' knot hole in his eye. So de ball come to a confusion den, an all de niggars exsited 'sept me, an I went home. I'de got to be such an unrully niggar, dat de old woman said I must do somethin to take care ob myself; so I set up as a student in an oyster cellar. Arter I had got along pretty well in an oyster line' an trusted out all de oysters to de niggars, I ax 'um for de pay, an dey said dey had took de benefit ob de axe. So I shut up shop and got my brudder musician niggar to larn me no [to?] play on de instruments; so dey fotch one to gib me a lesson; dey call'd it de Wioletusbrasstutus. When I ax how to make de notes, he sed I must go down wid a ladder to get de low notes, dive under de brige [bridge] for de middle notes, an take a pint of yeast to raise de high notes. It took a bullgine to wind up de screws, four pair of horses to draw de bow, an when dey wanted to stop it dey rolled on an omnibus. Byme-bye dey gin to blow de old instrument wid steam, an I turned bullgine niggar; so if dey get me off de track dis time, dey've got to grease it dat's all. Dey won't be no niggars, fore soon; dey'l hall turn to bullgines, all 'sept de little niggs, an dey'l turn to tea-kettles. Dar wont be any concasion for steam doctors, unless some ob de niggars bust dar bylers, an if dey do dat, dey'l scall demselffs to deff. Speakin ob dat puts me in mind of new byler I'be been getting into my sheanry; an for fear dat all de saftey valves ai'nt jis as dey should be, I'll raise de steam once more an gib 'um a trial. So clar de track, niggars, an look out for de cars when de bell rings. (Imitates a Locomotive.)[20]

The example is an informal narrative composed of a set of anecdotes chained together by little more than the forcefulness of the narrator's continuous emphasis on his own "character." Although the headnote refers to the piece as a recitation, the "reciter" or narrator identifies himself in the first few lines, where he also announces the controlling metaphor of the piece, namely, that the black speaker is being compared to a locomotive engine ("bullgine" in minstrel parlance). The persona centers the discourse on the alleged differences ("multiblycation ob de variation") between himself and the audience. Begging the audience's sympathy, the speaker sketches his general personality ("unfortunate"), his family background of parents and siblings, and the personal qualities that set him apart from his peers.

The example abounds in malaprops, puns, and rhetorical variations. The character *dissembled* (resembled) his father, a statement of obvious fact, and the relevant line includes a characteristic phrase inversion: *an so I did = and so did I,* the second item being technically redundant but typical of the repetitions found in public oratory, which employs parallels to clarify relationships or to create humor. Other examples of these parallel structures are "I didn't say nobody to nottin, nottin didn't say nobody to me" and "dey seed I was double jointed, but de gall sed my legs were hung on swibbles." The character poses as a know-it-all but is reasonably self-effacing in admitting that he really does not know any more than the people he imitates. The persona is rebellious, reflecting a dissatisfaction with social conventions that would have endeared him to his audience. The character shows little concern for personal courtesy or public decorum, even though he acknowledges the audience's existence when he "bows disgraceful to the president" and "retires in disguss."

The speaker is a disruptive presence not just because he is "brack" but because his statements reflect a distaste for the hypocrisy and social constraints that would inhibit his social behavior. The conflict between rights to individual self-expression and proprieties of social order recalls similar conflicts in examples drawn from the western "roarers" and Crockett types popular during the same period. The supremely "American" example is the nonconformist who flaunts convention and establishes a behavior pattern contrary to the norm. Behind all the regional dialects and racial caricatures lies a more vigorous resistance to the behavioral conventions imposed by life in an urban society and to the social organization required to create and enforce civic order.

The "Locomotive Lecture" moves on quickly to the major issues of the day: phrenology, abolition, temperance, miscegenation, race relations, and urban social life, each one ridiculed briefly to maintain the fast pace of the lecture. Phrenology becomes *pumbsologus,* but given the controlling metaphor, the speaker finds only the *bumbs ob de bullgine.* Just as the bull-plus-engine neologism pushes the connection between an agricultural image and the modern machine that transformed American transportation, so does the individualized naming process allow the speaker to dissemble legitimate advocacy organizations by giving them absurd titles. For example, the "mixation 'siety" probably refers to an abolitionist group that admitted the character only to disqualify him later for his disrespect of the organization's ideas.

The speaker disputes the prevailing but questionable assumptions held by other members of the club. Did the "sun stand still when Julycum Cezar fought his battles?" The performer can only *consplain (complain + explain)* and invoke a mechanistic metaphor suggesting a humorous chain of effects based on the heliocentric motion of the solar system: if the sun stood still ("on its axletrees"), all the rest of the planets would bump into each other causing a massive "train wreck" in the universe. The controlling metaphor of rail travel represents something the audience could easily understand, of course, and the "cars off the track" will later be associated with the Hutchinson Family's parody of Emmett's "Old Dan Tucker" known as "Get Off the Track." The "bullgine" was a powerful and unstoppable behemoth capable of both pulling a freight train *and* serving as an image of the forward motion of American life and commerce.

The speaker generally flits from one organization or relationship to another, his individualized and achronological experiences reflecting those of a vagabond traveler who observes life from its margins. His relationship to white society is particularly noteworthy when he introduces the possibility of an interracial marriage after a most casual and fleeting association, contrary to the accepted courtship patterns of the period. This reference to marriage plays on the white majority's fears about amalgamation. As in most of the satirical comments on contemporary society found in minstrel rhetoric, the subject is never addressed in a sustained and organized attack. The issue is simply displaced by a fairly weak metonym ("to see her hab *mournin* hangin on her arm"), with the black color of the character being mistaken for the dark mourning costume associated with public displays of grief. Marrying a black man could be considered a kind of social death—the mourning metaphor—but such a consideration is the absurd extreme for what is really a weak joke.

Although the tenor of the lines dealing with a black man in a white world may seem racist, the passage does capture the ambivalence found in later examples of minstrel show humor, namely, that "a white man is jis as good as a niggar if he only behabes himself." The comparison reinforces the common association of black and white with good and evil, however, just as the description of black women reflects similar negative attitudes about facial features and hair styles found in period songs. But the character in this lecture may be paying only incidental attention to the various physical characteristics of his alleged sexual conquests. The example, then, is similar to other examples of male boasting rhetoric of the period.

There are differences in the descriptions of the three women encountered in this lecture. The lecturer moves from the white woman whom he cannot marry to a black woman described in the most negative physical terms. The excursion into the reasons for that woman's death (circulatory complications) leads to an even more painful pun ("delirium triangles"). These references to the character's encounters are also characteristic of the male boasting tradition, even though the character's list mentions only three: the girl he loved but could not marry; the ugliest woman he met, whom he subsequently ridicules;, and his final conquest, the "gall" whose *mudturkle dove* eyes mock the *turtle dove* imagery of contemporary popular songs, just as her arrow mocks Cupid's arrows, which were part of the popular iconography of love in the mid-nineteenth century. The lecture shows the same generally negative and antisentimental attitudes toward women found in the blackface songs and sketches of minstrelsy's first decade.

The third encounter (beginning "I paid my distresses to annudder colored lady") introduces a humorous sequence of social activities typical of the period, for example, trips to the circus, where the speaker finds the pitchman's rhetoric nearly as absurd as his own; attendance at balls; and participation in events representative of contemporary society. The narrator's female companion is of course frightened by some of the circus animals. But the speaker quickly assumes the role of the omniscient male protector by pretending to know about all the exotic creatures he sees, thus continuing the same charade that opens the lecture. The structure, then, is tight even though the piece seems similar to a free association of randomly chosen episodes.

After the satire on music instruction methods—even in the 1840s piano and violin lessons were provided to young ladies and gentlemen—the imagery of the steam engine dominates the concluding lines of the lecture and leads to the instrumental effects used to imitate the typical sounds of a train. The final image—the one that probably related to the idea of "how the niggar raised steam"—finds the narrator firing up his "new byler" to make sure the "safety valves" are as "de should be." The act ends with the performance of a locomotive imitation, which some ensembles used as a transition into the "Railroad Overture," a combination of sound effects imitating the departure and arrival of a steam-drawn train.

The previously mentioned nonce word *pumbsologus* refers to one of the most popular set pieces of the antebellum burlesque lecture style, the "Lecture on Phrenology," a humorous rebuff of the "science" of identifying human behavioral traits by speculations on skull shapes and cranial topographies. Among the more dubious but nonetheless significant popular blends of anthropology and the emerging field of psychology ("Sykeschology" in minstrel parlance, after the character Sykes in comic plays of the period) during the nineteenth century was Orson Fowler's adaptation of Franz Gall and J. K. Spurzheim's theory of phrenology, known to blackface comedians by the less imposing names of "bumpology" or "freenology."[21]

Phrenology was so popular that seventy-two books on the subject were published between 1825 and 1855, a significant indicator of interest in a pseudoscience whose "concept of the individual reinforced the individualistic, democratic spirit of the age."[22] Nevertheless, there were skeptics of both phrenology and hypnotism among the many humorists and social critics of the era, whose creativity would almost certainly have been inspired by the following item from a daily paper:

Prof. Rogers' Experiments on "Human Magnetism"

Prof. Rogers has delivered over sixty lectures in this city, to public audiences and private classes, and magnetized nearly two hundred different individuals during the past four weeks—persons of highly respectable character, and most of them incapable of using any fraud or deception. . . . Twenty-three teeth have been extracted . . . while in the magnetic state, without causing any pain or movement of muscle. . . . Those experiments and many others that have been made by Prof. Rogers, have convinced us that amputation and other surgical operations may be performed while in the mesmeric state without any dread of pain to the individual and with more safety than they could be under any of the different preparations of aether or any other agent known.[23]

The subjects of phrenology and mesmerism were treated in several blackface lectures, at least one comic sketch by a leading southwestern humorist, and the Ethiopian skit entitled *Wake Up! William Henry*. There are many examples, but one of the most representative is the following extract from a burlesque Lyceum lecture published in 1846 as "A Black Lecture on Phrenology" in *Follitt's Black Lectures, No. 1*.

"My Frens" you dissemble here dis nite for hear lectar on Nalagy—nalagy, my frens, is de art ob telling de fief [thief] niggar from de bones niggar, de fool niggar from de wisdom niggar, de grug [grog] niggar from de water nigger; an how dat done I wonder? eh! why I tell you by the bumps on him "dam tick" skull—on dis side you may observ I hab cast of be head of a genelman ob color, an on de oder side I hab Cast ob de head ob a common white feller—berry well, here, my fren, I tink it rite to obserb, dat all great an clebber men of every nation are BLACK; fuss der was Aggamemnon an de Duke of Wellington, bof black; one all ober, an de oder only black heart; den der was Nerer de fiddler, Napolean de butcher, and Crumwell de brewer, all berry black indeed; den der was Robispir, Marat, Billy Waters, "George de Fort," an de debil, all black; but de LAST genelmam not so black as de rest. Dus you see, my frens, dat all great pipple are black; black-legs, black-hearts, and black-guards; and me furdder wish to obserb dat in my mumel obinion dat EBERY BODY was black once, ob course, during the DARK AGES.[24]

The play on black as a moral quality, however, is strongest when the speaker mentions characters from English and French history, as well as contemporaries ("Billy Waters"), or denigrates historical personages by linking them with specific trades ("Crumwell [Cromwell?] the brewer"), all of whom are ranked as worse than the "debil" himself.[25] The speaker compares them with the personification of evil, but *not* on the basis of their "bumps," because the "lectar" is really a pretext for the play on the word *black*. The application stressed in the charge is that all people share similar qualities ranging from skin color (though the lecturer takes pains to point out that the "*organ* of color is not to be found in BLACK PIPPLE kase black NO COLOR, nor in white kase dey hab no color") to the lack of conscience and from benevolence to amativeness, the choice of word or behavior depending apparently on those the speaker can transform into puns.

The example from *Follitt's* illustrates the English skepticism about phrenology, but such doubts and comic responses to questions about the new science were echoed four years later (1850) in a collection of southwestern humor containing a story by Johnson J. Hooper (1815–62). Hooper created a hilarious scene in which an experiment in phrenological analysis provides a good evening's entertainment for a group of Alabama legislators assembled in the bar of a prominent Montgomery hotel. A character named "Staven O'Cargin, Frinnolygist and so forth," interrupts the group's songfest and business discussion by inquiring whether there "is here iver a gintleman here wud let me have the faalin' [feeling] ov his head, to help a poor man in his thrubbel, and amyuse the good company." O'Cargin conducts a "burlesque examination" of Mac, a character who "took a pride in being considered" ugly but whose "generous heart could cover the universe with its charity." The ugliness of Mac's head made him a fit subject for phrenology, but the reliability of the "science" was sure to be tried, given Mac's behavior during his occasional bouts of intemperance reported in Hooper's burlesque story entitled "The 'Frinnolygist' at Fault."

[O'Cargin places one of his hands on Mac's head.]

"Riv'rence, gintlemen, here's riv'rence. At laste, here's the hole in his head where the aurgin should be! He's no more riv'rence than a cow, gintlelmen, an' he'd make fire-wood of the Thrue Cross. But we'll pas on. Ah, self-estame. He's *that* be sure, as big as a turnip. Yes, gintlemen, he's the aurgin of *estame*, and the aurgin of '*stame*,'" touching Mac's nose with his forefinger—"beautful! He'll dhrink like a fish and srthrut like a paacock!"[26]

Hooper's Irish "frinnolygist" is another outsider with a "florid complexion, yellow *snaky* locks, and a battered hat" who speaks in a "most unctuous brogue" and whose diagnosis leads to a fight scene—the same physical "business" that so delighted minstrelsy's audience—between the professor and his subject. The dispute is resolved by an explanation of the pun on *stame* (steam organ for venting anger), after which everyone joins in a drink to toast the "palpable hit" O'Cargin has made with his performance. The target of the humor is the science of phrenology, which fit so well with the southwestern humorist's love of social rivalry among males and the entertainment value found in brutal sporting competition.

The Irish character's dialect contributes to the humor of the sketch because it ensures that only those qualities the group already appreciates about the stereotypic Irishman (lover of drink, fighting, and practical jokes) will be manifest, not other "negative" characteristics (social critic and supporter of social causes) that would fracture the relationships of the tight-knit group of politicians.

Although I was not able to find an example of a lecture on phrenology actually used in a minstrel show, I did find a representative example in the lectures that William Levison (1822–57) published in *Black Diamonds* (1855). Levison's mock lecture follows by almost a decade the first reference to phrenology in an early minstrel show. One of the major topics of this burlesque lecture is the phrenologist's assignment of functions to the various organs or parts of the brain based only on the surface characteristics of the skull. The Levison example identifies some of the stereotypic traits attributed to African American workers but with typical ambivalence proceeds to generalize about some of the characteristics and behaviors that transcend ethnicity, namely, the debilitating features of undisciplined romantic love.

Lecture on Phrenology

Freenology consists in gittin 'nolage free, like you am dis evening; it was fust discu-bered in de free schools, and was always looked 'pon by de larned as being closely connected wid "E Pluribus Unum." . . . De hump in a cullered man's hed . . . am siterated on de top, and called by de siantifick de cokanut bump; dis bump lays in a triangular form ober be bump of don't care-a-d—nativeness, which every black man's hed am vully blessed wid. . . . De bump dat am moss cultiwated in de cullered man hed, am call'd on Fowler and Wells' map ob de brane, "Amativeness." Dis am de bump dat plays de debil wid de fair sex, bekase dat am whar Kupid springs from; dis bump lays in de back ob de neck, near de coat collar; it am call'd de bump of *lub*. . . . It am de bump what all de selfishness and wickedness ob mankind lays; and I wod say a word to dem fellers as hab got an ober quantity ob it. Look out how you fool you time 'round de opposite sex, kase wen you fall in lub dis bump swells to such an 'xtent dat it overwellms de hole brane, common sense am kicked out do be drainum, and lub rain 'spreme till every ebenue leadin to de soul am oberflowed wid de milk ob human kindness, and it takes an "orfullpoletice," as we say in French, to traduce de swell'd bump to its proper size.[27]

The speaker steps outside the frame of the lecture to warn about fooling "'round de opposite sex" with a reference to a swelling organ *not* located in the brain. Levison's blend of racist opinion with moral warnings about uncontrolled emotion as the source of "all de selfishness and wickedness ob mankind" shows how the binary concepts of black and white can be exploited to convey conventional moral principles dear to the hearts of urban social reform organizations seeking to control human sexuality, especially its public manifestations in prostitution and homelessness.[28]

The fascination with phrenology was due in part to its promise of providing "scientific" explanations for racial traits and behavioral differences based on the relative sizes of "localized brain areas." Its greatest deficit was the lack of any real scientific evidence for the "brain maps" the phrenologists thought they had discovered. Phrenology was one of many attempts to justify the assessment of an individual's worth on the basis of dubious theories about brain weight, skull size, cranial thickness, and a host of other ill-formed differentials vague enough to convince a generation of hopeful patrons that distinctiveness was just a matter of hat size.[29] Blackface comedians, however, like the better scientists working in the field, recognized the fatal flaw in Fowler's "system" and ridiculed his attempt to devise a theory of behavior.

Even with the emphasis on color as an indicator of character flaws, burlesque speakers did not focus solely on the ridicule of black persons. Having made their point about the differences between blacks and whites, lecturers usually jumped to generalizations about widely shared characteristics or values held by the majority or dominant group. The premise of the phrenology lecture is that character can be discerned by examining the indentations and protuberances in the skulls of individuals, a procedure that even the speaker questions by pointing out that bumps can be caused as much by blows to the head as by genetics ("kase when people get into a row dey sometims get nock on de sconse and dat break one organ in two or free"). The general theory is soundly refuted when it can be shown that even a superficial injury can produce an artifact sufficient to mislead the best scientific "experts."

The English example from *Follitt's Black Lectures* reveals its topicality in the choice of the "heroes" or targets drawn from recognizable power groups of politicians or generals. Although ethnicity provided the context for the joke, the actual humor arises from the speaker's charges against some of the character types. In the American example, however, the topical element is less important than the exploration of American values and a stronger emphasis on the negative qualities the speaker ascribes to African Americans. By revising the pronunciation of the /e/ morpheme from the short *e* of *phrenology* to the long *e* of *freenology*, the persona is able to pun on American education and political slogans. Again, however, the highly selective catalog of "bumps" does not apply to blacks alone; all races share the same qualities. For example, "amativeness," which is located in the "bump of *lub*," is associated with "all de selfishness and wickedness ob mankind" because the debilitating qualities of the emotion can affect everyone regardless of color. The balance of Levison's lecture reflects his own racist views about blacks, but his applications suggest an equal disdain for lower-class whites as well because they share a "self 'steem" to be observed in "dere horror ob swasheatin wid de wite trash, and de manner in which dey 'steem up; kasionally, fully probes."

Theories are only as good as their ability to predict behaviors with some credibility based on solid scientific evidence. The antebellum comedians were skeptical of any pseudoscientific theory arguing that a simple blow to the head could transform a dunce into a genius or reduce the brilliant lecturer to a mere mumbler. The commonsense test that trauma, not transformation, is the more likely result of a cranial assault provides the most pragmatic refutation of the science of phrenology. But that would not be funny; one additional comic device is required.

Exaggeration offered the most effective way of ridiculing the theory of bumpology by allowing the performers to emphasize one side of the binary opposition of black and white, rich and poor, or low- and high-class. The wider the differences between the two contraries, the more likely that the association of *blackness* or Irishness could be used to enhance the lecture or story. The authors of the burlesque lectures assumed that black means difference with a deficit regardless of whether the term applied to the characters presented on the stage or to the white working-class idea that "blackness could be made permanently to embody the preindustrial past that they scorned and missed."[30]

Although bad science or pseudoscience served as a frequent subject for burlesque sketches, special professional languages were also victims of the blackface satirist's invention. Like the other burlesque lectures, however, there are relatively few published examples of sketches drawn directly from the minstrel repertory, which suggests that much of the minstrel repertory is not recoverable.

One of the best examples from an actual minstrel performance is the following excerpt programmed by the Christy Minstrels and published later in *CPM4*. The persona in the Christy piece is Judge Augustus Hannibal, the same name Levison used in his published burlesques of professional legal language.

> Gemmem ob de jury, a fellow sneakin' up to de door like a hyena, softly enterin' de habitation ob de peaceful and happy family, and in de most mendacious and dastarly maner strayn', stealin' or enticin' way that are yaller dog. I cannot, I will not dwell upon the monstrosity ob such a scene. . . . Arter a brief view of disere [this here] case, let me retreat ob you to make up your minds candidly and unpartially, and give us such a verdick as well might reasonably suspect from such an enlightened and intolerant body of our feller-citizens. Rememberin' de language ob brudder Nimrod, who fell at de battle ob Bunker Hill, better dat ten innocent men escape, dan one guilty should suffer. Adjourned sine die.[31]

Courtrooms were only one source for the exhibition of rhetorical skill. Americans also enjoyed patriotic speeches, religious (mainly revivalist) sermons, scientific lectures, and, given their love for the independent entrepreneur in the freewheeling nineteenth-century economy, the burlesque of the pitchman and circuit-riding preacher in "The Erasive Soap Man."

> "Gentlemen," he said, or rather sang, "gentlemen, I offer you a splendid article, a superb article, an incomparable article—magical, radical, tragical article!" [Here he displayed a cake of his soap.] "Magical, radical, tragical, *erasive* soap! . . . It cleans oilspots, removes stains, hides dirt, brightens good colours, and obliterates ugly ones!—such is the virtue of the all-healing, never-failing, spot-removing, beauty-restoring, health-giving, magical, radical, tragical, e-ra-sive Soap!" . . . Why, gentlemen, it clears the complexion of a Negro, and makes a curly-headed man's hair straight! It removes the stains from the breeches and spots from your coats—in like manner, it purifies the conscience and brightens the character! . . . It is the only cure, panacea, medicamentum, vademecum, in all globular creation. Then come up, tumble up, run up, and jump up, like hung'ry patriots, and buy my incomparable, infallible, ineffable, inappreciable, coat-preserving, health-restoring, dirt-removing, speech-improving, character-polishing, virtue-imparting, compound, ERASIVE Soap."[32]

The pitchman's love of the lexicon, the rhythm and assonance of word chains, the avoidance of any product description, and the obvious entertainment value of the excerpt are directly similar to the rhetorical excesses parodied by the blackface comedians in their own performances. The garrulous black character is not the sole practitioner of "sweet talk" but rather a member of a whole class of humorous types used in American comedy. Granting an audience's predisposition to believe that some African Americans misused Standard English, the blackface minstrel's attack on American communications customs is not merely an insult to black speech practices; it is a satirical comment on all speech that manipulates audiences through emotional appeals, extravagant claims, and clever distractions numbing natural skepticism about dubious products.

What the burlesque sermons and lectures were to the stage, mock reports of political meetings (with invented "minutes") were to the newspapers of the period. Recognizing the New York newspaper readers' interest in problems experienced by different racial and ethnic groups, the editors of the *New York Clipper* regularly provided comic stories in Black English, Hiberno-English, and any prestigeless social dialect characteristic of working-class groups. The first example, which signifies on Irish attitudes and speech mannerisms, is from the "Shamus McFudd Letters," a collection supposedly written by a fictional traveler to America whose purpose is to afford his readers with "as much amusement as did the notes of Dickens and other Trollopes." The McFudd letters were parodies of Dickens and the other travelers who criticized America in several notoriously negative travel books. The second example brings to public attention the "minutes" of a mock gathering of the so-called Bowery B'hoys. The group, represented by Mose, Lize, and the other lower-class characters, was featured in numerous sketches and plays set in New York's working class between 1848 and 1858, the period when burlesques of public oratory appear to have been most popular in newspapers *and* minstrel shows.

"Letter from Shamus McFudd" (*New York Clipper,* July 9, 1853)

After me an Tim had seen the illiphant, an exhamined his trunk to see how many klane shurts he had, we wint to see a grate big snake, wid a body the size iv a whale, an a tail that wud wind 3 times around Pat Clansey's cow stable. Och! sich a monster I niver want to clap me ises on agin. His mouth was so big that he cud take me an Tim at wan swaller widout openin it at all; and when his 2 jaws cum together, the Whole house wud shake as it is had a fit iv the ager. They feed him on broiled pavin stones, an whin he takes dhrink, feth he laves the river so dhry that all the ships ran aground. The divil a wurd iv a lie I'm telling ye.[33]

"Minutes" of B'Hoys Meeting (*New York Clipper,* May 21, 1853)

Josey Stinson [Speaker]: I had a talk with the petishners for this road, and I told 'em how we done these kind o' things, and what I thought it would cost 'em to get it put through. I told 'em we charged for rail roads at the rate of $2000 for each one of us, and if they didn't chose to give it, why we could get as many as we chose to that would. They kind o' didn't like it at fust but they found I was in earnest, and so they giv in at last. . . . The gentleman from the 6th [Ward] stated that this Five Points road was for the benefit of some fust rate fellers, and he thought everybody would like it after it was down. . . . The petishners want to start with a track to the Tombs to the Pints [Five Points], and another track from the Park to the Tombs for the benefit of the Alderman.

Spenser: I spose if all hands votes for it that the people will say we've been bribed. It's always the way. If a few of us votes agin it, it'll make the thing look about right, so I goes agin it.

Some dialect words were imported into the vocabulary to help establish some credibility for the "delineation" of stage characters, because language differences were among the primary indicators of otherness in real life. If the dialect samples were too extensive, however, the average listener unfamiliar with the dialect's deep structure as well as its surface features would probably not understand the performance. Dialect cannot, then, be a direct indication of the writer's or performer's intentions or beliefs. The difference is important because in the theater, the audience witnesses not a private communication but a public performance created with an anticipated humorous effect.

Regardless of whether the burnt cork comedians held racist beliefs themselves, they recognized (as the newspaper writers had also) some phonological similarities between Black English Vernacular (BEV) and lower-class or low-prestige dialects—for example, *'em* and *dem* for *them,* the pronunciation of *such* as *sich* (something apparently common in Hiberno- and Black English), and *arter* for *after* or *agin* for *again,* these last two terms being holdovers from Yankee dialect. The examples emphasize phonology (*slabe* for *slave*) and distinguish between the use of the /th/ phoneme by each group. The Irish speaker is characterized by the /dh/ to /th/ feature, the black is marked by the complete deletion of the word-initial /th/ in favor of the /d/ phoneme, and the B'hoys use the same abbreviated form of the objective pronoun in the *'em* for *them* substitution. All the texts highlight the phonological features (sounds) by highlighting orthographic peculiarities (spellings) rather than imitate deeper structural elements of grammar and syntax. Each of the examples shows some problems of tense agreement, shifts in voice, confused subordination, and run-on phrases, but the major issue seems to be that the speakers sound different or that they speak in a colloquial manner.

The common elements are the use of hyperbole to force the humor of the situation, the rationalizations that allow Shamus to mock Barnum's promotions, and the corrupt politician's ability to mask the lack of integrity behind the feigned opposition to the railroad while explaining how the bribery system worked. The connection between the different forms of bondage in Ireland and the United States is a recurring theme throughout the minstrel shows and the public rhetoric over slavery. It reflects an ethnocentric view and emphasizes the false analogy linking two forms of injustice an ocean apart. Regardless of the number of dialect elements exhibited in the examples, the significance of the texts lies not only in how they sounded to audiences but in what they actually signify. Each speaking character is placed among language "misusers" because vulgar statements are the most effective way to express the ironies embodied in their beliefs or experiences. The dialect attributed to the abolitionists in the "Negro Lecture on Locomotion" sounds like Black English and allows the author to rank them among the low-prestige African American language users whose cause they championed.

The minstrel repertory provides good examples of the ways foreign languages and American dialects were treated as indicators of difference irrespective of their function in particular sketches, sermons, or songs. The best examples of the conflicts between different languages in the minstrel repertory are the pastiches of Italian in the burlesque operas and the jokes about the French in comic narratives and lectures such as the one shown in the epigraph.[34] The use of a few sounds or phrases of a language reflect "the acoustic images formed by members of the in-group when they listen to a foreign language." The caricature of the target group is usually established "once a few features and sounds are identified as characteristic of that language."[35] Although these theoretical conclusions apply to stereotypes of foreign languages, they can also be used to investigate the ways in which various dialects may be exploited in a monolingual culture regardless of whether the speakers use clothing, body language, or other cultural markers to strengthen their portrayals of out-groups.

The pieces excerpted from the New York Clipper show how dialects and linguistic practices were displayed and illustrate the major genres of rhetorical satire. The lectures, sermons, and mock political addresses ridiculed American public oratory from the camp meeting to the temperance hall and from the outdoor political rally to the hallowed Lyceums. The scripts were parodies of the "educational" discourses that, as an editor of Putnam's Monthly observed, "have come to be one of the established winter institutions; not in the cities only, but in many country towns, both large and small."[36]

The burlesque lecture had its counterpart in the mock sermon, which was based on the examples created for the urban revival movement and for the preacher circuits in rural America. Preaching was one of the most public forms of rhetoric, and published sermons were popular with nineteenth-century readers. Many clerics "preached" in lecture halls and other public spaces about the major issues of the day. Henry Ward Beecher's sermons at Plymouth Church were "printed weekly in the Plymouth Pulpit . . . and read by thousands." Religious magazines (New York Evangelist, the Presbyterian New York Observer, and the dozen or so other weekly religious newspapers) also printed sermons delivered by local or visiting preachers.[37] The sporting papers (the New York Clipper and the New York Spirit of the Times) also included humor among their many offerings. The colorful styles of the revivalists and the emotional intensity with which they delivered their messages were well represented by the published works of popular preachers and demonstrated in the style of Jedidiah Burchard's description of hell. "Do you know what hell is? Well, I'll tell you. . . . An ocean of liquid burning brimstone . . . walled in by great walls guarded by devils armed with pitchforks. High on the crest of the waves of fire, the damned soul is swept toward this wall, where the sinner thinks he may gain at least temporary rest, but when at last he has managed to climb part of the way out of this sea of fire he suddenly finds himself pitch-forked back and swept out by the receding tide."[38]

With the new waves of immigrants from the countryside and abroad, the cities had become fertile ground for the Lord's cultivators, and the "religious press for any week in the forties, fifties, or the sixties would reveal news of grace abounding from East Troy, Wisconsin to Parsippany, New Jersey." The blackface comedians recognized, as did the more serious critics of the older revival movements, that "too much emphasis might be placed on the actual experience of conversion and not enough on the formation of a Christian *character*." The concentration on emotional effects provided the appropriate trigger for a burlesque sermon, which only inspired the minstrels more because the popular revivals of the 1840s "took on the style of popular journalism," which was combative, sensationalist, provocative, and of doubtful accuracy.[39]

Journalists and editors entered the debates over the appropriate means for expressing religious fervor or over the moral issues affecting public life. James Gordon Bennett, the racist and antiabolitionist editor of the *New York Herald,* published lampoons of Jacob Knapp's revivalist sermons.[40] Knapp, whose sermons were filled with "little tales about stubborn animals and children," earned at least $2,000 a year with "pathetic pleas for free-will offerings during worship, as he cited an ill wife or pointed to the shabby clothing imposed on him by vows of poverty." The extravagance of Knapp's "pathetic pleas" for money contrasted with the vilification other clerics heaped on the theater profession, something guaranteed to inspire contemporary comedians to create burlesque sermons. Noting that the New York clergy's attacks on the theater contained "such perversions of fact, unjust conclusions, and wickedly uncharitable expressions," the editors of the *New York Clipper* thought about "having bound copies of the rules governing the prize ring presented to the clerical pugilists."[41]

Some revivalist sermons were shaped by a controlling image that governed the choice of ideas and guided the development of the symbolic or suggestive language required to make the message more compelling, as shown in the excerpts quoted from an example created by the Reverend Thomas De Witt Talmadge, a popular New York preacher. "Religion is sweetness, and perfume, and spikenard, and saffron, and cinnamon, and cassia, and frankincense, and all sweet spices together. . . . It counteracts all trouble. Just put it on the stand beside the pillow of sickness. . . . It sweetens the cup of bitter medicine, and throws a glow on the gloom of the turned lattice. . . . And it is good for rheumatism and for neuralgia, and for low spirits, and for consumption; it is the *catholicon for all disorders*."[42]

The flower or herb garden replaced the waves of fire and the burning brands of hell for audiences in the 1850s, suggesting some theological compromises that minstrel performers, rooted as they were in the past, could use to exploit religious rhetoric in the same humorous ways they dealt with medical chicanery, spiritual "rappings," mesmerism, laughing gas, and other panaceas for all human ills. The images Talmadge used to describe the healing effects of religion very nearly overwhelmed his message.

The burlesque sermon presupposed the creation of an imaginary religious or quasi-religious setting in which those attending the performance were expected to behave temporarily as a "congregation." Now transformed temporarily into "worshipers," audiences could recall the experience of being preached to and inhabit the appropriate symbolic environment (the theater) in which burlesque creations replaced the religious rhetoric of the chapel. The actual religious affiliation of the congregation was largely irrelevant. The mock sermons were recognized as general *burlesques* of the preacher types and not necessarily as imitations or impressions of specific figures. The preachers whose behaviors made them the objects of ridicule were almost always stereotypes of evangelical or fundamentalist types, the only requirement being that the preacher character's fervor be fueled by highly emotional appeals and his rhetoric be cleverly contrived to engage the audience.

The number of burlesque sermons available for study today is relatively small, making the samples especially valuable for their specific style characteristics and cultural significance. Dan Emmett's "Negro Sermon" is probably a typical example of the type and follows the Mathews model. The opening statement of Emmett's "Negro Sermon" (1860, although probably performed many times before its publication) establishes the preacher's role and defines his status within the imaginary congregation characterized as "bredren and sistern." Emmett's salutation addresses the audience as if its members were hearing the words in a church: "Bredren in de lamb an sistern in de church, when a preacherman rises up to undress de congregashum, he am conspected to stan right sqarr up an dressed, and took he tex jis as soon as he finds it; an heah am mine, yoa fine it by lookin arter it, if you look long nuff in de right place. *I run till I got it; picked it up but couldn't fine it; den froed it down an went away wid it.*"[43]

The malaprop *undress* [address/undress] and the portmanteau word *conspected* [conspectus + expected] reveal Emmett's ability to play on the ambiguity of words for comic effect. Neither word is a likely choice for an uneducated preacher seeking a religious rather than a comic effect. Emmett exploited the "simultaneity of two or more words within one meaning," and he used the word *undress* because its immediate meaning revealed it as a substitute for *address* while its suggested yet simultaneous connotation (*undress* the congregation) played on possibilities inherent in the preacher's lust and the audience's sense of privacy. The puns in this example do not contradict the syntax of the sentence, yet they divert attention away from the possibility that this example will deliver any kind of moral argument.

Following the introduction, the burlesque preacher usually promises to "'gins dis sarmon by commencin as fur back as de firs part o'de tex . . . an arter I git goin, jis watch de applicashum." The real or mock biblical text serves as a theme that generates excitement through its repetition and brings the speaker back to his subject after mandatory digressions. Emmett's preacher persona promises to interpret the apostle's statement and then offers an alternative that frustrates the hearer's expectation for some obvious and meaningful application. Beginning, as he promised, with the first part of the text, the preacher continues his explorations of the text.

> *I run till I got it,* what a splendid desertion to go to bed to; "dars millums in it." 'Twill do to sleep on: 'twill do to dream on, an will barr siften clarr to be bottom. When you look at 'um from de "five points" ob de compuss; you bear a little to de leeward, an den luff right up agin 'um, and if yoa git shipracked in de lustrification, den you skull yoaseff ashoa wid a jacknife. Den yoa see de meanin of de 'postle when he say: de "archiloozikus winky-wamity, an reelderackerus weltigooberous am too flamity bango, for de crackaboolity ob its own watchafalarity."

The digressions, always intriguing mental exploits in the hands of an experienced preacher, are clever flights of lexical fancy and rhetorical invention. The "Five Points" reference is to the First, Fourth, and Sixth Wards of New York City, which James McCabe described as "a terrible and wretched district," "the realm of Poverty" where "want and suffering, and vice hold their courts" and "where the poorest of the city can stand (at the intersection of Park and Worth Streets) and gaze into Broadway with its marble palaces of trade, its busy, well-dressed throng, and its roar and bustle so indicative of wealth and prosperity."[44]

The dream traveler meditating on the text *I run till I got it* is *shipracked* (a pun on *shipwrecked* and *racked* or wracked, which refer to storm clouds, destruction, and upset). He is subsequently caught in the *lustrification,* another pun derived by combining the verb *lustrate* (by way of the Latin *lavare,* meaning "to wash or purify ceremonially," or *lustrare,* "to purify") with the noun *purification.* Lustration, though not likely to be understood by the audience, was one of the rituals that the Roman people underwent after the five-year population censuses and a ritual that Roman Catholic women underwent after childbirth. Catholics also celebrated the Feast of the Purification of the Blessed Virgin Mary annually on February 2.[45]

Journeying on his path from the Five Points, the victim is given nautical directions as he first turns *leeward* (away from the wind) and then "luffs" (for *luff up,* meaning to sail closer to the wind). The only escape Emmett's imaginary victim has from such wretchedness is to *skull* (for *scull,* which means to use one oar for propulsion) himself "ashoa wid a jacknife," truly an unworkable proxy but all the more fascinating as a humorous substitute for a functional oar. The sailing terms are consistent as the controlling image around which the sermon is organized. The rest of the example *seems* to reflect the babble of tongues spoken among the inhabitants of Five Points, but the apparent nonsense of the script hides a more subtle form of wordplay in which grandiloquent display is equated with social importance and lexical complexity with critical thought.

The structure of Dan Emmett's antebellum sermons is deceptively simple.[46] He follows the same "controlling image" method identified earlier as a feature of the examples created by Mathews and Talmadge but exaggerates both the nautical terminology and rhetorical imagery by creating nonce words allowing the performer (or reader) considerable freedom to play the scene by emphasizing the speaker's emotional transport.[47] If language is viewed as a form of domination, then the ability to manipulate language gives the user temporary control over a situation, something folklorists have recognized in the use of words rather than fists as a means of attaining importance within a social group.

None of the burlesque sermons was meant to be taken literally—the vocabulary prevents that—and the example was probably successful only as long as the preacher was able to incorporate an effective level of symbolic discourse that often crossed racial, religious, and regional boundaries. The authors and performers of the blackface burlesques must have realized that the same emotional and playful elements found in their sermons were part of a similar preacher jest tradition that Johnson James Hooper captured in "The Captain Attends a Camp-Meeting": "Then he tried to argy wi' me—but bless the Lord!—but he couldn't do that nother! Ha! Lord! I tuk him, fust in Old Testament—bless the Lord!—and I argyed him all thro' Kings—then I throwed him into Proverbs!—and from that, here we had it up and down, kleer down to the New Testament, and then I begun to see it work him and then we got into Matthy, and from Matthy right straight along to Acts; and *thar* I throwed him! Y-e-s L-o-r-d!" Hooper argued ingenuously that "no disrespect [was] intended to any denomination of Christians," especially the Methodists, "whose respectability in Alabama is attested by the fact that *very* many of its worthy clergymen and lay members, hold honourable and profitable offices in the gift of the state legislature; of which, indeed, almost a controlling portion are themselves Methodists."[48]

Most of the mock sermons suggest that the preacher's persona was related to that of a relatively low-status character with little education working in rural areas or traveling the frontier. Such a conclusion is wrong. City preachers were also frequent targets of satire. Even William Levison's Julius Hannibal character recognized that the primary indicators of a preacher's success were his ability to attract an audience, to gain the ego gratification associated with public adulation, and to make a profit on his oratorical talents. Those characteristics are illustrated by the references to Horace Greeley and Henry Beecher in the following lecture: "Brudder Greeley and Brudder Beecher hab boff lectur'd an' dey never ax'd me a tall; an har I hab been lecturin' to de peeple for de lass year an' a haff, an' I'll bet a hunderd clams dat I spoke to fifty times as menny folks as edder one of dem."[49]

Levison's text, which was intended to ridicule Beecher and Greeley, whom Julius Hannibal particularly detests, reveals that some features of Black English (BE) phonology correspond quite accurately with the conventions of minstrel show dialect. The /th/ phoneme is seldom found in BE or its sources (WAPE); instead, BE speakers often substitute /d/ or /dd/ for /th/ between vowels, as in *brudder*. Such a substitution may have been conventional when Levison published his burlesques, but BE was still the sound source for the word. The substitution of /f/ for /th/ in *boff* is common in the dialect also. The word-final /t/ in *last* is replaced by the prolongation of the /s/ in *lass*, and the common transcription of *hab* for *have* reflects the pidgin pronunciation pattern of replacing voiced stops and aspirants in word-final position with voiceless endings.[50] But some of the other elements (e.g., *edder, menny, peeple*) seem more characteristic of eye dialect, intended for readers rather than listeners.

The success of the burlesque sermon depended on more than phonological features, however. The listener would also have needed to have some knowledge of an actual or at least a typical revivalist "script," because the burlesque text functioned as a form of criticism casting doubts on the efficacy and sincerity of religious speech making. Given the differences in religious expression and the association of social behavior with class differentiation among the various American denominations, the revivalist styles of salvation, "testifying," and "mourning at the bench" would probably have been poorly suited to more sophisticated converts or to those whose rituals assumed passive participation.

There is a wide range of evidence that both whites and blacks appreciated what is known in African American culture as "preacher jests," which poke fun at religious oratory.[51] The examples quoted previously show that the burlesque sermon was common among white and black Americans. Given the fact that Emmett and the other blackface character actors were the impressionists or mimics of their day, each apparently had the talent of hearing and imitating dialects and examples of nonstandard American speech. The emergence of various forms of American English and the distinctions among the classes that used them are the real subjects of the blackface excursions into burlesque sermons.[52]

Blackface entertainers were well aware of the differences in behaviors and communal ritual practices among various black and white religious groups. Religion and religious issues appeared often in minstrelsy both as objects of ridicule and as subjects for quotation in a variety of verbal or musical parodies. The following example, "Trip to a Nigga Meeting" (*NFM1*, 216), calls attention to the sheer emotional and physical power unleashed by the African American preacher's sermons.

When I got to de meeting house,
Dey say you better go,
Kase you come to raise de debil here,

And jump Jim Crow.
So I creep though de window,
And sat myself a down,
Broder Clem gub de text—
Den dey hand de plate around.
In de ninty-lebenth chapter
Ob de new Almanack,
Dar it tell you all about dare,
De white man and de brack.
He says dat Cane was de fuss man,
Julycome Cesar was de toder;
Dey put Adam on de treden mill,
Kase he kill him broder.
And den dat Mr. Samson,
Was de man who build de ark,
Mr. Jonas was de fisherman,
Who swallowed down de shark.

Negative stereotypes of African American worshipers are certainly present in this song. Blackface preacher jests seldom refer to particular preachers but do appeal to one of the most telling indicators of cultural difference, namely, religious practices different from the forms of worship generally known or assumed by the audience. The number of all-black congregations in New York increased between 1820 and 1850 from just a handful to fifteen Negro Methodist and five Baptist churches because most of the major religious denominations practiced racial segregation.[53]

Religion was a powerful example of difference, and the burlesque sermons, regardless of which religious group was the butt of the joke, seem critical of theatrical or charismatic forms of preaching. The previously quoted texts emphasize the charismatic role of the African American preacher and confirm one characteristic element of the burlesque sermon, namely, the creative conflation of different biblical texts through a free-association process acceptable in practice because it illustrates that the preacher is being moved by the Spirit into incongruous pairings of characters ("Cane was de fuss man, Julycome Cesar was de toder").

The printed sermons always deal with types, that is, with preachers who view the congregation as a group of sinners or skinflints and usually address the audience in the "brothers and sisters" rhetoric typical of evangelical Methodists or Baptists. The sermon assumes some knowledge of the Bible, and the verbal connections are sometimes so clever that the text should not be considered mere nonsense. Even if the black vernacular dialect was exploited for little more than local linguistic color, the brief excursions into alternative forms of English were enjoyed because they were not seen "as affecting the evolution of the hegemonic American English." It is generally true that even some of the most obviously racist and linguistically troublesome examples reflect rather strong and often quite narrow opinions about a variety of contemporary subjects.[54]

The contexts for the burlesque sermon or stump speech appear to be broader than the imagined circumstances of the black church or black speaker's talk before a fictional African American benevolent association, because the dialect was used for purposes other than "delineating" African Americans. Some Americans probably could not tolerate the fact that articulate black speakers such as Frederick Douglass demonstrated a great command of Standard English. Such facility would provide convincing evidence that language adaptation and learning have more to do with desire and discipline than with race as a marker of intellectual ability. Dialect use, however, was simply assumed for any unacculturated Americans, but especially for African Americans, because of the prevailing racist theories that linked difference with some form of deficiency.

My discussion of preacher jests assumes that audiences understood the convention and could interpret the rhetoric rather easily. How did they hear the performance in the typical theater? Did the audiences have sufficient information to translate the speaker's vocabulary and decode the typical sermon script at the first hearing? Theoretically speaking, the audience's comprehension would definitely be improved if the listeners were already familiar with the conventions of the burlesque sermon, that is, (1) if they knew from their direct experience what revivalist preachers did, (2) if they heard enough secondhand information about different styles of preaching to imagine the experience, or (3) if they had attended other performances so that they understood the general "script" underlying the particular joke.

The examples were related to divergent rhetorical practices including the techniques some black ministers reserved for speaking to an all-black congregation; the emotional styles associated with rural white ministers; and the hellfire-and-brimstone rhetoric used by urban evangelical revivalists, social activists, abolitionist speakers (a particularly despised group), and labor organizers. Although there are few antebellum descriptions of the performance practices for these sermons, later instruction manuals reminded performers that "a negro stump speech, being only a burlesque, admits of any peculiarities you may choose to introduce" and that "monologuists have a wide license in selecting their topics or *chatter*."[55] Even with that freedom, the choices made by blackface comedians and southwestern humorists are relatively narrow with respect to the subjects that appear in the extant material, and the sermons are more in the style of monologues or lectures because there are no stage directions encouraging audience participation. This is especially noteworthy because the burlesque sermon would have provided a great opportunity to ridicule the practice of speaking in tongues (glossolalia) or other forms of spiritual manifestations practiced by some marginal nineteenth-century religious groups. The only other group singled out for a burlesque treatment was the Shakers, and then only because of the number of apostate groups who decided to "go commercial" and publicize the sect's activities through performances at Barnum's American Museum and other houses on the typical itinerary of traveling entertainment troupes.

Sermons were probably the most common rhetorical experience that nineteenth-century Americans shared. Preaching played a significant role in structuring the religious values embodied in the American character. The blackface comedians recognized that religious charlatans victimized the gullible and exploited the emotions of their audiences for personal gain. The burlesque sermons ridiculed the behaviors of the charlatans as well as the legitimate preachers who relied on emotion as the primary persuasive force in public rhetoric. These mock sermons were also subversive texts, forms of rhetorical criticism extending beyond the ridicule of African Americans. There was also a regional and class bias underlying the comic sermon. African American preaching styles differed from those of *some* white churches in the North, but southern camp meetings often admitted racially mixed groups and included virtually all forms of preaching.

Lectures and sermons appear to have been closely related genres with respect to their contents and the comic devices used to satirize their authors. The mock sermons appeared less often in the antebellum minstrel repertory than did the burlesque lectures, but there was another rhetorical genre that inspired blackface comedy, namely, those forms of public oratory associated with holidays, patriotic events, and public celebrations.

Parades, militia musters, and public celebrations occurred often enough to generate numerous songs, marches, and quicksteps, each with dedications to the local militia unit and its commanders. Meetings of the militia were golden opportunities for male display, especially for political figures seeking greater prominence in public life. When James Henry Hammond of South Carolina attended the State Rights Convention in February 1832, he appeared "resplendently attired for his role of the governor's aide-de-camp in new uniform of dark blue, lace framed collar, gold epaulettes, red sash, cocked hat with white plume, white gloves, and 'State Rights badge.'"[56] In Connecticut the Governor's Foot Guard, originally founded by "forty-four leading young men of Hartford in 1771," was immediately recognizable for its uniform of "scarlet coat, faced with silver braid, buff knee-breeches, black velvet leggings, and fur hat," while the Albany Burgesses Corps was "quite a social group . . . renowned for its military glamour, its precision drilling, and its sumptuous entertainment."[57] The militia movement and the bands associated with it were important elements in the social rituals of nineteenth-century American life.[58]

The militia drill became a subject for comedy in urban centers and rural districts of the North and South. There are numerous accounts of burlesque parades and comical exhibits, but one of the funniest examples is William Cullen Bryant's recollection of the event he witnessed during his 1843 visit to the Barnwell District of South Carolina:

From the dances a transition was made to a mock military parade, a sort of burlesque of our militia trainings, which the words of command and the evolutions were extremely ludicrous. It became necessary for the commander to make a speech, and confessing his incapacity for public speaking, he called upon a huge black man named Toby to address the company in his stead. Toby, a man of powerful frame, six feet high, his face ornamented with a beard of fashionable cut, had hitherto stood leaning against the wall, looking upon the frolic with an air of superiority. He consented, came forward, demanded a bit of paper to hold in his hand and harangued the soldiery. It was evident that Toby has listened to stump-speeches in his day. He spoke of "de majority of Sous Carolina," "de interest of de state," "de honor of ole Ba'nwell district," and these phrases he connected by various expletives, and sounds of which we could make nothing. At length he began to falter, when the captain with admirable presence of mind came to his relief, and interrupted and closed the harangue with a hurrah from the company. Toby was allowed by all the spectators, black and white, to have made an excellent speech.[59]

Speeches similar to Toby's were part of the oratorical context the minstrel comedians caricatured in their own creations, and of the few remaining examples of this comic form, Charley White's "Peabody's Lecture at the Great Soger Camp-Meeting"[60] and Christy's "Jim Brown's Address to He [His] Sogers" are representative. The Christy burlesque of the public commendatory oration, published in *CPM3*, was created as an extension of a scene based on the "Jim Brown" song of 1835.

FELLER-CITIZENS AND BRUDDER SOGERS!

I hab de super infilicity ob undressing a few words of millumtary tictacs to your magnamimously insignificant and superbly extinguished corpse. Brudder sogers! from dem days of de future *dark* ages, wat has passed down de ascending stream of neber-to-be-forgotten oblibium, to de long-past moments of de resent time, de darkies, from whom dem coming periods took their names, was, as your illiterate mental compacities will clearly obliterate de origin, and confounders ob dat perceptible and distinctly invisible human greatness, which to use a well-known panelelgoloram is as clear and transparent to de opake vision, as a pellucid thousand ob de werry thickest kind ob hard-baked bricks.

"Jim Brown's Address to He Sogers" displays several interesting parallels to other forms of political address. The speaker revels in the relationships between ancient and modern heroes, conventions popularized in the academies through the study of the classics and of Greco-Roman history. American political rhetoric still contained references to classical characters and virtues. Minstrel speeches and songs were comic scripts based on the humorous rewriting of historical events. Compressing chronological time, mixing contemporary characters with ancient heroes, and

parodying the great travelers' reports of far-off lands by jumbling geographical locations were among the techniques used in another section of "Jim Brown's Address": "Let me compress upon you detrimental incapacities, de justly celebrated
speech of Captain Julius Caesar, wot he made to Ensign-General Napoleon
Bonaparte, when he soccombed to, and vanquished Pompey de Great at the imme-
morial Battle ob de Nile—which, you know, gem'en and scholars, was fought among
dem wonders of de vegetable world—de 'Egyptian Pyramids,' at de summit ob de
wallye obe de inexcusable Alps—dese was dem berry identical words—'It will never do to gib it up so, Mr. Brown!'"

"Jim Brown's Address" is a highly contextualized and topical example, not an
isolated instance of musical comedy. The reference to the contemporary song "'Twill
Nebber Do to Gib It Up So" (1844) and the similarities to the ostentatiousness that
James Kirke Paulding captured in Nimrod Wildfire's famous speech from *The Lion
of the West* (1830) reveal the relationships between blackface comedians and performers in other forms of theater. The similarities between Jim Brown and the characters found in the popular *Sketches and Eccentricities of Colonel David Crockett*
suggest that the frontiersman and the African American were related.[61] Many notable blackface characters—Pompey Smash, Old Dan Tucker, Jim Crow, Zip Coon,
and Gumbo Chaff—stood "between civilization and savagery." These characters
manifested their larger-than-life personas through "extraordinary feats of oral prowess" represented in words and pictures by "grinning, biting, laughing, and eating"
mouths capable of such ferocity that they were among the most "formidable weap-
ons in the Western arsenal."[62]

Jim Brown cautions "de New York niggers not to stop my way, for if he play de
fool wid me in de gutter lay," a challenge that again resounds with the bravado of
Nimrod Wildfire:

> Mister, says he, I'm the best man—If I ain't, I wish I may be teetotaciously exflunctified!
> I can whip my weight in wild cats and ride strait through a crab apple orchard on a
> flash of lightning. . . . Poh, says I, what do I keer for that? I can tote a steam boat up
> the Mississippi and over the Alleghany mountains. . . . He was a pretty severe colt, but
> no part of a priming to such a feller as me. I put it to him mighty droll—tickled the
> varmint till he squealed . . . bellowed "enough" and swore I was a "rip staver." . . . My
> name's Nimrod Wildfire. Why, I'm the yaller flower of the forest. I'm all *brimstone* but
> the *head,* and that's *aky fortis.*[63]

The boasts of Wildfire, Crockett, Mike Fink, and the other frontier roarers typified the flamboyant style of public rhetoric used among the more adventurous
public speakers of the period. This style of "tall talk" was a way of asserting the pioneering spirit of the American male by means of "a form of utterance ranging in
composition from striking concoctions of ingeniously contrived epithets, expressing disparagement or encomium, to wild hyperbole, fantastic simile and metaphor,

and a highly bombastic display of oratory, employed to impress the listener with the physical prowess or general superiority of the speaker."[64] The ego display involved in such public speaking calls attention to the preacher or lecturer as a public figure and suggests, on the part of the parodist, an understanding of the distinction between rhetoric as a tool of persuasion and as an object of ridicule.

"Jim Brown's Address" exists in the same rhetorical context as does the public commendatory oration and the proclamation of idiosyncratic identity found in *The Lion of the West*. The attribution of verbal extravagance to African Americans is based on more than the assumption that black speakers were imitating frontier rhetoric. Some blackface comedians found that blacks and whites shared a fascination with wordplay and what is now called "fancy talk" or "reaching" in Black English. Both forms of speech not only existed in the antebellum era but have continued among West African speakers, who typically use loan words or multisyllabic synonyms in highly creative ways, especially in contact situations with whites of high status or authority.[65] Some minstrel performers probably discovered the fancy talk behavior during their travels in the South, even though documentary evidence that the "talk of the African abounds in metaphors, figures, similes, imaginative flights, humorous delineations and designations" did not begin to be assembled until after the Civil War.[66] The minstrels may have misinterpreted the fancy talk phenomenon because they could not recognize its cultural implications, but they saw the humorous potential in coining nonce words and using complex figures of speech in that such activities could serve as ways of mocking class differences in American culture.

Returning to the "Jim Brown" example with those thoughts in mind, it is only within the broader context of militia activities and public rhetoric that the speech can be understood. Regardless of whether African American parade units were being ridiculed or the blackface burlesque was connected with any jealously over the black bandsmen's extravagant pretensions, the "Jim Brown" act used ethnicity as a means of attacking the whole artificial world of bombastic rhetoric and deflating self-glorifying statements. The black character may not have been the equal of whites in the real world, but the ridicule with which that figure was associated also reflected on the ideals that the Jim Brown type sought for himself. Jim was, however, a white man in black face; his identity was known just as his role as comedian lessened the seriousness of his attacks on the social behaviors of military and paramilitary organizations.

In the songster edition, "Jim Brown's Address" served as a prelude to the revival of the "Jim Brown" (1835) song, which contains boasts, threats, and political or topical references similar to those in Rice's "Jim Crow."[67] Both "Jim Brown" pieces were intended as burlesques of the militia system at a time when street comedy and public celebrations or demonstrations were gradually being replaced by institutionalized commercial theater. The Jim Brown songs also suggest public parades by

African Americans as sources. African American parades were apparently well known in some parts of New York and New England.

"First of August" celebrations in New England were reported in Garrison's *Liberator* and a number of other publications.[68] The appearance of brass bands in the celebrations has been documented throughout New England, principally in Boston, Providence, New Bedford, and Lowell. Similar occurrences involving music and "street theater" were held on "Lection Day," which was scheduled for various dates in the different states and which was "the most important ceremony for New England blacks."[69] The ceremonies associated with the day seem to have continued into the 1830s and could have provided important sources for interaction between whites and blacks, the kind of interaction in which different costumes, languages, and musical activities would have been observed.

The comic costuming seems to have gone both ways. In Philadelphia costumed groups known as "fantasticals" and representing white working-class groups frequently paraded during the 1850s. Their actions often led to violence, and evidence presented at an 1857 inquest described one group as wearing "white costumes, plumes and hats, blackface, and gold earrings."[70] With costumed groups of both races performing in the streets, it is likely that African American groups satirized whites, who in turn viewed the events as sources for comic songs and stories about blacks.

For whites who wanted to create burlesques of blacks, the Pinkster festivals in New York State were good sources for information about African Americans. Specific links have not been established between Pinkster and Ethiopian comedy, nor have solid connections been made between parades such as the 1827 New York event sponsored by the New York African Society for Mutual Relief and the burlesque parades found in the minstrel shows.[71] But the lack of strong connections at this stage of popular culture studies may well be more the result of the general neglect of African American culture by historians than a reflection of the conditions existing in early nineteenth-century cities, where racial interaction was not as strongly regulated by social custom or prejudice as it was after the Civil War. Although it is not clear how much blackface comedians might have known of the so-called men-of-words on some plantations,[72] some minstrel comedians must have read reports of parades such as the one described in James McCune Smith's *Memorial Discourse.*

As the New York African Society . . . the Wilberforce Benevolent Society and the Clarkson Benevolent Society followed each other down the street to the music of their bands "splendidly dressed in scarfs of silk with gold-edgings"—the men and boys five abreast beneath painted and lettered banners—there was "full-souled, full-voiced shouting for joy" from the sidewalks . . . crowded with the wives, daughters, sisters, and mothers of the celebrants, representing every state in the Union, and not a few with any bandanna handkerchiefs, betraying their West Indian birth: neither was Africa itself unrepresented, hundred who had survived the middle passage . . . joined in the joyful procession.[73]

The relationship between the realities of the street and the ordered artificiality of the theater reinforced the growing belief in the importance of codes of social behavior as indicators of class, privilege, or education, because "by the early nineteenth-century, the educated and propertied classes viewed plebeian dramas and customs as rude and quaint . . . or as barbarous, irrational evidence of the degenerations of the lower orders."[74] There may have been some reluctance to tolerate the boisterous performances of the "lower orders" in parades, but there was little hesitation to bring the street into the theater either by the blackface ridicule of militia activities or by William Mitchell's productions of Francis Chanfrau's presentation of the Bowery B'hoys' parades and fire drills in *A Glance at New York* (1848).

National holidays presented special opportunities for public orations celebrating American accomplishments. The Independence Day oration was a staple of public rhetoric in the United States. Most speakers attempted to remind their audiences about the ideals that inspired the establishment of American democracy, but the more pragmatic reveled in turning patriotic fervor into exercises in stand-up comedy, as shown in the following example:

> And what is the cause of this general rejoicing, this universal hilarity, this amiable state of feeling, this love and veneration for this particular day of all days in the year . . . a day that our German population respects and speak of as "more better than good"—a day which Pat, who believes one man is as good as another and a mighty sight better, reverences as he does "Saint Patrick's day in the morning"? . . . In this great and desirable country, any man may become rich, provided he will make money, any man may be well educated, if he will learn, and has money to pay for his board and schooling; and any man may become great, and of weight in the community, if he wlll take care of his health, and eat sufficiently of boiled salmon and potatoes. . . . Any man in this country may marry any woman he pleases—the only difficulty being for him to find any woman that he does please.[75]

Minstrel comedians found models for their burlesque speeches in the orations offered at militia assemblies and public holidays because these events were reported in local newspapers or invented by enterprising writers for the entertainment of their readers. For example, the following published report refers to a formal address allegedly delivered by a Captain Vincent, whose "brilliant, eloquent, and instructive address to the corps of Light Infantry and Boston Light Guards will ever be remembered and cherished by them as the noblest incentive in the hour of need, to fight for their beloved country, and to feel proud that they are embodied in the citizen soldiery army of our great and glorious Republic."[76]

It is not difficult to understand why the blackface comedians found such rhetoric funny or why they were led to the types of inventions illustrated by the following excerpt from "Brother Bones 4th of July Oration," performed by Buckley's New Orleans Serenaders on July 5, 1852.[77]

FRENS AND FELLOW CITIZENESES:

De day which was to habb arribed, habb arribben. Yes, de day of our great national jubilum is here. The day ob which so much had been conscribed and spoken had arribed! De glorious fourth of Independence when de fus' circumlocution . . . scratch wid de goose quill told de tiranific pot-en-tate ob de mudder gubberment dat we was *bound* to jump out of de political sauce-pan and break de yaller pine stick ob de oppressor ober de knee of dungence and contribution: when our faders leabing de possum foot frying in de griddle, de homony untouched in de cupboard, and de pork sassingers dangling in a string ober de fire place to waste dar fragrance on de desart air, seezed de pitchfork and de poker and wid one farwell blubber over dar wibes and children rushed with busticacious ramifacation upon de enemy and impedimented dar progress wid a discharge of baked apples wiggeonllay delibered into their massive and unbroken ranks.

The butt of this rhetorical hyperbole is not an imaginary black orator whose style has been exaggerated into a vehicle satirizing the speeches of all vacuous Fourth of July speakers. The Buckleys showed their ability to treat topical material inventively and capture the comedy in pretentious public orations. The "Brudder Bones" example was performed along with a mock militia drill (Buckley's "Dutch Drill") in a program that concluded with the "Star Spangled Banner." But many other New York companies played the same number, and *The Dutch Drill* was probably a set piece ridiculing the preparations for a militia parade. In 1850 the Virginia Serenaders presented a sketch described as "The New Laughter Provoking DUTCH DRILL," which included "Trouble among the Darkies. Arrival of Recruiting Officers, Greer and Grevare," but the playbill provides little information about the content or the performers' identities.[78]

The Dutch Drill was also performed by Pierce's Minstrels in August 1850, with Eph Horn and Pierce playing the principal parts. The Buckleys had it in their repertory in 1852 but called it "A Burlesque on The Dutch Drill," which suggests an existing source was used for the parody. By August—the start of the new season in New York—Wells's Minstrels had converted the skit into a blackface German piece featuring two characters called Captain Vodheirkelstricker (S. A. Wells) and Corporal Benenhamersteiner (W. Birch) in the portion of the evening featuring the "Peculiarities of the Darkies of the South."[79] The piece continued to appear through the 1850s, and the number of performers had increased to four by November 12, 1857, when Sanford's Opera Troupe presented Cool White as SergtSaurkrautmispecklagerbeermitpretsels [sic], Edward Dixey as Innocent Jerry, James Unsworth as the recruit, and the rest of the company as the Grand Army.

Although the contents of the sketch have not been recovered, *The Dutch Drill* ridiculed the process of militia training and the recruit's ineptness during the early stages of learning the conventions of the military drill. The references in the playbills to one officer or higher-ranking enlisted man and an innocent young man or "raw recruit" suggests that one character was taken through a comic drill routine after which the entire company joined in with some stage business.

The militia parades and demonstrations were opportunities for male display rituals and focused on the prerogatives men assumed as part of their responsibilities as citizen-soldiers. Minstrelsy's treatments of male display rituals and of the authoritarian attributes of military life are only two examples of male roles as defined in the typical minstrel show. Blackface comedy's images of women, however, ranged from sentimentalized objects of male affection to subjects of sexual exploitation, from idealized mothers whose subservience allowed men a fictionalized childhood to cantankerous shrews whose desire for legal equality became a threat to male sexuality and dominance.

Women's rights advocates received a great deal of interest from the minstrels, and that interest had little to do with blackface caricatures of African American women. White performers may have reflected society's general ambivalence about blacks, but they showed an equal disdain for those women who gave public lectures and argued for an increase in women's roles in politics and business. Such lectures began at least as early as 1829, when Frances Wright (1795–1852) became "the first woman in America to ascend a speaker's platform before a mixed audience, an act which (along with her unorthodox sexual life) earned her the epithet Priestess of Beelzebub."[80] The Grimke sisters (Sarah and Angelina) addressed antislavery meetings, and the number of women speaking out on human rights issues increased especially after the Seneca Falls "Declaration of Sentiments" (1848). Lectures on women's rights were advertised in the same columns that displayed the offerings of various minstrel companies in New York. Readers of the amusements section of the newspaper could find examples of serious *and* burlesque lectures, such as the following series:

THE FUTURE OF WOMAN IN AMERICA.—A COURSE of lectures will be given at Mozart's Hall, 863 Broadway, opposite Bond street, on the following subjects.

WOMAN AND HER LEGAL DISABILITIES—Hon. James T. Brady. Thursday, April 1.

FAIR PLAY FOR WOMAN—Geo. W. Curtis, Esq. Thursday, April 8.

WOMAN AND HER WORK—Rev. E. J. Chapin. Thursday, April 15.

WOMAN AND THE ELECTIVE FRANCHISE—Mrs. Lucy Stone, Thursday, April 22.

BENEFIT TO WOMEN OF ORGANIZED EMIGRATION—Hon. Eli Thayer.

These lectures are given in aid of the Shirt Sewers and Seamstresses Union, No. 1 Astor Place. The lecturers have generously undertaken the series in view of the importance of the subject to be discussed.[81]

Wood's Minstrels featured a burlesque entitled "Lecture on Woman's Rights," by J. T. Huntley, on October 8, 1853. One week later Wood advertised another burlesque lecture on women's rights, this one by "Mrs. E. Oakwood Smith."[82] The parody was probably performed by William W. Newcomb (1823–77), who appeared regularly in a old-fashioned woman's bonnet and Pilgrim dress to ridicule the lectures of Mrs. Elizabeth Oakes Prince Smith (1806–93), the independent spouse of the cantankerous downeast humorist Seba Smith.[83] Smith entered the lecture business because her family depended on her income. Those lectures and her *Woman and Her Needs* (1851) made her a subject for blackface parody even though she argued that "woman's highest position . . . is not on a pedestal, as in medieval times, but it is as man's helpmeet in the outside world of thought and action as well as in the home. . . . Her plea, she makes plain is for the good of the race, not for woman or for man, but for humanity."[84]

Smith advocated extending the franchise to women. She believed that voting was no threat to femininity, as some of the opponents of women's voting rights argued, because "the fact of [a woman's] dropping a ticket into a receptacle of the kind, does not look hazardous to her femininity; she might seem to do this with little or no commotion, and return in conscious dignity to her household, and there infuse a braver cheer, and instil into the immature judgments of those committed to her care nobler lessons of life." Smith's call was based on the belief that the ennoblement of her gender depended on the empowerment conveyed by the ballot. "I confess there is something humiliating in this cry of Women's Rights. . . . Unless we can do, as well as talk, it were better to be silent. God forbid I should encourage a race of vixens, it is because I desire to see woman nobly beyond these poor, mean tendencies that I urge her to the full demand of her being."[85]

Newcomb's costume probably identified Mrs. Smith as an old-fashioned New Englander in black dress and bonnet, but a contemporary observer, Robert Grant White (1821–85), wrote that her "bearing was majestically grand, her manners refined and dignified, yet cordial, and taking her all in all, she looked, acted, and moved the born patrician." Henry Clay described her as "the perfect model of the American matron, and a decided ornament to the country that gave her birth. Seldom has a woman of any age acquired such ascendancy by the mere force of a powerful intellect. Her smile is the play of a sunlit fountain."[86]

Smith's lectures and the dress reforms of Amelia Jenks Bloomer (1818–94), who also lectured frequently in New York on suffrage, temperance, gender equality, and education, were parodied in a song known as "Woman's Rights": "A Right Good Ballad Rightly Illustrating Womans [*sic*] Rights" (1853) and "Dedicated Without Permission to Mrs. Oakwood Smith and Mrs. Amelia Bloomer."[87]

Verse 1
'Tis "Woman's right" a home to have
As perfect as can be,

But "Not her right" to make that home
To ev'ry lover free;
'Tis "Womans right" to rule the house
And petty troubles brave,
But "not her right" to rule the head
And treat him as her slave.

Verse 3
'Tis "Woman's right" to dress as gay
As she can well afford,
But "not her right" in doing this
To ruin quick her lord.
'Tis "Woman's right" to claim sole love
From those who with her link,
But "not her right" when troubles come
To change, and from them shrink.

Songs, mock lectures, and comic sermons dealing with women's desires to "speak as commentators" inspired the minstrels to step up their ridicule as the agitation for women's rights increased during the 1850s. The popular press joined the fray, and William Levison published a burlesque women's rights lecture in which Judge Julius Hannibal discovers that "de most remarkable ob all de mankind lecturers am de woman-kind, who cum 'mong us and trow down the gimblet, or gauntlet . . . an openly declar' war wid de Lord ob Creation for de breeches, and spout 'bout wot dey call Woman's Rights."[88]

Julius's position was that "dese womans all want to be Captains, when ole Human Nature formed em spressly for mates!" The problem, as Julius saw it, was that "when a sailor captain ships a mate, he ships a mate, he don't ship a captain." By the late 1850s, the Woman's Rights issue and Shakespearian burlesques were linked in Dan Gardner's (1816–80) sketch entitled "Seven Ages of Women," in which he played seven different roles. Gardner, a cross-dressing comedian who had played female roles for several years, had such success that his creation was taken up by other companies in Philadelphia and New York.

Dan Gardner's Seven Ages of Women

FIRST AGE: The Infant; introduced by Mrs. Brown, a well-known Nurse of South Street.

SECOND AGE: Miss Jenkins, a School Girl in love with Romeo Thompson, with the song "The Life of a Wench."

THIRD AGE: Miss Betsy, a Schoolmistress from Manayunk with a Descriptive Imitation of Colored Children of a Boarding School.

FOURTH AGE: Miss Ellen Simpson, the Belle of the Ball-Room, a Coquette with the Song "I am in Love."

FIFTH AGE: Mrs. Smith, a Mother of Nine interesting youths who toils for her living, assisted with the wash tub.

SIXTH AGE: Miss Parrot-Cage, a meddlesome Old Maid, one who knows everybody
and everybody's business, with a song Introducing Jenny Doolittle, a romantic
reader of Novels and the *New York Ledger* with the song "The Maid that Loved a
Youth."

SEVENTH AGE: Joyce Heath, the Slave of General Washington, late of Barnum's
[Museum] with a short Sketch of her Life and Travels.

INTRODUCTORY FINALE: Fanny Elssler[89]

Gardner's act characterizes the only married person as a workingwoman "who
toils for her living" and presents a stereotypic old maid "who knows everybody and
everybody's business." Two of the characters are single women, one a schoolgirl in
love and the other the belle of the ballroom, roles that continue the blackface tradition's convention of treating women as the objects of courtship. Courtship often
puts the woman figure in a passive-aggressive role or portrays her as a foil for the
male suitor, who is often characterized as a bumbling incompetent whose actions
are obnoxious and ridiculous. There are relatively few extant examples of actual
minstrel show performances, but the following two selections are representative of
the minstrels' concerns about courtship. The first is known as "Brudder Bones's Love
Scrape," which was performed by Wood's Minstrels:

[Prior to the excerpt quoted, Bones narrates the events leading up to his breakup
with Sarah Gruttsy.]

You see I went down de oder night to see dat gal, pulled de string, went in sat down
beside de gal, and began to pour forth some of de words of de foreign poets, when
in come de old man; says he, "Bones, *dar's de door!*" So I got up and *shut de door,*
come back, sot down beside de gal, pressed *her lips,* and de old man sings out again,
"*Bones, dar's de door!*" So I got up, and dis time *I opened* de door. Den de old man
says, "Bones, if you don't empty dis building of your presence, I shall not be responsible for your early decease." So I got up, and when I saw his cowhide boots raised,
I started. When I got out de moon shone most elephant from behind a cloud; de star
didn't shine, 'kase it neber rained harder since de deluge. . . . I could hear nothing
but be beatings of dis poor darkey's heart. And as I went along something whispered
in my ear, "*Onward, Bones!—*dere is prospects ahead."

[Bones arrives home but is unable to sleep. He reports the following to the audience.]

Yes I couldn't sleep; so I took de banjo and tho't I'd give de gal a serenade. So I got
to de house, and played one of dose soul-stirring airs, when all at once de window
histed [hoisted], de shutters opened, and dere she stood in a silk-light form—she
looked 'zactly like Power's Greek Slave, only de Greek Slave was white and she was

black—and wid her hair floating to de breezes, and her eyes like two diamonds shining, in de voice of an angel she exclaimed, "If you don't go away from under dat
window, I'll scald all de wool off your head!"[90]

The second selection is from a comic piece entitled "A Serenader Cut Short" from
the *New York Clipper* (May 21, 1852) but found often enough to have been used
inside and outside minstrelsy.

A "gent" of mind romantic . . . stopped beneath the window of a mansion in the
South . . . [and] touched his instrument, which echoed to his lay of love . . . as he
sung: "Ah! tell me where is *fancy bred?*" And no farther did he sing; for a domestic
of the sex feminine and of Afric's line . . . did the window open and thus addressed
the minstrel: Look heah, you, dar b'low! we'se had two monkeys, two organs, tree
tamboreens, and a triangle heah to-day, young missus think dat quite nuff. If you
want to know whar de sell *fancy bread,* guess if you go to Mass Nichols, corner Camp
and Natchez street, you git it dar in any quantity. Whoo! Go away white man![91]

The examples utilize dialect and various personae to enhance the effectiveness of
the stories. The female characters turn the tables on the men, the courters demonstrate their ineffectiveness, and the joke captures the casualness of encounters in the
contemporary city. The minstrel characters describe the power of music and its function in courtship, the physical features of the woman as object ("she looked 'zactly
like Power's Greek Slave"), the role of the protective father or old male relative, and
the woman's role in determining whether the encounter developed into anything.

The distinctive use of expressive behaviors ranging from language to social dancing and from oral communication to physical forms of greeting were significant in
all forms of nineteenth-century American humor. The lectures debunked pseudoscientific claims or complicated social issues. Very little of the material dealt with
the major point of conflict between blacks and whites, slavery in the South and dis-
crimination in the North. Such avoidance of direct confrontation is symptomatic
of commercialized, commodified popular culture. The black preacher may have
been the object of jest in some sermon examples, and white audiences may have
indeed thought they were witnessing a satirical attack on African Americans, but
that is not at all clear in the limited subject matter covered in the mock sermons.

The burlesque sermons ridiculed strong emotions and occasional excesses of
religious enthusiasm because the success of the typical public preacher had only a
transient effect on belief or behavior. Minstrels viewed the public rhetoric on religion or religious revival as bogus or at least questionable because physical excitement replaced rational argument and principled conviction. The sermons reflected the blackface performer's preferences for less charismatic religious ritual or no
religion at all.

The intensity of different forms of religious experience suggested a theatrical element suitable for satire, given that religious behaviors were based on sometimes intense denominational differences among Christians that manifested themselves in mainstream Protestant opposition to Roman Catholicism and to a variety of sects, notably the Shakers. Some African American religions were even more culturally distinctive because they emphasized community solidarity and encouraged a stronger participatory emotional working out of religious conviction than did other American denominations. Feelings about the need for privacy and the exclusivity of religious ritual among antebellum Americans may have provided strong motivation for using humor as a means of exploring why different groups followed such divergent worship practices. Curiosity about ritual was probably a motivating force behind the adoption of the sermon or oration as a comic vehicle.

Probably few Americans thought much about African American culture as a distinctive element for the interpretation of the American experience, because there was still precious little to identify as "typically American" in the 1840s. The early minstrels found it convenient to emphasize the marginality of blacks in the mainstream of American culture, but at least they recognized the significance of American dialects as important forms of creative expression within various ethnic groups. At the same time, even the comedians realized that black plantation workers and urban hire-outs, northern free persons of color and southern slaves from the Georgia Sea Islands to the Texas fields, retained features of their respective African dialects.

The denial of any linguistic interaction between blacks and whites on the stage or in real life is incorrect, especially if it is based on the conviction that no African Americans "talked" as the minstrels depicted them. There are too many examples of African American phonology, vocabulary, syntax, and other features of Black English Vernacular that refute such denials, even when it is conceded that the minstrels did not fully comprehend how black Americans demonstrated their creative approach to language use through their own dialects. Although some scholars argue that "plantation dialect was fairly uniform throughout the country," that conclusion is weakened severely by sociolinguists' discoveries of many regional variations both in the root African languages that some slaves retained and in the contact situations or discourse communities in which blacks and whites functioned.[92]

Black English was a constantly changing dialect. Now that its fundamental principles have been described, it might appear that there was uniformity across various regions and social classes, but that is not the case. Some African Americans may never have spoken the dialect at all; others, depending on whether they came to the United States directly or through various Caribbean countries, would have reflected various stages of language acquisition, including the use of WAPE, creolized dialects of French and English, and various forms associated with the dialects used in Jamaica or Haiti.[93] Dialect use could get quite complicated and highly dependent on ethnic contexts when blackface comics involved in imitating "Negroes" spoke in Hiberno-English or Dutch dialects. In those circumstances, minstrelsy's burlesque view of American life became even more obvious to the audience.

The blackface minstrel borrowed as little or as much as was necessary to achieve just such a level of illusion as was necessary to make the character "work" on the stage. From a relative high incidence of Black English in early minstrelsy to a low in the late 1850s, the dependence on dialect in the stories, jokes, songs, and sometimes the sermons decreased to the extent that at least one minstrel guidebook recommended that companies should "not use dialect, nor allow it to be used, as it spoils the stories and is often unintelligible to the audience."[94]

The connections between social status and language skill or between the dependence on dialect and social or racial pathology are generally discounted today or at least viewed with serious skepticism, making it possible to consider attestations of BEV in a fresh light and see them as evidence of cultural interactions without necessarily assuming that the appearance of dialect "signifies" disdain.[95] The burlesque sermons and orations used in blackface comedy suggest that dialect use was part of a much more complex process involved in the development of a commercially viable form of popular entertainment; it was part of the same process of cultural appropriation that resulted in the creation of American comedy. In the final analysis, however, the claims of authenticity are better judged against the commercial desire to guarantee that audiences would receive relatively competent entertainment for their money rather than an accurate depiction of behavior. It is not in the nature of comedy to deal with all aspects of the human personality; rather, it deals only with those aspects that will translate into reasonably funny situations in theatrical contexts intelligible to the widest range of participants.

The emphasis on dialect assumed that the audience, especially for the sermons, was also capable of entertaining the conceit that allowed both the performer and the audience to suspend the common connections with their own culture and tolerate criticisms of American values. African American culture and Black English Vernacular differ from the general culture and standard dialect not because the former were deficient in some way but because they preserved elements of African and Caribbean culture in the midst of the stresses associated with life in the United States. In their own curious ways, the minstrel show writers recognized the significance of cultural differences and admitted into the mainstream of American culture elements that, regardless of whether they were viewed negatively, might otherwise have been ignored.[96]

Moreover, dialect and literary theory studies have advanced to a point where it is possible to recover aspects of African American culture and literary style through more sophisticated analyses of major authors, as well as through the investigation of folklore and slave narrative collections. Such investigations have revealed examples identical to those appearing in the minstrel repertory, thereby refuting the idea that the so-called minstrel show dialect was a totally artificial creation of malevolent or misinformed entertainers. Although the relationship between the stage dialect and black vernacular may range from a completely superficial resemblance to a relatively accurate rendering, depending on the particular minstrel company or the decade within which the group was performing, it appears that some of the claims about authenticity do have a basis in fact. These ideas are still hotly debated, however, with a recent study of Early Black English arguing that "the linguistic character of Earlier Black English and, subsequently, of present-day Black English is predominantly determined by its descent from nonstandard British and American English of the colonial period. A vast majority of its forms and structures can be identified as and traced back to diachronically older elements of such dialects, some of which have died out by now in standard English."[97]

Even if minstrel show dialect was an invented stage lingua franca adapted for a variety of characters, the existence of that dialect in examples does not necessarily confirm the claim that the minstrels were always portraying black Americans. Blackface comedy was one means of bringing material from one urban social stratum or cultural region to another. Most of the materials performed in American theater (in distinction to the largely unsuccessful ethnic theater in antebellum New York) had to have some elements *all* Americans would recognize. The interchangeability of the material and the transferability of stereotypic traits across racial and ethnic barriers indicate that (1) the minstrel comedians used virtually everything available to them to entertain their audiences and (2) blackface comedy, for all its flaws, is central to the study of American humor.

3   Opera for the Masses: Burlesques of English and Italian Opera

There was an old woman who somewhere did dwell,
Who was burnt for a witch as the op'ra doth tell,
A daughter she had too, a gypsy so bold,
Who went to a house where an infant she stoled.

(*Chorus* in the Italian language, relative to the way she hooked it)
Singing tooral, toledo and in dormio,
Allegro andanty and sempre amo,
O giorno dottore! mia madre you know,
With fata crudele funeste & Co.[1]

Blackface adaptations of operas, operatic scenes, and other stage works were an important part of the minstrel repertory. Burnt cork comedians invested their creative energies in burlesques of contemporary English theater pieces. They borrowed scripts and copied performances of the vehicles created by Thomas D. Rice (most of which were taken from works created by Charles Mathews or comedies performed at London's Adelphi Theatre). The more inventive and musically talented ensembles created clever burlesques of a limited number of English and Italian operas (usually but not always those presented by English companies), principally Michael Balfe's *Bohemian Girl* (1843) and Vincenzo Bellini's *La Sonnambula* (1831) and *Norma* (1831). Even the first American grand opera, William Henry Fry's (1813–64) *Leonora* (1845), provided three of the most frequently used choruses for blackface burlesques, and virtually every minstrel company averaged at least one or two Italian opera choruses per evening after 1846.

Burlesque filled every section of the minstrel show. Dramatizations of song texts, such as the "Boston Favorite Extravaganza of Miss Lucy Long," vied with adaptations of Rice's so-called Ethiopian operas. Rice's *Negro Assurance; or, Life in Old Virginny*, which was undoubtedly based on Dion Boucicault's *London Assurance*

(New York, 1841), was played as a blackface sketch throughout the 1850s. *Oh, Hush!;*
or, The Virginny Cupids was the most popular vehicle used in the antebellum minstrel shows, but unlike many of Rice's other Ethiopian items, *Oh, Hush!* was not
taken from any English model. It was a dramatization of George Washington Dix-
on's song "Coal Black Rose" (ca. 1830), which Rice had presented earlier as *Long-
Island Juba; or, Love in a Bushel* (1833).

Oh, Hush! remained in the repertory of several major minstrel ensembles from
1845 through the mid-1870s. The Buckleys performed it regularly during the 1846
season. Christy and Wood's Minstrels performed Rice's *Oh, Hush!* under the title
The Virginia Cupids; or, The Rival Darkies in 1853 with virtually the same text Rice
had used in the 1830s. George Christy played it often with other ensembles in the
mid-1850s following his departure from Edwin Christy's organization, and Rice
himself continued to offer it in the nonminstrel (but still blackface) theater well into
the 1850s. These pieces established Rice as one of the links between English and
American popular theater.[2]

Rice's *Jim Crow in London* (1837) was a burlesque of William Moncrieff's *Tom
and Jerry in London* (1823), and Rice transformed William Bayle Bernard's (1807–
75) farce *The Mummy* (1833), one of the many such works created by the American-born English playwright, into *The Virginia Mummy,* which was also known as
The Sarcophagus.[3] Among Rice's most noteworthy rewrites of an English source was
his revision of Maurice Dowling's burlesque of Shakespeare's *Othello,* which Rice
purchased during a visit to London in 1836–37.[4] But Rice's successful pieces were
not the only sources that burnt cork comedians imported into their shows.

William Mitchell's (1798–1856) productions at the Olympic Theater presented especially choice models for blackface adaptations, and William E. Burton (1804–
60) provided wonderful burlesques for the minstrel repertory at Burton's Chambers Street Theater between 1848 and 1856. The point is that most of the blackface
creations used in minstrel shows were derived from English or French melodramas
and farces because "popular British melodramas, often derived from French originals, outnumbered successful American ones by perhaps 5:1. The ratio for *popular* comedies, burlettas, and farces was probably closer to 2:1."[5]

The most popular Rice vehicle for minstrel comedians and ensembles was *Bone
Squash Diavolo* (1835). This extended sketch is not an adaptation of Auber's *Fra
Diavolo* (Paris, 1830; New York; 1832), a misidentification Wittke made in his entry on Rice in the *Dictionary of American Biography.*[6] *Bone Squash* is a comic melodrama in which Bone Squash, a chimney sweep, decides that the only way to escape
his dirty occupation is to sell his soul and live out his life as a wealthy gentleman
with all the financial and personal advantages of the upper class. The piece is important because *Bone Squash* relates directly to a common theme in American popular culture, namely, the desire for instant wealth and peer-group respect, the same
theme found in Dan Emmett's *Hard Times* (1855).

The cast of characters for *Bone Squash* is important too, because some of the same names appear later in the burlesques of Italian operas and other Ethiopian sketches. The principal character, originally played by Rice himself, joins other well-known comedy characters from the New York stage, namely, Mose, one of the Bowery B'hoys usually played by Frank Chanfrau (1824–84), and Sam Switchell, the Yankee devil, a character obviously related to the *diavolo* of the title.[7]

MEN
Bone Squash
Spruce Pink
Jim Brown
Mose
Juba
Caesar
Pompey Ducklegs
Sam Switchell, the Yankee Devil
Amos
Niggers, Sweeps, Watchmen

WOMEN
Junietta Ducklegs
Jenna Snowball
Milly
Black Ladies

Bone Squash is actually a ballad opera that includes frequent references to New York locales, such as the National Theater (where Rice appeared frequently), the Five Points district, and the lower Manhattan area around the Bowery. The songs used in the 1873 published version—apparently no earlier manuscript copy or printed edition exists—include "Jim Brown" (the Rice "Dandy" vehicle), "Sich a Getting Up Stairs," and for the overture, an adaptation of "The Drunken Sailor/Ten Little Indians" fiddle tune, all of which were published and performed before 1843.[8] The songs in the 1873 version were distributed as shown in table 2. An asterisk marks the items I have been able to locate in antebellum songsters or sheet music editions.[9]

The example illustrates the strong relationship between the English ballad opera, a genre "in which spoken dialogue alternates with songs consisting of new words fit to traditional and familiar tunes," and Ethiopian opera, in which the blackfaced actors presented the same kind of material but substituted American texts and topical references.[10] The principal forms of English and Italian opera containing new and original music were no less important than ballad operas in the development of popular musical theater, which presented excerpts from the latest operas, condensed versions of opera arias or concert solos, and combinations of operatic material and contemporary blackface hits. Finally, English opera burlesques, which some American managers saw during their tours of the United Kingdom, also provided examples for American managers to adapt for presentation back home. Samuel Sanford, who served as the Buckleys' manager during their tour of England in 1846, "saw Anna Bishop as Amina in *Lossnomula* [*sic*] *Poor House* at Liverpool's Theater Royal."[11]

Table 2. Overture: Medley of Songs and Incidental Music from *Bone Squash*

Location	Title	Characters
1. act 1, sc. 1	"Oh, Hurrah!"	Brown, Mose, Amos, and Juba
2. act 1, sc. 1	"Jim Brown"*	Jim Brown
3. act 1, sc. 1	"Oh, I Wish I Could"	Bone Squash
4. act 1, sc. 1	"I'm Beginning For to Fill Like a Baltimore Clipper"	Bone Squash and Devil
5. act 1, sc. 2	"Let Me Go"	Spruce, Junietta, Mose
6. act 1, sc. 3	"Come, Saw upon de Fiddle'	Chorus
7. act 1, sc. 3	"It Was de Oder Morning"	Bone Squash
8. act 2, sc. 1	"In a Chimney Tight"*	Bone Squash and Chorus
9. act 2, sc. 1	"Smile My Fortune"	Mose and Chorus
Incidental Music (accompanies business between Bone Squash and the Devil)		
10. act 2, sc. 3	"Listen While I S'plain"	Bone Squash, Devil, and Chorus
	"Farewell, All My Calculation"*	Bone, Squash, Devil, and Chorus
11. act 2, sc. 4	"Oh, Ladies, Pray Don't Tease Me So"	Bone Squash and Ladies Chorus
Finale		
12. act 2, sc. 5	"Save me! Save me!"	Bone Squash and Chorus

The burlesque sections of *La Sonnambula* were popular because the opera it-self was a hit in the United States from its first performance (in English) in 1835. The great success of William Mitchell's *Roof Scrambler* (1839), which ridiculed the plot of Bellini's opera and the exploits of the sleepwalking Amina, did not affect the popularity of the original. Performances of *La Sonnambula* continued during the 1840s, and George Templeton Strong, who heard the Havana Opera Company's performance on June 30, 1847, argued that the work was "worth three of *Norma.*"[12]

The burlesque operas were just as popular as the originals and just as profitable. P. T. Barnum was so interested in the profits to be gained from burlesque opera that he commissioned the authors of *New York in Slices* (George Foster) and *Lucy Did Sham Amour* (Dr. William K. Northall) to produce a version entitled *The Sleep Walker,* which the *New York Tribune* (Dec. 14, 1848) described as "a dark version of the popular opera of SONNAMBULA, with a choice selection of music of that and other popular operas, and the favorite Ethiopian melodies."

Since minstrelsy was an entertainment devoted to short excerpts rather than to sustained creative adaptations of complete works, the most prevalent operatic sources were solos and choruses that could be adapted to the vocal abilities of the various minstrel ensembles. However, the number of operatic sources used on the minstrel stage was surprisingly small given the variety of English, French, German, and Italian titles produced in New York alone during the antebellum period.

The sources of the most popular parodies of opera choruses, that is, those that appeared at least twice in the survey of 100 playbills, are shown in table 3. The big-gest hits of the period, however, were "See, Sir, See," introducing "Lucy Neal," from "Vi ravviso, o luoghi ameni," and the "Phantom Chorus" ("A fosco cielo"), both

Table 3. Most Popular Operatic Parodies Identified on 100 Playbills

Title	Opera Title (American Premiere)	Company	Year
"Darkies Bride" ("Come with the Gipsy Bride")	*The Bohemian Girl* (New York, 1844)	Ethiopian Serenaders	1845
"Come With the Darkey Band" ("Come with the Gipsy Bride")	*The Bohemian Girl* (New York, 1844)	Ethiopian Serenaders Christy's Minstrels	1845 1853
"Darkey Gal's Dream of Home" ("I Dreamt I Dwelt in Marble Halls")	*The Bohemian Girl* (New York, 1844)	Christy's Minstrels Christy's Minstrels	1847 1847
Solo/Chorus: "Virginia Rosebud"	*The Bronze Horse* (New Orleans, 1836)	Christy's Minstrels Ethiopian Serenaders Sable Harmonists Virginia Serenaders Rainer and Donaldson	1849 (twice) 1849 1849 1850 1851 and 1852
"Phantom Chorus"[a] (A fosco cielo")	*La Sonnambula* (New York, 1835)	Ethiopian Serenaders New Orleans Serenaders Ordway's Aeolians Rainer and Donaldson Christy and Woods Harmoneons White's Serenaders George Christy's Minstrels	1849 1850 1851 1851 and 1852 1851 1851 1852 1859
"Colored Fancy Ball" ("Through the Halls Resounding")	*Leonora* (Philadelphia, 1845)	Ordway's Aeolians White's Serenaders	1852 1852
"Dinah's Wedding Day" ("Fill up the Vine-wreathed Cup")	*Leonora* (Philadelphia, 1845)	White's Serenaders Parker's Opera Troupe Ordway's Aeolians Virginia Serenaders Rainer and Donaldson	1849 1850 1851 1852 1851 and 1852
Solo: "See, Sir, See" ("Vi ravvisso," from act 1, sc. 1)	*La Sonnambula* (New York, 1835)	Christy's Minstrels Pierce's Minstrels Ethiopian Serenaders Wood's Minstrels Christy and Woods Christy and Woods Bryant's Minstrels	1849 1850 1851 1852 1854 1855 1857

a. Also known under other titles, e.g., "Darkies Apparition," on some playbills.

from the burlesque versions of *La Sonnambula;* "The Virginia Rose Bud," from *Le Cheval de bronze;* and several airs and choruses from *The Bohemian Girl,* most notably "In the Gypsies Life You Read."

Most of the burlesque operas performed from 1840 to the mid-1850s featured men in all roles, but that was not always the case. After the first complete New York performance (1844) of *La Sonnambula* in Italian, a group calling itself the Ethiopian Minstrels joined with the Sable Sisters for a series of opera parodies that included examples from that opera. The *Spirit of the Times* noted that this performance marked the "first introduction of female voices" into minstrelsy, which had "the effect of enlivening the music and dispelling the monotony so often perceptible in their [the men's] songs and choruses."[13] During the mid-1850s the Buckley Serenaders often featured Eva Brent and Julia Gould in various female roles, Mrs. Nelson Kneass often joined her husband's companies when a strong soprano lead was required, and various ensembles employed women as dancers or comedians. By the 1860s the lead female roles in Samuel Sanford's burlesques of *La Sonnambula* (August 25, 1861) and other operas were played by women, including Julia Sanford and one famous Amina identified as Miss M. A'Becket, a relative of Thomas A'Becket, who played Rudolfo (Count Rodolfo).[14]

Buckley's New Orleans Serenaders performed their "first complete burlesque opera [*La Sonnambula*] for the benefit of the Western Literary Association on January 21, 1850." Nelson Kneass and one of the groups known as the Sable Harmonists performed a *La Sonnambula* burlesque under the title of *The Sleep Walker*. One of the most likely sources for the musical text was the arrangement Kneass made from "a script used by the Seguins" for his own company's production of *La Sonnambula in Three Parts* at Philadelphia's Cartee's Lyceum (later called the Eleventh Street Opera House) in 1855.[15] If it was the Seguin version, the blackface burlesque was probably taken from Sir Henry Rowley Bishop's (1786–1855) London adaptation of Bellini's opera. Now that most of these early nineteenth-century classics are performed in musically accurate editions with historical notes documenting the performance history, it is difficult to compare modern translations of the librettos with the blackface burlesques or to determine what portion of the original music the minstrels chose for their parodies.[16] The music for the most frequently burlesqued items was also available in sheet music editions in most cities, even though much of it is difficult to locate today.

Just as the burnt cork comedians claimed that their presentations of African American life were "authentic," so did some ensemble managers, especially James Buckley of the New Orleans Serenaders, argue that "the Music rendered by the Buckleys in their Burlesque Operas, is the music of the Opera itself, with here and there negro interpolations, which drive away the dullness of too close an observation of the original text." The New Orleans Serenaders (also billed as Buckley's New Orleans Serenaders) advertised that one of their opera parodies was to "be introduced in Burlesque, retaining all its Gems as in the original Libretto, interspersed with Ethiopian Airs, Scenic Effects, and Witticisms." When the engagement allowed them several extra evenings, the ensemble announced: "The New Orleans Opera Troupe will tonight commence their comical burlesques of the leading and favorite operas. *La Sonnambula* will be given this evening in regular Ethiopian style, with the original music considerably Africanized, and embellished after the peculiar manner of each of these distinguished and inimitable artists. Those who love music as a fine art, or laughter as a specific against the ills that flesh is heir to may enjoy it this evening."[17]

There were probably several burlesque versions and musical arrangements circulating simultaneously. This conclusion comes from the character lists from the *La Sonnambula* burlesques created by Buckley's New Orleans Serenaders, Sanford's Opera Troupe (*La Sum-Am-Bull-Ah*), and the various ensembles directed by Nelson Kneass.[18] A comparison of the Buckley and Sanford playbills with both the contents of the piano vocal score and Joan Sutherland's London recording with Luciano Pavarotti illustrates how the so-called Ethiopianizing process worked (see table 4).[19]

Table 4. Character Lists for *La Sonnambula* Burlesques

Bellini (1831)	Buckley (1850)	Sanford (1853)	Kneass (1855)
Amina	Dinah	Dinah Crow	Dina Grese-ano
Count Rodolfo	Dan Tucker	Dan Tucker	Dan Tucker Funny-Sara
Elvino	Gumbo	Gumbo	Jumbo Marry-oh
Alessio	Lazy Joe	Joe	Lazy Joe Low-riney
Lisa (Elisa)	Susanna	Susannah	Susanna All-bong
Notary	Deacon Ducklegs	Dean	Pompey Ducklegs Bad-ally
Theresa	Aunt Sally	Aunt Sally	Aunt Sally Patti-pan

The characteristics of the blackface parody choruses that most obviously distinguished them from either Bellini's original opera (Milan, 1831) or Sir Henry Bishop's adaptation (London, 1833) were (1) the use of two American English dialects, that is, Standard and Black English; (2) the transformation of the characters into the typical burnt cork personae; and (3) the combination of two apparently contradictory musical styles that contrasted the phrase and period structures of European vocal music and sometimes sophisticated harmonies (German sixths, augmented sixths, diminished seventh chords, and passing chords) with the three-chord accompaniment patterns and sometimes irregular phrasing of the many minstrel songs.

Bellini, La Sonnambula	*Buckley's Serenaders Travestie* *[of* La Sonnambula*]*
Act 1, Scene 1	*Act 1*
1. Chorus: "Viva Amina" ("Hurrah for Amina")	1. Chorus: "Viva Dinah"
2. Lisa: "Tutto è gioia, Tutto è feste . . ." ("All is gaiety, all is celebration"), with Alessio's "Ah! non sempre" ("Not forever will you fly from me")	2. Lazy Joe: "Oh! Susa let us married be"
3. Chorus: from "In Elvetia non v'ha rosa" ("Switzerland can boast no rose"), with Alessio, Lisa, and Amina, to Amina's "Sovra il sen la man mi posa" ("Place your hand upon my breast")	3. Dinah: "While heart with joy revealing" (original scene probably cut severely)

4. Amina and Chorus: "Come per me serena" ("How brightly this day") and "Sovra il sen la . . . posa"

5. Elvino and Amina: "Prendi: l'anel ti dono" ("Accept this: this ring I give you")

    4. Amina/Dinah and Elvino/Gumbo: "Take now this ring"

6. Rodolfo: "Vi ravviso, o luoghi" ("Again I see you pretty places"), and "Tu non sai" ("You do not know"), with Lisa, Teresa, Elvino, and Chorus

    5. Rudolph (Dan Tucker): "As I view these scenes"

7. Elvino and Chorus: "A fosco cielo" ("When all is dark"), and Elvino, Lisa, and Teresa with Villagers, "Il ciel vi guardi!" ("God forbid you should seek it")

    6. Phantom Chorus: "Beneath an overcast sky at dead of night"

8. Elvino and Amina: "Son geloso del zeffiro errante" ("I am jealous of the casual breeze") through "Ah! costante nel tuo, nel mio seno" ("Ah, constant in both our hearts")

    7. Elvino/Gumbo and Dinah/Amina: "Good night, go hide yourself"

Act 1, Scene 2

9. Principals with Amina, Elvino, and Chorus of Villagers: "Davver non mi dispiace" ("Truth to tell, I'm glad") to concluding quintet, "D'un pensiero e d'un accenta" ("Neither by a thought or a word"), including "Cielo, al mio sposo io giuro" ("To my husband I swear, oh heaven")

Act 2

8. Grand Quintette: "Hear me swear," Amina/Dinah, Elvino/Gumbo, and Chorus[20]

Act 2, scene 1

10. Chorus: "Qui la selva è più folta ed ombrosa" ("Here the wood is thick and shady")

11a. Elvino, Amina, and Chorus: "Tutto è sciolto" ("All is over")

11b. Elvino: "Ah! perché non posso odiati, infedel" ("Oh, why can I not hate you")

Act 3

9. Elvino/Gumbo: grand aria, "All is Lost"

10. Elvino/Gumbo: "Still so gently"

Act 2, scene 2

12. Lisa and Alexis: "Lasciami" and
"De'lieti auguri a voi" ("Leave me
alone" and "I am grateful for your
good wishes")

13. Chorus with Alessio, Elvino, Lisa,   11. Amina/Dinah: Prayer, "Oh, Dinah?"
Teresa, and Amina, including
Amina's prayer "Gran dio, non mirar
il mio pianto" ("Lord God, do not
heed my tears")

14. Elvino: "Signor! che credar deggio?"   12. Finale: Amina/Dinah and Chorus:
("O Lord, what am I to believe") and   "Ah! Do not mingle"
Amina: "Ah! non giunge uman
pensiero" (Ah! beyond all human
thought")

Opera burlesques offer unique opportunities to explore connections between the various elements in the typical minstrel ensembles' repertories. Why did the blackface comedians pick specific scenes? Why, given the number of comic possibilities in Italian opera plots, did so many groups decide on one scene from *La Sonnambula*? The answer is that the scene was the subject for a most interesting parody linking a newly composed blackface song with one of the finest arias in the opera, namely, "See, Sir, See," or "Vi ravviso, o luoghi ameni," and "Lucy Neal," a cross-dressed Lucy/Amina being in the tradition of New York opera burlesque since Mitchell's celebrated *Roof Scrambler*.

The stage directions in the original opera libretto indicate that Amina is still onstage when Rodolfo sings "Vi ravviso," and the text assumes that she is present just so that Rodolfo can comment on her beauty. There is no reason to believe the Amina/Lucy character would be absent from the burlesque, especially since the playbills assert that the scene "introduces Lucy Neal." Assuming that "Lucy Neal" replaced Rodolfo's "E gentil, leggiadra molto" ("She is charming, most attractive"), the minstrel song is a great foil to the pining nostalgia of "Vi ravviso," which in Christy's version could also have been sung by a bass.[21] The "Lucy Neal" chorus replaces the music allocated to the villagers of the original with the blackface quartet writing used in minstrel songs. The short scene would probably have been much more effective if the audience knew its derivation or understood that "See, Sir, See" was a stereotypic scene from Italian opera or a solo number in a vocal recital.

The examples illustrating the following discussions of the originals and the burlesques show the texts of the numbers in side-by-side format followed by the most widely distributed sheet music or piano vocal editions of the burlesques (see music example 1).

Example 1. "Vi ravviso," from Bellini's *La Sonnambula* (Kalmus edition).

"See, Sir, See" from *CPM2* (1853), 70–72, and *La Sonnambula,* Act 1, Scene 1[22] ("Vi ravviso, o luoghi ameni")

Burlesque Opera

First Voice: See, sir, see!
Second Voice: Oh, what can this be?

Third Voice: Yes, the mill there, the rocks and the treeses,
  And the duck pond and the geeses!
  As I view these scenes so charming,
  With fond remembrance my heart is warming,
  Of days long vanished, of days long vanished;
  Oh, this chest!—oh, this chest is filled with pain,
  Finding darkies that still remain,
  While those days and those nights,
  And that must never come again.
First Voice: Ah, who is he sir? can you tell?
Second Voice: He surely knows this place full well.
Third Voice: Finding darkies that still remain,
  While those days and those nights,
  And that must never come again.
  Oh! that form there brings sweet remembrances,
  Gentle darkies—oh, what strong resemblance!
First Voice: To whom?
Second Voice: To my poor Lucy Neal, to my poor Lucy Neal,
  And if I had her by my side, how happy I should feel.
Chorus: To his Lucy Neal, to his poor Lucy Neal,
  And if he had her by his side, how happy he should feel.

La Sonnambula

[Enter Rodolfo and two mounted attendants. He recognizes the inn. Lisa invites him to stay for the evening.]
Rodolfo: Ah! I remember it.
Lisa: You do, sir?
All: Who can he be?
Rodolfo: The mill . . . the spring . . . the wood . . .
  And the farm nearby.
  Again I see you pretty places, in which the happy carefree days passed so serenely when I was still a child.
  Dear places, you I have found again.
  Dear places, you I have found again, but those days are beyond recall!
  Again, I see you pretty places

Villagers: He seems to know the village well enough; when can he have been here?
Rodolfo: But here, if I am not mistaken, some festivity is afoot.
Villagers: We're celebrating a happy marriage.

Rodolfo: And the bride? is that her?
  [Referring to Amina, the sleepwalker.]
Villagers: That is her.
Rodolfo: She is charming, most attractive . . .
  Let me look at you. Oh! what a pretty face.
  You do not know how sweetly those lovely eyes touch my heart
    nor what memories they stir of a beauty I adored.
  She was just like you in the tender bloom of youth.

Third Voice: Away down in Alabama, not
far from Old Mobile,
There dwelt a pretty yellow girl, her
name was Lucy Neal;
Her coal black eyes, her curly locks,
around her neck did steal,
Which early taught my heart to love my
pretty Lucy Neal.
Chorus: To his Lucy Neal, etc.
Third Voice: Oh, what a strong
resemblance!
Yes, those black eyes are impressing,
Fill my breast with thoughts
distressing—
Long since dead, long since dead, and
passed away.
She was like thee about the heel,
Was my lovely Lucy Neal.
Chorus: To his poor Lucy Neal, to his poor
Lucy Neal,
And if he had her by his side, how
happy he would feel.

She was just like you in the tender
bloom of youth.
Lisa: She gets all the compliments.
Elvino: She's enjoying his admiration.
Rodolfo: She was in the tender bloom of
youth . . .
Villagers: What graceful, pleasing
manners, city dwellers have!

Ensemble

The song was presented "in character," that is, by a cross-dressed male, but the scene had to be set up to maximize the comedy of "introducing Lucy Neal." How that worked in practice is not clear, although when the Christys performed the number, the playbill stated that it was played by "E. P. Christy and Chorus." Edwin Christy may have been featured in the role of Rodolfo even though he was not generally known as a bass singer, and George Christy, one of the leading female impersonators of the period, probably played the Lucy role. Did the group introduce *only* the song, which was already well-known, or a character who then became the object of the group's admiration? The latter idea would have been an effective device even if the Lucy role was a nonspeaking one. The "Third Voice" and use of the third person in the text suggest that the Lucy character was introduced with the lines "She was like thee about the heel, / Was my lovely Lucy Neal." There is, then, no indication that the minstrels treated "See, Sir, See" very differently once it entered the opera parody.

"Vi ravviso" probably made its transition into minstrelsy through the Nelson Kneass arrangement of *La Sonnambula.* The combination of "Vi ravviso" with "Lucy Neal" brought together two different characters from two distinct cultural traditions to satirize a scene based on Arthur Edward Sheldon Seguin's (1809–52) performances of Rodolfo's aria during his vocal recitals or appearances as the Count in *La Sonnambula,* as well as Anne Seguin's performance of Amina during the six years (1841–47) that the Seguin Opera Troupe dominated the American operatic stage.[23] The parody is of a specific style, of the highly artificial setting of the original opera, and of Rodolfo's nostalgic reminiscences of a happy childhood.

The phrase "introducing Lucy Neal" implies that the blackface plantation woman, whose only gender-defining characteristics are those attributed to her by the male narrator, appears in the opera segment to exploit the satirical possibilities in cultural and class contrasts.[24] The melodies of Rodolfo's "Vi ravviso" and Amina's "Ah! non giunge" and the haunting staccato chords of the chorus in "A fosco cielo" are very different from the mainly pentatonic vocal or fiddle parts of early minstrelsy. But the stylistic differences are not always that strong because the Italian cavatinas and arias were easily reduced to the simple three- or four-chord harmonization patterns of American song and the sixteen- or thirty-two-bar phrase structure that was the bedrock on which even Emmett's "Old Dan Tucker" was based. Stripped of their vocal ornamentation and dramatic functions in a complicated opera scene, the Italian melodies have a strong affinity with the sentimental solo songs and generally three-part choral writing that found an acceptable home in minstrelsy and antebellum popular music.

The minstrel performers and their arrangers could announce whatever they wanted to their audiences, but the Italian choruses were essentially Italian regardless of what the performers wore. The minstrels exploited the peculiar musical affinities between Anglo- and African American modality and German or Italian tonality and inadvertently perhaps reinforced the European dominance of the struggling American musical style. That these styles could be combined so easily suggests that the differences between them were definitely not contradictory. Even if the three- and four-part settings of minstrel song choruses and the Italian opera examples no longer seem different stylistically, such a distinction still seems reasonable in any study of the confluence of musical practices available during the period regardless of what one thinks an American style was during the 1840s. The writing of the higher choral parts in thirds in "Vi ravviso" and "Lucy Neal" is noteworthy, as is the absence of the *alla ottava*, or "8va," marking indicating that the tenor sounds an octave lower than is written (see music examples 2a and b). In many respects the aria's style is similar to the popular musical style of the period, and the piece undoubtedly provided a model for minstrelsy's sentimental songs, especially those using arpeggiated accompaniments.

The choruses generally have a fairly uninteresting bass line, are often written in three parts, and are usually syllabic, that is, one note or chord sonority for each syllable of text. Although the Italian examples invariably avoid open sonorities, that is, triads without a third, the American ones often show them in the *published* material. There is absolutely no guarantee that the missing intervals were not performed, however. The confusion over the role of the tenor or baritone parts— American arrangements often seem to make them as irrelevant as the added alto

Example 2a. Four-part choral writing (SATB) from "Vi ravviso."

Example 2a. (cont.)

Example 2b. Four-part setting (TTBB) of "Lucy Neal," from *EGB1*. Used by permission of the Brown University Library.

part in southern folk hymnody—seems to come directly from carrying over Italian choral techniques to minstrelsy.

The "See, Sir, See" burlesque scene was performed by many different minstrel groups. The Christy Minstrels presented it often and included it in *CPM2* (70–72). Also performing it were the various ensembles managed by Nelson Kneass and, of course, Buckley's Serenaders, whose opera burlesques were among the most elaborate in minstrelsy. The Buckleys introduced their own *La Sonnambula* burlesque scenes shortly after their return from England in 1848 when, under the management of Dr. Charles Brown, they advertised a "series of entertainments" offering "a variety of Burlesque Operatic Music in Ethiopian character."[25] Within two years, however, they moved from offering a few selected opera scenes to presenting what their playbills described as complete works, the first of which was *La Sonnambula*, which was scheduled for New York's Western Literary Association on January 21, 1850.[26]

The Buckleys' claim that they performed burlesques of complete works is somewhat dubious because one of their most popular offerings described as an "Italian opera" in the playbills and newspapers advertisements (Dec. 14 and 26, 1848) was actually "Grand scenes from La Sonnambula, Lucretia Borgia, and all the 'Italian' operas, with imitations of Jenny Lind, Madame Grisi, Madame Alboni, Signor Lablache, Sig. Mario, Sig. Gardioni, Madame Bishop and others."[27] The Serenaders performed scenes from Henry Bishop's arrangement of Rossini's *Cinderella,* which included popular tunes, hornpipes, and some of the original music probably borrowed from or related to William Mitchell's burlesque of the same work now transformed into *Cinderella: or, A Foreign Prince and a Large Glass Slipper* (Mar. 7, 1842).[28]

During the next several years, the Buckelys presented burlesques of *Cinderella, Lucia di Lammermoor, L'Elisir d'amore, La Chalet; or, The Cottage,* and *La Fille du regiment,* but it is still unclear exactly what they actually offered their audiences.[29] Whatever their actual contribution turns out to have been, Buckley's New Orleans Serenaders seem to have had such a corner on the burlesque market that even *Dwight's Journal* (Apr. 21, 1855) remarked that the "Buckleys were doing as much for the elevation of musical taste of the people as the Philharmonic [was] doing in the higher sphere."[30] And Edwin P. Christy, recognizing the effect that the Buckleys' programs were having on the repertory, accused them of "ruining minstrelsy with their emphasis on operatic and musical performances."[31]

Samuel Sanford's burlesques were even more comical than those produced by his former employers because the magician, dancer, punster, and general comedian provided clever copy to the press wherever his ensemble appeared. Two of the better examples are shown in the following excerpts from a typical Sanford playbill.[32]

Introducing scenes from Norma, Lucretia Borgia, Lucy-do-lam-her-more [Lucia di Lammermoor], and Lend-her-de-sham money [Linda di Chamounix], etc.

Prima Donna, Mad[ame] Big Gourd	Max Zorer
Sig. Cesaro	Sig. J. H. Collins
Syncopatis	S. Sanford
Cavetino	Sig. G. Swaine
De Big-nees [Guiseppe de Begnis]	Ole Bull
De Poor-goose	J. Burke
Crotchiatio	C. Lewis
Conductor Max Mutton-sac [Max Maretzek]	Sig. N. Kneass

Introducing the Grand Over-Shoe from De-Fried-Sheep and opening chorus from Norma, Cavitino, Cast-at-eve-a, solo from Linda, "Oh, Dearest Why," and duet "Lady, Look on this Pale cheek." Chorus—"Long, Long, Ago," "See Cesar Comes," "Long Live the Darkey Bride," Duet from Norma, "Come to These Arms."

These examples illustrate how often the real subject of the burlesques and choral parodies was the English and American distaste for opera as a theatrical genre. For many American audiences, the simultaneity of musical events detracted from their understanding of opera as sung drama, and the plots, filled with the intrigues common to Italian opera of the period, seemed incongruous. For Henry Watson

(1818[?]–75), the English-born New York music critic, *La Sonnambula* was not even a good opera because it was "about on a par with the English ballad operas of fifty years before; melodious, but little more."[33] But whatever its dramatic elements or its flaws, *La Sonnambula* was well known to New York concertgoers because of the great patriotic fervor surrounding the New York debut of the American-born soprano Eliza Biscaccianti (1824–96), whose performance of "Ah! non giunge" at the Astor Place Opera House in 1847 led Robert Grant White to write that "personal predilection, national pride, and perhaps good musical taste, found sufficient reason for such an outbreak of applause that one not present during the first act would have imagined the debutante successful beyond expectation."[34] Vera Lawrence viewed the battle of Biscaccianti's performance as played out in the New York papers as being "a kind of class struggle." That was the point with the blackface minstrel companies, who seized on every opportunity to demonstrate the humor rather than the pathos of their own products.

The Italian opera in the minstrels' hands was essentially an American ballad opera composed out of native *and* foreign materials. Blackface became the intermediary for bringing Italian musical practice into the growing vocabulary of American music. The cuts made by the various burlesque opera companies were not unlike those used in England, where a typical evening's vocal entertainment by one of the great divas of the period at Drury Lane or Covent Garden was likely to consist of an act or two of Rossini's *Il Barbiere di Siviglia* followed by an act or short excerpt from *La Sonnambula,* concluding with dance selections, character pieces by comic actors or actresses, or a short farce.[35]

The blackface opera burlesques were produced at a time when audiences seemed willing to patronize several different versions of the same work ranging from the reasonably authentic to the simply silly. The performance history of *La Sonnambula* in New York provides a good example. The English version of *La Sonnambula* was presented by Mr. Joseph Wood (1801–90) and Mrs. (Mary Ann Paton) Wood (1802–63) at the Park Theater on November 11, 1835. The first U.S. performance in Italian was at Palmo's Opera House on May 11, 1844. During the nine-year period between these two events, Mitchell's highly successful production of Henry Horncastle's burlesque entitled *The Roof Scrambler* (New York, 1837; Olympic Theater, 1839) was still being performed at the Olympic Theater. Mitchell *himself,* dressed in suitable feminine attire, played the beautiful young sleepwalker Amina, "under the English, if not more euphonious name of *Molly Brown.*"[36] The Olympic players knew *La Sonnambula* quite well because they had performed in James Wallack's production at the National Theater, where Italian opera (including *La Sonnambula*) had a great success during the 1837–38 season.

Other adaptations of Bellini's work appeared in several English-language productions presented by Michael Rolphino Lacy (1795–1867) during his company's ill-fated visit to New York in 1845. Maria Caradori Allan (1800–1865) and company offered English pastiches of Italian opera at the Park (1838) during the portion of her two-year American tour that she spent in New York. Caradori Allan's troupe had great success with a work known as *The Elixir of Love,* which was patched together from liberal borrowings from Mozart, Donizetti, Rossini, and Herold. The Seguins (Anne Childe and Arthur Edward) and Jane Shireff presented *Fra Diavolo* and *La Sonnambula* many times during the 1840s. The Seguins' operatic successes at the National Theater were "nothing less than phenomenal." Bellini's *La Sonnambula* or some variation on it appeared in almost every theatrical and musical venue in New York City between 1835 and 1850.[37]

When Christy's Minstrels or Buckley's New Orleans Serenaders performed the "A fosco cielo" scene (the "Phantom Chorus") from *La Sonnambula,* they changed very little of the music. The Christys used an arrangement prepared by the French-born pianist and conductor Leopold Meignen (1793–1873), who conducted the world premiere of Fry's *Leonora.* Meignen retained the E♭-major key of the original and virtually the same accompaniment. Although nominally "arranged for four voices," the piece is in not four parts but three, all of which were written in the treble staff for unclassified but obviously male voices. The fourth part is set for the bass solos that move the narration forward. (See music examples 3a and b.) The major changes occurred in the text because the scene was excerpted from its place in the opera.[38]

Bellini, La Sonnambula, *act 1, scene 1* ("A fosco cielo")	Christy's *"Phantom Chorus" Parody* (Philadelphia: Fiot, Meignen and Co., 1848)
Part I: Introduction Teresa: You know the hour is approaching when the dread phantom appears.	*Part I: Introduction* Amina: Look yar Sar! As slowly comes de night: Den dese poor darkies am almost friz'd with fright:
Villagers: Oh yes, it's true. Soloists/Chorus: It's a mystery . . . an object of horror. Rodolfo: Nonsense. Teresa/Villagers: What are you saying? If only you knew, sir . . . Rodolfo: Tell me about it.	Trio: Tis true indeed Sar! Tis true indeed Sar! Tis de debil or some Bugaboo dat goes about at night. What dat Sar? look yar: hold you jaw, jus lisen.
Part II (Chorus I) Villagers: Listen. Beneath an overcast sky at dead of night, in the faint uncertain light of the moon, to the dulled sound of distant thunder down the hill towards the plain, a shade appears.	*Part II: Chorus I* (Three Parts TTB) When work am done Sar, den home we run Sar, For fear dis debil might be oncivil, We all shake so Sar, from top to toe Sar, Oh! we fear he'll come wid horns an tail, wid horns an tail.

Wrapped in a slipping white sheet,
with dishevelled hair and burning eyes,
like a thick mist stirred by the wind it
advances, grows bigger and seems huge.

Rodolfo: Your superstitious fancy depicts
and presents it to you.

Amina, Teresa: Oh, it's no silly tale, it isn't
fright . . . everyone sees it; it's true.

Elvino: Truthfully!

Part III (Chorus II)
Chorus: Wherever it passes with slow tread
a terrifying silence reigns. Not a breath
stirs, not a blade of grass moves; the
brook stays as if frozen.
Even the cowering dogs drop their
eyes and haven't a bark left in them.
Every now and them from deep down in
the valley alone the fetid screech owl
screams.

Amina, Lisa, Teresa, Elvino: It's the truth!
Rodolfo: Your credulous fancy!
Villagers [repeating Chorus II in
background]: Even the cowering dogs
[previous lines repeated]
Rodolfo: I should like to see it some time
or other . . . and find out what it does.
Amina, Elvino, Teresa, Lisa: May heaven
preserve you, it would be tempting
fate.
May heaven keep you from going in
quest of it!

From all Vargini each Pickaninny wid
berry long face on;
Wid prespiration, Dere wool am
dripping
As home dere skipping afraid to poke
dere noses in de dark Sar, I'll go bail.
Bass Solo: Tis some ole Cow Sar, or big
Bow-wow sar,
It arnt de Debil.
Trio: Oh no it arnt no Cow Sar, nor big
Bowwow, for Gingers' seen him, an
dat we know.
Tenor Solo: Yes dat I'll swear.
Bass Solo: Oh! Sar.

Part III: Chorus II (TTTB)
Quartet: Oh dear! oh dear me! I tink he's
near me,
whene'er de dog bark, An 'tis at all
dark,
Our teeth dey chatter, wid sitch a clatter
dat you'd tink five pair of castinets
was being playd.
Wid nose on ground Sar, a snuffing
round Sar,
Our ole dog Towser begins to howl.
Tis den wid fright Sar! we all turn white
Sar:
you'd tink each darky in his
shroud, has jus been laid.

Oh! dear me! dat's him I knows. Oh!
gracious, he's coming now. Oh!
[Eleven measures of bel canto solo
material deleted.]

Example 3a. "A fosco cielo" ("Phantom Chorus"), from *La Sonnambula* (Kalmus edition).

Example 3a. (cont.)

6

Example 3b. "Phantom Chorus" (Meignen arrangement for Christy's Minstrels). The author gratefully acknowledges the permission to reproduce minstrel songs from the Sheet Music Collection of the Free Library of Philadelphia.

Example 3b. (cont.)

The minstrel parody uses the same music as that of the opera. Some measures—the original scene is eighty-five measures long; the parody, only seventy-five—of solo material are deleted because the minstrel quartet could not handle the variety of vocal parts in the original ensemble scene (five soloists assisted by a mixed chorus), which typically closed with a cadenza for the female star. The "Phantom Chorus" parody was a stand-alone piece that, although obviously depicting African Americans as superstitious and fearful of the dark, played on the common Christian fear of the devil—the projection of the emotion onto the costumed others on the stage—instead of merely satirizing the sleepwalking young Amina of the original.

The Meignen version of the "Phantom Chorus" is an American appropriation of an Italian musical convention and illustrates yet another example of the incorporation of Italianate vocal and harmonic elements—diminished seventh and augmented sixth chords and chromatic passing tones—into American choral music. The parody clearly shows the dominance of Italian music in the American theater and highlights the differences between the Italian and German musical styles employed for those highly popular "scary" scenes that were among the great theatrical achievements of the romantic age of opera. Bellini's "Phantom Chorus" is in a major key (E♭), and the scene is devoid of any of the special instrumental effects that Carl Maria von Weber used effectively in the "Wolf's Glen" scene of Der Freischütz (1827), which did not have its American premiere until January 22, 1842.[39] The singers alone create the sense of foreboding critical to the dramatic effect of the forest scene in La Sonnambula, and the blackface comedians, especially the better singing groups, were capable of parodying the whole performance context of the imported musical style.

The character of the devil (undoubtedly costumed with horns and tail) lurks in the bushes for the unsuspecting travelers returning from work. This devil is not a mythic creature or chthonic deity associated with African American religious practice; he is the common representation of the devil type from Western Christianity and folklore. The characters react to their fear with "chattering" teeth, excessive perspiration, and a good deal of stage business in the Christys' creation of one of the popular stage conventions for the expression of fear. The "Ginger" referred to in the text is probably "Ginger Blue," one of the characters invented by Thomas Rice. The dog, Towler (sometimes Towser), although he does not seem to have appeared in the Christys' act, was apparently the Christy family's pet and is just one of the dogs referred to in the company's other songs. The arrangement concludes when a knock on the door signals the "devil's arrival," the characters "all start" and "tremble," and the harmony goes to four parts built on alternating tonic and dominant chords. Trills are marked for the entire six beats, and two of the chords are sustained to stress or perhaps emphasize the melodramatic effect.

The fear of ghosts, the devil, or evil spirits plays on one of minstrelsy's most prominent racist and contrary-to-fact conventions, namely, that excessive fright might turn black persons white, as white as a burial shroud, which is the equivalent of as "white as a sheet." But the "Phantom Chorus" projects anxiety about nighttime encounters onto the blackface characters, and it is there that the song connects with members of an audience who might have worried at some time about walking through the woods at night or through the dark streets and alleyways of the city. The setting is ill defined in contrast to the original—the only reference to a rural setting is the mention of a cow—so that the audience watches the dramatization of conventional fright responses through the vehicle of the burnt cork mask.

Most blackface minstrel companies during the mid-1840s seem to have selected individual numbers from popular Italian operas or works in the Italian style regardless of the nationality of the composer. Balfe's works (*The Bohemian Girl* and *The Enchantress*) were certainly in the Italian style. The desire to parody stage works extended to works by American composers, including the "first" American grand opera, by William Henry Fry.[40] The connection between Fry's work and minstrelsy is not as remote as might be presumed. The lead role was created for Anne Seguin, whose work had already been parodied in the blackface productions of *La Sonnambula.*

The most popular of the parodies from Fry's *Leonora* (1845) were "Dinah's Wedding Day," based on "Fill Up the Vine Wreathed Cup," and "De Colored Fancy Ball" (1848), derived from "Through the Halls Resounding." "De Colored Fancy Ball" is based on an original chorus of more than 240 measures. Fry's original chorus was set in E♭ major and scored for SATB and soloists. It was set in a tripartite design (ABA) with several sections, including a modulating middle part, and functioned as part of a grand stage scene in the opera's first act.[41] In the published parody the music was transposed to D major, the overall structure condensed (from 240 mm. to 89 mm.), the modulatory section simplified, and the second phrase (beginning with "To dance de Polka measure") rewritten. The accompaniment in the sheet music edition was completely reset with a simple bass tone and block-chord accompaniment or bass tone and arpeggiated chords for occasional contrast. (See music examples 4a and b.)

At 120 measures, "De Colored Fancy Ball" is one of the more extensive pieces of *minstrel* choral music available in print, ranking it with the "Phantom Chorus" from *La Sonnambula* and "Virginia Rose Bud" from Auber's *Le Cheval de bronze.*[42] The arranger literally recomposed the Fry original, focusing attention on the choral dance (waltz) section and simplifying the whole piece by limiting the more or less superfluous modulations that were the major pretensions of an American composer writing in an Italian style. Fry's chorus repeats the same text throughout while the music changes; the parody presents new words describing some of the characters at the mock ball while the music is repeated (see figs. 1a and b).

The strophic form of "De Colored Fancy Ball" supports the stage business that would have called for a repetition of the accompanying dance. The two other parts of the piece shown in figure 1b are also revealing because the texts are part of a

Example 4a. "Through the Halls Resounding," from *Leonora* (1845). Used by permission of the Pennsylvania State University Libraries.

Example 4a. (cont.)

Example 4b. "De Color'd Fancy Ball" (New York: William Hall and Son, 1848). Used by permission of the Brown University Library.

Example 4b. (cont.)

	Part 1	
Instrumental introduction 32 mm. in E♭ major, followed by choral intro. of 12 mm.: "'Tis mirth's welcome power, That rules the bright hours."	A 16 mm. male chorus (SATB), E♭ major: "Through the halls resounding, With melodious measure, Blended forms are bounding, Light with festal pleasure."	B 16 mm. solos, E♭ major: "'Tis the moment when beauty's fond smile, Gallant spirits sigh to share, 'Tis the moment when love may beguile, Virgin hearts its chain to wear."
		A 16 mm. (SATB), E♭ major: text of A repeated

	Part 2	
Musical transition 16 mm., modulation to A♭ major	C 16 mm., A♭ major: text of A repeated	D 34 mm., A♭ and other keys: text of B repeated

	Part 3	
Choral introduction repeated 12 mm., E♭ major	A' (A of part 1 repeated) 16 mm., E♭ major: text of A repeated	B' (B of part 1 repeated) 16 mm., E' major: text of B repeated
		A' (A repeated and extended) 16 mm., E♭ major: text of A repeated

Figure 1a. Design of "Through the Halls Resounding," from *Leonora* (1845), act 1, sc. 3; ABA'CDA'B'A' (ternary form) of 198 mm.

Part 1 (first time)

Prelude, 16 mm., D major: piano accompaniment, waltz meter established

A

Three-part male chorus (TTB), 16 mm., D major:

"Oh what enchanting pleasure,
On de light Bombastic toe,
To dance de Polka measure,
And thro' de waltz to go.//"

A'

Three-part male (TTB) chorus, 16 mm., D major:

"Specially wid de Venus
Dat holds your heart in thrall,
What sweet words pass between us,
At de Colored Fancy Ball.//"

B

Tenor solo with ascending and descending scale passages like original source, 16 mm., D major:

"Now den Gemblemen please to be quiet,
De Ball am gwarn to begin,
If you dair make a mus or a riot,
'Twill cost you a kick on de shin.//"

C

Three-part male chorus, modulating from D to C major and back:

"Now de music sweetly sound,
Dark eyes now are glancing,
Chassez croisez prombernade,
Oh de joys ob dancing!//"

C'

Three-part male chorus, 16 mm., D major:

"Now 'tis de time to whisper soft tings,
Sigh as if gwain to expire,
Talk ob dat little blind boy dats got wings,
Den sweat dat your heart am on fire.//"

A

Three-part male chorus, 16 mm., D major: text of A repeated

Postlude

8 mm.; music returns to the introduction to round off the song

Part 2: Additional Verses for Strophic Song

Prelude, 16 mm., repeated

(Like other strophic songs of the period, this parody returns to the beginning and runs through the second verse accordingly.)

A

16 mm.:

"Observe dat lubly Juno,
Wid de luxurant head ob wool;
She beats all de gals day you know,
I guess above a jug full.//"

A'

16 mm.:

"Jus look how she toe and heel it,
As she ballensays to de crowd;
And dat color'd gent seems to feel it,
For no gobbler was ever so proud.//"

B

16 mm.:

"See he offers a glass ob Ice cream,
Wid a real silver spoon just stuck in it;
She takes it but surely I dream,
For by golly 'tis gone in a minute.//"

C

16 mm.:

"See dat Nigg in de blue satin vest.
Wid his heel sticking out feet sirs;
Cutting such capers and doing his best,
To charm ev'ry gal dat he meet sirs.//"
Postlude
repeated, as before

C'

16 mm.:

"Sich a darky as dat has not right at de ball,
Tell him to quit and be off;
He had two years in Sing Sing and came out last fall,
For picking up tings on de wharf.//"

132 •

Figure 1b. "De Colored Fancy Ball" (1848). AA'BCCA' design of 120 mm. without internal repeats. The diagram is meant to be read from left to narrative commenting on the persons attending the ball and providing an opportunity for individual performers to exhibit their costumes and participate in the accompanying stage business. The song was a parody of fancy balls in general because they were held by all classes (with significant differences, of course), but it was probably aimed at African American dances in particular.

The performance may have included some instrumental interludes not published in the sheet music version of the song. The result is a good introduction to the ways in which American music was destined to develop. The stylistic contrast is between the strophic or repetitive techniques of popular music and the through-composed style of a European-derived practice. The minstrel style accommodates the waltz form, a simplified melodic design, and an accompaniment pattern acceptable to the skills of a modest amateur.

There are some textual references in the parody that the contemporary audience would have recognized easily. Pilfering ("picking up tings on de wharf") applies primarily to the longshoremen probably of the New York area who by this time were almost certainly not black. The dances mentioned (polkas, waltzes, line dances) are important also because the minstrel playbills show how common parodies of social dancing were. The popularity of those dances is reinforced by the number of polkas in banjo tutors, which indicates the polka's distribution among musicians after its introduction to the United States in the 1840s. By midcentury the various national dances from Europe used in American formal balls included polkas, waltzes, mazurkas, galops, and schottisches, whose rhythms were incorporated into American song. The Christys often included a "Burlesque Cachuca" or a "Burlesque on the popular and fashionable POLKA" in the regular programs as an example of their continued interest in ridiculing imported material.[43]

Who were the subjects of the satire in "De Colored Fancy Ball"? Were they African Americans who strove to imitate the manners of urban whites? That is a plausible reading and would certainly fit with some whites' feelings of superiority and the theory that such texts should be classified as racist disparagement humor. There is evidence that whites repeatedly ridiculed African Americans whose social and class aspirations as *Americans* were equivalent to those of whites. The white-on-black social critiques often appeared in caricatures and cartoons published in *Atkinson's Saturday Evening Post* (Philadelphia) between January 7 and April 7, 1832, *De Darkies' Comic All-Me-Nig* (Philadelphia, 1846), and other occasional publications of the 1830–40 period, that is, close enough to the origins of organized minstrelsy to have some potential connection.[44]

Social dances were part of the acculturation process for young people of all races and ethnic groups. The text of "De Colored Fancy Ball" ridicules both the male and female characters at one such dance among blacks and notes that antisocial behavior (the "muss" or "riot"), although common enough to be mocked, should not be tolerated at any dances held by any group; the point is that the dance was yet another occasion for male rivalry and sexual conquest. That made the "muss" a real possibility, especially among groups known for their belligerence. Admission to such balls, already satirized in *The Hop of Fashion*, was expected to be restricted so that the ex-convict (the pilferer) and similar persons could be excluded from polite society, especially on the occasion of a fancy ball.

Figures 1a and b show how the arranger reduced the original example from over 200 measures to 120 by dropping the instrumental transitions and avoiding the extensive modulations and repeats used in Fry's choral dance. This is a recomposition that simplifies Fry's example while retaining some of its attractive melodic features. The diagrams and the musical examples reveal a far more sophisticated style than that of the simple strophic songs typical of early minstrelsy and reinforce the argument that minstrelsy was a site for style assimilation regardless of its racial overtones.

The minstrel adaptations continue the double masquerade with cross-dressed men representing women and blackface makeup disguising white curiosity about how the "others" behaved at what were certainly segregated social events. The focus of the text is curious because the first verse is a general introduction, and the others mention only three characters, one couple and the ex-convict; it contains stereotypic references to wool, heels, and the speed with which the woman consumes the ice cream.

"De Colored Fancy Ball" characterizes the "others" attending a single-race event and projects what occurred to some of those attending. The men mentioned are not squabbling over a woman; the couple behave as any couple might at any similar social event. There are no differences between the white and black fancy balls other than the physical characteristics attributed to the black participants. Missing from the satire is an emphasis on the negative traits or deficiencies of the target group. Christie Davies has argued that the primary characteristic of an ethnic joke is that the "joketellers ascribe human deficiencies to other ethnic groups in an excessive or ludicrous fashion."[45] Using Davies's definition, "De Colored Fancy Ball" is not a successful ethnic joke unless the persons who heard it connected the parody with minstrelsy's tendency to take the broadest possible swipe at the customs and behaviors of contemporary social life. There are very few songs mocking the behaviors of any ethnic or racial groups during the antebellum era, a period of intense class awareness and significant competition for social position or respectability. The physical characteristics of burnt cork and cross-dressed characters were presented as African American because American musical comedy did not attack the pretensions of white upper-class society directly; masquerade was the more acceptable way of treating the whole issue obliquely. Why, for example, are the major satirical commentaries on social issues limited to the creations of blackface comedians allegedly masquerading as urban blacks? Judging matters on the basis of "De Colored Fancy Ball," it appears that the subject went well beyond a satire of African American social gatherings to include all the fancy dance and social dancing customs of the 1840s and 1850s. White audiences would probably have rejected the masquerade if the jokes had been addressed directly to them; instead, they accepted the performance because it is always the "others" who look ridiculous decked out in costumed finery. The comic device is based on a sense of racial difference, which is the reason for references to heels, but the "others" become the vehicles protecting white egos from disparaging jokes about themselves.

"De Colored Fancy Ball" ascribes a social ineptness to the blackface characters that may have focused attention on African Americans as the victims of this form of humor. The social ineptitude described in the chorus applies across the races, however, because the inherent problems are associated with class and with the mishaps likely to occur at the many balls or dancing events that took place in the modern city. The references to eating ice cream, the clothing worn by both sexes, and the flirtations of the guests surely suggest that other young men and women often overacted in these situations. In other words, although the parody portrays only black people behaving in the ways described, the point is that anybody can look silly in trying to attract a partner for dance or for life.

This parody of a chorus from Fry's *Leonora,* alleged in its own day to be the first American grand opera, emphasizes that neither this chorus nor the entire opera had anything to do with an American subject and was most certainly *not* composed in an "American" style. *Leonora* was deemed a failure "because it was derivative," even though it contains any number of fine solo and choral numbers.[46] Why parody a piece most of the audiences had never heard unless "Through the Halls Resounding" possessed useful features making it attractive as "American" music? The most likely answer is that, like the other Italian choruses used by the minstrels, it was not the source of the style that mattered so much as its suitability in a stylistic context that had already adapted itself to a different type of choral music.

A revival of *Leonora* was attempted in New York in 1858.[47] Although the opera failed to capture public attention, some of the music was apparently known in the musical community. The choruses, however, must have been known either from the few performances or from the piano-vocal score. How Christy got the material and why he thought it worthy of performance by his group remain mysteries. The opera's libretto was a "contemporary comedy of social manners, about class and money, two subjects of perennial interest to American audiences."[48] The opera provides an interesting insight into the interdependence of the minstrel show and the opera.

The second most popular parody from *Leonora* was "Dinah's Wedding Day," which, although it was published under Edwin Christy's name, was probably not arranged by him. Fry's original opera was presented at Philadelphia's Chestnut Street Theater on June 4, 1845, and given some sixteen additional performances, including four at the Walnut Street Theater. The lead soprano role was written for Anne Seguin, whose husband's performance of "Vi ravviso" was parodied in the "See, Sir,

See" example discussed earlier. Again, minstrelsy was tuned to the topical; its burlesques and parodies derived from the theatrical and concert events of the moment, with blackface used as the vehicle for nativist envy regarding the success of foreign performers. Christy's parody (based on "Fill Up the Vine Wreathed Cup") takes all the music from the original (including the prominent descending diminished seventh chords characteristic of the opera), retains the move to the relative minor even though his version is transposed down a minor third to C major, and includes the solo-chorus interchanges. The original was written mostly for three-part mixed chorus, whereas the Christy example was arranged for four male voices, as is clear from the directions for the tenor and bass solos clearly indicated in the parts. The musical style and performance practice are therefore quite close in spite of the different venues. (See music examples 5a and b.)

Many significant stylistic questions and ironies emerge from parodies like this one, for Fry wrote in his preface to the piano-vocal score that "the public attention given to the first American work of this kind induces the trust that in this country, which has been accumulating wealth, taste, and knowledge conferred by freedom and peace, and a coincident prosperity, there may a rapid, and at the same time, a vigorous growth of this branch of Art. . . . It is a matter of regret that English genius, so fertile in letters and arts, should have neglected this complete form of opera, or attempted only in 'burlesque' what should have been accomplished with sobriety and truth."[49] The irony is that Fry's "American" opera was generally considered a flop because it was derivative, and the minstrel show became the "only distinctly American contribution to the theater," its success directly proportional to its parodies, burlesques, and caricatures of real or imagined cultural and ethnic stereotypes.

The Dinah of "Dinah's Wedding Day" is a reluctant bride, but her situation is not the focal point for what is obviously a choral piece that usually served as a finale to one section of the minstrel show. The solo parts clearly indicate that the arranger intended four different voices to have roles in the song, partly because "Dinah's Wedding Day" is a parody and partly because such an arrangement would have given each member of the group an opportunity for a solo. Since the song deals with male rivalry, it is appropriate that the different soloists act out their parts. The narrator clearly emphasizes the male rivalry theme characteristic of masculine relationships expressed in minstrel shows. The characters of Pomp (Pompey) and Cuff (Cuffee) are mentioned by the bass voices in the second part of the song just prior to the repetition of the opening chorus. As a "Wenus from de south," Dinah is an object of desire, but again the rivalry ends with the marriage and the generally celebratory mood of the number. The references to corn, hoecakes, gumbo, cream, and the wedding cake "on which each dark must dream" suggest a relationship, whether real or invented, with African American wedding practices. For the most part, the other prominent characteristics of this particular example are the typical minstrel show references to the banjo, all-night festivities, and the male rivalry themes found elsewhere in the minstrel show.

Example 5a. "Fill Up the Vine Wreath'd Cup," from Fry's *Leonora*. Used by permission of the Pennsylvania State University Libraries.

Example 5a. (cont.)

Example 5b. "Dinah's Wedding Day" (New York: Bassford and Brower, 1852). Used by permission of the Brown University Library.

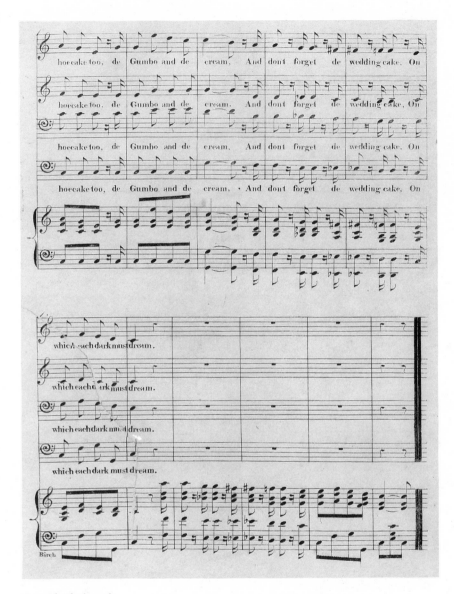

Example 5b. (cont.)

The *Leonora* chorus is set for three parts that grow to four or five when the soloists join for an ensemble number, the general rule for operatic choruses that do not serve as finales for acts or scenes. The Christys' arranger added a fourth part, the second tenor, to the SATB format designated in the sheet music edition. The parody, however, was set for four male voices, regardless of what the sheet music indicates, and the tenor part typically crosses the soprano line, which was probably sung by another tenor. The sheet music indicates that the song was to be performed twice with identical choral sections. Two solos were inserted immediately before the last statement of the final choral section. The original labels those solos "verse 1" and "verse 2":

"Dinah's Wedding Day"

Verse 1
Tenor Solo: Dinah's de prettiest gal dat ever you did see,
 And dar was once a time, she show'd sheeps eyes at me,
 But now those days are past, and dis poor child's forsaken,
 Alas and well a day.
Bass Solo: You Pomp fetch back dat Bacon

Verse 2
Tenor solo: First hear dat darkey shut up dat are mouf,
 Wed with you my Dinah dear, my Venus from de South,
 Come let us dance and sing, laugh and be jolly,
 Dinah dat sweetest gal.
Bass Solo: Has married Cuff by Golly.

The celebratory character of "Dinah's Wedding Day" is apparent. When the parody is detached from the opera, the audience misses the sentimental material that surrounds the drinking song in the original. Heard separately, then, in the context of the minstrel show, the parody is a very different work. Figures 2a and b illustrate the points raised in the discussion of "De Colored Fancy Ball." Both examples are three-part (ABA design), with the middle section modulating to the subdominant (A♭) in the original, but the parody is much less imaginative harmonically. There is a modulation, but it simply moves from D major, through the subdominant G to C major, and back again. The overall sectional form of the *Leonora* chorus is In–Pr–A–B–A–T–C–D–Pr–A'–B'–A', where everything but the introduction (32 mm.) and choral prelude (12 mm.) is 16 measures long, for a total of 200 measures. The extent of the design changes and simplification of the entire piece is displayed graphically in figure 2b. The sectional design is Pr–A–A'–B–C–C'–A–Po, with every section except the postlude (8 mm.) being 16 measures long and the total length being 120 measures; once the sectional repeats (indicated by the prime symbol in the figure) are discounted, however, the entire song is really an ABCA form. There are five repeats of the same text in "Through the Halls Resounding," but the

Prelude
8 mm.

Section A (24 mm.)

Chorus A, 8 mm., E♭ major:
"Fill up, fill up the vine wreathed cup
And drain its golden well,
Where truth lies deep,
And bright thoughts sleep,
And dreamy mem'ries dwell."

Chorus B, 8 mm., E♭ major:
"Fill up, and bring the ruby spring,
To lips whose kindred glow,
Full well may prove,
How wine and love,
Make earth a heav'n below."

Chorus C, 8mm., C and G minor to E♭ major:
"Grim care we flout, with merry shout,
Hurrah! Hurrah! Hurrah!
And while we quaff, blend song and laugh,
Ha-ha, ha-hah! ha-hah! ha-hah!"

Section B (12 mm.)

Transition, 4 mm., modulation back to E♭ major:
"Fill up! Fill up! Fill up!
Hurrah! hurrah! hurrah!"

Chorus B, 8 mm., E♭ major:
text of B repeated

Section A (16 mm.)

Chorus A, 8 mm., E♭ major:
text of A repeated

Figure 2a: William Henry Fry's "Fill Up the Vine Wreathed Cup," from *Leonora*, act 1, sc. 1 (part 1 only); overall design of part 1: Pr–A–B–C–X–A–B (8–8–8–8–4–8–8 = 52 mm.).

Part 1

Prelude,
8 mm.,
C major

Chorus A, 8 mm., C major:
"Huzzah, huzzah, de day is come,
Miss Dinah's to be married,
Oh, glad am me, for dats a fact,
For bery long she's tarried."

Tenor Solo and Chorus B, 12 mm., A minor to G^7:
Solo: "For we will dance and sing all night,"
Chorus: "Huzzah, huzzah, huzzah,"
Solo: "An play de Banjo till daylight,"
Chorus: "Ha. ha, ha, ha, ha, ha, ha, ha."
Solo: "We'll dance and sing, like any ting,"
Chorus: "Huzaah, huzzah, huzzah,"

Chorus A, 8 mm., C major:
text of A repeated

Chorus A', 8mm., C major:
"Bring out de corn, de hoe cake too,
De gumbo and de cream,
And don't forget the wedding cake,
On which each dark must dream."

Chorus A, 8 mm., C major:
text of A' repeated

Transition to Part 2
4 mm., descending diminished seventh chords to V^7–I cadence

Figure 2b: Christy's parody "Dinah's Wedding Day" (part 1 only); overall design of part 1: Pr–A–B–X–A–A (8–8–8–4–8–8 = 52 mm.).

first section is repeated only once during the first complete presentation of "De Colored Fancy Ball." The wedding song burlesque is characteristic of the ways other operatic choruses were presented on the minstrel stage. The musical material was generally retained, and the sheet music editions were usually published in easy keys for singers and accompanists. The choral writing was not difficult and for the most part copied the Italian style. In this respect there is little difference between the stylistic details; it is the performance practice that must be assumed to have differed, for the perception of the presentation would surely have been different if pantomime were employed in front of a stationary chorus. The Dinah of the number would then be presented before an audience as the obvious prize for the male of her choosing just as a bride at a wedding ceremony would be introduced to her spouse—depending, of course, on the practices appropriate for the various social classes during the period.

Opera burlesques were not limited to the borrowing of one or two sections of contemporary material. In some cases ensembles with gifted singers attempted much more elaborate performances. These attempts illustrate the distinctions between the average ensembles and those with a much higher level of professional skills. The New Orleans Serenaders continued to present burlesque operas, especially after Henrietta Sontag's successful production of *La Sonnambula* at Niblo's Garden in January 1853.[50] They toured the western United States during 1852, and in 1853 they reestablished themselves in New York, where they remained for three years. In November 1853 the Buckleys brought out their "Grand New Burlesque on the Opera of *Norma*," and less than one-half year later (Apr. 22, 1854) they presented their "version" of Donizetti's *Lucia di Lammermoor* (1835), whose first American production occurred in New Orleans (May 28, 1841). The New York premiere (Sept. 15, 1843) was so bad that the local papers panned the pickup "Italian" opera company.[51] The incompetence of the performers could itself have been suitable material for any comic burlesque. This is how the burlesque was announced on the playbill:

Part III

Grand Burlesque Opera of *Lucia di Lammermoor*

Edgardo [Sir Edgar Ravenswood]	Swaine Buckley
Lucy [Lucy Ashton]	Waddleton
Ashton, Papa to Lucy	Percival
Sig. Numskull, bodyguard to Ashton	R. Bishop Buckley
Sig. Santa Anita Gadsden Bill I Anto	Mullen
Sig. Life Perserverantiti	Lonsdale
Sig. Poco Tempo Californiatiti	Stevens
Sig. Petite Uncletomscabininahorn	J. Buckley
Sig. Le Compra Ova	R. Carroll
Leader of the Orchestra	F. Buckley[52]

The Buckleys provided the model for other groups entering the blackface business, for example, Josiah Perham's Ethiopian Troupe and Great Burlesque Company, who presented their "Burlesque Extravaganza Operatic of *Norma; or, The Injured Princess*" (Feb. 13, 1855) and a "Burlesque Opera of the *Barber of Seville* Plot Laid in Boston with Local Hits" (July 31, 1856). The Buckleys schooled several performers, such as Samuel Sanford, who continued the Buckley traditions after the deaths of Fred (1864) and Richard (1867) by using their material at his ill-fated Twelfth Street Opera House (Aug. to Dec. 1853) and later at the famous Eleventh Street House (1859–62).[53]

The critical significance of the burlesque versions of Bellini or the other English arrangements of his work, over and above their expressed disdain for the conventions of Italian opera—recall Buckley's statement about driving "away the dullness of too close an observation of the original text"—is in the use of blackface as a means of "Americanizing" the material. The English versions did not provide the local color or the American environment that some audiences demanded. Once opera was seen as an art form for the upper class or at least for those with a strong allegiance to European or English color, authors of burlesques transformed the settings and characters of opera by mixing them with local color and stage types. When the operas were presented in this form, Americans seemed capable of enjoying Bellini, Donizetti, and Rossini among the Italians and contributions of the Frenchmen Auber and Scribe. The burlesques were popular precisely because they made the operatic material accessible to American audiences, an observation confirmed by a *New York Tribune* writer on October 8, 1855, who concluded that "to those lovers of music for whom the Opera is too intricate, the Oratorio too dull, the Concert too scientific, and all too expensive, Ethiopian Minstrelsy is a melodious benefaction coming within reach of both their appreciation and their pockets."[54]

One of the Buckleys' burlesques of *The Bohemian Girl* shows the lengths to which the company went to ensure that they included the original musical material in their longer programs. The following example compares the contents of a Buckley Serenaders' playbill of October 30, 1854, with the libretto of the original opera. It shows how the musical numbers match up and reveals the unfortunately small amount known about the ways in which the Buckleys handled the spoken dialogue, what musical instruments provided accompaniment (White's groups were using the piano for this purpose), and how the plantation setting contrasted with Count Arnheim's sumptuous estate.

The cuts in the burlesques appear to have been quite lengthy, and many questions present themselves about how the piece would have looked to the audience. For example, why did the Buckleys delete the hit chorus "In the Gypsies Life You Read" from the first act? And how did the choral and orchestral material from the scene (if it was actually used) match with the "Life on the Old Plantation" material? It appears that the Buckleys introduced at least two period blackface songs, "Hit Him in the Eye

Ball, Bim" and the Rice vehicle "Sich a Getting up Stairs" (184?), to mimic the stage business associated with the pursuit of the kidnappers in the original opera.[55]

Balfe, *The Bohemian Girl* (1843)	Buckley, *Bohemian Girl Burlesque* (1854)
Act 1, Scene 1 (Celebration of Austrian Victory in Poland, Count Arnheim's Estate in Presburg)	*Act 1, Scene 1* (Celebration of Lucy's Third Birthday, Corn Cob's Plantation)
Chorus: Up with the Banner	Chorus: Up with the banner
Count: A soldier's life	Corn Cob: A Darkies life
Thaddeus: 'Tis sad to leave our Fatherland	Lemuel: 'Tis sad to leave one's fatherland
Gipsies: In the gypsies life you read	
Devilshoof and Thaddeus: Comrade your hand	Lemuel and Possum Heel: Comrade your hand
Florestein: Is no succour near at hand?	
[Rescue of Arline occurs here.]	[Rescue of Lucy from wild coon occurs here.]
	Lemuel: I left my home some time ago
	Lemuel [Corn Cob?]: Stranger accept my galvanic thanks
Orchestra: Waltz and Dance Scene	Life on the Old Plantation [unidentified]
Thaddeus and Chorus: Down with the daring slave who disputes the right	Lemuel: The toast disdained [Character refuses the toast.]
[Scene includes Thaddeus's refusal to toast the Austrian emperor.]	
Orchestra: Galop [during which Arline is kidnapped]	
Count and Chorus: What sounds break upon the ear?	Chorus: Rise old Corn Cob (Hit Him in the Eye Ball, Bim)
Chorus: Follow, follow [All players exit in pursuit of Devilshoof and Arline.]	[Character Unidentified]: Oh golly, I am a gonner
	[Character Unidentified]: Carry me to my palet [*sic*]
	[Character Unidentified]: Sich a Getting Up Stairs
	Chorus: Follow, follow.
Act 2, Scene 1 (Street in Presburg by Moonlight)	*Act 2, Scene 1* (A Plantation by Moonlight)
Gipsies: Silence, the lady moon	Chorus: Silence lady moon
[Long scene with Florestein, Devilshoof, Queen of the Gipsies, and others.]	

Arline: I dreamt I dwelt in marble halls
Thaddeus: The wound upon thine arm
Arline and Thaddeus: The secret of her birth
Arline: What is the spell hath yet effaced
Arline: Listen while I relate the hope of a Gipsy's fate
Gipsies: In the gipsy's life you read

Scene 2 (Another street in Presburg)
Chorus: In the gipsies life you read
Arline: Love is the first thing to clasp

Scene 3 (A Grand Fair in the Public Square of Presburg)
Chorus: Life itself is at its best
Quartet [Arline, Queen, Thaddeus Devils-hoof]: From the valleys and the hills

[Arline ends up with a medallion previously stolen from Florestein. He confronts Arline and Thaddeus and accuses her. Thaddeus rushes to her aid.]

Thaddeus: Tear them assunder

Scene 4 (Interior of Count Arnheim's Apartment)
Count: The heart bow'd down [Arnheim, contemplating a portrait of Arline, recalls his loss while background scene shows Arline in jail. The prisoner is brought before the count for judgment. Facing the loss of her freedom, Arline draws a dagger from beneath her scarf and is about to stab herself.]
Count: Hold! hold! We cannot give the life we take

[Scene continues with the reunion of Arline and her father; Thaddeus and Arline are reunited also.]

Lucy: I dreamt I dwelt in Chinese hall[56]
Lemuel: That wound upon thy arm,
Lemuel and Lucy: The secret of her birth

Lucy: Lemuel my lark

Chorus: Happy and light.

Scene 2 (A Wood)
Chorus: In the darkies life you lead.

Scene 3 (Fair Scene)

[Most of the original scene appears to have been cut.]

[As in the original, Lucy/Arline is arrested for stealing Billy Bean's property. Lemuel/Thaddeus defends her.]

Lemuel: I can whip any darkie on the ground.

Scene 4 (Interior of Corn Cob's House)

Corn Cob: The heart bow'd down

Corn Cob: Hold, hold

[Corn Cob notices a mark on Arline's arm and questions her.]
Corn Cob: How came that mark. [Arline reveals the origin of the mark, and the reunion is ensured.]

Count: Mine own, my long lost child!

Thaddeus and Arline: On heaven! Prais'd be the will of heav'n whose light o'er me smiled

Count, Devhilshoof, Thaddeus, and Arline: Prais'd be heaven

Count: 'Tis thy Daddy stands before thee

Chorus: Praised be heaven.

Act 3 (Splendid Saloon in Arnheim's Castle)

Arline: The past appears to me but a dream

Thaddeus: When other lips and hearts their tales
... then you'll remember me

Thaddeus, Arline, and Devilshoof: Through the world wilt thou fly love

Chorus: Welcome the present

Thaddeus, Count, Queen, Arline, and Florestein: Though every hope be fled

Arline: See at your feet a suppliant one

Thaddeus: When the fair land of Poland

Arline, Thaddeus, Count: Let not the soul for sorrows grieve

Arline and Chorus: Oh! What full delight.

Act 3, Scene 1 (Corn Cob's Chamber)

[Lucy is discovered meditating.]

Lemuel: Then you'll remember me

Lemuel, Possum Heel, and Lucy: Through the world wilt thou fly love

Quintette: Tho' every hope

Lucy: See at thy feet a suppliant one

Lemuel: The fair land of Virginia

Chorus: What full delight

The Buckleys apparently had a much shorter version of the burlesque that served sometimes as an afterpiece in their regular shows. The following extract from a playbill from March 6, 1854, shows a typical "highlights" program without intervening dialogue linking the various songs into a consistent narrative.[57] That may have been added in the performance, or the audience may have been expected to fill in the gaps from their own knowledge of the opera, which had been performed in New York many times.

Part III: Grand Operatic Burlesque of *The Bohemian Girl*

Cast

Lemuel, a banished Dukie

Lucy, Supposed to be Contralto, searching for her Papa

Count Corn Cob, an elderly gent, looking for his daughter

Heeltoe, friend to Lemuel

Possumheel

Clara Snowdrop

Gumbo Twolips

Aunt Debby, a fortune teller

Programme of Music

Silence the lady moon .... Lemuel
I Dreamt I dwelt in marble halls................................... Lucy
You'll Remember Me .... Lemuel
That wound upon thine Arm .... Lucy and Lemuel
Through the world wilt thou fly love .... Lucy, Lemuel, and Possumheel
Happy and light of heart are those...................... Chorus [Company]
The Heart bow'd down .... Corn Cob
In the darkie's life you lead .... Chorus [Company]
They stole my child away .... Corn Cob and Chorus
What visions... Corn Cob and Lucy
When the niggars in Virginia .... Lemuel
What full delight .... Lucy and Chorus

The most parodied item among the hits from *The Bohemian Girl* was Arline's dream of home as captured in "I Dreamt I Dwelled in Marble Halls," the air so despised by Richard Grant White (see music examples 6a and b).[58] Not only is this a classic example from English opera of the period, but it is also part of a lingering theme in mid-nineteenth-century culture: the poverty-stricken young maiden of regal hopes dreaming for the life of a princess and the adoration by a host of suitors.

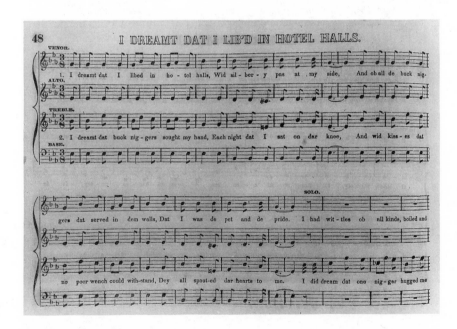

Example 6a. "I Dreamt Dat I Lib'd in Hotel Halls," from *EGB1*. Used by permission of the Brown University Library.

I Dreamt That I Dwelt in Marble Halls

From BALFE's "Bohemian Girl"

Example 6b. "I Dreamt That I Dwelt in Marble Halls," from *Heart Songs* (1909).

I Dreamt That I Dwelt in Marble Halls

Example 6b. (cont.)

The subject of this parody and the reason for its lingering presence is its obvious trivialization of the original's sentimentality. The blackface revisionists replaced the romantic castle settings and the hope of upward mobility with the practical life of the rooming house and the desire for a better diet. Arline's love of low-status deer meat and humble accommodations linger as memories of her life among the Gypsies and common folk after her restoration. There is a mixture of sentimentality and skepticism in the linking of the castle and hotel (or rooming house) metaphors. For most of the young women who came to the cities to work, the thought of liberation through love or elevation through the discovery of a noble and loving prince were just that; something earnestly to be hoped for but unlikely to be fulfilled. The following compares the original to the parody:[59]

Michael William Balfe, "I Dreamt I Dwelt in Marble Halls," from The Bohemian Girl

Minstrel Parody of "Marble Halls" (EGB1, 48)

Verse 1
I dreamt I dwelt in marble halls,
With vassals and serfs at my side,

Verse 1
I dreamt dat I libed in hotel halls,
Wid silbery pans at my side,

And of all who assembled within those
walls,
That I was the hope and pride.
I had riches too great to count
Could boast of a high ancestral
name,
But I also dream'd, which pleased me
most,
That you lov'd me still the same,
That you lov'd me, still the same,
That you lov'd me, you lov'd me, still the
same. .

Verse 2
I dreamt that suitors sought my
hand,
That knights upon bended knee,
And with vows no maiden heart could
withstand,
They pledged their faith to me,
And I dreamt that one of that noble
host,
Came forth my hand to claim;
But I also dreamt, which charmed me
most,
That you love'd me . . . lov'd me, still the
same.

And ob all de buck niggers dat served in
dem walls,
Dat I was de pet and de pride.
Solo: I had wittles ob all kinds, boiled and
roast,
And dishes too many to name,
Chorus: And I also dreamed, what
charmed me most,
dat I lobed Coon still de same.
And I also dreamed, what charmed me
most,
Dat I lobed Coon, dat I lobed Coon, still
de same.

Verse 2
I dreamed dat buck niggers sought my
hand,
Each night dat I sat on dar knee,
And wid kisses dat no poor wench could
withstand,
Dey all spouted dar hearts to me.
Solo: I did dream dat one nigger hugged
me close,
Brought sassage and oder roast game,
Chorus: (repeat from verse 1)

The presentation of this text, which was set to one of the most beloved melodies of the period, focused directly on the masking metaphor of blackface comedy. The voices of the despised are represented by a soloist and male chorus in the *Ethiopian Glee Book* version (see music example 6a), but the part of the young woman was probably played in drag, making the parody a burlesque of the whole concept of marrying above one's class. And class mattered in marriage, because "the onset of political democracy appeared to have no effect on the kind of family partners desired by New York City's oldest and most admired families. In the new era as in the old they bound themselves to families of distinction." That general pattern did not change when the newly wealthy came to choose spouses; that is, the marriages "owe[d] at least as much to considerations of the marketplace as to expectations of romantic bliss, paired wealth with wealth."[60] The literal meaning of the parody text describes a servant class—service employees—and shows the idea of love among them being no less dear than among any other New Yorkers.

There is every reason to believe that most audiences were familiar with the story of Arline, who knew she was not a Gypsy but a lost aristocrat looking for happiness and a secure community to replace the vagabond life of Devilshoof, the Gypsy queen, and the other characters of the original *Bohemian Girl*. Americans recognized the beauties of Balfe's melodies, the musical qualities of the choruses, and the melodramatic effectiveness of the operatic treatment. The burlesque, an obvious exaggeration of the sentimentality of the original, explored courtship difficulties, personal jealousies, societal involvement in marriage choices, misunderstood motives, and all the typical intrigues of the operatic stage. Although Americans could accept those features of the work—they were the lingua franca of nineteenth-century melodrama—many of those who believed that Americans must create their own culture could not publicly admire something as un-American as an Italianate opera. As the *New York Clipper* put it: "The Italian Opera has *gone in*, or, what is precisely the same, *just stepped out*. No loss to the public." Furthermore, it claimed, "The only *Italian opera* that can succeed in this country will be an *American* one."[61]

The American ambivalence toward opera was part of a shared concern about whether the United States had or could have a national culture. The compromise answer and easy escape from the question was to promote the enjoyment of the more popular aspects of the opera by masking and mocking the original materials or accomplishing what in folk culture is known as "signifying" on the original sources: appropriating the useful elements and linking them, however loosely, to new or different non-European performance styles, namely, borrowed or invented African American music. That is why the Buckleys described their burlesques as "Ethiopianized," that is, transformed from objects of class adulation to commodities for public enjoyment.

The parodies of English and Italian plays and operas reflected Americans' insecurities about their own culture and their inability to predict what its significant accomplishments might be. Burlesques played a significant role in encouraging the absorption of styles that took place whenever Italian music was memorized or arranged. The Italianate melodies of Stephen Foster are just as much a part of the history of American music as they are examples of the extension of Italian vocal traditions into Anglo-American culture, something Whitman acknowledged when he wrote: "The English opera, the tunes of the ballads, &c. sung by the various bands of 'minstrels,' and indeed all modern musical performances and compositions are, to all intents and purposes, but driblets from Italian music. —True they are bequeathed to use, from other quarters, some fresh and original tunes, as the native songs of Scotland, Ireland, and one or two other lands."[62]

The burlesque opera or travesty was an act of criticism by imitation or mimicry. The playbills and texts tell us what the minstrels thought was wrong about Italian opera. The Americanization of the material occurred by assigning the story to masked characters—the blackface comedians—whose performance of English and

Italian song styles in the guise of surrogate outsiders merely reinforced the foreign domination of American song. Although the minstrels proclaimed their alleged dependence on African American music, they were incorporating other styles into their productions, usually via this parody process.

The criticism displayed in the opera burlesques had social as well as musical origins. The social origins stem from the fact that support for imported opera was linked to the conscious attempts by New York's elite to use European cultural forms as a mark of class membership. The elites enforced the social rituals appropriate for concert attendance and demonstrated not only their wealth but also their acquisition of cultural products considered appropriate to "better" persons. Appearance at the opera was part of a social ritual designed to display status more than it was an excursion for furthering aesthetic pleasure in a form of entertainment whose plots differed little from the spoken melodramas of the period.

The difference in the audiences for "true" and "burlesque" operas may have been related directly to a kind of "ritual mystification" associated with attendance at a form of entertainment (Italian opera) that "served the social function of helping unify a New York patriciate badly divided in Jacksonian times along professional, ethnic, and religious lines." The elite socialites or nouveau riche who attended Palmo's Italian Opera House or the Academy of Music reinforced "a code of behavior appropriate to opera's social exclusiveness . . . [namely] formal attire, reserved seating in a box or in the parquette, and polite chatter with fellow socialites of both sexes during intermissions."[63] Attendance at the opera brought with it the cultivation of behaviors different from those tolerated at the Bowery Theater or Mechanics Hall, behaviors characterized by restraint, respect for the performers, detachment from direct involvement with the stage action, and other customs associated with social distinctiveness and class superiority.

Italian opera became an object of blackface ridicule because "by the 1850s, opera-going facilitated elite solidarity in New York City, helping to shape a genuine power base that would reach its fullest expression in the 'Gilded Age' of American society." When the minstrels recognized that attendance at the opera "provided upper-class Gothamites with the class consciousness and highly rationalized training necessary to manipulate the social order of a modernizing America," they incorporated opera excerpts and class criticism into their performances.[64] When the heroes and heroines of Italian opera became the Dinahs and Dan Tuckers of blackface burlesques, the transformation was more than a move from the Italian countryside to the southern plantation; it emphasized that the enjoyment of musical theater or vocal music did not have to be limited to those who could underwrite the costs and participate in the social exclusiveness associated with the performances of imported singers in foreign-language vehicles. The minstrels inverted that social order by exalting the American vernacular both in language and music and by criticizing class exclusiveness because it ran contrary to the egalitarian philosophy underlying the blackface comedians' sense of an egalitarian social order.

The full-scale opera burlesque merged ballad opera—the people's music—with the elements of Italian opera. The opera burlesques appeared infrequently until after Italian opera had established itself in New York and elsewhere in the early 1850s. Between 1845 and 1850, moreover, most minstrel groups performed only short excerpts from opera, usually no more than two or three choruses or solo numbers during which the burlesque element was primarily a satire on operatic conventions. For example, the Christys' burlesque of Verdi's *Il Trovatore* was concerned less with "fidelity" to the original than with a comic summary of the opera's plot "rendered in the vernacular by Signor Villikins," with a fine ear for the macaronic potential inherent in the alliterative nature of the original language but also characteristic of the limerick.

There was an old woman who somewhere did dwell,
Who was burnt for a witch as the op'ra doth tell,
A daughter she had too, a gipsy so bold,
Who went to a house where an infant she stoled.

(*Chorus* in the Italian language, relative to the way she hooked it)
Singing tooral, toledo and in dormio,
Allegro andanty and sempre amo,
O giorno dottore! mia madre you know,
With fata crudele funeste & Co.

Now arter they'd burnt up the old gipsy mother,
The daughter came by with her own child and t'other;
When she saw her marm burning, it woke up her ire,
And she slung the stole baby smack into the fire.

(Sizzling *chorus* deskriptive [sic] of the burning)

Now when this poor baby was all of a bake,
She found out she'd burnt up her own by mistake;
And she felt bad at the deed she had done,
She brought up the other and called him her son.

(*Chorus* in the barrow-tone style.)[65]

The blackface comedian criticizes the utter simplicity of most Italian opera plots and the length of time needed to work them out by reducing the plot to a few stanzas of rhyming couplets. Given the musical structure of operatic scenes and the recitative-aria conventions, as well as the convolutions and unmasking of secret identities found in many of the plots of the period, opera simply took too long for the average American's attention span; involvement in opera was thus a cultivated taste, whereas popular culture demands immediate accessibility for its success. The fast pace, variety format, and quick gratification of popular comic theater made the enjoyment of it quite different from the longer, more elaborate, and hence delayed pleasure of hearing the favorite operatic "hits."

Minstrelsy's selective use of Italian and English operas shows that blackface opera burlesques were highly derivative forms. The dramatic or comic pieces presented in the shows exemplify the typical ways emerging or immature popular cultures develop their own identities. The Italian and English opera burlesques were cross-cultural encounters, the Anglo-American sense of realism reacting against the narrative and sung tradition of Italy. The parodists and their audiences accepted ridicule as a technique for a nativist critique of foreign cultural imports that were the markers of the growing consciousness of class distinctions based on wealth and taste similar to those common to England. Yet English sources continued to dominate the American theater scene, and blackface comedians satirized those theatrical forms precisely because of their dominance of the slowly emerging American popular style. Blackface comics and their arrangers satirized the theatrical forms of the home country (England) because of their dominance of the American theater scene.

The relative speed with which current cultural styles became available for popular consumption was part of minstrelsy's contribution to the formation of popular culture and one reason burlesque is a far more complex matter than at first meets the eye. Opera was one of the first cultural possessions Americans craved. The desire for demonstrating respectability by appropriating the European products respectable people seemed to enjoy was part of the same need for class distinction that motivated Americans to accumulate goods and arrange social events for the public display of their acquisitions. Minstrelsy exploited class distinction so often that Italian operatic music was as much as a part of the whole burnt cork routine as any borrowed plantation dance. Therein lies the popularity of the highly selective operatic routines found in most of typical minstrel entertainments.

4 Ethiopian Sketches of American Life: Skits, Farces, and Afterpieces

> It is one of the best Farces in the language, and abounds in all sorts of *ludicrous situations, grotesque positions,* and *mirth-provoking dialogue.* It is, moreover, peculiarly adapted to the wants of small companies, requiring but *three persons to fill the parts;* and in troupes where the *Dramatis Personae* cannot be furnished for a large two act Drama or Farce, this piece will be found "just the cheese"— and especially when they cannot be spared in the Acts of a "second part" of a Minstrel performance.[1]

"Ethiopian" sketches or farces were usually performed in blackface by characters who wore the burnt cork mask to "conceal, reveal, confuse, or falsify" their real-life identities.[2] But it is not clear how many of the characters actually appeared in blackface in any particular skit because the "Cast of Characters" sections of the published Ethiopian sketches rarely indicate whether all the characters blacked up or only those with identifiable African American roles. In Charles White's *Hop of Fashion,* for example, one actor played two or more of the major roles. In the published version of White's *Mazeppa* (ca. 1856), the frontispiece shows two dark-skinned or blacked-up characters, but the cast list describes only one such character, Castiron of Hoboken, "a darkey full of airs, living above his means." *The Mischievous Nigger* (ca. 1856) includes Antony Snow, "a mischievous nigger," but the other characters are Monsieur Fripon, a French barber; Jimmy Ducks, an Irishman; and Mrs. Morton, a widow and mother of twins.[3]

The sketches were also adaptable to various ethnic groups through slight changes in costuming or dialect. Among the stage directions for various pieces are the following suggestions: (1) the sketch "can be played all white [but Pompey], if desired, or all black"; (2) "although the language of the manuscript favors the 'Live Injin,' parties wishing to alter it will find no difficulty whatever, except in changing talk and properties"; (3) "all the characters, except Peter Pipes, can be played in whiteface if desired"; and (4) "the parts can be played in White or Black . . . the whole may appear in blackface, or only Mat and Lulu; or those can be in dialect, Irish or Dutch."[4]

No matter how popular minstrelsy may have been, it was never the *only* venue available for audiences seeking entertainment that exploited ethnic or regional differences. During minstrelsy's heyday, stage Yankees still commanded serious public attention, and America's largest immigrant group—the Irish—was featured in at least twenty-one different "Paddy" plays produced in New York between 1843 and 1850. Local urban characters (the Bowery B'hoys and their hero, Mose) were also staples of the broader comic fare in New York for at least five of minstrelsy's most significant years, the 1848–1853 seasons. Mose (Chanfrau) and his sweetheart, Lize (played by the talented Mary Taylor, who was considered the "Shirley Temple of her day"),[5] also appeared in blackface in a number of "Ethiopian" sketches, showing that parody and burlesque were applied even to popular stage characters who themselves were stereotypes based on white, usually Irish, working-class people.

The sketches seem to have achieved their greatest popularity during the mid- to late 1850s, when the minstrel shows emphasized variety and when some New York theaters—for example, the New Olympic—returned to the burlesque offerings of Mitchell and Burton. Under Francis S. Chanfrau's management in 1857, the New Olympic set out to "revive, as near as possible, William Mitchell's Old Olympic, the motto being Mirth, Music and the Dance." Chanfrau promised much, but what he delivered were old standbys, *Grist to the Mill*, Burton's *The Stage-Struck Barber*, *Mother and Child Are Doing Well*, and *The Happy Man*.[6] Similar titles show up later among the Ethiopian sketches presented by Charles White and George Christy.

These preliminary remarks establish part of the context for a repertory of generally short sketches qualified by the adjective *Ethiopian* because they featured at least one blackface character. The repertory included a great variety of material, much of it unpublished until after the Civil War. Sketches did not appear in all minstrel shows during the antebellum period, and the playbill record shows a greater distribution of this type of comedy after 1849. The occasional references to opera in the title of a particular example suggests that some of the sketches included instrumental or vocal music. The list of sketches reveals the relative infrequency of Shakespearian burlesques in the antebellum minstrel repertory.[7] Although previous studies have suggested a relatively large number of pieces based on Shakespeare, there are relatively few antebellum examples in the minstrel playbills. (See table 5.)

One of the first Ethiopian sketches mentioned in period playbills was Charles White's *Going for the Cup; or, Old Mrs. Williams's Dance*, which was performed at White's Melodeon in 1847. White appeared as Old Mr. Rogers, Dan Emmett was Know-all (a "consequential Darkey"), Jack Danger was played by Neill Hall, and Ikey Van-jacklen (the barber's boy) was played by Master Juba, that is, William Henry Lane (ca. 1825–53), the most famous African American dancer of that time and an occasional member of White's company from 1846 at least until 1850. Juba learned some of his skills from the legendary Uncle Jim Lowe, the "black jig-and-reel dancer of unusual talent who was well-known in tenderloin districts of northern and southern cities."[8]

Table 5. Titles and Performance Dates for Selected Ethiopian Sketches, Interludes, or Afterpieces

Title	Type	Date	Company	Source
1. 1845–48 (5 Items)				
Love and Jewilrums	Ethiopian sketch	??/??/45	Ethiopian Serenaders	Playbill HTC
Gone to Texas	Farce	01/08/45	Buckley's Serenaders	Playbill HTC
Negro Assurance; or, High				
Life in Old Virginny	Ethiopian sketch	02/04/45	Ole Bull Band of Serenaders	Playbill HTC
"Cobbler's Daughter"	Pantomime	03/13/45	Sable Brothers	Playbill HTC
Prognosticators	Ethiopian sketch	03/26/45	Ethiopian Serenaders	Playbill HTC
2. 1850–55 (63 Items)				
Returned Volunteer	Ethiopian sketch	05/22/49	Sable Harmonists	Playbill HTC
Barber Shop in an Uproar	Ethiopian sketch	05/29/49	Sable Harmonists	Playbill HTC
Oh! Hush; or, The Rival				
Darkies	Ethiopian sketch	12/26/49	Virginia Serenaders	Playbill HTC
Returned Volunteer	Ethiopian sketch	12/28/49	Virginia Serenaders	Playbill HTC
Oh! Hush; or, The Rival				
Darkies	Ethiopian sketch	12/28/49	Virginia Serenaders	Playbill HTC
Negro Assurance	Ethiopian sketch	02/11/50	Virginia Serenaders	Playbill HTC
Negro Assurance (London				
Assurance?)	Ethiopian sketch	08/12/50	Parker's Opera Troupe	Playbill HTC
Returned Volunteer	Ethiopian sketch	09/12/51	Wood's Minstrels	Playbill HTC
Sam's Courtship	Ethiopian sketch	??/??/52	White's Serenaders	Title page
Darkey in the Bag; or,				
The Mysterious Sack	Ethiopian sketch	04/16/52	White's Serenaders	Playbill HTC
Old Folks at Home	Ethiopian sketch	04/16/52		
		05/03/52	White's Serenaders	Playbill HTC
Stage Struck Tailor	Ethiopian sketch	06/12/52	Rainer and Donaldson	Playbill HTC
Returned Volunteer	Ethiopian sketch	08/22/53	Wood's Minstrels	Odell 6:357
Dutch Drill	Ethiopian sketch	08/30/52	Well's Minstrels	Playbill HTC
Uncle Tom's Cabin	Ethiopian burlesque	08/20/53	Sanford's Opera Troupe	Baines, 120
Uncle Tom's Cabin	Ethiopian burlesque	07/29/53	Sanford's Opera Troupe	Baines, 111
Uncle Tom's Cabin	Ethiopian burlesque	10/10/53	Sanford's Opera Troupe	Baines, 122
Black Cupids (Virginny				
Cupids?)	Burlesque sketch	12/19/53	Christy and Wood's Minstrels	Odell 6:327
Oh! Hush; or, The Virginny				
Cupids (Rice)	Ethiopian sketch	12/22/53	Christy and Wood's Minstrels	Odell 6:583
Mistakes of a Night	Ethiopian sketch	??/??/54	Christy and Wood's Minstrels	Playbill HTC
Uncle Tom's Cabin	Burlesque opera	04/??/54	Wood's Minstrels	Odell 6:327
Uncle Tom's Cabin	Operatic burletta	04/10/54	Christy and Wood's Minstrels	Playbill HTC
Musical Chowder	Burlesque opera			
(Fra Diavolo parody?)	excerpt	04/22/54	White's Serenaders	Playbill HTC
Black Blunders; or,				
Forty Winks	Ethiopian farce	09/??/54	Christy and Wood's Minstrels	Odell 6:406
Darkey's Dodge	Ethiopian sketch	10/11/54	Wood's Minstrels	Playbill HTC
Black Blunders; or				
Forty Winks	Ethiopian farce	10/16/54	Christy and Wood's Minstrels	Playbill HTC
African Brothers	Burlesque sketch	10/18/54	Wood's Minstrels	Playbill HTC
Magic Penny	Ethiopian sketch	11/??/54	White's Serenaders	Odell 6:408
Mummy (Virginia Mummy)	Farce	11/13/54	Christy and Wood's Minstrels	Odell 6:406
Uncle Tom's Cabin	Ethiopian burlesque	01/01/55	White's Serenaders	Odell 6:408
Black Statue	Ethiopian sketch	01/26/55	White's Serenaders	Odell 6:408

Table 5 (cont.)

Title	Type	Date	Company	Source
Burlesque Tragedy of				
Damon and Pythias	Ethiopian sketch	01/26/55	White's Serenaders	Playbill HTC
Two Pompeys	Ethiopian sketch	02/26/55	Buckley's Serenaders	Odell 6:407
Damon and Pythias	Ethiopian sketch	03/12/55	White's Serenaders	Odell 6:408
Last Excursion	Ethiopian sketch	03/12/55	White's Serenaders	Odell 6:408
Old Dad's Cabin	Ethiopian sketch	03/12/55	White's Serenaders	Playbill HTC
Oh! Hush (Virginny Cupids)	Ethiopian sketch	03/12/55	White's Serenaders	Odell 6:408
Robert Makeairs	Ethiopian burlesque	04/19/55	Sanford's Opera Troupe	Baines, 144
Matrimonial Speculations	Ethiopian sketch	05/14/55	Buckley's Serenaders	Odell 6:407
Oh! Hush; or, The Virginny				
Cupids (Rice)	Ethiopian sketch	08/04/54	Backus's Minstrels	Playbill HTC
Black Shoemaker	Ethiopian sketch	08/06/55	White's Serenaders	Odell 6:494
Black Shoemaker	Ethiopian sketch	08/11/55	White's Serenaders	Playbill HTC
Oh! Hush; or, The Virginny				
Cupids	Ethiopian sketch	08/23/55	Sanford's Opera Troupe	Baines, 150
Black Statue	Ethiopian sketch	08/27/55	Sanford's Opera Troupe	Baines, 150
Le Bal Masque (The Hop of				
Fashion)	Interlude	08/27/55	Sanford's Opera Troupe	Baines, 150
Spirit Rappers	Burlesque	08/27/55	Buckley's Serenaders	Odell 6:494
Count Shanghai				
and His Man	Farce	09/07/55	White's Serenaders	Odell 6:494
Wanted: 1000 Milliners				
for Haiti	Burlesque	10/??/55	Christy and Wood's Minstrels	Odell 6:494
Oh! Hush; or, The Virginny				
Cupids	Ethiopian sketch	10/08/55	Sanford's Opera Troupe	Baines, 151
Black Shoemaker	Ethiopian sketch	10/11/55		
		12/12/55	White's Serenaders	Odell 6:408
Black Blunders; or				
Forty Winks	Ethiopian farce	10/15/55	Sanford's Opera Troupe	Baines, 151
Black Shoemaker	Ethiopian sketch	10/22/55	White's Opera House	Odell 6:494
Mistakes in the Dark	Ethiopian sketch	10/22/55	White's Opera House	Odell 6:494
Mystic Spell	Ethiopian sketch	10/22/55	White's Opera House	Odell 6:494
Robert Macaire [Makeairs]	Ethiopian burlesque	10/22/55	Christy and Wood's Minstrels	Odell 6:494
Uncle Tom's Cabin	Ethiopian sketch	10/22/55	Sanford's Opera Troupe	Baines, 151
Box and Cox	Ethiopian sketch	10/23/55	Sanford's Opera Troupe	Baines, 150
Black Statue	Ethiopian sketch	10/29/55	White's Opera House	Odell 6:494
Mummy (Virginia Mummy)	Ethiopian sketch	11/12/55	Christy and Wood's Minstrels	Odell 6:495
Villikins and His Dinah	Ethiopian sketch	11/17/55	Buckley's Serenaders	Odell 6:495
Villikins and Dinah	Ethiopian sketch	12/10/55	Sanford's Opera Troupe	Odell 6:583
Dancers	Ethiopian sketch	12/11/55	White's Serenaders	Odell 6:494
Sambo's Dream	Ethiopian sketch	12/24/55	Christy and Wood's Minstrels	Odell 6:495
3. 1856–62 (38 Items)				
Hop of Fashion	Ethiopian sketch	??/??/56	White's Serenaders	Copyright date
Black Statue	Ethiopian sketch	01/10/56	White's Opera House	Odell 6:494
Nigger in the Bag	Ethiopian sketch	01/10/56	White's Serenaders	Odell 6:494
Masquerade Ball (Hop of				
Fashion?)	Ethiopian sketch	01/14/56	Christy and Wood's Minstrels	Odell 6:495
Good for Nothing	Ethiopian sketch	01/31/56	Christy and Wood's Minstrels	Odell 6:495
Hop of Fashion	Ethiopian sketch	01/31/56	White's Serenaders	Odell 6:496

Table 5 (cont.)

Title	Type	Date	Company	Source
Happy Man; or, Treaty with Japan	Ethiopian sketch	02/11/56	Christy and Wood's Minstrels	Odell 6:495
Le Bal Masque (The Hop of Fashion)	Interlude	02/11/56	Sanford's Opera Troupe	Baines, 162
Virginia Mummy	Ethiopian sketch	03/03/56	Sanford's Opera Troupe	Baines, 162
Ethiopian Court Scene	Ethiopian sketch	03/26/56	Sable Harmonists	Playbill HTC
Macbeth	Burlesque	03/??/56	Christy and Wood's Minstrels	Odell 6:495
Mazeppa	Burlesque	03/??/56	White's Serenaders	Odell 6:496
Double-Bedded Room	Ethiopian sketch	04/??/56	Christy and Wood's Minstrels	Odell 6:495
Sambo's Dream	Ethiopian sketch	04/??/56	Christy and Wood's Minstrels	Odell 6:495
Villikins and His Dinah	Ethiopian sketch	04/14/56	Sanford's Opera Troupe	Baines, 166
Nicaragua State Secrets	Burlesque	04/21/56	Christy and Wood's Minstrels	Odell 6:495
Jocko: The Mischievous Monkey	Burlesque	05/12/56	Christy and Wood's Minstrels	Odell 6:495
Bone Squash Diavolo	Ethiopian burlesque	09/01/56	George Christy's Minstrels	Odell 6:583
Weffo, the Sensible Monkey	Burlesque	09/11/56	Christy and Wood's Minstrels	Odell 6:583
United States Mail	Ethiopian sketch	01/19/57	White's Serenaders	Odell 6:587
Stage Struck Barber [Darkey]	Ethiopian sketch	01/29/57	Christy's Minstrels	Odell 6:587
Negro Assurance; or, Jersey Impudence	Ethiopian sketch	02/09/57	Sanford's Opera Troupe	Baines, 170
Bone Squash Diabolo (Rice)	Ethiopian extravaganza	02/15/57	Sanford's Opera Troupe	Baines, 170
Mr. and Mrs. Snuffgrass	Farce	02/28/57	White's Serenaders	Odell 6:587
Black Camille	Ethiopian sketch	03/09/57	White's Serenaders	Odell 6:587
Mazeppa	Burlesque	03/30/57	White's Serenaders	Odell 6:587
Uncle Jeff	Ethiopian sketch	04/06/57	White's Serenaders	Odell 6:587
Virginia Cupids	Ethiopian sketch	04/06/57	White's Serenaders	Odell 6:587
Old Clock	Burlesque	11/24/57	George Christy's Minstrels	Odell 6:408
Black Shoemaker	Ethiopian sketch	12/25/57	White's Serenaders	Odell 6:587
Mummy (Virginia Mummy?)	Ethiopian sketch	12/25/57	White's Serenaders	Odell 6:587
Wreck	Ethiopian sketch	12/25/57	White's Serenaders	Odell 6:587
Laughing Gas	Ethiopian sketch	??/??/58	Wood's Minstrels	Title page
Soiree d'Ethiope; or, The Masquerade Ball	Unknown	08/25/58	Bryant's Minstrels	Playbill HTC
Spirit Rappings	Ethiopian sketch	09/01/58	Sanford's Opera Troupe	Playbill HTC
Miss Bloomer at the Soiree	Ethiopian sketch	08/19/59	George Christy's Minstrels	Playbill HTC
Wake Up! William Henry	Ethiopian sketch	03/24/62	White group	Title page
Black Chemist	Ethiopian sketch	06/16/62	White's Serenaders	Title page

Note: The genre/type classifications are based on the titles' identifications in the sources, but the terms *sketch, burlesque, burletta, Ethiopian opera, farce,* and others were used interchangeably and quite inconsistently during the antebellum period. Some sketches contained enough songs or incidental material to have been called "Ethiopian operas." The exact nature of these pieces deserves further investigation.

White built the sketch around Juba's dancing and linked that to the themes of male competitiveness, duplicity, and bodily display. Knowall and Danger rig a dance contest by soaping the floor. All the contestants will slip except Ikey Vanjacklen, who is guaranteed to win the silver cup. The characters bet on Vanjacklen knowing that he can beat any of the other dancers of the period. The "fixed bet" theme is common in popular comedy, but the underlying subject is male competition and the ethical conflicts inherent in using any means to gain an appropriate end. The remaining characters believe that they are decent dancers and decide to hold their own contest. Mr. Rodgers, who serves in the dual role as judge and contestant, escapes with all the wagers while the other characters end up with his empty pocketbook as their prize.

White's *Hippotheatron; or, Burlesque Circus* (1848) was performed as a circus burlesque. Minstrelsy always retained its connections with the circus, and later productions of this sketch featured Tony Pastor (1837–1908) as an equestrian director and Charles White as a clown. The circus characters in Ethiopian sketches included an American Hercules, a strong man who stuffs his sleeves and tights to look bigger; the Revolving Globe, an act in which the character revolves a large pumpkin on the soles of his feet while lying on his back; and the Motley Brothers, who specialize in posing and posturing as living statues. Another of the featured minstrel specialty acts was entitled "Walking the Ceiling," where one character suspends the other upside down and "walks" him along a board. White's sketch also contains some blackface characters who come to the apron and are allowed to sing any song they wish to the accompaniment of the tambourine, banjo, and bones.[9]

The combination of variety entertainment and circus acts was only one source for the Ethiopian sketches commonly used in the minstrel shows after 1847. The closing numbers, or "finales," were often dramatizations of song lyrics, such as the popular "Boston Favorite Extravaganza of Miss Lucy Long." "Jim Crow" Rice's contributions were significant, but a number of other theater pieces also served as models or provided the appropriate contexts for the references found in Ethiopian sketches. These plays featured specific domestic locales, stereotyped African American and foreign characters, contemporary fashions, and behaviors of newly wealthy social climbers who had accumulated the servants and goods representative of their new economic status as conspicuous consumers but lacked the "class" and "culture" of a true aristocracy. American audiences seemed to recognize that financial success, preferably the sudden acquisition of wealth *and* the excellent chance for retaining it, might allow people to "show off."[10] Rose's curtain speech in Wilkins's *Young New York* captures the prevailing conclusion of these plays that "the rich are not to be censured by the poor for being rich, nor the poor by the rich for being poor; but that every man and woman is to be tried by the standard of their acts alone; and upon them is to stand or fall."[11] Such conclusions, presented as they were in so-called society plays, are moralistic judgments designed to pacify audiences who might be offended by the portrayals they have just witnessed.

The most representative example of society plays is Anna Cora Mowatt's *Fashion; or, Life in New York* (Mar. 24, 1845), which features a number of stereotypes, including French maids, African American porters (notably, Zeke, who has been called "the first truly 'minstrelized' figure in American legitimate drama"),[12] Irish servants, and other natives or immigrants whose speech consists of phonological borrowings rather than a true dialect, something Mowatt must have believed was sufficient to support the portrayal of a "character." *Fashion* was fresh and new because "many of the men and women who attended Mowatt's play went to laugh at the fashionable pretensions of their own class"; "what was new about Mowatt's sentimental critique was its broad sense of humor about social issues that had been the source of profound anxiety a few years earlier."[13]

Mowatt's *Fashion* includes a scene in which Zeke serves as the "ticket taker" and announces the guests as they arrive at Mrs. Tiffany's ball.[14] The character named Adam Trueman refers to Zeke as "a nigger tricked out in scarlet regimentals." Mrs. Tiffany replies that Zeke's costume is appropriate because such "liveries are all the fashion," but Trueman, who cares more for freedom than fashion, declares that it is wrong "to make men wear the *badge of servitude* in a free land." Zeke and the other servant stereotypes in the play subvert the pretensions of the foreign dignitaries and American parvenus. Mrs. Tiffany rationalizes her employment of Zeke by complaining that she can't get anybody else to do the job: "I'm rather sorry that he is black but to obtain a white American for a domestic is almost impossible; and they say this a free country!" (act 1, sc. 1). The convention of the African American butler, "manservant," or waiter was established long before *Fashion* because it presented a character whose status was deemed lower than that of those likely to attend the theater and whose presence could then serve as a comic foil for the principals. The casting of servants was directly related to social status among the immigrants or urban poor, because maids are usually Irish or French, depending apparently on the relative wealth of the household.

Neither the maid nor the butler always has a subservient role, however. In White's *Mischievous Nigger,* for example, Antony (apparently not *Anthony*) is constantly upsetting the household with his tricks, while Fanny is always finding ways to escape to her boyfriend, Jimmy Ducks. The framing device is the courtship ritual, but the circumstances are varied so that the lower-status individuals use their wits to gain some personal freedom of action. Unfortunately those actions also fit the stereotypic conceptions middle- or upper-class characters had of their servants. The significance of the plot convention also allowed those lower-class audience members to revel in the blackface comedians' ability to outwit the domineering employers or incompetent bosses.

As *Fashion*'s Mrs. Tiffany sees it, the subservience associated with domestic labor makes a person less free, an attitude perhaps captured in the frequent references that artisans and laborers made to themselves as victims of "wage slavery." In the domestic sphere, however, Mrs. Tiffany's attitude reflected the changing status of domestic service from the Jacksonian period, when young women migrated from the farms to the cities, to the mid-1840s, when the pool of desperate immigrants and free blacks fundamentally changed the way mistresses looked at their "help." The 1850s were a period in which the physical and psychical distances between servants and families increased.[15]

Another typical exchange shows Mrs. Tiffany's false assumption of dominance when she renames Zeke something "more aristocratic," and Zeke, low-status but ironical "character" that he is, foils the pretentiousness of his mistress with adroit disdain for her misuse of a "perfectly charming" and "genteel" French word.

> Mrs. Tiffany: . . . Your name is Ezekiel. I consider it too plebeian an appellation to be uttered in my presence. In the future you are to be called A-dolph. Don't re-ply,—never interrupt me when I am speaking. A-Dolph, as my guests arrive, I desire that you will inquire the name of every person, and then announce it in a loud, clear tone. That is the fashion in Paris.
>
> Zeke: Consider de office discharged, Missus.
>
> Mrs. Tiff: Silence! Your business is to obey and not to talk.
>
> Zeke: I'm dumb, Missus.
>
> Mrs. Tiff: A-dolph, place that fowtool [Fr., *fauteuil*] behind me.
>
> Zeke: (Looking about him.) I habn't got dat far in de dictionary yet. No matter, a genus gets his learning by nature.
>
> Mrs. Tiff: You dolt! Where have you lived not to know that *fow-tool* is French for *arm-chair*. What ignorance! Leave the room this instant.
>
> Zeke: Dem's de defects ob not having a libery education.[16]

The traditional reading of this scene is that Zeke is the stereotypic Negro servant, a subservient role designed to demean African Americans. That judgment misses the point of the play. All the characters in *Fashion* are stereotypes; all exist in the artificial world Mowatt created to ridicule Americans (especially New Yorkers) caught up in the imitation of French social customs and culture.[17] Zeke's costume is the one assigned by Mrs. Tiffany rather than one of his own choosing. The assumption that American servants wear livery is in direct contrast to the custom of previous generations, when such customs only emphasized the classism of European, principally English, society. Although he may be treated as a low-status character, Zeke mocks both his employer and the French maid with whom he works. Regardless of his dialect, Zeke represents the ways in which characters at each level of society maintain their own sense of self regardless of what others think of them.

Zeke is just as disdainful of Mrs. Tiffany as she is of him. Their relationship is based on her power and wealth, a relationship that raises questions about the artificiality of "society" versus the natural wisdom of the uneducated servant. Mrs. Tiffany's foolish aspirations are revealed by her inability to pronounce *fauteuil*, thereby making her the victim of Zeke's facetious statements and feigned ignorance, which result from his lack of a "libery" education. The absence-of-an-education joke is based on the double pun of *libery* for both *livery* and *liberal.* There is no question about the way Zeke is presented. He is treated poorly, but he is also a servant character who plays a comic role in the context of a play dealing with American skepticism about adopting the superficial social behaviors of French society.

Fashion and plays like it are part of the context in which the Ethiopian sketches must be viewed. The social practice caricatured in the sketches was borrowed directly from plays and etiquette books of the period in order to parody the undemocratic artifice of the wealthy. In Karen Haltunnen's words, "For Mowatt and her republican hero [Adam Trueman], fashionable social forms were the cultural remnants of a corrupt and decadent Old World aristocracy; all attempts to ape foreign manners undermined American independence from Europe."[18] *Fashion* provides a good context for the sketches because it illustrates some of the period's class distinctions and styles that the blackface comedians chose to satirize. The class distinctions in the popular stage plays were just as prominent in the Ethiopian sketches.

Some of the sketches included parodies of scenes from contemporary stage plays and melodramas. Several such scenes were linked together in what I call a "parade play." The parade play displays a variety of characters drawn from contemporary life, popular stage personalities, and classic personae from Shakespearian plays, all of whom make brief appearances highlighted by an identifying speech or action; after the audience had time to recognize the parody, the actor playing the particular part moved briskly off stage for a costume change and reappeared in another burlesque role. Such plays could have been vehicles for talented mimics who, while they could not sustain themselves in a full-fledged burlesque, could successfully master a variety of traits, actions, or postures in the same way a modern variety-show impressionist does.

The parade plays are usually set in the context of a contemporary social event, typically a masquerade ball, and feature walk-ons by a variety of exotic or eccentric players. The ball setting was probably chosen because of the popularity of such events among all social classes, from the "Crow" clubs of Philadelphia to the Upper Ten Thousand of New York.[19] Characters from popular melodrama and the most famous Shakespearian dramas often join a motley cast of stock stage types common to American comedy ever since Thomas Rice sang "Jim Crow" or George "Yankee" Hill played "Brother Jonathan" during interludes or entr'actes to plays performed a decade or two before the parade plays appeared.[20] The main distinctions among the various types of parade plays rest on whether the plays display odd characters in satires about social events, such as masquerade balls or parades, or feature ridiculous representations of characters likely to appear in courtrooms, employment offices, or other quasi-official public venues.

One such parade play, Charles White's *Hop of Fashion; or, The Bon-Ton Soiree* (ca. 1856), may have been adapted from Rice's unpublished play *The Masquerade; or, The Ticket-Taker Outwitted,* which appeared at Philadelphia's Walnut Street Theater in 1837. Another possible source was "Mr. W. R. Pelham's *Masquerade Ball; or, Tickets on Tick,*" which Emmett's original Virginia Minstrels performed at the Adelphi Theater in Glasgow in June 1844.[21] White's sketch features an unlikely cast: Richard III, Mose (one of the Bowery B'hoys in another genre of popular comedy), a French gentleman, a drunken Irishman, and a stage-struck youth (named "Pops") who speaks of Rome, "the Queen of Cities," where "there is not a palace on those hills that has not been bought by blood." These characters join Macbeth and Lady Macbeth as guests at a masquerade ball hosted by Captain Slim (a newly made lottery ticket millionaire). The comic premise of the sketch is that characters drawn from Shakespeare's plays, contemporary melodrama, and urban life "parade" before an unsuspecting doorman who must screen their admission to Captain Slim's home.[22]

Nineteenth-century American authors created social comedies that often "uphold social standards imposed by common sense . . . and ridicule or otherwise oppose false standards."[23] By ridiculing what they considered to be false standards and hypocritical displays, the authors of social comedies emphasized what they believed were the true American values of modesty, honesty, and sincerity. The concern over status, class, and the display of American prosperity reflected an increasing consciousness of the relationships between wealth and social station. The newly wealthy were subjects of particular public interest because the prospect of instant riches was already fondly fixed in the American mind. No wonder, then, that one of the most popular types of Ethiopian sketches dealt with the nouveau riche in a typical social dance or masquerade ball setting, the latter chosen because of the humorous possibilities for costuming and mimicry.

The Hop of Fashion satirizes the social rituals of upper- and middle-class life and capitalizes on the audience's fascination with questions about "other" people's lifestyles and its unbounded curiosity about the customs of other classes and societies. The format of the parade play varies, but there is usually a controlling character who does not play double roles and can remain on stage while the other cast changes occur; in *The Hop of Fashion,* it is Anthony, who remains on stage during the various entrances and exits. Two quotations will illustrate how the odd combinations of characters fit into the overall parade or promenade format of White's sketch:

Anthony: I don't know whether dat ticket is right or not; it's most as big as de New York Herald.

Lady Macbeth: [*Enters.*] Go wash your hands. Put on your nightgown. Look not so pale. I tell you Banquo's buried. He cannot rise from his grave. Come, there's a knocking at the gate. Come, come, come, to bed, to bed, to bed! [*Macbeth*, V:i, 65–67, 69–72] [*Exits.*]

Anthony: Well, dat is de most singular thing in the world; dar, she's gon in de ballroom widout a ticket. De old man said dat if I didn't get a ticket from every one, he'd discharge me. Well, I think di ticket is most too large. [*He tears the ticket in two pieces.*] Now I think, that ticket is large enough for any reasonable ball. (10–11)

. . .

Macbeth: What? can such things be, an' o'ercome us without our special wonder [*Macbeth*, III:iv, 111–12.], and now I do behold you keep the natural ruby of your cheek, while mine is balanced with fear [*Macbeth*, III:iv, 114–16]. Approach thou like the rugged Russian bear, or Hulcan [Hrycan] the armed rhinoceros—take any other shape but that [*Macbeth*, III:iv, 100–102].

Anthony: I neber took a sheep in my life.(11)

The pun in the last line seems a long way to go for a joke, but there are more subtle things at work in this quoted excerpt. Anthony's role seems only marginally related to the others; he functions as a gatekeeper. At the same time, however, his own comments about the size of the ticket are related to the contemporary practice of controlling admission to private dances and some hosts' pretentiousness in designing elaborate admission tickets. The setting for these balls and the social life of the "fashionable" can be understood somewhat better from the following two notices from the March 16, 1858, issue of the *New York Herald:*

NOTICE. THE GRAND CHARITY FESTIVAL WILL take place at Mozart Hall on Wednesday evening, March 24, and will be a most attractive affair. Tickets, $1, can be procured at all the hotels, music, and book stores.

GRAND SOIREE TONIGHT AT MME. SAUVAGEAU'S Dancing Academy, 665 Broadway, opposite Bond street. Every stranger should visit this elegant establishment, the headquarters of fashionable young New York. Several new danseuses engaged. Les Lanciers and all the other fashionable dances.

The burlesque Macbeth's lines were taken from the ghost scene in act 3, but they are as hopelessly mixed up as Hamlet's and Macbeth's speeches are in another of White's popular sketches, *100th Night of Hamlet*. Shakespeare's text and Anthony's malaprop (*sheep* for *shape*) are both at home in the new environment of blackface farce. White also created a caricature of Claude Melnotte ("Melnot" in White's version), the principal character in two contemporary plays entitled *Claude Melnotte*

(1844) and *Pauline* (1845), both of which were American adaptations of Edward Bulwer-Lytton's (1803–73) *Lady of Lyons; or, Love and Pride,* a popular (nearly 400 American performances between 1838 and 1851) play originally written for Macready's Covent Garden theater.[24] *The Lady of Lyons* was presented at New York's Park Theater in 1838 and at the Olympic during the 1842 and 1846 seasons and was also burlesqued unsuccessfully by Mitchell in 1845. Bulwer-Lytton's play and three others like it—namely, Louisa Medina's (Thomas Hamblin's second wife) adaptations of Bulwer-Lytton's *Last Days of Pompeii* (1835) and Richard Montgomery Bird's *Nick of the Woods; or, The Jibbenainosay, A Tale of Kentucky* (1837), together with Joseph S. Jones's *Carpenter of Rouen; or, The Massacre of St. Bartholomew* (1837)—are representative of over one hundred scripts popular with working-class audiences during the 1835–50 period.[25]

The minstrels picked portions of *The Lady of Lyons* as subjects for parodies because the courtship scene fitted nicely with the antisentimental strain in blackface entertainment and probably because the play featured some of the most important actors of the period, including Edwin Forrest and Charlotte Cushman. In the original play, Pauline Deschappelles, the beautiful but spoiled daughter of a wealthy merchant, is courted by Claude Melnotte, a low-born but refined gardener's son. Some of Pauline's rejected wealthy gentlemen suitors contrive to have Claude woo pretty Pauline to repay her for her many rejections of their own suits, a plot that backfires several times as the two fall in love, marry, plan to divorce, and eventually are reunited when Claude's princely origins and war exploits are revealed. The play reinforces the marriage-within-one's-class rules of late eighteenth-century French society—the period in which the play is set—as well as the sentimental attitudes characteristic of early Victorian society's approach to marriage.

Bulwer-Lytton's preface captures the chief themes of the play and reveals the class issues that made Claude's part such a logical subject for blackface satire: "For during the early years of the first and most brilliant successes of the French republic, in the general ferment of society, and the brief equalization of ranks, Claude's high placed love, his ardent feelings, his unsettled principles (the struggle between which makes the passion of this drama), his ambition, and his career, were phenomena that characterized the age, and in which the spirit of the nation went along with the extravagance of the individual."[26] Similarly, White's *Hop of Fashion* characterized the blackface comedians' views of the pretentiousness exhibited by the new socially mobile Americans during the 1850s, as well as the exaggerated styles of those theatrical performers whose melodramatic performances were rivaled only by the excesses of popular preachers in their overblown rhetoric.[27]

In the typical minstrel company tradition, one performer played many parts. In *The Hop of Fashion* Charles White appeared in three roles: Captain Slim, a millionaire; Mose, one of the Bowery B'hoys; and Claude Melnot, a character played by every major American actor of the antebellum era. Another member of the company, an otherwise unidentified person identified only as "Mr. Vincent," played the roles of Pauline and Lize, the former essentially a walk-on who utters her seven words and, after listening to Claude's speech, is never seen again. Claude never returns to the sketch, because the parade play format simply presents characters serially, establishes some pretext for their posturing, and allows a character sole control of some portion of a scene that may have only two or three other players. The original speech from *The Lady of Lyons* and White's parody are shown below in parallel columns for easy comparison. In the sketch Claude's speech interrupts the couple's passage into the ball, the same format used for all the characters' appearances; in the original Claude describes the honeymoon site and future residence he and Pauline will inhabit after their marriage.[28]

Charles White, *The Hop of Fashion; or, The Bon-Ton Soiree*	Bulwer-Lytton, *The Lady of Lyons; or, Love and Pride*
	Act 2, Sc. 1
Claude: Ah, there's the door keeper. How to get by him?	Pauline: Sweet Prince, tell me again of thy palace by the lake of Como; it is so pleasant to hear of thy splendours since thou didst swear to me that they would be desolate without Pauline. . . .
Pauline: Whither would you lead me, dear Claude?	
	Mel: Nay, dearest, nay, if you wouldst have me paint
	The home to which, could love fulfil its prayers
	This hand would lead thee, listen! A
Claude: I'd take thee to a deep wale shut out by old pine treeses,	deep vale
	Shut out by Alpine hills from the rude world;
Near de big pond what floats the ducks and geeses.	Near a clear lake, margin'd by fruits of gold
Persimmons sweet and sweet potatoes grows,	And whispering myrtles; glassing softest skies,
And de perfume of de sunflower salutes de nose.	As cloudless, save with rare and roseate shadows,
	As I would have thy fate!
	Pauline: My own dear love!
In a little log hut made out ob pine,	Mel: A palace lifting to eternal summer,
All kibered ober wid de mornin' glory's vine,	Its marble walls, from out a glossy bower,
	Of coolest foliage musical with birds,
	Whose songs should syllable thy name!
Dar, lub, we'd sit and often wonder,	At noon
If anything could tear asunder.	We'd sit beneath the arching vines, and
Two loving hearts like ours.	wonder

We'd know no darks 'cept them dat had
    de dollars,
And dem dat wore fine clothes wid de
    largest kind ob big shirt collars;
Read police reports and then we'd
    see
How many colored men there be
Sent by his honor for thirty days
At public expense to mend their ways
And then the telegraph reports we'd
    read of darkies killed in showers,
And laugh to think what a happy fate
    was ours.
While lard oil lamps from Cincinnati
    straight
Should help to keep us wide awake;
And every wind that passed the still
    house on the green,
Should come loaded with whiskey made
    of the best fourth-proof camphene,
Breathe sighs of love, stars and moon,
While eating supper off of roasted coon;
To such a home I'd take you, love, if
    thou woulds't like.
My picture's finished. How likest thou
    the story?
Anthony: I'll take your ticket, if you please.
Claude: Ah, yes sir, I've left it in my
    overcoat pocket in the hat room. I'll go
    get it and return immediately. [Exits.]
    (12)

Why Earth could be unhappy, while the
    Heavens
Still left us youth and love! We'd have
    no friends
That were not lovers; no ambition,
    save
To excel them all in love; We'd read no
    books
That were not tales of love—that we
    might smile
To think how poorly eloquence of
    words,
Translates the poetry of hearts like ours!
And when night came, amidst the
    breathless Heavens
We'd guess what star should be our
    home when love
Becomes immortal; while the perfumed
    light
Stole through the mists of alabaster
    lamps,
And every air was heavy with the sighs
Of orange-groves and music from sweet
    lutes,
And murmurs of low fountains that
    gush forth
I' midst of roses!—Dost thou like the
    picture? (130–32)

Claude's original speech in *The Lady of Lyons* must have been known to members of the audience because Bulwer-Lytton's play was performed often in New York and because it must surely have been a paradigm of the hyperbolic, sentimental courtship speeches of contemporary melodrama. In the parody, while Claude describes the idyllic setting he envisions for Pauline, the couple seem proud of their position as better off than those others who lie below them in the socioeconomic order. But the indicators of difference are incongruous with such high station: "lard lamps from Cincinnati" rather than those made of tallow; "fourth-proof . . . camphene" whiskey—a mixture of 2 percent alcohol—which was essentially fumes from the stillhouse or cheap wood alcohol; and roast raccoon, a low-prestige food added to the diet of those living at a subsistence level. The humor, then, rests not only on the how the characters in the original play are satirized by their reappearance in a new environment but also on the incongruity between their claims to class and the examples they use to indicate their superiority. The speech also reflects attitudes about African American couples who were interested in the same domestic dreams attributed to respectable middle-class whites and parodies the courtship scenes of contemporary melodramas.

The parody serves a dual purpose: it reinforces class differences and it emphasizes the intricate irony inherent in two seemingly "black" characters who may represent a race the audiences believed to be inferior but who in reality espouse the same middle-class values and behaviors shared by many black and white people of the period. The inherent comparisons between classes characteristic of upward social mobility are expressed in something apparently as simple as a parody of a popular play, which shows that Americans did not really believe the myth of the classless society as the product of a democratic form of government.

Claude's value system sets him apart, and his speech suggests, just as many of the period's nonblackface plays do, that romantic love and financial security are the mythical keys to marital happiness and social respectability. Claude says as much when he describes his love for Pauline after she discovers his lower-class status:

Bulwer-Lytton, *The Lady of Lyons*

Act 3, Sc. 2

Melnotte [to Pauline]: From my first years my soul was fill'd with thee:
    I saw thee midst the flow'rs as the lowly boy
    Tended, unmark'd by thee—a spirit of bloom
    And joy and freshness, as if Spring itself
    Were made a living thing, and wore thy shape!
    I saw thee, and the passionate heart of man
    Enter'd the breast of the wild-dreaming boy. . . .
    I thought of old tales that by the winter hearth
    Old gossips tell—how maidens sprung from kings
    Have stoop'd from their high sphere; how love, like death,
    Levels all ranks, and lays the shepherd's crook
    Beside the scepter. Thus I made my home
    In the soft palace of a Fairy future. (145–46)

By putting the typically romantic values of the original plays into the mouths of a blackface gentleman and his cross-dressed companion, White satirized the romantic idealism embodied in *The Lady of Lyons,* Dion Boucicault's *Poor of New York* (1857), and a host of other lesser period offerings.[29] The point is not that the burnt cork comedians portrayed only black Americans as unrealistic dreamers but that they used the blackface disguise to reveal how ridiculous the sentimental idealism embodied in contemporary melodramas could be.

The idea that blacks were more likely than others to be engaged in criminal activity "rested on nothing more substantial than selective perception, pervasive racial antipathies, and an almost complete lack of continuing contact with the black community."[30] Unfortunately African Americans made up a disproportionate part of the urban prison population, and contrary to what seems to be a popular opinion among historians, "a larger percentage of black than white prisoners (by a ratio of more than 4:3) were jailed for violation of minor city ordinances," the types of "crimes" that generated the thirty-day sentences referred to in Claude's speech.[31] Persons aspiring to gentility in major urban centers would not admit to participating in such minor crimes for fear that their association with such lower-class activities would jeopardize their status as respectable citizens.

The reference to crime statistics shows how respectable Claude and Pauline think they are; they are modern people who get their news from a daily newspaper—the police log—not from direct observation. Claude uses that information as evidence that he and Pauline are much better than the uncouth people below them. That is what white lower-class audiences could get out of White's parody of Claude Melnotte's declaration to Pauline.

Regardless of the severity of the crime, however, criminal activity was often "treated as a cultural aberration rather than a symptom of class inequality," something Leonard Curry confirmed when he observed, "It was hardly coincidental that the most economically deprived elements of the cities' populations tended to commit a disproportionate number of crimes against property and that in each city the crime rates among free persons of color were roughly related, in an inverse fashion, to the levels of black occupational opportunity."[32] Claude's gloss on the honeymoon couple's vision in *The Lady of Lyons* seems rooted in observable facts but uses the information to distinguish the costumed couple from other period types.

The irony of the burlesque scene could have reminded lower-class or new middle-class persons in the audience of the perceptions middle- to upper-middle-class groups shared about crime rates among new immigrants, for there has been a pattern of "ethnic succession in all areas of crime, beginning with the Irish, who were the first identifiable minority to inhabit urban slums." Using an 1860s *Harper's* claim that "the Irish have behaved themselves [so badly] that nearly 75% of our criminals are Irish, that fully 75% of the crimes of violence committed among us are the work of Irishmen," Steinberg observed that just as later writers were to attribute the crimes African Americans committed to their ethnic distinctiveness, so too the majority culture of the 1860s attributed the Irishmen's tendency toward violence to "the intemperate disposition of the Irish race," something revealed in the Irishman's role in White's play.[33]

The Irishman who appears at the door of Captain Slim's ball is also an extension of the belligerent, uncouth article Steinberg described, as shown in the following exchange with Anthony:

Anthony: Well, you can't trot there without a ticket.
Irishman: A ticket is it?
Anthony: Yes, sir a ticket.
Irishman: The devil save the ticket have I, but that. [*Pointing stick in Anthony's face.*]
Anthony: That ticket won't pass me.
Irishman: I'll pass it across the bridge of your nose.
Anthony: Then, I'll burst you in the nose.
Irishman: You'll do what?
Anthony: I stubb'd one of my toes, sir.
Irishman: Then, I'll stubb the other one for you.
Anthony: I guess I'll have to talk louder to him. . . .
Irishman: You're the very man I've been looking for, for this last five days. Now, then; I'm going to give you what we call Bally Hooley.
Anthony: Well, then; I'll give you what we call Hooley Balley. [*They fight—Anthony down.*]
Irishman: Take that, you blackguard. [*Exits.*]
Anthony: [*Gets up and looks about.*] Well, I guess I must have knocked him clear out of sight. Well, there's one Frenchman gone. I kind o'think them tickets is too large yet. [*He tears another one in two.*][34]

The exchange, played in blackface, highlights the stereotype of the Irishman whose behavior is intimidating and unreasonable. It is apparent that both the Irishman and Anthony are treated as low-class individuals. Their dialogue seems to have been adjustable to whichever group the minstrel sketchwriters attacked, especially when the framing device is a social event at which a certain decorum is expected. The Irishman is a party-going gate-crasher who explains his presence by saying, "Dennis Bull Gutridge told me that the widow Maginis was going to have a Raffle for a stove."[35]

The American predisposition toward creative individualism can be seen in the portrayal of Claude as inhabiting a class different from that of the characters he describes in his short speech. He *assumes* a dignity and quality of character that set him apart from his economic class or ethnic group, those traits being the ones Pauline finds most attractive in a potential spouse, despite the fact that Claude's promises are ironic. The whole point is his insincerity, which is revealed in a knowledgeable drinker's in-joke: 2 percent alcohol wafting on the breeze may be better than nothing, but it is a far cry from a dram of 80-proof Kentucky bourbon or the thick texture of Bass's ale, something most of minstrelsy's male audience would certainly have known.

The character list in the published version of Griffin's *Ticket Taker; or, The Masquerade Ball* (1856) includes Mose (and a bogus Mose, for the contrast between type and stereotype could be made explicit if both characters appeared at the same time), Macbeth, Richard III, an Irishwoman, a "Man in Basket Horse," and a character called Previous Difficulties, whose gatekeeper role is similar to Anthony's part in White's play. Both masquerade ball examples illustrate the differences between plays chosen as vehicles for a particular company to demonstrate some of its specialties—Shakespearian takeoffs or Mose imitations, for example—and those that deal more broadly with developing patterns of class consciousness.

The parade plays were directly related to the middle-class audiences' pursuit of respectability, as well as to their desire to exhibit and display the property that their financial successes had helped them acquire. The variety format inherent in the "walk-on" style of the parade also served as a blackface counterpart to the exhibition strategies that popular nineteenth-century museums and circuses used to satisfy public curiosity for physical, cultural, and racial differences. The parade, or slice-of-life, format also reinforced the upwardly mobile person's need to achieve some measure of social distinction and respectability.

The distinction between wealth and class (defined by the appropriate social etiquette) was also maintained by social critics who recognized that ostentatious displays typically indicated individuals of sudden wealth, not persons whose acquisition of commodities was accompanied by an understanding of social graces or a love for allegedly sophisticated cultural events. James McCabe characterized the groups of the suddenly wealthy as the "New Rich" or the "Shoddyites," who "occupy the majority of the mansions in the fashionable streets, crowd the public thoroughfares and the Park with their costly and showy equipages, and flaunt their wealth so coarsely and offensively in the faces of their neighbors that many good people have come to believe that riches and vulgarity are inseparable."[36] The newly rich "whose respectability is built on wealth and not on the qualities known by others as signs of a more established merit" constituted "a class whose chief claims to eminence are that they are rich enough to be ostentatious, and insolent enough to set their feet upon the poor man's neck."[37] These "Shoddyites," not the black urban wealthy *or* poor, were the objects of ridicule in *The Hop of Fashion* and its companion pieces.

The topicality of blackface sketches was as important as the timeliness of the issues discussed in the burlesque sermons and lectures. Minstrelsy attuned itself to public rhetoric and fashionable discussions of such hot topics as phrenology, mesmerism, spiritualism, and similar excursions into alternative forms of spiritual experience. Those subjects also found their way into sketches that dealt with parenting, domestic life, and child development, one of which, Charles White's *Wake Up! William Henry* (1862), links a parent's inability to discipline a child with a satirical attack on Orson Fowler's "science" of phrenology.

Young William Henry cannot be motivated to perform better in school or show respect for his parents. The boy's father (Mr. Hemmingway) contracts with a "professor" (Prof. Fowler) who guarantees that phrenological analysis and hypnosis are the most effective remedies for the son's aberrant behavior:

> Hemmingway: Professor, what is de reason dat his head am so much harder dan any other head in de family?
>
> Professor Fowler: Simply because the valetudinary hypothesis of the cram disorganizes the currency functions of the digestion pad, which causes great moisture and elasticity in the external velocipede, and fills up the rotary antelope with a dusenberry compound of culinary impediments.
>
> Hemmingway: (Astonished.) My gracious! I neber know'd dat he had that. What do dey call it?
>
> Professor Fowler: Chop-valve-us Bass beer-us—that is the European term. It is an epidemic very prevalent among the higher class of business men.
>
> Hemmingway: Well, I'm glad dat I found out. What would you advise me to do wid him?
>
> Professor Fowler: I'll tell you; and if you follow my directions, I think he will get over it in a short time. Now, you take the boy home, send him to school, and see that he goes to bed every night at nine o'clock, and don't feed him on roast turkey, quail, broiled oysters or fancy pastry, and, take my word for it, he will be well in less than thirty days.[38]

Like the other cure-alls and pseudoscientific theories that caught public attention during the nineteenth century, phrenology and hypnotism were popular subjects for satire. Apart from referring to the possible relationship between the skulls of blacks and those of apes, *Wake Up! William Henry* does not deal with black families or with child rearing in black homes. It focuses instead on the gullibility of a parent who out of desperation accepts an irresponsible external agent or miraculous remedy as a treatment for his stereotypic teenager's behavior problems.

One of the other significant topics of the day was spiritualism, which also entered the list of satirical subjects that humorists used to ridicule public curiosity and uncritical acceptance of persons who made extravagant claims about their special abilities. Plays and sketches dealing with spiritualism were common in the 1850s. The sketch known as *Spirit Rappings*, for example, was probably based on Rice's *Rochester Knockings*, a burlesque of an earlier short play entitled *Mysterious Knockings* and produced by William Burton in 1849.[39] All these pieces were comic responses to the reports and demonstrations of the Fox sisters (Margaret and Kate) from Hydesville, New York, who claimed to have communicated, on March 31, 1848, with a spirit of a murdered peddler inhabiting their father's farmhouse. The girls later moved to Rochester with their older sister, Leah Fox Fish, where they began to communicate with spirits "through a 'spiritual telegraph' who rapped at appropriate intervals as the Foxes called out letters of the alphabet."[40] The Foxes toured the country in the late 1840s and 1850s demonstrating their special abilities and playing on their audiences' interest in contacting the departed spirits of family members and friends. The Fox sisters were members of a movement that blossomed quickly and "attracted national attention (much of it critical) as a nineteenth-century miracle promising a religious and even social millennium, and as an empirical demonstration of the soul's immortality in an age of growing doubt."[41]

The *Spirit Rappings* sketch was probably based on a Thomas Rice vehicle. Rice's library of comic sketches and burlesques was gradually absorbed into minstrelsy during the 1850s, especially through the arrangements and editions brought out by Charles White. White's edition of *Bone Squash Diavolo* links the behavior of Jim Brown, an outstanding fiddler, to cranial size and to the appearance of tell-tale bumps that explain Jim's musical abilities. Jim tells his friends that whereas nature "made me de great musician, she make you a common mechanic. From de fiddle to de drum, I am what you white folks call *de-ficient en mass.*" The pun is self-reflexive, refocusing the expression on the negative qualities of the stereotypically inferior black. But the Brown character is set up that way to introduce a song created to mock the pseudoscientific quality of phrenology. The "deficient en mass" figure is the vehicle used to criticize "popular" science.

> Brown: You ideas are so indirectly ober de way from one anoder, owing to your professions, dat it puts me in mind ob de Park orchestra, trying to play an overture. The horn takes up de superana [soprano], de triangular takes up de alto, and leab nothing but de solo for de brass drum. And in condition to dat, hear what de doctore of Physgne Combobologist say: he says, dat on de back of de head, just in de middle ob de craneum, de organ ob music am very strong enveloped in de great Pagganimincy. Now, I've got a bump dar, big as de great watermelon.
> Mose: How you get dat bump? buttin' down de fence?
> Brown: No natur gib um to me. Battin' down de fence?—what you take a musician for, you saucy nigger? Now leff me feel you head; you isn't got no bump like de one I is. You is got a berry big bump, just ober de ear. Ah, dat's de sign you black de boots. [*ALL laugh.*][42]

The exchange is followed by the performance of the "Jim Brown" (1835) song and an ensemble dance. The scene mocks the conclusion that a person's life is predestined by cranial topography, while it also suggests that, given the general inability to explain artistic abilities, phrenology's explanation is about a good as anything else. If this scene dates back to the years when Rice produced *Bone Squash* (late 1840s) as a regular item in his own shows, it would show the persistent interest in phrenology through some thirty years of blackface comedy. The minstrel sketches mocked phrenology's claims to predict behaviors as well as its potential as the basis for social reform. Phrenology offered answers to questions about whether abil-

ities were inherited or could be learned and—of considerable worry to most dem-
ocratically minded Americans—postulated "a hierarchical functionalism of apti-
tudes . . . [that] would help in 'applying the great masses of people to the work by
which each can best serve his family.'" Such an interest in ability classification and
the application of conclusions about the value of individuals by phrenologists "anticipated the personality and IQ assessments of the twentieth century, with all
their debatable utility and potential for abuse."[43]

Minstrel show managers demonstrated their ability to utilize issues of the day
as subjects for their sketches, and no issue seemed more important to workers than
economic security. Economic issues provided the content for a number of sketches
written in the decade that was marked by the panics of 1853, 1855, and 1857. The
best-known example is White's arrangement of Dan Emmett's successful *Hard
Times: A Negro Extravaganza* (1855), which shared the same general theme with
Stephen Foster's popular "Hard Times Come No More" (1855), to which the sketch's
opening lines refer. Emmett borrowed a familiar plot device from contemporary
drama and opera, namely, a poor character's sale of his soul in exchange for some
material goal.

Popular wisdom had it that the temporary release from need or desire for fame
is not a sufficient reason to risk eternal damnation *unless* the potential victim has a
foolproof plan to outwit the Devil. Old Dan Tucker has such a plan and is willing
to risk his own eternal life to obtain coal, food, and clothing for his family, as he
confesses in the sketch's opening lament:

Hard Times! hard times! an' worse a comin';
Hard times thro' my old head keeps runnin';
I'll cotch de nigger make dat song.
To shake him well would not be rong. . . .
Ob him dat's rich, I won't be jealous,
For don't de big book 'spressly tell us—
And tells us, too, widout much fussin',
Whedder we're white or color'd pusson—
"Bressed am dem dat's berry poor,
Dey'll nothing get, dats berry sure?"
Take ort from ort an naught remains;
But "you're a damn fool for your pains."
My wife an' children are most froze,
For want ob fire, food an' clothes,
I'd sell myself, both body an' soul,
For jist a peck ob fire coal![44]

The sentiments expressed in this excerpt deal with the frustration many white
small-business owners shared with poor and lower-class people. Tucker complains

that effort goes unrewarded and that hopelessness is the true lot of the poor. The paraphrase of a proverbial phrase or biblical beatitude ("Blessed are the poor in spirit, for theirs is the kingdom of heaven") is a common device in minstrel speeches and sermons. It contrasts the hope that the poor will receive some reward with the reality that they are doomed to a life of need. The skepticism embodied in the blackface rewrite of the Christian message reflects the comedian's view that the economic disparities of American life afflict all poor people, regardless of color.

The theme of soul selling as a means of mortgaging earthly needs against the possibility of eternal damnation is found in several sketches. Bone Squash sings the following song in the Ethiopian opera of the same name.

Oh, if I could sell myself to de debbil,
I'd cut a splash to kill old people;
I wish I could sell myself to de debbil,
And leff off patent sweeping,
I'll go and buy a suit of clothes,
Ruffle shirt and 'rocco shoeses,
Striped cravat, and whitewashed hat,
And spectacles for de noses.
Oh, I wish I could sell myself to de debbil,
Crowd in, move off, and pass through dem all.[45]

The theme reappears in White's *Magic Penny*, where Joe, a destitute character, makes the following statement and proceeds to sing his own parody of the song from *Bone Squash.*

I wish I could find some one dat wants to buy a nigger like me, 'case I'll sell myself berry cheap. I woun't care if it was de devil himself.

I wish I could sell myself to de debil,
I wish I could sell myself to de debil,
I wish I could sell myself to de debil,
Den I would habe lots of cash.
I'd have houses, I'd have horses,
Say farewell to all my bosses,
Wear fine clothes,
Be de pink ob beaux
And mingle wid de fust class s'iety.
I wish I could sell myself to de debil etc.

When the Devil does appear, Joe claims, "Dis is one of my rich relations come here in disguise. Just in de bery *nick* of time." Mephistopheles tells Joe that all he has to do is make a wish, and when Joe does so, someone hurls a purse onto the stage. The purse contains a magic penny and comes with the usual conditions associated with magical elements in American folklore.

'Tis but a cent—yet guard it well
For if it's lost, 'twill break the magic spell
And if there's aught that you require,
Rub the cent at your desire—
Rub it till it bright and clear
And all you wish will then appear!
Body and soul, you have been sold—
Remember all, Look quick—behold.[46]

Joe eventually loses his soul, and Mephistopheles wins in this conflict between immediate material comfort and eternal salvation. The underlying concern of these comedies is the human desire for economic security and pride in being a productive member of society. The characters are desperate enough to seek extraordinary solutions different from the nineteenth-century work ethic created by manufacturers and commodity producers to justify a production economy. For those on the periphery of employment, pacts with the Devil or other miraculous solutions to the problems of subsistence living were hoped-for fantasies reflecting a reverse image of benevolent grace from a God pleased with human effort.

Financial success seemed so randomly distributed that Americans placed their hopes in dubious get-rich-quick schemes. Popular plays and pamphlets encouraged individuals and families to invest their hopes in lotteries, new inventions, clever real estate deals, and a whole range of scams designed to bilk the unwary. The accumulation of wealth by middle-class families in the 1850s was "due as much to chance as to their innate morality."[47] Tucker's pact with the Devil thus makes sense only when it is seen as the last desperate act of a person who has not profited from good luck or adherence to traditional American moral values. Tucker's plight seems to capture the feelings of New Yorkers affected by the Panic of 1855, which, "contemporaries felt, forced many of the respectable lower-middle-class into tenement apartments."[48] That is why the conversion of a biblical axiom into a cynical aphorism could provide the rhetorical foundation for a comedy about communal economic misery and, at the same time, reinforce the hard-work ethic of middle-class audiences.

The sheer quantity of sketches about medical charlatans suggests strong public concern about the quality of medical care—although, as is the case with many other kinds of popular comedy, any financially successful routine was bound to be copied. Doctors, pharmacists, scientists, salespeople, and any others who hoped to profit by the invention of new machines or collusion in common frauds were satirized in blackface sketches; some of these sketches focused on the promoters of particular products or new scientific discoveries, whereas others ridiculed the products themselves. The presence of quack doctors and patent medicine vendors led James Mc-

Cabe to pass along the following warning received from his own "expert": "A prominent dealer in drugs once said . . . that the progress of a certain 'Bitters' could be traced across the continent, from Chicago to California, 'by the graves it had made.' The 'Elixirs of Life,' 'Life Rejuvenators,' 'Vital Fluids,' and other compounds sold to revive worn out constitutions are either dangerous poisons or worthless draughts."[49]

Whether searching for a quick cure for an embarrassing ailment or looking for a product designed to guarantee success, many Americans were gullible enough to patronize charlatans. In White's *Laughing Gas* (1858), for example, a quack professor tries to convince a group of stock characters (a singer, tragedian, etc.) that inhaling his invention will enhance their natural gifts:

> Ladies and gentlemen . . . doubtless you have seen the flaming posters on the walls announcing the exhibition of laughing gas. Perhaps a few of my auditors are aware of the component parts of laughing gas. No doubt you have observed the gas burning in the street lamps as well as in your houses. That's not the gas I purpose giving you tonight. Observe, I hold in my hand a silken bag. The gas contained in this bag is composed of four different ingredients, viz., hydrogen, oxygen, Holland gin and other gin—more of the latter than the other.[50]

Laughing Gas deals with the delicate balance between the desire of talented or skilled people to achieve public acclaim and the dubious means of taking whatever shortcuts are available to attain that end. Those behaviors are not depicted as bound to racial or ethnic backgrounds. Indeed, fancy-talking representatives for products or services of questionable value were admired for their verbal agility as well as their clever promotional schemes. At the same time, those very traits were considered extravagant and when suitably enhanced with appropriate comic hyperboles were quite successful as comic subjects.

The fourth-largest collection of sketches focuses on courtship, marriage, child rearing, and other domestic issues. The plots are limited to the same ones audiences might have expected in nonblackface comedies or comic operas of the period, with the rituals of courtship being the most common subject for ridicule. The most prominent plot device is a suitor's deception of a young woman's father, a theme found in scores of European comedies from Plautus to Molière. As David Grote has observed, "There is no doubt that . . . comedy has used humor as the bludgeon with which to assault the rigid, authoritarian, and hypocritical aspects of public society, as personified in the characters and events that block the lovers from each other."[51]

The most familiar object of ridicule in this type of comedy is the young woman's father, who always objects to the suitor, goes to extravagant lengths to protect his daughter, and is always outwitted by that suitor or his agent. The "protection of the eligible daughter" theme is found in several sketches that resemble one another because they feature family settings in which (1) a domineering authority figure (usually the father) abuses a child, servant, or deliveryman simply through a general maliciousness or as an assertion of a property right to protect the daughter from a suitor; (2) a young man seeks the hand of the daughter, who is seldom described as having any especially attractive qualities and who seems to enter quite willingly into the liaison; and (3) the most common method of enforcing domestic order is the liberal use of a strap or a cane.[52]

The sketches on this theme include White's adaptations/arrangements of *The Black Statue* (1862), which was probably based on Rice's *Black and White; or, The Protean Statue* (1837); *The Black Shoemaker* (ca. 1858); *The Darkey's Stratagem* (1875); and *Gettin' de Bag to Hold; or, The United States Mail* (1855), which was also known as *United States Mail; or, The Mysterious Sack of Taters* (1856) when White presented it at Sanford's in Philadelphia.[53]

These sketches seldom confront any racial matters directly. They do reflect some strong beliefs about race, class, and gender, although less through explicit statements made by the characters than through an exhibited tolerance for unflattering and inconsiderate behaviors. In *The Black Statue* Old Squintum, the father of the bride, physically threatens everyone around him; in *The Black Shoemaker* Mr. Brown knocks his son senseless for every minor misadventure; in *Gettin' de Bag to Hold* Post Office Sam, the Negro letter carrier (the U.S. male/mail pun does appear), is ridiculed by the very plain Lucy because he cannot read the address on her letter; and in *The Darkey's Stratagem* Old Cruncher, who censors his daughter's mail, hounds his black servant, Cupid, because he finds various ways of resisting the old man's orders. In almost every case, however, the abused victim turns the tables on the cantankerous father or authority figure at the end of the sketch. In sum, many of these sketches show the same comic intemperance that characterized the television program *All in the Family* over one hundred years later.

In *The Darkey's Stratagem* (1874), the miserable father (Old Cruncher) is eventually outwitted by his clever servant (Cupid), who succeeds in humiliating his boss and helping the couple. Under the guise of telling Cruncher a story about his former employer, Cupid carries out his clever plan to ensure the young lovers' escape from the old man's control:

> Cupid: Come, sit down, and I'll tell you about it. (They sit. . . . Every time "snoozer" is said Cruncher jumps up.) Well, you see, this old snoozer I used to work for . . . he had a daughter just like you, and there was a young feller used to come to see her, but the old man didn't like him, and wouldn't let him come in the house; so, one day he (this young man) made a bargain with the servant, just like me, to get the girl out of the house. Then the old man locked the girl in her room and put the key in his pocket. Well, this servant . . . got the old snoozer to sit down to tell him a story. Then the servant went down in the old man's pocket and took out the key of the door. (He does so.) Well, the signal agreed upon by the young man and the servant was a whistle, just like this. The young feller came in. The

servant put the key over his right shoulder. The lover came and took the key. [More dialogue follows and the young people leave.]

Cruncher: What a d____d old fool he must have been!

Cupid: Wasn't he!

Cruncher: They couldn't fool me that way.[54]

The comic premise in most of these sketches lies in the various methods devised to outwit the father, who, having established his protective demeanor in the opening scene, usually disappears for at least part of a scene. Mr. Brown goes to "buy leather and a glass of beer," Old Squintum goes to town "on business," Old Cruncher departs abruptly in a fit of frustration over the lack of respect shown by Cupid, and other characters are conveniently offstage or out of sight while the diversion is designed.

Although the broad structure of the business is the same, the means vary from sketch to sketch. In *The Black Statue* the comic premise hinges on disguising a suitor to help him gain access to an old curmudgeon's young daughter.[55] In some sketches the comic business depends on the father's interception of a letter that a suitor sends to the daughter announcing the former's imminent arrival to arrange or stage an elopement. In others various exchanges of clothing or hiding places create the fun. For example, if the suitor or anyone else arrives during the father's or mother's absence, the visitor is usually hidden away in a sack in *Gettin' de Bag to Hold,* a large cradle or a flour barrel in *The Black Shoemaker,* the statue in *The Black Statue,* and feminine garb in *The Darkey's Stratagem.* In spite of the father's protection, the young lady always decides to marry the romantically inclined caller—usually dressed as a dandy gentleman—and the couple's intentions are often confirmed by an official document or an elopement. None of the sketches mentions a "breach of contract" situation, none deals with interracial marriage, and only one raises the issue of a dowry. When the sketch includes the young lady's mother (Mrs. Brown in *The Black Shoemaker,* Mrs. Squintum in *The Black Statue,* and Mrs. Nipper in *Gettin' de Bag to Hold*), she is usually old, and her role in most of the antebellum pieces was played by a cross-dressed male actor.

The assumed social order in these sketches is usually the nuclear family: the daughter lives in a stereotypic two-parent situation, and her parents expect her to "marry up" or "out" of the trade, agricultural, or shopkeeper environment in which she was reared. As the New York social observer James McCabe put it bluntly in 1872 when he described marriage customs in New York society: "Only wealthy marriages are tolerated in New York society. For men or women to marry beneath them is a crime society cannot forgive."[56] The Ethiopian farces usually link the young lady with a companion of some means, except for Pete the gardener in *The Black Statue,* whose background is never revealed—he could have been another Claude Melnotte—and never question the source of the suitor's income. The mother/old woman figure usually defers to her husband but sometimes presents herself as an authority figure whose real power seems limited to controlling the inhabitants of the home or shop by physical force or emotional manipulation. The chief object of ridicule in these burlesques seems to be the authority figure who tries to prevent the young couple from courting or marrying. Minstrelsy assumes a male-dominated environment because it is only against the background of unreasonable behaviors that the ludicrous actions of tyrants can appear sufficiently comic.

The sketches that migrated from one company to another seldom suffered any major changes. The "cast of characters" in the printed version of White's *Black Statue* and the Carncross and Dixey Minstrels' playbill are the same, with the exception that White lists the traveling salesman as "Dr. Pilgarlic," whereas Carncross has "Dr. Garlick." The only obviously blackface character related to an African American background is Jake, "a mischievous servant" in White's printed version. The Carncross and Dixey playbill states that Pete is "a sentimental Dark, always in love," but does not mention the "white mask for the statue" that a black Jake would need in order to assume Pete's place on the pedestal.

The Black Statue combines the courtship between Pete and Rose with the role-reversal convention in which the blackface trickster Jake avenges himself on Old Squintum. The stereotypic charlatan Pilgarlic's talent for misdirection matches Squintum's passion for cheap curiosities. Pete and Jake are employed as hands on Squintum's farm. Pete is lazy: "I don't care for old Squintum—I wouldn't go to work if he was to tell me to." Jake, although industrious, is a fun-loving character who enjoys a good joke or game: "A game of blindman's *bluff*. . . . I'd like to see some blind man play bluff with us. Oh, how we would skin him."[57] Both are willing to take advantage of Squintum's absence to pursue their diversions and create a situation for Pete's courtship of Rose, which, in the conventions of blackface comedy, involves little more than a simple request and an immediate consent. Rose agrees to play blindman's bluff because her father is gone. As is the case with all these comedies, the workers always play when the boss or authority figure is away. She has "no objections, although it doesn't look very nice to be so familiar with colored people" (4). Pete's rejoinder, although it may be ironic, also recognizes Jake as his equal: "Oh, nonsense, Rose. I would as lieve associate wid Jake as with any brother I have. Jake is an honest feller if his skin is dark" (4).

The three adults play the children's game with abandon ("Why dat's what de little boys play; but it ain't no matter") and to make things more sporting agree to a wager ("de one dat get cotched fust must gib a shilling"). The blindfolded Jake is abandoned by the others when they see Old Squintum, and Jake runs right into the old man. When caught, Jake adopts a deferential behavior and attempts to explain why he was running around with a handkerchief over his eyes. When Squintum threatens him ("Now, you black devil, if you don't tell me what's been going on here, I'll break every bone in your body"), Jake tells the truth. The game was Pete's idea, and the revelation leads to his dismissal in the following dialogue.

Squintum: Look here sir; how dare you presume to take the liberty of getting my
daughter out here to play with fellows on the farm, and that too, with such company! Come here, sir. (to Pete). Go right into the house . . . I don't want you any
longer.
Jake: Say, Mr. Squintum, don't turn him away.
Squintum: Hold your tongue you black rascal, or I'll turn you away. (5)

Jake is not fired, and even though he was threatened by Squintum, he remains loyal
to Pete.

Jake: (begins to cry). Pete, dat was all my fault.
Pete: Never mind, Jake, I forgive you.
Jake: Say, Pete, I'll come to work wid you wherever you go. I always liked you, Pete;
'kase when we used to sleep together you kept me so warm. (5)

Pete's dismissal sets the stage for his return as the statue, since he will use any
means to pursue his courtship of Rose. When Pete and Pilgarlic meet along the road,
Pilgarlic proposes that their collaboration will ensure that each can achieve his goal.
Pete agrees to masquerade as the statue, which Pilgarlic will sell to Old Squintum
for $1,000. Throughout the scene Jake is treated as an object of derision, as a lazy,
bumbling character who is retained only because he is so cheap to maintain. At the
same time, however, he is given three chances to strike back and takes good advantage of those opportunities. Early in the play he hits Old Squintum with a sack of
flour, and he turns the tables a second time when he fills the perspiring Squintum's
handkerchief with flour. Later, after Pete abandons his statue disguise to run away
with Rose, Jake assumes the disguise (including probably the white "marble" mask)
and pummels Old Squintum and his wife "with a large stuffed club." Obviously the
planned disorders of low comedy, that is, the disguises, flour sacks, special effects,
and mock beatings, are important features of this sketch.

Squintum eventually forsakes his opposition to the union and suggests a "blow-
out" in the couple's honor featuring "two cents' worth of dates, and a penny's worth
of peanuts." By this time White has exhausted all his comic involvements and resorts
to a deus ex machina, namely, the destruction of Squintum's home by lightning and
fire. The final tableau shows Jake as a volunteer fireman being hoisted with a bucket
of water above the players so that he can douse the fire and all the characters below.

Some of the black characters in these sketches are stereotypes who are treated
poorly; others are so unrealistic as to be completely incongruous. The black letter
carrier in the United States Mail could not have been illiterate. Even in the graft-
ridden postal service of New York City, the screening process, the bonding requirements, and the political affiliations would make a "real" Post Office Sam unlikely.[58]
But the black characters are not the only ones subject to ridicule in these sketches,
some of whose characters may or may not have been played completely in burnt

cork. In this "theater of misrule," the mischievous Jake controls events from behind his various disguises, and Cupid makes a fool of Old Cruncher. The sketch assumes not only that Jake is low status but that he lives in an environment where Old Squintum, because of his behavior, is constantly the butt of other people's jokes. Squintum is too stupid to recognize Pete's disguise (something Jake does immediately), too cheap to realize Pilgarlic's fraud, and finally, too vainglorious and insensitive to understand that no one really fears him. Rose and Mrs. Squintum are mere objects, the wife the provider of meals and the daughter, played by a cross-dressed male actor, the purveyor of transvestite comic business.[59]

The protective-father theme allowed for many variations, including the transfer of parenting responsibility to the young woman's servant. In *Sam's Courtship* (1852) the result is a combination of the verbal trickster's techniques shown in the previous examples with mistaken identity and physical comedy. The protector here is not the woman's father but her servant, Cesar Cicero Anthony Snow. After reconciling himself with Sarah's suitor, Sam Simple, Cesar turns the tables on the unsuspecting Sam by devising a clothes-switch ruse to make sure that Sarah is not deceived by the unworthy suitor. The stage directions indicate that "as they embrace to elope, CESAR raises his arms to hug SAM, and his skirt drops off." Meanwhile Sarah pulls a string attached to Cesar's bonnet, which also flies off, and the sketch concludes with a typical chase scene. The ruse begins as follows.

> Sarah: Now, Mr. Simple, if you will wait for a few minutes, I will return with my hat and shawl and fly with the man I adore.
> Sam: Durn that nigger, I say. If that physic killed the old mare how on earth did he expect I was going to stand it? [Cesar tried earlier to poison Sam—*au.*] What will Eph say when I bring the gal home? What will Lize Britton say? Here she comes.
> [Enter Cesar, dressed in female attire, supposed to be Sarah.]
> Sarah: Come, come Mr. Simple, take me to your arms, and, ere I leave the roof of my happy home, let this empty room hear the echo of my future husband's kiss, and then farewell.[60]

Again, in *Sam's Courtship* the primary subject appears to be the ridicule of the servant type rather than of the black servant alone. White's "notice" to the printed edition reads that "the parts of Sam and Sarah can be played either in White or Black; or Sam can be played in Dutch."[61] The statement goes to the heart of White's intent: if racial specificity is not the principal object of the burlesque, this particular example of disparagement humor is directed at another object, such as the social ritual of courtship, in which the father played a major role. Old Cruncher is not very different from Brabantio in George Griffin's 1866 burlesque of *Othello.*[62] Sam wishes to preserve his daughter for a wealthy suitor, whereas Griffin's Brabantio wants to market his property to the circus. In both cases the daughter is the object of parental greed, which is displaced when the father gives in to his daughter's choice.

The burlesque courtship sketches subvert the domestic melodramas of the period by mocking the patterns those plays sought to reinforce. Since "domestic melodrama is by its very nature conservative, however subversive its underlying message, it argues for the preservation of the family and its traditional values—a binding in of the errant son or unforgiving father or wayward daughter." Just as Victorian drama should be seen "as a vehicle for some of the most powerful fantasies and desires of the time," so too should the trivial blackface sketches be interpreted as mocking the conventions of the social order.[63]

These examples force the question about whether blackface comedy provided "portraits" of African Americans or whether race should be considered the primary subject matter of all forms of blackface minstrelsy. Even though racism was its underlying reason for exploiting the low status of African Americans as a comic device, blackface comedy stressed the use of caricatures and stereotypes because they provided the best vehicles for criticizing the differences between what society promised and what it delivered. The sketches overemphasized the importance of perceived and real racial differences to ridicule the contradictions lower- or middle-class Americans found in their daily lives and the fads many Americans accepted at face value.

Most of the references to African Americans are brief or often incidental, especially when the plays (1) focus on political satire; (2) explore cultural differences, that is, demonstrate how "other" people live; (3) create satirical or irreverent treatments of the public's enthusiasm for fads, cures, and "scientific" theories; and (4) parody other theatrical genres, such as Shakespeare or contemporary comedies of manners. The sketches were closely linked to other forms of popular theater, and those connections seem to have fluctuated throughout the history of minstrelsy, often depending more on political and economic fears of the moment than on long-standing racial antipathies.

Nevertheless, those antipathies were always obvious. In Charles White's *Mischievous Nigger*, for example, there is no question about Antony Snow's place in the social hierarchy of the multiethnic home in which he is employed. The sketch includes Colonel Flutter (the nominal patriarch), Mrs. Morton (his currently unmarried sister), Monsieur Fripon (French barber and first suitor), Fanny Nibbs (Irish maidservant), Jimmy Ducks (second suitor), and Antony Snow (black manservant). The characters speak at least three different dialects, two (French and Black English) attributed to two male characters and an Irish brogue (Hiberno-English) for the female nurse and her boyfriend, Jimmy Ducks.

The plot consists of three contrived situations during which the characters interact and one final disclosure scene. As the sketch opens, the widowed Mrs. Morton and her brother are headed for a ball. Fanny Nibbs, a nurse employed to care for the Morton children, plans to go to the theater with Jimmy Ducks, her Irish boyfriend. The dialects offer numerous opportunities for malaprops and blatant homophonic puns such as *ladder* for *lather.* Jimmy Ducks's lines reflect the Irish stage dialect: "Oh, murder! look at that. That nagur knew I was dyin' wid hunger, and brought me this [a piece of chicken intended for Flutter]. Here goes! (*Sits down and eats.*) 'Pon my sowl, that chicken is nice—little tough, trifle too old—tay is beautiful." And Fripon's pseudo-French is even worse: "Oh, yes, I know zat she was married before, but if zat black negar put his elbow on me, look out, zat's all. . . . But, *ma cherie amie,* you know I love your mistress. . . . I love her as I do my four little bears zat I am making fat for de bear's grease."[64]

Regardless of the dialects' authenticity, the language and costumes are the primary features announcing the identities of the various characters. Nonetheless, all the characters in the typical Ethiopian sketch are stereotyped, not just the ones identified as "ethnic." All possess negative behavioral characteristics and language patterns on which the verbal exchanges and physical business are based. Again, the text only hints at what the performers might have done. The audience would have been clued to accept the identity of the character on the basis of readily observed elements announcing the specific type. The social events are typical activities for members of both groups even though the class distinctions are not necessarily maintained in all the interactions among the various characters. Colonel Flutter, for example, may think he is in charge of the activities within the household, but his power is relative to Antony's clever pranks and Mrs. Morton's ability to create situations so that she and Antony can free themselves from Flutter's domination.

The relationship between Antony and Colonel Flutter is also based on two stereotypes: the black servant and the retired soldier-gentleman who is little more than an intemperate crank. Antony is a practical joker who takes everything he is told literally *if* it fits with his general sense of superiority to the people who employ him. The master-servant relationship is maintained in *The Mischievous Nigger* as a general structure governing the interaction of the characters, but each of them is allowed to break the structure temporarily to advance the comedy. The inversion of the master-slave relationship is especially clear in the following passage, in which Antony explains why he borrowed Colonel Flutter's shaving brush to shave the family's Siamese cat.

> Flutter: Speak or I'll choke you. Why did you do it?
> Antony: Ha! Ha! Ha! I told you how it was dat cat came in ebery morning, and while I was eating my breakfast in the kitchen, she always 'teal piece of meat off the plate. Hold on, I said, when I cotch you I'll fix you, and dis morning I cotched her, lathered her all over wid hot water, then I shaved all de har off de cat's back. Ha! yah! yah!
> Mrs. M: Where is the cat now?
> Antony: Ah, I don't know, she never come back here again, 'cos when she found all her hair was off, she was so 'shamed of her 'pearance, dat she clear right out. ha! ha! (6)

Flutter maintains his relationship with Antony by threats of beatings, dismissal, and name-calling, behaviors suggesting that Flutter controls the situation. In reality Flutter is similar to the stereotypic "colonels" in contemporary melodrama who are invariably victims of their own faults. Threats of beating such as the following seem to reinforce Antony's low status, but he always manages to create a new trick to foil his employers.

> Flutter: I've a great mind to beat you black and blue.
> Antony: I golly! wish you would beat me white, 'cos I don't think you can make me much blacker dan I is. (7)

Antony's retort that while a beating might hurt, it won't change his color or his behavior foils Flutter's threat and allows Antony to continue his assault on his master by whitewashing the old man's coat. In his role as the family's servant, Antony performs assignments that appear to be clearly within the normal tasks of a domestic. Yet he is only too willing to protest the assignment of any additional duties not in keeping with his understanding of his responsibilities: "See here, old man. I want to know if you t'ink I am chamber-maid—fust you tell me to black yer books—den you tell me to clean de knives and forks—den you tells me to brush your cost—den you tell me to whitewash—now you tell me to bring up yer supper. Now I tell *you* dat I won't do it" (7).

The final complication occurs when Antony, frustrated by his inability to calm Mrs. Morton's infants, decides to give them paregoric ("baleygorick") and throw them under the bed. The other characters are convinced that the children have been kidnapped and that Antony should be dismissed. The comic business involves the usual surprise discovery of hidden suitors (Jimmy) and sheet-dressed ghosts (Fripon), as well as the fainting servant (Antony) who revives in time to escape burial, after which everyone is concerned with the whereabouts of the babies, who are in the big bed with Fripon.

At the end of the play, the courting pairs are joined, leaving Antony to contend with Flutter, who says: "Now, you story-telling specimen of African human nature, I discharge you! Leave the house! Go, or I'll kick you out." Faced with the prospect of Antony's dismissal, Fanny exclaims, "Two words to that, If he goes, I'll go too," a threat that, if executed, would leave the household without any domestic help. Having failed to get a positive reference from any family members, Antony breaks the frame of the play and directs his request to the audience. "Won't you ladies and gentlemen, give me recommendations? (Applause) Dar, old man, der's de recommendations. Like to hear, and if our little sketch afforded *you* any amusement, I will never repent having been called the 'MISCHIEVOUS NIGGER!'" (17)

The Mischievous Nigger exploits typical features of the courtship farce: stray letters that fall into the wrong hands, characters who get caught in compromising situations, dominant/protector relationships between the father/older brother and a spinster daughter/sister. In these and other examples, such as *The Black Shoemaker* and *The Black Statue,* the comic business involves getting a character into a compromising situation, such as hiding under a table or in a closet, jumping into a barrel, or assuming some disguise to avoid discovery by an authority figure or rival. The device also allows for an offstage or hidden voice to participate in the dialogue.

> Fripon: I must return to my shop, I have left somebody in ze shaving-chair wiz ze ladder on his face.
> Mrs. M: A ladder on his face—gracious goodness!
> Flutter: (off stage) All right, give me my umbrella.
> Mrs. M: Here comes my brother. Hide, my dear Fripon, or you'll be murdered.
> Fripon: Where ze devil s'all I go? under ze table? [He cannot hide there because Fanny's suitor, Jimmy Ducks, is already under the table.]
> Mrs. M: No, my dear Fripon. Here, in the bed, and cover yourself with the curtains.
> (Fripon gets into the bed and draws the curtains.)

The sketch also belongs to a family of pieces in which the "sassy nigger" character appears to win temporary verbal victories against white protagonists who cannot match the servant's ability to manipulate situations through language. White's *Uncle Jeff* (1856?) features the same type of character who, because of his low status, is blamed for every domestic mishap: "I was in a debble of a hurry—'cos if dere was anything done wrong, dey used to say dat I done it. Who set fire to de barns? Uncle Jeff. Who gib de pigs julap in deir swill? Uncle Jeff. Who tied de tin kittle to de cat's tail? Uncle Jeff. Who stole de eggs? Uncle Jeff.—dat's de way it use to be."[65]

In Griffin's *Troublesome Servant,* the servant is named "Handy Andy" (full name: Andy Rooney), after the character Samuel Lover (1797–1868) introduced to popular fiction in 1842.[66] Handy Andy is a bumbling Irishman who "revels in deadlocks and quandaries . . . and mixes low-comedy with false romanticism."[67] The part, which was played by George Christy, is that of a prankster who makes an old man's life miserable with one practical joke after another and generally refuses to cooperate with any of the household help except the female servant. This treatment of the female is typical; regardless of the situation or whether the sketch is performed in black or white, female servants are usually objects of male lust, even though most of the attempts at seduction are ineffective.

The matter is not so simple, however, because the characters often break the plane of the stage, step out of character, and make specific pleas to the audience, which is asked to participate by saying a few lines or allowing itself to be considered essential to the working out of the plot. At the end of *The Mischievous Nigger,* the actor *playing* the black servant receives the audience's favor, not the Antony character in the play. The actors move so easily from discourse among themselves to speeches directed at the audience and back again that the sketch should not be taken literally.

The Mischievous Nigger functions in a make-believe framework to which the individual members of the audience may join if the scenes are accepted as "temporary situations to be discarded when the humorous exchange is over."[68] That does not mean the sketch is escapist entertainment or that sheer pleasure is the only consequence of the dialogue. The characters are different enough to suggest some more compelling reasons for the sketch's humor. Take the cat-shaving joke, for example. Antony's action is a fiction all the more funny because of its improbability. He acts out of guile, not stupidity: the human's cruel revenge for feline creativity. This explanation agrees with some humor research that suggests that a listener may "be willing to suspend his disbelief temporarily in order to enjoy the humor of the joke."[69]

Another typical scene is the setup for Antony's story about the two infants assigned to his care. Unfortunately for him, he does not know that Fripon has moved the children to greater safety, and the audience has to be convinced that none of the males in this sketch are good babysitters. This is one of the genre's conceits that reinforce attitudes about gender responsibilities typically accepted by antebellum Americans, regardless of ethnic background or color.

> Mrs. M: (*kindly*) Do come down Antony, and tell what has become of my dear twins.
> Antony: Now yer ain't mad, is yer? 'cause if yer is, I ain't a goin to cum down.
> Mrs. M: . . . Now Antony, tell us all about it.
> Antony: (*comes to c.*) I tell you all about it; fust dar was fourteen robbers cum in wid swords—one ob dem got me by de wool—sez he, I want your money or dem babies—den de oder nineteen took my wool, and de hull forty-five said all at once, one after de odder, gib us yer money or dem babies. Take de babies, sez I—I didn't say dat—I said, take my money 'cos I didn't hab a red cent, you know. Den de fust t'ing dat I knowed, de hull fifty ob' em knocked me down—about one hundred and fifty jumped on me, carried off de Siamese Twins—and dat's all. (15)

The preposterous story is a tall tale, made funnier because the audience knows that the children are safe and that all will be revealed when Fripon is discovered.

Antony is cast as a servant, a role commonly assigned to African Americans in nineteenth-century theater pieces. The tendency to restrict African Americans to these low-status roles was contemporaneous with but not necessarily caused by blackface comedy. Zeke's role in *Fashion* was discussed earlier, but similar roles were written for Cuffee in John Brougham's *Life in New York; or, Tom and Jerry on a Visit* (1856) and Tom Scott in Preuss's *Fashions and Follies of Washington Life* (1857).

Blackface comedians seldom implied that their audiences lived "like" slaves or that the role-reversal sketches suggested any long-term benefits of a real inversion of class or ethnic differences. In the theater, however, symbolic inversions are visualized as occurring in a world governed by misrule and instability. The extent to which the average person enjoyed watching the working out of role reversals was probably inversely proportional to the likelihood that any of those events would ever happen. The servant would never replace the master, the criminal would never unseat the judge, and the hierarchical order would probably never change except in the imaginary world of the theater. American sketch writers seem never to have discovered the true comic potential in the slave or servant character as a means of exploiting the low-status comic in the ways Plautus used his slaves as vehicles for ridiculing Roman society. Ralph Ellison and other African American critics recognized that flaw when they argued that neither American comedy in general nor minstrelsy in particular could have drawn strength from any deep awareness of African American humor.[70]

The Ethiopian sketches were popular because they reinforced widely shared beliefs that things would not change much. The dysfunctional households of the sketches were comic because they contradicted American notions of well-run, organized, and efficient domestic environments. In these ideal households daughters were to be protected against lecherous males, and parents usually controlled their children. In the dysfunctional ones husbands generally beat or threatened to beat their spouses, married life was a living hell, raising children was the penalty for sexual pleasure, and life for the common person without status or money was a great trial.

The sketches and afterpieces show that the minstrel comedians did not neglect some of the tried-and-true subjects of comedy to focus on race or racial conflict as the primary foundation for their humor. Yet blackface comic conventions depended in some ways on the general view of African Americans as low-status individuals, especially among "lower-class whites who longed for some assurance of their own status, a sense that they were superior to someone, if only by virtue of the color of their skin."[71] The idea that there was some inherent declaration of white superiority is not so clear in the forms of blackface entertainment reviewed here, however. Class and gender seem to be just as significant as race in the various Ethiopian sketches and other types of afterpieces presented by the major minstrel companies. This seems to be valid regardless of whether the class issues on which the burnt cork mask reflected were those of whites or those of blacks, for the two groups shared some of their conceptions of class.

All the analyses offered thus far bring my conclusions closer to those suggested by Wilentz, Stowe, Grimsted, and others who argue that minstrelsy was about more than white supremacy, an opinion David Roediger challenged recently in *Wages of Whiteness*. Roediger believes that when Wilentz and the others argue

> that racism was subverted by the variety of images of minstrel entertainers—the beautiful, graceful, the ignorant, the savvy, the lonely, the wronged and the villain— they put aside the extent to which audiences knew that these were white entertainers, playing thinly blacked-up white stock characters. When arguing that blackface was a slight veneer providing the "distance" necessary to do effective social satire, they minimize the extent to which the mask seemed real to the audience and subverted the social criticism being expressed.[72]

The problems with Roediger's conclusion are (1) the reliance on the metaphor of the mask and (2) the assumption that minstrel audiences were extremely gullible. No one knows for sure what audiences believed; there are fewer than a dozen testimonials in the literature indicating that individual white observers were duped, whereas the antebellum audiences numbered in the tens of thousands. As the sketches show, blatant racism sometimes led to the denigration of African Americans, but just as often the comedians offered messages that had little to do with the costumes or makeup they were wearing. If the burnt cork comedians were accepted as surrogate black persons, there is no good explanation of why so little of what blackface characters did or said could be identified with African American life.

Disparagement humor, even demeaning humor, seldom functions in univocal ways. Even racial comedy has implications that go beyond the ascription of traits to fictional characters. The issue in most racial disparagement humor found in early minstrelsy is often one of class masquerading as race or ethnicity. Given audiences who equally disliked African Americans as a group and any other group of Americans belong to a higher class, social station, or profession, it is likely that jokes about class issues would not depend entirely on the dislike of African Americans to provoke laughter.[73] The factor of class would explain why some black Americans in various regions of the country during the antebellum era found humor in the class distinctions within white society. As John Blassingame has shown, "Poor whites, looked down upon and treated with contempt by the slave holders, were viewed by the slave as lower in the scale of humanities than he was." The persons of color who would associate with the "'po white trash' were practically outcasts, and held in very great contempt."[74] The Ethiopian sketches could be played to a large variety of black and white audiences precisely because the issue of class, represented on the stage by a group of characters sharing values or aspirations similar to those of the audience, provided opportunities for audience members to feel superior in some way or to feel secure that their positions, however bleak, were at least reasonably acceptable.

The contents and character treatments of the sketches discussed in this chapter suggest that behind the masks and the stereotypes lay serious concerns about social, cultural, and economic issues. The Ethiopian sketches certainly show that class rather than race, individual self-worth rather than conformity to a code or system, and an insatiable curiosity about physical or ethnic differences provided a rich selection of subjects for the sketch writers. What is often surprising (because revisionist studies would not lead readers to expect it) is how often the blackface servant, employee, or dandy outwits his antagonist. The humorous effect of that comic reversal was apparently one of the major reasons for blackface comedy's success among the working-class audiences.

Business-class audiences could entertain a very different reading by considering how they were to be sure that their servants were their inferiors if the rational ordering of life presented in contemporary melodramas was taken seriously. That order did not *have* to be taken seriously in the blackface sketches because the characters already had two markers identifying them as inferiors: their burnt cork masks and their "unrespectable" behaviors. The characters were still threats to the social order, however, not because they were seen as "real" African Americans but because they were the clever instruments of the egalitarian audience's need to feel some form of superiority with respect to other classes or races. Given the mask of respectability worn by unscrupulous businesspeople, there was always the chance that business dealings or a changed economy could ruin a family whose fortune was its only claim to membership in a social hierarchy.

Captain Slim in *The Hop of Fashion* may have been nouveau riche because of the fortune he had won in a lottery, but he was not so different from his social superiors, whose wealth may have been accumulated from unwitting victims excluded from established business associations.[75]

The blackface burlesques "paraded" examples of all social types for inspection and parodied the widespread interest in fashion, etiquette, and education. Once the sketch writers recognized the efficiency of the parade format in allowing for an ever-changing cast of walk-on characters—the model perhaps was the popular promenade of fancy balls and Sunday strolls—they were content to use a relatively restricted number of social rituals as the settings for their burlesques. The minstrel comedians took their cues also from the journalists of the period whose "satirical and at times tasteless treatments of the Upper Ten" filled the pages of the *New York Herald, Putnam's Magazine* (Curtis's *Potiphar Papers,* 1853), *Harper's Weekly,* and other New York magazines.[76]

Many of the sketches found in minstrel companies' repertories reflect contradictory attitudes about the legal, social, and economic implications of conflicts based on race, gender, and class equity. The ambivalence is often manifested in foggy language and sometimes veiled by the physical business of the comic action, submerged under the proclamations of male superiority, or revealed in statements about the nobility and simple generosity of the lower classes. Few of the sketches ever deal directly with the pragmatic questions that concerned most members of the minstrel show's middle- and lower-class audiences. The significance of the sketches rests more in the oblique ways they used burlesque comedy to mediate the audience's attitudes toward wealth, power, marriage, and social values while at the same time avoiding provocative opinions likely to antagonize large segments of the audience.

The Ethiopian sketches generally followed the same indirect approach to satirizing democratic values and the concerns of different racial or ethnic groups found in other forms of minstrelsy. There were several distinct types of sketches, however, one of the most popular of which was a group of pieces known as parade or processional plays that performed an important educational function, because the sketch writers often incorporated new images of city life, introduced ideas about the increasingly diverse immigrant groups, offered views (usually negative) about scientific inventions and economic theories, and explored contrasting or competing social or political philosophies. The sketches show how blackface stereotypes worked in concert with other comic elements to create a complex vocabulary for comedians to satirize manners, customs, and gender roles within acceptable limits. The black (and blackface) male servant reinforced his low status and his mischievousness—a masking behavior consistent with the contempt servants usually hold for their employers. Blackface comedy provided those moments when, through the power of humor, audiences could entertain the possibility (but not the probability) that a true social hierarchy might be based on the quality of the individual.

5 Blackface Minstrelsy, Masculinity, and Social Rituals in Vocal and Choral Repertories

> Although first published at the North, you know nothing of the power and pathos given them here. The whites first learn them—the negroes catch the air and words from once hearing, after which wood and fields resound with their strains—the whites catch the expression of these sable minstrels—thus Negro Melodies have an effect here not dreamed of at the North.[1]

Minstrel show playbills confirm that songs were an integral part of the whole enterprise of blackface entertainment. Copies of the most popular song texts were easily obtained from vendors at the doors of minstrel halls, from mail-order houses, or at local stationery stores. For those with pianos and parlor organs, piano arrangements of low to moderate difficulty could be purchased from music dealers. Minstrel show music was also accessible in the many instrumental tutors published principally by Elias Howe and Oliver Ditson of Boston, adaptations and variations for piano, and ensemble numbers arranged for brass or quadrille bands. Those distribution systems were not the only ones, however, because the most popular numbers were transmitted orally along the major transportation systems of the South and West.[2]

Minstrel songs were popular because they ranged from vigorous, participatory dance numbers emphasizing what initially appear to be nonsense lyrics to slow narrative pieces dealing with lost loves and nostalgic feelings about childhood; from male display and boasting songs about women to tall tales about hunting, fishing, and horse racing; from descriptions of traditional agricultural activities to accounts of seasonal festivals associated with harvests; and from parodies of popular Italian opera choruses and hits of the period to topical songs lampooning politicians and contemporary entertainers.

Topical songs were among the most popular items in the minstrel repertory because they dealt with contemporary social and political problems. Representative examples include the several versions of "The Maine Boundary Question"

(1844), which describe ongoing disputes about Maine's borders with New Brunswick and fishing rights off the coast (*BDS1, NFM1, NFM2, NSO1*).[3] There are war songs held over from the War of 1812 and newer pieces about the Mexican-American War ("General Taylor" in *NSO1* and *WNB1*) that reflect the growing ethnocentrism in the United States as Mexicans became "yellow skins" and "greasers."[4]

Minstrel tunes became part of the common musical experience by serving as source tunes for the Hutchinson Family's "Get Off the Track" (1844), William Wells Brown's *Anti-Slavery Harp* (1848 and 1854), and countless now-forgotten parodies. Many songs were adapted by the performers themselves to localize the events described in a topical text. "Ole Bull and Dan Tucker" has a local version entitled "Philadelphia Ole Bull and Old Dan Tucker" (*WBA1*, 5), and Charley White's "Westchester Nigga Song" (*CNS1, NSO1, WBA1*), found in New York–based songsters, describes the commute on the then new railroad line from lower Westchester Country to Manhattan.

Some songs contain only one or two nonsense verses that refer to a particular event, political character, or contemporary issue, such as new clothing styles. The combination of bitter satire with what appears to be nonsense is characteristic of the evolving nature of American humor in the 1840s and 1850s, as illustrated by the following verses from Dan Emmett's "Jordan Is a Hard Road to Travel" (1853).

Verse 4
If I was de legislator ob dese United States,
I'd settle de fish question accordin,
I'd give de British all de bones and de Yankees all de meat,
And stretch de boundary line to de oder side of Jordan.

Verse 5
Der's been excitin times for de last month or two,
About de great Presidential election,
Frank Pierce got elected and sent a hasty plate of soup,
To his opponent on de oder side of Jordan.[5]

Just as the Ethiopian sketches, burlesque sermons, and opera parodies seem to have been limited to a number of distinct types focused on relatively few themes, so also were the song types used in the antebellum minstrel show. Most of the shows contained at least one example of following types.[6]

1. Solo Male Display/Boasting/Roarer Type or "Character" Songs:
    "Jim Brown" (1835): male display with topical verses
    "Ginger Blue" (184?): male display
    "Jim Along Josey" (1840): male display with topical verses
    "Walk Along John" (1843): unconventional "roarer" type of black male

"Old Dan Tucker" (1843): carouser/party male type

"Dandy Jim of Caroline" (1844): male display in monogamous family

"Ole Bull and Dan Tucker" (1844): male rivalry over skill

"Picayune Butler" or "Ahoo! Ahoo!" (1848): male display (Tucker type)

2. Narrative Songs (Table Turners, Tricksters, and Others Exploiting Class or Status Differences)

    a. Master-Slave Relationships

        "Blue Tail Fly" (1846): role reversal

        "Come Back Steben" (1848): deceptive slave who escapes punishment for disruptive behaviors

    b. Animal Allegories (Hunt Songs/Animal Adversaries)

        "Old Tare River" (1840): black man as clever hunter

        "Corn Field Green" (1844): probable parody and animal allegory; hungry "coon" eats green corn and dies

        "Uncle Gabriel" no. 1 (1848): black male hunter

    c. Historical or Mock Historical Events

        "Uncle Gabriel" no. 2 (1848): garbled slave insurrection story

3. Mock Courtship Songs (Male-Female Relationships with Male Narrator)

    "Whar Did You Come From" (1840)

    "Lucy Long" (1843): male versus female rivalry

    "Stop Dat Knocking" (1843)

    "Goin Ober de Mountain" (1843)

    "Black Eye'd Susianna" (1846)

4. Social Scenes (Dances, Sporting Events, Parties, Nonwork/Leisure Time or Escapist Activities)

    "Clare de Kitchen" (1832)

    "Sich a Gettin Up Stairs" (ca. 1834)

    "Jenny Get Your Hoe Cake Done" (1840)

    "Walk Jaw Bone" (1840)

    "De Boatman's Dance" (1843)

    "Oh Lud Gals Gib Me [Us] Chaw Tobacco [Tebackur]" (1843)

    "Bowery Gals and Buffalo Gals Variants" (1844)

    "Sing, Sing, Darkies Sing" (1846)

    "Walk in de Parlor," or "History ob de World" (1847)

    "Colored Fancy Ball" (1848)

    "Camptown Races" (1850)

    "Dinah's Wedding Day" (1852)

5. Work or Mock Work Songs (Boating, Corn Shucking, Fishing, Hunting)

    "Old Tare River" (1840)

    "Jonny Boker," or "De Broken Yoke in de Coaling Ground" (1840)

    "'Twill Nebber Do To Gib It Up So" (1843)

"Old Pee Dee" (1844)

"The Jolly Raftsman" (1844)

6. Sentimental Songs (Emphasizing Expressiveness over Humor or Ironic and Humorous Treatment of Sad Subject)

a. Forced Separation (Slavery or Death)

"Cynthia Sue" (1844): male lover sold into slavery

"Lucy Neal" (1844): love partner sold

"Rosa Lee," or "Don't Be Foolish Joe" (1847): death of female lover

"Mary Blane" no. 1 (1847): spouse kidnapped

"Virginia Rosebud" (1849): child kidnapped for slavery

"Darling Nelly Gray" (1856): love partner sold into slavery

b. Courtship Difficulties (Travel, Distance, Restrictions on Movement or Leisure Time, Desire for Better Life)

"Dearest Mae" (1847): distance between plantations or work sites

c. Nostalgia (Lost Homes, Childhood/Innocence, Old Age)

"Carry Me Back to Old Virginny" (1847)

"Uncle Ned" (1848)

d. Local or Regional Pride (Real and Imagined Locales and Mythologized Interpretations of the South as a Region)

"Old Virginny State" (ca. 1845): parody of "The Old Granite State"[7]

Male display and boasting songs presented the costumed performer to the audience, identified the subject (usually through costume and physical action) in the direct style required to capture the audience's attention immediately, and, since the emphasis in minstrelsy was often on the soloist, permitted the clearest definition of the persona's stage attributes. The song paraded the minstrelized version of the male body in many of its characteristic aspects and demonstrated which masculine qualities were deemed most suitable for treatment in stage comedy.

Male "character" songs usually open with declarations of the individual's identity and descriptions of the contents of his "text." These stage conventions antedate minstrelsy and are related directly to the frontier adventurers, sailors, or other exotics presented in "characteristic" solo acts by specialty performers. One representative example from preminstrelsy is Thomas Dartmouth Rice's "Ginger Blue," which is seldom addressed in any discussions of minstrelsy but which showed up regularly on playbills from 1844 to 1851.[8] The "Ginger Blue" character first appeared in Rice's Ethiopian opera, *Bone Squash Diavolo,* and returned in a number of other Rice vehicles through the early 1850s. The song may have changed when it entered the minstrel show genre and may have been shortened somewhat, since it then became part of a variety show rather than an extended solo act. How the performance worked is uncertain, but the following example illustrates the combination of sung and spoken sections characteristic of the "Ginger Blue" act, as well as the mixture of eye dialect and Black English elements typical of the early minstrel shows.

"Ginger Blue" (Ethiopian Serenaders's Version): Song, Narrative, and Chorus

Verse 1
My name is ginger blue and wat I tell yous mity true,
I come from the Tenessee mountains,
My paragraf is short and my words they are as true,
As the waters what flows from the fountains,
The first thing that I sed, when I could raise dis nigger head,
To the darkies all on the plantation,
[*Chorus/Refrain*] Was walk chalk ginger blue get over double trouble Old Virginia neber tire.[9]

Verse 2
One night Peter Williams was going to have a dance,
For the niggers are round that quarter,
Sez he ginger blue I want you to come,
And then you shall have my daughter.
He no sooner sed the word and I was up like a bird,
Then my feelings began to Fangolire.[10]

Spoken: Yes, yes I did feel rather preserpertatious about dat time dats a fac but sez I look here Pete how do you expect I can hab dat Daughter ob yours when Clem Greene is a troing [throwing?] his affections at her and a nother thing he is such a consequencial nigger dat he caries so much musk and colone water about him dat you can smell him a half a mile off any time but how someever I went into the Ball room and come tree or four quartilion steps and I tell you what it is I made old Clem Greene [*Chorus/Refrain*] Walk chalk ginger blue get over double trouble Old Virginia neber tire.

Verse 3
When the dance it was all over we began to lumber home,
And between you and me whe [*sic*] had a splutter,
Whe looked for all the world just like a flock of ducks,
A squambling and paddling in the gutter,
I was going cross old master farm Roseciana under my arm,
There was something that struck my obsication.

Spoken: Yes dar was de President and Secretari ob de temtation 'ciety and its no use of talking da was both so drunk dat you could not tell dar heds from a bag of wool no how you could fix it, but if dem old niggers had to fool dar time wid me I bet you I'd made them [*Chorus/Refrain*] Walk chalk ginger blue get over double trouble Old Virginia neber tire.

Verse 4
Then I got on bord a boat and went to New Orleans,
And landed rite on the lebe [levee],

There was a big nigger there sez he I will gib you beans,
But I gess he found that I was rather heby,
I up with my fist and struck him on the head,
Then the folks all began to diskiver.

Spoken: Well its no use ob talking bout dat fight for when I struck dat nigger in de countenance dar was a mity large crowd began together round dar bout dat time and dar was one wite gemmen stept up to me sez he look here nigger you have hut dat man might bad de lord nows you habe vell sez I told him if he dident lebe be I would broke his jaw and so I did I gib him a little what I call [*Chorus/Refrain*] Walk chalk ginger blue get over double trouble old Virginia neber tire.

Verse 5
Then I thought I would leave New Orleans and go to New York,
For there was such a muss about that quarter,
So I worked my passage on board of a ship,
And come clear over by the water,
And when I got there I landed on the warf,
I tried to cut a mighty figure.

Spoken: Dats a fac when I landed at the foot ob Dover Street where the little niggers was inking lasses I did try to cut a mity swell before the white folks but it was no go the old foot was too big too much like a jay bird the bigest toe struck clar out behind but while I was promonading round ar was some sailors come up from the quarintine ground and sed dar was a ship just rived from New Orleans and had De John De arms [gendarmes?] on board not dad [that] I felt any ways skerd but I had a little business up town so I thort it was time to begin [*Chorus/Refrain*] Walk chalk ginger blue get over double trouble old Virginia neber tire.[11]

The phrases "walk chalk ginger blue," "get over double trouble," and "Old Virginia neber tire" or their respective fragments appear in other period songs. Each of the phrases suggests a particular dance or dance step the singer performed before resuming the verse. The phrases "cut a figure," "get in a muss," "feel rather preserpertatious," "but sez I," and "he is such a consequencial nigger" also appear in other songs, sermons, and stump speeches. They refer to street behaviors and aggressive personal expressions captured also in the expression "to lumber home," which evokes a particular gait and recalls the opening phrase of "Buffalo Gals": "As I was lumbering down the street."

The Ginger Blue character in this song is a roarer type blacked up for a typical male display or presentational song. The song's text manifests the same strong interest in male sexual desire that characterizes songs about the minstrel dandy. The reference to the character's feet ("the old foot was too big too much . . . the bigest toe struck clar out behind") is common in minstrelsy and identifies the speaker as an aggressive street persona, that is, one who uses his foot or feet to block access to doorways or routine passage. But this Ginger is an unsuccessful character because he cannot cut a figure with the street people he meets in one of the city's worst districts. He remains an outsider, a symbolic representation of the new group of single males in antebellum American cities, and the account of his activities is characteristic of the presentational songs associated with men's sexual pursuit of women in a changing urban environment of unmarried young people.

The music of "Ginger Blue" is also characteristic of early minstrelsy in that the four musical phrases are similar melodically (a formulaic use of interlocking thirds) and harmonically in spite of the break created by a modulation to the dominant at measure 12, where the chorus begins (see music example 7). The first repetition of the melody contains a D against a C^7 harmony (m. 11), probably a misprint, since every other statement shows an $E\flat$ at this point. The harmonies in the published example suggest an overarrangement of the piano accompaniment. The song is printed in the key of $B\flat$, and the progression is $E\flat–F^7–Cm–Edim^7–F–B\flat$ (IV–V^7/ii–ii–vii^7/V/–V–I), followed by the passing diminished sevenths. There is scarcely any other song in the whole repertory showing secondary sevenths and dominants or diminished seventh chords; most minstrel songs use the typical primary triads of antebellum popular music. The melody and the accompaniment do not seem to fit together stylistically, especially since the following eight-measure phrase labeled "reel" is harmonized entirely with tonic and dominant seventh chords.

The repeated sixteenth notes set to the verse are typical of a "talk" or patter song, and the music actually works well at a moderate to fast tempo. In a live performance, however, the tempo of the whole piece would have to be set carefully to ensure that the sung and spoken parts fit with the dance section. The dance and the repetition of the eight-bar reel would have allowed the players to demonstrate the dance steps, change positions, and present their characters if they chose to perform the song as an ensemble number.

These promenade songs emphasize how important the presentation of the male body and masculine interests had become in popular song. The "roarer" type symbolized the masculine urge for gratification but sheltered the moral doubts associated with the exercise of such behaviors by exaggerating the qualities performers displayed in the specialty songs. Such presentations of self represented one extreme of a range of male social behaviors that were significant features of courtship rituals and sexual access strategies in the new urban environment. As important as the display of male prerogatives was to women, however, it was also significant that the presentation of self to other men now allowed on the stage included those prestige-seeking behaviors valued by members of the same sex.

Urban centers must have been seen as arenas for male self-promotion and display, for there are virtually no minstrel songs dealing seriously (or comically, for that matter) with men (black or white) who go about the business of life with gentlemanly refinement or common decency. Many young male characters in minstrelsy are dandies and street-wise promenaders, objects of ridicule because of their own exaggerated behaviors. Nonetheless, blackface songs do not always or primarily project white male fantasies onto a black man's body or revel in displays of great sexual prowess or desire.[12] Such fantasies could be celebrated vicariously through the conquests and unbridled behaviors of the roarer characters in the Mike Fink and Davy Crockett tradition, whose tales provided an entertaining and gratifying context for those males who, instead of participating in the sexual liberties available in the New York demimonde, preferred to observe the unrepressed social displays presented on the minstrel stage.

Early minstrel songs were presented on the stage during the same period that new social structures were being identified in the contemporary urban environment and class distinctiveness was being designated as much by fashion as by the conspicuous consumption of personal wealth. New Yorkers in particular did not define their neighborhoods distinctively along economic lines; rich and poor might well live within the same wards or districts. But men out on promenade did define themselves by their costumes and their consciousness of the types of male behavior appropriate for public display.

These male display songs called attention to the physical features of their characters and defined public presentations of masculinity in aggressive terms because conventional attitudes held that a "real man" could not (or at least should not) take urban culture passively. Maleness itself became a subject for blackface parody as minstrel comedians recognized the potential hypocrisy in all social behaviors and sought to exploit them for humorous ends. This potential hypocrisy seems to have been seen as especially significant when the subjects made claims or assumed poses contrary to their normal stations in life.

One of the most representative and common subjects of the male display songs was the so-called northern dandy, a persona who came in whiteface and blackface versions and who became an important character in minstrel parodies during the 1840s. The dandy was a composite stereotype drawn from the uncivilized and marginalized "characters" of the theatrical world itself, the "sporting men" whose leisure time was spent in the pursuit of pleasure and all manner of legitimate and illegitimate sports, the nonurbanized newcomers to the eastern manufacturing centers, unconventional frontier types noted primarily for their mock heroic exploits or general belligerence, the immigrant populations (principally Irish "outsiders") who had not been acculturated to American life, and the upper-class male aristocratic population whose attire suggested a high degree of affectation.

Songs about dandies focus on humorous portrayals of *all* young males. Older men, however, are never portrayed as "on the make" and are usually presented as desexualized characters regardless of their race. The most common type of dandy caricature is based on humorous and pretentious examples of nineteenth-century courting behavior ascribed to single white men whose social parading was one method of seeking eligible female partners outside the typical environments of church, fraternal organizations or social clubs, theaters, and political parties. "Dandies," "fancy men for the upper ten-thousand," and "fancy men for the lower million" were common expressions in New York City, where "sporting male sexual activity consistently challenged and often confused emerging divisions based upon social class, work, and education."[13]

The urban dandy stereotype satirizes male display behaviors in the same way that the blackface rhetoric treated the militia muster and the social activities of other fraternal organizations. The dandies shown in figure 3 are displaying themselves to the city's streetwalkers, whose increasing presence after the 1840s shows the growing commercialization of sex at least in New York City.[14] Gilfoyle's description of the type is especially illustrative of the style of male display particularly significant at the time that minstrelsy's satires of urban dandies were most popular.

> The quintessential dandies were fastidious in dress and detached in manner. They were known for their flashy outfits, finger rings, watch chains, leather boots, and "fashionable behavior." They aspired to be part of the "upper crust" and "the bon ton." They displayed the "polished manners" and "the ways of a gentleman." At the same time, they were described as "knaves" or "rascals." Critics castigated them as part of the "Puppy order" and "conceited fops." Indeed, the dandies moved between the "respectable" world of elite society and the criminal underworld of Gotham. Indulging in wine, women, and pleasure, "the fast boy of Young America" was, according to Charles Astor Bristed, "dressy, vulgar and good natured."[15]

The dandy stereotypes are, as Jane Tompkins has argued about female stereotypes in nineteenth-century American sentimental novels, "the instantly recognizable representatives of overlapping racial, sexual, national, ethnic, economic, social, political, and religious categories; they convey enormous amounts of cultural information in an extremely condensed form."[16] The idea that assuming the superficial characteristics of sartorial style and etiquette will somehow bring gentility is one of the great tropes of American popular culture. That is the point of the following preminstrel song (1841) performed by Dick Pell (Richard Pelham of the original Virginia Minstrels).

Some have de mockazins and some haves none,
But he dat habs a pair of boots he tinks himself a man.
Wid his big Brass button and his long tail Blue,
Dem what we call de dandies of de carolina crew.[17]

The various (and different) dandy caricatures should not be confused. The "Dandy Broadway Swell" and "Zip Coon" (he claims to be from "Tuckyhoe" or some

Example 7. "Ginger Blue" (London: T. E. Purday, n.d. [1840s]). Used by permission of the Brown University Library.

raise dis nigger head. To the darkies all on the plan...ta...tion, Was

walk chalk ginger blue get o..ver double trouble old Vir...gi..nia ne..ber tire.

REEL.

2

One night Peter Williams was going to have a dance
For the niggers all round that quarter
Sez he ginger blue I want you to come
And then you shall have my daughter
He no sooner sed the word and I was up like a bird
Then my feelings began to Fangolire.

(SPOKEN) Yes yes I did feel rather preserpertatious about dat time dats a fac but sez
I look here Pete how do you expect I can hab dat Daughter ob yours when Clem Greene
is a troing his affections at her and a nother thing he is such a consequencial nigger
dat he caries so much musk and colone water about him dat you can smell him a half
a mile off any time but how someever I went into the Ball room and come tree or four
quartilion steps and I tell you what it is I made old Clem Greene (CHORUS) Walk chalk
ginger blue get over double trouble old Virginia neber tire.

Example 7. (cont.)

Figure 3. Dandy Jim illustrations from selected antebellum sheet music covers. Courtesy, American Antiquarian Society.

Figure 3. (cont.)

Figure 3. (cont.)

other non–New York locale) are not the same type, and both differ from "Dandy Jim of Caroline." But they all reflect the parvenu or nouveau riche convention that was a typical and efficient method for parodying class distinction. The minstrel performers' choices of material were probably not governed primarily by a *need* to display racist attitudes even though minstrelsy was based on them. Neither racial aversion nor desire is by itself a concept sufficient to explain the relationships shared by performers playing for an American audience of whites and blacks, both of whom found something funny in the minstrel caricatures.[18] The satirized dandy figure is a pretender, a charlatan, a confidence man who is insincere and ignorant of the values associated with social station or power. The blackface dandy embodies the same feelings of disdain coupled with class envy captured in the epithets heard outside the Astor Place Opera House the night when firebrand orators urged the crowd to "Burn the damned den of the aristocracy!" and complained, "You can't go in there without . . . kid gloves and a white vest, damn 'em."[19]

Sheet music illustrations often have no relationship to the songs' actual texts, and the interpretations of any text must never be restricted to a strictly literal reading. Michael Pickering and Tony Green captured my caveat well when they argued: "We should not assume that we can simply read off song content as an inscription of the social values, attitudes, norms and beliefs of particular groups. Indeed, song content may in part or in whole be discordant with the moral community, but of value precisely because it offers a self-legitimating counterpart to that community."[20]

The dandy songs, then, refer not always and everywhere to African American males but to the broader context of male presentation and display that was part of the new urban communities of the 1840s and 1850s. The "Dandy Jim" stereotype must be interpreted within the broader contexts of American male culture. That culture and those contexts do not have simple conceptual boundaries. There are any number of possible meanings, although the number of probable meanings for any of the "Dandy Jim" examples may be relatively small. Not only it is impossible to know which version most audiences knew, but it is also imperative to allow that the song's meanings depend on the contexts in which it was heard as well as those in which it is interpreted today. In the discussions that follow, several probable contexts are suggested, and most of them complicate the sometimes superficial implications of the literal text.

The dandy stereotype was envied for his assumed sexual prowess, but the characters presented on the stage represented those males who used clothing in the same way that confidence men used faulty logic to dupe potential customers. Both types of upper-class characters were apt subjects for satire, as were their working-class counterparts, including the "Bowery B'hoys," who "equated sexual promiscuity and erotic indulgence with individual autonomy and personal freedom."[21] The blackface comedians realized that men who aspired to the status of the dandy could appear ludicrous in their attempts to mimic the dress and behaviors of a basically amoral social type.

"Dandy Jim of Caroline" is a quintessential portrait of the dandy type in minstrelsy. The song is much more representative of minstrelsy's treatment of the dandy character than is "Old Zip Coon," which appears only once as a vocal number in over 100 different playbills.[22] "Dandy Jim" has been criticized often as a stereotypically racist song that demeans black males because it reflects poorly on all those industrious African American men who, condemned by racism to work in menial jobs, attempted to support their families in northern urban centers. But the behaviors depicted in the various song texts are seldom related to any forms of physical or mental labor and focus instead on courtship, sexual aggressiveness, narcissistic self-indulgence, and male boasting, traits associated with the urban dandies of both races. "Dandy Jim" is the poster boy, the male model, for men who think their personal qualities rank them above the common and whose exploits are the envy of the less aggressive and attractive. "Dandy Jim" also differs from his "Jim Crow" counterpart in what Cockrell has defined as an "aesthetic of opposition"; that is, both types embody the contrast between comedic and dramatic characters representing the conflicts between urban and rural, elite and common, white and black in American folk theatricals and on the legitimate stage.[23]

Most of the sheet music editions of "Dandy Jim" open with the same or similar first verse and define the persona the performer presents.[24] Those presentations depended on the skills of the soloist and his interactions with other members of the companies associated with the "Dandy Jim" character, namely, the Virginia Serenaders, Virginia Minstrels, Ethiopian Serenaders, or similar ensembles. Cool White, S. [Sam?] Johnson, J. Richard Myers, Dan Emmett, Barney Williams, and Samuel Sanford specialized in "dandy" characters, and each brought something different to the song he performed. Cool White offered the song with a chorus and company band, and Barney Williams encountered some difficulties playing this blackface role convincingly because of his Irish brogue. Regardless of the specific qualities of each character, the performer sang the opening verse to attract audience interest, display the costume prominently, and define himself as the eponymous dandy. In the quotations that follow, Jim is identified by his allegedly southern origins or connections with a southern "type," his "fine" qualities as compared with South Carolina's major export (yellow pine), his status ("hansome niggas are boun to shine"), or his regional reputation as a ladies' man; subsequent verses identify him by those physical characteristics that the character thought might be considered attractive to women.

"Dandy Jim from Carolina" No. 3 (New York: Firth, Hall, and Pond, 1844)

Verse 1
Oh white folks jis as sure as fate,
Dat Carolina is de nullify state,
It hab de finest nigger and de best yellow pine,
An a tall sample is dandy Jim ob Caroline.

"Dandy Jim of Caroline" No. 4 (London: D'Almaine, 1844)

Verse 1
I've often heard it sed ob late,
Dat sout Carolina am de state;
Whar hansome niggs are boun to shine,
I'm Dandy Jim of Caroline.

"Dandy Jim from Caroline" No. 5 (Philadelphia: A Fiot, 1844)

Verse 1
I've often heard it said ob late,
Dat souf Carolina was de state,
Whar a handsome nigga's bound to shine,
Like Dandy Jim from Caroline.

"Dandy Jim of Caroline" No. 7 (Philadelphia: George Willing, 1844)

Verse 1
I've often heard it said ob late,
Dat Souf Ca'lina was de state,
Whar handsome nigga's bound to shine,
Like Dandy Jim of Caroline

"Dandy Jim of Caroline" No. 8 (Boston: Charles H. Keith, 1844); reprinted in EGB2 (7).

Verse 1
Dar's dandy niggers in each place,
Wid beef stake lips dat wink wid grace,
But none among de galls can shine,
Like dandy Jim ob Caroline.

"Dandy Jim from Carolina" No. 10 (Baltimore: F. D. Benteen, 1844)

Verse 1
I've often heard it said of late,
Dat Souf Carolina was de state,
Whar handsome Niggars bound to shine,
Like "Dandy Jim from Caroline."

The capitalization and punctuation differ in most of the versions, syllable elisions and spellings are inconsistent, and the various texts suggest that the soloists had considerable freedom to improvise during their performances. The different versions share a common chorus, although the words and spellings also change slightly ("jus" for "just," "I'm" for "I'se," "I'se" for "I was," "niggas" for "niggars" or "niggers") from one edition to another. The chorus confirms and reinforces the physical attributes of the character; he and his master are the sole judges in the symbolic beauty contest that Dandy Jim wins. The more or less standard chorus (the section is not always marked "chorus" in the examples) is typically repeated after each verse in every version.

"Dandy Jim of Caroline" No. 10

Chorus
For my ole massa tole me so,
I was de best lookin Niggar in de County O,
I look in de glass an I found it so,
Jus what massa told me O.

In some of the versions (nos. 8 and 11), "Dandy Jim" defines his character as a sociable male familiar with women and comfortable in their presence. These texts emphasize the broader range of Jim's potential preaudit with a larger group of potential women, especially the version associated with the performances by one of minstrelsy's most successful blackface performers, Cool White (John Hodges).

"Dandy Jim ob Caroline" No. 8

Verse 2
I went one ebenin to de ball,
Wid lips combed out an wool quite tall,
De ladies eyes like snowballs shine,
On dandy Jim ob Caroline.

Verse 3
Dey squatsied to me an advance,
To foot it wid me in de dance,
Yet none could toe but Ginger Dine,
Wid dandy Jim ob Caroline.

Verse 4
An when I cut de pigeon wing,
I fan de ceilin wid my fling,
De ladies all fell in a swine [swoon],
For dandy Jim ob Caroline.

Verse 6
An when I started to go home,
De ladies sighed and tried to come,
But none could go but Molasses Dine,
Wid dandy Jim ob Caroline.

Verse 7
Den from my head each gal did pull,
A lock of my fine silken wool,
Dey plat [plaited?] it into letters fine,
Ob dandy Jim of Caroline.

Although "Dandy Jim" seems to define himself as a successful playboy in the Keith edition, most of the other texts (nos. 3, 5, 6, 7, and 10) describe him as pursuing only one woman (Dinah) in rather routine ways.

"Dandy Jim from Caroline" No. 5

Verse 2
I drest myself from top to toe,
And down to Dinah I did go,
Wid pantaloons strapped down behind,
Like Dandy Jim from Caroline.

Verse 3
De bull dog cleared me out de yard,
I tought I'd better leave my card,
I tied it fast to a piece ob twine,
Signed "Dandy Jim from Caroline."

Verse 4
She got my card an wrote me a letter,
An ebery word she spelt the better,
For ebery word an ebery line,
Was Dandy Jim from Caroline.

The "Dandy Jim" persona in versions no. 7 and 10 is nearly identical with the character in most of the other examples, that is, he is not an unsophisticated plantation hand imitating the behaviors of "city folk." Regardless of his origins in "souf Carolina," he is a courter who narrates the history of his courtship (down to the custom of leaving a calling card and writing to his sweetheart) and declares the legitimacy of his current relationship with Dinah. Respectability and legitimacy are prominent in nearly all the texts, as Jim and Dine take pains to ensure the salvation of their offspring by baptizing each and every one.[25] For all his arrogance, the song-and-stage version of "Dandy Jim" seems to accept the conventional behaviors associated with respectability. As the following verses from "Dandy Jim" no. 7 show, Dandy Jim is actually quite monogamous and adheres to the generally accepted courtship and marriage practices of the period.

"Dandy Jim of Caroline" No. 7

Verse 5
Oh, beauty is but skin deep,
But wid Miss Dinah none compete,
She changed her name from lubly Dine,
To Mrs. Dandy Jim of Caroline.

Verse 6
An ebery little nig she had,
Was de berry image of de dad,
Dar heels stick out three feet behind,
Like Dandy Jim of Caroline.

Verse 7
I took dem all to church one day,
And hab dem christen'd widout delay,
De preacher christen'd eight or nine,
Young Dandy Jims of Caroline

The presentation of a character possessing great sexual prowess (many children connoted that) was stronger in some versions of the song than others. The song's female character, however, "swines" for her lovely beau and as a compliant companion accepts his expressions of affection. The dandy presents himself as the center of women's attention, the focal point of her physical desires. This is most apparent in one of the variants performed by Cool White, where the "My old massa told me so" chorus is replaced with the following lines:

"Dandy Jim ob Caroline" (NSO1, 210–11)

All color'd virgins tell me, oh!
I'se the best lookin' nigger in the country, oh,
I looked in the glass an' found it so,
Just as the virgins tell me, oh!

The melody for most versions of "Dandy Jim" is a two-strain, sixteen-bar (AB) structure and is usually a pentatonic (D–F♯–G–A–B or F–G–A–C–D) or hexatonic design (D–E–F♯–G–A–B) or (F–G–A–B♭–C–D). The examples (nos. 1–6) that focus on C and F as the principal notes were published in the key of F major, use F as the final for the melodic cadence, and avoid the seventh scale degree (E). The versions that focus prominently on D and A (nos. 7–11)) have a D-major key signature and D for the melodic cadence and use the seventh scale degree (C-sharp) for little more than a passing tone. All versions use the signature motive (5–8–5–6–5–7–5 in D or 5–8–5–6–5–3–5 in F), and that melodic idea is easily identified as the primary characteristic of the source tune. The motive suggests that the melody must have been conceived with the open strings of the banjo in mind. It seems likely also that an extensive study of the stemma of "Dandy Jim" would reveal that the pentatonic structure was the formula from which every adaptation arose.[26]

The banjo version of the tune is notated in D major even though the pitches of the melody lie entirely in G major (see music example 8a). That is because the D-major signature puts the tune on the banjo's open strings in the G-tuning (d-G-D-F#-A) recommended in *BBI*.[27] The banjo player's left hand remains entirely in the first position, and the first and second fingers need only to stop the D and A strings to create pitches E and B for the hexatonic versions of the "Dandy Jim" verse and chorus.

Because the minstrel-period banjo practice emphasized the single-tone melodic style of playing described by Winans and Ayers, the banjo could have generally doubled the voice but with idiomatic patterns usually designed to keep the two somewhat separate.[28] An instrumental break would certainly maintain that distinction. The doubling of the vocal line and repetition of foreground (melodic) and background (accompaniment) motives, however, connected the melody to folk traditions and possibly to an African American performance practice. As Peter Van der Merwe has argued, "In European folk music, as in African music, the repeated cycle . . . might be closed, that is, come to an end in the familiar way, or open (or, as it is sometimes put, circular), where instead of coming to a close, the tune simply repeated itself indefinitely. This scheme was common in British popular music during the early eighteenth century."[29]

In "Dandy Jim" no. 3, the arrangement for piano and voice features a Pr–A–B–Po design (4–8–8–8), with the postlude marked *vivace* doubling as an interlude and, after the last chorus, as a conclusion.[30] Example 8b features an opening phrase similar to the D-major examples cited previously, but the harmonies are much more elaborate because of the insertion of a passing secondary dominant (V⁷/V, or G⁷/C) in mm. 14 and 16.

Example 8a. "Dandy Jim," from *Briggs' Banjo Instructor*. Used by permission of Tuckahoe Music.

Example 8b. "Dandy Jim from Carolina" (no. 3) (New York: Firth and Hall, 1844). The author gratefully acknowledges the permission to reproduce minstrel songs from the Sheet Music Collection of the Free Library of Philadelphia.

Example 8b. (cont.)

The four-part arrangement in *EGB* follows the F-major versions of "Dandy Jim," with the notable difference that the block harmonies regularize the rhythm even more (see music example 8c). The text differs from the other F-major versions because it contains verses from the Keith edition (no. 8), notably the one referring to the "pigeon wing." The melody of the first phrase, the A portion of the song, is the same as found in most of the versions regardless of the keys in which they were set. This setting was also conceived as a four-part TTBB arrangement because each part is identified by the name "tenor" or "base." The harmonization is not especially interesting or clever because the first phrase of the chorus is in unison and is not repeated. The line "me so, I's de best lookin nigga in de" is in octaves, and the arrangement reveals open fifths, doubled and tripled roots, and entire phrases set primarily in thirds over a doubled root in the bass. Both of the song's phrases end with octaves rather than complete triads. These harmonies are similar to those used by the Hutchinsons and seem well within the typical style patterns of the period. Moreover, just because the arrangement is found in the *Ethiopian Glee Book* does not mean that this particular style of harmony was widespread in blackface minstrelsy. All the published arrangements of "Dandy Jim" neutralize many of the song's original characteristics by eliminating most of the vocal inflections or gestures that would probably have been employed in a live performance.

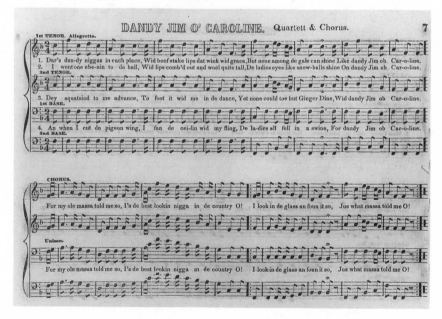

Example 8c. "Dandy Jim o' Caroline" (no. 11), from *EGB2* (7). Used by permission of the Brown University Library.

Although the melody of the verse seems relatively stable from edition to edition, the refrains are not so regular because portions of the tune in the chorus are more likely to follow the outlines of the chords chosen by the arranger. The verses of the Willig arrangement (Pr–A–B–Po [8–8–8–4]) follow the pentatonic version (D–F♯–G–A–B) of the melody closely (see music example 8d). The first four bars of the solo phrase (mm. 9–14) in example 8d are supported by the tonic triad, with the subdominant (G major) and dominant (A major) leading the phrase (mm. 15–16) back to the tonic. The chorus, although not marked as such in this edition, begins with "For my ole massa." The melody is controlled by the underlying harmonies as the accompaniment reiterates the I–IV–I–V triads in measures 17–20. The last four utilize the I–IV–V⁷–I chords that lock this melody into the major key harmonizations typical of most 1840s popular music. The Willig version outlines the subdominant triad in measures 18 and 22 (on the words "tole me so" and "found it so"), a parallelism that distinguishes this version from the others, each of which ends with a slightly different melodic pattern. The primarily modal features of the melody are lost.

The Keith edition differs from the other versions because of the second inversion G-major triads that accompany the repeated Bs in the first phrase (see music example 8e). The chorus/refrain is labeled clearly to distinguish it from the verse, thereby clarifying the song's organization. Finally, the refrain differs melodically from all the other D-major versions, especially in the "told me so" and "foun twas so" phrases. The underlying melodic structure is elaborated slightly, perhaps for a more agile voice, but the last melodic descent avoids the E and sticks to the same pentatonic formula (8–5–6–5–3–1–1) that concludes the refrain.

Finally, the instrumental interlude between the verses, which serves as a postlude after the last repetition of the chorus, is of some interest because it is a variant of the melody that could have been played on a banjo or fiddle. The phrase was probably used to accompany a stage dance if any of the piano arrangements were actually linked to Cool White's act, something suggested in at least one version of the text.

"Dandy Jim of Caroline" No. 9 (Boston: Charles H. Keith, 1844)

Verse 5
De fiddler he so much admired
Life "Ole Bull" he got ginspired,
An ebry note he sawed so fine,
Said, "Dandy Jim ob Caroline."

The structure of the Benteen piano-vocal version shows a four-measure prelude, two different eight-measure phrases, and a four-measure postlude (Pr–A–B–Po) (see music example 8f). The chorus contains the highest degree of variation of all

Example 8d. "Dandy Jim of Caroline" (no. 7) (Philadelphia: George Willig, 1844). The author gratefully acknowledges the permission to reproduce minstrel songs from the Sheet Music Collection of the Free Library of Philadelphia.

tole me so, I'm de best looking nigga in de county oh, I look in de glass an I found it so,

ral

Just as mas—sa tell me oh.

tempo.

2

I drest myself from top to toe,
And down to Dinah I did go,
Wid pantaloons strapped down behind,
Like Dandy Jim of Caroline.

       For my ole massa &c.

3

De bull dog cleared me out ob de yard,
I tought I'd better leabe my card,
I tied it fast to a piece ob twine,
Signed "Dandy Jim of Caroline."

       For my ole massa &c.

4

She got my card an wrote me a letter,
An ebery word she spelt de better,
For ebery word an ebery line,
Was Dandy Jim of Caroline.

       For my ole massa &c.

5

Oh, beauty is but skin deep
But wid Miss Dinah none compete
She changed her name from lubly Dine,
To Mrs. Dandy Jim of Caroline.

       For my ole massa &c.

6

An ebery little nig she had,
Was de berry image ob de dad,
Dar heels stick out three feet behind,
Like Dandy Jim of Caroline.

       For my ole massa &c.

7

I took dem all to church one day,
An hab dem christen'd widout delay,
De preacher christen'd eight or nine,
Young Dandy Jims of Caroline.

       For my ole massa &c.

8

An when de preacher took his text,
He seemed to be berry much perplexed,
For nothing cum across his mind,
But Dandy Jims of Caroline.

       For my ole massa &c.

Dandy Jim of Caroline. 2.

Example 8d. (cont.)

Example 8e. "Dandy Jim ob Caroline" (no. 8) (Boston: Charles H. Keith, 1844). Used by permission of the Brown University Library.

lyrics under music: told me so, I's de best lookin nigga in de country, O! I look in de glass an foun twas so, Just what mas-sa told me, O! 8va----

2.
I went one ebenin to de ball,
Wid lips combed out an wool quite tall,
De ladies eyes like snowballs shine
On dandy Jim ob Caroline,
        For my ole massa, &c.
3.
Dey squatsied to me än advance,
To foot it wid me in de dance,
Yet none could toe but Ginger Dine,
Wid dandy Jim ob Caroline,
        For my ole massa, &c.
4.
An when I cut de pigeon wing,
I fan de ceilin wid my fling,
De ladies all fell in a swine,
For dandy Jim ob Caroline,
        For my ole massa, &c.
5.
De fiddler he so much admired,
Like 'Ole Bull' he got ginspired,
An ebry note he sawed so fine,
Said 'Dandy Jim ob Caroline,'
        For my ole massa, &c.

6.
An when I started to go home,
De ladies sighed an tried to come,
But none could go but Molasses Dine,
Wid dandy Jim ob Caroline,
        For my ole massa, &c.
7.
Den from my head each gal did pull,
A lock ob my fine silken wool,
Dey plat it into letters fine,
Ob dandy Jim ob Caroline,
        For my ole massa, &c.
8.
Next to a concert I did go,
An soon as I my figger show,
An ebery singer change each line,
To dandy Jim ob Caroline,
        For my ole massa, &c.
9.
Oh! music it hab charms all know,
But beauty clipses all below,
For de people turned from strains so fine,
To dandy Jim ob Caroline,
        For my ole massa, &c.

10.
Dey say dat beauty's but skin deep,
My skin's so thick twill always keep,
An till I die I'll live an shine,
The dandy Jim ob Caroline,
        For my ole massa, &c.

238 – 2

Example 8e. (cont.)

Example 8f. "Dandy Jim from Caroline" (no. 10) (Baltimore: F. D. Benteen, 1844). The author gratefully acknowledges the permission to reproduce minstrel songs from the Sheet Music Collection of the Free Library of Philadelphia.

best lookin Niggar in de County O, I look in de glass an I found it so,

Jus what massa told me O.

2.
I drest myself from top to toe,
And down to Dinah I did go,
Wid pantaloons strapp'd down behine,
Like "Dandy Jim from Caroline."
  For my ole massa &c.

3.
De bull dog clar'd me out ob de yard,
I tought I'e better leabe my card,
I tied it fast to a piece ob twine,
Signed "Dandy Jim from Caroline."
  For my ole massa &c.

4.
She got my card an wrote me a letta,
An ebery word she spelt de betta,
For ebery word an ebery line,
Was "Dandy Jim from Caroline."
  For my ole massa &c.

5.
Oh, beauty it is but skin deep,
But wid Miss Dinah none compete;
She chang'd her name from lubly Dine,
To Mrs. Dandy Jim from Caroline.
  For my ole massa &c.

6.
An ebery little one we had,
Was de berry image ob he dad,
Dar heels stick out tree feet behine,
Like "Dandy Jim from Caroline."
  For my ole massa &c.

7.
I took dem all to church one day,
An hab dem christened widout delay,
De Preacher christened eight or nine,
Young Dandy Jims from Caroline.
  For my ole massa &c.

8.
An when de Preacher took he tex.
He seem'd to be berry much perplex,
For noting cum across he mine,
But "Dandy Jim from Caroline."
  For my ole massa &c.

221

L. W. Webb.

Example 8f. (cont.)

the various versions of the "Dandy Jim" tune. The first phrase of the Benteen edition is similar to the other D-major versions except that the right-hand accompaniment doubles the melody line. The second, however, is different. The subdominant triad is not used on the "tole me so" phrase, and the IV–V–I concluding formula is avoided by another melodic variant emphasizing the tonic harmony. All the versions of "Dandy Jim," then, show a two-strain, strophic song, the structure being typical of most of the early minstrel tunes. The pentatonic or modal character of the melody seems to disappear, however, as the song was adapted by various house arrangers for sheet music editions that brought "Dandy Jim" from the streets and theaters into the American home.

The topical references to fiddlers, dancers or dancing, courtship practices, and public rituals in some of the "Dandy Jim" songs were tied to the promenade scenes on New York streets, that is, the typical male and female display activities that took place on Sundays and holidays on lower Broadway and the Bowery where young unmarried persons often met. The minstrel theaters themselves provided some of the best opportunities for promenades during the intermissions, at least in those theaters that permitted such displays, as described in the following announcement: "An Intermission of 16 minutes for promenade in the Vestibule will be given, where Ice Creams, Confectionary [*sic*], Pastry, and Iced Soda Water of all kinds may be obtained."[31]

Many of the textual references in the song are still somewhat obscure. "Dandy Jim" *appears* to have very little to do with South Carolina. Jim is an "outsider," referred to in the third person as a character spoken "about." The song's persona refers to himself in some versions as "like Dandy Jim *of* Caroline" and in others as "like Dandy Jim *from* Caroline."[32] If this song had a topical basis, it could be that Dandy Jim was a caricature of James ("Dandy Jim") Hammond, the governor of the South Carolina between 1842 and 1844, rather than a fictional persona developed exclusively for the minstrel stage. Most editions of the song were published during the 1842–44 period. Governor Hammond, as his most recent biographer notes, behaved in a manner likely to have provoked his slaves to satire. He treated "plantation management as theater, with Hammond starring as a paternalist and the blacks all assembled as [a] captive, if not appreciative, audience."[33]

Hammond's political opinions about the North and northern workers aroused public sentiment and animosity among New Yorkers when the governor visited that city during the 1840s. His views did not change during the next decade, and his "Mud-sill Speech," delivered before Congress in 1858, defended the southern system of social stratification as well as the paternalistic philosophy of southern slave holders. Hammond's words were likely to be remembered in a class-sensitive society where immigrant workers ("wage slaves") were often compared with African American slaves:

In all social systems, there must be a class to do the mean duties, to perform the drudg-ery of life, that is, a class requiring but a low order of intellect and but little skills. Its requisites are vigor, docility and fidelity. Such a class you must have, or you would not have that other class which leads to progress, refinement and civilization. It con-stitutes the very mud-sills of society and of political government. . . . Fortunately for the South, she found a race adapted to that purpose to her hand. . . . We are old-fash-ioned at the South yet; it is a word discarded now by ears polite; but it will not char-acterize that class at the North with that term; but you have it; it is there; it is every-where; it is eternal.[34]

The class whose lot it was "to do the mean duties" attended the minstrel the-aters on the Bowery. Many of them agreed that Hammond was not far off the mark in arguing that the "whole class of manual laborers and operatives, as you call them, are slaves." These were the same laborers who often opposed emancipation on the grounds that they might come to be treated like African Americans. They were also the class that George Fitzhugh, one of South's most outspoken proslavery theorists, described as "the poor hardworking people, who support everybody, and starve themselves." Hammond certainly did not endear himself to political philosophers, Republican party spokespersons, or the working class in the North, but his state-ments "elicited essentially no negative response from the South or Southwest."[35]

James Hammond could have been a source for "Dandy Jim" or a "Dandy Jim" parody. The hypothesis has some circumstantial probability and might explain the song's name. But since I have cautioned against reading song texts too literally, I do not wish to make more of this evidence than it may be worth. "Dandy Jim of Caroline" is actually a song type describing a flashy, attention-getting male whose boasts about his attractiveness to women set him apart from the typical male. There are additional connections that New Yorkers might have recognized, namely, pos-sible references to local characters known to all, such as Michael Walsh (1798–1859), the so-called "workingman dandy—with his disheveled clothes, diamond ring, and silver-tipped cane."[36] The dandy type, however, regardless of class, was more complex in antebellum culture, and it may well be the type itself that Dandy Jim embodies.

The blackface dandy persona would not have been as funny or as conventional as it was if black men had been its only subjects or the exclusive objects of derision. The dandy gentleman, who was already a subject of disdain by the lower classes, dropped another prestige level when fitted out with blackface makeup and mis-matched attire. The whole caricature struck at the American distaste for pretentious-ness and enhanced the pleasure derived from ridiculing those who claimed to be what they truly were not. The Dandy Jim stereotype's real problem is that he is ba-sically a hypocrite who uses lures to ensnare female victims—he is a confidence man whose goal is pleasure—and personifies the "middle-class American's desire to set himself or herself apart from the democratic masses by establishing artificial social distinctions." Just as those who desired "to distinguish themselves from the egalitarian masses below them . . . wielded invitations and calling cards to barricade the vulgar from their social presence," so too did the "vulgar"—Dandy Jim and his colleagues—aspire to middle-class social practices to make themselves more attractive to women.[37]

There were characters like that in the audience, individuals who craved the attention directed at those who aspired to the dandy status and the pursuit of the illicit pleasures of the city. As Stuart Blumin has noted, "Fancy men of the wealthier classes slummed at workmen's theaters and other disreputable places in the wrong parts of town, and some voluntary societies . . . brought workers into seemingly egalitarian relations with men of the nonmanual sector." Fanny Fern (Sara Payson Parton) observed in her *Fern Leaves from Fanny's Port-folio* that "half the married men should have their 'licenses' taken away. . . . They can't expect to come down to town and peep under all the ladies bonnets the way they do. . . . It's none of *my* business, but I question whether their wives, whom they left at home stringing dried apples, know how spruce they look in their new hats and coats, or how facetious they grow with their landlady's daughter, or how many of them pass themselves off for bachelors, to verdant spinsters."[38]

"Dandy Jim" was one of minstrelsy's real hits. In addition, it is considered a paradigm of the negative, demeaning, stereotypic songs characteristic of minstrelsy's worst racist perceptions about African American men. This study of its context confirms that there are very few minstrel songs presenting positive images of the adult male African American. But it also demonstrates that there are relatively few hit songs presenting any positive features of white American males during the 1840s.[39] The display songs must have been important cultural artifacts defining types of male public behavior for both black and white men during the antebellum period and exploring the forms of sexual aggression admired or accepted by period audiences.

The blackface characters in male display songs often appear as outsiders, usually newcomers, who are not accepted into the imaginary communities the songs present to the audience. Emmett's Old Dan Tucker is such a character. Tucker's social attachments reflect his difficulties in adapting to new environments and moral codes. He also identifies himself by repeating the first-person pronoun in the first verse but shifting repeatedly to the third person in the others. The song is *about* Tucker and his exploits. The singer describes his exploits in the first person and tells audience members how they should judge his accomplishments.

These pronoun shifts break the unified frame of the narrative and introduce a different performance style into the theatrical songs of the period. This "participant persona" device allows the singer to maintain the fictional context of the entire song, relate the character to the mock heroic genres of folk and popular culture, and guarantee that the unconventional behaviors will be noticed.[40]

"Old Dan Tucker" (Boston: Charles H. Keith, 1843)

Verse 1
I come to town de udder night,
I hear de noise an saw de fight,
De watchman was a runnin roun,
Cryin Old Dan Tucker's come to town.

Chorus ("Gran' Chorus")
So get out de way! Get out de way!
Get out de way! Old Dan Tucker.
Your to late to come to supper.

Verse 2
Tucker is a nice old man,
He use to ride our darby ram,
He sent him whizzen down de hill,
If he hadn't got up he'd lay dar still.

Chorus

Verse 3
Here's my razor in good order,
Magnum bonum—jis had bought 'er,
Sheep shell oats, Tucker shell de corn,
I'll shabe you soon as de water get warm.

Chorus

Verse 4
Old Dan Tucker an I got drunk,
He fell in de fire an kick up a chunk,
De charcoal got inside he shoe,
Lor bless you honey how de ashes flew.

Chorus

Verse 5
Down de road foremost de stump,
Massa make me work de pump;
I pump so hard I broke de sucker,
Dar was work for ole Dan Tucker.

Chorus

The text contains vagrant verses, that is, lines of text that interrupt the narrative and force it into a different context. Such variations reinforce the performance aspects of many of these repertory items. What the "Old Dan Tucker" song was each evening depended on the singer who presented it and on his ability to act out the part identified with his comic persona. Narrative interruptions are strong stylistic features emphasizing the humorous elements in the material. The "Sheep shell oats" line in verse 3, for example, is an illogical but nonetheless satisfying phrase that does not contribute to the story; its purpose is to extend the rhyme or the patter scheme.[41] The instrumental interludes were important parts of the performance because, like the verbal inventions and improvised verses, they also illustrated the performer's skills and were intimately linked to the character type being presented on the stage. These demonstrations were part of the whole pattern of male competitiveness, which was celebrated in minstrel show songs and dances just as strongly as it was in real-life sporting events.

Many examples of the first generation of minstrel songs (1843 and after) show that the works with the strongest links to black culture were composed by or attributed to Joel Sweeney, Cool White, or Dan Emmett. Their songs share remarkable similarities with preminstrel examples known to have been part of the African American vocal music tradition. One of those songs, "Long Time Ago; or, Shinbone Alley" (1833), describes two common themes, the master-slave relationship and male rivalry or competition over a woman usually named "Dinah" or "Sally." The song uses the call-and-response pattern of African American and Anglo-American communal singing in the folk tradition, a characteristic captured in William Clifton's arrangement of the song years before the practice became part of the minstrel style, as seen in examples such as Christy's "Uncle Gabriel, the Negro General" (1848).[42] Such a precedent is important because musicians tend to work with what they have performed and use patterns that have proven effective for other songs.[43]

"Long Time Ago" (Baltimore: John Cole, 1833)

Verse 1
O I was born down ole Varginee (Solo), Long time ago (Trio)
O I was born down ole Varginee (Solo), Long time ago (Trio)
Massa die an make me free (Solo) Long time ago (Trio)
Massa die an make me free (Solo) Long time ago (Trio)

Joel Sweeney's "Ole Tare River" (1840) illustrates a possible adaptation of two traditions of black communal music: (1) the call-and-response style and (2) the use an instrumental break between lines of text suggesting the voice-instrument dialogue known later as the talking blues style, where the instrument substitutes for the voices of listeners/participants. The piano-vocal score makes the example appear more regular than it would sound in a live performance. The diagonal lines in the following example represent the bar lines of the four-measure musical phrases shown in the sheet music edition.

Verse 1
On de banks of / Ole Tare river / banjo / banjo/
I go from dar to / Alabama / banjo / banjo /
For to see my / ole Aunt Hannah / banjo / banjo /

Postlude (four measures)

    The interludes (in the 1840 edition of "Sweeney's Virginy Melodies") occur while the text is being presented and actually interrupt the narrative continuity of the song with a characteristic musical tag, just as they do in a Frank Brower song known as "Old Joe" (1844).[44] "Old Tare River" is a twenty-eight-measure design (Pr–AB–Po), but each of the text sections (A and B) features two-measure text statements followed by a two-measure presentation of an instrumental phrase on the banjo, making the song appear to move forward by fits and starts. In most of the other early nineteenth-century dance songs, the dance sections occur during the symphonies or interludes, that is, *between* the verses, not within the individual phrases. A two-measure interruption of a four-measure vocal phrase is relatively rare outside the blackface songs of the early 1840s. The instrumentalist-singer combination was unique to blackface entertainment and the slave behavior on which it may have been based.[45]

    The performance practice used in songs such as "Old Tare River" may be another feature Sweeney borrowed from the black musicians he heard in Virginia. These combination songs are different from the prevailing Anglo-American styles of the period. It is not that they are incompetently written or appear to be "products of shallow minds." Rather, they appear to be a new form of dance song composed in the composite style of the folk tune in which the disparity between the strains may be the result of a performance practice where continuity was not so important. If the instrumental portion of the phrase was intended to display the banjo or a dance step, both these activities and the words associated with them would not necessarily have to connect with the first part of the phrase. Such a feature would be especially appropriate if the dance steps themselves were derived from those observed on southern plantations or presented as different from the prevailing styles of solo or set dancing of the period in northern urban settings.

    The early blackface, or "Negro," songs are not through-composed according to the composition practices of the English stage or Italian opera but may be the direct result of a different tradition of composite melody making, that of Anglo- and African American folk practices.[46] By the late 1840s, however, most of the songs containing odd phrase lengths, instrumental breaks, and odd word chains had become regularized, with eight-measure phrases for a soloist and a harmonized chorus for other members of the minstrel company. Textual implications may have been lost, too. For example, later performers using "Old Tare River" may not have understood the tradition at all or, given their own attitudes about race, could easily have missed the animal symbolism characteristic of African American culture, the very features that make Sweeney's song seem more authentic. These conclusions are suggested by the following textual comparisons between two versions of "Old Tare River."[47]

"Old Tare River" (Boston: Henry Prentiss, 1840)

Verse 1
Way down in North Carolina,
On de banks of de Ole Tare River.
I go down dar to Alabama,
For to see my Old Aunt Hannah.

Verse 2
Raccoon and possum got in a fray
Fought all night until de next day
When de day broke de Pos[s] cut to de hollow
Old Coon says I guess I better follow.

Verse 3
Day met next on de top ob de hill
For to settle dis great diffikil
Possum seized de Coon by de tail
Make him wish he was on a rail.

Verse 4
Ole nigger cum along wid his dog
Possum cut for de hollow log
Coon he looked and saw day nig
So up de tree he den dig.

Verse 5
De ole dog watch, smelt all around
He found the Coon jest lef de ground
Den he bark rite up de tree
De ole Coon says you cant ketch me.

Verse 6
De ole dog bark, de nigger blow his horn,
Ole coon begin to tink he was gone
Ole nigger cum he cast up his eye
On a big limb dat coon did lie.

"Original Ole Tar River" (NFM1, 56)

Verse 1
Oh, way down in ole Tare riber,
Hu hu lu a hu ahoo,
On de banks of Alama,
Lum tum tum tum Toddy um de da,
Dar's ar I see my ole Anna,
Oh hu hu lu a hu ahoo.
Gwaine away to ole Lusianna,
Lum tum tum tum Toddy um de da.

Verse 2
She grin dis nigga too good bye,
Oh hu hu lu a hu ahoo,
I gib her hand a good bye shaken,
Fur lu ah ahoo,
Twas hot enough to bake a cake on,
Lum tum tum tum Toddy um de da.
I ride upon de rollin riber
Hu hu lu a hu ahoo,
Wid a sail made ob a waggon kiver,
Lum tum tum tum Toddy um de da.

Verse 3
I go down to de dismal swamp,
Hu hu ahoo!
War alligator's ghosts do romp,
Lump tum tum.
I dance wid dem all in de mash, ah!
Hu hu ahoo!
It make de trees turn all goose flesh, ah!
Lum tum tum,
I sing a song to massa raw bone,
Hu hu ahoo!

Verse 7
Nigger went to work and cut de tree down,
De ole Coon he could not be found
De Coon cut stick he was afraid ob de dog,
He run slap in anoder hollow log.

Verse 8
De Pos says Coon get out ob dis log
Lay rite still for I believe I hear de dog
De nigger den cum and stopt up de hole
And day couldn't get out to save dar souls.

Verse 9
Now Miss Dinah I'm going to leave you,
And when I'm gone dont let it grieve you,
First to the window den to de door,
Looking for to see de banjo.

Verse 4
I'm gwaine to de wild goose nation,
Hu hu ahoo,
For to complete my educashin,
Lum tum tum tum Toddy um de da.
To England on a raff I'll scull, ah,
Hu hu hu,
Den I'll print notes about John Bull, ah,
Tum tum tum,
I'll larn em how to eat dar pickens,
Hu hu hu,
And dey call me de Yankee Dickens,
Lum tum tum.

Verse 5
Den I'll turn a weather gauger,
Hu hu hu,
By rule ob star shine like old Hague, sa,
Hu hu ah ahoo,
Clar thro' de stone fence of de futah,
Lum tum tum, toddy um de da.

The nonsense syllables in the filler text function like the banjo interludes in the earlier versions of this song, but the rest of the text is not so illogical as it first appears. The narrative is somewhat disjointed, but it is not utter nonsense. In verse 2 of the songster version, for example, the woman waves good-bye—the waves are characterized as "too good bye"—the male shakes her hand, and the day is so hot that a cake could be baked without an oven. The narrative continues with the male persona taking a river "ride" on a small sailing dinghy of the type used to transport tobacco down the James River.

Some of the minstrel songs dealing with animals probably refer to the exploits of slaves who had to supplement their diets by raiding fields, trapping, or fishing. Other songs seem linked to black folklore, especially those that include references to mammals, birds, and insects, which recur often enough in blackface song to raise questions about why the minstrel entertainers would have chosen them. This group of songs includes "Walk Jaw Bone" (1840), with its chorus of "Jenny come along";[48] "Wild Goose Nation" (1844); "Wild Raccoon Track"; "Blue Tail Fly" (1846); and "Gray Goose and Gander," which is also known as "The Ole Gray Goose" (1844) because both songs have the same text. Other examples are "Uncle Gabriel" no. 1 (1848) and "Corn Field Green" (1844), which is about a raccoon that eats too much green corn. There are animal and insect songs dealing with cats ("White Cat and

Black Cat"), eels, alligators, frogs, locusts, and dogs. These songs have no apparent relation to the white commercial song traditions of the period and seem more closely tied to the folk materials characteristic of rural areas in the North and South.

The most popular song in the group was "The Blue Tail Fly" (also known as "Jim Crack Corn"), which appears some twelve times in the songsters, whereas "Wild Goose Nation" and "Wild Raccoon Track" are each found only six times.[49] The Benteen edition of "The Blue Tail Fly" has often been considered a nonsense song, but its contents suggest otherwise. The event described in the song is the planter's or master's inspection of his domain and the slave's obvious pleasure in knowing that a person of such power is brought low by a common insect. The song refers to the world-turned-upside-down or role-reversal theme common in the Marster John stories and already discussed as an important feature of the Ethiopian sketches.

By the time the 1846 sheet music edition appeared, "Jim Crack Corn" had a regular melody not unlike "Lucy Long" and a four-part chorus that functions as a refrain. Different versions of the song exist, however, so it is not easy to determine which company performed the song first. The most notable difference between Emmett's "Blue Tail Fly" (1844 or 1846) and the Benteen version is the easy singability of the latter because of its simple melodic construction and G-major tonality. The Emmett example is modal—notated oddly in B♭ but obviously in C Dorian mode (C minor) and hexatonic because of the C–D–E♭–F–G–B♭ pitch classes of the tune—and although it can be learned without great difficulty, it would still be hard for the average listener to learn it quickly.

The "Jim Crack" referred to in the Benteen chorus but not in the version attributed to Emmett is probably an allophone for *gimcrack*, which signifies something showy but of little worth. The expression thus refers to poor quality yellow corn or popcorn; it is not a noun-verb combination referring to an action ("Jim cracked [the] corn" or "Jimmy cracked corn"). The song's persona does not care about the quality of the corn because "the master's gone away."

The performance styles for this song are not known, but the repetition of the chorus could serve a variety of functions, especially if the choral version included some additional stage business.[50] The setting favors a voicing of three tenors and a single bass with the second tenor crossing the melody line (see music examples 9a and b). The voices on the first and third staves harmonize the melody line in thirds; the second-staff voice completes the harmony by doubling or filling in the missing pitches required to complete the triad or double the root. The melodic substructure of the song is the familiar chain of thirds (G–B, F♯–A, G–B, [A]–C, B–D, C–E), presented linearly, but the tune is harmonized at the third above or below, in the style typical of Italian operatic choruses. The entire song is built on the primary triads implied in the tertian structure of the melody. Incidentally, the differences between the Benteen edition and those commonly found in post-1950s collections

Example 9a. "Jim Crack Corn; or, The Blue Tail Fly" (Baltimore: F. D. Benteen, 1846).
Used by permission of the Brown University Library.

2.
Den arter dinner massa sleep,
He bid dis niggar vigil keep;
An' when he gwine to shut his eye,
He tell me watch de blue tail fly.
   Jim crack corn &c.

3.
An' when he ride in de arternoon,
I foller wid a hickory broom;
De poney being berry shy,
When bitten by de blue tail fly.
   Jim crack corn &c.

4.
One day he rode aroun' de farm.
De flies so numerous dey did swarm;
One chance to bite 'im on the thigh,
De debble take dat blu tail fly.
   Jim crack corn &c.

5.
De poney run, he jump an' pitch,
An' tumble massa in de ditch;
He died, an' de jury wonder'd why
De verdic was de blue tail fly.
   Jim crack corn &c.

6.
Dey laid 'im under a 'simmon tree,
His epitaph am dar to see:
'Beneath dis stone I'm forced to lie,
All by de means ob de blue tail fly.
   Jim crack corn &c.

7.
Ole massa gone, now let 'im rest,
Dey say all tings am for de best;
I nebber forget till de day I die,
Ole massa an' de blue tail fly.
   Jim crack corn &c.

Example 9a. (cont.)

Example 9b. "De Blue Tail Fly" (Boston: Keith's Music Publishing House, 1846). Used by permission of the Brown University Library.

Example 9b. (cont.)

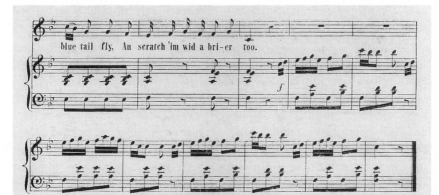

3

When I was young, I used to wait
On Massa's table an hand de plate;
I'de pass de bottle when he dry,
An brush away de blue tail fly,
    An scratch 'im &c.

4

Den arter dinner massa sleep,
He bid me vigilance to keep;
An when he gwine to shut he eye,
He tell me watch de blue tail fly,
    An scratch 'im &c.

5

When he ride in de arternoon,
I foller wid a hickory broom;
De poney being berry shy,
When bitten by de blue tail fly,
    An scratch 'im &c.

6

One day he rade aroun de farm,
De flies so numerous did swarm;
One chance to bite 'im on de thigh,
De debble take dat blue tail fly,
    An scratch 'im &c.

7

De poney run, he jump, an pitch,
An tumble massa in de ditch;
He died, an de Jury wonder why,
De verdict was de "blue tail fly,"
    An scratch 'im &c.

8

Dey laid 'im under a simmon tree,
His epitaph am dar to see;
Beneath dis stone I'm forced to lie,
All by de means ob de blue tail fly,
    An scratch 'im &c.

9

Ole Massa's gone, now let him rest,
Dey say all tings am for de best;
I neber shall forget till de day I die,
Ole Massa an de blue tail fly,
    An scratch 'im &c.

10

De hornet gets in your eyes an nose,
De 'skeeter bites y'e through your close,
De gallinipper sweeten high,
But wusser yet de blue tail fly,
    An scratch 'im &c.

449   5

Example 9b. (cont.)

of folk and popular music are noteworthy because in the latter the song has been simplified even further to accommodate a typical three-chord (I–IV–V–I) guitar accompaniment.

In the first example the first phrase (mm. 1–8) consists of essentially one four-measure unit. The second phrase, labeled "chorus," reverses the upward skip from G to B. The release on the third "I don't care" combined with a change to the subdominant chord relieves the potential monotony of the alternating melodic thirds and tonic-dominant harmonies. Note that the tune as sung and notated today is somewhat different melodically and rhythmically, a result of oral and written transmission as well as the change of "jim crack" to "Jimmy crack[ed] corn." Both versions of the song are made up of interlocked thirds spelled in linear (solo part) and harmonic (chorus) forms of the primary triads or the dominant seventh (D^7 in G major). The Benteen version is easier to sing and harmonize because of its limited pitch content, derivation from primary triads, and overall repetitiveness. In example 9c the upper stave system shows the Benteen melody, and the lower shows the motivic and phrase design, with beams linking the significant melodic components.

The two-measure phrases of example 9b are stated four times prior to the tag or refrain line "An scratch 'im wid a brier too." Example 9d shows that the melodic pattern falls in the C-minor hexatonic scale without the sixth degree ($A\flat$). The melody of the first phrase focuses on C as a reciting note, and the final half-phrase (mm. 14–15) drops onto C an octave below to conclude the vocal portion of the song. The arranger took the C as the fifth of an F-major triad and had difficulty figuring out what key fit the melody best. The modal elements, the repetition of a melodic formula, the two-measure breaks, and the sometimes weak text underlay suggest strongly that the melody originated in a folk tradition, one that I suspect was African American. Finally, the evidence suggests that the song was originally conceived for voice or banjo alone. Since the minstrel banjo was not played in a chordal style, harmonization would not have been an issue.

The "Blue Tail Fly" songs begin with an acceptance of the paternalistic master-slave situation but challenge the morality of that relationship by inverting the roles of the characters. The resulting role reversal puts the slave in temporary control because he understands the natural ecology of the place. The master is a deserving victim of chance, not a tragic character whose intrinsic worth to his community or plantation makes his death a real loss to his neighbors. The master-slave power relationship is symbolically dissolved through the encounter with an insect and the ludicrous behavior of the authority figure. The role reversal is more than a simple inversion; the song rejects the whole paternalistic pattern of nineteenth-century power relationships by using an apparently simple comic narrative as a vehicle to mock the social order. What makes it humorous is the improbability of the slave ever having more than temporary power on the plantation or in the city.

Example 9c. Melodic structure/phrase design of "Jim Crack Corn."

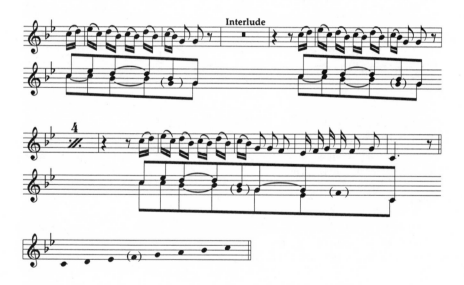

Example 9d. Melodic structure/phrase design of Emmett's "Blue Tail Fly."

"Jim Crack Corn or The Blue Tail Fly" (Baltimore: Benteen, 1846)

Verse 1
When I was young I us'd to wait
On Massa and hand him de plate;
Pass down de bottle when he git dry,
And bresh away de blue tail fly.

Chorus
Jim crack corn, I don't care,
Jim crack corn, I don't care,
Jim crack corn, I don't care,
Ole Massa gone away.

Verse 2
Den arter dinner massa sleep,
He bid dis niggar vigil keep,
An' when he gwine to shut his eye,
He tell me watch de blue tail fly.

Verse 3
An' when he ride in de arternoon,
I follow wid a hickory broom;
De poney being berry shy,
When bitten by de blue tail fly.

Verse 4
One he rode aroun' de farm,
De flies so numerous dey did swarm;
One chance to bite 'im on the thigh,
De debble take dat blu [*sic*] tail fly.

Verse 5
De poney run, he jump an' pitch,
An' tumble massa in de ditch;
He died, an' de jury wonder'd why,
De veric [verdict] was de blue tail fly.

Verse 7
Dey laid 'im under a 'simmon tree,
His epitaph am dar to see:
"Beneath dis stone I'm forced to lie.
All by de means ob de blue tail fly."

Verse 8
Ole massa gone, now let 'im rest,
Dey say all tings am for de best;
I nebber forget till de day I die,
Ole massa an' dat blue tail fly.

The slave-over-master inversion theme in "Jim Crack Corn" is also found in "Come Back Steben" (1849, but possibly as early as 1843), which is shaped as either a dialogue or a soliloquy with the singer enacting two different roles. The "participant persona" or self-reflexive role assigned to the performer is also obvious in this example.[51] Steben outwits the master by combining deference and deceit, mental cunning with physical business. Contrary to Dennison's contention that slaves showed no concern for the master's property rights, it appears that this slave knows only too well that property is an extension of the master's domain, for which some slaves were the stewards. Steben's cunning is revealed in his understanding of how vandalism or outright destruction of the master's property can be disguised as chance occurrences or staged accidents. He recognizes how broken equipment can wreak havoc with the master's overall productivity. Even when an accident may have a bad outcome for the responsible agent, the whole subject can be viewed humorously once the audience perceives the subtle inversion process set in play when the slave takes control of the situation.

"Come Back Steben" (Philadelphia: Lee and Walker, 1848)

Verse 1
Come back Steben, come back.
Come back Steben, come back.
I'm a com' [special vocal effect]
Oh come back Steben for you am de berry man,
What stole massa's blue coat,
Now fotch back de money.

Chorus
Oh lord ladies don't you mind Steben,
Steben am so decebin,
Dat his daddy wont belieb him.

Verse 2
Get out ob dat, get out ob dat you bones,
Get out ob dat, get out ob dat you bones,
You am de berry man,
What stole massa's sheep head,
For to make dem dar bones out ob.

Chorus

Verse 3
Good news Steben, good news.
Good news Steben, good news.
What is em?
Why Massa bought a new wagon,
Pompey was de driver,

And he run agin a gate post,
And smash em all to nofen.[52]

Chorus

The text of "Come Back Steben" describes, in what I believe are favorable terms, the clever trickster whose thieving ways show a rebellion against the system of slavery. Steben gets away with his crimes, and the characterization of him as a deceiver, while contributing to the negative portrayal of blacks as two-faced, also describes behaviors indicative of persons acting against oppression. The messages of this song may be mixed, then, and both interpretations would be acceptable to an audience disposed either to perceive a liar or to appreciate a rebel.

"Come Back Steben" presents "massa" as a loser, just as in the "Blue Tail Fly." The key element of both songs is the shattering of the physical and mental bondage inherent in the master-slave relationship. This is the dominant message conveyed by the happy-go-lucky character disguised as a plantation hand. Reading the texts only as examples of a slave's incompetence or generalizing about the reduced capabilities attributed to African Americans misses the point that vandalism on the job was a key form of rebellion for northern "wage slaves" as well as southern plantation workers.

The narrative song collection also includes several examples that deal with misreadings of recent historical events. One of Edwin Christy's "Uncle Gabriel" songs ("Uncle Gabriel, the Negro General") was associated with the Southampton insurrection of Nat Turner (1831), even though the name "Gabriel" links the text to Gabriel Prosser, the leader an earlier rebellion of 1800. The Christy Minstrels announced the number in their programs as "Uncle Gabriel, the Negro General, an original Refrain, descriptive of the Northampton Insurrection."[53] That announcement meant that the text was not an *accurate* narration of the events.

The "original refrain" of "Uncle Gabriel" was performed by E. P. Christy himself accompanied by a four-part chorus in a style similar to that of the Italian opera parodies the Christy Minstrels had been performing since their years with Palmo's Burlesque Opera.

"Uncle Gabriel" (New York: C. Holt, 1848)

Verse 1
Solo: Oh, my boys I'm bound to tell you
Chorus: Oh!
Solo: Listen a while and I will tell you.
Chorus: Oh!
Solo: I'll tell you little bout Uncle Gabriel
  Oh! boys I've just began.
Chorus: Hard times in Old Virginy

Verse 2

Solo: Oh don't you know Old Uncle Gabriel

Chorus: Oh! Oh!

Solo: Oh! he war a niger General,

Chorus: Oh! Oh!

Solo: He war Chief of de Insurgents
    Way down in Southampton.

Chorus: Hard times in Old Virginy.

Verse 3

Solo: It war a little boy betrayed him,

Chorus: Oh! Oh!

Solo: A little boy be the name of Danel,

Chorus: Oh! Oh!

Solo: Betrayed him at de Norfolk landing,
    Oh, boys I'm gettin done.

Chorus: Hard times in Old Virginy.

Verse 4

Solo: Says he de do my Uncle Gabriel

Chorus: Oh! Oh!

Solo: I am not your Uncle Gabriel

Chorus: Oh! Oh!

Solo: My name is Jim McCullen
    Sometimes called me Archey Mullin.

Chorus: Hard times in Old Virginy.

Verse 5

Solo: The whites dey fought him and dey caught him.

Chorus: Oh! Oh!

Solo: To Richmond Court House dey did brought him

Chorus: Oh! Oh!

Solo: Twelve men set up on de jury,
    Oh! boys I'm most done

Chorus: Hard times in Old Virginy.

Verse 6

Solo: Dey took him down de Gallows

Chorus: Oh! Oh! Solo: Dey drove him down, wid four grey horses.

Chorus: Oh! Oh!

Solo: Bryce's Ben, he drove de wagon
    Oh! boys, I'm almost done

Chorus: Hard times in Old Virginy.

Verse 7

Solo: And dere dey hung him an dey swung him,

Chorus: Oh! Oh!

Solo: And dey swung him and dey hung him,
Chorus: Oh! Oh!
Solo: And that war the last of the Niger General,
 Oh! boys I'm just done.
Chorus: Hard times in Old Virginy.

Christy or whoever wrote the words mixed up the aborted "revolt" led by Gabriel Prosser on August 30, 1800, which ended in the Brook Swamp outside Richmond, with the insurrection led by "General" Nat Turner on August 21–29, 1831. The latter event took place in Southampton county in southeastern Virginia near the North Carolina border.[54] The betrayers of Gabriel Prosser were two slaves named Tom and Pharaoh who were rewarded with their freedom by Governor James Monroe. Neither Gabriel Prosser (1776–1800) nor Nat Turner (1800[?]-1831) was very old at the time of his death, and neither was commonly referred to as "Uncle" in any of the contemporary sources. Finally, Turner was not tried in front of a twelve-person jury, although he was hanged "at the usual place of execution," an old tree located near the Old Southampton County Jail.

With so many historical inaccuracies, Christy's "Uncle Gabriel" must be a mock heroic tale that, while it appears to sanction the harsh penalty that the insurgent receives, distorts the history of Turner's insurrection so much that the significance of the slave revolts is trivialized. The choral exclamations, "Hard Times in Old Virginy," for example, refer to events scarcely two decades old and still in the memory of the over-thirty generation. Regardless of the factual distortions, "Uncle Gabriel" no. 2 emphasizes the necessity of preserving the American social order by enforcing sanctions on those revolutionaries who might disrupt the fabric of society.

This version of "Uncle Gabriel" is unusual for a number of reasons. First, the piano introduction is not closely related to the soloist's melody, although the cadential motif in measures 7–8 is repeated later in measures 15–16. Most minstrel songs begin with the melody of the principal strain. Second, the juxaposition of the soloist and chorus in a call-and-response practice is also different. The appearance of the interjection after the soloist's phrase is also noteworthy because the cadence completes the phrase musically and dramatically. Most minstrel songs follow the verse-refrain pattern of period folk and popular music. Third, the performance practice shown here antedates the mock spirituals that appeared in the early 1860s and after the publication of *Slave Songs of the United States* in 1867. The third interruption by the chorus is also worth observing because the phrase "Hard times in Old Virginy" was frequently used in early minstrelsy in what appears to be a lament. These interruptions occur relatively infrequently in the minstrel repertory, suggesting that this song may be a mock serious imitation of African American performance practice, something that on further investigation of the repertory raises questions about the sources for Christy's performance practices. (See music example 10.)

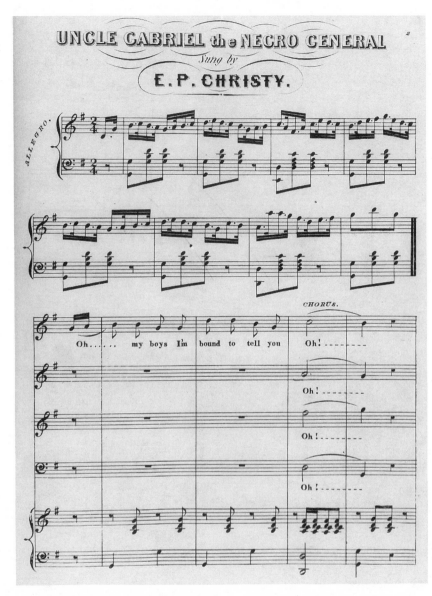

Example 10. "Uncle Gabriel" no. 2, from *Music of the Christy Minstrels*. Used by permission of the University of Pittsburgh Library.

Example 10. (cont.)

Oh dont you know Old Uncle Gabriel,
Chorus Oh! Oh!
Oh! he war a niger General,
Chorus Oh! Oh!
He war de Chief of de Insurgents,
Way down in Southampton.
Chorus. Hard times in Old Virginy.

3
It war a little boy betrayed him,
Chorus Oh! Oh!
A little boy by the name of Danel,
Chorus Oh! Oh!
Betrayed him at de Norfolk landing,
Oh! boys I'm gettin done.
Chorus. Hard time in Old Virginy.

4
Says he how de do my Uncle Gabriel,
Chorus Oh! Oh!
I am not your Uncle Gabril,
Chorus Oh! Oh!
My name it is Jim Mc Cullen,
Some dey calls me Archey Mullin.
Ch. Hard times in Old Virginy

5
The whites dey fought him and dey caught him,
Chorus Oh! Oh!
To Richmond Court House dey did brought him,
Chorus Oh! Oh!
Twelve men sot up on de jury,
Oh! boys I'm most done.
Chorus. Hard times in Old Virginy.

6
Dey took him down to de Gallows,
Chorus Oh! Oh!
Dey drove him down, wid four grey horses,
Chorus Oh! Oh!
Brice's Ben, he drove de wagon,
Oh! boys, I'm most done.
Chorus. Hard times in Old Virginy.

7
And dare dey hung him an dey swung him,
Chorus Oh! Oh!
And dey swung him and dey hung him,
Chorus Oh! Oh!
And that war the last of the Niger General,
Oh! boys I'm just done.
Chorus Hard times in Old Virginy.

S. Ackerman.

Example 10. (cont.)

The facts could have been garbled in the songwriter's memory, but that seems unlikely. The song was purposefully contrived to treat history humorously, in the same way that the creation story in Genesis 1 is mistold in "De History ob de World" (1847). The same song was also known under titles taken from the first line of its chorus, "Walk in de Parlor" or "Walk into the Parlor."[55]

"De History ob de World" (Boston: Oliver Ditson, 1882)

Verse 2
Oh, dis world was made in six days,
And den dey made de sky,
And den dey hung it oberhead,
And left it dar to dry;
And den dey made de stars out ob nigger wenches' eyes,
For to gib a little light,
When de moon didn't rise.

Chorus
Walk into de parlor,
And hear my banjo ring,
Watch my lightning fingers,
As they play upon the strings.

Verse 5
O, lightning is a yellow gal,
She libs up in de clouds,
And thunder he's a black man,
For he can hollow loud;
When he kisses lightning,
She dodges off in wonder,
Den he jumps and tares his trowsers,
And dat's what makes de thunder.[56]

The other version of "Uncle Gabriel" (no. 1), which contains no references to a general, is a hunting song with some of minstrelsy's most popular animals prominent in the text. Songs of this type tell stories similar to those found in the African American oral tradition, where the hunter is a clever trickster, understands the secrets of nature and the behavior of his prey, and utilizes limited resources to accomplish his goal. These elements are present in the animal-hunt song text of "Uncle Gabriel" (1847).[57]

"Uncle Gabriel" (New York: William Hall and Son, 1847)

Verse 1
As I was gwan to Sandy point de oder arternoon,
Dis niggers heel cum'b out ob joint a runnin arter a coon;

I thought I see'd him on a log, a lookin might quar,
When I cum'd up to de log, de coon he was'nt dar.

Chorus
O come along, O Sandy Boy, now come along O do;
O what will Uncle Gabriel say,
Ya eh eh eh, ya eh eh eh,
What will Uncle Gabriel say,
Why Jinny can't you come along too.

Verse 2
I blow'd de horn, I call'd de dog, and tell him for to bark;
I hunt all night in de hollow log,
But de coon he still keep dark:
At last I hear de ole coon sneeze, de dog he fly around;
And on to him he den did frieze and pull him to de ground.

Chorus

Verse 3
De coon he lay upon de ground, as stiff as any post;
I Knock him den upon de head, and he gabe up de ghost;
I took him to de old log house, as soon as he suspire;
He look'd just like a little mouse, and we roast him on de fire.

Chorus

Verse 4
De niggers dey come all around, and kick up a debil of a splutter;
Dey eat de coon and clar de ground, to dance de chicken flutter,
Day dance all night till de broke of day, to a tune on de old banjo,
And den dey all did gwan away, before de chicken crow.

Chorus

The song is a verse-chorus type with the third male part written on the bass staff, reflecting the convention of writing the part in the octave in which it actually sounds rather than using the treble clef and assuming that the singer will understand the transposition. The structure is Pr–A–B–Po (8–8–8–8), for a total of thirty-two measures, with an A section consisting of two identical eight-bar phrases and the B section—the harmonized chorus—comprising a single phrase. The phrase endings strongly suggest a pentatonic melodic structure, but the harmonization forced on the tune by the piano arrangement gives the song a strong tonal organization. The chorus establishes B♭ as a secondary tonic via a ii–V–I cadence, a not entirely convincing movement given the musical structure and textual content of the main phrase.

Uncle Gabriel's story, however, ends with the type of festive chorus suggesting that the plantation slaves celebrated often and, in the typically self-referential style of the minstrel song, provides a pretext for the demonstration of specific dances ("dance de chicken flutter") or for the excitement of closing a number with a variety of stage business. Such festive choruses were often linked to the mistaken notion that slaves lived in some agrarian paradise characterized by fun rather than work. Some plantation situations could be read that way—corn-shucking parties or holiday celebrations, perhaps—but it was the fantasy of leisure time that must have fascinated the minstrel show audiences. Those fantasies were contrary to the prevailing ideology that social improvement and economic success depended on free labor and the industriousness of the individual. The ascription of a lack of industry to an enslaved "other" living on a plantation is so unrealistic that it could only have been the result of a mythic view of the South. It is also a stage contrivance analogous to the happy sailors, peasants, soldiers, and others groups in the serious and comic operas of the period.

The interpretive conclusions offered about the animal songs, mock heroic narratives, stylistic aspects of the narrative shifts, and other new features of early minstrel songs have not been linked directly to documented cultural exchanges between blacks and whites. My hypotheses have assumed that such exchanges occurred in contact situations, but however convincing the circumstantial evidence may be, the documentation largely remains to be discovered. Some evidence has been recovered by Roger Abrahams in *Singing the Master,* but there is still much work to be done to establish the links between Anglo- and African American cultures in the marketplace of nineteenth-century popular theater.

Minstrel shows were communal events; they existed in the context of public participatory and shared experience. Audiences must have expected some specific pleasures as they lined up for the shows. Entertainment or diversion figured into the equation required for a successful excursion, and every show involved some comic business based on social practices of the period. Since popular entertainment could tolerate many different approaches to the symbolic gratification of fantasy, blackface comedians created songs and scenes that encouraged audiences to contemplate the pleasures of lives without responsibility. Burnt cork comics offered highly energetic performances based on competitiveness, burlesques of social activities, and presentations that displayed a light-hearted attitude toward all serious issues as substitutes for the tedium of everyday labor and life.

The celebration of such leisure activities as social dancing, drinking, and fantasizing about women occurred in a context in which the minstrels signified on their own labors. It is natural that working and partying would be combined in the same song because they were coupled as the principal activities in a single person's life. The partying theme is one of the principal features of the best-known festive minstrel song, namely, Dan Emmett's "Boatman's Dance" (1843).[58] The first of the following two examples is taken from the version performed by the Ethiopian Serenaders; the second, attributed to Dan Emmett, has several different verses connecting it more closely to the boasting song genre. The placement of what I call the tag line is different in the two editions also. In the Emmett version, the tag line or chorus precedes the verse-refrain section. If the publications can be taken as relatively reliable, they confirm that different performance practices were employed by various minstrel groups.

"De Boatman's Dance"
  (Ethiopian Serenader's Version, 1843)

Verse 1
De boatman dance, de boatman sing,
De boatman up to eb'ry ting,
An when de boatman get on shore,
He spends his cash and works for more.

Refrain
Den dance de boatmen dance,
O dance de boatman dance,
O dance all night 'till broad daylight,
and go home wid de gals in de morning.

[Interlude]
Tag line: Hi, ho, de Boatman row,
  Floating down de riber on de Ohio [*repeated once*]

Verse 2
De boatman is a thrifty man,
Da is none can do as de boatman can,
I never see a pretty girl in all my life,
But dat she was some boatman's wife.

Refrain + Interlude + Tag Line

Verse 3
When you go to de boatman's ball,
Dance wid my wife or not at all;
Sky blue jacket an tarpaulin hat,
Look out my boys for de nine tail cat.

Refrain + Interlude + Tag line

Verse 4
When de boatman blows his horn,
Look out old man you hog is gone;
He steal my sheep, he cotch my shoat [young hog],
Den put em in bag an toat em to boat.

Refrain + Interlude + Tag Line + Postlude

"De Boatman's Dance"
    (Boston: Charles W. Keith, 1843)

Chorus
High row, de boatmen row, floatin down de river de Ohio.

Verse 2 (Solo)
De oyster boat should keep to de shore,
De fishin smack should venture more,
De schooner sails before de wind,
De steamboat leaves a streak behind.
Den dance de boatmen dance,
O dance de boatmen dance,
O dance all night till broad daylight,
    an go home wid de gals in de morning.

Verse 3 (Solo)
I went on board de odder day,
To see what de boatmen had to say,
Dar I let my passion loose,
An dey cram me in the calaboose.
Den dance de boatmen dance,
O dance de boatmen dance,
O dance all night till broad daylight,
    an go home wid de gals in de morning.

Verse 4 (Solo)
I've come dis time, I'll come no more,
Let me loose I'll go ashore;
For dey whole hoss, an dey a bully crew,
Wid a hossier mate an a captin too.
Den dance de boatmen dance,
O dance de boatmen dance,
O dance all night till broad daylight,
    an go home wid de gals in de morning.

Emmett's boatmen have their counterparts in comparisons between sailors, rail-road workers, canal laborers, and other, usually agricultural, workers. The compari-son is explicit in the popular "Life by the Galley Fire" (1848), which is a parody of Henry Russell's "Life on the Ocean Wave" (1838). Under the former title it appears no fewer than nine times in the songsters and at least five times in the playbills dur-ing the 1845–50 period alone.[59] The song lyric compares the job of tending the galley fire in a caboose to the life of a cook aboard a ship, subject to the incessant and re-lentless power of the sea. The railroad worker in the song, who cannot be black be-cause specific references within the text require otherwise and because blacks were seldom employed on the railroads until considerably later in the nineteenth century, prefers his occupation to other more adventurous and probably hazardous choices.[60]

"A Life by the Galley Fire" (New York: William Hall and Son, 1848)

Verse 1
A life by de galley fire,
A home in de good ole ship,
Whar de waves roll higher an' higher,
Like a nigger's under lip.
Like a coon in de cage I pine,
While on de stan' still shore,
Gib me de pickle brine,
An' de black caboose once more.

Chorus
A life by de galley fire,
A home in de good ole ship,
Whar de waves roll higher an' higher,
Like a nigger's under lip.

Verse 2
In de ole caboose I sit,
Among de fire an' pot,
An' dar I hab comman,'
Ob de wittles smoking hot.
I sit an' toast my shins,
An' work on my ole jaw bone,
An' when de storm begins,
I sing him dis yar toon.

Chorus

Verse 3
Wid a slice ob good fat ham,
Cooked brown as a nigger's skin,
My wittles chest I cram,'
An' like a shark I grin.
An' when eight bells hab struck,
Away I goes to roos,'
An' sleep like a black sea duck,
An' dream of de ole caboose.

Chorus

"A Life on the Ocean Wave" (New York: James L. Hewitt, 1838)

Verse 1
A life on the ocean wave!
A home on the rolling deep,
Where the scatter'd waters rave,
And the winds their revels keep!
Like an eagle cag'd I pine,
On this dull unchanging shore,
Oh, give me the flashing brine,
The spray and the tempest's roar.

Chorus
A life on the ocean wave!
A home on the rolling deep!
Where the scatter'd waters rave,
And the winds their revels keep!

Verse 2
Once more on the deck I stand,
Of my own swift gliding craft;
Set sail! farewell to the land,
The gale follows fair abaft.
We shoot through the sparkling foam,
Like an ocean bird set free,
Like an ocean bird our home,
We'll find far out on the sea.

Chorus

Verse 3
The land is no longer in view,
The clouds have begun to frown,
But with a stout vessel and crew,
We'll say let the storm come down!
And the song of our hearts shall be,
While the winds and the waters rave,
A life on the heaving sea!
A home on the bounding wave!

Chorus

The parody chorus sings of a ship's galley in a "good ole ship" and contrasts the threat of the ocean waves to the placid conditions of rail travel. As a trope for rising waves, the "nigger's under lip" is difficult to visualize and a poor, demeaning metaphor even by antebellum standards, although one perhaps justified in the parodist's mind by the need to make a rhyme with *ship*. The epithet nonetheless ties the parody to the threatening circumstances of life at sea.

The image of the caged eagle, an otherwise wild and free bird of prey, is replaced with that of the imprisoned raccoon; the wily and resourceful raccoon often appears as the victor of confrontations in African American folklore and minstrel hunting songs. The exciting and romantic life of a wealthy yachtsman who spends his leisure time testing his masculinity against the elements with his faithful crew contrasts with the blue-collar labors of the railroad worker. The threats of storms and sudden squalls, however adventurous for the captain in his *own* boat, are challenges the working-class persona can avoid by accepting the comforts of his secure and sturdy caboose.

The character seeks what workers called a "situation," a job that was not too demanding and that came with such perquisites as a comfortable place to sleep, reasonably good food on demand, and shelter during inclement weather. The dominant image of the happy-go-lucky urban worker—many minstrel song characters seem to sing through their workday as if labor were leisure—was invested with the same characteristics attributed to slaves and free persons of color working in the agricultural economy of the South. But the illusion that African Americans were generally happy workers because they were observed singing during labor or celebrating during corn shucks did not take into consideration the total experience of slavery. The minstrel show conception of happy slaves allowed audiences to rationalize the true conditions of an oppressive system and dismiss the negative accounts of that oppression published with increasing frequency during the heyday of antebellum blackface comedy.

The types of work mentioned in minstrel show songs—corn husking, rowing, harvesting various crops, and transporting tobacco—reflect some of the common socializing experiences among black field workers in the South. These work-related songs include crop-harvesting examples, such as "Away to the Tobacco Fields" (*CNS1*) and "Oh Down in de Tobacco State" (*WBA1*); postharvest husking songs, such as "Huskin' de Corn" (*ESB1, CNS1, CNS2,* and *RNS1*) and "To the Corn Fields" (*BHW1, CPM4, NSO1, ESB1, CNS2,* and *NNB1*); and transportation songs, such as "Lynchburg Town" (*BHW1, CNS1, CNS2, RSB2, JJO1, NSO1, UNS1,* and *WNB1*) and its variants, along with other titles about labor in river transportation, such as "De Boatman's Dance."[61] In Coosa County, Alabama, "It was generally understood that a corn shucking was free to any who wished to come, so that if the familiar sound of a number of negroes singing corn songs at one place was heard, any negro man or boy felt he had a right to go, and they generally went, for they expected two things that appealed strongly to the negro, and that was a good dram and a good supper."[62] The point of this claim (in spite of the characterization concerning the free meal) is its author's recognition of the social significance of an event that allowed persons of different communities relatively free passage to dance, sing, court, and enjoy each other's company.

The corn shuck was also known quite well in the North, where it "was part of the rural scene from New England to Georgia as early as 1790, and by 1825 it had replaced the fodder pulling and topping almost completely and dominated the corn belts." The southern corn belt included all the slave states; the northern, most of the states along the eastern seaboard up to Maine. The corn shuck was one of the "overwhelming themes" of the "American landscape through the nineteenth and early twentieth century in the fall and winter."[63] These were common elements in the lives of agricultural workers in both regions, so that workers would have understood the references to corn harvesting and crop commerce in minstrel songs such as "Walk Jaw Bone."

The rural characters in the various versions of "Walk Jaw Bone" define themselves by statements such as "I husk de wood an' I chop de corn," the reversal of logic (husk the corn and chop the wood) creating a strong comic image. That song has a counterpart in another type of plantation song known as "Old Jaw Bone." "Old Jaw Bone," which has many variants, is an African American adaptation of an English ballad known as "The Mistletoe Bough."[64]

"Walk Jaw Bone" (MSON, 210)	*"Old Jaw Bone" (Boston: Henry Prentiss, 1840)*
Verse 1	*Verse 1*
In Caroline, whar I was born,	De Jaw Bone hung on de kitchen wall,
I husk de wood an' I chop de corn,	Jaw Bone he is berry tall,
A roasted ear to de house I bring,	De Jaw Bone ring, Jaw Bone sing,
But de driver cotch me and he sing:	Jaw Bone tell me eberyting.
Chorus	*Chorus*
Walk jaw bone, Jenny come along,	Walk Jaw Bone wid your turkey too,
In come Sally wid de bootees on.	Neber mind dat buger bu.
Walk jaw bone, Jenny come along,	
In come Sally, wid de bootees on.	
Verse 3	*Verse 3*
Dey fasten me up under de barn,	De lute string blue it will not do,
Dey feed me dar on leaves ob corn;	I want a string to tie my shoe,
It tickled my digestion so,	A cotton [string] it will not do,
Dat I cotch de cholerophoby, oh.	A cotton string will break into [in two]
Chorus	*Chorus*

Verse 5
Next come a hungry eagle down,
Oh! gosh, thinks I dis nig's done drown,
But he winked an' cried, "I'se de bird ob
   de free,
And won't eat de meat ob slabery."

Chorus

Verse 6
Next come a weasel for my juice,
An' he gnawed till he untied me loose,
An' den I made off wid a quick alarm,
An' lef' him be widout a dram.

Chorus

Verse 7
Den down de bank I see'd a ship,
I slide down dar on de' bone ob my hip,
I crossed de drink an' yare I am,
If I go back dar, I'll be damn!

Chorus

Verse 3
As I was cum from Tennessee,
My hoss got mired up to his knee,
I whipped him till I saw de
   blood,
Den he hauled me out ob de mud.

Chorus

Verse 4
There was a little man he had a little hoss,
Went to de riber couldn't get across,
I fed my hoss in de poplar troff,
Old Cow died ob de hooppin coff.

Chorus

Verse 5
De niggers at de south dont dress berry
   well,
Day walk about and try for to cut a swell,
In de night day meet for to play,
Dance all night until de next day.

Chorus

Some of the behaviors described in "Walk Jaw Bone" did indeed occur, according to evidence Roger Abrahams gathered for his discussion of the African American style in *Singing the Master*.[65] The choice of an African American celebration as
an object of satire was inspired by the same general spirit of parody commonly
mentioned in field observations, travel narratives, and adventure stories describing the customs of different American groups. Such parodies were also created by
African Americans to ridicule the manners of their masters, that is, to signify on the
customs of the planter class. The following account of mutually reinforcing performance practices at one plantation is an especially revealing example of an African
American signifying activity: "The slaves, given entrance to the plantation mansion
and plied with food and drink, did not content themselves with effusive thanks, but
performed sly, satiric songs and skits about the lords' and ladies' behavior."[66]

The imagined role reversals and power inversions embodied in the slaves' technique of coping with the power of the slaveowner "through the act of mimicry or
some other form of grotesquerie . . . created a world of imitational possibilities that
became a part of the cultural process of breaking out" from the burdens and restrictions imposed by the culture of slavery.[67] Is the tendency to satirize differences
between blacks and whites what the early blackface performers found in African

American musical practices and converted into a vehicle for similar treatment of northern urban life? Why were the celebrations that the minstrels attributed to people in bondage so popular among the northern working class? The common element had to have been some deeply felt sense that labor as an expression of the human need for survival and compensation can have a comic side when those who control the flow of labor and the quantity of the product can have their authority questioned with impunity or maligned with irony.

Roger Abrahams assembled many testimonials from former slaves and other observers that convincingly support the argument that minstrel performers' imitations took place in a context that included some knowledge, however limited, of African American folk practices.[68] In one case a correspondent reported that "white people husk corn, negroes shuck it—wonderful difference between the two processes is there—quite as much as between a white man playing on his violin and a negro playing on his fiddle." Another observer reported,

> In all your life did you ever hear such fine voices—some as clear and strong as Kent bugles and others as soft as a German flute. . . . Hear them as the leader, in a clear strong voice, calls out.

> [Solo] Massa is in de grate house countin' out his money
>   *Chorus:* Oh, shuck dat co'n an' trow't in de ba'n,
> [Solo] Mistis in de parler eatin' bread an' honey
>   *Chorus:* Oh, shuck dat co'n an' trow't in de ba'n,
> [Solo] Sheep shell co'n by de rattle of his ho'n,
>   *Chorus:* Oh, shuck dat co'n an' trow't in de ba'n,
> [Solo] Send to de mill by de whipperwill.
>   *Chorus:* Oh, shuck dat co'n an' trow't in de ba'n.

> And then a hundred voices would ring out half a dozen times or more, repeating the chorus until the leader would call out:

> Ole Dan Tucker he got drunk,
>   *Chorus:* Fell in de fiah an' kick'd up a chunk,
> A red-hot coal get in his shoe,
> An' oh, lawd me, how de ashes flew,
> Marster and Missus look' might fine—
> Gwine to take a journey, gwine whar dey gwine,
> Crab grass a-dyin', red sun in de west,
> Saturday's comin', nigger gwine to rest.[69]

The festival recounted in the narrative dates from sometime during the 1850s. Many similar accounts are repeated over and over again in various literary genres by white authors—for example, travel books, magazine articles, and journals—and in various slave narrative collections. One traveler (1850) observed: "The rural custom of *corn husking* or *corn shucking* is peculiar to the southern States. It occurs at night, in the autumn of the year, is participated in by negroes alone, and has for its main object the husking and the gathering into barns of the yellow maize or corn."[70] These and other attestations confirm that the original sources for corn-husking songs lie within southern culture itself and include opportunities for African Americans to practice their own cultural traditions with subtleties that many white observers would almost certainly have missed.

Some minstrel companies, such as Buckley's New Orleans Serenaders, toured portions of the South and lower Midwest during the corn-shucking season and thus could have heard for themselves the singing styles of African American workers. This is one of the most contested and vilified arguments in minstrelsy studies. Nonetheless, the Buckleys' railroad trips have been documented; indeed, all the major groups followed the train tracks into the South. The denials that whites knew anything about black music in either the South or the North are narrow and myopic. Even if the minstrel companies misinterpreted what they saw and heard, they incorporated some remnants of their experience into their entertainments. The fact that contemporary cultural historians know little about the events that took place on the road, rail, and water routes before the Civil War does not mean that exchanges could not have occurred as professional and semiprofessional performers traveled throughout most of the United States.[71]

Wherever they went and whatever they saw, the blackface songwriters produced songs that mention eating corn, husking corn, and activities related to harvesting corn, cotton, tobacco, sugarcane, and a minuscule number of other agricultural products. There are at least fifteen different songs with corn in their titles—not including "Jim Crack Corn" or "Jinny Crack Corn"—the majority of which specifically describe corn husking, work in the corn fields, problems caused by eating green or unripened corn, and the pleasures of snacking on hot corn (popcorn) or other corn products.[72]

The songs about corn and tobacco are related directly to their counterparts in the plantation culture and contradict the opinion that "none of the music performed on the minstrel stage before the Civil War had any connection with the music of black slaves or freemen."[73] Given the attestations about singing, instrumental music making, and dancing at the corn-shucking or other harvest events, there must have been significant musical and social contacts between blacks and whites in many parts of the country during the preminstrel era. How those contacts manifested themselves in the practice of minstrelsy is still somewhat of a mystery because the many musical styles found in the blackface repertories seem incompatible. Simple strophic songs appear in the same context as do complicated operatic parodies, sophisticated English theater numbers are mixed with nonsense songs whose texts seem to make no sense, and sentimental tearjerkers vie with clever social satires on topical issues. However contradictory they might at first appear to be, these styles represent the range of offerings available in the new consumer-oriented urban world that cared little whether the songs that proclaimed the happy state of plantation slaves turned out to be parodies of popular Italian opera choruses, English solo songs, or imitations of those styles.

The projection of happy fraternity and community in the mock work songs carried over into the minstrels' characterization of themselves as entertainers and crowd pleasers. Songs linked the minstrel enterprise to the same type of fraternal conviviality found in "Dance, Boatman, Dance" and other songs about leisure time. These performance songs come directly from a theatrical setting rather than a mythical plantation, from blacked-up comics, not imitators of African American workers. That is the case with one of the popular versions of "Sing, Sing, Darkies, Sing" (1846), an original song composed in the style of an opera chorus.[74] In the following example, the chorus is sung before and after each of the verses to create a rounded binary design, ABA, with B designating the verse. The version in *EGB*, however, is different because it has a third phrase (c) with a different melody set for the solo voice, after which the chorus is repeated. This is an ABACA design, or a minirondo, similar to English glee or theater music. A comparison of this number with Christy's version of "Uncle Gabriel" shows how different the latter piece is in the minstrel tradition.

"Sing, Sing, Darkies, Sing" (Philadelphia: Lee and Walker, 1846)

Chorus
Sing, sing, darkies, sing,
Don't you hear the banjo ring,
Sing, sing, darkies, sing,
Sing for the white folks, sing.

Verse 1
Since music am de meat ob love,
Made by old 'Pollo from above,
De sweetest wittles ob de kine,
Am in de darkies strain divine.

Chorus

Verse 2
Dar's Dandy Jim of Caroline,
An oder airs dat's quite as fine,
Dar's Daniel Tucker, Lucy Neal,
Dat makes de frame all over feel.

Chorus

Verse 3 [from *EGB1* (1848), 16–17]
With 'lodious voice An' eber suple hand,
Come raise de noise, An' make de wool straight stand,
An' shake de bones, An' scrape de fiddle leine [*sic*],
Come twang de banjo, shake de tambourin.

Chorus

The minstrel show version is a self-reflexive parody establishing the blackface singers' stage presence in a variety show. The song titles mentioned in the second verse were staples of the minstrel repertory up to 1846, reinforcing the self-referential nature of the text because the "darkies" mentioned here were professional performers with no apparent connection to plantation life. They performed for "white folks" because the audiences in most urban centers were whites who were largely unaware of life in the South.

"Sing, Sing, Darkies, Sing" is a short (forty-measure) piece with a prelude and postlude of eight measures each (Pr–ABA–Po); the first musical and text phrases are repeated to round off the song (see music examples 11a and b). The ABA phrase structure suggests that different types of minstrel material could be based on the same musical patterns without materially affecting the style or meaning of the song. The meaning could be affected in other unpredictable ways, however, for "Sing, Sing, Darkies, Sing" appears later in an account of a corn shucking in Robert Criswell's *Uncle Tom's Cabin Contrasted with Buckingham Hall, the Planter's House; or, A Fair*

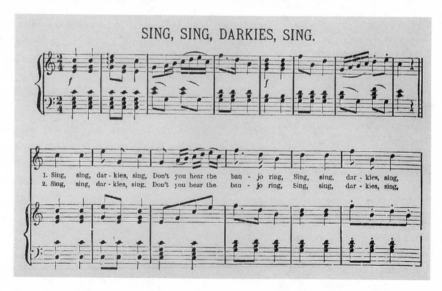

Example 11a. "Sing, Sing, Darkies, Sing," from *MSON*. Used by permission of the Pennsylvania State University Libraries.

Example 11a. (cont.)

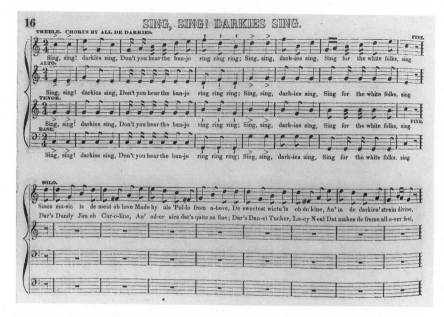

Example 11b. "Sing, Sing! Darkies, Sing," from *EGB1*. Used by permission of the Brown University Library.

View of Both Sides of the Slavery Question (1852). The example was probably imported from minstrel performances to convince readers that there was little difference between work and play.

> Around the large corn heaps were seated over two hundred men and women, (many of whom were from the neighboring plantations), tearing off the husks and throwing the ears into separate piles; and in the midst of their employment all were chattering, laughing, singing, and telling stories, much to the amusement of themselves and the young gentlemen, who were seated a little apart, observing the proceedings. . . . One of the songs ran thus:
>
> > The lubly Moon is shine so bright,
> > We doesn't want no oder light,
> > > *Chorus:* Sing, darkies, sing!
> > De man up dere, he look at us,
> > He think we make a great, big fuss,
> > > *Chorus:* Sing, darkies, sing!
> > Possum dog he cotch a coon,
> > Nigger skin him pretty soon,
> > > *Chorus:* Sing, darkies, sing![75]

The presence of dubious attestations of the transfer of texts across racial and regional boundaries—"Sing" was published in the North prior to its first appearance in the southern novel—does not refute the argument that minstrel material occasionally moved from African American culture into the primarily Anglo-American theater. But the differences among the various musical styles were also frequently recognized by contemporary observers of the American scene. David Hunter Strother, writing as Porte Crayon in "Adventures of Porte Crayon and His Cousins" (1855), noted the stylistic differences between Anglo- and African American music and observed that musical code switching—that is, the ability to play proficiently in several different styles—was already common among black performers in the 1840s and 1850s.

> The music and manner of singing were thoroughly African, and as different from the negro music of the day as from the Italian opera. The themes were humorous, gay, and sad, drawn for the most part from the incidents of plantation life, and not infrequently from the spontaneous effusions of the moment. The melodies were wild and plaintive, occasionally mingled with strange, uncouth cadences that carried the imagination forcibly to the banks of the Gambia, or to an encampment of rollicking Mandingoes.[76]

Strother's comments imply that there was a style performed by African Americans that was distinct from the conventions of minstrelsy *and* from the English/Italian melodic styles of the day. The style Strother described may not have fit with the conventions of the theater and may have required modification by blackface entertainers to fit the phrase structures and accompaniment patterns dictated by the tunings and techniques of the two melody instruments, the banjo and fiddle, in the usual minstrel ensemble. The short melodic phrases and communal responses of some African American music were imitated easily because the style encompassing those techniques was not unlike that found in other folk practices and because it fit the vigorous give-and-take style of ensembles reconstructing social rituals or communal events.

The following account of a corn shucking confirms Strother's observations and reveals what some minstrel performers knew and others could have witnessed.

> On the summit of the pile, sat a person, selected for his skill in improvisation, who gave a line in a sort of rapid chant, at the end of which the whole party joined in a chorus. The poet seemed to have no fixed object in view, but to sing. He passed from one subject to another without regard to the connection. I have retained in memory the following lines, which may serve to give some idea of their style of composition, They seldom use the sign of the possessive case:
> Oh, Jenny, gone to New-town
>   *Chorus:* Oh Jenny gone away!
> She went because she wouldn't stay,
>   *Chorus:* Oh Jenny gone away!

She run'd away, an' I know why,
Chorus: Oh, Jenny gone away![77]

The minstrels parodied the Anglo-American tradition because, as postcolonialist and sometimes nativist entertainers, they imitated the styles they enjoyed but also resisted dependence on English material. The African American materials were respected for their uniqueness as well, but the recognition of the musical creativity was controlled by a generally racist attitude toward the people whose music promised so much.

If Anglo-American styles and their Italianate relatives were the norms for a maturing musical culture, the first signs of a shift in the melodic and textual structures of theatrical songs might be expected in the "Jim Crow" and "Zip Coon" titles of the 1830s. The difference, assuming that those who created those tunes were reasonably capable musicians—something that is often doubted because of the formulaic and repetitive nature of the melodies—should manifest itself in examples that differ significantly from other music of the period. The same criteria of difference should apply to the texts that have been criticized as disjointed declamations or strings of nonsense phrases rather than logical (and comical) narratives. Many of the songs do have an internal consistency—the music remains the same, for all the songs are strophic—while the text allows disruptions of narrative continuity.

Regardless of the musical styles of the various songs discussed thus far, it is clear that early minstrel shows created an essentially male-dominated performance environment both in the subjects treated and in the control performers exerted over the treatment of class, gender, and race. The songs about male display and competitiveness reflect the contrasts in musical styles and texts among songs initially created by practical musicians whose composition and performance interests were governed by a need to establish a blackface repertory during minstrelsy's early years. As blackface entertainment developed, the number of male display songs declined, as did the overt exhibitions of male competitive behaviors. The absence of such songs is notable in the playbills of the Buckley, Campbell, Christy and Woods, and White ensembles from 1849 to 1855.

The presentation of women, when it did occur, was also totally under male control, because blackface impersonators chose the aspects of female behavior they wished to use as subjects for satire. The male display songs deal with typically masculine characteristics: male competitiveness ("Ole Bull and Dan Tucker"), achievements of tricksters and huntsmen ("Walk Along John," "Come Back Steben," and some versions of "Ole Tare River"), mock work activities or adventures relating to work ("Jolly Raftsman," "Boatman's Dance," and "Jonny Boker"), and the male displays associated with the dandy type ("Dandy Jim of Caroline" and "The Dandy Broadway Swell"). But minstrelsy's songs deal more often with women than with men, and those songs reveal how deeply blackface entertainers were committed to maintaining male prerogatives while cultivating increasingly misogynistic values in a form of entertainment long believed to have concentrated primarily on race. The following chapter addresses this issue.

6   Blackface Minstrelsy and Misogyny in Vocal and Choral Repertories

"What kind of time would the women have, were there only one man in the world?" Why, they'd resort to *arms* of course! What kind of time would they have? What is *that* to me? They might "take they're own time," every "Miss Lucy" of 'em, for all *I* should care; and so might the said man himself; for with me, the limited supply would not increase the value of the article.[1]

The minstrel theater was a gendered domain where American men acquired knowledge about women from watching depictions of gender in sketches and songs performed by cross-dressed male actors and from observing the respectable and unrespectable ladies in the audience during performances and intermission promenades. Minstrelsy was certainly not the primary educator of males in antebellum society, but its commodified images of women reinforced existing attitudes about sexuality, prostitution, courtship, marriage, gender equality, and domestic responsibility. I explore those images in this chapter, using the most frequently performed and published songs as the basis for an investigation of the ways minstrel shows embodied negative and sentimentalized attitudes about women.

For every negative stereotype of an African American male in minstrelsy, there are as many if not more stereotypes of black and white women generated as much by misogyny as by racism and all the more powerful because those images were encoded in the sentimental language of the antebellum period. Minstrelsy offered an alternative to the sentimental image of woman that Nicholas Tawa has argued took precedence over "the more masculine active concept of divinity," presenting both images simultaneously, as the playbills show. The masculine concept was replaced "with the soft-toned worship of Catholicism's Virgin Mary" in whose image American women became the "spiritual and moral ideal against which to measure the rightness and wrongness of every action."[2] Whether that hypothesis is valid or not—the United States was primarily a Protestant nation—blackface comedians controlled the delineation of women by imagining them as objects of male desire, as dominating personalities or complaining shrews, as defenseless victims of abduction or early death, and as ideal subjects for sentimental veneration.

These images of women often reinforced male homosociality and provided a protected space for homosexual performers to express aspects of their own sexuality through the double masks of race and gender.[3] These issues are new to the discussion of minstrelsy. They raise deep questions about the nature of the repertory as a mix of racist songs about African American men, serious sentimental ballads about women or children, and nonsense and topical material inspired by blackface comedians' satirical take on contemporary life. In reality, when it came to songs about women, minstrelsy dealt with a relatively limited number of subjects: (1) kidnapped spouses, wives, or lovers and the resulting disruption of the normal patterns of courtship and family life; (2) the positive and negative conceptions associated with courtship; (3) the blackface constructions of the feminine/unfeminine female, from "yaller gal" to shrew; (4) the effects of lost innocence, urban life, and early death on the mid-nineteenth-century male's conception of women as companions and nurturers; and (5) the sometimes contradictory and comic roles of women in public life or "polite" society.

These songs appeared in a variety of formats that used the same narrative styles found in the "serious" sentimental or pathetic ballads and the parodies whose special effects depended on an even greater emotional indulgence than was found in the original tearjerkers.[4] Blackface comedians also presented nonsense songs about women and wrote throwaway lines containing implicit judgments about women, as well as offering a seamier, more sexually cognizant type of song that reflected the more typical interests of the young male audience. That characteristic is represented by songs containing "reports" about sexual exploits that emphasize the boastful character of the male desire for pleasure and gender dominance, for example, "The yellow rose of Texas beats the belles of Tennessee." "Black Eye'd Susianna" (1846), "Belle of Baltimore (1848), and "I'll Throw Myself Away" (1852) introduced audiences to male fantasies about sexual freedom or the debilitating effects of passionate love. The texts of "Buffalo Gals," "Philadelphia Gals," "Boston Gals," "Charleston Gals," and a host of others invited women rhetorically to join men in the playful spirit minstrels projected from behind their burnt cork masks.

"Black Eye'd Susianna" is a particularly good example of minstrelsy's male boasting songs because it opens with a reporting formula establishing the persona as an experienced observer of women.[5] The text's conventions—the report of the persona's travels, samplings of social life, and fantasies about exotic ladies—are common to male courting songs in both the folk and popular traditions.

"Brack-Eyed Susianna" *(Philadelphia: A. Fiot, 1846)*

Verse 1 (Solo)
I been to de east,
I been to de west,
I been to Souf' Car'lina,
And ob all de gals I lub de bes,
Is my brack ey'd Susianna.

Four-Part Chorus (first part; includes instrumental breaks)
She's brack, dat's a fac,
She's brack, dat's a fac.

Four-Part Chorus (second part; repeats verse 1 melody and text)
I been to de east,
I been to de west,
I been to Souf Car'lina,
And ob all de gals I lub de bes,
Is my brack ey'd Susianna.

Verse 2 (Solo)
I courted a gal way in de wes,
Her name it was Jemima,
But I still had a feelin in my bres,
For my brack-ey'd Susianna.

Chorus

Verse 3 (Solo)
A letter to my lub I wrote
When I was in Indiana
Eb'ry sentence dat I spoke,
Was brack ey'd Susianna.
Is my brack-ey'd Susianna.

Chorus

Verse 4 (Solo)
Home I started to my lub,
Her promise to remind her,
Soon herself to me she gub,
Dat brack-ey'd Susianna.

Chorus

Verse 5 (Solo)
I lub her now wid all my heart,
My 'fections grow sublimer,
Nebber more from her I'll part,
Sweet brack-ey'd Susianna.

Chorus

Verse 3 ("Eb'ry sentence dat I spoke, / Was brack-ey'd Susianna") is similar to verse 5 of the Fiot edition of "Dandy Jim" (1844), which reads, "For ebery word in ebery line, / Was 'Dandy Jim of Caroline.'" The texts of "Belle of Baltimore" and "I'll Throw Myself Away" are also comparable, and the regional (Baltimore) and local (Broadway) references are more specific.[6]

"Belle of Baltimore" (Boston: E. H. Wade, 1848)	"I'll Throw Myself Away" (New York: William Hall and Son, 1852)
I've been through Caroline,	I've seen the beauties of the South,
I've been to Tennessee,	Likewise the East and West,
I sailed the Mississippi,	And thought this was a happy land,
For Massa set me Free.	By such dear angels blest.
I've kissed lubly Creoles,	But when I saw the New York belles,
On Louisiana's shore,	That promenade Broadway,
But I nebber found de gal to match,	I gosh I thought that I should take,
De blooming Belle of Baltimore.	And throw myself away.

The "participant persona" in these songs surveys all the women in the various regions and implies that his experience also extends to sexual intimacy. In "Black Eye'd Susianna," "feelin'" and "'fections" are acceptable demonstrations of true romantic love. In the sentimentalized discourse of the period, love is seldom characterized as anything deeper than an overpowering and disabling feeling. It causes blackface comedians to "drap right to the floor." Although, according to popular mid-nineteenth-century beliefs, a man in the throes of love's powerful emotional effects would have great difficulty controlling himself, the male suitor in "Black Eye'd Susianna" and the "Belle of Baltimore" proclaims that he will be true to his sweetheart back home because the moral code of the period assumes that fidelity is the standard. But men traveled and boasted about their exploits to other men because their sexual curiosity and profligacy were acceptable, even if they were only a fantasy captured for a blackface masquerade.[7]

The music of "Black Eye'd Susianna" is of interest because of its phrase structure: Pr–A–B–A–Po = 40 mm.; that is, the overall design is a rounded binary form A:BA, the last two phrases (B–A) in the sheet music arrangement being set in four-part harmony. The other version from *BBI* is set for solo voice with banjo accompaniment but concludes with the same chorus (see music example 12). The first phrase (A) serves the double burden of providing music for the verse and for its repeat after the seven-bar chorus (B). The accompaniment patterns illustrate the easy way in which the octave jumps are handled on the banjo and why that accompaniment is idiomatic for that instrument. The suggested tuning of the Briggs banjo (D–G–D–F♯–A), where the first D is the short fifth string and G is the bass or fourth string, makes the performance in the key of G major rather easy. The triplet pat-

2	4
I courted a gall away in de Wes',	Home I started to my lub,
Her name it was Jemima,	Her promise to remind her,
But I still had a feelin' in my bres,	Soon herself to me she gub,
For my brack-ey'd Susianna.	Dat brack-ey'd Susianna.
I been to de East, &c.	I been to de East, &c.
3	5
A letter to my lub I wrote,	I lub her now wid all my heart,
When I was in Indiana,	My 'fections grow sublimer,
Eb'ry sentence dat I spoke	Nebber more from her I'll part,
Was brack-ey'd Susianna.	Sweet brack-ey'd Susianna.
I been to de East, &c.	I been to de East, &c.

Example 12. "Black Eye'd Susianna" with banjo accompaniment, from *Briggs' Banjo Instructor*. Used by permission of Tuckahoe Music.

tern, which integrates the downstroke of the index finger and the thumb pull on the fifth string, can be executed by placing the first finger of the left hand on the F♯ string (second) and the second finger on the A string. The alternation of the arpeggiated G and D chords is then easily accomplished. The stopped strings produce G and B, and the others sound D-G-D. The D-major arpeggio lies naturally on the open strings. The double stops beginning in measure 13 are played just as the separate notes were earlier. The rolled chords in the chorus are played "by the first finger alone, which is done by sliding the finger rapidly over the strings, beginning with the lowest note" (*BBI*, 9). All this is accomplished while playing in the first position or, in the case of a fretted banjo, in the first and second frets. The only contrast in the overall rhythmic flow of the song is in the first part of the chorus (B), with its emphasis on the "She's brack, dat's a fac" line, which reiterates the suggestion that love (at least in this context) transcends the color line. The piano arrangement, probably created by a house arranger, captures something of banjo style in the combination of broken chord and repeated note patterns that do *not* double the four-part setting. But the point of presenting this brief technical description is to show that the melody was idiomatically conceived for the banjo even though the banjo part serves as an accompaniment for a solo song.

Songs were the primary vehicles for constructing and representing gender on the minstrel stage. The most frequently performed and published sentimental songs fall into the somewhat predictable types popular in the United States during the antebellum era, that is, songs based on themes "about home, loved ones, the beloved, adversities of adult life, death, and the hope of an afterlife."[8] Although those subjects called for the vocabulary of symbols required to sustain the emotional and spiritual life of the American popular culture community, minstrelsy's portraits of women used another, darker, and much more complicated lexicon. Here is where male audiences found allusions to the sexual freedom available to the burgeoning populations of major urban centers and the breakdown of the traditional kinfolk relationships that provided the normal communal environment for dating and courtship.

Men on the make were often referred to as "dandies," but women inhabiting or passing through public spaces were "gals," whose behaviors in their new social environments encouraged more open liaisons. The "social profiles of prostitutes" in antebellum New York shows them to have been not the "demimondes listed in the gentleman's guide to elegant brothels, but . . . women who had to ply their trade in public places," among which were the theatrical districts of major cities.[9] Songs about women "whose feet took up the whole sidewalk" usually took the name of a city or a section known for free associations among men and women, hence the number of songs about "Buffalo gals" or "Bowery gals."

The tune of "Buffalo Gals" was a musical parody of Cool White's popular "Lubly Fan Won't You Come Out Tonight" (1844), which Samuel Foster Damon described as "evidently the long-lost original of 'Bowery Gals.'" Damon also noted that "the girls in the [minstrel show] audience were an excellent substitute for Lubly Fan; and the minstrel companies invited the New York Gals, or the Philadelphia Gals, or the gals of whatever city they were performing in, to come out and dance by the light of the moon." The Christy Minstrels, who were originally from Buffalo, included "Bowery Gals" in their shows and listed it among their songs on sheet music covers as early as 1847. The Ethiopian Serenaders performed the song in their pre-1848 programs and copyrighted their version in 1848 but never identified any composer.[10]

"Buffalo Gals" has sometimes been considered a folk tune because the melody exists in the oral tradition, but it was published in 1848 as a minstrel song. It was already well known in Mobile in 1846, where a woman who had once been "'a flower, innocent and beautiful but long since torn from its stem, trampled, soiled and desecrated[,]' was arrested for drunkenly singing 'Mobile Gals, Won't You Come Out Tonight?' on the streets."[11] If this story was reported correctly, the possibility that "Lubly Fan" had traveled south by 1846 and picked up lyrics associated with fallen and exploited women fits with the social contexts that I am suggesting are the most appropriate for the song.

Most references to "Buffalo Gals" confirm that the song and its variants did not appear often on period playbills after 1847, about the time the various minstrel companies began to emphasize their respectability and the elimination of all vulgarity from their shows. Why did the practice of enticing the ladies of the audience to "dance by the light of the moon" stop? Why did one of minstrelsy's potentially hit songs apparently disappear from most playbill collections in the late 1840s? Some of the answers lie in the texts of the various "gal" songs themselves; others emerge only from the contexts in which they were performed. Samples of each of the texts in question follow.

"Buffalo Gals" (1848; text from Heart Songs *[1909], 366)*

Verse 1
As I went lumbrin' down de street,
Down de street, down de street,
A lubly [pretty colored] gal I chanc'd to meet,
Oh! she was fair to view.

Chorus
Oh! Buffalo gals, will ye come out tonight.
Will ye come out tonight, will ye come out tonight,
Buffalo gals, will ye come out tonight,
And dance by de light of de moon.

Verse 2
I ax'd her if she'd hab some talk,
Hab some talk, hab some talk,
Her feet cover'd up de whole side walk,
As she stood side by me.

Chorus

Verse 3
I'd like to make dat gal my wife,
Gal my wife, gal my wife,
I would be happy all my life,
If I had her by my side.

Chorus

"Original New York Gals" (from NSO1, 72)

Verse 1
I is come from Baltimore,
To see de sights dat can be saw,
But nothing makes my bosom swell,
Like de sight at dese New York gals.

Verse 2
As I was going down de street,
A handsome gal I chanced to meet,
We stopt awhile and had some talk,
And her heel covered up de hul sidewalk.

Verse 3
We went down to an oyster cellar,
Setting by a stove a talking to a feller,
A gal come in to get a shilling stew,
And her foot was so big she couldn't wear a shoe.

Verse 4
And she went out with her silk and satins,
Turned up hat and short-legg'd mittens
And for de want of nature's mussell [*sic*],
Wore a double-breasted bustle.

"Charleston Gals" (from CAW1, 54)

Verse 1
I'm a nigger from de Souf,
I come from dare in time ob de drouf,
Times so hard in dat dare place,
De nigger dare not show his face.

Chorus
Hi, ho de Charleston gals,
Hi, ho de Charleston gals,
Dey am so high, dey am so low,
Dey git no money for to come to de show.

Verse 2
When I got in I took my seat,
A Charleston gal axed me to treat,
She found it no go, an gin a frown,
Dat's de way wid de gals in Charleston town.

Chorus

"New York Gals" (from CWS1)

Chorus
New York gals, pretty faces,
Dress'd to death and trimm'd with laces,
Ankles small and waists so slender,
Ha, ha, ha, goodbye John.

The "Buffalo Gals" or "Lubly Fan" melody is probably the source tune used for most of the texts quoted, although "De Boatman's Dance" may have been used for "Charleston Gals" since the latter's text does not fit "Lubly Fan" very well. But what does the title mean? "Buffalo Gals" and the other "gals" songs are not harmless nonsense numbers. They are not to be read just as humorous invitations to the women in the audience. The word *buffalo* had some specific meanings, and its appearance in the title of this song is not mere chance.[12] *Buffalo* sometimes referred to black women, just as *yaller gals* also identified women of mixed race.

The term *yellow* or *yaller* was common for men *and* women born of African American and white parents. *Yellow* applied to young people of both sexes in New York City, as is shown in George Foster's comments about Pete Williams, Esq. (in *New York by Gas-Light*), "a middle-aged, well-to-do, coal-black negro, who had made an immense amount of money from the profits of his dance-house." Williams "glories in being a bachelor—although there are something under a dozen 'yellow-boys' in the neighborhood who have a very strong resemblance to Pete, and for whom he appears to entertain a particular fondness—frequently supplying them with sucks of candy, penny worths of peanuts, and other similar luxuries for the most part enjoyed only in dreams by the juvenile population of the Points."[13] "Yaller gals" are mentioned often in minstrel songs as desirable sexual partners. Much is left unsaid in the texts, especially since the official records show foreign-born prostitutes in Boston, New York, and Philadelphia outnumbering native-born ones, although immigrants were a minority of the total population.[14]

The references to "yaller gals" in minstrelsy are interesting because seldom do the blackface songs refer to black, brown, or mulatto women in terms of behaviors, attitudes, knowledge, or experience seen from the woman's point of view.[15] The tragic octoroon, who was not necessarily referred to as "yellow," was a convention in novels of the period, for example, Joseph Holt Ingraham's *Quadroon* (1841), Henry Wadsworth Longfellow's "Quadroon Girl" (1842), Mrs. E. D. E. N. South-worth's *Retribution* (1849), Harriet Beecher Stowe's *Uncle Tom's Cabin* (1852), and William Wells Brown's *Clotel; or The President's Daughter* (1853). The same tendencies are found in Dion Boucicault's melodrama *The Octoroon* (1859), which shares a similar function with novels, for the purpose of all the examples was "to arouse pity for the oppressed slave: the flogging, the separation of families, the cruelty of ruthless traders, the squalor and misery of the slave huts that contrasted so sharply from the gaiety and luxury of the 'big house' were all stock elements of this genre."[16]

The context for the "gal" songs of the period was the world of single working women, including those driven to prostitution, which "by midcentury made New York the carnal showcase of the Western world for native-born Americans and foreign visitors alike."[17] Reformers and respectable persons lamented that "houses of prostitution proliferated throughout the city" and that "there were sexual service stations even in middle-class and elite neighborhoods."[18] Whether the young single women were known as Broadway "gals" or "Bowery g'hals," these "young women, who took their name from that street, . . . were fluent in the language of street sociability. They had their own way of perambulating through the crowds, a distinctively brisk and bouncing gait."[19] Identified also by their overt behaviors, these young women, ranging in age from twelve to forty, "could be identified by the ankle-length skirts, bright-colored clothing, and painted faces—all fashions shunned by respectable women."[20] Single men and women found Broadway between Spring and Canal Streets the "axis" of a "new entertainment and sex district" that housed Christy's Mechanics Hall (now occupied by the Bryant brothers), Fellow's Opera House (featuring Campbell's Minstrels) in Mitchell's Olympic Theater, and Wood's Marble Hall.[21] On these streets and those of other antebellum cities, the "comings and goings of women in the walking city were marked by class and sexual distinctions more than those of gender. While wives and daughters of the elite were singled out for patriarchal protection, escorted through the streets by their kinsmen, poor and unprotected women were likely to be sexual prey of upper-class dandies" as well as working toughs and street gangs.[22]

The men referred to earlier as "dandies" in the discussion of "Dandy Jim of Caroline" could stroll down the streets of the Bowery and meet pretty "gals" of many hues "because antebellum New York had few parks and little public space," and the "broad thoroughfares and small, open squares functioned like the formal malls and parade grounds in major European cities. Each provided an open, public space for men to meet prostitutes or prospective lovers."[23] In those public spaces, especially in the Bowery, these women "wore bright-colored clothing that accentuated their figures," walked with a "swing of mischief and defiance," and "met at ice-cream parlors, dance halls, or at the Bowery Theater, apart from the watchful eyes of kin." The Bowery Theater "was nationally known for its sexual excursions from propriety"; both men and women could be observed there "in strange and indecent positions in the lobbies, and sometimes in the boxes."[24] The aggressiveness of some of the young women was captured in the phrase "her feet covered up the whole sidewalk," an expression that referred euphemistically to sexual commerce in urban locations such as the Bowery. That is the appropriate context for "Bowery Gals" "as sung by W. [William] B. Donaldson, the celebrated Jawbone player."

Verse 3
I'd like to kiss dem lubly lips,
Dem lubly lips, dem lubly lips,
I think dat I could loose my wits,
And drap right on de floor.

Chorus

Verse 5
I danc'd all night and my heel kept a rocking,
O my heel kept a rocking,
O my heel kept a rocking,
And I balance to de gal,
Wid a hole in her stocking,
She was de prettiest gal in de room.

Chorus

These songs refer to the active social life available to young persons of both sexes in the changing cities. In New York, where most of these songs were performed for the first time, theaters existed in an environment that included a number of attractions. Brothels were often located adjacent to theaters—Palmo's and the Park Theater, for example—and dance halls, where "men could entertain themselves at clubs that offered *tableaux vivants* [the statue dances often mentioned on minstrel playbills], forerunners of the strip show." One establishment in the theater and minstrel hall district seems especially noteworthy. "The Melodeon, a 'concert saloon,' on Broadway in New York City featured 'waiter girls' in short-skirted theatrical costumes who performed 'Gaities,' served drinks, and sometimes joined customers at their tables."[25]

The interpretation of "Buffalo Gals" and its variants becomes complicated once its social contexts are explored, but the musical qualities are less complex. The verse and chorus are virtually the same melodically and harmonically with the exception of a few divided beats required to carry text. The syncopations in the first phrase of the chorus shift the rhythmic emphasis on the following italicized words: "won't you *come out* tonight, won't you *come out* tonight." The syncopations, brief though they are, were one of the notable characteristics of blackface songs since Dan Emmett's "Old Dan Tucker."

The most commonly printed "Buffalo Gals" melody is built from arpeggiated major triads spelling out sequences of thirds (see music example 13a). Such sequences also provide the vocabulary for typical harmonizations of the melody in thirds and sixths over a static bass line using only the roots of the tonic and dominant seventh chords. The series of interlocking thirds are directly related to the tonic and dominant seventh harmonies on which the melody is built, as shown in music example 13b. The melodic phrases of the verse are shown in the first, single staff; the brace below reveals the tertian formulas and the underlying harmonic structure of the song. Although the melody certainly allows for the harmonization of the third (C-E) with the subdominant triad, the arranger used only the tonic (I) and the dominant seventh (V^7) to support the melody.

The melody of "Buffalo Gals" also uses a typical cadential formula that avoids the third of the key or mode; that is, the melody at the end of the verse is 8–7–5–4–7–1, and the ending phrase of the chorus is 8–7–5–4–2–1. These melodic cadential formulas are also characteristic of some period banjo tunes, for example, "Black Eye'd Susianna" (5–4–2–1), suggesting connections with the earlier melodies published or performed by Joel Sweeney. The simplicity of "Buffalo Gals" is consistent with the requirements for a stage performance. The differences between the published version of the 1840s and those sung today reflect a further refinement of the tune through oral transmission.

Reports on the social life of young males in New York and other majors cities suggest that some of the young dandies "lumberin' down the street" were likely to meet ladies who were "magnificently attired with their large arms and voluptuous bosoms half naked, and their bright eyes looking invitingly at every passer-by hailing 'How do you do, my dear? Come, won't you come home with me.'" When the young gents went out for the afternoon or evening, they entered the same locations featured in minstrel sketches and songs: cheap theaters, masked balls, oyster cellars, grog shops, concert saloons, and brothels. The last mentioned were places, in the words of one contemporary critic, "whose specialized function was to permit dangerous women to entrap vulnerable men" and that in New York alone employed some 17,000 women in 3,000 establishments.[26] In 1858 Dr. William Sanger estimated "that there were six thousand prostitutes, or one for every sixty-four men, in New York City,"[27] his statistical report being published when minstrelsy emphasized sentimental songs, basket horse acts, opera burlesques, and Ethiopian sketches.

Minstrel songs seldom dealt with the outcomes of the freer relationships between the sexes during the antebellum period. But the working class apparently "joked openly about the flirtations of unmarried men and women, even as reticence in-

BUFFALO GALS.

Example 13a. Common version of "Buffalo Gals," from *MSON*. Used by permission of the Pennsylvania State University Libraries.

Example 13a. (cont.)

G: I   V⁷   I   V⁷   I   I   V⁷   I   V⁷   I

Example 13b. Underlying harmonic structure and tertian melodic formulas in "Buffalo Gals."

creasingly characterized middle-class sexual etiquette."[28] Against lusty, demonstrative, and single "Buffalo gals" and "Bowery gals," minstrelsy juxtaposed the chaste and properly fashioned models from *Godey's Lady's Book,* who then became targets of burnt cork burlesque when cross-dressed men appeared in elaborate caricatures of women's fashions.[29] "Gals" (or "g'hals") were also the subjects of significant interest among the readers of pulp novels such as Ned Buntline's *Mysteries and Miseries of New York* (1848) and *G'hals of New York* (1850) and George Thompson's *G'hals of Boston* (1850).[30] Given the public interest in "gals" generally, the minstrel songs about "yaller gals" assume greater significance for several reasons.

In the first place, the idea that learning about sex was distinct from understanding romantic love was not just a class-bound male fancy. Prostitution was accepted as a legitimate form of premarital sexual "learning," but "the emphasis on speedy orgasm, the lack of emotional connection, and the absence of any expectation of mutuality made commercialized sex a poor training ground for middle-class bridegrooms."[31] Second, the songs in question serve to indicate male conceptions of the public roles of women. Married and unmarried women's social lives and opportunities for public activity were circumscribed by custom and by law in what Mary Ryan described as the "social geography of the big city"; that is, they were limited to the areas where unescorted women would not be accosted by young men or where sexual solicitation was unlikely to occur.[32] Songs containing direct references or indirect allusions to the sexual marketplaces of American cities are only one of the subject areas in a relatively underinvestigated aspect of the minstrel song repertory. Examples containing sexual allusions and encouraging free associations with women seem to recede as minstrelsy changed and emphasized the respectability of its presentations during the 1849–54 and 1855–60 periods of its development.

The minstrel show had its share of serious songs on sentimental themes, especially when it dealt with abductions or deaths of children, sweethearts, and wives. Two of minstrelsy's most popular songs, "Mary Blane" and "The Virginia Rose Bud" (sometimes known as "We Hear the Hoofs"), deal with one of the Victorian era's most persistent themes, namely, the "pattern of the distressed female in apparent need of rescue by a resourceful male."[33] Two of the other most frequently performed songs, "Lucy Neal" and "Lucy Long," explore marriage and courtship, the sexual freedom of males both inside and outside marriage, the status of women in apparently affectionate relationships, and—in those situations when "Lucy Long" was presented "in character"—the cross-dressed male as an object of desire.

Blackface comedians composed and presented original songs and parodies based on (1) sentimental tales of sold or abducted female children, fiancees, or lovers; (2) nostalgia for lost loves; (3) youthful sexual exploits or the types of courting behaviors commonly discussed among single men; (3) negative aspects of marriage or the consequences of extramarital relationships; (4) observations about women's dress and the differences between the sexes; and (5) typical behaviors of both genders at mixed-sex social events such as dances, cotillions, and wedding celebrations.

The preceding thematic summaries are based on the appearance of specific songs and their variants on period playbills and in the minstrel songsters published before the Civil War. The biggest hits were "Mary Blane," "Lucy Neal," and "Lucy Long"; in the case of "Mary Blane," there were variant texts and completely different tunes. The list includes several other representative songs that mention women in their texts but not in their titles, for example, "De Boatman's Dance," "Stop Dat Knocking," and "Camptown Races." Songs dealing with masculine exploits, such as "Old Tare River," "Old Dan Tucker," and "De Old Jaw Bone," generally ignore women altogether, reinforcing the gender roles presented in minstrelsy, where women are much more restricted in their behaviors than are their counterparts in the "roarer" traditions of Davy Crockett and Mike Fink. The most popular example in songster, playbill, and sheet music editions is "Mary Blane" and its many variants, most of them of the sentimental and pathetic type based on the same kidnapping or captivity themes found in period melodramas, novels, and operas.

Most of the "Mary Blane" texts foreground two of minstrelsy's most common conceptions of gender roles, namely, the woman as a silent (and silenced) victim or object and the man as the pathetic subject lamenting "his" loss in a highly sentimentalized expression of grief. The same sentimentality envelopes the separation of children from their fathers in "The Virginia Rose Bud," a title that appears less often in the songsters because, like the "Phantom Chorus" or "Dinah's Wedding Day," its performance was more complex than that of a straightforward strophic song.[34]

The "Mary Blane" songs were not only the most popular of all the blackface laments about the loss of a lover but also the examples with the greatest variety of comic texts. That observation explains how minstrelsy's ambivalence about subjects usually worked. Individual minstrel companies and composers chose the material they wanted to perform, material that reflected their particular attitudes or allowed them to play to their own performance strengths. The "ambivalence" results from the aggregation of the many different meanings of the various texts and represents the range of opinions likely in a popular culture patronized by very different audiences.

Which version of the song was best known? Which example can be considered representative enough to be worth the labor of interpretation? In most cases, it is virtually impossible to determine whether a particular ensemble performed the text attributed to it in the songsters or noted on sheet music covers.[35] The texts themselves were not stable—there are at least five different versions of "Mary Blane." Some verses cannot be taken literally because they have migrated from one example in the cycle to another, and others are stock lines that appear in a large number of entirely different songs and constitute the lingua franca of the antebellum popular song.

On the other hand, the presence of omnibus or nonsense verses in the "Mary Blane" songs should not hinder attempts to interpret the meanings of the various examples. Popular music often depends on conventions and stock expressions for its effects. Most country songs written in the last three decades use the same expressions, repackage the same stock phrases, and still lose none of their effectiveness, for they repeat the emotionalized vocabulary that audiences expect. So-called nonsense verses may appear to make little sense when they are read, but their function was sometimes to fill time on stage while the meaning was expressed by physical movement or stage business. In addition, nonsense verses should not be dismissed as meaningless when it can be shown that their purpose is to disrupt logical discourse or juxtapose unlikely chains of ideas for comic effect.[36]

The musical texts of "Mary Blane" are based on only two different melodies, which I have labeled "A" and "B."[37] Most A versions are thirty-six to forty measures long (Pr–A–B–C [3pt. chorus]–Po), the total number of measures depending on the lengths of the preludes or postludes. The other tune (melody B) is the source for at least two variants, the first in *EGB1* (1848 and 1850) and the second in *Briggs' Banjo Instructor* (1855), but its appearance in those two sources does not necessarily mean that that version was the most popular in the antebellum shows. (See music examples 14a–d.)

Example 14a. "Mary Blane" no. 1, melody A, in G major (New York: Firth and Hall, 1847). Used by permission of the Brown University Library.

Example 14a. (cont.)

2

While in de woods I go at night
A hunting for some game
A nigger came to my old hut
And stole my Mary Blane
Long times gwan by it griebᵈ me much
To tink no tidings came
I hunt de woods both night and day
To find poor Mary Blane.
CHORUS.

3

I often askᵈ for Mary Blane
My Massa he did scold
And said you saucy nigger boy
If you must know she's sold
If dats de case she cannot live
Thro'—out a weary life
Oh let me die and lay me by
My poor heart broken wife.
CHORUS.

4228

T. Halliday.

Example 14a. (cont.)

MARY BLANE.

SONG.

Example 14b. "Mary Blane" no. 3, melody B, in A major (New York: William VanDerbeek, 1847). The author gratefully acknowledges the permission to reproduce minstrel songs from the Sheet Music Collection of the Free Library of Philadelphia.

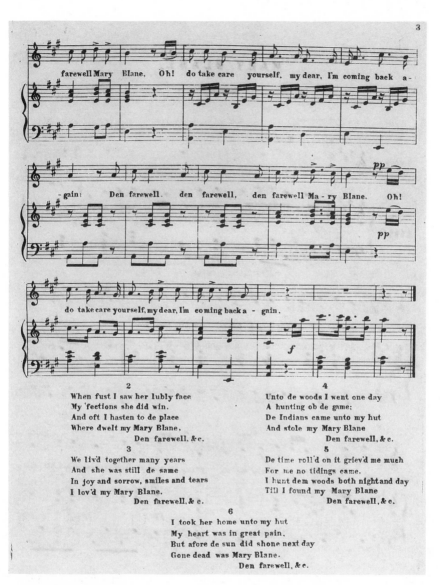

farewell Mary Blane, Oh! do take care yourself, my dear, I'm coming back a-

-gain: Den farewell. den farewell, den farewell Ma - ry Blane. Oh!

do take care yourself, my dear, I'm coming back a - gain.

2
When fust I saw her lubly face
My 'fections she did win.
And oft I hasten to de place
Where dwelt my Mary Blane,
  Den farewell, &c.

3
We liv'd together many years
And she was still de same
In joy and sorrow, smiles and tears
I lov'd my Mary Blane.
  Den farewell, &c.

4
Unto de woods I went one day
A hunting ob de game;
De Indians came unto my hut
And stole my Mary Blane
  Den farewell, &c.

5
De time roll'd on it griev'd me much
For me no tidings came.
I hunt dem woods both night and day
Till I found my Mary Blane
  Den farewell, &c.

6
I took her home unto my hut
My heart was in great pain,
But afore de sun did shone next day
Gone dead was Mary Blane.
  Den farewell, &c.

Example 14b. (cont.)

Example 14c. "Mary Blane," melody B, in F major, from *EGB1*. Used by permission of the Brown University Library.

Example 14d. "Mary Blane," melody A, in G major, from *Briggs' Banjo Instructor*. Used by permission of Tuckahoe Music.

"Mary Blane" (Melody A) No. 1 (1847) and No. 2 (1848[?])

"Mary Blane" No. 1
Words by F. C. German; Arr. by J. H.
* Howard (New York: Firth and Hall, 1847)*

"Mary Blane" No. 2 ("The New Mary
* Blane")*
Words by W. Guernsey; Music by George
* Barker (Boston: Ditson, 1848[?])*

Verse 1
I once did know a pretty Gal,
And took her for my wife
She came from Louisiana,
And I lik'd her as my life.
We happy lib'd togethder
She nebber caus'd me pain,
But on one dark and dreary night
I lost poor Mary Blane.

Verse 1
I once did lub a pretty gal,
I lub'd her as my life,
She came from Lousiana,
And I made her my dear wife;
At home we lib'd so happy,
Oh free from grief or pain,
But in de winter time of year,
I lost my Mary Blane.

Chorus (Three Part)
Oh, Farewell, Farewell poor Mary Blane
One Faithful heart will think of you
Farewell, Farewell poor Mary Blane
If we ne'er meet again.

Chorus (Four Part)
Oh fare dee well poor Mary Blane,
One feeling heart bids you adieu,
Oh fare dee well my Mary Blane,
We'll nebber meet again.

Verse 2
While in de woods I go at night,
A hunting for some game,
A nigger come to my old hut,
And stole my Mary Blane.
Long times gwan by it grieb'd me much,
To tink no tidings came
I hunt de woods both night and day,
To find poor Mary Blane.

Verse 2
I went into de woods one day,
To hunt among de cane,
De white man come into my house,
And took poor Mary Blane;
It grieb me berry much to tink,
No hope I entertain,
Of ever seeing my dear gal,
My poor Mary Blane.

Chorus

Chorus

Verse 3
I often ask'd for Mary Blane,
My Massa he did scold,
And said you saucy nigger boy,
If you must know she's sold.
If dats de case she cannot live
Thro'out a weary life,
Oh let me die and lay me by
My poor heart broken wife.

Verse 3
When toiling in de cotton field,
I cry and say goodbye,
Unto my broder comrades,
Dat oh soon, oh soon, I die;
My poor wife gone I cannot lif
Amidst dis world of pain,
But lay me in de grabe,
To find out my poor Mary Blane.

Chorus

Chorus

"Mary Blane" (Melody B) No. 3 (New York: William VanDerbeek, 1848) and No. 4 (EGBI, 33–34)[38]

VanDerbeek Edition

Verse 1
I once did love a yallow gal,
I'll tell you all her name,
She came from Old Virginia, and
They call her Mary Blane.

Chorus
Den farewell, den farewell, den farewell
Mary Blane,
Oh! do take care yourself my dear,
I'm coming back again. [Repeated.]

Verse 2
When fust I saw her lubly face,
My 'fections she did win,
And oft I hasten to de place,
Where dwelt my Mary Blane.

Chorus

Verse 3
We liv'd together many years,
And she was still de same
In joy and sorrow, smiles and tears,
I lov'd my Mary Blane

Chorus

Verse 4
Unto de woods I went one day,
A hunting ob de game;
De Indians came unto my hut,
And stole my Mary Blane.

Chorus

Verse 5
De time roll'd on it griev'd me much
For me no tidings came,
I hunt dem woods both night and day,
Till I found my Mary Blane

Chorus

Version from EGB1

Verse 1 (Solo)
I once did love a yellow gal,
I'll tell you what's her name;
She came from old Virginia,
And they call her Mary Blane.

Chorus (Four Part)
Den farewell, den farewell, den farewell
Mary Blane,
O do take care yourself my dear,
I'm coming back again.

Verse 2 (Solo)
They've sung of charming Lucy Neale,
They've sung of pretty Jane,
But I will sing of one more fair,
My own sweet Mary Blane.

Chorus

Verse 3 (Solo)
Saint Louis boasts of pretty girls,
But Oh! 'tis all in vain,
They have no gal that fills my eye,
As does my Mary Blane.

Chorus

Verse 4 (Solo)
We lived together many years,
And she was still the same;
In joy and sorrow, smiles and tears,
I loved my Mary Blane.

Chorus

Verse 5 (Solo)
I was taken very sick one day,
It give my Mary pain;
Oh! den I learn'd how kind she was,
My own sweet Mary Blane.

Chorus

Verse 6
I took her home unto my hut,
My heart was in great pain,
But afore de sun did shone next day
Gone dead was Mary Blane.

Chorus

Verse 6 (Solo)
The doctor gave me medicine,
But said 'twas all in vain;
He said that I must surely die,
And leave my Mary Blane.

Chorus

Verse 7 (Solo)
Oh! Mary, now before we part,
Come smile on me again;
'Tis you can ease this dying heart,
My own sweet Mary Blane.

Chorus

Most "Mary Blane" songs assume that the couple are husband and wife or that they lived together long enough for their union to be sanctioned by society and common law.[39] The text defines the couple's relationship by emphasizing the male's romantic and protective role: Mary is the victim. Most of the serious "Mary Blane" songs move from the happiness of the courtship or living circumstances to the loss of the wife, from the causes of their separation to its results in personal lamentation or morose self-indulgence, and finally from confusion about the entire situation to a resolution with the return of the victim or the discovery of the woman's death.

These texts and their musical accompaniments are sentimental songs; it is difficult to conceive how any of these versions could be performed to contradict that classification, although performance practices for the "Mary Blane" songs are still somewhat of a mystery. The narrators in both "Mary Blane" versions, A and B, describe their fruitless searches for their loved ones. The pathetic husband in "Mary Blane" would rather die—the melodramatic flair is worthy of note—than deal with the separation. The song could be overplayed, but the singer would have to overact so that the deeper sentiments of loss would be replaced by awareness that the whole pathetic framework could be rendered absurd by excessive self-indulgence.

The textual variants may be regional or local versions of the song aimed at specific audiences and reflecting the differences among the various minstrel groups. There are some variations in the identities of the kidnappers and some bitter statements about the "rescue" activities of some abolitionists, but all the examples emphasize the kidnapping theme.

"Mary Blane" No. 5 (NSO1, 119)
"Composed and sung by Charles White"

"Mary Blane" No. 6 (NSO1, 201)

Verse 1
When first I fell in love wid her,
Her 'fections I did gain,
I courted her for seben years,
Before she was Mrs. Blane.

Verse 1
I once did lub a yaller gal,
I'll tell you all her name,
She came from Old Virginia,
An dey called her Mary Blane.

Verse 2
De niggars all went out one night,
A hunting for dar game,
Dey den come to my peaceful hut,
And stole poor Mary Blane.

Verse 2
I went out hunting one fine night,
Arter coon and game,
When de Abolitionist came to de house,
And stole my Mary Blane.

Verse 3
I found my lub tied to a tree,
She was in berry great pain,
De niggars had tarr'd and feadered her,
And so left Mary Blane.

Verse 3
Dey took her on board a ship,
De Nancy was her name,
'Twas about persimmon time,
When I lost my Mary Blane.

Verse 4
I den did take my lub strait home,
To relieve her from her pain,
But afore de sun did shine next day,
Stiff and cold was Mary Blane.

Verse 4
De time rolled by it grieved me some,
To think no tiding came,
So I started off for Boston town,
To find my Mary Blane.

Verse 5
I found my love in prison,
She was in berry great pain,
Dey didn't gib her anything to eat,
Case she wouldn't tell her name.

Verse 6
I went up to the squire's house,
He axed me what's my name,
Den he gib me a warrant,
For to get my Mary Blane.

White's "Mary Blane" no. 5 text treats the Mary Blane character to great indignities that eventually lead to her death at the hands of renegades. The second parody ("Mary Blane" no. 6) tells an antiabolitionist story in which northern "liberators" steal a man's wife and create the same type of family disruption attributed to the slave dealers of the South. The different versions of "Mary Blane" reveal the variety of ways that minstrel composers, performers, and audiences approached the public presentation of ideas about personal relationships, social activism (the treatment of the abolitionists' actions), and criminal acts against women. The women or children in these songs are twice victims. First, they are kidnapped, lost, or abandoned. Second, minstrelsy's blackface singers provided no voice for the woman to sing or speak of *her* suffering, in part because "women of the time raised no objection to the male-orientation in most lyrics to songs. The question of gender-usage had not yet arisen, and it remained a widely accepted convention."[40]

The texts of three of the "Mary Blane" songs focus attention on the feelings of the male narrator rather than on the experience of the kidnap victim.[41] One variant, however, emphasizes the male character's decision to run away rather than accept his master's decision of a forced removal to a different state. The song's theme is still *separation,* but the story focuses on the male's actions and his pledge of fidelity to his companion.

"Mary Blain" (Melody B) No. 7 (GEM2, 208)

Verse 1
When niggers meet it's a pleasure,
But when they part it's pain,
I can't forget, oh never,
My lovely Mary Blain.

Chorus
Den farewell, farewell,
Farewell, poor Mary Blain
Do take care of yourself my dear
I'se coming back again.

Verse 2
One morning I lay snoring,
Ole Master says to me,
Sam get up I'se going,
To take you to Tennessee.

Chorus

Verse 3
I cotch our horse old Barley,
So nice I comb his main,
I heard somebody call me,
'Twas lovely Mary Blain.

Chorus

Verse 4

Now, Mary, I'se going to leave you,
Now Mary don't complain.
I never will deceive you
For I'se coming back again.

Chorus

The farewell choruses echo themes of parting that embodied the same sentimental view of life found in blackface and vernacular entertainment. There are few songs about found victims or resolved kidnappings, however, because the convention dwells on the *hope* that the relationships will be restored and the more realistic (and commercially viable) view that such reunions seldom if ever occur. The genre simply does not tolerate happy endings. Songs about life in the home after reunion are also relatively rare. The "home songs," for example, "My Old Kentucky Home" (1853) or "Old Folks at Home" (1851), belong to a different convention involving nostalgia for a place, parents (usually a mother), and childhood memories or longing for a blissful refuge from urban life.

The most sentimental example is a "new version" of "Mary Blane" newly constituted as a "pathetic" tomb song. The songster (*ESB1*) does not indicate which tune was used for this version, but it scans best with the Guernsey and Barker version (melody A).

"Mary Blane" No. 8 (ESB1, 33–34)

Verse 2

I've nothing left to live for now,
I weary of my life;
Then take and lay me gently by,
My poor heart-broken wife.
I wander sadly through the world,
But find my sorrow's vain;
These tears can never bring to me,
My darling Mary Blane.

Verse 3

I buried her at dead of night,
'Neath de persimmon tree;
De snow was falling thick and white,
On her dear grave and me.
And often since in dreams I see,
Her well-known form again,
As when I laid her in de grave,
And wept o'er Mary Blane.

Verse 4
Then raise no tomb-stone on de place,
But lay me by her side,
The best, the kindest of her race—
My faithful constant bride.
I'm ready now to leave this life,
To join her once again;
Beneath the old persimmon tree,
Where sleeps my Mary Blane.

The "separated lovers" theme of the "Mary Blane" song cycle is also found in most versions of "Lucy Neal," a number that usually features a female beloved who is sold by a wicked master. The theme of the enslaved woman as victim is closely linked to the pro-abolitionist novels of the period. The abduction or forced separation represents the action of oppressors concerned with exercising dictatorial control over their employees and slaves. This theme may provide an analogy to the practices of paternalistic capitalism showing that arbitrary displays of power characterized the corrupting influence of both real slavery as practiced in the South and the forms of "wage slavery" working persons believed were common in the North.

The most common sheet music edition of "Lucy Neal" is the 1844 version reprinted in *MSON* (1882). It differs in three respects from the version of "Miss Lucy Neale; or, The Yaller Gal" (1844) performed by the Congo Melodists, the original name of Buckley's Serenaders.[42] The order of the verses is different in the Buckleys' version, two of those verses (6 and 7) are variants, and the melody is more elaborate than in the *MSON* version; that is, the later edition is a simplification of the one performed by the Buckleys. The variant verses follow.

"Miss Lucy Neale; or, The Yaller Gal" No. 2 *(Cincinatti: S. Brainard, 1844)*

Verse 6
My boat it was a pine log,
Without a rudder or a keel,
And I floated down the ribber,
Crying poor Lucy Neale.

Verse 7
Miss Lucy she was taken sick,
She eat too much corn and meal,
De Dockter he did give her up,
Alas, poor Lucy Neale.

The version of "Lucy Neal" in *MSON*, like many of the other minstrel songs, had omnibus verses used by different groups. The melodies varied in pitch content, but the underlying chord progressions remained essentially the same as those shown in example 15a. Although the publication date is late (1882), the text is virtually the same as most of the 1844 versions.

"Miss Lucy Neal" No. 1 (MSON, 155–56)[43]

Verse 1
I'se born in Alabama,
My master's name was Meal,
He us'd to own a yaller gal,
Her name was Lucy Neal.

Chorus
O, poor Miss Lucy Neal,
O poor Miss Lucy Neal!
If once I had her in my arms,
How happy I should feel.

Verse 2
She us'd to go out wid us,
And pick cotton in de field;
And dar is whar I fell in love,
Wid pretty Lucy Neal.

Chorus

Verse 3
Miss Lucy she was handsome,
From de head down to de heel;
And all de niggers fell in love,
Wid pretty Lucy Neal.

Chorus

Verse 4
De Niggers gave a ball,
Miss Lucy danced a reel,
And no one could at all compare,
Wid pretty Lucy Neal.

Chorus

Verse 5
I ask'd her would she have me,
How glad she made me feel,
For then she gave to me her heart,
Sweet, simple Lucy Neal.

Chorus

Verse 6
My Massa he did sell me,
Because he said I'd steal,
And that's de way he parted
Poor me and Lucy Neal.

Chorus

Verse 7
Miss Lucy she was taken sick,
And mourn'd for me a deal;
The doctor he did give her up,
Alas! poor Lucy Neal.

Chorus

Verse 8
One day I got a letter,
And jet black was the seal;
And dere de words did tell me,
Ob de death ob Lucy Neal.

The "Lucy Neal" melody in *MSON* has several interesting features, one of which is the implied I–vi–V–I progression suggested by the melody; that is, the melody in measure 11 could have moved onto an E minor (vi) chord. The arranger chose instead the subdominant on C, resulting in a I–IV–ii–I–V–I progression. The pitch content of the *MSON* edition is diatonic in G, and the overall phrase structure is Pr–A–A'–Po (8–8–8–4), an essentially sixteen-bar, two-phrase strophic song with the chorus being a variant of the first phrase. That phrase, and especially the first measure, is focused on a reciting note, as are many narrative songs, but it is arpeggiated into a G-major triad at the beginning of the chorus. The same device is used for measures 5–6 in music example 15a.

Although the song may seem simple, the melodic elaboration makes it attractive to play, and the arpeggiations in the chorus create a more interesting sense of melodic movement. The version of the song shown in example 15b is different in several respects. The most notable melodic difference occurs in the song's refrain, which is in the uppermost voice (tenor 1) of the four-part setting. This setting is interesting in itself because the octave doublings, the exposed fifths, the virtually static bass line, and the voice leading do not show much influence of the Italian choral style that entered minstrelsy with the arrangements of Nelson Kneass.[44]

The version shown in example 15b is in C major and has a different but not unrelated melodic structure, with ornamentation in measures 3–4 that decorates the reiteration of the C by circling it with upper and lower neighboring notes. The second phrase in the chorus differs from the sheet music edition, but the key

LUCY NEAL.

Example 15a. "Lucy Neal" no. 1, from *MSON*. Used by permission of the Pennsylvania State University Libraries.

Example 15a. (cont.)

Example 15b. "Lucy Neal," from *EGB1*. Used by permission of the Brown University Library.

structural elements of the melody are generally recognizable in all the variants, including the one printed in *EAI* and *BBI* (see music example 15c).[45] There is only one syncopation, namely, on the second beat in the penultimate measure of the printed chorus (the sixteenth and dotted eighth note combination).

Example 15c. "Lucy Neal" no. 2, from *Briggs' Banjo Instructor*. Used by permission of Tuckahoe Music. Key signature is incorrect in original.

The *EGB1* version of "Lucy Neal" includes a strong abolitionist sentiment that may be indicative of regional (New England) attitudes about slavery. Verse 6 condemns the white slave trader for kidnapping wives and destroying relationships inherent in the couple's family and community. This is true even though another verse stresses minstrelsy's comic obsession with the woman's physical qualities: "I nebber should hab known her, / I soon cognized [recognized] her feet." If the figure of Lucy was played by a male in costume, the reference to the feet, especially the size of the feet, would have been an important comic clue calling attention to the disguise and suggesting that the text was not to be taken literally. Few versions of the song state the case against the manifest injustice of forced separation so strongly as the one quoted in the following extract. But even those that do include the kidnapping motif always emphasize the destructive effect of the separation.

"*Miss Lucy Neal*" *(EGB1 and Winans,* The Early Minstrel Show*)*[46]

Verse 1
Come listen to my story,
You can't tell how I feel,
Ise guine to sing the lub I hab,
For poor Miss Lucy Neal.

Chorus

O poor Miss Lucy neal,
Den, O poor Lucy Neal
O if I had you by my side,
O den how good I'd feel.

Verse 2
When I do come to Danville,
I take my horn and blow,
An den you see Miss Lucy Neale,
Cum running to de door.

Chorus

Verse 3
Miss Lucy dress'd in satin,
Its O, she looked so sweet,
I nebber shoud hab known her,
I soon [re]cognized her feet.

Chorus

Verse 5
Oh! tell me, dearest Sambo,
Whar hab you been so long,
Dey say dat you had leff me,
An cross de sea was gone.

Chorus

Verse 6
I told her dat it was not so,
And I'd leave her no more;
O den poor Lucy kiss me,
An fell faintin' on the floor.

Chorus

Verse 7
Oh! dar's de white man comin,
To tear you from my side,
Stan back! you white slave dealer,
She is my betroth'd bride.

Chorus

Verse 8
Dis poor nigger's fate is hard,
De white man's heart is stone,
Dey part poor nigger fro his wife,
And brake up dar happy home.

This "Lucy Neal" mentions Danville, a town in southcentral Virginia, almost directly south of Lynchburg, and one of the leading tobacco centers in the United States. The appearance of Lynchburg, Danville, and other economically important towns in minstrel songs suggests important connections linking what are now obscure references to preexisting textual and musical sources. There are some telltale inheritances reflecting Black English (BE) expressions or syntax that are not essential to the meaning of the song but do reveal connections with period attestations of spoken dialect. For example, the clause "when I do come to Danville" contains two present tense markers, /do/ plus /come/, for the past tense /came/. The combination of auxiliary verb forms /have/ and /had/ in the active indicative mood, for example, /had leff/, and the passive indicative past tense /was gone/ raise the question about whom the singer/narrator is addressing. The verb forms are probably storytelling conventions from folk traditions but suggest a performance practice in which the singer(s) address other onstage characters using the narrator switches already noted in other minstrel songs.

The singer mentions "the lub I hab" rather than the love he had for his partner, with the implication that he still loves her, wherever she is. The /d/ for /th/ consonant substitution is captured in /dar/ for /there/, /dat/ for /that/, /dey/ for /they/, /de/ for /the/, and /den/ for /then/. The dropped final /d/ before words beginning with /b/ or /d/ is also consistent throughout this text in phrases such as /an blow/, /an den/, and /stan back/.

These characteristics are complicating factors for interpreting the texts. If the early blackface performers were committed to modeling themselves on African Americans, they were able to do so by their selection of specific BE characteristics. How did that modeling take place? Where did the published versions of the songs come from? Where did the performers hear these songs or texts? Someone had to have had a good enough ear (and memory) to learn the material; someone else, the skill to put everything into the form of a song. At present there is no theory explaining the retention of BE characteristics in early minstrelsy, even though songs such as this version of "Lucy Neal" clearly illustrate features available only through imitation.

This text, at least, must have been composed or compiled by someone sensitive to the dialect and concerned enough about projecting a reasonably believable character to have preserved some authentic dialect features. In a minstrel show performance, the Lucy Neal story is told "in the character" of an African American; the amount of dialect in the example is sufficient to support that performance characteristic, just as the other versions of "Lucy Neal" reveal descriptors suggesting local and regional variants. One version of "Philadelphia Lucy Neal" is illustrative of the ways minstrel songs may have been adapted for particular audiences. The dialect elements are inconsistent and completely inauthentic, and the text commands a very different reading from the other examples because it reflects the demonstrably more negative environment for African Americans in Philadelphia compared with New York, Baltimore, or Boston.[47]

"Miss Lucy Neal" No. 3, or "Philadelphia Lucy Neal" (NSO1, *292*)[48]

Verse 1
Oh, down to Quakerdelphy,
I walked upon my heel,
I met a 'lasses color'd gal,
Dey called her Lucy Neal.

Chorus
Oh, Lucy Neal,
Lord bless her head an' heel,
If she was between my arms,
How maggitized I'd feel.

Verse 2
Her eyes was like a dumpling,
Made out o' white corn meal,
An' when she turned it up at me,
My gizzard danced a reel.

Chorus

Verse 3
Her lips war like red 'taters,
When they begin to peel,
An' when I bit a buss from her,
'Twas sweet as a fried eel.

Chorus

Verse 6
But when I took her to her home,
How flat my nose did feel,
A nigger with a wooly lip,
Kotch'd hold of Lucy Neal.

Chorus

Verse 8
He called her "breach of promise,"
And pull'd out a cane of steel,
An' run himself right into it,
'Fore me and Lucy Neal.

Chorus

Verse 9
I wink'd at Lucy with my shin,
And off from dare we steal,

An' soon I tied de marriage wool,
Along with Lucy Neal.

Chorus

Verse 10
Soon Lucy had a infant,
Marked with a cane of steel,
And wool upon its upper lip,
Den I left Lucy Neal.

The characters in this song differ from those in the other "Lucy Neal" texts. Unlike the woman in those versions, who is little more than a voiceless, passive companion, this Lucy Neal maintains two relationships and a very active social life— she acts like a man. In the end she is abandoned. Lucy accommodates her men sexually even though the child is born after her marriage to the song's narrator. Few minstrel songs mention promiscuity so clearly, acknowledge the results of sexual activity as openly, and relate so directly to social conditions contemporaneous with the song's performance.

"Philadelphia Lucy Neal" existed in a depressing economic and social environment. The Philadelphia that this Lucy called home was marked by "a decline in the percentage of two-parent households for the poorest fifth of the population from 70 percent in 1838 to 63 percent ten years later, and, for the poorest half of the black population, the decline was from 73 percent to 68 percent. In other words, among the poorest half of the community at mid-century, roughly one family in three was headed by a female."[49] The Lucy of this song is more deeply rooted in the poverty associated with her (northern) city's racial oppression than are any of her namesakes in those songs set in the South. The "poor" Lucy Neal of the Philadelphia version is a victim of male lust and abandonment, her plight tied to a different kind of slavery (exclusion from employment) and a potent form of social marginalization.

The Philadelphia version was not the most widely distributed example of the "Lucy Neal" type, but it does reveal the presence of local and regional song traditions in minstrelsy. That is consistent with the generally topical nature of minstrelsy. For example, the Lucy character changes dramatically when she is moved from the plantation, where she is an occasionally cherished lover, to the city, where she becomes a chastised and abandoned outcast. The other Lucys range from the maiden in the "See, Sir, See" scene in the *La Sonnambula* burlesque to the pathetic partner in an interrupted relationship, from an apparently cherished lover to an emotionally abused victim of urban poverty. Regardless of the comic elements and the presentation of this specific character as a victim, the images of Lucy Neal confirm the generally negative views of women in the overall minstrel vocabulary.

The variations on the Lucy types of women included an even more complicated character when costumed males expanded the "Lucy Long" song into skits for the final act of the show, where the more elaborate sketch or dance versions were usually identified with announcements such as "The Concert will conclude with the Boston Favorite Extravaganza of LUCY LONG."[50] Miss Lucy must have been a pantomime rather than a speaking part, performed "doubtless in skirts and pantalettes," even though "it seems to have been done by the Virginians [the Virginia Minstrels] without the appropriate costume."[51] Both cases involved female impersonation, however, which was an essential part of minstrelsy from its first months.

Versions of "Lucy Long," or "Miss Lucy Long," appear in most songsters and playbills published between 1843 and 1854. Regardless of how it was presented, "Lucy Long" has many different texts but relatively few melodic variants. In most of those texts, the song's male persona refers to himself; when the number was performed by an ensemble, the singer performing the part would have referred to himself *and* to the theater audience. This narrative method identifies the singer's purposes as a storyteller and entertainer, creating interesting questions about how antebellum musical theater experiences functioned for the performer as well as for the audience. These observations can best be explored in the following two key "Lucy Long" texts, each of which is found in two different performance traditions. The song on the left is from the 1842 versions as reprinted in *MSON*, and that on the right is from Joe Ayers's recorded performance on *Old Dan Tucker.*[52]

"Lucy Long" No. 1	"Lucy Long" No. 2
Verse 1	*Verse 1*
Oh! I just come afore you,	I've come again to see you,
To sing a little song;	I'll sing another song,
I plays it on de Banjo,	Just listen to my story,
And dey calls it Lucy Long.	It isn't very long.
Chorus	*Chorus*
Oh! take your time Miss Lucy,	Oh! take your time Miss Lucy,
Take your time Miss Lucy Long;	Take your time Miss Lucy Long,
Oh! take your time Miss Lucy,	Oh! take your time Miss Lucy,
Take your time Miss Lucy Long.	Take your time Miss Lucy Long.
Verse 2	*Verse 2a* (Double Verse)
Miss Lucy she is handsome,	I went to see Miss Lucy,
And Miss Lucy she is tall;	I got her to consent,
To see her dance Cachucha,[53]	And up to Deacon Snowball,
Is death to Niggers all.	Dis child and Lucy went.
Chorus	[No chorus]

Verse 3
Oh! Miss Lucy's teeth is grinning,
Just like an ear ob corn;
And her eyes dey look so winning!
Oh! would I'd ne'er been born.

Chorus

Verse 4
I axed her for to marry,
Myself de toder day;
She said she'd rather tarry,
So I let her habe her way.
Chorus

Verse 5
If she makes a scolding wife,
As sure as she was born,
I'll tote her down to Georgia,
And trade her off for corn.

Chorus

Verse 2b
He axed what we wanted,
I told him he knew best,
He pulled our hands together,
I cannot explain the rest.

Chorus

Verse 3
And now that we got married,
I expect to have some fun,
And if Lucy doesn't mind me,
This fellow will cut and run.
Chorus

Verse 4
Miss Lucy she is handsome,
Her teeth as white as snow,
And when she rocks da cradle,
I plays de ole banjo.

Chorus

Verse 5a (Double Verse)
Pray turkey buzzard,
Now lend to me your wing,
'Til I fly o'er de river,
To see Miss Sally King.

Verse 5b
When I got over de river,
Miss Sally she was gone,
If I had known she sob me so,
I'd stop with Lucy Long.

Chorus

The opening verses of both examples are conventional introductions not unlike narrative examples found in folk songs or ballads. The verses announce what the performer intends to do and promise that the performance will be relatively brief. The first chorus does not explain why Lucy must "take her time," but that becomes clear when some of the mock courting verses appear later. The physical characteristics attributed to Lucy in verse 3 of "Lucy Long" no. 1 are her height, her shining teeth (which the singer compares to white corn), and her "winning eyes." The other version uses the synecdoche of her white teeth as the only easily identifiable characteristic the persona presents.

Lucy Long no. 1 is also the object of the male persona's unfruitful courtship. He proposes marriage, but she is reluctant to accept his offer (verse 4). That offer is coupled with the typical male sanction of casting off the wife (verse 5) if she questions her husband's prerogatives. The refrain leaves the decision about the relationship in the hands of the woman, hence the repetition of the line "take your time, Miss Lucy, take your time Miss Lucy Long."

The other version shows the couple as legally married. The arrangement and commitment place no limits on the male's behavior, for he still has the freedom to "fly o'er de river, / To see Miss Sally King." The woman may acquiesce to a marriage proposal or some other promise, but such an assumption is ironic because verse 5 clearly shows the husband in a dominant power role. The song reinforces a patriarchal relationship in which the man treats his partner as if she were a simple child rather than a mature women and makes the singer appear victorious even though the "female" character he is addressing in most of the "in character" versions of the song is actually another male. The performance convention would certainly admit of an liberal dose of dramatic irony; the audience would have known that Lucy was a dress-up character even if the song's male persona played the part quite straight.

Lucy's social role as a single woman in version 1 is limited to various forms of dancing, as shown in the reference to the cachucha, the triple-time dance introduced by Fanny Elssler (1810–84). "Lucy Long" no. 2 shows the male's freedom to carry on extramarital liaisons and behaviors that some men believed to represent their prerogatives. Although audiences may have attributed such behaviors to the demoralizing effects of slavery or even to the alleged moral inadequacies of black Americans, the deeper issue transcends race. Marital fidelity might have been the preferred ideal relationship between men and women, given the American ideas about the family as a primary social structure. Nonetheless, many married and unmarried men believed that marital happiness could be achieved only after sexual dalliance because "aspects of masculinity, social status, and self-esteem rested on demonstrating a promiscuous, heterosexual orientation." This orientation helped men to bond with each other, and "glorification of male heterosexual freedom and bachelorhood permeated not only New York but much of America."[54] It would be highly unlikely that sporting men, dandies, artisans, working males, and curious youth, the major audience for early minstrelsy, would have missed the references to "gals" in blackface songs.

The real issue in this song is gender difference. Males, regardless of color or ethnic background, attributed to themselves the freedom to behave as they saw fit while relegating women to a subservient role in marriage, sexual relationships, and public life. The freedom attributed to Lucy Long is relatively limited, reflecting the boundaries within which men expected women to live. With the exception of her dancing, the public space in which Lucy Long dwells appears to be only what her "husband" allocates to her. In one text she stays at home to "rock the cradle," the domestic territory that women felt was their special preserve and that some male moralists believed was their primary purpose in life.

"Lucy Long" was intended to be a comic song, especially in those programs where the dance business and "statue scenes" featured "Lucy Long and Statue Dance by the Company." Although it has not been possible to reconstruct the performances antebellum audiences saw or to interpret any of the materials in anything like their original contexts, it is likely, given the participatory nature of minstrelsy's early shows, that the typical performance was probably interrupted by some dialogue or stage business. That was the procedure in other dance songs known as "Virginia breakdowns" and in the following example that occurred between verses 5a and b of the previously quoted version of "Lucy Long."

> Frank: She had a ticklar gagement to go to camp me[e]tin wid dis child.
> Dan: Hah! You went down to de fish Market to daunce arter eels. Mity cureous kind ob camp meetin dat!
> Frank: I[t] wasn't eels, it was a big cat fish.
> Dan: What chune did you dance?
> *Chorus* [both singing]
> Take your time Miss Lucy,
> Take your time Miss Lucy Long
> Rock de cradle Lucy,
> Take your time my dear.
> Frank: I trade her off for bean soup.
> Dan: Well, you is hungrest nigger ever I saw. Your satisfied widout your tinken bout bean soup all de time.[55]

Minstrelsy's approach to marriage is generally negative, portraying marriages as getting worse the longer they last. Marital conflict is one of the most popular blackface tropes, the exact reverse of the sentimental portrait of marriage as the fulfillment of the natural order. Blackface comedy stresses the hierarchical relationship implied in American marriages and follows the negative views in contemporary British and European popular texts, where "marital discord is usually cast in terms of female resistance to male authority." The scolding wife character argues against that hierarchical arrangement by constantly criticizing her husband's small faults, thereby provoking his retaliation ("tote her down to Georgia, / And trade her off for corn"). The threat is hyperbole, of course, but that is what makes the "Lucy" type of song a parody of all those "insurgent women . . . who choose to pass the bounds of respectful exhortation."[56]

"Lucy Long" is not mere escapist entertainment, nor is it a mere charade. The texts and the performance practices are public expressions of male resentment toward a spouse or lover who will not be subservient, a woman's indecision, and the real or imagined constraints placed on male behaviors by law, custom, and religion. These characteristics commonly support rationalizations of male misogyny.

The "Lucy Long" character appears to have been performed in pantomime; there are no indications that "Lucy" spoke or sang in any of the extravaganzas, statue dances, or sketches. What, then, did the character mean to audiences of the period? Eric Lott observed recently that "in acts such as 'Lucy Long,' the misogyny occurs through the degradation of the male singer who expresses his love for such a distasteful object of desire; he praises Lucy's huge feet and corncob teeth." But minstrelsy's misogyny is revealed and confirmed not by the degradation of the male character but rather by the reduction of the female persona to the physical attributes selected by impersonators who often wore men's shoes with their ball gown ensembles and displayed an appealing (and exaggerated) smile as an indicator of "feminine" allure. The "Lucy Long" persona represented a male construction of female behavior and a satire on the ritual of courtship as a prelude to male expectations of free sexual expression after marriage. That is why the male character sings, "And now that we got married, / I expect to have some fun."

"Lucy" is not only played by a male performer, however; the character is also in blackface, wearing as it were a double disguise. Minstrelsy's presentation of the blackface male and the cross-dressed wench suggested that "the blackface male is after all a figure for the audience's looking, however ridiculous he is made to appear; the 'wench' encompasses in her person male and female both; and the relationship between the two figures is foregrounded. The singer's most ridiculous impulse is indeed to proclaim his love for such an unworthy object as blackness."[57] It may be, however, that blackness and its racial implications were not the most important factors because audiences knew they were viewing a female impersonator. It was the male wench's presentation of female promiscuity and the allure of sexual freedom (at least in fantasy) that attracted interest. For what men feared most (and blunted by controlling the portrayal of women) was the power that women could exercise in marriage, power over sexuality and reproduction during a period when "the American middle class idealized male sexual control and depicted women as 'passionless'" and when some men of all classes pursued illicit pleasure without restraint.[58] And that is why the male character sings, "And if Lucy doesn't mind me, / This fellow will cut and run."

The male singer was not degraded because he looked ridiculous or loved a black woman; his spouse was only temporary anyway. After all, many minstrel songs praise the love of a "yaller gal." The story he tells is one of obtaining pleasure without responsibility or any serious commitment to his partner. Sexual satisfaction without commitment is a significant male fantasy, and Lucy seems to satisfy that need for a time. But the fact that Lucy Long is a *he* creates many more possibilities for humor, especially those based on physical comedy. In the final analysis, Lucy Long should not be viewed as a metonym for black women; she symbolizes a more general male desire for sexual access to and control over *all* women. Blackness is the cover under which the male fantasy of exercising complete control over women is played out in the seemingly innocuous comic scene.

Whereas generally respectable young women are the subjects of sentimental and mock sentimental ballads performed by blackfaced males, the songs featuring cross-dressed characters allowed men to use the nearly exclusive male domain of the minstrel show to criticize women publicly and give broader public expression to private male conversations about gender (see figure 4). Fashioning themselves in the women's costumes shown in *Godey's Lady's Book,* performers of the "Lucy Long" burlesque disposed of the issue of class by ridiculing the dress and deportment of middle-class women.[59] Whereas *Godey's* "was dedicated to advancing the middle class and its values," "Lucy Long" was committed to trivializing and inverting them, a point made clearly in the husband's threat "to take her down to Georgia / And trade her off for corn" or to replace the disobedient Lucy with her value in beans.

Cross-dressing was a common feature of American theater during minstrelsy's early days. Robertson Davies identified one of the most popular period examples as *The Rosebud of Stinging Nettle* (1862), a burlesque in which "the leading comedian played a female role, and the hero was represented by a pretty girl with a striking stage personality and excellent legs."[60] The practice was not restricted to comedians, however, because cross-dressing was not uncommon among both white and black men during the antebellum period. Peter Sewally, alias Mary Jones, who was wearing female attire when he was arrested in 1836 for grand larceny, said that he "attended parties among the people of [his] own color dressed this way."[61] The burnt cork masks, costumes, and wigs of early minstrelsy's best female impersonators— Maximilian Zorer (famous for his Jenny Lind roles), William Newcomb (noted for his appearances as Mrs. E. Oakwood Smith), and George Christy (renowned for his "wench" characters)—did not represent women any more accurately than did the cross-dressed characters of Mose—the Bowery B'hoy—and his companions portrayed working-class women of the Bowery and Broadway in Benjamin Baker's *Glance at New York* (Feb. 15, 1848), where Mose, Harry, and the country boy George disguise themselves as ladies for a pleasure trip to a Ladies Bowling Saloon. The real ladies see through the disguise immediately, and Mose, who is "a man and no mistake—and one of de b'hoys at dat"—makes a pass at Mrs. Morton to show his manly aggressiveness.[62]

Cross-dressing was part of the humor of the sequel *New York As It Is* (Apr. 17, 1848), which appeared the same year that William Burton achieved one of his greatest successes in a comedy called *The Toodles* (Oct. 2, 1848) at the Chambers Street Theater. The latter is a burlesque of *The Broken Heart; or, The Farmer's Daughter* and features Mrs. Toodles, a woman who buys useless things at auctions and tries to convince Timothy Toodles, her skeptical and long-suffering husband, that the

Figure 4. Transvested male wench characters: (a) Rollin Howard (in wench costume) and George Griffin (ca. 1855), used by permission of the Harry Ransom Research Center, University of Texas; (b) playbill of Perham's Opera Vocalists (1856), used by permission of the Brown University Library; (c) Rollin Howard (1840–79) in wench costume, used by permission of the Lawrence Senelick Collection; (d) Eugene d'Ameli as minstrel wench, used by permission of the Lawrence Senelick Collection.

(b)

(c)

(d)

"junk" will eventually prove useful. The Christys delivered a burlesque afterpiece entitled *The Toodles, with Curtain Lectures* in 1857, with the major role (Mrs. Toodles) played in drag by the great George Holland (1791–1870), the star of the American premiere of the *Hamlet Travestie.*[63]

George Christy was famous for his "wench" roles, especially when he was with E. P. Christy and afterward when he headlined with Griffin's company. "As early as 1835" Dan Gardner (1816–80) performed as a "wench character . . . and was the first performer to do a female part in blackface. And he was absolutely the first to do Lucy Long, a famous characterization in early minstrelsy."[64] J. T. Huntley, of Sanford's Opera Troupe during the late 1850s, "dressed and looked the part of" Amina in the troupe's burlesque of *La Sonnambula* and "managed to get through the music in the 'falsetto used by male performers to personate females.'"[65] Nelson Kneass, one of minstrelsy's most important composers and arrangers, played the part of Aunt Chloe (his daughter Annie played Eva) when he appeared as a guest in Christy and Wood's Minstrels parody of *Uncle Tom.* Other blackface comedians are known to have had great success playing "skirt" parts. Henry Wood of Wood's Minstrels played Mrs. Puffy in a popular afterpiece. Marshall S. Pike (1818–1901) began his career in *whiteface* as a member of the Albino Family Troupe in the early 1840s, a group that was known as the Harmoneon Family and later as the Harmoneons. Pike was "one of the first female impersonators" and appeared during the 1850s with songs such as "I Hab Leff Alabama" (1849) and "The Indian Warrior's Grave" (1850).[66]

The extent of female impersonation in minstrelsy is obviously a rich subject, for "female impersonators were usually comics who both belittled women and set standards for their dress and behavior."[67] The primary issue is that with so many men dressed up, the references to African American women's feet and eyes go well beyond a fixation with sexualized parts of the body. As Paskman and Spaeth wrote, "The traditional climax of mirth [in the minstrel show] has always come when the simpering 'lady' suddenly displayed a pair of huge feet, emerging from dainty skirts, and preferably topped by unmistakably masculine trousers."[68]

The texts tell more about male conceptions of women. The rhetoric suggests that the battle between the sexes was perceived as an important arena for comedy because of the nineteenth-century male perception that women were weaker than men both physically and emotionally and hence were worthy of protection from harm.[69] David Roediger argued that "songs showing promiscuous Black women were probably more popular than those emphasizing the sexuality of Black men."[70] The evidence from period playbills and songsters does not show such a concentration on "promiscuous black women," however, because blackface cross-dressing was the vehicle by which males ridiculed the sentimentality of the age, criticized the emerging definitions of women's roles in society, and satirized the relationships between men and women in courtship and marriage.[71] The songs also indicate that black women were not nearly as promiscuous as the male characters depicted in minstrel songs. Women are portrayed either negatively as targets (usually "yaller gals") of sexual interest or so idealistically as to become sacralized objects.

"Lucy Neal" is a "yaller gal" who suffers the loss of her lover; when Pompey, the principal character in "Cynthia Sue" (1848), gets to New Orleans, he ends up with women who will not let him return. References to mulattoes or "yaller gals" seem even more common in minstrel show songs than those to black or brown women. Perhaps the mulatto was an acceptable character because she was the result of the same illicit unions that men were describing to their friends in tall tales, songs, and pornographic literature. Although white males played the parts of black women and women in general, the characters portrayed are seldom referred to as "mulatto," "mixed blood," "octoroon," "maroon," or any of the other terms commonly found in the fiction of the period.

"Yaller gals" are sometimes mentioned in nonminstrel sources, such as Melville's *Pierre; or, The Ambiguities* (1852), but minstrelsy pays little attention to subtle distinctions in its portrayals of women. In the Melville citation, for example, the novel's hero, Pierre Glendinning, lives in the country, which is "not only the most poetical and philosophical, but . . . the most aristocratic part of the earth." During a visit to his wayward and dissolute cousin, Glendinning Stanly, Pierre and his wife, Isabel, encounter the following cast of characters near a watch-house "in the city":

> In indescribable disorder, frantic, diseased-looking men and women of all colors . . . were leaping, yelling, and cursing around him. The torn Madras handkerchiefs of negresses, the red gowns of yellow girls, hanging in tatters from their naked bosoms, mixed with the rent dresses of deep-rouged white women, and the split coats, checkered vests, and protruding shirts of pale, or whiskered, or haggard, or mustached fellows of all nations, some of whom seemed scared from their beds, and other seemingly arrested in the midst of some crazy and wanton dance. On all sides, were heard drunken male and female voices in English, French, Spanish, and Portuguese, interlarded now and then, with the foulest of all human lingoes, that dialect of sin and death, known as the Cant language, or the Flash.[72]

Melville's "yellow girls" were representatives of the lower cultural life of the city, belonging to a group ("mulatto") the census of 1850 had counted for the first time as "people in whom mixed ancestry was visible." Mulattoes were sometimes characterized as the result of unions produced by the "midnight marauding of lower-class white males," that is, "poor whites, itinerant Irish laborers, and Yankee overseers." But well-to-do southern males were just as profligate as poor whites; the signs of their liaisons were "all too often for the integrity of an idealized southern society, whose settlements were losing the color line in a welter of browns, yellows, and reds."[73] Racial mixing must have been occurring at a fairly substantial rate, for some northerners claimed that "amalgamation was worse, by far, than sodomy."[74]

The attraction to "yaller gals" and the suggestion about interracial liaisons in New York show up so often in minstrel songs that they confirm Timothy Gilfoyle's observations that "the sharp spatial boundaries typical of black prostitution later in the century were absent in antebellum New York" and that the notion of racial separation modern readers might project back into the previous century is wrong because "the racial divisions characteristic of much nineteenth-century America vanished in this mixture of promiscuity, poverty, and loneliness."[75] Such feelings could certainly be attributed to the large number of single men between the ages of twelve and forty flocking to the city for employment.

Racial mixing was much stronger in some parts of the city than in others. Some of the brothels and saloons in the Five Points offered the "most racially integrated milieu in antebellum New York," and many "accommodated black and white prostitutes and a similarly mixed clientele." Rev. Samuel Prime observed a "motley multitude of men and women, yellow and white, black and dingy, old and young . . . male and female Baccahanals dancing to the tambourines and fiddle; giggling and dancing . . . and making 'night hideous' with their lascivious orgies." There seems to have been a natural affinity, as the New York Herald reported, for "the strange and disreputable anomaly of theaters, churches, and houses of ill-fame all huddled together in one block."[76]

References to "yaller" also appeared on the Broadway stage outside minstrelsy but within the working-class theater of the period. The best evidence is a parody of "Oh Lud Gals Give Me Chaw Tobacco" in Benjamin Baker's Glance at New York in 1848. Preparing for an evening out at the Vauxhall Gardens, Mose's "gallus gal" Lize and her friend Jenny parody a blackface song usually performed by men:[77]

> Lize: Here we are, as you diskiver,
>   All the way from roaring river,
>   My wife dies—I'll get another,
>   Pretty yaller gal—just like t'other,
>   Oh Lud gals, give me chaw tobacco.
> Jenny: Oh, dear fotch along de whiskey,
>   My head swims when I get tipsy.

Buntline's Mysteries and Miseries offered much helpful information for those who wished to experience the differences and pleasures of New York's many social environments. Describing an underground nightclub located in the Five Points district, Buntline wrote:

> And yet wider opened he his eyes, when he stepped within. He saw a sight! Not less than two hundred negroes, of every shade, from the light, mellow-cheeked quadroon,

down to the coal-black were there. Some were dancing to music made by a fiddle, a tambourine, and an exceedingly ancient looking guitar; all of them played with more strength than sweetness; and speaking of this latter the atmosphere was not tinctured with much of it. Those who were dancing, of course, kept neck and neck with the music; to do so, it was impossible not to sweat some, and the odor raised therefrom, was less agreeable than some of the perfumes which Goraud has invented.[78]

One of the most striking conclusions suggested by the frequent references to "yaller gals" is that during the antebellum period there was a class of mixed-race women who were the objects of male desire precisely because they were considered inferior and exploitable. The blackface minstrel companies' views of women, then, included a strong interest in those who were sexually available, deference to those who were objects of desire but discreet representatives of true and moral womanhood, and sorrow for all those who passed away before reaching some fulfillment in this life. Such ambivalence would explain the wide divergence in minstrel songs from the pathetic ballads to the suggestive songs or from the tearjerkers about mothers and kidnapped children to the idealized conceptions of chaste love.

The themes of courtship, marriage, and death in songs about women have their appropriate counterparts in the minstrel repertory. The first two have already been considered at length. Death was no less important as a subject for public attention during the antebellum period. High mortality rates for persons under fifty were part of everyone's consciousness about the unpredictability of death irrespective of class and gender, but there are few songs about the deaths of men over eighteen until the Civil War. The number of songs dealing with the deaths of women is large and well known: natural disruptions, such as a child's death (as in Foster's "Gentle Annie" [1856]), and a spouse's death in childbirth or from disease (as in Foster's "Nelly Was a Lady" [1849], Lynch and Crosby's "Dearest Mae" [1847], and Thompson's "Lilly Dale" [1852]) were common enough to be the topics of popular songs and objects of sentimental experience for both sexes.[79]

The evidence for early mortality is as overwhelming as it is sad. In London during the 1830s, for example, "the average age at death was estimated at forty-four for gentry, professional persons, and their families; at twenty-five years for tradesmen, clerks and their families; and at twenty-two for laborers and their families."[80] For the United States, Jack Larkin estimated that the "years of childhood and adolescence, now the safest of all, were also a time of high mortality . . . meaning that one white child out of every four or five would not survive from birth to maturity," a statistic only slightly worse than the disheartening estimate that "one white infant in six or seven did not survive to age one."[81] The mortality rates for African American children were even higher.

The numbers do not tell the whole story, however; the antebellum ways of death were different from those of the late twentieth century. In the antebellum era people usually died at home, among family and friends, and the immediate community participated directly in the preparations for burial before the funeral business expanded and employed professional directors to "handle everything" in special parlors and mourning rooms. The memory of a death at home lingered as a presence within the home, especially for Irish Americans, who held wakes there, and for years afterward the family could recall the images of death and grieving associated with the passing of a family member. For those middle-class families with a parlor, the very piano around which the family gathered for pleasure could have been the same instrument on which the final hymns were played as the departed was taken from the home for the last time. These customs were part of the "protocols of dying in the nineteenth century," and the "large number of popular songs may not reflect a preoccupation [with death] so much as familiarity."[82]

Such statistics and the intimate nature of funeral and burial preparations led songwriters to see deaths of female children and young women as important subjects for theatrical songs and church or folk hymns. The sentiments were strong enough that the "mourning" song was just as likely to apply to urban residents as to persons living on farms and to be equally significant for any community, whether slave or free. The plantation setting, however, provided a locale where the likelihood of separation by kidnapping or the sale of a companion or spouse severely ruptured the stability of a social network within the black family and the slave community. Such critical disjunctions were often the subject of blackface songs because the sense of loss depicted in the expression of the burnt cork singer could apply across racial barriers to white families, as it must have done, for the audiences were primarily white.[83] The primary controlling image for these songs was the sanctity and integrity of marriage and the family, irrespective of the partners' race or ethnicity.

Courtship and marriage are the most typical themes in which gender conflicts were worked out. The blackface comedian's general opinion about marriage was seldom positive. Youthful marriages often end with the death of the young woman in these songs, hence the many laments about young lovers or brides sleeping in bowers and meadows. In older marriages the wife is usually a shrew who forces her values on her henpecked husband, who complains about his experiences in songs whose contents are similar to the negative portrayals of women in the Ethiopian skits and sketches. "De Old Jaw-Bone" (from the first line of the first chorus) is an example of the first type (it is also found in an instrumental version known as "Kick de Debbil on de Holiday" and in a song entitled "Young Bowshin's Bride" [1843]) that tells the tragic story of a young woman who decides to play hide-and-seek with her husband and his friends. Unfortunately for the young lady, her hiding place ("an old log all covered wid brush . . . found in de swamp") is not discovered. Her heartbroken husband searches for many years, only to find "her colored bloom, all faded away in de old log tomb." The 1843 sheet music edition of the song ends with a repeated tag line "Oh! de old Jaw bone! Oh! de old Jaw bone!"

The song was a parody based on the source tune "The Mistletoe Bough" and entitled "A Pathetic Ballad as sung in the Opera of 'Sin De'Ella; or, Black Fairy and Leather Slippers,'" that is, the Rossini/Bishop version of *Cinderella*. The thoroughly English melody is one more example demonstrating the stylistic variety that minstrelsy could accommodate so easily.

"De Old Jaw Bone," or "Young Bowshin's Bride" (1843)[84]

Verse 1
De "Jawbone" hung in de kitchen hall,
De cornstalk shine on de white wash wall,
Old Possum's brack friends lub fun and were gay,
And kick up de debil on a holiday,
Old Possum he see'd wid a fader's pride,
His own color'd child young Bowshin's bride,
And she wid her white eyes seem'd to be,
De new moon ob day company.

Chorus
Oh! de old Jaw bone! Oh! de old Jaw bone.
Now just tink ob dat ere Nigger and weep!
Whar! Whar!! Chaw!!! Whoo! oo!! oooo!!!!

Verse 2
"I'm tired of dancing now," he cried;
"So put up de Banjo! I'll hide, I'll hide.
While I hide myself from your grinning face."
Away she ran, and her friends began,
To find his here nig!! If any ob 'em can.
And young Bowshin cried, "Oh! whar bouts you hide?
I can't lib widout you, my own brack bride."

Chorus

A later version performed by Wood's Minstrels in 1855 changes the text so that the "brack friends" become "niggers" and the young woman's eyes are changed from "white" to "black," but the same tragic outcome befalls the overly playful young woman. The original stage directions, which read "'Take Your Time' ad lib with much effect" and "with much expression," are replaced with an entirely new verse similar to the "Phantom Chorus" from *La Sonnambula* and probably accompanied by newly designed special effects.[85]

"De Old Jaw Bone" (Wood's Minstrel's Songs, 32–33)

Verse 4

About twelb o'clock, or de hour ob one,
A figure appears, and it strikes you dumb!
It has no flesh upon its bones'
It shakes its teeth—it laughs—it groans!
It seizes you by de wool ob de head,
And shakes you about till your almost dead!
It rings in your ears, "I was murder'd thar!"
And this is what dey call de old nightmar!

"De Old Jaw Bone" is another example of material borrowed from Italian opera by way of an English adaptation migrating into blackface comedy. The music is the same regardless of the theatrical environment in which it appeared. But what of the text just quoted? The song's narrator captures the grief of the poor old man, who looks back on the seemingly innocent game with great regret and remorse for his own pride. The pathetic victim entombed because she took the game of hide-and-seek too seriously becomes a second subject of an antisentimental satire directed at the highly melodramatic story. The concern over the plight of the couple, especially the loss of the young woman, is the same general theme found in the various versions of "Mary Blane" and "The Virginia Rose Bud."

The number of songs about courtship or companionship exceeds by far the number of titles dealing with a happy marriage. It appears that most of the songs are narratives describing the male's activities and sometimes recounting in an ironic way the circumstances under which the couple work out their relationship. Minstrel show courters are always males. They usually appear as dandies and cultural travelers who report on the types of women they have encountered or would like to have met in particular locales. The songs reflect a world in which men enjoyed a period of sexual freedom before choosing the supposedly monogamous relationships considered the norm in mid-nineteenth-century America. For the young women they married, however, there was a different perception of marriage. Whereas the men lost some of their sexual freedom, the young ladies lost their sense of romance, something a Philadelphia girl observed in her diary: "And now these pages must come to a close, for the romance ends when the heroine marries."[86]

There are virtually no blackface songs about "regular" young men who meet women in normal social ways, through churches, benevolent organizations, business relationships, formal balls, and other social occasions sanctioned by nineteenth-century society. Public announcements about minstrelsy always seem to stress its "respectability," even though much of the material refers to what were illicit behaviors. The good guy seldom appears to get the girl, because it is the "dandy" types whose behaviors captivate the highly emotional "gals." This view of women was not exclusive to minstrelsy. Once again, blackface comedy only reflected some of the male conventions found in other forms of theater, the context within which minstrelsy functioned best.

The pathetic ballads served as foils for the comic treatment of nostalgia, courtship, lost love, and personal insecurity. Minstrelsy often presented both a parody and a sentimental model in the same program, the two different types playing off against one another and perhaps providing a balance to avoid too serious an assault on the period's song conventions that the public held so dear. The words of these songs "seem designed to elevate the urban middle class by presenting a mock-aristocratic approach to courtship[,] but . . . the specific images and allusions in these songs tended to intensify the different position of the sexes, showing active men in a sordid and violent outside world, while passive women occupied a secluded and untainted domestic realm."[87] Courtship may well have taken place that way, but the proper social behaviors surrounding courting also delayed the couple's establishment of a sexual relationship. Minstrelsy seems to have argued for the pleasure of more direct relationships in part because such arguments undoubtedly ran counter to the public morality of sexual restraint.

The presentation of women in one-on-one relationships is only part of minstrelsy's construction of the woman on the stage. Since the minstrel stage was a public forum, however, it cannot be separated from other sites where women expected to be welcomed, have their constitutional rights respected, and watch their concerns dramatized or satirized. But just as women's civic expectations were frustrated by the failure to extend the franchise to females, so also their roles were restricted in blackface comedy. Although the development of women's roles in nineteenth-century culture has been explored in Ryan's *Women in Public,* Matthews's *Rise of the Public Woman,* and other studies, there is still a need for a more thorough exploration of the depictions of women in blackface and nonblackface comedy, both forms of which seem to have been conservative in their opposition to the expansion of women's rights.

Women's life and attire intrigued men. Cross-dressing focused men's attention on women's presentations of themselves. The physical characteristics of women, as revealed in song, provide some insight into those perceptions. That is why we find Buckley's Serenaders (May 7, 1852) including a "Fanny Bloomer Dance" for J. J. Mullen as a regular offering in the second part of the show, White's Serenaders (Apr. 16, 1852) presenting a "New Bloomer Dance," Backus's Minstrels (Aug. 1, 1854) staging a "Fanny Bloomer duet" for two male comedians, and George Christy's Minstrels (Aug. 19, 1859) presenting "the very laughable Interlude, called MISS BLOOMER AT THE SOIREE" at the Musical Fund Society Hall in Philadelphia.[88]

Minstrel songs seldom deal with the image of the domestic nurturer popular during "The Golden Age of Domesticity" (1840–60) because the comedians preferred to refer to spouses as cantankerous shrews.[89] In contrast to the moral model of the dutiful middle-class Christian wife of Catherine Beecher's *Treatise on Domestic Economy, for the Use of Young Ladies at Home, and at School* (1841), married women became objects of derision. If blackface songs and skits are to be believed, most marriages were sad affairs where men were ruled by domineering and unhappy wives. If the wife dies in these songs, the man resumes life with another partner, and the relationship between the couple is reduced to something that appears to be no more romantic than a living arrangement. Those ideas are underscored in the blackface song usually called "Old Grey Goose and Gander."[90]

"Old Grey Goose and Gander" (NFM1, 57)

Verse 1
When I was a single feller,
I lived in peace and pleasure,
But now I am a married man,
I'm troubled out of measure.

Chorus
Den look here, look dare,
And look over yonder,
Don't you see the old grey goose,
A smiling at de gander.

Verse 2
Every night when I go home,
She scolds or its a wonder,
And den she takes dat pewter mug,
And beats my head asunder.

Chorus

Verse 3
My old wife was taken sick,
De pain ob death came on her,
Some did cry, but I did laugh,
To see de breff go from her.

Chorus

Verse 4
Saturday night my old wife died,
Sunday she war buried,
Monday was my courting day,
On Tuesday I got married.

Chorus

Verse 5
My old wife has gone abroad,
Some evil spirit guide her,
I know she has not gone to church,
For de debil can't abide her.

The stereotyping of women in minstrelsy has been demonstrated in this review of minstrelsy's most popular songs. Just as minstrelsy stereotyped males of both races, it also treated women in very generalized ways with scarcely any real conception of women as persons living in the complex and changing social world of the mid-nineteenth century. Women and men had to contend with the conflicting forces of domesticity and women's employment outside the home, with the public perceptions of women's rights in general and suffrage in particular, and with the prominence of religion as a controlling influence in conceptions of women as being the key forces in the moral education of children, especially in the increasingly secular urban world where minstrel shows first introduced songs and sketches about women to mixed audiences.

Blackface comedians chose to treat these aspects of women in the songs that embraced all women, regardless of color or ethnicity. They worked out the theatrical presentation of some of those ideas by playing the women's roles themselves. They were better able to control the caricatures and, based on costume, demeanor, and ridicule, to present only those images of women they felt would be successful in popular entertainment. Some actors or companies may also have incorporated critiques of male homosexuality in their cross-dressed acts. Eric Lott has argued that "implicit or explicit appreciation of black male sexuality could always slip into homoerotic desire," that "male desire for black men was everywhere to be found in minstrel acts," and that some songs "allowed white men to image same-sex desire even more freely than when virile black men were represented."[91] But the most common and apparently successful images of women were those that conformed more or less to what audiences had already come to expect from the presentations of women in magazines, newspapers, self-help books, educational primers, popular theater and novels, and the often more subtle but nonetheless persuasive world of fashion.

Women were not excluded from minstrelsy, however. Female roles were played by women in some companies, so some of the generalizations about cross-dressing must be qualified. Julia Gould (1824–93) appeared regularly as a character in the Buckleys' operatic burlesques. As Rice put it, "She essayed the principal female roles in the great operatic burlesques that made the Buckleys famous."[92] Thayer's Band of Minstrels (Boston) announced (July 19, 1848) that they would feature a "Miss Stephens in the much admired Song of 'Oh Susanna Don't You Cry for Me' as sung by her in the popular Extravaganza entitled A GLANCE AT NEW YORK." Jeannie

Reynaldson appeared with White's Serenaders during part of the 1852 season, and White also seems to have hired some female minors (as well as males, it should be noted), according to the convention of allowing young children to appear in novelty acts throughout most of the antebellum period. Wood's Minstrels used young girls, usually called "La petite Melissa" or "La petite Jeanne," in dance numbers.[93] Samuel Sanford featured his children in many of his productions, even billing his son as "Young America" in some of the Sanford's Opera Troupe playbills.

However much the minstrels may have ridiculed women, they certainly wanted mothers and their children in the audience. Women and families were encouraged to attend minstrel shows, and their attendance at "family entertainments" may have been one reason the programs began to change from mocking attacks on sentiment before 1850 to a general tolerance for sentimentality during the 1850s. Some playbills stated that "front seats [were] reserved for Ladies and Families," and others indicated that the material to be performed was "respectable" enough for families to enjoy.[94] Portraits of some companies showed them in standard evening dress on sheet music covers, declaring that although the performers did blackface, their aspirations were to move up to legitimate theater.

Foreign visitors noted that one difference between American and European audiences was that in the United States, "Women of all social classes felt freer to sit where they wished. Most ticket prices meant that middle-class women of no social standing could afford box seats. Even the 'pit,' heretofore a masculine preserve, had been invaded by women. The sight of 'several females of respectability comfortably seated' there suggested that this 'innovation [would] become universal.'"[95]

Despite these observations, however, there is little minstrel material related to families, except for the songs about kidnapped or lost children, death, and nostalgia for a sheltered life away from the city. There are some differences between married and single women in the songs, but the same cult of sentimentalism found in popular fiction is also found in the antebellum songs. The conventions used to present women were so well established that some recent scholarship suggests the practice reflected males' concerns about their own sexual identities.[96] Transvestism may also have been related to the acceptability of public expression of male homosexuality through characters representing both male and female types. These suggestions are not at all clear from the evidence, however.

The list of song types and the number of sentimental songs dealing with dead, dying, lonely, or heartbroken women or men and with women whose courtship patterns are interrupted by the departure of a companion sold by a heartless master suggest that the abandoned lover motif was popular in every genre of song during the antebellum period. The pathetic affect extended beyond the surface level of the song—the rupture of the persona's relationship by the thoughtless master—because the "master" in these contexts was a symbolic figure for anyone holding the authority over another, whether slave or wage earner. Even songs that focus on broken relationships among slaves do so not necessarily out of sympathy for those suffering slaves but from the memory or prospect of similar disruptions, broken promises, or breaches of contract among members of the audience. Such sentimentality may also be related to an underlying guilt that slaves were after all people, too, and felt the pains of separation just as strongly as did members of the racially dominant group. Sentimentalizing the practice of breaking up slave couples was a means of avoiding the consequences of such actions by transforming them into superficial, publicly expressible conventions rather than facing the disruption caused by the external control of an individual's most personal relationships.

The distinctions between the "Negro" songs, "plantation" songs, and any of the other song types of the day were never really neat, for minstrelsy always treated some male-female relationships in highly sentimentalized and sometimes evasive or deeply symbolic ways. Songs about the breakups of love relationships, a genre that dominates blackface entertainment, cannot be taken literally, because although the literal message may emphasize the grief of separation felt by one of the song's characters (usually the male), the broader meaning does not necessarily attribute any special or distinctive qualities to African American personal relationships. The black characters are not representative of slaves so much as they are objects in which white audiences found examples of their own sense of loss made manifest in the songs directed at cross-dressed males rather than tragic female characters. These feelings were not projected onto black representatives—the characters were masked whites, not authentic blacks. But the feelings displayed by the characters and embodied in the conventions of the songs were capable of touching audiences unsympathetic to the conditions of slavery. The underlying themes of these songs are generally the conquest and possession of sexual partners (and eventually spouses), one of the principal realms of male competitiveness and one of the frequent subjects of minstrel songs. So many songs express this theme, in fact, that it is invalid to claim that "most blackface contacts between men and women occurred in happy, but decorous, love songs or in sentimental laments for loves lost."[97]

The blackface presentation of black and white women, although it seems to degrade only African American women, actually embodies complex attitudes toward gender that are offered up in satires, parodies, and comic songs that were seldom considered as anything more than mere diversions. In reality they were effective enforcing mechanisms ensuring that unenlightened male attitudes were confirmed by the genderized status quo underlying their texts. When the minstrel comedians presented their interpretation of a courtship ritual between a costumed blackfaced male playing a female and a suitor dressed as a dandy, the audience was not always witnessing the depiction of love relationships among African Americans. Once the cross-dressing convention became a known and common feature of the performance practice, any allusion to authenticity was replaced by the conventions of burlesque, and the whole courtship process became available for comedy. However, the songs that featured female impersonators seldom exploit the conceit that the character is really a man in masquerade unless the specific performances permitted exaggerations associated with revealing the man's foot—a very common reference in minstrel songs—or referring to other masculine characteristics that the costume could not hide.

The truly compelling conclusion to be drawn from trying to reconstruct the image of a woman from what the blackface comedians created is that the conventions required that the "dream girl" provide companionship and sexual pleasure, comply with male plans and desires, and tolerate all manner of demeaning behaviors if she were to remain an ideal woman, regardless of color or class. In these portrayals, courtship is hardly ever happy because it seldom leads to lasting relationships, and even if marriage does occur, it inevitably leads to the imposition of limits on male freedom, something blackface comedians and their real world counterparts could not accept. However much blackface comedy demeaned and insulted African Americans, its usually sentimental and often hostile values reinforced the limitations on freedom and equity for American women even more.

Conclusion

From the very first African captives, through the years of slavery, and into the present century black Americans kept alive important strands of African consciousness and verbal art in their humor, songs, dance, speech, tales, games, folk beliefs and aphorisms. They were able to do this because these areas of culture are often the most persistent, because whites tended not to interfere with many of these culture patterns which quickly became associated in the white mind with Negro inferiority or at least peculiar Negro racial traits, and because in a number of areas there were important cultural parallels and thus wide room for syncretism between Africans and Europeans.[1]

Blackface minstrelsy was a complex commercial and cultural enterprise. The sum of its many parts added up to more than the commercialized exploitation of racial imitation or the commodification of ethnic or racial envy and white superiority. From the contents of the shows to the organization of the programs, from the allegedly authentic "delineations" of African Americans to the representation of women, and from the curious banjo songs of the 1840s to the sophisticated opera parodies of the 1850s, antebellum minstrelsy established a now familiar pattern in American popular culture. Musical material borrowed from the cultural periphery establishes itself as a viable commercial product and develops into a respectable mainstream entertainment purged of any features that would complicate unduly the audience's perceptions of the need (or lack thereof) for radical changes in American attitudes toward race, gender, and class.

Race played a fundamental and undeniably primary role in the development of minstrelsy because racial and ethnic differences were defining features of American comedy, just as they are still significant factors in American political and social life. Although the notion of racial inferiority may have been a motivating factor in the selection of blackface as a medium of comic expression, the expression of racial attitudes in minstrelsy was always more complicated than Bernard Bell believed when he argued that blackface minstrelsy exemplified the "psychological distancing of whites from their personal responsibility in their tragic perversion of American principles."[2] Minstrelsy was also more psychologically multidimensional than Nathan Huggins realized when he argued that the "minstrel 'Negro' . . . [was] a symbolic scapegoat *alter ego* into which whites projected sinful, guilt-provoking wishes otherwise suppressed by puritan consciences" or that "the white man [who] . . . put on the black mask modeled himself after the subjective black man . . . which whites carried within themselves and harbored with both fascination and dread."[3]

Huggins's identification of the "mask" as a key symbol for minstrelsy is particularly significant because it invests the burnt cork makeup with the same powerful religious and metaphorical forces that carved facial and body masks share in African or Asian cultures. But the blackface mask of the American minstrel show was one of those symbols whose complex meanings did not depend on its self-evident but only occasional significations of blackness. After looking behind the mask to determine the many purposes and functions it served, I have struggled to understand how the blackface comedians used "the original, actual minstrel mask . . . to remind whites of the African Americans' ostensible lack of humanity, their supposed irresponsibility, and their willingness to accept ill treatment."[4]

The minstrel's task of "putting on a character" and the structure of racial depiction involved more than blackface makeup. When the minstrels "put on" blackface or whiteface, they assumed other traits to disidentify themselves, assume a new aspect, and become different characters. Depiction or "delineation" required that the minstrel show personalities had to work with dialect; perform in costume; assume various serious and comic poses; sing, dance, or play an instrument; demonstrate some comic or imitative talent; and, unless they specialized in one particular type of act, possess some general acting or musical ability.

The blackface mask could be a powerful vehicle for racial depiction, but it is a mistake to assume that burnt cork makeup worn by white men functioned as masks do in African or other non-Western cultures. The assumption endows the makeup with the magical and symbolic properties of totems and sacralized objects and ignores the fact that the theatrical effectiveness of the minstrel mask depended very much on who wore it and what the idea of the "mask" really conveys. Ellison argued that the "racial identity of the performer was unimportant, the mask was the thing . . . and its function was to veil the humanity of Negroes thus reduced to a sign, and to repress the white audience's awareness of its moral identification with its own acts and with the human ambiguities pushed behind the mask."[5] It is just those ambiguities and their consequent complexities that make generalizations about the minstrel show so complicated.

The playbills and the various examples of minstrelsy's repertory show, as Ostendorf argued, that "what makes minstrelsy work is the race, class, and caste polarity: black and white, primitive and civilized, rich and poor, urban and rural."[6]

That is certainly true, but minstrelsy's meanings are still more complex culturally than any listing of simple binary polarities can convey. That is why Ellison's "Change the Joke" essay must never be discounted in minstrelsy studies; it moved the discussion of blackface comedy away from the focus on racial ideologies and politics. Antebellum blackface comedy was more than a convenient rationalization for the white oppression of blacks. Ellison's critique, although applicable in some respects, is not based on any historical understanding of the development of white imitations of African Americans or on the multiple linkages between minstrelsy and other forms of popular entertainment.[7] If minstrel comedians "put on" character with their makeup, then, the real issue is how that newly created persona functioned in blackface comedy, a theatrical form that quickly established the viability of variety entertainment as a staple of American commercial culture and the open-ended format as an efficient and flexible presentation structure.

Minstrelsy demonstrated that the practice of "putting on" racial characteristics (dialect, costume, and real or invented behavioral patterns) was among the basic ingredients of American popular entertainment since the late eighteenth century and may indeed be an essential feature of humor in a multicultural society. As a form of popular, vernacular entertainment, minstrelsy confirmed specific patterns for presenting male and female bodies through mimicry, presentations that were usually described as "delineations" or "personations" and are commonly called "impressions" in contemporary comedy. For all its interest in race as a subject for popular humor, blackface comedy made gender a dominant issue because, as a form of entertainment created and controlled by men, it embodied deeply held concepts about the power relationships between the sexes.

All these characteristics are complicating factors that make generalizations about minstrelsy ineffective guides to understanding its real complexities, some of which are inextricably linked to problems with the kinds of evidence available for the study of popular culture. Much of what is available for the critical study of antebellum blackface entertainment has to be reconstructed from published material—insufficient evidence at best in a form of theater whose meanings for antebellum audiences have yet to be verified from prompt books, scripts, eyewitness accounts, and more thorough assessments of the theater criticism from the major newspapers and magazines of the period.

Essential to discussions of what minstrelsy meant to audiences of the antebellum period are two fundamental observations about the development of popular culture in the United States. The first observation is that cultural and musical syncretism could and did occur in various aspects of the minstrel show. Such syncretism is demonstrated by all the comparative studies of the forms of popular humor incorporated in the narratives, burlesque sermons, and jokelore of the typical antebellum minstrel show. The second observation is that minstrelsy's musical styles were representative of a postcolonialist adaptive process involving not only European, Anglo-American, and African American music but also other cultural products imported from abroad, all these ingredients being mixed in various ways by forces as diverse as class envy, racial politics, commercial exploitation, and sometimes even instinctive recognitions of the quality of the music itself. The minstrel show was, after all, a form of musical theater, dominated by song and instrumental music.

The evidence offered in earlier chapters shows that the term *minstrel show* is a convenient generalization; it covers a variety of acts and parts of longer performance routines and programs presented by different ensembles rather than a relatively rigid format in a tightly organized type of theater. The "typical" show's structure was not a closed rhetorical action at any time during the antebellum period; variety was the primary feature of the minstrel show's organization. A survey of even a small number of playbills and programs confirms that conclusion even though the most recent authoritative discussion of the matter still accepts the tripartite organization of the minstrel show and infers from that a series of symbolic consequences for antebellum American culture: "Armed with an array of instruments, usually banjo, fiddle, bone castanets, and tambourine, the performers would stage a tripartite show. The first part offered up a random selection of songs interspersed with what passed for black wit and japery; the second part (or 'olio') featured a group of novelty performances (comic dialogues, malapropistic 'stump speeches,' cross-dressed 'wench' performances, and the like); and the third part was a narrative skit, usually set in the South, containing dancing, music, and burlesque."[8]

The analyses of the contents and performance practices of the shows reveal that the organization of most of them were flexible and open-ended, dependent more on styles of different companies than on any preset formulas, closely related to the specialty acts of particular "stars," and linked to the other theatrical styles or events, especially burlesques, of the antebellum period. Even if as many as 50 percent of the playbills or cards follow the tripartite formula just summarized, one might well question the appropriateness of deducing all the rhetorical and symbolic consequences of blackface entertainment from a template that applies to only half the material.

Some minstrel shows did not have any designated plantation sections, and many companies restricted the so-called darkey routines to instrumental solos or dances in the second of what were often four-part programs, regardless of where the intermission occurred. The Ethiopian sketches, when they did occur, were seldom set in the South, and dances or novelty numbers were just as likely to appear as successful wrap-ups for the entire variety show as they were for the second part. The settings for some Ethiopian operas—*The Virginia Girl*, for example—migrated to the South because the blackface conventions and the interpolations of minstrel songs in Balfe's work required the removal from the eighteenth-century locale of Pressburg. The burlesque created as many opportunities for ridiculing the feudal social hierarchy of European life as it did for mocking the analogous organization of southern plantation life.

Some of the most popular minstrel song texts applied equally to southern or northern locales regardless of the songs' positions in the typical minstrel show. Both "Dinah's Wedding Day" and "De Colored Fancy Ball," parodies based on William Fry's *Leonora,* refer to urban activities and not to African American plantation wedding rituals. These songs were presented in various parts of the minstrel shows between 1842 and 1852 rather than being featured specifically in sections referring to northern or southern life.

Songs such as "De Old Jaw Bone" or "See, Sir, See," whose texts suggest a plantation or rural setting, are usually found in the first part of the show, which sometimes referred to the contrasts between northern and southern "darkies" even though the material seldom went beyond the most superficial distinctions. Stephen Foster's "Old Folks at Home" seldom if ever appeared in the third part of the minstrel show, where such an expression of nostalgia for the old plantation might be expected. "Old Folks" usually appeared as a pathetic ballad in part 1 without any strong indication that the nostalgia the song evokes had much to do with the "Dandies [not Darkey Dandies] of the North," which some commentators take to be the principal material of part 1.[9]

The titles of the so-called plantation scenes varied from "Representing the Peculiarities of the Southern or Plantation Negroes" to "Saturday Afternoon in Old Virginia" or "DOWN IN CAROLINA: Introducing the Cornshucking or Festival DANCE." Local or regional specificity is seldom applicable to minstrel materials regardless of the song's geographic setting. If "authenticity" had ever been the true goal of "Negro delineation," the minstrels would have chosen something more concrete than the quasi-mythical setting of "Old Virginia." The locale was little more than a convenient backdrop for playing out the song text and establishing a setting for dancing.

Minstrelsy did not create the plantation myth; rather, it participated in the commodification of the escapist notion that forced labor differed little from supervised play. The dances that took place on minstrelsy's plantations were not part of "the romantic myth of gentility" or the "abolitionist plantation myth of barbarity" because the material attributed to African Americans preserved only as much a sense of style as was necessary to make the entertainment work, not to make the caricatures authentic.[10] The minstrels recognized that borrowing from African American culture was one way of gaining independence from the English and Irish domination of American folk and theater music.

The plantation burlesques were inspired by the same desire that motivated writers and composers to burlesque Shakespeare or borrow from already successful ventures and repackage them for a populist audience. The minstrels' arguments about "authenticity" as a mark of verifying the integrity of their programs was really intended to convince audiences that the shows were worth the price of admission. All arguments about "authenticity" aside, the humor of the antebellum minstrel show was embodied in a vocabulary of symbols with special significance for the formation of American popular culture.[11] No matter how energetic or innovative the "plantation" scenes may have seemed to audiences in the 1840s, those fictive locales seldom ventured far from the songs, banjo solos, dances, and instrumental numbers of the first blackface acts. The idea of the plantation never changed, never developed into a "real" place. It remained a convention where the "make believe" southern slaves dwelt. The plantation of minstrelsy's making was essentially a burlesque environment, just as the blackface operas were a domain for fantasized social pleasure. It was a setting celebrating a sense of conviviality and community that the ever-changing minstrel show audience could imagine as applicable to their own lives, a theatrically effective site for burlesque improvisation, specialty dancing, and the mimicry of the culturally other.

The plantation environment of the typical minstrel show could never have served (as its twentieth-century critics would like it to have done) as the principal site for a critique of the effects of racial oppression. To the extent that the fictional creations of northern entertainers may have reinforced the myth that slavery was not oppressive, minstrelsy's creators were similar to other managers of popular culture, for they allowed sentimentality and shallowness to substitute for critical and comic assessments of the human condition.

Minstrelsy moved away from its early characterizations of African American culture because the performers and managers recognized the inherent limitations of a style based on the imitation of a people marginalized by disfranchisement and systematic economic subjugation. One of the ironies involved in the rehabilitation of Black English as a positive characteristic of African American distinctiveness during the last thirty years is that the early blackface comedians' attempts to use the dialect for satirical purposes can now be investigated more seriously even though that dialect, which virtually vanished from the minstrel shows of the 1850s, was only one feature in the whole minstrel package of burlesque entertainment.

Within a performance context, the appropriation of a prestigeless dialect into a different linguistic environment is a masking act. It proclaims that the actor is "in character" and notifies the audience that such language use is only temporary. Dialect use, however, served as a vehicle for several comic purposes in nineteenth-century published humor without disturbing the dominance or preference for a standard spoken and written English among elite users. Many different and nonstandard forms of dialect were respected (and exploited) among all classes during the antebellum era, demonstrating Noah Webster's theory that "the presence of local vocabularies may be admitted as long as they do not pass into the standard national language." That "national language" or dialect should be based on a "standard polite usage shared by the educated and influential classes in all parts of the republic."[12]

Webster's principle made minstrel show dialect a powerful tool for satire in blackface comedy because the dialect *did not* adhere to standard polite usage; it allowed subjects to be treated without privilege or prestige in the two major genres of spoken humor, the burlesque sermon or preacher jest and the ludicrous lecture or stump speech. The burlesque lectures outnumber the preacher jests in antebellum minstrel playbills, so the basis for the satire does not seem to have been linked exclusively to African American traditions of educational, religious, and political rhetoric.[13] Both the lecture and the sermon were solo specialty items, but neither appeared often in the plantation set pieces of the minstrel show, the most obvious locus for the presentation of African American characteristics. The basis for the genre's significance must lie in the audiences' experiences with similar forms of persuasive preaching or lyceum lecturing, even if the vehicle for the satires was the class- and race-based assumptions about folk preachers or fancy-talking lecturers. The only way the minstrels' patrons could have functioned effectively as symbolic lyceum audiences or congregations was if they viewed the lectures as exaggerations of styles with which they were already familiar.

Whether the minstrel show material came from the *New York Picayune,* some forgotten comic almanac, or a recent lecture by a prominent male or female entertainer or public speaker (say, the inimitable Dr. Valentine or Elizabeth Oakes Smith),[14] blackface comedians were quick to import the burlesque rhetoric into their acts. Most of the acts confirm that "the *real* essence of minstrelsy was burlesque . . . in every aspect of the show" and that "the blackface minstrel, by taking on theatrically some form of the black image, whether rudely stereotyped or ethnographically scrupulous, had consciously or unconsciously entered into a many layered satire of Anglo-American life."[15] The dialect comedians of the early 1840s might have exploited the great richness of African American spoken humor and folklore, but the course of dialect use in minstrelsy was similar to the development of the music and other theatrical business. Although the blackface comedians' adaptations of Black English originally showed great promise as devices for exploiting the immense creative potential of linguistic practices linking African American and Standard English dialects in positive ways, by the end of the 1840s those adaptations were gradually reduced to a number of conventions in the songs and sermons. Minstrel performers discovered that only a hint of dialect was needed to "get into character," and comedians usually exploited linguistic differences only when they reinforced the conflict between some innovative idea—for example, women's rights—and the social status quo or between two individuals, because rivalry and mock contests were the principal rhetorical techniques in much of male-dominated blackface humor.

The spirit of burlesque identified minstrelsy as derivative and capable of accepting much more interesting and entertaining material than just cheap racist caricatures. The purpose of the Italian opera parodies was not to show that African Americans could not sing opera, even if some Americans believed such a foolish idea. When they sang Italian opera choruses or Tyrolean refrains, the blackface quartets or octets measured themselves against what they perceived as a standard for musical performance established by some of America's European guests. American performers recognized quality but expressed their frustration with the attention foreigners received by making fun of the imported traditions and the highly paid artists who performed them in the United States. For Americans in general and blackface comedians in particular, making fun of foreign performers diverted attention from a growing sense of cultural inferiority that led to the ridicule of European cultural products.

The blackface comedians showed how American culture reacted to the influx of foreign-born performers who brought new musical styles to a country without a definable music tradition and helped expand the range of music available. But foreigners were also rivals for American attention and compensation; there was no small amount of jealousy about the pay differentials between European and American musicians. The minstrels recognized the disdain that most foreigners held for American culture because most Europeans still thought of the United States as a colony, or at the very least a former colony, without an indigenous national culture. That culture was acknowledged in minstrelsy's adaptations of the products of popular and elite music making among various social classes.

Minstrelsy has already been revealed as a heavily derivative genre; its very derivativeness strengthens its claim as a critical player in the formation of an American popular style. In large measure, the popular or vernacular style is just a mixture of those materials from a variety of sources that cross over various market segments to become fairly universally known.[16] The instrumental solos in the musical portions of late-1850s minstrel shows differed from those of the 1840s because the earlier performers had to have depended on some black players and on one another for tutoring in the various instrumental styles. The movement of banjo players from one group to another facilitated the development of banjo-playing techniques, and as minstrelsy moved toward the format of the variety show after 1855, instrumental tutors, beginning with *Briggs' Banjo Instructor* (1855), provided some guidance to beginning players. With the improvements in the instruments and the development of virtuosos such as George Swaine Buckley and Charley Fox in the early 1860s, banjo styles reached heights earlier performers could never have imagined.[17]

Some of the musical exchanges were described in detail, especially in the parodies that blackface instrumentalists created in response to the performances of professional musicians. But what marked the differences between the songs of Dan Emmett and Joel Sweeney and those of Thomas Moore and Michael Balfe? How was it that some African American musical material could fit into the variety of music offered by minstrels in the mid-1840s, and how could that material be identified?

The arguments about African musical remnants in minstrelsy and the recognition that African Americans "signified" on European styles of dance and art music cannot be dismissed just because minstrelsy left a legacy of lingering negative images about African American culture. Many of the steps and figures in blackface specialty acts were borrowed from African American culture, from black parodies of white social dancing, or were invented to distinguish American folk or popular dances from those of Europe.

There is simply no questioning the fact that there was such a black dance culture and that whites borrowed from it. As John Blassingame noted, the plantation slave "held onto many remnants of his African culture, gained a sense of worth in the quarters, spent most of his time free from the surveillance by whites, controlled important aspects of his life, and did some personally meaningful things on his own volition."[18] The fact that antebellum black culture is still somewhat of a mystery at the end of the twentieth century makes it difficult to document in detail the synthesizing activities that took place in contact situations between black and white musicians at the time minstrelsy became popular.

Those points are important to investigating why the new blackface songs of the 1840s were different from European stage music imported into the United States all through minstrelsy's formative years. The minstrel songs were often "composed" and performed by the singers themselves, who were required to move about on the stage and in some cases accompany themselves while they sang and danced. Those activities require that the performance material be simpler than examples in which the performer simply sings to the accompaniment of a piano, ensemble, or orchestra. The performance styles could easily accommodate the patterns established by Joel Sweeney and could also accept importations of African American styles. The relationships between African American and the predominantly Anglo-American musical cultures existed in the early 1840s when minstrels' publicists claimed that blackface comedy delineated the "sports and pastimes of the Negro race." The evidence of the songs confirms the differences between Emmett's early songs and contemporary British examples, especially in the former's limited melodic compass, modal pitch structure when performed with the banjo-fiddle instrumentation, and frequent interruption of the vocal line for instrumental breaks designed to accompany new forms of stage business and theatrical dancing.

There are examples where the stylistic characteristics we now know to be related to African American musical culture were incorporated into an evolving popular music tradition at a time when both white and black musicians *shared* a number of common musical repertories, some of which have now been recovered in Cecilia Conway's and Joyce Cauthen's studies of late nineteenth-century musical exchanges.[19] This "sharing of repertories" or "common repertory" theory is not a romantic concept of a "people's music" untainted by racism. Even if a pattern of white-over-black dominance prevailed at the social and political level, and even if black fiddlers provided much of the occasional music on the practical level in some urban environments or at some plantation locations, musicians usually play what audiences request, and performers often share material for their own pleasure.[20] The belief that musical exchanges occurred across racial barriers does not imply that practicing musicians living in the distant past of the early nineteenth century inhabited some idyllic world where only music mattered. What is implied is that, in their daily practice as performers, musicians were more likely to find a melody or playing style suitable to a particular performing environment than to remain aloof to influences from African American instrumentalists or singers. The experiences I describe were not always documented, or if documented, they have not always been discovered by historians. But Solomon Northrup, who described himself as the "Ole Bull of Bayou Boeuf," wrote, "My master often received letters, sometimes from a distance of ten miles, requesting him to send me to play at a ball or festival of whites. He received his compensation, and usually I also returned with many picayunes jingling in my pocket—the extra contributions of those to whose delight I had administered. In this manner I became more acquainted than I otherwise would, up and down the bayou."[21]

The theory that musical exchanges went only one way is false; Levine's argument in the epigraph debunks such a theory. Where there were distinct differences between white and black culture, the tendency has been to discount the observations of eyewitnesses who reported such differences to the reading public. If William Cullen Bryant's corn-shucking account is read as a white supremacist's report on behaviors associated with an inferior group rather than an observation about alternative social behaviors, it is easy to miss the point that his report supports the authenticity claims made by minstrel show performers. Although blackface comedians are unlikely to have understood the evidence of African cultural practices being shared by the plantation workers at the corn shucking, they could have easily concluded that African Americans practiced a decidedly different work ethic. To outsiders, the enslaved people may have seemed happy in their labors, not because slavery was benevolent, but because the labor provided an opportunity for social exchanges that the masters tolerated because corn shucking was essential to the plantation or agricultural economy. "The light wood fire was made, and the negroes dropped in from the neighboring plantations, singing as they came . . . . and the negroes began to strip the husks from the ears, singing with great glee as they worked, keeping time to the music and now and then throwing in a joke and an extravagant burst of laughter. The songs were generally of a comic character; but one of them was set to a singularly wild and plaintive air, which some of our musicians would be well to reduce to notation."[22]

American musical history might be easier to write if Bryant's suggestions had been taken, but the continued intensive explorations of African American culture in cities and on plantations suggest that the denial of musical influence across the black-white cultural barrier is another example of the general ignorance about pre-twentieth-century black music and its relationships to the dominant culture. The practical world of music making does not require that performances be reduced to notation to be kept alive. Musicians, as I have argued, absorbed each others' work through a natural process of exchange. To deny African American musicians a role in the creation of earlier American music is just as flawed an argument as the one supporting the contention that all black culture was derivative and that, until the late nineteenth century, there was precious little African American music from which whites *could* have borrowed.[23]

The banjo, which contributed the unique melodic sound to the minstrel show, was an instrument that had been played principally by Africans, both bound and free, in the South and probably in the North as well. The development of an idiomatic instrumental practice takes time, and the transmission of styles across homogeneous and heterogeneous groups (in this case, other black players and early white imitators of blacks, respectively) involves contact situations of some duration. It is simply impossible for there to have been no body of banjo technique and no repertory of material in the late 1830s and then for both to have appeared suddenly when the first white players hit the stage in the early 1840s. This is especially telling given that the drop-thumb downstroke style of frailing has no counterpart in any known style of playing European fretted or unfretted instruments.

This hypothesis would also explain why minstrel material found its way back into African American culture easily; the tunes were already constructed to fit the primarily melodic styles of the antebellum banjo and fiddle, and since these playing styles were dependent on a preexisting African American tradition, their development could easily have been taken up by the black players who were already playing in some of those styles. This ethnomusicological argument is related to a recent prediction that "when social scientists and historians begin to investigate systematically the survival of African culture among European-Americans they will discover that as much African culture survives in the United States now among whites as among blacks."[24]

Hans Nathan demonstrated that many of the earliest blackface songs were parodies of existing tunes, a truly significant observation about early American musical culture. The parody process was a form of cultural appropriation symptomatic of the first stage of a cultural separation from British song. Because the United States was a postcolonialist entity, American musicians sought to define themselves and their repertories as different from English culture to equalize the cultural, political, and economic relationships between the two countries. Those declarations of difference varied from defiantly nativist to decidedly assimilationist. To escape the paternalistic role in which the English cast themselves in their dealings with the United States, American artists in particular transformed the shared cultural models, songs, ballads, and musical theater pieces by subtle irony and sarcastic wit.

The musical examples could be shared easily because, as Charles Rosen has recently argued, much of what is now considered high European art music from the nineteenth century was in fact "trash"; that is, it was once really the common popular material of its day and a counterbalance to the notion some nineteenth-century musicians and critics held about music's aspirations to being the highest art. That theory explains the Italian domination of American vocal music as a consequence of "the fact that the Italian operatic tradition was more openly and comfortably vulgar than the historical novel or the more grandiose salon paintings." Rosen argues that "only the tension between the vulgarity of the genre and consistent high aspiration of the composers can enable us to understand the frequent disparagement of Bellini's music by French and German critics," the same Bellini whose La Sonnambula appears so often in blackface burlesques.[25]

Some of the parodies of Italian opera choruses from Ernani, La Sonnambula, and Masaniello, as well as the English choruses in the Italian style from The Bohemian Girl and The Enchantress, were just as popular on the minstrel stage as the original music was in opera houses. Blackface parodies did nothing to weaken the appeal of the music, and little was done to change it. Even after the "antebellum elite rejected egalitarianism for class exclusiveness," they were unable to restrict access to operatic hits, which must have been respected, for the parodies deal primarily with the texts. There are very few if any parodies of the music and no attempts to render the songs (at least in the published ones) in the disjointed self-reflexive styles found elsewhere in minstrel show music. The parodies, then, were used to provide music that the minstrel composers could not have created themselves or to ridicule the conventions of their Italian and French musical sources.[26]

Those sources never lost their importance for minstrelsy. When the minstrels moved from primarily solo songs to harmonized (usually three-part) choruses in the mid-1840s, the harmonies did not demonstrate any fusion of African American and Anglo-American musical elements, at least as far as the published arrangements are concerned. Comparison of the Italian opera choruses by Bellini and Donizetti with the arrangements used by the Hutchinson Family or the quartet style of the EGB1 (1848) do not reveal any significant stylistic differences. Minstrelsy's choral style seems squarely in the realm of contemporary popular choral practice and not something new or innovative.[27]

The whole minstrel enterprise, regardless of its early roots in cultural imitation, eventually ended as a theatrical style when "the minstrels turned from racist humor to mocking the arrogance, imitativeness, and dim-wittedness of the upper classes in 'permissible' ways."[28] But minstrelsy's appeal was not so class-linked as it might first appear; the male working class and lowlife of the city were not the only ones who treated women with disdain or as objects of sexual desire. That was a gender prerogative, not one of class, although the mechanisms by which male dominance was preserved depended on financial worth, property, social standing, and family relationships.

Class envy manifested itself as a natural outcome of the progressive American ideals of self-improvement, economic security, social elevation, and the typically postcolonialist belief of achieving status somewhat comparable with the perceived class structures of European society.[29] The minstrel style was compatible with American song because it appealed to vernacular *and* reasonably cultivated audiences. Unlike some of their European counterparts, however, minstrel composers did not aspire to create high art in the same way that Italian composers occasionally did. The former were delighted to capture popular attention and respectable sales, whereas the latter were at their best when they were able to elevate "trash" to the musically sublime.

Minstrelsy's distinctive musical *sound* did not pretend to the sublime. The original and unique instrumentation of banjo, violin, bones, and tambourine distinguished it from other music of the period. It was not uncommon to double the banjos or the fiddles, but there is no evidence of the way that the parts were divided when the number of melody instruments increased. When that early instrumentation changed from the fiddle-banjo combination of melody instruments with two contrasting percussion instruments, minstrel music itself had to change also. The presence of the piano in the minstrel hall together with the use of the accordion or concertina and additional fiddles would have led to simplifications in the tunes themselves. The inclusion of brass bands in the minstrel show would also have changed the ways the original melodies were played. The use of equal tempered keyboard instruments and three- or four-part harmony quickly undermined the modal nature of tunes originally featured on the fretless banjo and promoted the development of that instrument from its folk roots to its eventual acceptance as the "classical" banjo in the hands of performers such as George Swayne Buckley, Thomas Briggs, James Unsworth, and the other early minstrel professors.[30]

The publication of arrangements for piano, guitar, brasswinds, and other instruments makes it even more difficult to evaluate the early songs and instrumental numbers of Joel Sweeney, whose techniques were never documented. The translation of African American folk practices into the primarily white world of minstrelsy is still a matter of dispute, but for stylistic reasons a number of early tunes do not require the fourth (bass) string of the banjo. Conway argues that "the evolving repertory of tunes using all five strings took two decades or more" to develop after the premiere of the first minstrel show in 1843.[31] What might have been an African American or Anglo-American modal melody could easily have been absorbed into an emerging "American" style as the tune was subjected to multiple performances and arrangements. The modal, pentatonic nature of the tunes, which could have easily been accommodated in the minstrel ensemble of two melody and two percussion instruments, was lost in a piano or brass band arrangement. This is analogous also to the decrease in the number of different tunings early banjo players used to accommodate their instrument, an argument often heard in discussions of mountain banjo styles.[32] These are stylistic arguments operating within the domain of the prevailing musical practice, which, although it may have been conditioned by the demands of various classes for music befitting their own social rituals, also involved practical decisions by musicians in which the alterations of tunes was more a matter of how the melody lay for the instrument or how it could be arranged as part-music for four voices given the limitations of the typical tenor and bass parts.

The contrasts among musical styles in minstrelsy can best be seen in one of its favorite forms, the burlesque virtuoso act. A blackface fiddler would not have needed to be able to play one of Ole Bull's virtuosic operatic medleys note for note to ridicule the American audience's admiration for brilliant technical display. Even though "Little Ole Bull" Buckley or "Ole Bull" Myers were outstanding fiddlers, the Ole Bull burlesque required only that blackface performers mimic the stage manners or musical style by choosing an appropriate Anglo-American tune, say, the "Sich a Getting Up Stairs" quadrille from the *Jim Crow Quadrilles* (Philadelphia, 1837), and creating a variation set to demonstrate the superiority of the blackfaced rustic fiddler over the foreign violin virtuoso. The variation sets in the banjo and fiddler tutors, which reduced to notation and hence to duplication tunes such as "Yankee Doodle," pointed the way for a banjo performer to learn conventions employed by the touring European virtuosos. The burlesque performance questioned not Bull's skill (although his repertory certainly reflected the worst of nineteenth-century potpourri recitals) but rather the envy native-born musicians held for foreigners.

The traditions from which a real American "Ole Bull" could draw would have been the Irish and European fiddle tunes that were transformed into new combinations by the American demand for set dances. The two-strain AB tune built out of eight- or sixteen-bar repeatable phrases did not furnish enough music for the more intricate sets, so additional strains, typically from three to six, were required. The added material could have been based on the tune itself but more likely was an interpolation from another melody sharing similarities with the existing material. The references to "Jenny Get Your Hoe Cake," "Old Virginny Nebber Tire," "Clare de Kitchen," and other tunes within other songs illustrate one way in which musical material was constantly being recirculated and refashioned.

Going beyond the blackface minstrels' contributions to American music, minstrelsy's role in defining other aspects of popular entertainment in the United States is evident in the short skits that simplified the dramatic conflicts found on the legitimate stage into primitive rivalries over women or contests over position in male power groups. The replacement of the subtleties and complexities in interpersonal relationships by a few sentimental conventions is characteristic of the quick psychological gratification inherent in vernacular cultures. Blackface comedy captured the skepticism most Americans shared about the sincerity of preachers, the integrity of philanthropy and charitable reform, the effectiveness of politics, and the equity of a capitalistic system that guaranteed unequal distribution of wealth and political power. Minstrelsy also dealt, albeit obliquely, with an even deeper fear about the many changes predicted for the immediate future. Minstrel humor was derived from the same motivation David Reynolds attributed to other forms of popular comedy and satire when he argued: "Beneath the lighthearted satire of the urban humorists lurked a dark anticipation of impending social chaos. The retreat to humor represented a withdrawal from volcanic forces such as dark reform, women's rights, and pseudoscience."[33] Many of those fears were captured in the sketches that argued for maintaining the status quo.

The sketches satirized the democratic values of different racial or ethnic groups. The sketch writers often incorporated new images of city life, introduced ideas about the increasingly diverse immigrant groups, offered views (usually negative) about scientific inventions and economic theories, and explored contrasting or competing social or political philosophies. The result was that blackface stereotypes worked in concert with other comic elements to create a complex vocabulary for comedians to satirize manners, customs, and gender roles within acceptable limits. The black (and blackface) male servants in some sketches complicated their low-status roles with their mischievousness—a masking behavior consistent with the contempt servants usually hold for their employers.

The typical minstrel show did not focus *exclusively* on black men as subjects of ridicule (contrary to the claims of Ellison, Huggins, and other African American scholars). The evidence shows that blackface entertainment also reinforced negative perceptions of women, regardless of their color or class. Nonetheless, minstrelsy was generally as ambivalent about gender as it was about race. The ensemble minstrel show (unlike the solo or duo acts before 1843) openly contradicted the values of American sentimental culture, a culture that was itself a construct designed to rationalize gender competition. Even in its most sentimental songs (and there were many), minstrelsy embraced antebellum ideologies about women; in its antisentimental moments, it underscored the limits of male tolerance toward equality for women.

Minstrelsy was a generally negative style of comedy; it was complaining, critical, skeptical, denigrating, misanthropic, misogynistic, and suggestive. It questioned and defied logic, but it also affirmed American values by insisting that its comic inversions never seriously threatened to upset the social order and by reinforcing existing political power relationships. The fictional world minstrelsy offered was a "theater of misrule" that considered alternatives but did not argue forcefully for their adoption. Minstrel comedy contributed to patterns of racial and gender disparagement humor that, however deplorable, were also inescapable consequences of the changes that threatened the male control of the political and social order.

Race and gender were linked in minstrelsy, links that seem clear because depictions of women clearly dominated the programs. Women of all races and classes were the most frequent victims of blackface comedians' humor. The images of women that emerge from minstrel songs and sketches are decidedly negative because "the urban imagination encoded class and racial differences in the categories of the dangerous and endangered and played out these social distinctions within the female sex."[34] Many of the women described or characterized in minstrel songs were treated as victims or as pleasure-seeking companions, for example, the kidnapped child or spouse, the sold companion or lover, and the "yaller gals" willing to provide a good time for a price.

Songs about courtship, dying young women, and marrying and establishing a home all had a strongly moralistic tone in the antebellum period. Those genres correlate quite well with the treatment of women in melodrama, where goodness and virtue are found in the "passive suffering of the virtuous characters, while evil is embodied in the villain." The villain in most minstrel songs is the master who sells a slave spouse, a kidnapper who steals a child or lover, and death, the ultimate thief, which robs a loving relationship by "taking" the young woman. The songs demonstrate that the "villain's greed and sensuality are outward manifestations of a desire to control others. By preying upon a beautiful woman (or foolish man), whose allegiance is or should be to her father, lover, or husband, he gains control over all the men around her."[35] The pathetic personae in "Lucy Neal," "Mary Blane," and the "Virginia Rose Bud" are melodramatic characters because the female victim is subject to the actions of tyrannical or thoughtless slaveowners while the male character usually goes on about his life.

The male voice or persona speaks through the blackface song, and it is usually the male's suffering that takes primacy in the texts. Women were potential threats to male prerogatives, and the most frequently threatening situations were conventionalized in minstrel comedy. From the "yaller gals" who accosted men on urban streets to the wives who placed limits on acceptable behaviors in marriage, male fear of a disgruntled spouse or of an aggressive "lady" appears frequently in minstrelsy's repertories. The burlesque of women was, therefore, "largely a male-dominated form of discourse that privileged male voices and experiences of the community while muting, even silencing, its women."[36]

When the minstrels chose to depict women through the cross-dressed convention of the "Lucy Long" dance, they presented aspects of the feminine ranging from the display of the female body as an object of male ridicule to sentimentalized portrayals of chaste companions "sleeping" in bowers and valleys. Women were partners in relationships that included casual sexual associations and the most intimate family transactions. And women were treated idealistically as a class whose arguments for human rights were interpreted generally as an assault on a male-dominated social structure. In the final analysis, blackface minstrelsy cannot be divorced from the world its comedy created and the sentimentality its songs about women espoused. Mary Ryan has observed that "although male writers posed primarily as protectors of women's acute sensibilities to public insult, they clearly felt personally threatened as well" and that "the fearful possibility of meeting death by female hands was conjured up around dance halls and low-class dives, public spaces where men and women came together to transact sexual commerce."[37] This was the new world that young people encountered when they arrived in large cities. The minstrel comedians recognized the comic potential embodied in the disillusionment and disappointment that new urban dwellers felt by contriving the fictive escapist worlds of the convivial plantation and the freewheeling city.

The differences between rural life and the mid-nineteenth-century American city created serious conflicts for young men and women who had to re-create supportive communities different from the kinship relations that characterized small-town and rural life. Minstrel shows and blackface songs could offer some solace in the artificial environment of the theater, where they could heal the "split between production and personal life . . . in which people no longer worked close to or in their homes, but in factories or workshops at the hours set by their masters."[38] Family and kinship relationships were replaced by new types of associations and living arrangements that made the family environment a subject for pathetic songs.

The subject of family disruption was a serious concern because the culture was intent on defining the nuclear family as the essential substructure of American society. The breakup of family relationships caused by the exodus to urban manufacturing and business centers led songwriters to reinforce the values associated with stable family life and sketch writers to revive the popular overprotective father figure in the courtship skits.

There were constant assaults on the sanctity of the domestic life of the nuclear family, however, because young women were taking up employment outside the home and the communities of their birth. Yet minstrel ensembles seldom dealt with working women—the real world—because it was assumed that women were somehow primarily objects of courtship and humor. The ideal woman as minstrel songs envisioned her was very different from the new urban public woman, who had to negotiate her way through difficult circumstances. The structured roles of the ideal parents, the appropriate nurturing for young people, and other qualities reinforced by the domestic melodramas of the period appear as objects of parody and sentimentality in the blackface songs associated with "home."

Some groups were far more negative than others in their depictions of women, for example, White's Serenaders during the mid-1850s. Other ensembles lacked the skill to produce consistently good plantation scenes or imitations of dancing or other allegedly African American activities. These companies—for example, Buckley's New Orleans Serenaders—generally limited themselves to a greater variety of clever burlesques or hired guest artists when the need arose. Ordway's Aeolians, because of their Boston location, seems to have programmed fewer songs associated with sexual commerce or cross-dressed libidinous characters than appeared in the shows produced by New York–based ensembles. Wood's Minstrels regularly programmed burlesque lectures against women's rights, for example, William Newcomb's lecture in the persona of Mrs. E. Oakwood Smith. In those cases individual performers and companies simply reflected the wide diversity of opinion in the United States on important social issues.

Minstrel performers usually avoided intellectually difficult issues, preferring instead more direct approaches to their comic material. The suggested displays of the "female" body via the cross-dressing conventions were similar to those that occurred in the social contexts surrounding the minstrel show. The exhibitions of women in tights posing as Venus or Diana titillated the male body gazers in northern cities. The urban context for displays of the female body had more to do with the commercialization of sex than with the aesthetic qualities of Greek and Roman statues. The transfer of statuary exhibits to the mythical plantation was the ultimate trivialization of the classical ideal of beauty in the eyes of the minstrel companies because the plantation represented the domicile of the ultimately powerless.

In the cross-dressing situations, the humorous convention depended on the implication that the character would reveal something. The lifting of the skirt or the prominence of the foot (whether heel or toe really did not matter) was suggestive. So, too, were the live imitations of classic statuary and contemporary American sculpture that the minstrels parodied by placing men in most of the roles. The Christy Minstrels' exhibits of statuary in "Down in Carolina, introducing Specimens of ETHIOPIAN STATUARY," provided an opportunity for members of the company to demonstrate their dancing abilities and still ridicule Dr. Collyer's Living Models.[39] The unlikely juxtaposition of parodied black dancing and exhibitions of statuary emphasizes how important burlesque was to the typical minstrel show.

There are some clear class and role distinctions among women represented in the minstrel repertory illustrating how class differences fit with the minstrel comedians' choice of targets for satire. The sketches, operatic choruses, dances, Dutch drills, and cross-dressed acts show how often the nouveau riche were caricatured because they pretended to be better than they were. Those individuals, it appeared, based their sense of individual moral value on the demonstration of personal wealth, usually in the extravagant attire the minstrels used to ridicule white and black urban dandies. For the less public miscreants who were thought respectable, Charles White offered some typical advice:

A little thieving is a dangerous part,
But thieving largely is a noble art,
'Tis vile to rob a hen-roost of a hen,
But thieving largely makes a gentleman.[40]

White's cynicism was repeated by other urban humorists, such as Mortimer Neal Thompson, who attributed the same failings of sincerity and integrity to politicians when he described a moral training academy as a place "where American reformers and statesmen are trained in their favorite activities, drinking, swearing, lying, and confidence games."[41]

Role reversal and status inversion were the typical techniques blackface comedians used to level the class distinctions that gradually weakened the American belief in an egalitarian society. The blackface disguise may have "homogenized cultural opposition so facilely that it could express the ethos of both respectable and rowdy working class culture at once, or perhaps so facilely that it could fully express the ethos of neither."[42] Whose ethos did it express then? And were those *ethoi* the same if they were captured by *middle-class* comedians? How much of an ethos could a genre of popular culture be expected to express given the inherent limitations of a commercial product directed at audiences who themselves could not articulate a consistent set of principled beliefs?

The audience is now the issue in minstrelsy studies. Given the evidence from the shows themselves and the amount of material unrelated to African Americans or their culture, the emphasis on respectability and the appropriateness of blackface entertainment for audiences of women and children, and the prominence of contemporary references in what has been supposed to have been a form of comedy based on belittling one racial group, the question remains: what did the audiences internalize about the issues of the day? What evidence is there about what audiences believed?

Minstrel companies generally avoided controversial issues or approached them only tangentially. That behavior was consistent with popular culture's dependence not only on income but on the ways the theater reinforced the ambivalence many persons felt about the economic and social issues of the period. In this respect the managers of the blackface minstrel companies were not unlike "the urban humorists [who] opposed slavery but were horrified by the hyperbolic, often seamy language of extreme abolitionists."[43]

Minstrelsy in general was never associated with a particular party line or class ideology; the evidence indicates that virtually all points of view can be found somewhere in the repertories of blackface comedy. Individual groups may have espoused specific political views, but the genre never demonstrated a uniformity of social purpose or a desire to achieve universality within popular culture as a whole. Yet minstrelsy also reflected the same consciousness of class differences found in Mowatt's *Fashion* (1845) and translated into the Ethiopian sketch known as *The Hop of Fashion*. In that respect minstrelsy "helped constitute a break (and thus an anxious discourse about the break) between elite, genteel, and low cultures which would be fundamental by our century."[44] Blackface comedians may have been conscious of class, but the recurrent themes in their songs, sketches, and burlesque rhetoric were not so much about class as about the pretentiousness that accompanied American elitism. Since the possession of wealth and its consequence of privilege became the principle on which Americans attempted to define class difference, and since those who achieved that financial prosperity exhibited their success as a means of demonstrating distinction, minstrel comedians usually depicted the newly wealthy as characters who disdained the poor—who had only yesterday been their peers. That was the point of *The Hop of Fashion.*

Minstrelsy did not define the contents of the shows on the basis of class because all classes were its patrons as well as its targets, the term *targets* meaning the array of hypocrites, parvenus, and confidence men of all classes and social stations. Even a song such as Foster's "Old Folks at Home" became a vehicle for blackface comments on class distinction when White's Serenaders concluded their show with "the laughable Burlesque entitled Old Folks at Home" (May 3, 1852) and Buckley's Serenaders presented G. Swaine Buckley in a "Scientific Banjo Solo, The Second Edition of the 'Old Folks at Home' or how it is sung among the Upper Crust" (Nov. 23, 1853).[45] Minstrelsy's characterizations of the "upper crust" were not so frequent as to mark blackface comedy as a totally class-based phenomenon, however, and its meanings for American culture cannot be fathomed solely on the basis of a class-based method of interpretation. Minstrelsy's desire to achieve respectability is evident in the following account of the changes George Christy and Henry Wood made when they opened Henry Wood's new 1,660-seat theater at 444 Broadway. As the patrons entered the theater, they passed through a large corridor to discover the ladies room at their right "furnished in the most luxurious style, with toilette appliances, useful in cases of sudden illness or fainting, to which latter disability . . . the belle sex is often subject, where there is a large crowd to see them do it gracefully." The main auditorium displayed "all the features of a well-regulated theater: spacious aisles and lobbies, an able orchestra, a profusion of mirrors and painted decorations, and . . . two 'elegant and spacious' private boxes on either side of the proscenium 'gloriously done,' like the ladies dressing room, in 'rosewood, brocatel [a heavy figured fabric], Brussels [carpet], and lace.'"[46] By the 1854–55 season Christy and Wood's programs "were replete with new musical gems, new character dances, and new burlesques: 'The Hutchinson Family' and 'Ten Minutes at the Academy of Music,' with some new, quaint, quizzical, and quiet bon mots—in fact a little of everything for everybody."[47]

As the contents of the shows demonstrate, minstrelsy's conventions were so firmly established by 1853 that, far from being the singular attraction of the working classes, some blackface ensembles presented programs that mirrored the higher-class theaters of Broadway, a world of rarefied racism where politeness and practiced distance minimized the potential that political and moral issues might be confronted directly. The notion of minstrelsy as primarily a working-class entertainment breaks down here because neither popular music nor any other form of theater could ever "fully express," much less capture the essence of, any group's feelings.

If the *content* of blackface performances identifies "their particular appeals as expressions of the longings and fears and hopes and prejudices of the northern Jacksonian urban working class, especially the artisanate,"[48] how did content alone express all that, given the diversity shown in the playbills and the continuing problem of even defining who the "urban working class" was during the antebellum era. The issue is not which class was the most racist, however, or which bought the minstrelized forms of copy most quickly. The real issue is making assumptions about the way that audiences of the period understood what they were seeing and recognizing that they did not view blackface entertainment with the same sensitivities that some modern audiences bring to it.

It is certainly reasonable to argue that white racism was the primary meaning of minstrelsy and to accept all the arguments made by Houston Baker, Ralph Ellison, Nathan Huggins, and the many others already quoted. Nonetheless, if minstrelsy exploited blacks as scapegoats for white guilt, imaged blacks as comic surrogates for repressed white sexuality, or substituted blackfaced victims to accomplish a cathartic release of white hatred, how can we "reconcile the fact that aggression purportedly *disguised* or otherwise made acceptable in humor is often consciously expressed in non-humorous ways?"[49] One answer is certainly that racism was not the primary and exclusive purpose of every minstrel burlesque.

But the same question can be raised about the theory that some minstrel ensembles consciously subverted racist ideologies by presenting antislavery arguments and painting sympathetic portrayals of black victims. David Roediger recently argued against the subversion theory because it puts "aside the extent to which those audiences knew that these were white entertainers, playing thinly blacked-up white stock characters." The antislavery messages did not depend on the color of the messenger or the fact that the performers who delivered them appeared in makeup and costume.

Roediger also offered a telling criticism of the notion that blackface was a disguise serving other comic purposes by pointing out that those who argue that "blackface was a slight veneer providing the 'distance' necessary to do effective social satire . . . minimize the extent to which the mask seemed real to the audience and subverted the social criticism being expressed."[50] That is, those who believed that white comedians were creating reasonably effective impressions of blacks would never have taken the satirical comments seriously because they would have seen the comments as coming from African Americans. But Roediger's two arguments cancel each other. Some members of the audience probably knew that the performers were white; others were no doubt taken in completely and, believing that the players were black, paid little attention to the criticisms of contemporary society. Both statements are based on a lack of evidence about what audiences actually thought, however. If the minstrel show patrons were truly fooled, they would have had to conclude that African American males held the same misogynistic attitudes they themselves did. In that case nothing was really subverted, for the players and the payers were essentially in complete agreement. That agreement, however, means something else. It means that both the performers and the audience held a common skepticism about the nature of relationships between men and women.

There have been no compelling arguments demonstrating that the "mask" seemed real to the vast majority of the audiences, in spite of the puffs describing various minstrel performers as true representatives of Negro eccentricities. Of what value is the "mask of blackness" as a racist marker when the minstrel is burlesquing the yodels of the Tyrolese minstrels, the songs of the Hutchinson Family, or the styles of Jenny Lind and the Seguin Opera Troupe? Minstrelsy was too complex in its various significations to be understood only as an entertainment in which whites masqueraded as blacks. Minstrelsy did not subvert the importation of foreign manners and cultural products so much as it revealed nativist assertions of cultural independence.

Mask or no mask, the true object of minstrelsy's subversive texts was the overthrow or replacement of the dominant culture, for much of what it offered was imposed from outside the body politic, something only partially true, as the number of Italian and English examples on the minstrel playbills shows. Worrying about the effectiveness of the disguise or the authenticity of portrayals of African Americans misses the implications of social mobility and status inversion as principles in blackface comedy. The inversion theory played out in the skits and sketches explains why a good portion of American society seems to have delighted in and identified with the spectacle of powerless blackface characters outsmarting or commanding the powerful. Compare, for example, the two texts of "Blue Tailed Fly" or "Jim Crack Corn" (1846) and "Down in Alabama," which was later published as "Get Out De Wilderness" (1858). These texts clearly show the rebellious nature of the plantation character. The characters in the respective songs rejoice at the deaths of their masters, the one from an insect bite and the other from dropsy.

As the first manifestation of a form of entertainment initially associated with the vulgar lower classes, minstrelsy was generally praised or disdained according to the critics' social or class status and the strength of their dedication to European or American cultural traditions.[51] Yet minstrel composers and arrangers created the first form of commercially acceptable popular music based on the commingling of folk and popular traditions, which were different both from the "scientific music" based on central European musical practice and from the English traditions of song.

Blackface minstrelsy seems to have been attentive to most of the major concerns of the antebellum period. Deconstructing or reconstructing the ways in which it was so have proven difficult because of the recurring concerns about the vehicles blackface comedians used to reach their audiences, such as the burnt cork makeup and the way it was used, the image of the disguise as a device for expressing hidden feelings, the metaphor of the mask as an indicator of symbolic communication that protected creator and listener alike from the truth about the conditions of the people who were represented in the racial masquerade, and the conflicts allegedly resulting from whites who felt guilty about their roles as racial mimics.

David Reynolds suggested that "the great lesson of American humor" was that "one could register democracy's disruptions but at the same time distance oneself from them and thus strip them of their terror."[52] The terror was probably more a fear of change or of a reduction in the number of perceived prerogatives. The sense of "democracy's disruptions" was ultimately a recognition of the contradiction that the full freedom of the individual as the logical extension of a radical and liberal philosophy would inevitably lead to chaos and a potential reversal of an economic and social order that needed to be changed but not necessarily overturned. Depending on the particular fear each individual experienced, the anxiety about change could be extended to a world that intemperate abolitionists might somehow control and to the social changes likely if emancipation were a real political and social goal. Minstrelsy could not resolve those problems any more than the political powers could; entertainment was a sensitizing force but not a fundamental power in antebellum popular culture.

These conclusions lead to one final corollary based on a burlesque lecture written by William Levison:

> Ef a furiner wus to belebe all he hear on his ribal [arrival] to dis kedenty [country], he wood put us doun in he scrach book, for a nation of quacks. . . . Wen you hear a preecher-man take he *tex* from de scriptur, and *preech* from de newspapers, and when he use de words ob our Saviour, to probe [prove] his politikal doctren in de pulpit, you may in safty bet your dinner dat he am a quack! and I don't noe a more contempable man in de site ob de Lord and man, dan a quack in religion. When you hear a lawyer talk 'bout sacrificin he konshunce to he business, and offerin to stake his existence on de result ob your case in de ward cort, and at de same time wants a V or an X for his 'pinion, and boasts ob he nolege ob Blackstone and Bluestone, ef you aint got a nose dat am too flat to smell, you can plainly smell quackery and bad gin, while he am talkin to you. . . . De quack artist am pretty easily seen fru, but it takes some little time to find 'em out, and dats de reason so menny ob de furener musicians and actors dat send money and ready written puffs ahed ob dem, draw one or two big houses afore de folks find out dere true merit.[53]

Levison's advice invites speculation about how the history of minstrelsy might have been written if antebellum audiences could tell us more about how minstrelsy looked and sounded. The testimony quoted in most investigations of burnt cork comedy is highly suspect because there is not much of it and because some of the most frequently quoted items are attributed to unknown authors whose credentials are just as murky; other quotations reflect a class bias against popular culture and mass entertainment, for example, *Dwight's Journal of Music*.[54] Blackface comedians may have been quacks when some of them tried to imitate African American life, but that does not mean that the performers were scapegoats for the audience's hidden fears or auteurs purging their own consciences before a congregation of paying witnesses.

Individual minstrels may well have been racist if they assumed that African Americans could be reduced to comic signs and stereotypic buffoons, but it is not the individual minstrels who matter. The materials they performed were simply too diverse to support the hypothesis that all burnt cork comedy focused on racial issues or that all the parts in a typical minstrel show were played by nothing more than "thinly blacked-up white stock characters." Many of the characters parodied in the shows were based on real people, for example, Ole Bull, Edward Seguin, Edwin Forrest, Elizabeth Oakes Smith, Amelia Bloomer, Dr. Collyer and his living statues, John Ericcson, and now forgotten lecturers and preachers. If this study has proven anything, it is that minstrelsy was directly connected to the culture of its own period, much of which has been lost because the events of everyday life are easily forgotten and hard to retrieve.

Early American comedy seems now to have been related to the creation of new forms of burlesque comedy, using that term in its nonliterary meaning. The literature on black Americans in the South clearly demonstrates that the practice of signifying or burlesquing the white power culture was a cultural trait of African immigrants. That same practice was also a convention in the burlesques of lower-class whites by the southwestern humorists. But the assumption that blacks and whites would not have laughed at some of the same things is also a naïve view of the broader American contexts in which both races dwelt. In other words, arguments based on that assumption take blackface humor to be racial or racist and fail to understand that humorous characters, if studied on a comparative basis, may transcend racial or ethnic barriers and be archetypical.

If the blackface comedians were not playing or could not play black people, what was the purpose of the disguise? Why did they have to dress up if they could fool only some members of the audience for part of the time? And if they were successful in convincing those few naïve patrons that they were surrogate African Americans, why was their material related so strongly to the sentimental and burlesque culture of the period? Why, finally, were the racial and ethnic masquerades of African Americans, Irish, Germans, and others during the antebellum period so prominent a part of American entertainment? White racism cannot be the answer to every form of comedy based on inhabiting the "other" and incorporating into comic performance traits selected for their denigrating references to the target groups.

Blackface comedy announced that the time for playful consideration of some social issues had begun in American mass culture, that what was to be said and sung on the stage was not always to be taken literally, and that with the protection of the disguise, whose negative impact has not been shown to be the cause of American racism, the players themselves did not need to be personally accountable for their utterances or actions. The costumes and makeup created characters who did not have to be "authentic" because the primary purpose of the genre was burlesque. That was the point of popular blackface humor: it could have no program for reform because its purpose, like the circus, the sideshow, and the museum of horrors, was to display, to criticize, to ridicule, to hold up to nature a cracked mirror showing only a partial reflection of the complexities of antebellum life.

Minstrelsy may well have been the "national art of its moment," but its impact on the future of American popular music now appears to have been quite significant. Minstrelsy appropriated elements of black culture with varying degrees of accuracy and with an overall purpose of creating a commercially popular product. It provided an early demonstration that Americans were committed to topical entertainment, were sentimental in their perceptions of much deeper emotional issues, misogynistic in their views of gender equality, and resistant to the portrayal of complex social problems in an environment devoted to play and diversion. In the end the minstrel show was a form of popular culture that, in its own imperfect and ambivalent ways, addressed (1) the unfairness of privilege and the growing exclusivity of class, whether based on accomplishment or the randomness of sudden wealth in a capitalist economy; (2) insecurity about emerging cultural forms borrowed from foreign countries; (3) the distrust of differences among groups other than one's own in a society where the ethnic mix changed rapidly in the 1840s; (4) questions about widely held convictions about family and courtship expressed in satirical fashion in sketches and other forms of spoken comedy; (5) the threats to male dominance of the economy and political power inherent in the extension of full and equal rights to American women; (6) fears of a power inversion if allegedly submissive slaves were emancipated and concerns over the potential loss of access to work or political power; (7) the sustenance of American-born performers in an environment where English and Europeans were able to command high salaries and public praise for often marginal musical skills; and finally, (8) the ways in which the means of cultural production as well as the subjects explored in public theater could be controlled by the market forces and audience demands. Blackface minstrelsy was one of the primary paradigms for the whole enterprise recognized now as the popular culture industry.

Appendix A: Representative Minstrel Companies and Personnel in Playbills and Newspaper Advertisements, 1843–60

Note: Asterisks identify performers who participated in more than one ensemble.

1. Various Virginia Minstrels and Serenaders Companies, 1843–50

Virginia Minstrels I (1843)
Daniel Emmett*
William Whitlock*
Frank Brower*
Richard Pelham*

Virginia Minstrels II (1844)
Barney Williams
William Whitlock*
T. G. Booth
Harry Mestayer*

Virginia Serenaders I (1844)
(Portland, Maine, group)
Cool White*
J. A. Carter
John Diamond*
Robert Edwards (Master)

Virginia Serenaders II (1843)
Samuel Sanford*
J. Richard ("Ole Bull") Myers
Master Mulroy (?)
Sam Johnson

Virginia Serenaders III (1843–44)
Anthony Winnemore*
William W. Newcomb*
Edwin Deaves*
Solomons (?)

Virginia Serenaders IV (1844)
Samuel Sanford*
J. Richard ("Ole Bull") Myers*
John Diamond*
Evan Evans ("Eph") Horn*
Edwin Deaves*

Virginia Serenaders V (1849)
William ("Billy") Birch*
J. Farrell
Edwin Deaves*
J. Kavanaugh*
Evan Evans ("Eph") Horn*
Hy Rumsey
C. Clarke

Virginia Serenaders VI (1850)
Anthony F. Winnemore*
J. Richard Myers*
Edwin Deaves*
J. Sanford
Warrington (?)

Winnemore's Serenaders (1850)
Anthony F. Winnemore*
D. W. Lull
J. Rudolph
F. Solomon
W. D. LaConta
T. Barrymore
Little Juba

2. Ethiopian Minstrels or Serenaders Groups, 1843–51

Boston Minstrels (1843)
Original Ethiopian Serenaders I
Francis Germon*
A. [Anthony] F. Winnemore*
Moody G. Stanwood*
J. Baker
O. Wilson

Ethiopian Serenaders III (1844)
Francis Germon*
Richard Pelham*
Moody Stanwood*
George A. Harrington
George W. White*

Ethiopian Serenaders V (1845)
Amidon ("Bije") Thayer*
F. Crawford
Edward Gray
C. Wheeler
William W. Necomb*
John G. Brown
Master Lemons

Ethiopian Serenaders VII (1851)
Sherwood Campbell*
J. B. Farrell
Evan Evans ("Eph") Horn*
Thomas F. Briggs*
William ("Billy") Birch*
S. A. Wells [Sam Welles]*

Ethiopian Melodists (1848)
Cool White*
Robert Edwards
Philip Rice
W. Howard
Dan Leon

Ethiopian Serenaders II (1844)
(Palmo's Opera House group)
Francis Germon*
Gilbert W. Pell*
Moody G. Stanwood*
George A. Harrington
Cool White*

Ethiopian Serenaders IV (1845)
Thomas Briggs*
Gilbert Pell*
Moody Stanwood*
Charley Howard
S. A. Wells* [Sam Welles]

Ethiopian Serenaders VI (1849)
(Dumbleton's Band)
Moody G. Stanwood*
Charley (?) Howard
George W. White*
Parker (first name unknown)
Jerry Bryant*
S. A. Welles*

Ethiopian Minstrels I (1847)
J. A. Carter
Harry Mestayer*
W. Donaldson*
Jerry Bryant*

3. Buckley and New Orleans Serenaders Groups, 1845–56

Buckley's Congo Melodists (1844)
James Buckley
Richard Bishop Buckley
G. Swaine Buckley
Frederick ("Ole Bull") Buckley
John G. Brown

Buckley's New Orleans Serenaders (1848)
James Burke [James Buckley]
J. Rainer [R. Bishop Buckley]
J. Swaine [G. Swaine Buckley]
Master Ole Bull [Frederick Buckley]
S. [Samuel] L. Sanford*

Buckley's Serenaders (1850)
Richard Bishop Buckley
Frederick Buckley
G. Swaine Buckley
W. Percival
T. S. Waddletown [Waddington*?]
G. Simpson
R. Carroll
J. J. Mullen

Buckley's Serenaders (1855)
Richard Bishop Buckley
Miss A. Eleanor
Miss Heywood
W. Percival
J. A. Lonsdale
T. S. Waddington*
J. A. Basquin

Buckley's Serenaders (1845)
James Buckley
Richard Bishop Buckley
G. Swaine Buckley
Frederick Buckley
Samuel Sanford*

New Orleans Serenaders (1850)
J. C. Rainer [James Buckley]
Frederick ("Old Bull") Buckley
F. Burk
Nelson Kneass*
J. H. Collins
Max Zorer*
C. D. Brown
Samuel Sanford*

Buckley's Serenaders (1853)
Richard Bishop Buckley
G. Swaine Buckley
J. J. Mullen
J. A. Londsdale
T. S. Waddington*
Evan Evans ("Eph") Horn*
Thomas F. Briggs*
W. Percival

4. Edwin P. and George Christy Groups, 1843–56

Christy Minstrels I (1844–45)
Edwin P. Christy
George Christy*
Thomas Vaughan*
Lansing Durand
R. M. Hooley*

Christy Minstrels III (1847)
Edwin P. Christy
George Christy*
Earl Pierce
S. A. Welles*
Thomas Vaughan*
Thomas F. Briggs*
C. Abbott

Christy Minstrels II (1845)
Edwin P. Christy
George Christy*
Earl Pierce
S. A. Welles*
R. M. Hooley*

Christy Minstrels IV (1848)
Edwin P. Christy
George Christy*
Thomas Vaughn*
J. W. Raynor
J. Upson
C. Abbott
H. Donnelly

Christy Minstrels V (1849)
Edwin P. Christy
George Christy*
Thomas Vaughn*
J. W. Raynor
E. [Earl] Pierce

Christy Minstrels VI (1850–51)
Edwin P. Christy
George Christy*
Thomas Vaughn*
J. W. Raynor
E. [Earl] Pierce
W. A. Porter
Napoleon Gould
Max Zorer*

Christy Minstrels VII (1853)
John B. Donniker
Thomas Christian
E. [Earl] H. Pierce
Thomas Vaughn*
Napoleon Gould
Lewis Mairs
B. Mallory
August T. Vass
Philip B. Isaacs*
J. Simpson

George Christy Minstrels I (1859)
George Christy*
Sherwood Campbell*
J. K. Edwards
R. H. Hooley*
J. A. Herman*
Master Eugene [Eugene D'Ameli]
Master Gus Howard

5. Charles ("Charley") White's Ensembles, 1848–55

White's Serenaders I (1848)
Charles T. White*
H. Neil
W. D. Corrister
B. F. Stanton
G. Wray
Master Marks (R. M. Carroll)
Nelson Kneass* (musical director)

White's Minstrels II (1849)
Charles T. White*
H. Neil
W. D. Corrister
B. F. Stanton
G. Wray
Master Marks (R. M. Carroll)
Mickey Warren

White's Serenaders III (1851)
Charles T. White*
H. Neil
W. D. Corrister
W. Donaldson*
George W. White*
Master Marks (R. M. Carroll)
P. B. Isaacs*
T. Waddee
William ("Billy") Coleman

White's Serenaders III (1852)
Charles T. White*
D. Price
S. H. Denman
W. Donaldson*
George W. White*

White's Serenaders IV (1852)
Charles T. White*
Edwin Deaves*
Dan Bryant*
Bowers [Edward Bowers?]
George W. White*
Master Marks (R. M. Carroll)

White's Serenaders V (1853)
Charles T. White*
Daniel Emmett*
Dan Gardner
James Budworth*
George (full name not known)
R. M. Carroll ("Master Marks")
Master Witters

White's Serenaders VI (1854)
Charles T. White*
James Budworth*
James Carroll
P. B. Isaacs*
Daniel Emmett*
J. Sweeney
J. Niel
W. Llwellen
J. D. Pell

White's Serenaders VII (1855)
Charles T. White*
James Budworth*
James Carroll
P. B. Isaacs*
J. T. Huntley
George Wood
Tim Norton
M. Vincent
La Petite Christine

6. Samuel Sanford's Companies and Opera Troupes, 1853–57[a]

Sanford's Minstrels I (1853)
Samuel Sanford*
W. Pearson ("Punch") Collins
Joseph H. Kavanaugh*
Julian A. Von Bonhorst
Professor Nosher
James Lynch
Barney Williams*
Master Sanford (Sam's son)
Richard ("Dick") Sliter*
Lindsay [R. Lindsey?]
Nelson Kneass*
Master C. and Prof. Schmitz
Signor Foghel

Sanford's Opera Troupe I (1853)
Samuel Sanford*
W. Pearson ("Punch") Collins
Joseph H. Kavanaugh*
J. C. Rainer
Edward F. Dixey
James Lynch
Cool White*
Master Sanford
Richard Sliter*
C. Perry
Buruff (first name unknown)

Sanford's Opera Troupe III (1856)
Samuel Sanford*
W. Pearson ("Punch") Collins
Joseph H. Kavanaugh*
J. C. Rainer
Edward F. Dixey
Pete Lane
Cool White*
Master Sanford
Dan Gardner
R. Lindsey
Frank Brower*
Professor Andrews
Miss Julia Sanford
J. Holden
Miss Ernestine de Fieber
Lafferty (first name unknown)

Sanford's Opera Troupe III (1857)
Samuel Sanford*
Edward F. Dixey
Julian A. Von Bonhorst
J. C. Rainer
J. H. Collins
Joseph H. Kavanaugh*
Cool White*
James Unsworth
W. Jackson Rudolph

Sanford's Minstrels IV (1858)
Samuel Sanford*
Edward F. Dixey
Julian A. Von Bonhorst
J. C. Rainer
Hugh Dougherty
Joseph H. Kavanaugh*
Cool White*
O. Perry
J. Holden
P. Strum
Sanford children

Sanford's Minstrels V (1859)
Samuel Sanford*
Edward F. Dixey
Julian A. Von Bonhorst
J. H. Carncross
Dan Gardner*
Joseph H. Kavanaugh*
J. Finnie
O. Perry
J. Holden
Dick Sliter*
T. A. A'Becket and Sanford children

7. Henry Wood's Companies, 1852–59

Wood's Minstrels I (1851)
M. Campbell
J. A. Herman*
Evan Evans ("Eph") Horn*
Thomas F. Briggs*
Winchell (first name unknown)
Master Malatrat
Max Zorer*
Henry Wood (manager)

Wood's Minstrels II (1852)
Amidon ("Bije") Thayer*
J. A. Herman*
Evan Evans ("Eph") Horn*
Thomas F. Briggs*
M. Mitchell
S. A. Welles*
Richard Sliter*
Henry Wood (manager)

Christy and Wood's Minstrels III (1853)
M. Campbell
J. T. Huntley
George Christy*
George Griffin
Dan Bryant*
Master Eugene [Eugene D'Ameli]
C. Keene
Henry Wood (manager)

Wood's Minstrels IV (1858)
Charles H. Fox
James Lynch*
J. H. Collins
Charles T. White*
Frank Brower*
Thomas Vaughn*
Ned Davis
James Budworth*

Wood's Minstrels V (1859)
Evan Evans ("Eph") Horn*
James Lynch
David S. Wambold
Charles T. White*
Master M. Lewis
Thomas Vaughn*
Ned Davis

8. Bryant's Minstrels and Family Ensembles, 1857–58

Bryant's Minstrels I (1857)
Jerry Bryant*
Dan Bryant*
Neil Bryant*
T. B. Prendergast
S. E. Clark
William P. Lehr
Charles ("Charley") Fox
Ben Mallory

Bryant's Minstrels III (1858)
Jerry Bryant*
Dan Bryant*
Neil Bryant*
Seth Howard
W. Percival
H. Leslie
Ben Mallory
P. B. Isaacs*

Bryant's Minstrels II (1858)
Jerry Bryant*
Dan Bryant*
Neil Bryant*
Napoleon W. Gould
S. E. Clark
M. Lewis
H. Leslie
J. Butler
P. B. Isaacs*

9. Various Campbell Groups, 1847–55

Campbell's Minstrels I (1847)
Jerry Bryant*
Sherwood Campbell* [Coan]
J. W. Raynor
Matt Peel [Flannery]
James A. Carter
William B. Donaldson*

Campbell's Minstrels III (1849)
L. V. H. Crosby
Barry (full name unknown)
J. A. Herman*
Luke West [William Sheppard]
Matt Peel [Flannery]
(Five others unnamed
in Odell, *Annals*, 4:90)

Campbell's Minstrels V (1853)
D. Raymond
T. Waddee
Joseph Murphy
Matt Peel [Flannery]
Luke West [William Sheppard]
James Kendall

Campbell's Minstrels II (1848)
R. White
Sherwood Campbell* [Coan]
J. A. Herman*
Luke West [William Sheppard]
Matt Peel [Flannery]
J. Upson
Bishop (full name unknown)

Campbell's Minstrels IV (1853)
Sherwood Campbell* [Coan]
S. E. Clark
Evan Evans ("Eph") Horn*
Thomas B. Prendergast
Max Zorer*
William W. Newcomb*
Master T. J. Peel

Campbell's Minstrels VI (1853)
D. Raymond
T. Waddee
J. Murphy
H. Fenton
Luke West [William Sheppard]
C. C. Dickinson
H. E. Dickinson
Billy Wray

Campbell's Minstrels VII (1854)
Joseph Murphy
Matt Peel [Flannery]
D. Raymond
T. Waddee
Luke West [William Sheppard]
James Kendall

Campbell's Minstrels IX (1855)
F. M. Beler
J. H. Ross
H. Fenton
T. B. Prendergast
S. E. Clark
G. S. Fowler
J. H. Burdett
H. B. Nettleton
Dan Bryant*
William W. Newcomb*

Campbell's Minstrels VIII (1855)
(Murphy and Peel's)
Joseph Murphy
Matt Peel [Flannery]
Mike Mitchell
Hy S. Rumsey
J. Farrenburg
C. Keene
R. Moore

10. Other Prominent Local or Regional Minstrel Companies

Kunkel's Nightingales (1846)
George Kunkel
F. Stimmel
C. Little
H. Stimmel
J. S. Boswell

Ordway's Aeolians (1851)
John P. Ordway
George W. White*
S. B. White
Jerry Bryant*
Marshall S. Pike
J. R. Hector
F. B. Howe

Ethiopian Melodists (1848)
Cool White*
Robert Edwards
Philip Rice
W. Howard
Dan Leon
S. Clarke

Kunkel's Nightingales (1850–52)
George Kunkel
W. H. Morgan
J. M. Keach
William Lehr
Harry Lehr
Sam Johnson

Ordway's Aeolians II (1852)
John P. Ordway
George W. White*
S. B. Ball
Jerry Bryant*
F. H. Winchell
S. C. Howard
H. M. Williams
Daniel Emmett*

Ole Bull Band of Serenaders (1845)
Harry Mestayer*
Sam Johnson [Isaac Ray]
W. B. Donaldson*
G. H. Morgan
Thomas ("Pickaninny") Coleman

11. Various Ensembles Using *Sable* as Group Name, 1845–48

Sable Brothers and Sisters (1845)
John Brown
Frank Diamond
Mrs. Hood (?)
Master York
Mr. Hamblin
Mr. Belcher
Miss Lothrop
Miss Fenwick

Sable Harmonists II (1847)
J. W. Plumer
James B. Farrell
William Roark
R. H. Hooley*
J. Tichenor
Thomas F. Briggs*
S. A. Wells* [Sam Welles]
Miss Fenwick

Sable Harmonists IV (1847)
Sable Brothers and Sisters
Nelson Kneass*
T. W. Plumer
James B. Farrell
W. Jackson Rudolph
S. A. Wells* [Sam Welles]
William Roark
J. Tichenor
R. H. Hooley*
Thomas F. Briggs*

Sable Harmonists I (1845)
J. W. Plumer
James B. Farrell
William Roark
Archer (first name unknown)
J. Tichenor
Wall (first name unknown)
Cramer (first name unknown)

Sable Harmonizers III (1847–48)
(*Kneass's Original Sable Harmonists*)
Nelson Kneass*
J. W. Plumer
James B. Farrell
J. T. Murphy
J. Huntley
William Roark

Sable Harmonists V (1848)
Nelson Kneass*
J. W. Plumer
James B. Farrell
Ned Fitz Henry
Master Eugene* [Eugene D'Ameli]
William Roark
T. F. Archer
William Brown

---

a. Sanford left the Buckley family in 1851 and returned from Missouri to found several different companies, one of which was resident in Philadelphia; the others were touring ensembles.

Appendix B: Representative Concluding Numbers from Selected Minstrel Shows, 1843–60

Item Title	Ensemble	Date	Genre
1. Playbills, 1843–48 (11 Titles)			
"Lucy Long" Extravaganza	Virginia Minstrels I	03/20/43	Dramatized song
	Christy Minstrels I	04/18/44	
	Ole Bull Serenaders	02/18/45	
	Ethiopian Serenaders I	08/16/45	
"Cellar Door" Reel	Virginia Serenaders	??/??/43	Dance
Love and Jewilrums	Ethiopian Serenaders	??/??/45	Ethiopian sketch
Fireman's Chaunt	Buckley's Congo Minstrels	01/??/45	Choral number
Negro Assurance; or, High Life in Old Virginia	Ole Bull Serenaders	02/04/45	Ethiopian sketch
Burlesque Cachucha and Polka	Christy Minstrels	03/03/47	Burlesque dance
"Cobbler's Daughter"	Sable Brothers and Sisters	03/13/45	Pantomime
Prognosticators; or, Sleeping Beauties	Unidentified ensemble	03/26/45	Sketch
Railroad Overture	Female American Serenaders	05/19/47	Comic number with sound effects
Solo Dance Burlesque	Thayer's Band of Minstrels	07/19/48	Solo dance act
"Jenny Lind Polka"	Campbell's Minstrels	10/17/48	Burlesque dance
2. Playbills, 1849–54 (47 Items)			
"Down in Carolina" with Ethiopian Statuary	Christy Minstrels	02/26/49	Song and burlesque dance
"Camptown Hornpipe"	Sable Harmonists	05/22/49	Burlesque dance
"Lucy Long" with Classic Illustrations of "Nigger" Statuary	Sable Harmonists	05/26/49	Song and dance
"Lucy Long" Extravaganza	Ethiopian (Dumbleton's) Serenaders	07/06/49	Dramatized song
Burlesque of Distin Quartet	Buckley's Serenaders	09/11/49	Burlesque concert
"Congo Green" Dance with Ethiopian Statuary	Christy Minstrels	10/24/49	Burlesque dance
Burlesque Cachucha	Ethiopian (Dumbleton's) Serenaders	11/30/49	Burlesque dance

Item Title	Ensemble	Date	Genre
Oh! Hush; or, The Rival Darkies	Virginia Serenaders I	12/16/49 12/18/49	Ethiopian sketch
Negro Assurance	Virginia Serenaders	02/11/50	Ethiopian sketch
Burlesque of the Distin Quartet	Buckley's Serenaders	05/24/50 06/14/50	Burlesque concert
"Grape Vine Twist" with Locomotive Imitations	Pierce's Minstrels	08/01/50	Novelty number
Negro Assurance; or, High Life in Old Virginny	Parker's Ethiopian Opera Troupe	08/12/50	Ethiopian sketch
"Old Tar River" Dance	Kunkel's Ethiopian Nightingales	12/28/50	Burlesque dance
"Lucy Long"	Harmoneons	01/22/51	Song and dance
"Breakdown Hornpipe"	Ordway's Aeolians	??/??/51	Burlesque dance
The Black Shakers	Rainer and Donaldson's Serenaders	03/01/51	Burlesque
"Sugar Cane Reel"	Ordway's Aeolians	05/21/51	Burlesque dance
"Old Tar River" with Ethiopian Statuary	Ethiopian Serenaders	06/17/51	Song and dance
"Arkansas Walk-Around"	Wood's Minstrels	09/12/51	Novelty dance
"Congo Green" Festival Dance with Statuary	Ordway's Aeolians	02/19/52	Burlesque dance
Comic Step Dance	Wood's Minstrels	03/04/52	Burlesque dance
"Old Folks at Home"	White's Serenaders	04/18/52 05/03/52	Burlesque song and sketch
Brudder Bones's July 4th Oration and Patriotic Tableau	Buckley's Serenaders	05/07/52	Burlesque oration/ musical number
Stage Struck Tailor	Rainer and Donaldson's Serenaders	06/12/52	Ethiopian sketch
Alabama Festival Dance and Trial Walk-Around	Wells's Minstrels	08/30/52	Burlesque dance
Grand Trial Dance	White's Serenaders and Others	11/07/52	Dance contest number
Christmas Frolic	Campbell's Minstrels	07/18/53	Not known
Aromatic Brothers	Campbell's Minstrels	09/01/53	Sketch
Burlesque Chinese Dance	Campbell's Minstrels	11/07/53	Burlesque dance
Fanny Bloomer in Character	Buckley's Serenaders	11/16/53	Song and dance
Burlesque of *Norma*	Buckley's Serenaders	11/23/53 12/16/53	Burlesque opera excerpt
The Black Statue; or, The Marble Man	White's Serenaders	12/06/53	Ethiopian sketch
The Virginia Cupids; or, The Rival Darkies	Christy and Wood's Minstrels	12/22/53	Ethiopian burlesque opera
Mistakes of a Night	Christy and Wood's Minstrels	??/??/54	Ethiopian sketch
Burlesque of *The Bohemian Girl*	Buckley's Serenaders	03/06/54 10/30/54	Burlesque opera
Uncle Tom's Cabin	Christy and Wood's Minstrels	04/10/54	Operatic burletta
The Lost Child	White's Serenaders	04/10/54	Ethiopian sketch
The Musical Chowder	White's Serenaders	04/22/54	Burlesque opera excerpt

Item Title	Ensemble	Date	Genre
Burlesque of *Lucia di* Lammermoor	Buckley's Serenaders	04/22/54	Burlesque opera excerpt
Burlesque Characteristic Manouevres à la Hippodrome	Campbell's Minstrels	06/07/54	Circus burlesque
"Arkansas Walk/Around"	Wood's Minstrels	07/13/54	Burlesque dance
Oh! Hush; or, *The Virginny Cupids*	Backus's Minstrels	08/01/54	Ethiopian sketch
Darkey's Dodge; or, Two in One	Wood's Minstrels	10/11/54	Ethiopian sketch
Black Blunders; or, Forty Winks	Christy and Wood's Minstrels	10/16/54	Ethiopian sketch
African Brothers and Burlesque		10/18/54	
Scenes	Wood's Minstrels	10/24/54	Burlesque sketch
"Old Bob Ridley" Festival	Wood's Varieties	11/15/54	Song and dance
3. Playbills, 1855–60 (23 Items)			
Burlesque Tragedy of *Damon and Pythias*	White's Serenaders	01/26/55	Ethiopian sketch
Excursion Party and Express Train	Perham's Ethiopian Troupe	02/13/55	Railroad overture variant
Festival Dance	White's Serenaders	03/02/55	Burlesque dance
"Lucinda Snow" with Negro Eccentricities	Backus's Minstrels	06/20/55	Song, dance, and novelty number
Black Shoemaker	White's Serenaders	08/11/55	Ethiopian sketch
Ethiopian Court Scene	Sable Harmonists II	03/26/56	Ethiopian sketch
Burlesque of *Barber of Seville*	Perham's Opera Troupe	07/31/56	Burlesque opera
Plantation Number: "Down in Alabama"	Bryant's Minstrels	05/27/57 10/14/57	Song and dance
Horse Opera	Bryant's Minstrels	07/02/57 12/05/57	Sketch with basket horses
Terrific Horse Combat	Sanford's Opera Troupe	10/19/57	Sketch with basket horses
Motley Brothers	Bryant's Minstrels	12/25/57	Sketch
Stupendous Panorama and Burlesque of Fire Eaters	Wood's Minstrels	06/07/58	Novelty number[a]
Soiree d'Ethiope or Masquerade Festival Dance	Bryant's Minstrels	08/25/58	Dance number
Spirit Rappings	Sanford's Opera Troupe	09/01/58	Ethiopian sketch
Black Swan Burlesque	Sanford's Opera Troupe	09/01/58	Ethiopian burlesque sketch (evening)
Southern Life Illustrated by Tableau	Wood's Minstrels	12/13/58	Variety scenes and tableaux
Ball à la Musard; or, *The Dangers of a Door-keeper*	Nubian Troubadours	02/09/59	Ethiopian sketch
The Disappointed Lovers	George Christy's Minstrels	07/16/59	Ethiopian sketch
Miss Bloomer at the Soiree	George Christy's Minstrels	08/19/59	Ethiopian sketch
The Bedouin Arabs	Wood's Minstrels	09/19/59	Ethiopian sketch
Double Bedded Room	George Christy's Minstrels	07/17/60	Ethiopian sketch

Note: This list is based on the Harvard Theater Collection of playbills dating from 1843 to 1860 and representing most of the dated material but not including damaged sheets or those lacking some indication of the year of performance. If there were two examples, one lacking a verfiable date, the other, dated item was included in the sample. "Concluding" number means the last item performed, regardless of whether the show was in two or three parts or whether it had a designated finale.

a. Supposedly a 1,800-foot panorama with working steamboat.

Appendix C: Song Text Frequency in Selected Antebellum Songsters

Titles Appearing Six or More Times in Songster Collections

Song Title	1843–48	1849–53	184?–60	Totals
"Mary Blane"/"Mary Blaine"	4	2	16	22
"Lucy Long"	13	0	7	20
"Old Dan Tucker"	12	0	7	19
"Lucy Neal"/"Lucy Neale"	10	1	7	18
"Picayune Butler (Ahoo! Ahoo!)"	4	1	12	17
"Jim Crow" and parodies	9	0	6	15
"Blue Tail Fly"/"Jim Crack Corn"	4	1	10	15
"Carry Me Back to Old Virginny"	6	1	8	15
"Uncle Gabriel" and variants	4	3	7	14
"(Oh, Lud Gals) Gib Me [Us] Chaw Terbakur"	6	0	7	13
"Boatman's Dance"	10	0	3	13
"A Life by the Galley Fire"	4	1	8	13
"Dandy Jim of Caroline"	9	0	4	13
"Alabama Joe"	7	0	4	11
"Dearest May"	5	2	4	11
"Get Up in de Morning"	1	1	9	11
"Susey Brown"/"Suzy Brown"	2	2	7	11
"Cynthia Sue"	3	2	5	10
"Happy Are We Darkies So Gay"	4	2	4	10
"Jim Brown"	6	1	3	10
"Old Jaw Bone" and variants	3	3	4	10
"Whar Is de Spot We Were Born?"	5	1	4	10
"Come Back Stephen"/ "Come Back Steben"	2	1	7	10
"Jim Along Josey"	7	0	3	10
"Lynchburg Town"	1	2	7	10
"Clar de Track" ("Dan Tucker" parody)	2	0	7	9
"Jolly Raftsman"	5	1	3	9

Song Title	1843–48	1849–53	184?–60	Totals
"'Twill Nebber Do to Gib It Up So"	5	0	4	9
"Old Pee Dee"	3	0	6	9
"Old Tar River"	5	1	3	9
"Old King Crow"	1	1	7	9
"Bowery Gals" ("As I Was Lumbering")	4	1	3	8
"Black Eyed Susianna" and parodies	2	1	5	8
"Bowery Gals"/"Buffalo Gals"	4	1	3	8
"Jenny Get Your Hoe Cake Done"	5	0	3	8
"Rosa Lee"	2	2	4	8
"Sich a Gittin' Up Stairs"	3	0	5	8
"Stop That Knocking"	1	1	6	8
"At Night When de Nigga's Work Is Done"	1	1	5	7
"Charleston Gals"	4	1	2	7
"Far [Fare] You Well Ladies"	2	0	5	7
"Ginger Blue"	4	0	3	7
"Going Ober de Mountain"	3	0	4	7
"Gray Goose and Gander	3	0	4	7
"Hot Corn"	2	0	5	7
"Johnny Boker"	4	0	3	7
"My Old Aunt Sally"	3	1	3	7
"Philadelphia Gals"	5	0	2	7
"Old Dad"	2	0	5	7
"Singing Darkey of the Ohio"	2	2	3	7
"Sugar Cane Green"	1	1	5	7
"Sweep Oh!" and "Sweep Oh" refrain	0	1	6	7
"Who's Dat Knocking"	2	0	5	7
"To the Cornfields Away"	0	0	7	7
"Walk Jaw Bone"	3	0	4	7
"Wild Raccoon Track" ("In de/the")	5	0	2	7
"Guinea Maid"	1	2	3	6
"Bress Dat Lubly Yaller Gal"	3	0	3	6
"Dandy Broadway Swell"	1	1	4	6
"Dinah's Wedding Day"	0	2	4	6
"Jordan Am a Hard Road to Trabel"	3	1	2	6
"Jumbo Jum"	4	0	2	6
"Long Time Ago"	3	0	3	6
"Merry Sleigh Bells"	0	2	4	6
"Nigga General"	1	0	5	6
"Oh! Susanna"	1	1	4	6
"Old Joe"	1	0	5	6
"Ole Bull and Old Dan Tucker"	3	0	3	6
"Philisee Charcoal"	3	0	3	6
"Skeeters Do Bite"	1	2	3	6
"Suke of Tennessee"	1	0	5	6
"Virginia's Lubly Ground"	2	0	4	6
"Uncle Ned"	1	2	3	6
"Westchester Nigga Song"	3	0	3	6
"Whar Did You Come From"	3	0	3	6
"Wild Goose Nation"	2	0	4	6
"Old Zip Coon"	5	0	1	6

Notes

Introduction

1. Cantwell, *Bluegrass Breakdown*, 257.
2. Preston, *Opera on the Road*, 30.
3. Ibid., 94, 216–30.
4. Abrahams, *Singing the Master;* Szwed and Marks, "European Set Dances."
5. The first quotation is from Rogin's dustjacket comment on Lott, *Love and Theft;* the second, from Roediger, *Wages of Whiteness*, 118.
6. Preston, *Opera on the Road*, 100.
7. Cooper, *Notions of the Americans*, 2:122. See also Simpson, *Politics of American English*.
8. Crawford, *American Musical Landscape*, 75.
9. Cantwell, *Bluegrass Breakdown*, 261.
10. McConachie, rev. of Lott, *Love and Theft*, 175.
11. Levine, *Black Culture*, 444.
12. Douglass, "The Hutchinson Family.—Hunkerism," 1. *Hunkerism* refers to the Hunkers, a conservative branch of New York's Democratic party during the 1840s. They opposed antislavery positions and earned the ire of Douglass and other abolitionists. The Hutchinsons were pro-abolition, a position that earned them Douglass's unfailing support. Cass believed that citizens of the territories should determine whether they wished admittance to the Union as free or slave (the doctrine known as "popular sovereignty") and later supported the Kansas-Nebraska Act (1854). For more on Cass, see Woodford, *Lewis Cass*.
13. Ibid.
14. Robert Winans raised this issue when he noted that Lott made "inadequate use of the actual materials of minstrelsy" (Winans, rev. of Lott, *Love and Theft*, 111).
15. McConachie, rev. of Lott, *Love and Theft*, 176.

Chapter 1: Revisiting Minstrelsy's History

1. Nevins, *Diary of Philip Hone*, 710.
2. Lott, *Love and Theft*, 209.

3. This issue will be considered in the chapter on burlesque. One example here will illustrate my point. Fanny Elssler's (1810–84) New York appearance during the 1840–42 seasons made her "the most sensational performer up to that time seen on the American stage" according to Bordman, *Oxford Companion,* 229. For Elssler's life and career, see Guest, *Elssler.* Elssler's dancing was first treated to a hilarious burlesque entitled *La Mosquitoe* by William Mitchell in 1840 and later mocked by blackface entertainers who parodied her cachucha, *cracovienne,* and tarantella. Elssler's most popular dance, the cachucha (sometimes spelled *cachuca* in period sources) was performed by the Christy Minstrels (Mar. 3, 1847, and Oct. 24, 1847), the Virginia Serenaders (Dec. 23, 1849), and the Sable Harmonists (May 29, 1849). For Mitchell's career and influence on American theater, see Rinear, *Temple of Momus.*

4. None of the early blackface impressionists ever earned as much as the famous Austrian dancer Fanny Elssler, who received $500 per evening ($6,545 in 1992 dollars) during her 1842 Boston appearances. Jenny Lind earned ten times more for her first two American concerts in September 1850 and received an average of $1,903.00 ($24,739) for each of her ninety-three American concerts in 1851–52 until she broke her contract with P. T. Barnum. See Ware and Lockard, *P. T. Barnum Presents.*

5. "Ole Bull and Old Dan Tucker" (Boston: Charles Keith, 1844). The song occurs at least three times under various titles in the twelve songsters printed between 1843 and 1848 and on 19 percent (nine) of forty-two playbills published during the same period, according to statistics compiled in Winans, "Early Minstrel Show Music." My statistical summary of the songster evidence will be found in appendix C. Since there are currently no bibliographic controls for sheet music and since variations in punctuation, spelling, capitalization, and content are common in nineteeth-century popular music titles, I adopted the simplest and shortest title as a convention when faced with examples published by different publishers in the same year or the same publisher in different years. Whenever possible, I used the first verified publication of the title as the canonical source for a citation.

6. Moody, *Dramas,* 482–83. Sanjek reports a figure of $317,000 in *American Popular Music,* 2:174. My estimates about current dollar values are based on Greene, "Understanding Past Currency," 48. The figures are derived by dividing the current Consumer Price Index (CPI) by the older CPI to derive a multiplier and then multiplying the dollar amount by that figure. In this case the multiplier is 4.42. These figures are only approximations and admit a wide margin of error. But $100 a month would have been a big sum in 1850 for any working person.

7. Lawrence, *Reverberations,* 546n, reports the lower figure. All these figures are estimates, but the overall range of Christy's earnings suggests that minstrel managers could meet the middle-class status level described here.

8. Whitman, *I Sit and Look Out,* 245. The Christy figures are from Moody, *America Takes the Stage,* 45. Montrose Moses provided a context for interpreting theatrical incomes by reporting that John E. Owens (1823–86), an English-born actor most famous for his farcical adaptation of the Solon Shingle role from Joseph Jones's *The People's Lawyer* (1839), earned $250,000 over a thirty-year period, or roughly $8,333 ($36,832) per year. See, Moses, *Representative Plays,* 2:388. Owens copyrighted his version of *Solon Shingle* but acknowledged his debt to Jones. For a biographical sketch of Owens, see Bordman, *Oxford Companion,* 531–32.

9. Wilmeth and Miller, *Cambridge Guide,* 92.

10. Lawrence, *Resonances,* 530 (first quotation); Odell, *Annals,* 6:122, 5:220 (second and third quotations).

11. An example of a typical "trip to America" from March 25, 1823, will be found in Mathews, *Memoirs,* 3:342–43. The program was organized into three parts, each with several sections or character pieces separated from one another by popular period songs and bal-

lads. The third part concluded with one of Mathews's patented "monopolylogues" known as "All Well at Nachitoches," in which Mathews played all the characters.

12. *New York Daily Tribune,* November 3, 1845. Odell, *Annals,* 5:224, places Christy at the same location on April 24, 1846.

13. The cross-fertilization process that encouraged Kneass to share his talents as an arranger, manager, singer, and instrumentalist with each ensemble he joined demonstrates how groups learned from one another and why so many of the same items appear in the playbills of minstrelsy's first half-decade. The process is shown clearly in appendix A, which lists the personnel in each ensemble I tracked with indications of which individuals appeared with more than four different companies. Kneass shared his talents with a mixed company of singers in a project called *The Unrelated Family* (1846), billed as "the greatest entertainment ever given at Franklin Hall," in which he parodied the Rainer, Hutchinson, and other singing families from home and abroad. The date and contexts are verified in Odell, *Annals,* 5:394. The Original Kneass Opera Troupe expanded its repertory by engaging members of the Sable Harmonists, a group that claimed to have been founded in 1841 and to have traveled some 40,000 miles. Kneass was listed as a member of the Sables in 1847, and he reappears in 1850 on the title page of the *Melodies of the New Orleans Serenaders Operatic Troupe* with Max Zorer, the premiere female impersonator, Master Ole Bull (played by Frederick Buckley), and G. Swaine Buckley. In 1848 Kneass emerges as a principal in a new group known variously as Kneass's Great Original Sable Harmonists, Kneass's Ethiopian Band, and the Original Western and Southern Band of Sable Harmonists. Kneass's organizations and their names seem to have changed as often as they changed locations, but all of them were important factors in the business throughout the period. See Krohn, "Nelson Kneass."

14. Opera choruses were such popular subjects for ridicule and imitation that ninety-six choral parodies appear in 120 representative Harvard playbills, a higher percentage than for any other song type.

15. All the playbills in the text are based on originals in the Harvard Theater Collection or newspaper advertisements. Since some of the originals are fragile and the reproduction costs are high, I decided to standardize the format for each item. Playbills are cited with the permission of the Harvard Library.

16. Conway, *African Banjo Echoes,* 61, 62; see also Epstein, "The Folk Banjo" and *Sinful Tunes and Spirituals.*

17. Rice, *Monarchs,* 22. For example, "Where Did You Come From?" (1840), which appears on many early minstrelsy playbills, was the same "celebrated banjo song as sung with great applause at the Broadway circus by Mr. J. W. Sweeney" (quotation from the title page of the 1840 edition published by Firth and Hall).

18. "Jenny Get Your Hoe Cake Done" (New York: Firth and Hall, 1840). My reasons for accepting to some degree the contributions of Joel Sweeney will be argued elsewhere in this study.

19. The phrase is found in a narration from the slave narrative collection and quoted from Lester, *To Be a Slave,* which can be heard on the Tony Trischka section (tracks 24–28) of *Minstrel Banjo Style* (Rounder CD 0321).

20. One example will illustrate the point. "Why is a man snoring in bed, like music paper? Because it is sheet music" (*WNP1,* 66).

21. The punctuation is consistent with the original.

22. "Uncle Gabriel" (New York: William Hall and Son, 1848). The cover shows the Ethiopian Serenaders (Pell, Harrington, White, Stanwood, and Germon) holding (from left to right) bones, two banjos, concertina, and tambourine.

23. The tunes are virtually the same in both versions. Text 1 is a separated song sheet from the Brown University Library and may have been intended for group performance based on the first verse, "I just come out to sing a song, / I hope de Lord it aint too long, / And if you listen while we sing, / We'll make it on de banjo ring." Text 2 is attributed to Dan Emmett in *Old Dan Emmit's Original Banjo Melodies*. My quotations are from the sheet music edition (text 1) and the reprint (text 2) in Nathan, *Emmett*, 316–39.

24. Playbill dated March 21–22, 1843, from Brinley Hall (Worcester, Mass.) at HTC. The lecture itself will be discussed in chapter 2, but the expression "raise steam" or "raising the wind" may derive from a James Kenney farce entitled *Raising the Wind* (London, Covent Garden, 1803) or *How To Raise Wind* in the manuscript copy but now reprinted in Booth, *English Plays*, 39–74. This typical courtship farce introduced the famous Jeremy Diddler comic character as a suitor who outwits the family and his rival for the hand of Miss Plainway.

25. Virginia Serenaders playbill, September 22, 1849 (HTC).

26. The Emmett reference is from Hutton, *Curiosities*, 126; the quotation is from Odell, *Annals*, 5:396.

27. Two of the four Virginia Minstrels later gave conflicting testimony about the group's initial appearance. Whitlock told his daughter (Mrs. Edwin Adams): "The organization of the minstrels I claim to be my idea, and it cannot be blotted out. . . . The first time we appeared before an audience was for the benefit of Pelham at the Chatham Theater. The house was crammed—jammed with our friends; and Dick, of course, put ducats in his purse" (quoted in Hutton, "The Negro on the Stage," 140). Six months after the Virginia Minstrels' debut at the Bowery Amphitheater, the original quartet, which appeared as a unit in the United States *only* from February 6 to April 23, 1843, disbanded on July 14, 1843, after concluding its tour of the British Isles.

28. The number of minstrels increased from a couple of quartets and a few soloists in 1843 to a total of nearly 140 individual performers and at least forty different groups of male and female performers involved in "Ethiopian" entertainment for New York's half-million inhabitants by 1850. The count is based on a review of the index to the fifth volume of Odell, *Annals*. Few of those individuals or companies received more than five citations, and most were mentioned once or twice, just enough to show that minstrelsy was a strong and influential force in New York but not enough to establish a comparative basis for calculating its share of the entertainment market. Odell's information by itself provides an unstable basis for such a comparison because he frequently omitted items, misdated them, and generally dismissed many elements of popular culture.

29. Reports based on Christy's statements or advertisements in the *New York Tribune*, September 28 and November 2, 1848. Christy's claims appear (among other places) in *CPM1*. Christy reprinted "Triumphant Legal Decision," the judgment in a lawsuit he brought against George Christy after the latter's departure from the group, in *CPM5*, v. Edwin Christy believed the presiding judge validated his claim to have "organized and established the First Band of Ethiopian Vocalists and Delineators of Negro Characters in the world." More of Christy's "innovations" are discussed in Davidson, "The American Minstrel Show," 79–80. Dan Emmett questioned Christy's credibility in a statement published in *The New York Clipper* (May 19, 1877); see Nathan, *Emmett*, 285–86.

30. The song differs from the earlier "Goin Ober de Mountain," also known as "I'm Gwine ober de Mountains" (1843), which has several verses dealing with a slave's desire to visit his sweetheart and comic ones describing the disposal of his impossible old horse. See Nathan, *Emmett*, 298, 316–19.

31. Nathan, *Emmett*, 65.

32. The location of the Christys in New York has not been dated back this early. Rice found them in Albany during the 1844 season but not in New York City (*Monarchs*, 19). But the HTC playbill referred to here does bear the 1844 date.

33. William Mitchell's burlesque of *The Bohemian Girl* appeared in March 11, 1845, at the Olympic Theater as *The Bohea-Girl* with Florestein's name changed to "Floorstain" and Count Arnhein's changed to "Mr. Harniem." "Thaddeus" became "Thady" (an exiled tea merchant from the Bowery), "Devilshoof" was transformed into "Hoopingcough," and the role of Arline was divided to produce two different characters played by the Taylor sisters, the first a "fine specimen of Young Harlem" and the second twelve years her senior. The famous "I Dreamt I Dwelt in Marble Halls" became "I Dreamt I Had Money to Buy a Shawl." See Odell, *Annals*, 5:127.

34. "The Dandy Broadway Swell" song was published in 1853. The first verse runs: "You talk ob dandy Niggers, but you neber saw dis Coon, / Perambulating Broadway, on a Sunday Arternoon. / I'se de sole delight ob Yaller Galls, de envy ob de men, / Observe dis Nigger when he turns and talk ob dandies den." The chorus runs: "For I'se de kick, de go, de Cheese / As ev'ry one can tell. / De dark fair sex, I'se sure to please, / I'se de Dandy Broadway swell." "Picayune Butler" was originally attributed to John Butler (d. 1864) and performed by George Nichols, a black entertainer working in New Orleans, according to Southern, *Music of Black Americans*, 94. "Young Bowshin's Bride" (New York: James L. Hewitt, 1843) is a mock pathetic ballad from *Shin de Heela; or, Black Fairy and Leather Slipper*. The cover indicates that the arrangement for "'Forty Pianos' [forte piano] was made by Chomas Tomer," who was really Thomas Comer, the house arranger for a number of publishing firms. Comer was also the compiler of the music for Thomas Rice's *Bone Squash Diavolo* overture. The song's chorus, "Oh! de old Jaw bone," appears in many other period blackface songs. The young bride runs away to play an innocent game of hide-and-seek but gets trapped in a hollow log and dies. Her groom's inept efforts to find his beloved are described, and the melodramatic ending provides an excellent example of an early blackface burlesque of the sentimental song and romantic love.

35. The first performance may have been on January 3, 1845. Nathan, *Emmett*, 149, shows an illustration of the Buckleys from the cover of *The Celebrated Congo Minstrels' Songs* (Boston, 1844) with two fiddles, tambourine, banjo, and cymbals. The cover also suggests that the group was popular enough in the Boston area to get its songs published.

36. The Buckley Minstrels often used different names on their playbills. "J. L. Buckley" was James Buckley, "Sweeney" was George Swaine Buckley, "Little Ole Bull" was Frederick Buckley, and the final member of the quartet was Richard Bishop Buckley. The composition of the various Buckley groups from their first appearance as the Congo Minstrels to their final performance in 1867 is shown in appendix A.

37. The Buckleys were first known as the Congo Melodists and played in Boston as early as 1843, according to Rice, *Monarchs*, 15. "Old Granite State" (New York: Firth and Hall, 1843) was copyrighted by John Hutchinson, who also claimed that it was "composed, arranged, and sung by the Hutchinson Family." See Dichter and Shapiro, *Handbook*, 149. Cockrell noted that the hymn was "from a Second Advent hymnbook, set there to the text 'The Old Church Yard.'" For additional information, see Cockrell, *Excelsior*, 96, 415. The title page of Emmett's "De Wild Goose Nation" (Boston: Charles Keith, 1844) carries the note that Emmett had sung the song "with unprecedented success . . . both in Europe and America" and that the piece was dedicated to "Jim Crow" Rice. The only place the "wild goose nation" phrase appears is in the first verse of this character and animal song, the vocal part of which is only twelve measures long.

38. Lawrence, *Resonances,* 136. The "Pompey Nagel" listed on playbill 4 was probably a play on the name of John Nagel, the German violinist, also heralded as a new Paganini and as "Composer and Violinist to the King of Sweden." See Lawrence, *Resonances,* 118.

39. "Bless Dat Lubly Yaller Gal" (New York: Firth and Hall, 1845) takes its title from the first line of the song. It is also the first line of "Fi, Hi, Hi; The Black Shakers' Song," generally attributed to Evan Horn.

40. This playbill (at HTC) states, "This Band of Minstrels never introduce into their Concerts any thing offensive to the most fastidious."

41. Robert Toll's contention that "few famous troupes, in fact, traveled widely before the Civil War" (*Blacking Up,* 31) is not supported by the evidence. The Boston Ethiopian Serenaders and Dumbleton's Ethiopian Serenaders toured the South during the summer and fall of 1845, visiting Richmond, White Sulphur Springs, Lexington, Vicksburg, Natchez, and New Orleans with numerous stops in small towns along the Ohio and Mississippi Rivers, according to Baines, "Samuel S. Sanford," 15–20. The dates of the tours and other information on the travels of the other various ensembles mentioned is from Rice, *Monarchs,* 15–16, 26. Playbills located at AAS confirm that New York groups "toured" New England's major cities as early as 1844.

42. Christy replaced the term *Campanologians* with *Cowbellogians* (Odell, *Annals,* 5:154) to emphasize the parody of the Swiss Bell Ringers' performance at Palmo's Opera House in September 1845 for a series of concerts "assisted by Mrs. Timm and Master Sconcia; sometimes, also, the Angelesa Singers assisted" (ibid., 223). Mrs. Timm was Sarah Timm, wife of the conductor of the New York Philharmonic and an actress and singer of some note in New York. Master Giovanni Sconcia was an Italian child prodigy in a period noted for its admiration of youthful talent.

43. "Uncle Gabriel," in *Music of the Christy Minstrels.* The song describes briefly the capture, trial, and execution of "Uncle Gabriel," the "Chief of de Insurgents." I reviewed the following accounts to establish a context for this song: Aptheker, *Slave Revolts;* Tragle, *Southampton Slave Revolt;* Oates, *Fires of Jubilee* and *Our Fiery Trial.*

44. Lawrence mentions the two Pelham brothers (Gilbert and Richard), who were both prominent in minstrelsy, and Benjamin Pelham, who was "billed as 'the great Paganini Whistler'" (*Resonances,* 144).

45. Lawrence notes that Lind "was famous in the United States long before her visit in 1850. In 1848, for instance, at the Bowery Theater, both Mary Taylor [Lize in *A Glance at New York*] and Adelaide Phillips (1833–92), the English-born soprano whose European education had been sponsored in part by Jenny Lind, were cast as the Swedish Nightingale in an afterpiece billed as 'The Extravaganza of Jenny Lind'; a Jenny Lind novel was published; Jenny Lind beaver hats and bonnets were advertised by William Banta, at 94 Canal Street" (*Resonances,* 501).

46. Odell, *Annals,* 5:378. For more on *tableaux vivants,* see McCullough, *Living Pictures.* I am indebted to Don B. Wilmeth for this helpful reference.

47. Odell, *Annals,* 5:535; Lawrence, *Resonances,* 492.

48. References to the "statue" phenomenon are in the playbills already mentioned. The citation of the Ethiopian Melodists' burlesque is from the *New York Daily Tribune,* September 5, 1848. Some blackface comedians emphasized their own interpretations of the living statues phenomenon, with Charles White (1821–91), now of White's Serenaders, billing himself as the "Black Apollo."

49. Preston, *Opera on the Road,* 132.

50. The best discussions of this phenomenon are Preston, *Opera on the Road,* 99–148; McConachie, "New York Operagoing"; and Ahlquist, "Opera, Theatre, and Audience." Most

of the English troupes performed versions of Italian opera adapted for the English stage and audience by Henry Bishop (1786–1855) or Michael Rolphino Lacy (1795–1867).

51. Christy Playbill dated ca. 1845 (AAS). The playbill is a generic one with blank spaces for the insertion of specific concert information.

52. From unidentified clipping in HTC.

53. The quotations in this paragraph are from Davidson, "The Minstrel Show," 80–81, 82. The same point was made by a reviewer of the Buckleys' May 24, 1850, performance in Boston: "The New Orleans Opera Company are doing a tremendous business, notwithstanding the full houses of the Ravels, and the excitement of the Italian Opera, too, they come in for the largest share of patronage. . . . Here you can hear ballads sung by the best vocal performers in this country, and a comic song as it should be. . . . We advise one and all not to lose a chance of seeing these ebony artists, as their time among us is limited" (quoted in Baines, "Samuel S. Sanford," 79).

54. *New York Tribune*, August 30 and September 15, 1848.

55. Playbill reconstructed from Odell, *Annals*, 5:488–89. Complete playbill at HTC.

56. The Distins were in the United States from January to September 1849, that is, for two theatrical seasons, time enough to create just the kind of musical hubbub blackface minstrels enjoyed. Henry Distin eventually moved to this country (1877) and established a manufacturing plant in Williamsport, Pennsylvania, in 1887. For the Distins' reception in the United States, see Lawrence, *Resonances*, 593–95. This burlesque was copied by the Buckleys and inserted into the third part of an 1849 show that included some of the novelties mentioned earlier.

57. The references to "Tyrolean" in the programs point to minstrels' parodies of the performing styles of the various European singing groups that toured the United States in the 1840s and 1850s. Some of the songs based on Swiss or Austrian singing groups may have been yodels. Tom Christian (1808–67) of the Christy Minstrels was "one of the best to do Tyrolean warbling" (Rice, *Monarchs*, 23).

58. Quoted in *Dwight's Journal of Music*, July 24, 1852, and in Hamm, *Yesterdays*, 109, 211.

59. Baines, "Samuel S. Sanford," 70.

60. Playbill, October 24, 1849 (HTC). This playbill is in poor condition, but the contents I describe are still clearly visible.

61. Pierce's Minstrels Ethiopian Operatic Troupe claimed in their August 1, 1850, playbill (HTC) that they were performing the piece for the "275th time and received nightly with shouts of laughter."

62. The Shaking Quakers appeared at Barnum's from November 23, 1846, until mid-December, according to Odell, *Annals*, 5:233. "The Black Shaker's Song," or "Fi, Hi, Hi," as it was also known, was attributed to "Even [Evan] 'Eph' Horn" on the sheet music version published by Firth, Pond, and Co. (New York, 1851). The Black Shakers skit was still in the repertory, according to an Bryant's announcement printed in the *New York Herald*, January 17, 1858. The song also appeared under the title of "The Black Shakers' Song" or "Fi, Hi, Hi" in *WNP1*, *WNE1*, *CPM1*, and *ESB2*. An illustration of a minstrel adaptation of Shaker dancing will be found in Nathan, *Emmett*, illustration 33, 95. The opening line of the song, "Bress dat lubly yaller gal, de white folks call Miss Dinah," is the same as the title of another minstrel show song found in *NSO1*, *WBA1*, and *GEM2* whose first playbill appearance is on one for the Virginia Serenaders in 1850 (HTC).

63. *New York Daily Tribune*, September 7, 1846.

64. "Fi, Hi, Hi; The Black Shakers Song and Polka," written and composed by Evan Horn of Fellows Ethiopian Troupe (New York: Firth, Pond, 1851).

65. Odell, *Annals*, 6:76–77.

66. A Buckley Serenaders playbill for September 11, 1849 (HTC), shows the following finale: "We Dreamt We Dwelt in Kitchen Halls" and "GRAND MARCH by the Wonderful DIS-TIN-guished PERFORMERS, on their SIX RUSH-ING HORNS." The same example also appears as a concluding act in a May 17, 1850 playbill: "Burlesque of the MUSICAL PA-NOR-A-MA ON THE DIS-TIN HORNS Original with this Company and performed with great applause by several Popular Companies in New York" (quoted in Baines, "Samuel S. Sanford," 333).

67. "Jullien and His Orchestra" and "Jullien's Concerts," *Dwight's Journal of Music*, October 15, 1853, and October 29, 1853; quoted in Sablosky, *What They Heard*, 31–37.

68. The evidence for this conclusion will be found in appendix B. How White managed to acquire the rights to Rice's work is still unclear. Answers may be forthcoming, however, in W. T. Lhamon Jr.'s projected book on Thomas Dartmouth Rice.

69. Buckley's Serenaders playbill, New York, Nov. 23, 1853 (HTC). The "Kate" Hayes may have been Catherine Hayes (1825–61), the Irish-born soprano who toured the United States during the 1850s and whose "success in San Francisco . . . eclipsed [the] career for Eliza Biscaccianti, her American rival there" (Sablonsky, *What They Heard*, 297). Hayes apparently appeared often with all-women choruses, which may have been the reason for the Buckleys' burlesque.

70. Lawrence notes that Reynoldson, who was identified as "the much admired and talented Scotch Vocalist," appeared at the Minerva Rooms with the "veteran pop singers and blackface performers [Francis] Lynch and [Thomas] Kavanagh, . . . Nelson Kneass, and Austin Phillips, who both sang and presided at the piano" (*Resonances*, 537).

71. Preston, *Opera on the Road*, 144–45.

72. The playbills list this title in French, English, and permutations thereof. For consistency, it will be rendered in English throughout.

73. For performance dates, see Odell, *Annals*, 5:9, 19, 74, 164, 235, 312, 504, 583; Lawrence, *Resonances*, 364–65, 393–94, 540–41. It appeared as a violin, flute, or tin whistle solo in the Buckleys' programs of 1849, 1850, and 1854; as a flute solo performed by the Sable Harmoneons in 1851; and as an unidentified instrumental solo with orchestra by Backus's Minstrels in 1855.

74. The Argo recording gives the timings of the two acts as 64.37 minutes for the second act and 36.43 minutes for the third act, or slightly more than 90 minutes total. The stage business would add time. My source was the Argo recording of Balfe, *The Bohemian Girl*, Argo 433 324–2.

75. It is not true that Edwin Christy never performed after he lost his company and returned from San Francisco in 1855. He appeared rarely but did work with Sanford's Opera Troupe in Philadelphia (Christy's birthplace) for a two-week engagement in 1859, three years before his death. Christy appeared with Sanford in *The Double-Bedded Room* and with E. F. Dixey in *The Rival Comedians* (probably the piece known earlier as *The Rival Darkies*) and "played Ginger Blue" in T. D. Rice's *Virginia Mummy* (Baines, "Samuel S. Sanford," 198–99).

76. On October 28, 1853, George Christy placed an announcement (at least the second time he had done so) in the *New York Daily Tribune* "Amusements" section stating, "GEORGE CHRISTY, as professionally known for the last 12 years in connection with Ethiopian Minstrelsy, takes this method of informing his friends and the public that he has formed a co-partnership with Mr. H. WOOD of 'Minstrel Hall' No. 444 Broadway and that on and after Monday Evening next (the 24th of Oct.) he hopes to meet his friends in that magnificent and commodious Hall in his professional capacity. He hopes his endeavors to please will meet

with that success which his favorable and flattering prospects now promise. No effort on his part will be spared to merit the patronage a generous public have heretofore accorded him. G. N. Harrington, Professionally known as GEO. CHRISTY."

77. Playbills dated March 2 and November 7, 1852 (HTC).

78. *New York Daily Times,* October 4 and 17–22, 1853.

79. Dates for Foster's song are from Saunders and Root, *Music of Stephen C. Foster,* 1:459–65.

80. Both Winans and Hamm have commented on the changes in the minstrel show songs dealing with women, especially those items dealing with female slaves whose sale broke family relationships. The merging of the sentimental ballad tradition and the blackface treatment of women narrowed the focus on women to tragic heroines, argumentative shrews, or troublesome wenches.

81. Baines, "Samuel S. Sanford," 198, 215.

82. For "Dixie," see Fuld, *World-Famous Music,* 196–99. The story, performance data, and a copy of *Hard Times* will be found in Nathan, *Emmett,* 305, 415–28. For Christy's appearances with Sanford, see Baines, "Samuel S. Sanford," 198, 215.

83. *New York Clipper,* December 26, 1857. In September the *Clipper* also noted that the "old style of negro delineations takes much better than the new-fangled notions which some troupes attempt to palm off upon us as negro eccentricities" (*New York Clipper,* Sept. 12, 1857). Both citations are found in the "Amusements" section of the respective editions.

84. My conclusions are based on the HTC playbills I reviewed. I reiterate my disclaimer that it remains to be seen whether a broader sample of playbills will confirm my hypotheses about minstrelsy.

85. Rice, though infirm as the result of a stroke, continued to appear during the late 1850s. He played "Daddy Rice at Home with the Children" on August 2, 1858, and "Jumbo Jum" on August 7. Rice was back again at the Art Union Concert Hall (Oct. 24, 1859) as "Jim Crow" and was engaged for the Canterbury Concert Hall on July 28, 1860, for "six nights," his last appearance before his death on September 8, 1860 (Odell, *Annals,* 7:89, 284, 290).

86. *Spirit of the Times,* October 16, 1847, as quoted in Odell, *Annals,* 5:378. Emphasis added.

87. Cogswell, "Jokes in Blackface," 583.

88. Wilentz, *Chants Democratic,* 259.

89. Roediger, *Wages of Whiteness,* 118.

90. Winans, "Early Minstrel Show Music," 95; Cantwell, *Bluegrass Breakdown,* 261, 270.

Chapter 2: Blackface Parodies of American Speech and Rhetoric

1. "A Black Lecture on Language," lecture no. 6 from *Follitt's Black Lectures,* reproduced in Gates, *The Signifying Monkey,* fig. 13. Gates writes that the lecture is "a discourse on the representation of black spoken language, of the vernacular, and constitutes a Signifyin(g) parody in which the subject is not an antecedent text but a broader mode of spoken discourse itself" (92).

2. When the Buckleys toured England as the New Orleans Serenaders, they featured a "Burlesque Lecture on MESMERISM" at the Theater Royal, June 26, 1848 (Baines, "Samuel S. Sanford," 57).

3. Levy (*Grace Notes in American History,* 140–45) offers a brief discussion and extensive quotations from a song by Ossian Dodge, the famous temperance singer and Manifest Destiny advocate, entitled "The Magnetic Lecture." The example features a verse-and-chorus format interrupted by lengthy comic attacks on mesmerism similar to those commonly found

in minstrel performances. Mesmer's practices were also ridiculed in La Roy Sunderland's (1802–85) *Confessions of a Magnetizer Exposed: Exhibiting the following and falsehood of a recent pamphlet . . . showing the falsity of the notions prevalent in regard to what has been de-nominated "Mesmerism"'* (Boston: Redding, 1845). This piece contains dialect and nonce words, for example, *echperiments, mouves, candegular system, dorryophrizulous,* and *flambu-guziptionary nerves,* all of which are similar to "fancy words" in blackface burlesque sermons.

4. Nathan, *Emmett,* 44. Mathews's burlesque sermons may have provided the first *published* models of the type, which he claimed to have "collected" in Philadelphia or New York some-time during 1823. For Mathews's relationship to American culture, see Hodge, "Charles Mathews Reports."

5. Quoted in Dennison, *Scandalize,* 513.

6. Mathews, *Memoirs,* 3:353.

7. Francis, *Old New York,* 238. Also quoted in Young, *Famous Actors,* 2:775.

8. "Letter to James Smith," in Mathews, *Memoirs,* 3:390–92. The letter containing the ser-mon was written from Philadelphia in 1823, according to Nathan, *Emmett,* 44–46, which is my source for the quotation. The New York area that Mathews visited in 1824 had a tradi-tion of interracial religious celebrations known as the Pinkster (Pentecost) at least two de-cades before blackface entertainment became popular. Pinksterfest was outlawed by the Al-bany Common Council in 1811 because of "boisterousness, rioting and drunkenness," as well as because it fell prey to a general pattern of suppression of black culture in New York. Pink-ster has been revived as a spring season crafts and arts festival, according to the *Albany Times Union* (May 12, 1991). For additional information, see Williams-Myers, "Pinkster Carnivals"; and White, "Pinkster in Albany." Dennison reprints the complete text of Mathews's letter to Smith but notes the disdain Mathews showed toward African Americans by quoting a Janu-ary 7, 1823, letter from Mathews to his wife: "The pranks that are played in the 'nigger meet-ings,' as they are called, are beyond belief—yelling, screeching, and groaning, resembling a fox-chase much more than a place of worship" (in Dennison, *Scandalize,* 508).

9. Examples in Levison, *Black Diamonds.* Levison worked for the *New York Picayune* and published his lectures in 1855 and 1857 to ridicule "the prevailing follies of the time, and to draw a moral therefrom; and if some of the itinerant lecturers of the day should find them-selves satirized, none will stop to weep" (ii).

10. Dennison strongly (and wrongly) disagrees with Mathews's authenticity claims and cites the inconsistent treatment of word endings and phonology. He characterizes the dialect as rem-iniscent of "a poor Italian immigrant saying 'stim a boat,' or 'lend a to de poor,' or a German saying 'ven you go.' One can even imagine an Indian scout using the form, 'meetum-house.' All in all, Mathews's version of black dialect fell far short of realism" (*Scandalize,* 512).

11. A pidgin dialect is a "first contact" language used by speakers who share no common language and consequently communicate by blending elements of their native languages. West African Pidgin English was widely used among American slaves and in time developed its own grammar, a process commonly known as "creolization." See Traugott, "Vernacular Black English."

12. Such an example would be an idiolect, a form of a dialect containing a high number of idiosyncracies uncharacteristic of other users of the same dialect.

13. William Pipes found the same practice in the examples of African American preach-ing he collected during his field work in the 1940s in which the speaker acknowledges that he is aware of the change-making ploys used by churchgoers who take out more than they give when the basket is passed (Pipes, "Old-Time Negro Preaching," 16; cited in Holmberg and Schneider, "Emmett's Stump Sermons," 38n35).

14. West, *Gyascutus*, 216–18. West notes that the authenticity of this example is questionable. Stovall was a popular South Carolina preacher active during the 1830s and 1840s. If he was only a local preacher, it is difficult to understand how he knew about Abraham Lincoln. The example may be a parody of a Stovall sermon created for *Spirit of the Times*. The emphasis on the word *spirrit* in the text suggests a pun applicable to readers of the magazine.

15. See Garrison, "Battalion Day"; Holmes, "Pennsylvania Militia"; Smith, "Militia of the United States"; and Davis, *Parades and Power*, especially 49–72.

16. See Nickels, *New England Humor*, 58, 73, 86–87, for information on the Yankee burlesques of the militia muster. Nickels's book also contains an illustration (fig. 7 on p. 126) of David Claypoole Johnston's "Militia Muster" (1828), the original of which is located at AAS.

17. Longstreet, *Georgia Scenes*, and Emily Burke, *Pleasure and Pain*, representative portions of which appear in Abrahams, *Singing the Master*, 193–94.

18. Abrahams, *Singing the Master*, 192–93.

19. Harrigan and Hart's Mulligan Guard plays feature such groups, for example, *The Mulligan Guard* (1879). A song from this play features a "target excursion band" tune based on an eight-bar phrase followed by "a sixteen-bar chorus . . . in which the Mulligan Guard sang and marched" (Norton, "Nineteenth-Century American March Music," 19). See also, Appelbaum, *Show Songs*, 14–16. Of interest for the study of black-white interactions as depicted on the American stage is the conclusion of *The Mulligan Guard Ball*, which features a scene in which a black organization, the Skidmore Guards, stomps so wildly on the second floor of the ballroom the Mulligan Guards have rented that the floor collapses, and both groups end up in the same room (Bordman, *Oxford Companion*, 493).

20. *NSO1*, 128–32. I quote the example exactly as it appears in the original, with the unusual spellings and the odd use of apostrophes and commas. The Robert ("Bob") Edwards (1822–72) whose name is listed along with George "Great" Western's in the headnote may have been the same Edwards who performed a "Locomotive Lecture" for the Ethiopian Melodists in 1848. George Western was billed as "The Ethiopian Orator and Locomotive Imitator" at an "Ethiopian Concert" at Barnum's American Museum on August 21, 1843, according to a playbill at AAS.

21. Playbill at HTC.

22. Nye, *Society and Culture*, 335. For more on phrenology, see Reigel, "Early Phrenology," and "Introduction of Phrenology." Fowler's *Practical Phrenology* was published in 1849; his *Human Science of Phrenology*, in 1873.

23. *North Star* 1, no. 44 (Oct. 27, 1848).

24. I am indebted to WAY for copies of the London edition of the Follitt lectures (1846) that I compared with the American examples. *Wake Up! William Henry* was performed at the American Theater (New York) at least as early as March 24, 1862, according to the title page.

25. Billy Waters was a "one-legged musical negro who had fiddled . . . successfully through the streets of the metropolis, attracting attention by his quaint songs and ribbon-decked cocked hat. 'No lemon to him weal, no hoyster to him rump-steak, de turkey widout de sassages!' let out the secret of beggar luxury" (Mathews, *Othello*, 31n59). Waters, a street beggar, went to the poorhouse as a result of the portrayal of beggars as crooks in Pierce Egan's *Tom and Jerry in London*.

26. Quoted from West, *Gyascutus*, 179–84. Hooper's piece originally appeared in *Wheler's Magazine* 2 (Jan. 1850): 25–28. Irish characters appear in other examples of southwestern humor, for example, Lewis, "Cupping an Irishman," and Harris, "A Snake Bit Irishman." The sketch quoted was originally written for *Spirit of the Times* in Knoxville, Tenn., December 25, 1845, according to Griffith, *Humor of the Old Southwest*, 89.

27. Levison, *Black Diamonds,* Lecture 43, 140–43.

28. I am indebted to Smith-Rosenberg, *Disorderly Conduct,* for the connection between moral reform and male-centered definitions of human behavior.

29. See Gould, "Wide Hats," for this persuasive argument.

30. Roediger, *Wages of Whiteness,* 97. The ideas of whiteness and blackness as key symbols in the ideologies of class formation constitute an important consideration throughout Roediger's study, and my use of them will be most apparent in the material on minstrel songs.

31. *CPM4,* 69.

32. Hooper, "The Erasive Soap Man," as quoted in Tidwell, *American Folk Humor,* 199–200.

33. Hereafter, when full bibliographical information is given in the headnote of an example, no endnote will be used.

34. One good example is the parody of Giuseppe Verdi's *Il Trovatore* (1853) from *CPM5,* 59, in which Signor Willikins (the name was taken from "Vilikins and Dinah") gives a synopsis of the entire opera to the tune known as "Sweet Betsy from Pike."

35. Apte, *Humor and Laughter,* 120.

36. *Putnam's Monthly* 1, no. 1 (Jan., 1853): 107. See also Scott, "The Popular Lecture." Scott notes that "in New York City there were more than 3,000 advertised lectures between 1840 and 1860, and in 1846 the citizens of Boston could choose from twenty-six different 'courses' of lectures . . . [and] by the early 1840s there were probably 3,500 and 4,000 communities that contained a society sponsoring public lectures" (791).

37. McCabe, *Lights and Shadows,* 657. McCabe includes the *Observer, Evangelist, Methodist, Observer,* and *Independent* among "the most prominent religious journals" (256).

38. Quoted from Weisberger, *They Gathered at the River,* 135–36; Weisberger's source was Cross, *The Burnt-Over District,* 188–89. Russell Sanjek (*American Popular Music*), quoting an unattributed source, noted that Jedediah Burchard and his wife "made any church they entered 'become a theater'" (2:192).

39. Weisberger, *They Gathered at the River,* 137, 143, 158.

40. The information on Bennett is from ibid, 148. See also Crouthamel, *Bennett's New York Herald,* esp. 52–53, 72–73.

41. *New York Clipper,* May 13, 1857. The editors decided that a few satirical editorials would show the ridiculous behaviors of the clergymen named in their articles; see Sanjek, *American Popular Music,* 2:199. For more on Knapp and other revival preachers, see McLoughlin, *Modern Revivalism.* Knapp may have been the first American evangelist removed from the pulpit for investing his followers' gifts in unprofitable real estate ventures.

42. Quoted in Weisberger, *They Gathered at the River,* 172. Weisberger quotes from several different sermons, notably "The Ferry Boat over Jordan," "The Gospel Looking Glass," and "Religion an Antiseptic," in Rusk, *T. De Witt Talmadge,* 301, 372, 387, 410–11.

43. Daniel Decatur Emmett, "A Negro Sermon" (ca. 1860); quoted in Schneider, "Emmett's Negro Sermons," 73. Schneider did not include this example in his coded catalog of Emmett's sermons but listed it among the miscellaneous items in the Ohio Historical Society collection.

44. McCabe, *Lights and Shadows,* 398.

45. The word is not as ludicrous as it might appear because, as Sandra Sizer noted, "The revival was thus a strategy of purification, through repentance of individuals from the national signs of aggressiveness and lust for money. The community, understood as 'a people,' had to be cleansed, and this was done through the revival which brought individuals into the proper state of mind" (Sizer, *Gospel Hymns,* 144).

46. The Emmett collection at the Ohio Historical Society contains forty sermons and fifty-seven hymns. Most of the Emmett sermons were written after 1873 in response to a request from the *New York Clipper*. Most of the examples were never published. See Schneider, "Emmett's Negro Sermons," and Holmberg and Schneider, "Emmett's Stump Sermons." Schneider and Holmberg, whose expertise is in African languages and African American dialects, demonstrate that Emmett had a good grasp of BE.

47. Schneider conducted an analysis of word frequency in the Emmett sermons and reported that the big words used in this example do not recur elsewhere in the collection. I am indebted to Prof. Schneider for sharing the results of his research and for his advice on some of the more difficult problems I encountered in studying Emmett's sermons.

48. "The Captain Attends a Camp-Meeting," from *Some Adventures of Captain Simon Suggs* (1845), reproduced in Cohen and Dillingham, *Humor of the Old Southwest*, 234–35. *Adventures* went through eleven editions by 1856. Hooper's parody of the proselytizer's technique was matched by William Penn Brannan's classic burlesques of white preachers in *The Harp of a Thousand Strings* and the companion pieces published in 1855 and 1858. These satires, like much of southwestern humor, were directed at unsophisticated Americans who could be manipulated by bogus methods of persuasion. The southwestern humor examples flourished in newspapers of the 1840s and 1850s and are similar in all but dialect to the Emmett samples.

49. Levison, *Black Diamonds*, Lecture 19, "Long Ears," 65–67, 67. This lecture is about the different "varieties" of and "uses" for the "Rabbet," whose physical features and behaviors are contrasted with those of several types of human subjects.

50. The attribution of phonological elements to nineteenth-century Black English Vernacular is based on the number of attestations (examples) citing different treatments of consonants, consonant clusters, vowel combinations, and consonant characteristics found in a wide variety of private and public documents. I base my conclusions on Dillard, "Black English in New York," *Black English, All-American English*, and *Perspectives on Black English;* Stewart, "Acculturative Processes," "Continuity and Change," and "Sociolinguistic Factors"; and Labov, *Language in the Inner City*.

51. Some twentieth-century examples of these types of sermons will be found in Pipes, *Say Amen Brother!* 22–30, 25; Quad, *Brother Gardner's Lime-Kiln Club;* Burdett, *Negro Dialect Recitations;* and Cooper, *Brudder Kinkhard's Stump Speeches*, examples of which are quoted in Spalding, *Encylopedia of Black Folklore*. Spalding includes excerpts from *Poketown People*, a late nineteenth-century collection of dialect pieces that, he writes, provides "an entertaining and instructive insight into the daily activities of a village in which black people lived, loved, and worshiped and—yes—fought among themselves" (162).

52. Emmett expected his work to be published in the *New York Clipper* because the paper had been carrying "the exhortations of Brother Allen, a colored preacher in New York, and the exclamations of his excitable listeners" (Nathan, *Emmett*, 278).

53. Ottley and Weatherby, *The Negro in New York*, 55–56. A product of the Federal Writers Project, this volume is truly an "informal" history compiled by writers, not historians. It shows the manner in which many promising black writers of the 1930s viewed their own history and New York's role in African American culture.

54. Simpson, *Politics of American English*, 16.

55. Townsend, *Negro Minstrels*, 7; Dumont, *Witmark Amateur Minstrel Guide*, 80.

56. Faust, *James Henry Hammond*, 138.

57. Quotations are from Levy, *Picture the Songs*, 68, 64. Levy also provides examples of lithographed sheet music covers illustrating the importance of this genre as well as the frequency of satirical treatments of the militia movement. Of particular relevance to my discussion are

"Major Jack Downing's March" (ca. 1834), "The Burgesses Corps Parade March" (1844), "Foot Guard Quickstep" (1845), "Fifth Regiment March," and "Warren Guards Quick Step."

58. The possession of a band was "a status symbol" because, as William Henry Dana put it in 1878, "A town without a brass band is as much in need of sympathy as a church without a choir." In 1889 Leon Mead estimated that "there were over ten thousand military bands in the United States," the name *military* applying to "brass, town, military, para-military, amateur, and professional bands" (Dana and Mead quoted in Camus's review of Kreitner, *Discoursing Sweet Music*, 361). The original sources are Dana, *J. W. Pepper's Practical Guide*, 42; and Mead, "Military Bands," 785–88. For more on bands, see Hazen and Hazen, *The Music Men*.

59. Bryant, *Letters*, 2:207. The event referred to in this account took place after a corn shucking, a few hours of entertainment (dancing, singing, and comedy), and other social activities by people who had walked four to seven miles after working a full day.

60. *WNE1*, 76. *WNI1* lists "burlesque lectures" in full title and claims that the material was used by "Christy's, Campbell's, and Sable Brothers's" minstrel companies as well.

61. Clarke (attrib.), *Colonel David Crockett*, and Botkin, *American Folklore Stories*. It is worthwhile noting that there were few female heroes in minstrelsy and that most of the women depicted in antebellum songs are victims.

62. Norton, *Alternative Americas*, 205.

63. James Kirke Paulding, *The Lion of the West*, quoted in Cohen and Dillingham, *Humor of the Old Southwest*, 14.

64. Quoted in Marckwardt, *American English*, 109–10. Marckwardt notes that "this tendency toward the bizarre creation is a significant feature of American English which can be accounted for in terms of cultural history and linguistic tradition" (111).

65. Gilbert D. Schneider collected samples from an African in which the speaker says, "My mother constructed a conflagration in her domicile," when "My mother built a fire in the house" would have given the same information. Personal communication (May 14, 1991.)

66. Quoted from Harrison in Dillard, *Perspectives on Black English*, 187.

67. *CPM3*, 67. The "Jim Brown" song was published by Hewitt (New York, 1835) and appeared in ten different songsters, with the most appearances during minstrelsy's first five years. Dennison (*Scandalize*, 71) suggested that the model for "Jim Brown" could have been Francis Johnson (1798–1844) of Philadelphia, one of the first African American musicians to achieve international recognition. The most widely distributed edition in archives and libraries today was published in New York with a cover produced by the George Endicott shop. The evidence from the sheet music covers is inconclusive because two of the extant versions have very different designs. One shows a figure playing a lower brass instrument (probably a tuba or ophicleide); the other shows each of three uniformed players—only the front line is shown—proceeding past an audience of black *and* white listeners while holding generic heraldic trumpets (without valves) instead of period trumpets or cornets.

68. Some documentation is quoted in the appendix of Yizar, "Afro-American Music." Yizar's dissertation deals principally with Massachusetts and Rhode Island.

69. Stuckey, *Slave Culture*, 76. See also Greene, *The Negro in Colonial New England*, 246–55.

70. Davis, *Parades and Power*, 107.

71. See White, "Pinkster in Albany," 191–99; and Williams-Meyers, "Pinkster Carnival," 7–17.

72. John Pendelton Kennedy describes the set pieces performed by the slave Old Jupiter in *Swallow Barn*, according to Abrahams, *Singing the Master*, 187.

73. Stuckey, *Slave Culture*, 144.

74. Davis, *Parades and Power*, 76. Davis presents ample evidence of street theater in Philadelphia in the 1830s and 1840s, the best example being the story of the Northern Liberties (Philadelphia) Eighty-Fourth Foot Regiment's election of a deformed, deficient stable hand as a colonel to show that "even one in his low station was a better man with a clearer sense of honor than [the] titled and careerist officers" (79) drawn from the ranks of lawyers, merchants, and bankers. Similar military burlesques were common in New York City and Albany with notably large parades in 1831 and 1833.

75. Speech "Delivered . . . on Fourth of July, 1856, by John Phoenix, S.D., Sergeant Major, Eighty-Third Regiment, Oregon Territory Light Mules," reprinted without attribution in Falk, *The Antic Muse*, 173, 175.

76. *New York Daily Times*, October 18, 1853.

77. Playbill, July 5, 1852 (HTC). This particular show also included a grand performance of the "Star Spangled Banner" and a parody entitled "The Dutch Drill."

78. Playbill, February 11, 1850 (HTC). The same piece was also presented by the same group on March 2, 1850.

79. Playbill, August 30–31, 1852 (HTC).

80. Stansell, *City of Women*, 135. Wright's 1829 lectures were published as *A Course in Popular Lectures* (New York, 1829). One of the classic midcentury attacks on women's rights was entitled *A Book for the Times*. For a later but still representative example of a stump speech entitled "A Speech on Women's Rights" from *Dick's Ethiopian Scenes, Variety Sketches, and Stump Speeches* (1879), see Bean, Hatch, and McNamara, *Inside the Minstrel Mask*, 133–37.

81. *New York Herald*, March 31, 1858.

82. *New York Daily Times*, October 7 and 15, 1853. Rice considered Huntley "one of the early wench dancers of minstrelsy" (*Monarchs*, 43).

83. She was the wife of Seba Smith, himself the creator of the great Yankee humorist Major Jack Downing, and her writing for the *New York Tribune* in 1850 created enough attention to bring her great success on the lecture circuit, which she left in 1857 because of her health. See Wyman, *Two American Pioneers*. Smith's works were published as part of a series entitled *Women's Rights Tracts* and are available again in microfilm.

84. Wyman, *Two American Pioneers*, 206–7.

85. Both quotations from Smith, *"Woman and Her Needs,"* quoted in Wyman, *Two American Pioneers*, 191.

86. Ibid., 195.

87. The song was published in Boston by George P. Reed and in New York by Horace Waters (1853). A similar song with a text attributed to Fanny Fern and called simply "Women's Rights" (New York: William Hall, 1853) was performed by Wood's Minstrels during the mid-1850s.

88. Levison, *Black Diamonds*, 219.

89. Playbill, Sanford's Opera Company (Philadelphia), October 3, 1859 (TFLP). In a playbill (HTC) announcing a benefit for Frank Brower (Oct. 10, 1855), Gardner is described as "The Great Original Ethiopian Female Performer."

90. *WMS1*, 31, where the headnote says "Printed verbatim by permission of E. Horn, Esq., and told by him with tremendous applause at Wood's Minstrel Hall." A more accessible version is reprinted in Moody, *Dramas*, 485 without attribution to its nineteenth-century source. Most of the minstrel show material published in *Dramas* also appeared in Moody's earlier *America Takes the Stage*.

91. Davies (*Ethnic Humor*, 301–3) notes that there are a few ethnic jokes about bread, so that pun here is based on the homophone, which serves as a neat exit opportunity from the

class rivalry of the example. Home-baked bread may not be *fancy*, so those who want the product must be able to shop for it.

92. Spalding argued that "plantation dialect, as apart from the perversions of minstrelsy, was the nationally recognized language of the black man of yesteryear" and offered his collection of black folklore "with the dialect, and its descendant, black English . . . without apology—indeed, with a deep sense of pride" (*Encyclopedia*, xv).

93. See Mahar, "Black English"; Schneider, "Emmett's Negro Sermons"; and Holmberg and Schneider, "Emmett's Stump Sermons."

94. Dumont, *Witmark Amateur Minstrel Guide*, 8.

95. See Baratz and Baratz, "Black Culture," for an early 1970s statement of the New Social Science.

96. The following studies from the 1970s show the transformation of American attitudes toward language teaching and use: Stewart, "Acculturative Processes"; Dalby, "The African Element," 170–71; Labov, *Language in the Inner City;* and Stewart, "Continuity and Change" and "Sociolinguistic Factors."

97. Schneider, *American Earlier Black English*, 269. This is an English translation of Schneider's 1981 book originally published by Peter Lang.

Chapter 3: Opera for the Masses

1. Text from *CPM5*, 59. The Buckleys also produced an *Il Trovatore* burlesque in November 1855; see Lawrence, *Reverberations*, 742.

2. *Oh, Hush!* appears under its alternative title of *The Virginny Cupids; or, The Rival Darkies* in the following playbills: Parker's Ethiopian Operatic Troupe, August 12, 1850; Christy and Wood's Minstrels, December 22, 1853; and Backus's Minstrels, August 1, 1854.

3. Charles White's "arrangement" of *The Mummy* was performed by White's Serenaders and other minstrel groups. The piece remained in the minstrel repertory and the mail order catalog at least through the early decades of this century. Samuel Sanford was still featuring *The Virginia Mummy* at his Eleventh Street Opera House in 1861. Moncrieff may have created some specific scenes for Rice to perform during Rice's London appearances in 1836–37 and again in 1839–40. Bernard was an American-born playwright working in London. The information on Sanford is from a playbill for September 5 and 7, 1861, in Eleventh Street Opera House file at TFLP. A biographical sketch of Bernard will be found in Wilmeth and Miller, *Cambridge Guide*, 70.

4. See Draudt's introduction to Mathew's *Othello*, 30.

5. McConachie, *Melodramatic Formations*, xiii–xiv; emphasis added. French and English culture generated nearly all the formulaic conventions most American playwrights used to structure their melodramas, according to McConachie. My conclusion about origins is based on Rinear's assessment in *The Temple of Momus* and Stanley Wells's conclusion that "travesty, or burlesque, was a favourite form in the nineteenth-century theater, and the plays of Shakespeare, especially those in the regular repertory, were a natural target" (Wells, *Shakespearean Burlesques*, 5:vii).

6. In his *Dictionary of American Biography* entry on Rice (s.v. "Rice, Thomas Dartmouth"), Wittke wrote that "Bone Squash" was a burlesque of Daniel François Auber's popular comic opera *Fra Diavolo: ou, L'Hotelière de Terracine* (Paris, 1830; New York, 1832). My study of the opera and the Rice piece uncovered no similarities between the two works. For Rice's career, see Smith, *Theatrical Management*. Smith did not mention Rice in the earlier edition

(1846) of his memoirs entitled *The Theatrical Apprenticeship.* See also Hutton, *Curiosities,* 115–19; Ramshaw, "'Jump Jim Crow.'"

7. *Bone Squash,* arr. by Charles White (New York: Happy Hours, n.d. [ca. 1870]). Christy and Wood's playbill, August 17, 1853, New York (MFLP).

8. The identification of the "Bone Squash" tune was made from an edition of Hewitt's *Crow Quadrilles,* where it is the fifth of a series that Hewitt arranged for solo piano. Source at AAS and MFLP.

9. There is no thorough study of *Bone Squash,* a piece that seems to have introduced the soul-selling theme into blackface comedy. The only other song I have identified is "Sich a Getting Up Stairs," which was used for the act 2, scene 1, song. The "Farewell My Calculations" number contains the line "I'm bound for the wild goose station," which may bear some relationship to the "Wild Goose Nation" song attributed later to Dan Emmett.

10. The definition of ballad opera is from Randel, *Harvard Dictionary,* 68. The best characterization of what the word *opera* meant to nineteenth-century American audiences is in Lawrence, *Resonances,* 35.

11. Baines, "Samuel S. Sanford," 32.

12. Lawrence, *Resonances,* 444.

13. Ibid., 286.

14. Baines, "Samuel S. Sanford," 241; playbill for August 25, 1861 (TFLP).

15. Baines noted: "It is apparent from the cast that the burlesque paralleled the original opera rather closely in its personnel, but it was not beyond an occasional innovation such as 'Lucy Long.' The action of the burlesque was divided into three parts and included twenty-eight vocal numbers, including some stock minstrel songs" ("Samuel S. Sanford," 121). The information that Kneass used the Seguin script is from Baines, "Samuel S. Sanford," 120, and confirmed by Ahlquist, "Opera, Theatre, and Audience," 400, which lists a *La Sonnambula* in the form of an "English prompt book owned by Edward Seguin" (Philadelphia: Turner and Fisher, 1840) as being located at the University of Wisconsin–Madison, Mills Music Library, Tams-Witmark Collection. Blase Scarnati Jr. has shown convincingly that Seguin's copy was the Turner and Fisher libretto containing the English translation of Samuel Beazley Jr., which Henry Bishop used in his arrangement of the opera (Blase Scarnati, personal communication, Apr. 9, 1997).

16. There were many other *La Sonnambula* burlesques, because the story of the sleepwalking maiden was immensely popular in Europe even before the English translation of Pont de Vile's French comedy was published in 1778. Felici Romani, Bellini's librettist, based his story on a vaudeville by Eugene Scribe and produced at least one (possibly two) other libretto for Carafa's *Sonnambula* (Milan, 1825) and another for a version by Luigi Ricci (Rome, 1829). By 1828 William T. Moncrieff produced a comedy entitled *The Somnambulist; or, The Phantom of the Village* (Feb. 19, 1828), which was presented at New York's National Theater in May 1828. The setting is changed from Switzerland to Provence, "but the story is that of Bellini's opera, with a few trifling variations," according to the editor of the Kalmus piano-vocal score.

17. Quotations from playbills at TFLP and Baines, "Samuel S. Sanford," 120.

18. Note on Kneass from Baines, "Samuel S. Sanford," 120. The Buckley note is from a late (sometime between 1860 and 1872) playbill. According to a playbill for Cartee's Lyceum, January 16, 1855 (MFLP), Kneass was the musical director for Sanford while the troupe was at the Twelfth Street Opera House, so at least those dates for that particular version of the burlesque are secure. The Seguin Opera Company was another family group from England led by Arthur Edward Seguin (1809–52). For information on the Philadelphia theaters, see Glazer, *Philadelphia Theaters.*

19. Bellini, *La Sonnambula*. The various recitatives and choruses have been deleted to show the principal materials used by the Buckleys. I assume that most of the connecting material would have been deleted. The musical numbers from many Italian operas were available in sheet music editions with English texts from American publishers in most major cities. It is still not clear which version of *La Sonnambula* the Buckleys used. Librettos of the opera as performed by the various companies were published in the United States throughout the antebellum period: Edward Seguin's version, by Turner and Fisher (Philadelphia, 1840); Madame Anna Bishop's adaptation, by Berford and Co. (New York, 1847); and the Pyne and Harrison Company's production, by Samuel French (New York, 1854).

20. The only quintet in the original occurs at the end of act 1, after which Alessio continues singing with the basses of the chorus.

21. In her 1991 dissertation, Karen Ahlquist quotes an example of "Vi ravviso" in B♭ major set in the treble clef and probably intended for a tenor. The aria could be performed by a soprano, but Ahlquist acknowledges that Rodolfo was a "baritone or bass." For a discussion of the aria and its style, see Ahlquist, "Opera, Theatre, and Audience," 194–98.

22. The music and text for the number can be found in Bellini, *La Sonnambula*, 55–64. This translation differs from the version I quote from the London recording. A third translation will be found in the Kalmus piano-vocal score.

23. Preston, *Opera on the Road*, 218. Seguin is listed as a bass in Warrack and West, *Oxford Dictionary of Opera* (s.v., "Seguin, Arthur"), which contains an interesting note that he also became "chief of an Indian tribe" and was given a name signifying "the man with the deep, mellow voice."

24. This particular pairing of the song and the *La Sonnambula* parody almost always appears at the end of the first part of the minstrel show.

25. Baines, "Samuel S. Sanford," 66.

26. *Philadelphia Public Ledger*, January 21, 1850, quoted in Baines, "Samuel S. Sanford," 73.

27. Baines, "Samuel S. Sanford," 67.

28. The relationship between the Buckleys and Mitchell was confirmed by the *New York Clipper*, December 12, 1857, whose editor noted that "the Buckleys are back at their old quarters again, and promise a series of those burlesque pieces that crowned the old Olympic in its palmy days." As noted elsewhere, Mitchell managed the Olympic from 1839 to 1850.

29. The Buckleys' claim that they offered complete works cannot be evaluated on the playbill evidence alone. The burlesque operas were never numerous during the antebellum era, although it is likely that those I discovered in the playbill collection constitute only a portion of those that were performed. Comparisons of the following operas and the minstrel burlesques would be especially illustrative: *Barber of Seville* (Perham's Opera Troupe, July 31, 1856), *The Bohemian Girl* (Buckley's Serenaders, Mar. 6 and Oct. 30, 1854), *Lucia di Lammermoor* (Buckley's Serenaders, Apr. 22, 1854), *Norma* (Buckley's Serenaders, Nov. 16 and 23, 1853), and *Norma; or, The Injured Princess* (Buckley's Serenaders, Feb. 13, 1853). Renee Norris (University of Maryland) is currently investigating a number of opera burlesques.

30. Quoted in Lawrence, *Reverberations*, 640. The same positive opinion was seconded by *Spirit of the Times* (Dec. 8, 1855, p. 516), but other critics disagreed. Lawrence quotes Theodore Hagen's (1824–71) review of Buckley's *Il Trovatore* burlesque in the *Review and Gazette* (Nov. 29, 1856), where Hagan complains that Buckley's *Il Trovatore* burlesque was "absolutely cruel in its adaptation of beautiful music to barbarous words and worse acting" and that "the beautiful music of the *Anvil Chorus* [was] sung to such words as 'Fill up the lager.' . . . If they must give burlesques, why can they not select such music as they at least are capable of singing?" (in *Reverberations*, 725n20).

31. Baines, "Samuel S. Sanford," 69.

32. Ibid., 332.

33. Lawrence, *Resonances*, 444.

34. Quoted in Lawrence, *Resonances*, 463.

35. From playbills reproduced in the booklet accompanying Joan Sutherland's London recording (OSA 1365) of *La Sonnambula*.

36. Rinear, *Temple of Momus*, 15–16. Attributed (by Rinear) to another Englishman, Gilbert A'Beckett, and first presented at the Royal Victoria Theater (July 15, 1835), *The Roof Scrambler* finds Molly Brown (a pun on the name of Maria Malibran, the famous soprano) racing over the city's rooftops in search of her lover. Rinear notes that only one critic had difficulty with Mitchell's cross-dressed role, writing that "his farcical, low comic style of acting must have made his transvestite characters sufficiently unrealistic that they were not offensive, for he was never again chastised for playing a female role" (ibid., 16). The first American performance of Bellini's opera was given in English, not Italian, and in an arrangement by Sir Henry Bishop (Lawrence, *Resonances*, 36).

37. The facts and quotation are from Lawrence, *Resonances*, 45. For more on Shireff and her successful collaboration with John Wilson, see Preston, *Opera on the Road*, 44–98. Operas on sleepwalking subjects by Piccini and Paer appeared in Italy and Sweden by 1797, and at least one English travesty had also been presented in London under the title *The Sleep-Walker; or, Which is Which?* (June 1812) and again in New York one year later. The information about the other versions is from the preface to the Kalmus piano-vocal score.

38. There were at least three editions of the parody: (1) "The Phantom Chorus: A Parody from *La Sonnambula*" (New York: Firth, Pond, and Co., 1848); (2) "A Parody on the Phantom Chorus in *La Sonnambula*" (New York: C. Holt Jr., 1848), which is distinguished by its elaborately engraved cover; and (3) "The Celebrated Phantom Chorus 'When day light's going' in Bellini's Opera *La Sonnambula*" (Philadelphia: Fiot, Meignen, and Co., 1848). "Phantom Chorus" (a parody) appeared in *WNB1, CPM1, and ESB2* as well. It is likely that the Buckleys performed their own parody. The "Bugaboo" (derived from *goblin* and *boo*) was an "imaginary object of fright" or, as derived from Scots and English, a specter or goblin.

39. Lawrence, *Resonances*, 165–66.

40. For an easily accessible discussion of the premiere and Fry's claims, see Lawrence, *Resonances*, 336–39.

41. Although the sheet music edition has been associated with the Christy Minstrels, the HTC playbills do not show a Christy performance. The piece was presented by Ordway's Aeolians on February 19, 1852, in Boston and by White's Serenaders on March 3, September 23, and November 7, 1852, all in New York.

42. My conclusions are based on "De Colored Fancy Ball" (New York: William Hall and Son, 1848). The text-only version appears in *CNS1, CPS1, WMS1, WSS1,* and *CPM3.* The "Virginia Rose Bud" identification comes from the title page, but the idea to use the song probably came from yet another connection between the minstrels and William Mitchell's Olympic Theater, where *The Bronze Horse* was burlesqued as *The Flying Horse; or, The Patent Pegasus* (Lawrence, *Resonances*, 419). According to Odell (*Annals*, 5:215), Mitchell presented 107 different productions (surely a burlesquer's record) from September 1845 to May 1846.

43. Playbill, March 3, 1847 (HTC).

44. Young's *Darkies' Comic All-Me-Nig* contains a collection of dialect pieces and references to minstrel songs, for example, "Dandy Jim of Caroline," "Old Dan Tucker," and "Coal Black Rose." This title is a significant minstrel-era document, and there may be many more classified as almanacs, comics, and cartoon collections, such as *Tregar's Black Jokes*. These titles

suggest that further study of the connections between minstrelsy and cartoons or caricatures would be useful. Examples of white-on-black critiques are found in a set of etchings by David Claypool Johnston (1797–1865) entitled *Scraps for the Year* (1830) and now located at the Library Company of Philadelphia. The series consists of four plates of nine images, with each plate showing a different scene; the scenes are entitled "Weak Nerves" (pl. 1), "Stricken in Ears" (pl. 2), "Hot Corn" (pl. 3), and "African Mawworn." The last plate also contains an additional cartoon ("Sheet Contrived") about a flophouse that uses bedsheets for tablecloths.

45. Davies, *Ethnic Humor,* 307.

46. Dizikes, *Opera in America,* 101.

47. ibid.; Holden, Kenyon, and Walsh, *Viking Opera Guide,* 336.

48. Dizikes, *Opera in America,* 101, which gives a total of twenty performances for the two Philadelphia theaters. See also Preston, *Opera on the Road,* 225–26, where the number of Philadelphia performances is given as twelve not sixteen and the comments of New York and Philadelphia critics are mentioned.

49. Fry, *Leonora,* v.

50. The copy of the title page refers to *La Sonnambula* as an "opera in three acts," but the libretto is printed in the standard two act format and states that the performance took place in January 1853. See Bellini, *La Sonnambula* (New York: Sheridan [Corbyn], 1853). William Niblo (1798–1878) supervised the management of his Garden from 1839–48 and resumed that activity in 1849 after the Astor Place riots of 1848 forced him to give up his lease to the Astor Place Opera House (Wilmeth and Miller, *Cambridge Guide,* 343).

51. Lawrence, *Resonances,* 215–17.

52. Playbill, April 22, 1854 (HTC).

53. Baines, "Samuel S. Sanford," 67. The quotations are from notices in *Spirit of the Times,* January 30, 1840. Baines notes that many of Sanford's "specific attractions, such as *La Sonnambula, The Virginia Girl* (a burlesque of Balfe's *The Bohemian Girl*), and *Cinderella,* had first been presented in the old company with the Buckley family" ("Samuel S. Sanford," 94). Sanford's successors, Carncross and Dixey, continued to present the same burlesques for several years after Sanford lost the theater following a misunderstanding and subsequently bitter dispute with his lessors.

54. Lawrence, *Reverberations,* 640.

55. "Hit Him in the Eyeball, Bim" will be found in *NSO1, WNN1, NFM3, JJO1,* and *VSI1.* "Sich a Getting Up Stairs" was, according to its title page, the "Celebrated Niggar Song Sung by Mr. T. D. Rice" (Baltimore: George Willig, 184?).

56. This is a pun on the name of the theater where the Buckleys performed. The Chinese Hall was located at 539–41 Broadway and accommodated some three thousand persons. After the Buckely family left, the hall became Barnum's American Museum. It was the site of "The First Banjo Tournament in America" on October 19, 1857. For a report, see *Stewart's Banjo and Guitar Journal* 7, no. 2 [whole no. 58] (June/July, 1890), which was reprinted in its entirety in *The Tuckahoe Review* 1, no. 2 (Spring 1997): 2–3, 13, 15.

57. Some of the capitalization and spellings have been changed to simplify the presentation of this part of the program, which concluded the Serenader's performance for that evening.

58. Preston, *Opera on the Road,* 221.

59. Texts from the piano-vocal edition of *The Bohemian Girl* and *Heart Songs,* 244. Example includes all text repeats.

60. Pessen, "The Marital Theory," 396.

61. *New York Clipper,* January 7, 1854; *New York Clipper,* May 14, 1853.

62. Quoted in Austin, *"Susanna," "Jeannie," and "The Old Folks at Home,"* 63.

63. McConachie, "New York Operagoing," 185–6, 190, 191.

64. Ibid., 190, 191.

65. *CPM5*, 59; in the libretto by Cammarano and Bardere, after a play by Gutierrez. Set in northern Spain during the fifteenth century, the plot features a gypsy's daughter (Azucena) who kidnaps the brother of the conte di Luna and burns him to death in revenge for the execution of her own mother. Years pass, and the present conte di Luna falls in love with Leonora, who really loves Azucena's son, Manrico, a troubadour warrior with a mysterious past. Later Azucena admits that she killed her own son instead of the count's baby brother, who, it turns out, is none other than Manrico. In the end Leonora poisons herself rather than forsake Manrico, who is summarily executed as an outlaw, after which Azucena finally informs the conte di Luna that he has just executed his own brother.

Chapter 4: Ethiopian Sketches of American Life

1. Editorial preface to *Box and Cox;* quoted in Paskman and Spaeth, *"Gentlemen, Be Seated!"* (139), from the edition published under E. Byron Christy's (1838–66) name. Odell (*Annals*, 6:327) notes a performance of this piece during the summer of 1854 (actual date uncertain). Another edition of *Box and Cox* (New York: Dick and Fitzgerald, 1858) was still listed in that company's catalogs through the 1880s.

2. Cantwell, *Bluegrass Breakdown*, 262.

3. The dates are those assigned by the libraries that submitted cataloging information to the *National Union Catalog of Pre-1956 Imprints* and may not be the actual dates of publication or performance.

4. White, *Pompey's Patients* and *The Live Injin; or, Jim Crow*. Although the sketch was published (1875) after the period generally discussed in this study, it is likely that the practice of whiteface-blackface cast substitution had been a part of the Ethiopian sketches even earlier.

5. A biographical sketch will be found in Bordman, *Oxford Companion*, 656.

6. Odell, *Annals*, 6:585. The sources of these farces have not been identifed. *The Stage-Struck Barber* was probably a burlesque of Oliver Everett Dursivage's *Stage-Struck Yankee* (1840), which played throughout the 1840s at Mitchell's Olympic Theater. Burton's production *The Stage-Struck Barber* was probably the source for the Ethiopian sketch known as *The Stage-Struck Darkey.* Dursivage also wrote a burlesque of *The Lady of Lyons*, dubbed *The Lady of Lions*, which appeared "at the Bowery Theater in 1842, the Olympic in 1846, and in Baltimore, St. Louis and Albany after mid-century," according to Meserve (*Heralds of Promise*, 108).

7. The number of skits or burlesques based on Shakespeare in the antebellum minstrel shows may not have been as high as previously estimated in Browne, "Shakespeare," Haywood, "Negro Minstrelsy," and Mahar, "Ethiopian Skits." The Shapespearean burlesques outside minstrelsy during the same period far outnumbered those presented by blackface comedians. The relatively small but representative sample found at HTC contains only sixteen examples: four "Shakespearean Readings" by the Buckleys in 1853 and again in 1854, three by Bryant's Minstrels in 1857, four by Sanford's Opera Troupe between 1857 and 1860, and one by Carncross and Dixey in 1860.

8. Southern, *Music of Black Americans,* 121. The quoted statement was not included in the second edition of Southern's history, but she noted there that Lane "began his career in the notorious Five Points district of the city of New York" (95).

9. The clowns' lines in *Hippotheatron* are in minstrel show dialect. This edition also advertises a number of other items, including *Africanus Bluebeard,* a piece usually attributed

to Frank Dumont; the *Charge of the Hash Brigade;* and *Mr. Mikado; or, Japanese from the "Neck."*

10. Miller, "Image of Fashionable Society," 244.

11. Miller, *Bohemians and Critics,* 53.

12. Sherman, "The Diversity of Treatment," 239. The play was introduced at the Park Theater in New York on March 24, 1845, and ran for twenty performances, something of a record in its day. The text of *Fashion; or, Life in New York* is reprinted from a collation of the 1850 London edition and a Boston edition originally published with Mowatt's *Armand* in Quinn, *Representative American Plays,* 281–312. Mowatt's preface to the London edition states that her play is "a good-natured satire on some of the follies incident to a new country, where foreign dross sometimes passes for gold, while native gold is cast aside as dross; where the vanities rather than the virtues of other lands are too often imitated, and where the stamp of *Fashion* gives currency even to the coinage of vice" (quoted in Moses, *Representative Plays,* 537).

13. Haltunnen, *Confidence Men,* 151.

14. For a discussion of this and other "fashion" plays, see Blayney, "City Life," 99–128.

15. Matthews, "Just a Housewife," 97.

16. Reproduced in Quinn, *Representative American Plays,* 384.

17. Although the name of Mrs. Tiffany's daughter, Seraphina, does not seem very French, it may still have been unusual enough to have been perceived as foreign. The name also appears as "Seraphina Tell" in four minstrel songsters, *CPM2, CPM3, ESB2,* and *NNB1.*

18. Haltunnen, *Confidence Men,* 156.

19. These fraternal organizations were important because they sponsored fancy balls, social activities, and other events for both sexes. The following editorial from the *Philadelphia Ledger and Daily Transcript,* July 18, 1837, notes, "Our streets have been *enlivened* by certain masquerades, called the parades of the 'Crow clubs' and other associations of similar character." Defending the activities of those organizations, the *Ledger* also carried advertisements of club-sponsored events, such as the following example from February 17, 1838: "THE MARINER'S CLUB NO. 1 intends giving their Second Grand FANCY CITIZEN'S and CLUB DRESS BALL" or "UNION BALL: MILITARY CITIZENS and CLUB DRESS BALL. The Managers of the Union Ball respectfully inform their Subscribers of the Union Ball that it will take place on MONDAY EVENING, 19th of February, at the MASONIC HALL."

20. For the principal stage Yankees, see Francis Hodge, *Yankee Theater;* and Richard M. Dorson, *Jonathan Draws the Long Bow.*

21. The earlier sketch featured Richard III, Hamlet, Ophelia, Falstaff, Othello, and Lady Macbeth, who, according to Nathan's summary, appeared with "'Sambo Hit-Em-Hard, a negro doorkeeper' (Pelham), 'Spruce Pink and his Love' (Emmett and a Mrs. Wood), and 'Joe Break-Em-All, the Virginia Paganin' (Joel Sweeney)" (Nathan, *Emmett,* 139–40). No connection has been made between this sketch and Rice's 1837 piece, but given the derivative nature of minstrelsy, it is likely that one or both of the early sketches featured the parade format and served as a source for the later sketches.

22. The same plot can be found in Philadelphia sketches entitled *The Masquerade Ball* (Nov. 7 and 8, 1859), in which P. T. Barnum, Jenny Lind, Fanny Elssler, and Alfred "Highflyer" join a comic parade peopled with the characters from *The Hop of Fashion.* White's sketch also appears in one of the Bryant's Minstrels announcements published in the *New York Clipper* (Apr. 23, 1859). The word *hop* is a colloquialism for an informal dance or ball. *The Hop of Fashion* is reprinted in Bean, *Inside the Minstrel Mask,* 126–34.

23. Havens, *Columbian Muse of Comedy,* 4. Havens takes social comedy to include everything from "low farce through comic operetta, domestic drama (or dramas of sensibility),

sentimental comedy, with an occasional comedy of manners" (2). The Ethiopian sketches that deal with social events and the nouveau riche would probably fit at the low end of the social comedy scale.

24. Bulwer-Lytton, *Dramatic Works*, 103–76, which contains *The Duchess of Vallière, The Lady of Lyons; or, Love and Pride, Richelieu; or, The Conspiracy, Money*, and *Not So Bad As We Seem; or, Many Sides to a Character*. Another source for *The Lady of Lyons* is Brown, *Later English Drama*, 293–371. For a brief summary of the play, see Bordman, *Oxford Companion*, 413; for another synopsis of the *Lady of Lyons* and its sequels, see Dormon, *Theater*, 266–68. The play's popularity in New York is discussed in Ireland, *Records of the New York Stage*, 2:436–40.

25. McConachie, *Melodramatic Formations*, 124. Bird's novel was published in 1837. The play did not appear until 1838 but was unsuccessful until its 1839 revival at the New Bowery Theater, where it ran for twelve performances.

26. Bulwer-Lytton, *Dramatic Works*, 106.

27. White's parade play may have been taken from Griffin's *Ticket Taker; or, The Masquerade Ball*, which is reprinted in Engle, *This Grotesque Essence*, 78–84. It is more likely that both sketches were taken from a single English source. Lotteries and games of chance were important for nineteenth-century audiences, and many were taken in by confidence games. See Williams, *Lotteries, Laws, and Morals;* and Ezell, *Fortune's Merry Wheel: The Lottery in America*.

28. The Claude speech must have been a convention, for it appears in *Minstrel Gags and End-men's Jokes* as a separate set piece entitled "Shakespeare with a Vengeance," where the setup line identifies it as "taken from de Lady ob de Lions, whar Claude Meddlenot gets de gal so sweet wid his lies, dat she slopes [elopes?] wid him" (113–14).

29. Boucicault's play was an adaptation of a French original by Edouard Brisebarre and Eugene Nus set in New York and featuring scenes from the city, a burning house, and numerous allusions to the Panic of 1837. Minstrel burlesques were thus based on French as well as English originals. For a discussion of these plays, see Miller, *Bohemians and Critics*.

30. Curry, *The Free Black*, 113.

31. Ibid., 115.

32. Ibid., 119.

33. Steinberg, *The Ethnic Myth*, 117, 118.

34. White, *Hop of Fashion*, 15.

35. Ibid., 14.

36. McCabe, *Lights and Shadows*, 139.

37. Blayney, "City Life," 117. The second passage quoted is from Boker, *Glaucus and Other Plays*, 69.

38. White, *Wake Up! William Henry*, 5–6. Russell Nye noted that however foolish the idea of phrenology may appear today, "the concept of the individual that it projected reinforced the individualistic, democratic spirit of the age" (*Society and Culture*, 335). Blackface lecturers saw phrenology and mesmerism as related "sciences." For samples, see Levison, *Black Diamonds*, 140–43 (phrenology), 144–46. This publication is virtually identical to an English collection entitled *Irish Diamonds*.

39. Lawrence, *Reverberations*, 123.

40. Kerr, *Mediums*, 4–5.

41. Kerr, *Mediums*, 3. "Forty years later Margaret Fox was to confess that she and Kate had meant only to tease their superstitious mother by cracking their toe-joints against the bedstead," according to Kerr (4), who cites numerous contemporary sources and explores the influences of spiritualism on a number of prominent Americans.

42. White, *Bone Squash*, 4–5.

43. Staum, "Physiognomy and Phrenology," 461. Staum quotes from Jean-François Braun-stein's study (*Broussais et le materialisme, médecine et philosophie au XXXe siècle* [1986]) of the French materialist philosopher and member of the Paris Phrenological Society.

44. White, *Hard Times*, 3. *Hard Times* is also reprinted in Nathan, *Emmett*, 415–26. Note the number of instances of eye dialect in this piece, that is, words whose pronunciation is not affected by the misspelling, for example, *rong* for *wrong*. The similarity between *Hard Times* and *Bone Squash Diavolo* has already been noted several times and should be recalled here.

45. White, *Bone Squash*, 6.

46. White, *The Magic Penny*, 13 (both quotations). As with the other examples, the per-formance dates of this item have not been established.

47. McConachie, "Cultural Hegemony," 52.

48. Smith-Rosenberg, *Religion*, 179.

49. McCabe, *Lights and Shadows*, 808.

50. White, *Laughing Gas*, 3. This sketch may have been played as early as 1844, for an ad-vertisement for the Carolina Minstrels' performance at the New York Museum and Picture Gallery states that "*The Laughing Gas* will be administered" (*New York Daily Tribune*, Oct. 11, 1844).

51. Grote, *The End of Comedy*, 31.

52. The "protective father" theme may have been passed on from Didbin's *Padlock* (1768), the libretto of which Isaac Bickerstaffe based on Cervantes's *El celoso estremeno* (The jealous husband). In *The Padlock* the "protagonist was an old miser who kept his young bride-to-be (in Cervantes, his wife) shut up in his house, and, in order to forestall all sinful temptation, placed a padlock on the door" (Nathan, *Emmett*, 20). The libretto of the opera was published in 1815, and the main character in the play was the servant Mungo, not the father, Don Diego.

53. *The Black Statue* was also known as *The Statue Lover* (1862) when Carncross and Dix-ey presented it in Philadelphia on November 22, 1862, according to a playbill at TFLP. The plays attributed to Charles White often appeared on stage long before they were printed for the amateur minstrel companies. All the plays listed were already regular offerings by White at his various New York theaters as early as 1851, according to the playbills cited in Odell, *Annals*, 6. Whenever possible, the date shown in parentheses is the first performance or the first publication date.

54. White, *The Darkey's Stratagem*, 8. The same kind of comic twist occurs in White's *Black Chemist*. Pete Grabem, a poor, uneducated black character, outwits a pompous doctor-chem-ist by impersonating the son of Horace Greeley—a "noted bachelor," according to the script—and stealing the doctor's prize invention, the Secesh Soother, which is a storage battery ca-pable of killing 25,000 men. See White, *The Black Chemist* (perf. at the American Theater, June 16, 1862), 3.

55. The major differences between Rice's burlesque (1833) and White's sketch (ca. 1856) is that the former has longer and more entertaining scenes with some good comic exchang-es and a better assortment of characters (e.g., Captain Rifle of the Western frontier, the Irish-man O'Leary, and Ginger Blue), whereas the latter, consistent with its status as a sketch, has many fewer complications and much less subtle dialogue. White, who was known for his ability to strike classical and athletic poses, also transformed the mummy into a statue.

56. McCabe, *Lights and Shadows*, 166.

57. White, *The Black Statue*, 3 (subsequent citations will be made parenthetically in the text). This sketch was performed at least as early as 1856, according to playbill information

at TFLP. As I have noted several times before, Odell confirmed this piece as being in the repertory during the 1854–55 New York season.

58. McCabe described in some detail the requirements for postal workers in "The Letter Carriers" chapter of *Lights and Shadows,* 460–63.

59. Music was a part of the business in these sketches. It is difficult to know from the text alone how music fitted into these sketches, some of which have musical clues such as "light pantomime music" or "JAKE goes to the cottage in theatrical style (music)," whereas others have verses and choruses of songs without the identifying air, ballad, or song title. There are several places where songs might be inserted, and the playbills suggest that supporting players and some type of instrumental ensemble were available to provide an appropriate musical accompaniment. If the sketch served as an afterpiece, all the performers could have been assembled, and in houses with a resident orchestra, such as Sanford's, the musicians were already in their places to assist with the musical accompaniment whenever required.

60. White, *Sam's Courtship,* 7.

61. Ibid., 2.

62. Engle, *This Grotesque Essence,* 68–77. Brabantio sings: "I feed her up, to see if I could make her, / So far to see her dat people would pay. / Just as I think dat Barnum would take here, / Dis nigger comes [Othello], and takes her away."

63. Vicinus, "'Helpless and Unfriended,'" 184–85.

64. White, *The Mischievous Nigger,* 9. Subsequent citations will be made parenthetically in the text.

65. White, *Uncle Jeff.* The dates of the first performance and publication are uncertain. The hypothetical earliest date is 1856.

66. The performance date is unknown, but the title page of the sketch indicates that the piece was "performed by Griffin and Christy at the Fifth Street Opera House" in New York. The Griffin and Christy ensemble disbanded in 1867, and George Christy died in 1868, so the piece must have been presented in 1867.

67. Lover, *Handy Andy,* v. The quotation is from the introduction by John Sheridan.

68. Apte, *Humor and Laughter,* 145.

69. Middleton, "Negro and White Reactions," 180.

70. Ellison, *Shadow and Act,* 48.

71. Frederickson, *The Arrogance of Race,* 204.

72. Roediger, *Wages of Whiteness,* 123–24.

73. Zillman, "Disparagement Humor," 87–91.

74. Blassingame, *The Slave Community,* 202–3. The second quotation is from Anderson, *From Slavery to Affluence.*

75. McConachie's *Melodramatic Formations* (198–230) raises these questions very well and suggests that the exploration of class differences among minstrel show audiences could explain much of minstrelsy's ambivalence on many subjects.

76. Miller, "Image of Fashionable Society," 244.

Chapter 5: Blackface Minstrelsy, Masculinity, and Social Rituals

1. *Dwight's Journal of Music,* Feb. 26, 1853, quoted in Sablosky, *What They Heard,* 260–61.

2. Conway, *African Banjo Echoes,* offers numerous helpful suggestions on how the mapping of the transmission process might be accomplished and cites most of the major arguments about the connections among African American, southern white mountain, and blackface minstrel traditions.

3. The version found in *BDS1* is entitled "The New Jim Brown Song 'Bout de Disputed Territory."

4. Bowman cites a number of these songs from the undated *Rough and Ready Songster* but notes that "liberty and war songs had not yet linked up completely with the major genres in popular song, and compositions had not yet become original, unified, quality works of art" (*Voices of Combat*, 86).

5. Quoted in Nathan, *Emmett*, 336–39. The song refers to Pierce's 1852 victory over his Whig opponent, General Winfield Scott. Pierce's inability to resolve the issue of slavery in the territories made him a one-term president. The "hasty plate of soup" refers to one of the more comic elements in an otherwise boring campaign. Scott himself referred to "a hasty bowl of soup" in a letter to the secretary of war, William Henry Marcy, and the Democrats mocked the symbol whenever possible, reprinting, for example, a report of a Scott campaign stop in Pennsylvania during which "an immense 'soup bowl,' on wheels, containing a band, glee club, with flags, banners, and three or four live raccoons" played a prominent role in the festivities (quoted in Lawrence, *Music for Patriots*, 328).

6. My classification is based on the types Winans and Hamm used in their discussions. Any classification based on content is instructive, not definitive, because the texts and music of similarly titled songs varied considerably throughout the whole period. The songs discussed here were chosen on the basis of their frequency in songsters and sheet music editions, potential or real relationship to the African American song tradition, phrase structure or overall musical design, and the social or political contexts that influenced the contemporary interpretation of the texts.

7. Virginia is by the far the most frequently mentioned state in the songsters. Virginia (also spelled "Virginny" and "Wurginny") occurs much more often than do Kentucky, Louisiana, Mississippi, and South Carolina.

8. "Ginger Blue" appeared seven times in the forty-nine antebellum songsters and was performed by the Sable Brothers and Sisters (Mar. 13, 1845) and Ordway's Aeolians (May 20, 1851). The expression "walk chalk" occasionally appears in other minstrel songs. One of the variants of "De Boatman's Dance" shows the following opening verse: "Ole winter's walk'd his chalk so nice, / An' Massa Sun's unfriz de ice; / De canal's open wid de spring, / Canal boat niggers laugh and sing." Ginger Blue was a character in Rice's *Virginia Mummy*, which he performed regularly from the mid-1830s to the end of his career. See Odell, *Annals*, 4:77, 231, 244, 265, 306, 372, 484, 635, for the preminstrel show performances. For performances from 1843 and later, Odell provides references on 5:32, 39, 201, 220, 358, 372, 464, 511, 574, 577, showing that *Virginia Mummy* was a common source for minstrel sketch writers well into the 1850s; for example, it was the featured afterpiece (part III) of Christy and Wood's October 16, 1854, performance at Minstrel Hall, 444 Broadway.

9. There are several references in minstrelsy to a tune known as "Old Virginny Nebber Tire." One version, with words by T. Vaughn, was adapted by Edwin P. Christy and arranged by Thomas Spencer. It was published by Millet's Music Saloon (New York, 1851). A copy is at the Brown University Library. The tune does not appear in any of the three major banjo tutors.

10. The French feminine noun *fange* and the adjectives *fangeux* (m) and *fangeuse* (f) mean "mud, mire, filth; to live in degradation or to have a filthy mind" (*Heath's Standard French and English Dictionary*, sv. "fange").

11. The text is quoted from an undated London edition at Brown. The song and several of its variants appears in *NSO1, NPS1, NFM2*, and *CNS2*. Printed copies of a combined song, narrative, and chorus are unusual in early minstrelsy.

12. Lott argues, "Bold swagger, irrepressible desire, sheer bodily display: in a real sense the minstrel man *was* the penis, that organ returning in a variety of contexts, at times ludicrous, at others less so . . . invoking the power of 'blackness' while deriding it, in an effort of cultural control, through the very convention that produced its power—the greasepaint and burnt cork of blackface" (*Love and Theft,* 25–26).

13. Gilfoyle, *City of Eros,* 104.

14. Ibid., 104–5.

15. Ibid., 105. The source and date of the original are confirmed in Bristed, *The Upper Ten Thousand,* 6, 20.

16. Tompkins, *Sensational Designs,* xvi.

17. Quoted from "The Free Nigger As Sung by R.W. Pelham" in Nathan, *Emmett,* 57.

18. The idea that white Americans, particularly entertainers, had a love-hate relationship with black culture lies behind the title of Lott's *Love and Theft* and David Roediger's use of an aversion-desire hypothesis to explain working-class attitudes in *The Wages of Whiteness.* Michael Rogin has argued that by "admiring and expropriating African-American expressive power, minstrelsy split work from play, tied pleasure to shiftlessness, and deprived black and white workers alike of access to the collective, pre-industrial work rhythms of African-American labor" (Rogin, "Black Masks, White Skin," 145).

19. Quoted from the *New York Herald,* May 7–14, 1849, in Levine, *Highbrow/Lowbrow,* 64.

20. Pickering and Green, "Cartography of Vernacular Milieu," 3.

21. For the prevalence of the dandy type among all races and social classes, see Gilfoyle, *City of Eros,* 105–7.

22. According to the Harvard playbills and New York newspapers I reviewed, "Old Zip Coon" appeared in the Sable Brothers show on March 13, 1845, as "ZIP COON With grand variations on the Tamborine, by John Brown, received last night with Deafening applause," and was followed by the "Grand Trial Dance Between Frank Diamond and John Brown." "Dandy Jim" was performed by the following groups: Palmo's Ethiopian Opera Company (Nov. 11, 1845), Virginia Serenaders (1843; month and day unknown), Christy Minstrels (Apr. 18 1844), Ole Bull Band of Serenaders (Feb. 18, 1845), Sable Brothers and Sisters (Mar. 13, 1845), and Sanford's Opera Troupe (May 14, 1859). Winans ("Early Minsterl Music") found "Dandy Jim" ten times in forty-seven programs dating from 1843 to 1847.

23. Cockrell, *Demons of Disorder,* 54.

24. The uniform title for this song is "Dandy Jim from Caroline," but the usual title on the sheet music covers is "Dandy Jim of Caroline." There are at least ten sheet music editions, which I have numbered to clarify my discussion. The first six versions were published in F major, with the earliest appearing in 1843. No. 1 is "Dandy Jim from Caroline" (New York: C. G. Christman, 1843), a version attributed to J. Richard ("Ole Bull") Meyers and associated with the Ethiopian Serenaders and the Boston Minstrels. No. 2 is "Dandy Jim of Caroline" (New York: Firth and Hall, 1843), also attributed to J. R. Meyers. No. 3 is "Dandy Jim from Carolina" (New York: Firth and Hall, 1844), "as sung by B. Williams," that is, Bernard O'Flaherty, who had some difficulties playing a blackface role convincingly because of his Irish brogue. No. 4 is "Dandy Jim of Caroline" (London: D'Almaine and Co., 1844), which appeared as part of Emmett's *Celebrated Negro Melodies or Songs of the Virginny Banjoist.* No. 5 is "Dandy Jim of Caroline" (Philadelphia: A. Fiot, 1844; New York: Wm. Dubois, 1844), as arranged by J. Norton for the Virginia Minstrels, which is also attributed to J. R. Myers. No. 6 is "Dandy Jim of Caroline and Sam of Tennessee," as "Sung by the Virginia Minstrels" (Philadelphia: Lee and Walker, 184?), an arrangement attributed to F. Johnson. The next four examples are in D major. No. 7 is the arrangement of O. F. Slack entitled "Dandy Jim of Car-

oline" (Philadelphia: G. Willig, 1844). No. 8 is "Dandy Jim ob Caroline" (Boston: Charles Keith, 1844), with music attributed to Dan Myers and the words "written expressly for Cool White by S. S. Steele." No. 9 is "Dandy Jim of Caroline," arranged by J. W. Turner in the *Songs of the Virginia Serenaders* series (Boston: Keith's Music House). No. 10 is "Dandy Jim from Caroline" (Baltimore: F. D. Benteen, 1844), the title page of which associates this number with the Virginia Minstrels. Other arrangements of the song include "Dandy Jim o' Caroline," the four-part arrangement (in F major) from the 1850 edition of the *Ethiopian Glee Book*. "Dandy Jim" appears no fewer than sixteen times as a words-only text in the following songsters: once each in *BTS1, JJO1, LFM1, NFM1,* and *VSI1;* twice in *DJD1, DSN1, GEM1,* and *NFM2;* and three times in *NSO1.* The melody also appears in at least two of the instrumental tutors (*Briggs' Banjo Instructor,* 12 [henceforth abbreviated as *BBI*]; *Ethiopian Accordeon Instructor,* 12) that I examined.

25. The song is referred to occasionally as a courtship song in the playbills; for example, it is listed as "Dandy Jim—a Negro's Courtship" on an Ole Bull Serenaders playbill for March 18, 1845 (HTC).

26. A stemma is "a family tree that shows the interrelationships of various manuscripts," according to the *Harvard Dictionary of Music* (1986, s.v., "stemma"). In this case the stemma would be based on all published versions of "Dandy Jim," as well as on transcriptions of any attestations discovered in the oral tradition. Spitzer's study of the stemma of Foster's "Oh, Susanna" is an outstanding example of the method applied to a popular culture artifact.

27. *BBI* states, "The keys of G major, and D major, are called the *Natural* keys of the banjo" (3). The banjo is a tenor instrument, and although the melodies are written in the G, or treble, clef, they are heard an octave lower. The instrumental version will be found in *BBI,* 11. Incidentally, the tuning instructions and diagram in *BBI,* 8–9, is not what banjo players typically call G tuning (gDGBD), according to Conway, who has traced the various tunings used by African American and white mountain performers from the nineteenth through the twentieth centuries. See especially chapter 5, "The Transmission of Playing Methods and Tunings," in *African Banjo Echoes,* 194–237. For additional information based on arguments about the banjo published since the 1970s, see Conway, "Mountain Echoes," and the Adler, Bailey, Heaton, and Winans essays.

28. Winans, "The Five-String Banjo" and "Black Banjo-Playing"; Conway, "The Afro-American Traditions"; Rosenbaum, *Old-Time Mountain Banjo;* Heaton, "The 5-String Banjo." My own conclusions are based on the recommendations in *BBI,* where the melody is printed in D major. The Buckley banjo tutor recommends the A tuning, which would mean that the song would be written in E major, perhaps a more comfortable key for some tenors. The performance style is not so easy to re-create accurately, however. Bob Flesher's recent *Minstrel Banjo Stroke Style* argues that the banjo tuning of the 1830s and 1840s was 2½ steps (five semitones) below the present-day pitch (G), or a D tuning (D-g-d-f♯-a). Briggs mentions tuning the banjo with an A tuning fork but not whether the fork was set to the modern (A = 440) standard.

29. Van der Merwe, *Origins of the Popular Style,* 105.

30. The method for designating the structure of a song discussed in this and the subsequent chapter is as follows: Pr = prelude, A = first phrase, B = second phrase (and so on with other letters to show major sections), and Po = postlude (the instrumental close to the song). Each section is also identified by its total number of measures.

31. Playbill dated July 17, 1860, for George Christy's Minstrels, who were appearing at Niblo's Saloon (HTC). Some versions of the song contain verses suggesting that the performance tradition encouraged the addition of new material rhyming with the principal text,

as shown in the following quotation from the Charles Keith edition (Boston, 1844): "Next to a concert I did go, / An soon as I my figger [figure] show, / An ebery singer change each line, / To Dandy Jim ob Caroline."

32. Nathan, *Emmett*, 324, prints a London version (my "Dandy Jim" no. 4) that shows some additional differences in the second phrase. The famous *Life in Philadelphia* series, a collection of cartoons and caricatures now in LCP, is especially illustrative. For information on fraternal societies and church groups, see Curry, *The Free Black*, 174–96.

33. Faust, *Hammond*, 103.

34. The original can be found in *United States Congressional Globe*, 35th Congress, 1st Session, 961–62. My quotation is from Feldstein, *The Poisoned Tongue*, 93. The speech was made in the U.S. Senate (1858) and offered as a rebuttal to Senator William Seward, an antislavery advocate. Hammond was obviously still a figure in American political life. The speech and its relationship to northern labor are discussed in Foner, *Free Soil*, 66.

35. Faust, *Hammond*, 346–47. The Fitzhugh reference is to George Fitzhugh's *Sociology for the South; or, the Failure of the Free Society* (Richmond, 1854), as quoted in Foner, *Free Soil*, 66.

36. Wilenski, *Chants Democratic*, 332.

37. Haltunnen, *Confidence Men*, 62–63.

38. Blumin, *Middle Class*, 233; Fern, *Fern Leaves from Fanny's Port-folio*, 247–48.

39. The dandy stereotype carries through into other male display songs because snatches of verses migrate from one song to another, as in Andrew Evans's parody of "The Jolly Raftsman" (1844) that specifically mentions that Dine always described her raftsman lover "as a prettier nigger than Dandy Jim of Caroline" (Evans, "The Jolly Raftsman" [Boston: Henry Prentiss, 1844]).

40. "Old Dan Tucker" and its many variants occur in the following songsters: two versions in *BTS1*, *CNS2*, and *CNS1* and three versions in *DJD1*, *DSN1*, *EGB1*, *JJO1*, *NFM1*, *NSO1*, *LFM1*, and *VSI1*. "Old Dan Tucker" continued as a novelty number with "Irish, Dutch, and French verses" on the Virginia Serenaders' playbill for March 2, 1850. The large number of performances of "Dan Tucker" is confirmed in Winans's study "Early Minstrel Show Music." The sheet music editions of "Old Dan Tucker" include (1) "Old Dan Tucker" (New York: Millet's Music Saloon, 1843); (2) "Old Dan Tucker" (Boston: Oliver Ditson, 1843); (3) "Old Dan Tucker," in *Old Dan Emmit's Original Banjo Melodies* (Boston: Charles H. Keith, 1843), whose tune Nathan says was not by Emmett "even though he claimed it in later years" (*Emmett*, 301); (4) "Old Dan Tucker," arr. Thomas Comer (Boston: George P. Reed, 1843); (5) "Old Dan Tucker," *Emmit's Celebrated Negro Melodies* (London: D'Almaine and Co, ca. 1844[?]); (6) "Old Dan Tucker" (New York: Atwill's Music Saloon, 1843); (7) "Old Dan Tucker" (Philadelphia: George Willig, 184?); and "Old Dan Tucker" (Boston: W. H. Oakes, 1843).

41. Finson notes that "the musical content of 'Old Dan Tucker' hails from the traditional roots of minstrelsy. . . . The melody shares the parlando rhythms of earlier minstrel songs and punctuates the prosaic declamation with many syllables on one repeated pitch. The tune has a very flat melodic shape suited to its patter, and the refrain emphasizes a relatively new feature of blackface songs, syncopation in the phrase 'get *out* de way!'" (*Voices*, 180–81).

42. William Clifton may have been the house arranger for the New York song publisher George Endicott, who published this song as "Long Time Ago: A Favorite Comic Song and Chorus" (New York: George Endicott, 1836). According to Damon (*Old American Songs*, no. 18), this number was based on an 1833 original performed by Thomas D. Rice. The same call-and-response formula also appears in the song I refer to as "Uncle Gabriel" no. 2, which was published by Charles Holt Jr. as "Uncle Gabriel, the Negro General" (New York: C. Holt

Jr., 1848), an edition of which is now in the Foster Hall Collection at the University of Pittsburgh Library. "Uncle Gabriel" no. 1 (New York: William Hall, 1847) was performed by the Ethiopian Serenaders and is set on Long Island. Two representative verses are:

I was gwan to Sandy Point de oder arternoon,
Dis niggers heel cum'b out ob joint a runnin' arter a coon,
I thought I see'd him on a log, a lookin' mighty quar,
Wen I cum'b up to de log, de coon he wasn't there.

I blow'd de horn, I call'd de dog, and tell him for to bark,
I hunt all night in de hollow log, but de coon he still keep dark.
At last I hear de ole coon sneeze, de dog he fly around,
And onto him he den did freeze, and run him to de ground.

43. Damon says that the song "was rooted in the Negro past, and had already assumed a variety of forms when it burst into sheet music" (*Old American Songs*, no. 18). The song has at least two different texts and was used by Rice in an "Ethiopian Opera" (Damon does not identify which one) in 1833. It should be noted again how many of minstrelsy's earliest songs were arranged by William Clifton. The chorus is set for three parts, not four. There are several unisons, doubled notes (usually at the octave), and sixths built on only two chords, namely, the dominant seventh and tonic chords.

44. Ayers recorded "Old Joe" on the *Old Dan Tucker* cassette. The song refers to Joe's activities with a "yaller gal" and recounts how happy his wife and children are when he returns. Joe "kicks it up behind and before wide de yaller gal," another allusion to the double standard that tolerates extramarital liaisons for husbands.

45. "Old Tare River" was also known as "Old Tar River." It appears in five of the playbills I surveyed: Virginia Minstrels, January 20–23, 1843; Christy's Minstrels, April 10, 1844; Ethiopian Serenaders, June 17, 1851; and an undated but probably 1840s bill for the Virginia Serenaders. Winans found it in nine of forty-two playbills (19 percent) from 1843 to 1847. The song appears under the title of "Old Tare River" in nine of the forty-nine songsters I reviewed, with the largest number of citations (five) during the the 1843–48 years. "Old Tare River" and its many variants will be found in *DSN1, NFM1, WNE1*, and *NSO1*. Dichter and Shapiro call the song "more traditional" than the other song illustrations shown in their *Early American Sheet Music*, 54. The song's frequent appearances in minstrelsy's first decade confirm the influence of Joel Sweeney on early minstrelsy. Hamm gives Sweeney's dates as 1931–60, the former undoubtedly a misprint for 1813 (*Yesterdays*, 126).

46. *Through-composed* means "without internal repetitions, especially with respect to the setting of a strophic or other text that might imply the repetition of music for different words; thus, e.g., a song in which new music is composed for each stanza of text" (*Harvard Dictionary*, 1986, s.v., "Through-composed [Ger. *Durchkomponiert*]").

47. In *Old American Songs* Damon says the Prentiss edition is the "earliest known version." The title page seems to indicate that this song is one of "Sweeny's Virginy Melodies," "As sung with tremendous applause at Harrington's New Museum and at the principal theaters in the United States." The song also appears with different texts and under the titles of "Old Tar River," "Ole Tar River," and "Original Old Tar River" in *DSN1, NFM1* (twice), *BTS1, WNE1*, and *NSO1* (twice). Nathan reprints this version of the song but adds an "Ah" syllable in square brackets that is not found in the original sheet music edition. The second text is from Dennison's (66–67) reprinting of another version, called "Old Tar River (Wid a Little Local Salt

in de Wata)," from *NFM1* that includes the syllables "Hu hu lu a hu ahoo" and "Lum tum tum tum Toddy um de da" for the nontext passages in the 1840 Sweeney edition of the song.

48. This song describes a slave's treatment on a corn plantation and his escape. The apparently nonsense chorus, "Walk Jawbone, Jenny git along, in come Sally wid de booties on," contains lines from three other songs or dances, as is the case with the "Walk, chalk" chorus of "Ginger Blue" quoted earlier. Such choruses may have indicated dance numbers or musical quotations. A good performance by Bob Flesher appears on his *Minstrel Banjo*, side 2.

49. The Benteen edition of the song is entitled "Jim Crack Corn, or The Blue Tail Fly," and published in 1846, according to Fuld, *Book of World-Famous Music*, 312. Both versions of the "Blue Tail Fly" and "Jim Crack Corn" tell essentially the same story, but it is seldom clear from the playbills which of the versions might have been performed. Some versions of the "Blue Tail Fly" can be performed to the "Clare de Kitchen" melody. The original and variants, which are usually entitled "new," will be found in *BTS1, NFM1, WNB1, NSO1* (twice), *NFM3, CPM5, CNS1*; under the title of "Jim Crack Corn" it appears in *GEM2, CNS1*, and *NSO1*. "Wild Goose Nation" will be found in *BTS1, LFM1, NFM1, ESB1, NSO1, CNS1*; "Wild Raccoon Track," in *DSN1, NFM1, BTS1, NPS1, EGB1, NSO1*, and *CPM5*.

Neither the music nor the text has been attributed to anyone. Emmett's arrangement, entitled "De Blue Tail Fly" (Boston: Keith's Publishing House, 1844), has a different melody in the same two-plus-two-measure pattern of "Old Tare River." Contrary to Fuld's statement that Emmett's "Blue Tail Fly . . . has a completely different melody and words" (312n3), most of the verses after the first are quite similar to those in the Benteen edition. See Nathan, *Emmett*, 429–31, for that version, the first musical phrase of which is similar to Emmett's "'Twill Nebber Do To Gib It Up So" (1843). The Emmett song has a different minor mode melody of twelve bars without a chorus, gives the locale as South Carolina, and notes the time of year (August) when the blue tail fly hatches. Another version of the Emmett song, at AAS, indicates that the text was to be sung to "Clare de Kitchen"; its cover shows a highly agitated blackface character with a broom and banjo observing a gentleman's fall from his horse. The song is no. 3 of *Emmitt's Celebrated Negro Melodies or Songs of the Virginny Banjoist*. Nathan shows this as item g in *Old Dan Emmit's Original Banjo Melodies* (Boston: Keith's Publishing House, 1844) (Nathan, *Emmett*, 302). Bob Flesher's performance on his *Minstrel Banjo* illustrates the strong musical differences between the two examples. Emmett's modal melody seems strongly related to an Irish fiddle tradition and is not as easy to learn as the musically simpler Benteen song. There may have been some connection with African American music, for as Peter Van der Merwe argues, African melodies use interlocking thirds ("pendular thirds") in a variety of work and religious songs. See his *Origins of the Popular Style*, especially 120–31. The Benteen version is usually associated with the Edwin Christy group, which regularly added choruses to its songs, perhaps in imitation of the Hutchinsons.

50. A Christy playbill of March 3, 1847 (HTC), indicates that Edwin P. Christy was the soloist in this production but does not say how many other performers might have participated.

51. "Come Back Steben" appears in *CPS1* and *WNB1*; it appears as "Come Back Stephen" in *BHW1, BTS1, CNS1, NSO1, VSI1, CAW1, WSS1*, and *CNS2*. One sheet music edition was known as "Come Back Steben, Negro Cavatina as sung by a Kentuckian" (Boston, 1848). The special effect mentioned in the sheet music edition required the following special instructions: "To be sung in imitation of the mew [*sic*] of a Cow, by closing the mouth on the middle note and forcing the other against the roof of the mouth." The song will also be found in playbills of the Ethiopian Serenaders (1849), Rainer and Donaldson's Minstrels (1851), and White's Serenaders (1852).

52. Verse 3 borrows lines from "Pompey O'Smash," an earlier parody of Samuel Lover's "Rory O'Moore." The melodic organization and structure of "Come Back Steben" are somewhat unusual. The structure is prelude (10 mm.), verse (10 mm.), and chorus (5 mm. + 3 mm.), or Pr–A–B. The last three measures of the chorus serve as a short interlude between the repetitions of the verse. The chorus is unharmonized and was probably sung in unison. The playbills do not explain whether this was a solo song or the whole ensemble participated at key points—another example, then, of how little the sheet music edition of a song can tell about the performance practices of key blackface groups.

53. Christy Minstrels playbill, Mar. 3, 1847 (HTC). The Virginia Minstrels performed a song with the same title on March 20, 1843, but subtitled their version "Chapter on Tails." There is also an "authorized" sheet music edition featuring the Ethiopian Serenaders (Pell, Harrington, White, Stanwood, and Germon) that is entitled "Uncle Gabriel No. 1" (New York: William Hall and Son, 1847).

54. I reviewed the following accounts for background on the song: Aptheker, *Slave Revolts*, 293–324; Tragle, *Southampton Slave Revolt of 1831*, 71; and Oates, *Fires of Jubilee* and *Our Fiery Trial*.

55. The song is probably the item known as "Nigger's History of de World," which was performed by the Ethiopian Serenaders (1845), Thayer's Band of Minstrels (July 19, 1848), and the Harmoneons (Jan. 22, 1851). The "History" title is found in *NSO2, ESB1, NFM3, NSO1,* and *WNN1.* "Walk in de Parlor" and its variants appear more than eleven times in major period songsters.

56. *MSON,* 70–71. The melody of this example differs slightly from the typical banjo melody found in other sources. The song was recorded by Bob Flesher on his *Minstrel Show Banjo.*

57. "Uncle Gabriel" appears in *BHW1, CNS1, LFM1, NFM1, NFM2, NSO1, WNB1,* and *CNS2;* another song listed as "Uncle Gabriel; or, Sandy Point" occurs in *WMS1.* Another version, known as "Uncle Gabriel, the Negro General," appears in the songsters as "Uncle Gabriel the Darkey General" in *CPM2, ESB2, NNB1, ESB1,* and *RLS1.*

58. Nathan believes the words of the verse and refrain were by Emmett but that the chorus "was known in the twenties or thirties to Ohio boatmen" (*Emmett,* 291). "De Boatman's Dance" appears under that title in *BTS1, CNS2, LFM1, NFM2, NFM1, EGB1, NFM2, DJD1, NSO1, DJD1, JJO1,* and *GEM1.* It also appears on more playbills (slightly over 10 percent) than do most of the other "hits," namely, on those of the Virginia Minstrels, Sable Brothers and Sisters, Ole Bull Serenaders, Sanford's Opera Troupe, the Female Serenaders, and Wood's Minstrels. A performance of the song will be found on the New World Records minstrel album recorded by Robert Winans (*The Early Minstrel Show*).

59. One published version of the song bears no musical resemblance to Russell's song at all. See "A Life by de Galley Fire; or, A Home in de Good Ole Ship" (N.p.: White, Smith, and Co., 1848), attributed to Cuffy Josslin. This version uses an ascending F-major scale to mimic the activity of the waves. The parody can, however, be sung to Russell's song without any difficulty. See also "A Life by de Galley Fire" (New York: William Hall and Son, 1848), the cover of which lists the song as being sung by the Ethiopian Serenaders but carries an illustration showing the Campbell Minstrels.

60. The author of the parody text is unknown; Russell's lyricist was the poet Epes Sargent.

61. See Abrahams, *Singing the Master,* for supporting evidence. Other tobacco titles include "Away to the Tobacco Fields" (*CNS1*), "Gib Me Chaw Terbacker" (*NSO1, NFM3, CNS1, ESB1, NSO1*), and "Gib Us Chaw Tobacco" or "O Lord [Lud] Gals" (*BTS1, DSN1, NFM1, WNI1, WSS1*).

62. George Brewer, "History of Coosa County, Alabama," quoted in Abrahams, *Singing the Master,* 278.

63. Hardeman, *Shucks, Shocks,* 103.

64. Patterson ("A Different Drum," 168) notes that "Walk Jaw Bone" appears in the *Gems of Melody* (London, 1845), which may have been the model for the American edition cited as *GEM1.* "Walk Jaw Bone" appeared in only two of one hundred playbills, but it can be found in many songsters, namely, *CNS1, CNS2, DSN1, NFM2, NFM3, NSO1,* and *WNN1.* Other versions feature either "Sally come along" or "Jinny come along" as the second phrase after the opening chorus line of "Walk Jaw Bone"; see *BHW1, NFM1, DJD1,* and *MSON.* According to Nathan, the same tune was used for "De Ole Jaw Bone" (Boston: Henry Prentiss, 1840), sung with a similar chorus of "Walk Jaw Bone." The song may be related to those of Joel Walker Sweeney and is sometimes attributed to him. Winans lists "Ole Jaw Bone" among the top ten songs in the 47 programs of the 1843–47 period and the top fifteen songs of the 104 programs in the 1848–52 period but notes that the "second version is a distinctly different song from the first" ("Early Minstrel Show Music," 91). The differences are clear in Bob Flesher's recording, where he attributes the song to Joel Sweeney because of its early publication date.

65. Abrahams, *Singing the Master,* 83–106.

66. Kinser, *Carnival American Style,* 73.

67. Abrahams, *Singing the Master,* 88.

68. Abrahams quotes some 125 accounts of corn shucking in *Singing the Master,* 203–328.

69. Avirett, *The Old Plantation,* 140–46, as quoted in Abrahams, *Singing the Master,* 236–37. Although this account was *published* well after the antebellum minstrel era, it describes events that took place, according to Abrahams's note, in Orange County, North Carolina, during the 1850s. I quote it here to show how "Old Dan Tucker" migrated into the African American tradition.

70. Abrahams, *Singing the Master,* 225. According to accounts quoted earlier, the practice certainly was *not* specific to this area.

71. The tours of the minstrel companies deserve serious investigation. Their itinerary follows the same general path taken by the traveling opera companies and described in detail in Preston, *Opera on the Road.* What did the Buckleys do in Richmond from June to October of 1851, in Washington and Wilmington, North Carolina, during October 13–18 and 20–24, respectively, and Charleston and Columbia, South Carolina, during November 10–22 and 24–29? See Baines, "Samuel S. Sanford," for the Buckleys' itinerary prior to their break with Sanford in 1851.

72. Other examples include "Corn Husking" (*BEM4, WNN1,* and *NFM3*), "Cornfield Chorus" (*NSO1, ESB1, NSO1, CNS1,* and *CNS2*), "Corn Field Green" (*CNS2, NFM2, RLS1,* and *BEM1*), and "Yaller Corn" (*BEM1, EGB1, NFM1, NSO1,* and *CNS2*).

73. Hamm, *Music in the New World,* 104. Hamm observed that "the similarities between the early minstrel song and some of the oral-tradition music of the southern Appalachians are so numerous and striking as to be unquestionable," an observation that led him to conclude that "it is clear that one of the most distinctive American musical dialects, the banjo and fiddle style of the Appalachian region, was forged from the traditional music of two quite different (and sometimes antagonistic) groups who found themselves in the New World: Afro-Americans and Anglo-Americans" (ibid., 79, 81).

74. "Sing, Sing, Darkies, Sing" (Philadelphia: Lee and Walker, 1846) is my source from MFLP. The song appears as "Sing, Darkies, Sing" in *CNS1, EGB1, NFM1, NFM2,* and *NSO1.* The later publication date of the sheet music edition used here suggests that the song is a parody of an earlier piece. The musical style certainly supports that suggestion.

75. Robert Criswell's novel (New York: D. Fanshaw, 1852) is quoted in Abrahams, *Singing the Master,* 229–30. Criswell's account, which was written to counter Harriet Beecher Stowe's novel, may reflect a conflation of an existing minstrel song, namely, "Sing, Sing, Darkies, Sing," with an existing corn-husking tradition instead of being the authentic account Abrahams takes it to be. However, he quotes many other accounts whose accuracy can be verified.

76. Crayon, "Virginia Illustrated," 175.

77. *Family Magazine,* 1836, p. 42; quoted in Abrahams, *Singing the Master,* 209.

Chapter 6: Blackface Minstrelsy and Misogyny

1. Fern, "The Last Man?" 258–59.

2. Tawa, *Music for the Millions,* 77.

3. The term comes from Sedgwick, *Between Men,* where she uses *homosocial* to describe "social bonds between persons of the same sex" (1). Some of my ideas about male conceptions of women and gender are also based on Bonner, Goodman, Allen, James, and King, *Imagining Women;* and Senelick, *Gender in Performance.*

4. See Tawa, "Serious Songs 2."

5. The song was one of the first to use *Susanna* or *Susianna* in its title and seems to have been introduced by Kunkel's Nightingale Serenaders (1844–55) at least by the mid-1840s. The Campbells had the number on their New York playbill for October 17, 1848.

6. "Belle of Baltimore" (Boston: E. H. Wade, 1848; Boston: A. and J. P. Ordway, 1848). The song was scheduled for each of the following shows: Campbell's Minstrels, October 10, 1848; Sable Harmonists, May 22, 1849; Virginia Serenaders, February 11, 1850; and a Virginia Serenaders' show advertised in an undated playbill. "I'll Throw Myself Away" (1852) appeared on the following playbills: Buckley's Serenaders, November 23, 1853, and April 22, 1854; Backus's Minstrels, June 20, 1855; and Wood's Minstrels, September 19, 1859.

7. "Black Eye'd Susanna" may originally have been a parody of a song from the English melodrama *Black Eyed Susan,* which was performed at London's Surrey Theater in 1829. Ranked among the ten most popular melodramas of the 1830s and 1840s, *Black Eyed Susan* features a generally passive heroine (Susan) whose fidelity to her sailor husband (William) makes her a notable example of feminine virtue. Davies notes that Susan's primary "function in the play is to display from time to time the kind of purity for which Sweet William is ready to endanger his life" (*Ethnic Humor,* 53). The melodrama became a vehicle for Edwin Forrest after its introduction to the United States. The song confirms the importance of the male subject and his freedom just as the play assumes that a sailor can explore the pleasures of every port of call. Dudden, *Women in the American Theatre,* 72, is the source for my comment about the popularity of this play. The title of the song and the play should not be confused with the current occasional use of *black-eyed Susans* for contemporary African American women writers, as in the collection of short stories entitled *Black Eyed Susans.*

8. Tawa, "Songs 1."

9. Hobson, *Uneasy Virtues,* 86.

10. Damon, *Old American Songs,* no. 39.

11. Cauthen, *With Fiddle,* 14. The story originally appeared in the *Alabama Planter,* December 10, 1846.

12. There are several citations of *buffalo* as an adjective. *Buffalo gall* (1846) referred to the drink made from the bile or stomach fluid of the buffalo, which was also known as *buffalo cider* (*Dictionary of American Regional English,* s.v. "buffalo"). *Buffalo* was occasionally asso-

ciated with a black person, but the list of citations is not especially convincing except for the term *buffalo soldiers* (*Historical Dictionary of American Slang*, s.v. "buffalo"). In New York political slang, a buffalo was a member of the majority political faction in the Loco-Foco or Equal Rights Party (*Dictionary of American English*, s.v. "buffalo"). *Buffalo* was also the name of a shuffling tap dance, according to the *Random House Dictionary of the English Language* (1966, s.v. "buffalo"). Mencken (*The American Language*) cites the word as one of many expressions considered equivalent to *nigger* or *Negro*.

13. Foster, *New York by Gas-Light*, 72–76. The chapter entitled "The Dance House: Pete Williams's, or Dickens's Place" is reprinted in Southern, *Readings*, 138–41. "Pete Williams" is a character in several Ethiopian sketches and operas, namely, *Love and Jewilrums!; or, The Colored Lady in Difficulty, Negro Assurance; or, Life in Old Virginny*, and *The Virginny Cupids; or, The Rival Darkies*.

14. Hobson, *Uneasy Virtue*, 88.

15. *Yellow* was usually a "contemptuous and slang" expression "applied to Negroes and Indians of a brown or mulatto color," according to the *Dictionary of Americanisms* (s.v. "yellow") and Berrey and van den Bark, *The American Thesaurus of Slang* (s.v. "yellow"). *Yellow women* was a term sometimes associated with prostitutes, as in Mitford's references (1831 and 1873, respectively) citing "Much has been said about certain connections that are winked at with the yellow women of [New Orleans]" and "We plunge into the dark alleys lined by little cubby holes alive with yellow women." Another citation limited the term to "a mulatto woman or girl; a light skinned women of Negro blood" (*Dictionary of American English*, 4:2314 and 2519). Compare the opening line of Winnemore's "Stop Dat Knocking," which is printed as "Oh, how I lub'd a cullard gal" or "I once did lub a colored girl." In South Carolina African Americans referred to persons with Indian ancestry as "Yellow Hammers," "Yellow People" or "Yaller Nuttins." See Berry, *Almost White*, 33.

16. Berzon, *Neither White Nor Black*, 55.

17. Gilfoyle, *City of Eros*, 29.

18. Ryan, *Women in Public*, 88.

19. D'Emilio and Freedman, *Intimate Matters*, 133.

20. Ryan, *Women in Public*, 84.

21. Gilfoyle, *City of Eros*, 120.

22. Ryan, *Women in Public*, 66.

23. Gilfoyle, *City of Eros*, 120.

24. Stansell, *City of Women*, 27; D'Emilio and Freedman, *Intimate Matters*, 74.

25. Gilfoyle, *City of Eros*, 111, 130. The Melodeon (53 Bowery St.) shared its name with one of the several theaters Charles White (of White's Serenaders) managed during his many years in the minstrel business.

26. This estimate and the quotation are from George Ellington's *Women of New York*, as quoted in Scherzer, "The Unbounded Community," 324–25; the others are from Foster's *Gas-Light*, 6; and Ryan, *Women in Public*, 88, 104, 110. Ryan argues that prostitution was not a crime in nineteenth-century New York and that "the number of prostitutes arrested, around six thousand annually, would account, furthermore, for approximately two-thirds of all the women arrested under the disorderly conduct statute," making prostitutes the "third largest category in this rogues' gallery in the 1860s, trailing only laborers and the unemployed" (*Women in Public*, 110).

27. D'Emilio and Freedman, *Intimate Matters*, 133.

28. Ibid., 74.

29. See Kelley, Boydston, and Margolis, *The Limits of Sisterhood;* Stansell, *City of Women;* and Smith-Rosenberg's *Disorderly Conduct,* which I found helpful in dealing with the contexts most relevant to the treatment of women in song.

30. The impact of these novels is discussed in the chapter entitled "The Carnivalization of Language" in Reynolds, *Beneath the American Renaissance,* 441–83. See Buntline, *Mysteries and Miseries;* and George G. Foster, *Celio.*

31. D'Emilio and Freedman, *Intimate Matters,* 184.

32. Ryan, *Women in Public,* 61.

33. Donohue, "Women in Victorian Theater," 118.

34. My choice of songs for this chapter is based on the survey shown in appendix C.

35. The fact that the title of a song appears on the stencil of a sheet music cover associated with a specific performance group does not mean that the ensemble performed it. A signed, published review or reference in a diary should be required to confirm the performance of a text.

36. Stewart, *Nonsense,* argues effectively that nonsense is a disruption of the cognitive process resulting from the simultaneous perception of what appear to be different and conflicting narrative patterns.

37. There are several sheet music editions of "Mary Blane" based on either one of the two major melodies. The melody A family includes "Mary Blane" no. 1, "as sung by the Ethiopian Serenaders at the St. James Theater London and Palmo's Opera House New York," words by F. C. German [*sic*], arr. by J. H. Howard (New York: Firth and Hall, 1847). This version (in G major) is for three-part chorus in simplified operatic style and is the same as the edition published by William Hall and Son the same year. "Mary Blane" no. 2 is entitled "The New Mary Blane," with text by Wellington Guernsey and music by George Barker (Boston: Oliver Ditson, between 1844 and 1855). The music of no. 2 is the same as that of no. 1 (G major with four-part chorus), but the texts differ significantly because Guernsey attributes the kidnapping to a white man. Versions based on melody B include "Mary Blane" no. 3 (in A major), for solo voice and simplified piano accompaniment. This "Mary Blane" is sometimes referred to as "The New Mary Blane" and was allegedly "written and partly composed by Edwin P. Christy" (New York: William VanDerbeek, 1848). This edition appeared in a bound sheet music volume entitled *Christy's Minstrels and Other Ethiopian Melodies* (1846–53), item no. 7. "Mary Blane" no. 4 (in F major), in *EGB1,* 23–24, is arranged for solo voice and four-part chorus without any composer attribution. There are a number of different texts in the minstrel songsters. I have chosen the following: "Mary Blane" no. 5, from *NSO1,* 119; "Mary Blane" no. 6, from *NSO1,* 201, and attributed to Charles White; "Mary Blane" no. 7, from *GEM2,* 208; and "Mary Blane" no. 8, from *ESB1,* 33–34. Jon Finson refers to a "Mary Blane" by John Hill Hewitt (Baltimore: Benteen, 1848), which was the only one he found that "actually attributes a violent act to Native Americans" (*Voices,* 269). This text differs significantly from the others. The kidnappers are Indians, the man finds his lover eventually, and Mary dies a day after being rescued. Finally, "Mary Blane" no. 1 was republished in *MSON* and attributed to F. C. Germon with the arrangement by Howard.

38. This is a four-part setting in F major, but the alto part was apparently added later. The one harmonically interesting idea is the viidim^7/vi (C$\sharp$dim^7 of Dmin) on the second part of the second beat three measures from the end.

39. "Mary Blane" with various spellings is found in the following dated and undated collections: *GEM1, NPS1, CNS1, EGB1, NFM1, CPM1, WNP1, WNN1, ESB2,* and *CNS2* (dated); *ESB1, JJO1, BHW1,* and *VSI1* (undated). Several versions will be found in *NSO1* under

the titles "Mary Blain" (27, 84) and "Mary Blane" (113, 119, 201), the last item identified as "composed and sung by Charles White."

40. Tawa, "Songs 1," 8.

41. There are a few examples of blackface songs describing the sale of the male partner. One is James Carter's "Cynthia Sue" (1844).

42. I located the following editions but there are probably more: (1) "Miss Lucy Neal," arr. J. Buckley (New York: Firth and Hall, 1844); (2) "Miss Lucy Neal" (Boston: A. Thayer, 1844), whose title page links the song to the "Congo Melodists," one of the Buckleys' early names; (3) "Lucy Neale," adapted and arr. Charles VonBonhorst (Philadelphia: J. G. Osburn's Music Saloon, 1844); (4) "Miss Lucy Neale" (Philadelphia: A. Fiot, 1844), attributed on title page to "James Sanford," the name under which Samuel Sanford sometimes worked when he was with the Buckleys; (5) "Oh! Poor Miss Lucy Neale," arr. James W. Porter (Philadelphia: George Willig, 1844); (6) "Miss Lucy Neale; or, The Yellow Gal," also published by Willig; and (7) "Miss Lucy Neale; or, The Yaller Gal," arr. J. Barckley [sic] (Cleveland: S. Brainard and Co., 1844; New York: Joseph Atwill, 1844). The last two items are copies of the Buckley arrangement, for the title page contains the same headnote: "A Celebrated . . . Congo Melodists." The edition published in MSON (1882) is much simpler and must have come from an earlier song.

43. "Lucy Neal" and its variants also appear in BHW1 (twice), BTS1, CNS1, CNS2, EGB1, GEM1, JJO1, NFM1 (twice), NFM2, NSP1 (twice), NSO1 (twice), and VSI1. There are variants also for the identity of Lucy's owner, whose name is sometimes "Meal," "Deal," or "Mister Beale."

44. I assume that published versions regularize the variety found in the different performances of the original, especially if there has been some intervening oral transmission.

45. Bob Flesher has recently published this number and other minstrel songs in a tablature edition accompanied by an instruction guide and cassette tape in The Minstrel Banjo Stroke Style. "Lucy Neal" is no. 23 in the collection.

46. The version performed on Winans's album corrects some of the grammatical problems and makes the text clearer to the listener.

47. See Hershberg, "Free Blacks," for additional information on race riots, disfranchisement, and limited opportunities for education and employment among the African American population of the city.

48. The song is a parody of the other Lucy Neal items. The reference to children fathered by someone other than the song's male character also appears in NSO1, 269, where one verse states that "Miss Lucy had a baby, / Twas limber as an eel, / It was de image of its dad, / And looked like Lucy Neale."

49. Hershberg, "Free Blacks," 115.

50. Playbills containing this citation include Virginia Minstrels, Boston, March 22, 1843; Christy Minstrels, New York, January 8, 1844, and New York, February 16, 1849; Buckley's Minstrels, New York, January 8, 1845; Ethiopian Serenaders, New York, August 14, 1845; Ethiopian Serenaders, New York, month and day unknown, 1845; Ole Bull Band of Serenaders, New York, February 18, 1845; Dumbleton's Ethiopian Serenaders, Boston, July 6, 1849; Parker's Ethiopian Operatic Troupe, New York, August 12, 1850; and Wood's Minstrels, New York, October 18, 1854. "Miss Lucy Long and Her Answer" (1843) also appeared as a duet with texts for a bride and bridegroom similar to the dialogue song "Coal Black Rose," and the part of Lucy was played by one of the Virginia Minstrels. See Nathan, Emmett, 131.

51. Nathan, Emmett, 131. Nathan quotes a New York Clipper article of December 8, 1866, reporting that "George [Christy] was the first to do the wench business; he was the original

Lucy Long." Other sources, including Rice, *Monarchs,* indicate that the honor goes to Dan Gardner.

52. The 1842 publication date of the first version places it *prior* to the establishment of blackface minstrelsy even though "Lucy Long" achieved its greatest fame as a blackface song. The text of the second was transcribed from Joe Ayers's performance of the double verse version, wherein two verses are sung sequentially without an intervening chorus. The recording is entitled *Old Dan Tucker* and is available from Tuckahoe Music. *Heart Songs,* 289, contains another common verse, which usually appears at or near the end of the song: "My mamma's got de tisic, / My daddy's got de gout, Good morning, Mister [sometimes Doctor] Phisick, / Does your mother know you're out?"

53. The *cachucha* refers to the Spanish dance in triple meter that Fanny Elssler introduced to European theaters in *Le Diable boiteux* (1836) and popularized during her 1840–42 American visit. Elssler's version was a solo dance, though the cachucha (perhaps a different dance type) was also a couples dance, the best theatrical example of which is in act 2 of Gilbert and Sullivan's *Gondoliers* (American premiere, January 7, 1890). The example from *The Gondoliers* will be found in Bradley, *Annotated Gilbert and Sullivan,* 1:426–30, with the note that the *Topical Times* reported, "The chorus wore comparatively short skirts for the first time, and that gratifying fact revealed to a curious world that the Savoy chorus are a very well 'legged lot'" (428n265). The cachucha has never been mentioned as being popular in the South, but dances of the period made a quick transition from the dance hall or theater into the popular traditions even in remote areas. For the adoption of European dances by African Americans, see Szwed and Marks, "European Set Dances."

54. Gilfoyle, *City of Eros,* 115.

55. Nathan, *Emmett,* 130–31. The example is taken from an Emmett manuscript, which Nathan dates to about 1848 based on the internal evidence.

56. Wiltenburg, *Disorderly Women,* 97.

57. Lott, *Love and Theft,* 166. Here as elsewhere Lott argues back from his secondary source evidence. Olive Logan, the source for his comments on transvestism, wrote "The Ancestry of Brudder Bones" for *Harper's New Monthly Magazine* when postbellum performers seem to have achieved even greater freedom with their cross-dressing routines. It would take a much closer analysis of the sexual freedoms of the 1840s to read Logan's comments on the famous Leon back into the world of Billy Whitlock and the early transvestite blackface characters.

58. Gilfoyle, *City of Eros,* 114.

59. Baym, *Novels, Readers, and Reviewers,* 210.

60. Davies, *The Mirror of Nature,* 56. For pre-nineteenth-century cross-dressing, see Howard, "Cross-Dressing"; and Senelick, "Boys and Girls Together."

61. Quoted in Gilfoyle, *City of Eros,* 137–37; Gilfoyle also cites the original court case from which the quotation was taken.

62. Meserve discusses the Mose plays in some detail (*Heralds of Promise,* 122–26).

63. Paskman and Spaeth, *"Gentlemen, Be Seated!"* 91. Biographical sketches of Holland will be found in Wilmeth and Miller, *Cambridge Guide,* 235; and Bordman, *Oxford Companion,* 348–49. The reference to *Hamlet* is in Croghan, "New York Burlesque," 88.

64. Rice, *Monarchs,* 26. Four pages later, Rice says that George Harrington was the first to do the Lucy Long role.

65. Baines, "Samuel S. Sanford," 202.

66. See Rice, *Monarchs,* 28; and Paskman and Spaeth, *"Gentlemen, Be Seated!"* 92, for biographical information, including a reference to Pike's "Home Again" (1849). Jon Finson

points out the connection between Moore's "Believe Me If All Those Endearing Young Charms" and Pike's melody, again revealing the connections between Irish tunes and minstrelsy's nostalgia (*Voices*, 185–86). "Home Again" appears in only one songster, *WNN1* (1854), and on none of the playbills. Neither of the other songs seems to have been prominent in the minstrel repertory.

67. Dolan, "Gender Impersonation Onstage," 5. Dolan's essay originally appeared in *Women and Performance Journal* 2, no. 2 (1985).

68. Paskman and Spaeth, *"Gentlemen, Be Seated!"* 91.

69. Donohue discusses the "pattern of the distressed female in apparent need of rescue by a resourceful male" as one of the primary conventions in Victorian drama ("Women in the Victorian Theater," 118).

70. Roediger, *Wages of Whiteness*, 121.

71. Cross-dressing was not restricted to serious male actors or burnt cork comedians; the convention was very much of interest to women. Some great actresses of the period played male roles, for example, Charlotte Cushman (1816–76), who was famous for her characterizations of Claude Melnotte in *The Lady of Lyons*, Romeo in *Romeo and Juliet*, and Hamlet. See Shafer, "Women in Male Roles," 74–75.

72. Melville, *Pierre*, 16, 335–36. I am grateful to Stout's *Sodoms in Eden*, 131–32, for pointing out this connection.

73. Williamson, *The Crucible of Race*, 40–41. Sexual relationships between white men and black or yellow women were known to white wives and sweethearts nearly everywhere, as Fanny Kemble observed in her *Journal of a Residence on a Georgian Plantation in 1838–1939*.

74. The term *yaller dog* was the "Confederate infantrymen's term for a young staff officer who served as an aide to senior officers" (Lyman, *Civil War Wordbook*, 185). There may have been a similar class distinction surrounding the use of the word *yaller* in the antebellum period for women who served the sexual needs of men, but I could not confirm this in my survey of dictionaries. *WNP1* contains an explicit reference to miscegenation in a song entitled "De Pretty Yaller Gal Am a Warning." Verse 1: "Some loves white and some loves black, / In spite of nature's scorning, / But all de gals I ever did see, / Dat yaller gal was a warning." Chorus: "Dar am a gal in New Orleans, / Dat loves me to distraction, / And de reason I don't lub dat gal, / Am 'case of her complexion." See, Gilfoyle, *City of Eros*, 42, where his references come from the *New York Sporting Whip* (Jan. 28, 1843) and the *Whip* (Mar. 12, 1842), both of which are nearly contemporaneous with the invention of minstrelsy.

75. Gilfoyle, *City of Eros*, 41.

76. Ibid., 41, 34 (*Herald* quotation). Prime's *Life in New York* was published in 1847 at the same time that minstrelsy was attracting stronger attention from audiences in New York and Christy was assembling the first real "show." See also Hobson, *Uneasy Virtue*, 29.

77. The word *gallus* came originally from the corn harvest and refers to a brace formed by twisting several cornstalks together to form a supporting structure for the storage of the other stalks in the same row or square. The result was called a "horse," "gallows," or "gallus." By extension then, *gallus* referred to a tough, supportive companion. One of the materials used to tie up the shock and its contents was wild grape vine, which was twisted into strong ropelike tie cords. The references to the "Grape Vine Twist" or "Grape Vine" dance in minstrel shows probably come from the same agricultural vocabulary, one related to land clearing, which sometimes was a back-breaking job because dense stands of vines wove the forest together and resisted the clearers' efforts to remove logs for processing. Information from Hardeman, *Shucks, Shocks*, 55 and 104.

78. Buntline, *Mysteries and Miseries,* 89.

79. From the time it was published in 1852, "Lilly Dale" was featured by the following minstrel groups: Wells's Minstrels (Aug. 30–31, 1852); Campbell's Minstrels (July 18, 1853); Christy and Wood's Minstrels (Oct. 16, 1854); and Bryant's Minstrels (July 2, 1857). It also appeared in the following songsters: *WNN1, NFM3, CPM3, CPM4,* and *MPB1.*

80. Morley, *Death and the Victorians,* 7. The statistics have to be taken with reservation but are nonetheless startling, as in the report, for example, that in Manchester "more than fifty-seven out of every hundred working-class children died before reaching the age of five" (ibid.).

81. Larkin, *Everyday Life,* 75.

82. Finson, *Voices,* 83–84.

83. The kidnapping theme is found in the works of both male and female writers. As Shirley Samuels pointed out, in Lydia Maria Child's 1821 children's story "Mary French and Susan Easton," "two little girls, one white and one black, are kidnapped and sold into slavery. The white girl has been disguised; she appears black, but her tears gradually dissolve this surface identity, revealing the white body beneath the black surface, and she is restored to her family. Her friend's tears cannot accomplish a similar miracle: because they do not change her surface identity, she is left in slavery" ("The Identity of Slavery," 157).

84. This particular song is of singular interest. There are two sheet music editions of this version. One indicates James Hewitt as the publisher and the copyright date as 1843; the other is dated 1848 and published by Firth and Hall. The title page also attributes the words to T. Baines Haily, that is, Thomas Haines Bayley (1797–1839), the composer and novelist remembered today for "Long Long Ago" (ca. 1835); see Fuld, *World-Famous Music,* 338. To add to the confusion, there is an old version entitled "De Ole Jaw Bone" published in Boston by Henry Prentiss in 1840; see Nathan, *Emmett,* 464–65. The parody was undoubtedly related to Michael Rolphino Lacy's (1795–1867) adaptation of Rossini's *La Cenerentola,* the English title of which was *Cinderella; or, The Fairy and the Little Glass Slipper* (New York, Jan. 24, 1831). As Preston points out, Lacy's adaptation "included music from three of Rossini's other operas, *Armida, Maometto II,* and *Guillaume Tell*" (*Opera on the Road,* 12).

85. The harmonies of the 1843 version highlight the "Oh! de old Jaw bone" phrases. The first statement is harmonized the first time it appears with a somewhat colorful I–ii^6–V^7/vi progression, the second with a IV–V^7–I.

86. Welter, *Dimity Convictions,* 9. Welter did not identify her primary source.

87. Finson, *Voices,* 41.

88. Material from HTC playbills for dates listed in text.

89. Matthews, *Just a Housewife,* 35–65.

90. Under the title "Grey Goose and Gander" or "Gray Goose and Gander," this song appears in *NFM1, NFM2, CNS1, WSS1, NSO1, BHW1, JJO1,* and *CNS2.* Nathan (*Emmett,* 461–62) shows a sheet music edition (Philadelphia: A. Fiot, 1844) with additional verses dealing with a "bery fat" Miss Dinah Rose. Only the first and second verses Nathan reprints are similar to the version quoted here. The others refer to the Miss Dinah of that song as "fat" and as having a "great big hole right in her stocking" and make the usual references to the exposed heels of the blackface characters. This version was probably connected with a dance.

91. Lott, *Love and Theft,* 120, 163, 164.

92. Rice, *Monarchs,* 46.

93. Ibid. The Reynaldson evidence comes from an HTC playbill dated September 23, 1852, where she is identified as a Scottish vocalist. She may have been only a guest with White's group. The Wood reference is from an October 24–25, 1854, playbill (HTC), the same source as the Thayer citation.

94. Virginia Serenaders playbill, 1845 (HTC).

95. Quoted from the *National Gazette* (Philadelphia), September, 29, 1827, in Dizikes, *Opera in America*, 50–51.

96. Lott writes that "since women were a major presence in the 'legitimate' midcentury American theater, one must surmise that cross-dressing in the minstrel show was intended to clear a space in which homoeroticism could find halting, humiliated, but nonetheless public expression" (*Love and Theft*, 165).

97. Roediger, *Wages of Whiteness*, 21.

Conclusion

1. Levine, *Black Culture*, 444–45.

2. "Twain's 'Nigger' Jim,'" 12. Bell argues in the sentence leading up to my quotation that minstrelsy "was a national symbolic ritual of debasement of blacks for petty profit."

3. Huggins, *Harlem Renaissance*, 273–74.

4. Floyd, *Power of Black Music*, 88.

5. Ellison, *Shadow and Act*, 49.

6. Ostendorf, "Minstrelsy and Early Jazz," 577–78; see also Dormon's "Strange Career."

7. Ellison's view was essentially presentist, generated as it was by his own lived experience and by the significant upheavals in black-white relations during the 1960s. Lott and I agree that "reading off from a text the stereotypes that a historical moment is presumed to have required is typically presentist, and in viewing minstrelsy as the nail in the coffin of cultural containment . . . is rather narrowly functionalist" (Lott, *Love and Theft*, 8–9).

8. Lott, *Love and Theft*, 5–6.

9. Virginia Serenaders playbill, February 11, 1850 (HTC).

10. Quotations from George B. Tindall, "The Benighted South: Origins of a Modern Image," in Gerster and Cords, *Myth and Southern History*, 246.

11. See Abrahams, "Complex Relations." The best overview of these developments is Bronner, *American Folklore Studies*.

12. Simpson, *Politics of American Literature*, 106.

13. Only one of the preacher jests written by Dan Emmett was published before the Civil War. Few of Emmett's forty dialect sermons, all of which are at the Ohio Historical Society, were ever published, but all seem to have been intended for performance along with the fifty-seven hymns Emmett composed, according to Schneider, "Daniel Emmett's Negro Sermons," 71–72.

14. Valentine appeared with the Ethiopian Serenaders on July 6, 1849, in a collection of sketches, songs, imitations, and other elements for which he had established a solid local reputation. On October 24, 1854, "the celebrated Dr. Valentine" presented "a variety of Freaks, Follies, and Foibles, with Imitations of Quaint, Quizzical, Quiet and Quarrelsome People, Musical Sketches, and little of everything and everyday," according to a Wood's playbill. For a biography of the Valentine family, see Maynard, *The Valentines in America, 1644–1874*.

15. Winans, "Early Minstrel Show Music," 95; Cantwell, *Bluegrass Breakdown*, 261, 270.

16. Theoretical and practical studies of minstrel show audiences are essential if minstrelsy's significance is ever to be understood adequately. Too often scholars have adopted Gans's "taste culture" hypotheses and assumed that musical consumption is based on stratified social class defined by wealth and distinctiveness. See Gans, "Popular Culture in America."

17. Winans, Conway, and Ayers have all contributed valuable information about how playing techniques could have crossed the racial divide, which I think is social and political, be-

cause for performing musicians, the musical gap between the races is not so large as we have made it.

18. Blassingame, *The Slave Community,* viii.

19. See, Cauthen, *With Fiddle.* Of particular interest for students of minstrelsy is Cauthen's listing of "old-time" tunes that date back to antebellum minstrel days.

20. See Winans, "Black Instrumental Music" and "Black Banjo-Playing"; and Conway, *African Banjo Echoes,* especially chap. 5, "The Transmission of Playing Methods and Tunings," 194–237.

21. The situation I refer to is described in Northrup's *Twelve Years a Slave,* 156–66, 218–19.

22. Bryant, *Letters,* 2:205.

23. According to Charles Hamm, "none of the music performed on the minstrel stage before the Civil War had any connection with the music of black slaves or freemen" (Hamm, *Music in the New World,* 104).

24. Philips, "The African Heritage," 277.

25. Rosen, *Romantic Generation,* 605–6.

26. Pessen, *Riches, Class, and Wealth,* 245.

27. Stylistic fusion could have occurred along the lines sketched out in Nathan's *Dan Emmett,* which argued for the high probability of musical interactions among African American, Anglo-Celtic, and American music and showed some musical and textual connections among minstrel songs, instrumental numbers, and dances. Nathan, a pioneer in popular music studies, offered rich areas for future study, but his interpretations of the English, Irish, and African or African American sources for minstrelsy have often (and unjustifiably) been discounted because the melodic parallels were not always convincing. Blackface minstrelsy imitated African American spirituals after the Civil War, but to my knowledge there have not been any studies comparing examples from these diverse cultural sources.

28. Wilentz, *Chants Democratic,* 258.

29. McConachie, "New York Operagoing."

30. The banjo's history is explored thoughtfully in Linn, *That Half-Barbaric Twang.*

31. Conway, *African Banjo Echoes,* 228.

32. Conway quotes Art Rosenbaum, who wrote that fretless banjos "discouraged the early musicians from doing much noting above first position especially from trying to fret [stop] more than one string at a time high on the neck" (ibid., 231), difficulties raised also by the composition of the strings on the early minstrel banjos.

33. Reynolds, *Beneath the American Renaissance,* 479.

34. Ryan, *Women in Public,* 73.

35. Vicinus, "'Helpless and Unfriended,'" 181.

36. Cook, "'Cursed Was She,'" 203.

37. Ryan, *Women in Public,* 70–71.

38. Vicinus, "'Helpless and Unfriended,'" 175.

39. Christy Minstrels playbill, February 26, 1849 (HTC).

40. White, *Charley White's New Book of Black Wit,* 24.

41. Quoted in Reynolds, *Beneath the American Renaissance,* 473.

42. Roediger, *Wages of Whiteness,* 122.

43. Reynolds, *Beneath the American Renaissance,* 473.

44. Lott, *Love and Theft,* 64.

45. Information from HTC playbills for the dates mentioned. Elizabeth Greenfield "sang the ballad, 'Old Folks at Home,' giving one verse in the soprano, and another in the tenor

voice" (alto?) during her visit to London (Stowe, *Sunny Memories of Foreign Lands,* 1:284; see also 1:432). Alto and tenor lines are often swapped in choral music with the understanding that the tenor part lies an octave below. Additional information on Greenfield will be found in Cuney-Hare, *Negro Musicians.* The reference to singing in two registers acknowledges Greenfield's range of three and one-half octaves.

46. Quoted from the *New York Herald* in Lawrence, *Reverberations,* 642.

47. Quoted in Lawrence, *Reverberations,* 643.

48. Roediger, *Wages of Whiteness,* 115.

49. Oring, *Jokes and Their Relations,* 17.

50. Roediger, *Wages of Whiteness,* 124.

51. Austin quotes examples of the distaste some critics felt for Ethiopian and popular music, especially John Greenleaf Whittier and the Scotsman Charles Mackay, in *"Susanna," "Jeannie," and "The Old Folks at Home,"* 48, 51, and elsewhere.

52. Reynolds, *Beneath the American Renaissance,* 445. The context of the quotation is Reynolds's discussion of Washington Irving's style of humor in *Salmagundi.*

53. Levison, "Lecture LX: Quackery," in *Black Diamonds,* 198–201, 199.

54. Of particular concern are the unsigned, decontextualized comments of reviewers or correspondents for magazines and serials whose credibility cannot be established from either primary or secondary sources, notably the oft-quoted essays of Y. S. Nathanson and J.K., now identified occasionally and without verification as J. K. Kinnard Jr.

Works Cited

Abrahams, Roger D. "The Complex Relations of Simple Forms." *Genre* 2 (1969): 104–28.

———. *Singing the Master: The Emergence of African American Culture in the Plantation South.* New York: Pantheon, 1992.

Adler, Tom. "The Physical Development of the Banjo." *New York Folklore* 28, no. 3 (Sept. 1982): 87–208.

Ahlquist, Karen Ethel. "Opera, Theatre, and Audience in Antebellum New York." Ph.D. diss., University of Michigan, 1991.

Anderson, Robert. *From Slavery to Affluence: Memoirs of Robert Anderson, Ex-Slave.* Reprint. Steamboat Springs, Colo.: Steamboat Pilot, 1967 [1927].

Appelbaum, Stanley. *Show Songs from the Black Crook to the Red Mill.* New York: Dover, 1964.

Apte, Mahadev L. *Humor and Laughter: An Anthropological Approach.* Ithaca, N.Y.: Cornell University Press, 1986.

Aptheker, Herbert. *American Negro Slave Revolts.* Reprint. New York: International, 1969 [1943].

Austin, William A. *"Susanna," "Jeanie," and "The Old Folks at Home": The Songs of Stephen Foster from His Time to Ours.* 2d ed. Urbana: University of Illinois Press, 1983.

Avirett, James Belle. *The Old Plantation.* New York: F. T. Neely, 1901.

Bailey, Jay. "Historical Origin and Stylistic Developments of the Five-String Banjo." *Journal of American Folklore* 95 (1972): 58–65.

Baines, Jimmy Dalton. "Samuel S. Sanford and Negro Minstrelsy." Ph.D. diss., Tulane University, 1967.

Baratz, Joan, and Stephen Baratz. "Black Culture on Black Terms: A Rejection of the Social Pathology Model." In *Rappin' and Stylin' Out: Communication in Urban Black America,* ed. Thomas Kochmann, 3–18. Urbana: University of Illinois Press, 1972.

Baym, Nina. *Novels, Readers, and Reviewers: Responses to Fiction in Antebellum America.* Ithaca, N.Y.: Cornell University Press, 1984.

Bean, Annemarie, James V. Hatch, and Brooks McNamara, eds. *Inside the Minstrel Mask: Readings in Nineteenth-Century Blackface Minstrelsy.* Hanover, N.H.: Wesleyan University Press, 1996.

Bell, Bernard W. "Twain's 'Nigger Jim': The Tragic Face behind the Minstrel Mask." *Mark Twain Journal* 23, no. 1 (Spring 1985): 1–17.

Bellini, Vincenzo. *La Sonnambula.* New York: G. Schirmer, 1901.

———. *La Sonnambula: An Opera in Two Acts.* New York: Edwin Kalmus, n.d.

Berrey, Lester V., and Melvin van den Bark. *The American Thesaurus of Slang: A Complete Reference Book of Colloquial Speech.* 2d ed. New York: Crowell, 1953.

Berry, Brewton. *Almost White: A Provocative Study of American's Mixed Blood Minorities.* New York: Collier, 1969.

Berzon, Judith R. *Neither White Nor Black: The Mulatto Character in American Fiction.* New York: New York University Press, 1978.

The Big Heel and Woolly Headed Melodist. Boston: T. W. Strong, 185[?].

Black Apollo Songster. New York and Philadelphia: Turner and Turner, 1844.

Black Diamond Songster. Containing all the new negro songs . . . to which is added Rolland Forrester's address to his companions. New York: Turner and Fisher [1840?].

Blassingame, John. *The Slave Community: Plantation Life in the Antebellum South.* New York: Oxford University Press, 1972.

Blayney, Glen H. "City Life in American Drama, 1825–1860." In *Studies in Honor of John Wilcox,* ed. A. Doyle Wallace and Woodburn Ross, 99–128. Detroit: Wayne State University Press, 1970.

Blumin, Stuart M. *The Emergence of the Middle Class: Social Experience in the American City, 1760–1900.* New York: Cambridge University Press, 1989.

Boker, George Henry. *Glaucus and Other Plays.* Vol. 3 of *America's Lost Plays,* 20 vols., ed. Barret H. Clark. Reprint. Bloomington: Indiana University Press, 1963–65 [1940–42].

Bonner, Frances, Lizbeth Goodman, Richard Allen, Linda James, and Catherine King, eds. *Imagining Women: Cultural Representations and Gender.* Cambridge: Polity, 1992.

Book of a Thousand Songs. Boston: n.p., 1845.

Booth, Michael R., ed. *Farces.* Vol. 4 of *English Plays of the Nineteenth Century.* London: Oxford University Press, 1973.

Bordman, Gerald A. *American Musical Theatre: A Chronicle.* New York: Oxford University Press, 1978.

———. *The Oxford Companion to the American Theatre.* New York: Oxford University Press, 1984.

Botkin, Benjamin A., ed. *A Treasury of American Folklore Stories, Ballads, and Traditions of the People.* New York: Crown, 1944.

Bowman, Kent A. *Voices of Combat: A Century of Liberty and War Songs, 1765–1865.* Westport, Conn.: Greenwood, 1987.

Box and Cox. New York: Dick and Fitzgerald, 1858.

Bradley, Ian, ed. *The Annotated Gilbert and Sullivan.* 2 vols. New York: Viking/Penguin, 1982–84.

Briggs, Thomas. *Briggs' Banjo Instructor.* Boston: Oliver Ditson, 1855; repr., Bremo Bluff, Va.: Tuckahoe Music, 1993.

Bristed, Charles Astor. *The Upper Ten Thousand: Sketches of American Society.* New York: Stringer and Townsend, 1852.

Bronner, Simon J. *American Folklore Studies: An Intellectual History.* Lawrence: University of Kansas Press, 1986.

Brown, Calvin Smith, ed. *The Later English Drama.* New York: A. S. Barnes, 1898.

Browne, Ray B. "Shakespeare in American Vaudeville and Negro Minstrelsy." *American Quarterly* 12 (1960): 374–91.

Bryant, William Cullen. *The Letters of William Cullen Bryant.* 6 vols. Ed. William Cullen Bryant II and Thomas G. Voss. New York: Fordham University Press, 1975–92.

Buckley's Ethiopian Melodies No. 1. New York: P. Cozans, 1853.

Buckley's Ethiopian Melodies No. 4. New York. P. Cozans, 1857.

Buckley's Melodies No. 2. New York: P. J. Cozans, 1853.

Buckley's Song Book for the Parlor: A Collection of New and Popular Songs as Sung by Buckley's New Orleans Serenaders. New York: P. J. Cozans, 1855.

Bulwer-Lytton, Edward. *The Dramatic Works of the Right Honorable Lord Lytton.* Freeport, N.Y.: Books for Libraries, 1972.

Buntline, Ned. *The Mysteries and Miseries of New York: A Story of Real Life.* New York: Berford, 1848.

Burdett, James S. *Burdett's Negro Dialect Recitations and Readings.* New York: Excelsior Publishing House, 1884.

Burke, Emily. *Pleasure and Pain: Reminiscences of Georgia in the 1840s.* Reprint. Savannah: Beehive, 1978 [1850].

Camus, Raoul F. Review of Kenneth Kreitner, *Discoursing Sweet Music: Town Bands* (1990). *Journal of the American Musicological Association* 45, no. 2 (Summer 1992): 361–64.

Cantwell, Robert. *Bluegrass Breakdown: The Making of the Old Southern Sound.* Urbana: University of Illinois Press, 1984.

Cauthen, Joyce H. *With Fiddle and Well-Rosined Bow: Old-Time Fiddling in Alabama.* Tuscaloosa: University of Alabama Press, 1989.

Charley Fox's Bijou Songster. New York: Frederic[k] A. Brady, 1858.

Charley Fox's Ethiopian Songster. Philadelphia: A. Winch, 1858.

Christy's Negro Serenaders. Containing all the choice songs as sung by that inimitable band of Melodists. New York: Elton and Vinten, 184[?].

Christy's Nigga Songster. Containing Songs as are sung by Christy's, Pierce's, White's, Sable Brothers, and Dumbleton's Band of Minstrels. New York: T. W. Strong, n.d.

Christy's Panorama Songster. New York: W. H. Murphy, 1857.

Christy's Plantation Melodies No. 1. New York: Fisher and Brother, 1851.

Christy's Plantation Melodies No. 2. New York: Huestis and Cozans (on first title page); New York: Turner and Fisher, 1853 (on second title page).

Christy's Plantation Melodies No. 3. Philadelphia and New York: Fisher and Brother, 1853.

Christy's Plantation Melodies No. 4. New York: Turner and Fisher, 1854.

Christy's Plantation Melodies No. 5. New York: Fisher and Brother, 1856.

Clarke, Matthew St. Clair (attrib.). *Sketches and Eccentricities of Colonel David Crockett of West Tennessee.* New York: J. and J. Harper, 1833.

Cockrell, Dale, *Demons of Disorder: Early Blackface Minstrels and Their World.* New York: Cambridge University Press, 1997.

———, ed. and annotator. *Excelsior: Journals of the Hutchinson Family Singers, 1842–1846.* New York: Pendragon, 1989.

Cogswell, Robert G. "Jokes in Blackface: A Discographic Folklore Study." Ph.D. diss., University of Indiana, 1984.

Cohen, Hennig, and William B. Dillingham. *Humor of the Old Southwest.* 2d ed. Athens: University of George Press, 1964.

Come Day, Go Day, God Send Sunday: The Songs and Life Story of John Macguire, Tradi-

tional Singer and Farmer from Co. Fermanagh. London: Routledge and Kegan Paul, 1976.

Conway, Cecelia. *African Banjo Echoes in Appalachia: A Study of Folk Traditions.* Knoxville: University of Tennessee Press, 1995.

———. "The Afro-American Traditions of the Folk Banjo." Ph.D. diss., University of North Carolina at Chapel Hill, 1980.

———. "Mountain Echoes of the African Banjos." *Appalachian Journal: A Regional Studies Review* (Winter 1993): 146–61.

Cook, Susan C. "'Cursed Was She': Gender and Power in American Balladry." In *Cecilia Reclaimed: Feminist Perspectives on Gender and Music,* ed. Susan C. Cook and Judy S. Tsou, 202–24. Urbana: University of Illinois Press, 1994.

Cooper, George, ed. *Brudder Kinkhard's Stump Speeches and Droll Discourses.* New York: Wehman Brothers, ca. 1920.

Cooper, James Fenimore. *Notions of the Americans Picked up by a Bachelor.* 2 vols. Reprint. New York: Frederick Ungar, 1963 [1828].

Crawford, Richard. *The American Musical Landscape.* Berkeley: University of California Press, 1993.

Crayon, Porte [David Hunter Strother]. "Virginia Illustrated: Adventures of Porte Crayon and His Cousins." *Harper's New Monthly Magazine* 12 (1855–56): 158–78.

Croghan, Leland A. "New York Burlesque 1840–1870: A Study in Theatrical Self-Criticism." Ph.D. diss., New York University, 1968.

Cross, Whitney R. *The Burnt-Over District: The Social and Intellectual History of Enthusiastic Religion in Western New York 1825–1850.* Ithaca, N.Y.: Cornell University Press, 1950.

Crouthamel, Jake L. *Bennett's New York Herald and the Rise of the Popular Press.* Syracuse, N.Y.: Syracuse University Press, 1989.

Cuney-Hare, Maud. *Negro Musicians and Their Music.* Reprint. New York: Da Capo, 1974 [1936].

Curry, Leonard P. *The Free Black in Urban America 1800–1850: The Shadow of the Dream.* Chicago: University of Chicago Press, 1981.

Dalby, David. "The African Element in American English." In *Rappin' and Stylin' Out: Communication in Urban Black America,* ed. Thomas Kochmann, 170–71. Urbana: University of Illinois Press, 1972.

Damon, Samuel Foster. *Series of Old American Songs.* Providence, R.I.: Brown University Library, 1936.

Dana, Willam Henry. *J. W. Pepper's Budget of Wit and Humor.* Philadelphia: C. Marshall, 1849; New York: W. F. Burgess, 1850.

———. *J. W. Pepper's Practical Guide and Study to the Secret of Arranging Orchestra Music; or, The Amateur's Guide.* Philadelphia: J. W. Pepper, 1878.

Dandy Jim and Dan Tucker's Jaw Bone; or, Cool White's Nigga Minstrel. New York and Philadelphia, 1844.

Davidson, Frank Costellow. "The Rise, Development, and Decline of the American Minstrel Show." Ph.D. diss., New York University, 1952.

Davies, Christie. *Ethnic Humor around the World: A Comparative Analysis.* Bloomington: Indiana University Press, 1990.

Davies, Robertson. *The Mirror of Nature.* Toronto: University of Toronto Press, 1983.

Davis, Susan G. *Parades and Power: Street Theatre in Nineteenth-Century Philadelphia.* Philadelphia: Temple University Press, 1986.

Deacon Snowball's Negro Melodies. Philadelphia: Turner and Fisher, 1843.

D'Emilio, John, and Estelle B. Freedman. *Intimate Matters: A History of Sexuality in America.* New York: Harper and Row, 1988.

Dennison, Sam. *Scandalize My Name: Black Imagery in American Popular Music.* New York: Garland, 1982.

A Dictionary of American English on Historical Principles. Ed. William A. Craighe and James R. Hulbert. Chicago: University of Chicago Press, 1944.

Dictionary of Americanisms on Historical Principles. Ed. Mitford Matthews. Chicago: University of Chicago Press, 1951.

Dictionary of American Regional English. Ed. Frederic Cassidy. Cambridge: Harvard University Press, 1985.

Dichter, Harry, and Elliott Shapiro. *Handbook of Early American Sheet Music, 1768–1889.* New York: Dover, 1977.

Dillard, Joey Lee. *All-American English.* New York: Random House, 1975.

———. *Black English: Its History and Usage in the United States.* New York: Random House, 1972.

———. "Black English in New York," *English Record* 21 (Apr. 1971): 114–20.

———, ed. *Perspectives on Black English.* The Hague: Mouton, 1975.

Dixey's Songster. Philadelphia: A. Winch, 1860.

Dizikes, John. *Opera in America: A Cultural History.* New Haven, Conn.: Yale University Press, 1993.

Dolan, Jill. "Gender Impersonation Onstage: Destroying or Maintaining the Image of Gender Roles?" In *The Presentation of Difference in the Performing Arts,* ed. Lawrence Senelick, 3–13. Hanover, N.H.: Tufts University Press (University Press of New England), 1992.

Donohue, Joseph. "Women in Victorian Theatre: Images, Illusions, Realities." In *The Presentation of Difference in the Performing Arts,* ed. Lawrence Senelick, 117–40. Hanover: Tufts University Press (University Press of New England), 1992.

Dormon, James H. *Theater in the Ante-bellum South, 1815–1861.* Chapel Hill: University of North Carolina Press, 1967.

Dorson, Richard M. "Mose the Far-Famed and World-Renowned." *American Literature* 15 (1943): 287–300.

———. *Jonathan Draws the Long Bow.* Cambridge: Harvard University Press, 1946.

Douglass, Frederick. "Gavitt's Original Ethiopian Serenaders." *The North Star,* June 29, 1849. Reprinted in Philip S. Foner, ed., *The Life and Writings of Frederick Douglass,* 5 vols., 1:141–42. New York: International, 1950–75.

———. "The Hutchinson Family.—Hunkerism." *The North Star* 1, no. 44 (Oct. 27, 1848).

Dudden, Faith E. *Women in the American Theatre: Actresses and Audiences, 1790–1870.* New Haven, Conn.: Yale University Press, 1993.

Dumont, Frank. *The Witmark Amateur Minstrel Guide.* New York: M. Witmark and Sons, 1899.

Eby, Cecil B. *"Porte Crayon": The Life of David Hunter Strother.* Chapel Hill: University of North Carolina Press, 1960.

Elkins, Stanley. *Slavery: A Problem in American Life.* Chicago: University of Chicago Press, 1959.

Ellison, Ralph. "Change the Yoke and Slip the Joke." *Partisan Review* (1958). Reprinted in Ralph Ellison, *Shadow and Act,* 45–59. New York: Vintage, 1972.

————. *Shadow and Act*. New York: Vintage, 1972.

Emmit's Celebrated Negro Melodies or Songs of the Virginny Banjoist. London: D'Almaine and Co., n.d. (ca. 1844).

Engle, Gary D. *This Grotesque Essence: Plays from the American Minstrel Stage*. Baton Rouge: Louisiana State University Press, 1978.

Epstein, Dena J. "The Folk Banjo: A Documentary History." *Ethnomusicology* 19 (Sept. 1975): 347–71.

————. *Sinful Tunes and Spirituals: Black Folk Music to the Civil War*. Urbana: University of Illinois Press, 1977.

The Ethiopian Accordeon Instructor. Boston: Elias Howe, 1848.

The Ethiopian Glee Book. Containing the songs sung by the Christy Minstrels; with many other popular Negro melodies in four parts arranged for quartett [*sic*] clubs by Gumbo Chaff. Boston: Elias Howe, 1848–49.

Ethiopian Medley for the Piano Forte No. 2. Boston: Henry Prentiss, 1843.

The Ethiopian Serenader's Own Book. New York: Philip J. Cozans, n.d.

The Ethiopian Serenader's Own Book. New York and Philadelphia: Fisher and Brother, 1857.

Ezell, John Samuel. *Fortune's Merry Wheel: The Lottery in America*. Cambridge, Mass.: Harvard University Press, 1960.

Falk, Robert P., ed. *The Antic Muse: American Writers in Parody, a Collection of Parody, Satire, and Literary Burlesque of American Writers Past and Present*. New York: Grove, 1955.

Faust, Drew Gilpin. *James Henry Hammond and the Old South: A Design for Mastery*. Baton Rouge: Louisiana State University Press, 1982.

Feldstein, Stanley, ed. *The Poisoned Tongue: A Documentary History of American Racism and Prejudice*. New York: William Morrow, 1972.

Fern, Fanny [Sara Payson Willis]. *Fern Leaves from Fanny's Portfolio*. Buffalo, N.Y.: Miller, Orton, and Mulligan, 1854.

————. "Who Would Be the Last Man?" *Olive Branch*, June 4, 1853. Reprinted in *Ruth Hall and Other Writings*, ed. Joyce W. Warren, 258–59. New Brunswick, N.J.: Rutgers University Press, 1986.

Finson, Jon W. *The Voices That Are Gone: Themes in Nineteenth-Century American Popular Song*. New York: Oxford University Press, 1994.

Fisher, Judith L., and Stephen Watt, eds. *When They Weren't Doing Shakespeare: Essays on Nineteenth-Century British and American Theatre*. Athens: University of Georgia Press, 1989.

Flesher, Bob. *Bob Flesher's Old-Time Minstrel Banjo of the Civil War and Antebellum Period*. Cassette. Dr. Horsehair's Old-Time Minstrels.

————. *The Minstrel Banjo Stroke Style*. Peachtree, Ga.: Dr. Horsehair's Music Co., 1995.

Floyd, Samuel A., Jr. *The Power of Black Music: Interpreting Its History from Africa to the United States*. New York: Oxford University Press, 1995.

Folio, Fred [pseud.]. *A Book for the Times, Lucy Boston; or, Woman's Rights and Spiritualism, illustrating the Follies and Delusions of the Nineteenth Century*. Auburn, N.Y.: Rochester, Alden and Beardsley, 1855; New York: J. C. Derby, 1855.

Follitt's Black Lectures. London: Follitt, 1846.

Foner, Eric. *Free Soil, Free Labor, Free Men: The Ideology of the Republican Party before the Civil War*. New York: Oxford University Press, 1970.

Foster, George G. *Celio; or, New York Above-Ground and Under-Ground*. New York: Dewitt and Davenport, ca. 1850.

————. *New York by Gas-Light with Here and There a Streak of Sunshine.* New York: 1850.

Francis, John W. *Old New York; or, Reminiscences of the Past Sixty Years.* New York: Charles Roe, 1858.

Frederickson, George. *The Arrogance of Race; Historical Perspectives on Slavery, Racism, and Social Inequality.* Middletown, Conn.: Wesleyan University Press, 1988.

Fry, William Henry. *Leonora.* Philadelphia: E. Ferrett, 1845.

Fuld, James J. *The Book of World-Famous Music: Classical, Popular, and Folk.* 3d. ed. New York: Dover, 1985.

Gans, Herbert J. *Popular Culture and High Culture: An Analysis and Evaluation of Taste.* New York: Basic, 1975.

Garrison, J. Richie. "Battalion Day: Military Exercise and Frolic in Pennsylvania before the Civil War." *Pennsylvania Folklife* 26 (1976–77): 2–12.

Gates, Henry Louis. *The Signifying Monkey: A Theory of Afro-American Literature.* New York: Oxford University Press, 1988.

Gems of Song: A Selection of the Most Popular Songs, Glees, Duetts, Choruses Etc., Also a Great Variety of Irish, Scotch, Sentimental and Comic Songs and all the Favorite Negro Melodies. 2 vols. in one. New York: D. and J. Sadler, 1847.

George Christy and Wood's New Song-Book. New York: Philip J. Cozans, 1854.

Gerster, Patrick, and Nicholas Cords, comp. *Myth and Southern History.* New York: Rand McNally, 1974.

Gilfoyle, Timothy J. *City of Eros: New York City, Prostitution, and the Commercialization of Sex, 1790–1820.* New York: Norton, 1992.

Glazer, Irwin. *Philadelphia Theatres A-Z: A Comprehensive, Descriptive Record of 813 Theatres Constructed since 1724.* Westport, Conn.: Greenwood, 1986.

Gould, Stephen Jay. "Wide Hats and Narrow Brains." In *The Panda's Thumb: More Reflections in Natural History,* 145–51. New York: Norton, 1982.

Greene, Gary A. "Understanding Past Currency in Modern Terms." *Sonneck Society Bulletin* 13, no. 2 (Summer 1987): 48.

Greene, Lorenzo J. *The Negro in Colonial New England.* New York: Atheneum, 1968.

Griffith, Nancy Snell, comp. *Humor of the Old Southwest: An Annotated Bibliography of Primary and Secondary Sources.* Westport, Conn.: Greenwood, 1989.

Grote, David. *The End of Comedy: The Sit-Com and the Comedic Tradition.* Hamden, Conn.: Archon, 1983.

Guest, Ivor. *Fanny Elssler.* Middletown, Conn.: Wesleyan University Press, 1970.

Haltunnen, Karen. *Confidence Men and Painted Women: A Study of Middle-Class Culture in America, 1830–1870.* New Haven, Conn.: Yale University Press, 1982.

Hamm, Charles. *Music in the New World.* New York: Norton, 1983.

————. *Yesterdays: Popular Song in America.* New York: Norton, 1979.

Hardeman, Nicholas Perkins. *Shucks, Shocks, and Hominy Blocks: Corn as a Way of Life in Pioneer America.* Baton Rouge: Louisiana State University Press, 1981.

Harris, George Washington. "A Snake Bit Irishman: An Original Tennessee Hunting Incident." *Spirit of the Times,* January 17, 1846, pp. 549–50; *Yankee Notions* 1 (May 1852): 150–52.

Harrison, James A. "Negro English." *Anglia,* no. 7 (1884): 232–79.

Havens, Daniel F. *The Columbian Muse of Comedy: The Development of a Native Tradition in Early American Social Comedy, 1787–1845.* Carbondale: Southern Illinois University Press, 1973.

Haywood, Charles. "Negro Minstrelsy and Shakespearean Burlesque." In *Folklore and*

Society: Essays in Honor of Benjamin A. Botkin, ed. Bruce Jackson, 77–92. Hatboro, Pa.: American Folklore Society, 1966.

Hazen, Margaret Hindle, and Robert M. Hazen. *The Music Men: An Illustrated History of Brass Bands in America, 1800–1920.* Washington, D.C.: Smithsonian Institution Press, 1987.

Heath's Standard French and English Dictionary. Ed. J. E. Mansion. 2 vols. Boston: Heath, 1961–62.

Heart Songs Dear to the American People and by Them Contributed in the Search for Treasured Songs Initiated by the National Magazine. Boston: Chapple Publishing Co., 1909.

Heaton, Cherrill P. "The 5-String Banjo in North Carolina." *Southern Folklore Quarterly* 35 (1971): 62–82.

Hershberg, Theodore. "Free Blacks in Philadelphia." In *The Peoples of Philadelphia: History of Ethnic Groups and Lower-Class Life, 1790–1840,* ed. Allen F. Davis and Mark H. Haller, 111–34. Philadelphia: Temple Univeristy Press, 1973.

Hewitt, John, arr. *Crow Quadrilles.* Philadelphia: John F. Nunns, ca. 1840.

Historical Dictionary of American Slang. 3 vols. Ed. J. E. Lighter. New York: Random House, 1994–97.

Hitchcock, H. Wiley, and Stanley Sadie, eds. *The New Grove Dictionary of American Music.* 4 vols. New York: Macmillan, 1986.

Hobson, Barbara Meil. *Uneasy Virtue: The Politics of Prostitution and the American Reform Tradition.* Chicago: University of Chicago Press, 1990.

Hodge, Francis. "Charles Mathews Reports on America." *Quarterly Journal of Speech* 50 (1950): 492–99.

———. *Yankee Theatre: The Image of America on the Stage, 1825–1850.* Austin: University of Texas Press, 1964.

Holden, Amanda, with Nicholas Kenyon and Stephen Walsh, eds. *Viking Opera Guide.* London: Penguin, 1993.

Holmberg, Carl Bryan, and Gilbert D. Schneider. "Daniel Decatur Emmett's Stump Sermons: Genuine Afro-American Culture, Language, and Rhetoric in the Negro Minstrel Show." *Journal of Popular Culture* 19, no. 4 (Spring 1986): 27–38.

Holmes, Joseph L. "The Decline of the Pennsylvania Militia, 1815–1870." *Western Pennsylvania Historical Magazine* 57 (1974): 199–217.

Hooper, Johnson James. "The Captain Attends a Camp Meeting." In *Some Adventures of Captain Simon Suggs, Late of the Alabama Volunteers; Together with "Taking the Census" and Other Alabama Sketches,* 118–33. Philadelphia: Carey and Hart, 1845, 1846, 1848, 1850.

———. "The Erasive Soap Man." In *A Ride with Old Kit Kuncker and Other Sketches and Scenes of Alabama.* Tuscaloosa: M. D. J. Slade, 1849. Also in *The Widow Rugby's Husband: A Night at the Ugly Man's and Other Tales of Alabama,* 109–11. Philadelphia: A. Hart, 1851; T. B. Peterson, 1851.

Howard, Jean E. "Cross-Dressing, the Theater, and Gender Struggle in Early Modern England." In *Crossing the Stage: Controversies on Cross-Dressing,* ed. Lesley Ferris, 20–46. New York: Routledge, 1993.

Huggins, Nathan. *Harlem Renaissance.* New York: Harvard University Press, 1971.

Hutton, Lawrence. *Curiosities of the American Stage.* New York: Harper and Row, 1891.

———. "The Negro on the Stage." *Harper's New Monthly Magazine* 79, no. 469:131–45.

Ireland, Joseph N. *Records of the New York Stage from 1750 to 1860.* 2 vols. Reprint. New York: Benjamin Blom, 1966 [1866].

Irish Diamonds; or, A Theory of Irish Wit and Blunders. London: Chapman and Hall, 1847.

J. K[innard Jr.] [attrib.]. "Who Are Our National Poets?" *Knickerbocker Magazine* 26 (Oct. 1945): 331–41. Reprinted in *The Negro and His Folklore in Nineteenth-Century Periodicals,* ed. Bruce Jackson, 23–35. Austin: University of Texas Press, 1967.

Julianna Johnston's Own Colored So-lo's. New York: P. J. Cozans, 185[?].

Kelley, Mary, Jeanne Boydston, and Anne Margolis. *The Limits of Sisterhood: The Beecher Sisters on Women's Rights and Woman's Sphere.* Chapel Hill: University of North Carolina Press, 1988.

Kemble, Fanny. *Journal of a Residence on a Georgian Plantation in 1839–1939.* Reprint. New York: Knopf, 1961 [1864].

Kennedy, John Pendelton. *Swallow Barn; or, A Sojourn in the Old Dominion.* Reprint. New York: Putnam, 1854 [1832].

Kerr, Howard. *Mediums, and Spirit-Rappers, and Roaming Radicals: Spiritualism in American Literature, 1850–1900.* Urbana: University of Illinois Press, 1972.

Kinser, Samuel. *Carnival American Style: Mardi Gras at New Orleans and Mobile.* Chicago: University of Chicago Press, 1990.

Krohn, Ernest C. "Nelson Kneass: Minstrel Singer and Composer." *Yearbook for Inter-American Musical Research* 7 (1971): 17–41.

Labov, William. *Language in the Inner City: Studies in the Black English Vernacular.* Philadelphia: University of Pennsylvania Press, 1972.

Larkin, Jack. *The Reshaping of Everyday Life, 1790–1840.* New York: Harper and Row, 1988.

Lawrence, Vera Brodsky. *Music for Patriots, Politicians, and Presidents: Harmonies and Discords of the First Hundred Years.* New York: Macmillan, 1975.

———. *Resonances, 1836–1850.* Vol. 1 of *Strong on Music: The New York Music Scene in the Days of George Templeton Strong.* New York: Oxford University Press, 1988.

———. *Reverberations, 1850–1856.* Vol. 2 of *Strong on Music: The New York Music Scene in the Days of George Templeton Strong.* Chicago: University of Chicago Press, 1995.

Lester, Julius. *To Be a Slave.* New York: Dell, 1970.

Levine, Lawrence W. *Black Culture and Black Consciousness: Afro-American Folk Thought from Slavery to Freedom.* New York: Oxford University Press, 1977.

———. *Highbrow/Lowbrow: The Emergence of Cultural Hierarchy in America.* Cambridge, Mass.: Harvard University Press, 1988.

———. *The Unpredictable Past: Explorations in American Cultural History.* New York: Oxford University Press, 1993.

Levison, William H., ed. *Black Diamonds; or, Humor, Satire, and Sentiment Treated Scientifically . . . A Series of Burlesque Lectures.* Reprint. Upper Saddle River, N.J.: Gregg, 1969 [1855].

Levy, Lester S. *Grace Notes in American History: Popular Sheet Music from 1820–1900.* Norman: University of Oklahoma Press, 1967.

———. *Picture the Songs: Lithographs from the Sheet Music of Nineteenth-Century America.* Baltimore: Johns Hopkins University Press, 1976.

Lewis, Henry Clay. "Cupping an Irishman." In *Odd Leaves from the Life of a Louisiana "Swamp Doctor,"* 113–19. Reprint. Upper Saddle River, N.J.: Gregg, 1969 [1850].

Linn, Karen. *That Half-Barbaric Twang: The Banjo in American Popular Culture.* Urbana: University of Illinois Press, 1991.

Logan, Olive. "The Ancestry of Brudder Bones." *Harper's New Monthly Magazine* 58, no. 347 (1879): 687–98.

Longstreet, Augustus Baldwin. *Georgia Scenes: Characters, Incidents Etc. in the First Half Century of the Republic.* Augusta, Ga.: Press of the *States Right Sentinel,* 1835; repr., New York: Harper, 1840; Upper Saddle River, N.J.: Gregg, 1969.

Lott, Eric. *Love and Theft: Blackface Minstrelsy and the American Working Class.* New York: Oxford University Press, 1993.

———. "Racial Cross-Dressing and the Construction of American Whiteness." In *Cultures of United States Imperialism,* ed. Amy Kaplan and Donald E. Pease, 474–95. Durham, N.C.: Duke University Press, 1993.

Lover, Samuel Lover. *Handy Andy.* Reprint. New York: Dutton, 1954 [1842].

The Lover's Forget-Me-Not, and Songs of Beauty: A Choice Collection of Sentimental, Comic, and Temperance Songs, with All the Latest Negro Melodies. New York: N. C. Nafis, 1844; Philadelphia: John B. Perry, 1847.

Lull, James, ed. *Popular Music and Communications.* Newbury Park, Calif.: Sage, 1987.

Lyman, Darryl. *Civil War Wordbook Including Sayings, Phrases, and Expletives.* Conshohocken, Pa.: Combined, 1994.

Mahar, William J. "'Backside Albany' and Early Blackface Minstrelsy: A Contextual Study of America's First Blackface Song." *American Music* 6, no. 1 (1988): 1–27.

———. "Black English in Early Blackface Minstrelsy: A New Interpretation of the Sources for Minstrel Show Dialect." *American Quarterly* 37, no. 2 (Summer 1985): 260–85.

———. "Ethiopian Skits and Sketches: Contents and Contexts of Blackface Minstrelsy, 1840–1890." *Prospects: An Annual Journal of American Cultural Studies* 16 (1991): 241–79.

Mansion, Jean Edmond, comp. *Mansion's Shorter French and English Dictionary.* New York: Henry Holt, 1947.

Marckwardt, Albert H. *American English.* 2d ed., rev. J. L. Dilliard. New York: Oxford University Press, 1980.

Massa's Old Plantation Songster. New York and Philadelphia: Fisher and Brother, 185[?].

Mathews, Anne Jackson. *The Memoirs of Charles Mathews, Comedian.* 4 vols. London: R. Bentley, 1838–39.

Mathews, Charles. "Letter to James Smith." In Anne Jackson Mathews, *The Memoirs of Charles Mathews, Comedian,* 4 vols, 3:380–94. London: R. Bentley, 1838–39.

———. *Othello, the Moor of Fleet Street (1833).* Ed. Manfred Draudt. Tubingen, Germany: Francke Verlag, 1993.

Matthews, Glenna. *"Just a Housewife": The Rise and Fall of Domesticity in America.* New York: Oxford University Press, 1989.

———. *The Rise of Public Woman: Woman's Power and Woman's Place in the United States, 1630–1970.* New York: Oxford University Press, 1992.

Maynard, Thomas W. *The Valentines in America, 1644–1874.* New York: Clark and Maynard, 1874.

Matt Peel's Banjo; being a selection of the most popular and laughable negro melodies, as sung by the renowned Peel's Campbell's Minstrels. New York: Robert M. De Witt, 1858.

McCabe, James Dabney. *Lights and Shadows of New York Life; or, The Sights and Sensations of the Great City.* New York: National Publishing Co., 1872.

McConachie, Bruce A. *Melodramatic Formations: American Theatre and Society, 1820–1870.* Iowa City: University of Iowa Press, 1992.

———. "New York Operagoing, 1825–59: Creating an Elite Social Ritual." *American Music* 6, no. 2 (Summer 1988): 181–92.

———. Review of Eric Lott, *Love and Theft: Blackface Minstrelsy and the American Working Class. The Drama Review* 40, no. 1 (Spring 1996): 175–78.

———. "Using the Concept of Cultural Hegemony to Write Theater History." In *Interpreting the Theatrical Past: Essays in the Historiography of Performance,* ed. Thomas Postlewait and Bruce C. McConachie, 37–58. Iowa City: University of Iowa Press, 1989.

McCullough, Jack W. *Living Pictures on the New York Stage.* Ann Arbor, Mich.: UMI, 1983.

McLoughlin, William G., Jr. *Modern Revivalism: From Charles Grandison Finney to Billy Sunday.* New York: Ronald, 1959.

Mead, Leon. "The Military Bands of the United States." *Harper's Weekly Magazine* 33 (Sept. 28, 1889): 785–88.

Melville, Herman. *Pierre; or, The Ambiguities.* (1852). Vol. 9 of *The Standard Edition of the Works of Herman Melville,* 16 vols. New York: Russell and Russell, 1963.

Mencken, H. L. *The American Language.* [1935.] 4th. ed. New York: Knopf, 1965.

Meserve, Walter. *Heralds of Promise: The Drama of the American People during the Age of Jackson, 1829–1849.* Westport, Conn.: Greenwood, 1986.

Middleton, Russell. "Negro and White Reactions to Racial Humor." *Sociometry: Journal of Research in Social Psychology* 22, no. 2 (June 1959): 175–83.

Miller, Tice L. *Bohemians and Critics: American Theatre Criticism in the Nineteenth Century.* Metuchen, N.J.: Scarecrow, 1981.

———. "The Image of Fashionable Society in American Comedy, 1840–1870." In *When They Weren't Doing Shakespeare: Essays on Nineteenth-Century British and American Theatre,* ed. Judith Fisher and Stephen Watt, 243–52. Athens: University of Georgia Press, 1989.

Minstrel Songs Old and New. Boston: Oliver Ditson, 1882.

Moody, Richard, ed. *America Takes the Stage: Romanticism in American Drama and Theatre, 1750–1900.* Bloomington: Indiana University Press, 1955.

———. *Dramas from the American Theatre, 1762–1909.* Boston: Houghton Mifflin, 1969.

Morley, John. *Death, Heaven, and the Victorians.* Reprint. Pittsburgh: University of Pittsburgh Press, 1978 [1971].

Moses, Montrose. *Representative Plays by American Dramatists from 1765 to the Present Day.* 2 vols. Reprint. New York: Benjamin Blom, 1964 [1925].

Music of the Christy Minstrels. New York: Holt, n.d.; Boston: Oliver Ditson, n.d. [1848?].

My Dearest May and Rosa Lee's Song Book. Philadelphia: Turner and Fisher, 184?.

Nathan, Hans. *Dan Emmett and the Rise of Early Negro Minstrelsy.* Norman: University of Oklahoma Press, 1962.

National Union Catalog of Pre-1956 Imprints. London: Mansell, 1971.

Negro Dialect Recitations: comprising a series of the most popular selections in prose and verse. Ed. George Melville Baker. Boston: Lee and Shepard, 1888; New York: C. T. Dillingham, 1888.

The Negro Forget-Me-Not Songster. Philadelphia: Turner and Fisher, 1844.

The Negro Forget-Me-Not Songster. Philadelphia: Turner and Fisher, 1855.

Nevins, Allan, ed. *The Diary of Philip Hone 1828–1851.* 2 vols. in 1. New York: Arno, 1970.

New Negro Band Songster. Philadelphia: Fisher and Brother, ca. 1857.

The New Negro Forget-Me-Not Songster. Cincinnati: Stratton and Barnard, 1848.

The Negro Melodist. Cincinnati: U. P. James, 185?.

Negro Singer's Own Book, containing every Negro Song that has ever been printed. Philadelphia: Turner and Fisher, ca. 1846.

Nickels, Cameron C. *New England Humor from the Revolutionary War to the Civil War.* Nashville: University of Tennessee Press, 1993.

The Non-Pareil Songster; or, Singer's Pocket Companion. Philadelphia: John B. Perry, 1847.

Northrup, Solomon. *Twelve Years a Slave: The Narrative of Solomon Northrup, A Citizen of New York, Kidnapped in Washington City in 1841 and Rescued in 1853 from a Cotton Plantation near the Red River in Louisiana.* Ed. Sue Eakin and Joseph Logdon. Baton Rouge: Louisiana State University Press, 1968.

Norton, Anne. *Alternative Americas: A Reading of Antebellum Political Culture.* Chicago: University of Chicago Press, 1986.

Norton, Pauline. "Nineteenth-Century American March Music and John Philip Sousa." In *Perspectives on John Philip Sousa,* ed. Jon Newsom, 43–52. Washington, D.C.: Library of Congress, 1983.

Nye, Russell B. *Society and Culture in America, 1830–1860.* New York: Harper and Row, 1974.

Oates, Stephen B. *The Fires of Jubilee: Nat Turner's Fierce Rebellion.* New York: Harper and Row, 1975.

———. *Our Fiery Trial: Abraham Lincoln, John Brown, and the Civil War Era.* Amherst: University of Massachusetts Press, 1979.

Odell, George. *Annals of the New York Stage.* 15 vols. New York: Columbia University Press, 1927–49.

Old Dan Emmitt's Original Banjo Melodies. Boston: Charles H. Keith, 1843.

Old Dan Emmitt's Original Banjo Melodies. ["Second Series"]. Boston: Keith's Publishing House, 1844.

Old Dan Tucker: Melodies of Dan Emmett and the Virginia Minstrels. Cassette. Tuckahoe Music.

Oring, Elliott. *Jokes and Their Relations.* Lexington: University Press of Kentucky, 1992.

Ostendorf, Berndt. "Minstrelsy and Early Jazz." *Massachusetts Review* 20 (1979): 574–602.

Ottley, Roi, and William J. Weatherby, eds. *The Negro in New York: An Informal Social History, 1626–1940.* New York: Praeger, 1967.

Paskman, Dailey, and Sigmund Spaeth. *"Gentlemen, Be Seated!" A Parade of the Old Time Minstrels.* New York: Doubelday, 1928.

Patterson, Cecil L. "A Different Drum: The Image of the Negro in the Nineteenth-Century Song Books." Ph.D. diss., University of Pennsylvania, 1961.

Pessen, Edward A. "The Marital Theory and Practice of the Antebellum Urban Elite." *New York History* 53 (Oct. 1972): 389–409.

———. *Riches, Class and Wealth in Jacksonian America.* Lexington: D. C. Heath, 1978.

Philips, John Edward. "The African Heritage of White America." In *Africanisms in American Culture,* ed. Joseph Holloway, 225–39. Bloomington: Indiana University Press, 1990.

Pickering, Michael, and Tony Green. "Toward a Cartography of Vernacular Milieu." In *Everyday Culture: Popular Song and the Vernacular Milieu,* 1–38. Philadelphia: Open University Press, 1987.

Pipes, William Harrison. "Old-Time Negro Preaching: An Interpretive Study." *Quarterly Journal of Speech* 31 (1945): 15–21.

———. *Say Amen Brother! Old Time Negro Preaching: A Study in Frustration.* New York: William Frederick, 1951.

Pop Goes the Weasel Songster. Philadelphia: Fisher and Brother, ca. 1857.

Preston, Katherine K. *Opera on the Road: Traveling Opera Troupes in the United States, 1825–60.* Urbana: University of Illinois Press, 1993.

Quad, M. *Brother Gardner's Lime-Kiln Club.* Being the regular proceedings of the regular club for the last three years; with some philosophy, considerable music, a few lectures, and heap of advice worth reading. Chicago: Belford and Clarke, 1882.

Quinn, Arthur Hobson. *Representative American Plays from 1767 to the Present Day.* 6th ed. New York: D. Appleton–Century, 1938.

Ramshaw, Molly N. "'Jump Jim Crow': A Biographical Sketch of Thomas D. Rice." *Theatre Annual* 17 (1960): 36–47.

Randel, Don Michael, ed. *The New Harvard Dictionary of Music.* Cambridge, Mass.: Harvard University Press, 1986.

Random House Dictionary of the English Language. Ed. Stuart Berg Flexner. 2d ed. New York: Random House, 1987.

Reigel, Robert. "Early Phrenology in the United States." *Medical Life* 36 (July 1930): 361–36.

———. "The Introduction of Phrenology into the United States." *American Historical Review* 39 (Oct. 1933): 73–78.

Reynolds, David S. *Beneath the American Renaissance: The Subversive Imagination in the Age of Emerson and Melville.* New York: Knopf, 1988.

Rice, Edward Leroy. *Monarchs of Minstrelsy: From Daddy Rice to the Present.* New York: Kenny, 1911.

Rinear, David L. *The Temple of Momus: Mitchell's Olympic Theatre.* Metuchen, N.J.: Scarecrow, 1987.

Roediger, David R. *The Wages of Whiteness: Race and the Making of the American Working Class.* London: Verso, 1991.

Rogin, Michael. "Black Masks, White Skin: Consciousness of Class and American National Culture." Review of David R. Roediger, *The Wages of Whiteness,* and Melvin Patrick Ely, *The Adventures of Amos 'n' Andy. Radical History Review* 54 (1992): 141–52.

Rosen, Charles. *The Romantic Generation.* Cambridge, Mass.: Harvard University Press, 1995.

Rosenbaum, Art. *Old-Time Mountain Banjo.* New York: Oak, 1968.

Rusk, John. *The Authentic Life of T. De Witt Talmadge.* Chicago, 1902.

Russell, Henry. *An Evening with Henry Russell.* Sound recording. Nonesuch Records H-71338.

Ryan, Mary P. *Women in Public: Between Banners and Ballots, 1825–1880.* Baltimore: Johns Hopkins University Press, 1990.

Sablosky, Irving. *What They Heard: Music in America from the Pages of Dwight's Journal of Music, 1852–1881.* Baton Rouge: Louisiana State University Press, 1986.

Samuels, Shirley. "The Identity of Slavery." In *The Culture of Sentiment, Race, Gender, and Sentimentality in Nineteenth-Century America,* ed. Shirley Samuels, 157–71. New York: Oxford University Press, 1992.

[*Sanford's*] *Popular Ethiopian Melodies Including Many New and Favorite Songs as Sung at Sanford's American Opera House.* 3d ed. Philadelphia: McLaughlin Brothers, 1856.

Sanjek, Russell. *From 1790 to 1909.* Vol. 2 of *American Popular Music and Its Business: The First Four Hundred Years.* New York: Oxford University Press, 1988.

Saunders, Stephen, and Deane L. Root. *The Music of Stephen C. Foster.* Washington, D.C.: Smithsonian Institution Press, 1990.

Saxton, Alexander. "Blackface Minstrelsy and Jacksonian Ideology." *American Quarterly* 27 (Mar. 1975): 3–28.

———. "Problems of Class and Race in the Origins of the Mass Circulation Press." *American Quarterly* 36, no. 2 (Summer 1984): 211–34.

———. *The Rise and Fall of the White Republic: Class Politics and Mass Culture in Nineteenth-Century America.* New York: Verso, 1990.

Scherzer, Kenneth Alan. "The Unbounded Community: Neighborhood Life and Social Structure in New York City, 1830–1875." Ph.D. diss., Harvard University, 1982.

Schneider, Edgar W. *American Earlier Black English: Morphological and Syntactic Variables.* Tuscaloosa: University of Alabama Press, 1989.

Schneider, Gilbert D. "Daniel Emmett's Negro Sermons and Hymns: An Inventory." *Ohio History* 85 (1976): 67–83.

Scott, Donald M. "The Popular Lecture and the Creation of the Public in Mid-Nineteenth-Century America." *Journal of American History* 66 (1980): 791–809.

Sedgwick, Eve Kosofsky. *Between Men: English Literature and Male Homosocial Desire.* New York: Columbia University Press, 1985.

Senelick, Laurence. "Boys and Girls Together: Subcultural Origins of Glamour Drag and Male Impersonation on the Nineteenth-Century Stage." In *Crossing the Stage: Controversies on Cross-Dressing,* ed. Lesley Ferris, 80–95. New York: Routledge, 1993.

———, ed. *Gender in Performance: The Presentation of Difference in the Performing Arts.* Hanover, N.H.: University Press of New England, 1992.

Shafer, Yvonne. "Women in Male Roles: Charlotte Cushman and Others." In *Women in American Theatre: Careers, Images, Movements,* rev. and expanded ed., ed. Helen Krich Chinoy and Linda Walsh Jenkins, 74–81. New York: Theatre Communications Group, 1987.

Sherman, Alfonso. "The Diversity of Treatment of the Negro Character in American Drama prior to 1860." Ph.D. diss., Indiana University, 1964.

Simpson, David. *The Politics of American English, 1776–1850.* New York: Oxford University Press, 1986.

Sizer, Sandra S. *Gospel Hymns and Social Religion: The Rhetoric of Nineteenth-Century Revivalism.* Philadelphia: Temple University Press, 1978.

Smith, Elizabeth Oates. *Women's Rights Tracts.* New Haven, Conn.: Research, 1977.

Smith, Paul Tincher. "Militia of the United States from 1846–1860." *Indiana Magazine of History* 15 (1919): 19–47.

Smith, Sol. *The Theatrical Apprenticeship and Anecdotical Recollections of Sol Smith.* Philadelphia: Carey and Hart, 1846.

———. *Theatrical Management in the West and South for Thirty Years.* Reprint. New York: Benjamin Blom, 1968 [1868].

Smith-Rosenberg, Carroll. *Disorderly Conduct: Visions of Gender in Victorian America.* New York: Knopf, 1965.

———. *Religion and the Rise of the American City: The New York City Mission Movement, 1812–1870.* Ithaca, N.Y.: Cornell University Press, 1971.

Southern, Eileen. *The Music of Black Americans: A History.* 1st ed. New York: Norton, 1971.

————. *The Music of Black Americans: A History.* 2d ed. New York: Norton, 1983.

————. *Readings in Black American Music.* 2d ed. New York: Norton, 1983.

Spalding, Henry D., ed. *Encyclopedia of Black Folklore and Humor.* Middle Village, N.Y.: Jonathan David, 1972.

Spitzer, John. "'Oh! Susanna': Oral Transmission and Tune Transformation." *Journal of the American Musicological Society* 47, no. 1 (Spring 1994): 90–136.

Stansell, Christine. *City of Women: Sex and Class in New York, 1789–1860.* New York: Knopf, 1986.

Staum, Martin. "Physiognomy and Phrenology at the Paris Athenee." *Journal of the History of Ideas* 56 (July 1995): 443–62.

Steinberg, Stephen. *The Ethnic Myth: Race, Ethnicity, and Class in America.* New York: Atheneum, 1981.

Stewart, Susan. *Nonsense: Aspects of Intertextuality in Folklore and Literature.* Baltimore: Johns Hopkins University Press, 1979.

Stewart, William A. "Acculturative Processes and the Language of the American Negro." In *Language in Its Social Setting,* ed. William W. Gage, 1–46. Washington, D.C.: Anthropological Society of Washington, 1974.

————. "Continuity and Change in American Negro Dialects." In *Perspectives on Black English,* ed. Joey Lee Dillard, 233–47. The Hague: Mouton, 1975.

————. "Sociolinguistic Factors in the History of American Negro Dialects." In *Perspectives on Black English,* ed. Joey Lee Dillard, 222–32. The Hague: Mouton, 1975.

Stout, Janis. *Sodoms in Eden.* Westport, Conn.: Greenwood, 1976.

Stowe, Harriet Beecher. *Sunny Memories of Foreign Lands.* 2 vols. Boston: Phillips and Samson, 1854.

Stuckey, Sterling. *Slave Culture: Nationalist Theory and the Foundations of Black America.* New York: Oxford University Press, 1987.

Szwed, John F., and Morton Marks. "The Afro-American Transformation of European Set Dances and Dance Suites." *Dance Research Journal* 20, no. 1 (Summer 1988): 29–36.

Tawa, Nicholas E. *A Music for the Millions: Antebellum Democratic Attitudes and the Birth of American Popular Music.* New York: Pendragon, 1984.

————. "Songs of the Early Nineteenth Century. Part 1: Early Song Lyrics and Coping with Life." *American Music* 13, no. 1 (Spring 1995): 1–26.

————. "Serious Songs of the Early Nineteenth Century. Part 2: The Meaning of the Early Song Melodies." *American Music* 13, no. 3 (Fall 1995): 263–94.

————, ed. *American Solo Songs though 1865.* Vol. 1 of *Three Centuries of American Music.* Boston: G. K. Hall, 1989.

Tidwell, James, ed. *A Treasury of American Folk Humor.* New York: Crown, 1956.

Toll, Robert C. *Blacking Up: The Minstrel Show in Nineteenth-Century America.* New York: Oxford University Press, 1974.

Tompkins, Jane. *Sensational Designs: The Cultural Work of American Fiction, 1790–1860.* New York: Oxford University Press, 1985.

Townsend, Charles, ed. *Negro Minstrels with End Men's Jokes, Gags, Speeches, Etc.* Reprint. Upper Saddle River, N.J.: Gregg, 1969 [1891].

Tragle, Henry Irving. *The Southampton Slave Revolt of 1831: A Compilation of Source Material.* New York: Robert M. De Witt, ca. 1874.

Traugott, Elizabeth Closs. "Pidgin, Creole, and the Origins of Vernacular Black English." In *Black English: A Seminar,* ed. Deborah Sears Harrison and Tom Trabasso, 57–94. Hillsdale, N.J.: Lawrence Erlbaum, 1976.

Treagar's Black Jokes, Being a Series of Laughable Caricatures on the March of Manners amongst the Blacks. London: G. S. Treagar, 1834.

Trischka, Tony. *Minstrel Banjo Style.* Compact disk. Rounder CD 0321.

Tybout, Ella Middleton. *Poketown People; or, Parables in Black.* Philadelphia: Lippincott, 1904.

Uncle Ned's Songster. New York: Fisher and Brother, 1857.

Van der Merwe, Peter. *Origins of the Popular Style: The Antecedents of Twentieth-Century Popular Music.* New York: Oxford University Press, 1992.

Vaughn and Fox's Banjo Songster; or, Minstrel Time Melodist. New York: Frederic[k] A. Brady, 1860.

Vicinus, Martha. "'Helpless and Unfriended': Nineteenth-Century Domestic Melodrama." In *When They Weren't Doing Shakespeare: Essays on Nineteenth-Century British and American Theatre,* ed. Judith Fisher and Stephen Watt, 174–86. Athens: University of Georgia Press, 1989.

The Virginia Serenader's Illustrated Songster. Philadelphia: Turner and Fisher, 184?.

Wake Up! William Henry: A Negro Sketch, known as Psychological Experiments, Psychology, Bumps and Limps, Bumpology, Etc. Rev. and arr. Charles White. New York: R. M. De Witt, 1874.

Ware, W. Porter, and Thaddeus C. Lockard Jr. *P. T. Barnum Presents Jenny Lind: The American Tour of the Swedish Nightingale.* Baton Rouge: Louisiana State University Press, 1980.

Warrack, John, and Ewan West, eds. *Oxford Dictionary of Opera.* Oxford: Oxford University Press, 1992.

Weisberger, Bernard A. *They Gathered at the River: The Story of the Great Revivalists and Their Impact upon Religion in America.* Reprint. Chicago: Quadrangle, 1966 [1958].

Wells, Stanley. "Shakespearian Burlesques." *Shakespeare Quarterly* 16, no. 1 (1965): 49–61.

Wells, Stanley, ed. *American Shakespeare Burlesques (1852–1888).* Vol. 5 of *Shakespearen Burlesques.* 5 vols. London: Clarke, Doble and Brendan, 1978.

———, ed. *Nineteenth-Century Shakespeare Burlesques.* 5 vols. London: Diploma, 1978.

———, ed. *Shakespearean Burlesques.* 5 vols. Wilmington, Del.: Michael Glazier, 1978.

Welter, Barbara. *Dimity Convictions: The American Woman in the Nineteenth Century.* Athens: Ohio University Press, 1976.

West, James L. III, ed. *Gyascutus: Studies in Antebellum Southern Humorous and Sporting Writing.* Atlantic Highlands, N.J.: Humanities, 1978.

Whicher, George Frisbie. *This Was a Poet: A Critical Biography of Emily Dickinson.* Reprint. Ann Arbor: University of Michigan Press, 1957 [1938].

White, Charles T., arr. *The Black Chemist.* New York: Robert M. De Witt, ca. 1874.

———. *The Black Statue: An Operatic Olio.* New York: Happy Hours Co., n.d.

———. *Bone Squash.* New York: Happy Hours Co., n.d. [ca. 1870].

———. *Charley White's New Book of Black Wit and Darkey Conversations.* New York: Dick and Fitzgerald, ca. 1856.

———. *The Darkey's Stratagem.* New York: Robert M. De Witt, n.d.

———. *Hard Times: A Negro Extravaganza in One Scene,* by Daniel D. Emmett. New York: De Witt Publishing Co., 1874.

———. *Hippotheatron; or, Burlesque Circus. An Extravagant Funny Sketch.* New York: De Witt Publishing House, 1875.

———. *The Hop of Fashion; or, The Bon-Ton Soiree*. New York: Frederick A. Brady, ca. 1856.

———. *Laughing Gas*. New York: Robert M. De Witt, n.d.

———. *The Live Injin; or Jim Crow. A Comic Ethiopian Sketch in Four Scenes*, by Mr. Dan Bryant. Chicago: Dramatic Publishing Company, n.d.

———. *The Magic Penny. A Negro Farce*. New York: Frederick W. Brady, ca. 1856.

———. *Mazeppa: An Equestrian Burlesque in Two Acts*. New York: Frederick A. Brady, ca. 1856.

———. *The Mischievous Nigger*. New York: Frederic[k] A. Brady, n.d.

———. *Pompey's Patients (Sometimes Called Lunatic Asylum)*. New York and Chicago: Dramatic Publishing Co., n.d.

———. *Sam's Courtship*. Chicago: Dramatic Publishing Co., n.d.

———. *Storming the Fort. An Ethiopian Burlesque Sketch in One Scene*. New York: Robert M. De Witt, 1874.

———. *Uncle Jeff: A Negro Farce in One Act and Five Scenes*. New York: Frederick A. Brady, n.d.

———. *Wake Up! William Henry*. New York: Robert M. De Witt, n.d.

White, Shane. "Pinkster in Albany, 1803: A Contemporary Description." *New York History* 70, no. 2 (Apr. 1989): 191–99.

White's New Book of Plantation Melodies. New York: H. Long and Brother, 1849.

White's New Ethiopian Song Book. New York: H. Long and Brother, 1850.

White's New Illustrated Melodeon Songbook. New York: H. Long and Brother, 1848.

White's Serenaders' Song-Book. New York: H. Long and Brother, 1854.

Whitman, Walt. *I Sit and Look Out: Editorials from the Brooklyn Daily Times by Walt Whitman*. Ed. Emory Holloway and Vernolian Schwarz. New York: Columbia University Press, 1932.

Wilentz, Sean. *Chants Democratic: New York City and the Rise of the American Working Class, 1788–1850*. New York: Oxford University Press, 1984.

Williams, Francis Emmitt. *Lotteries, Laws, and Morals*. New York: Vantage, 1958.

Williams-Myers, A. J. "Pinkster Carnivals: Africanisms in the Hudson River Valley." *Afro-Americans in New York Life and History* 9 (1985): 7–17.

Williamson, Joel. *The Crucible of Race: Black-White Relations in the American South since Emancipation*. New York: Oxford University Press, 1984.

Wilmeth, Don B., and Tice Miller, eds. *Cambridge Guide to American Theatre*. New York: Cambridge University Press, 1993.

Wiltenburg, Joy. *Disorderly Women and Female Power in the Street Literature of Early Modern England and Germany*. Charlottesville: University of Virginia Press, 1992.

Winans, Robert B. "The Black Banjo-Playing Tradition in Virginia and West Virginia." *Folklore and Folklife in Virginia* 1 (1979): 7–30.

———. "Black Instrumental Music in the Ex-Slave Narratives." *Black Music Research Newsletter* 5, no. 2 (Spring 1982): 2–5.

———. *The Early Minstrel Show*. Sound Recording. New World Records NW338.

———. "Early Minstrel Show Music, 1843–1852." In *Musical Theatre in America: Papers and Proceedings of the Conference on the Musical Theatre in America*, ed. Glenn B. Loney, 71–98. Westport, Conn.: Greenwood, 1984.

———. "The Folk, the Stage and the Five-String Banjo in the Nineteenth Century." *Journal of American Folklore* 89, no. 354 (Oct.-Dec. 1976): 407–37.

————. Review of Eric Lott, *Love and Theft: Blackface Minstrelsy and the American Working Class*. *American Music* 13, no. 1 (Spring 1995): 109–12.

Wittke, Carl. "Rice, Thomas Dartmouth." In *Dictionary of American Biography*, ed. Dumas Malone, 8:545–46. New York: Scribner's, 1935.

————. *Tambo and Bones: A History of the American Minstrel Stage*. Reprint. New York: Greenwood, 1968 [1930].

Woodford, Frank B. *Lewis Cass: The Last Jeffersonian*. Reprint. New York: Octagon, 1973 [1950].

Wood's Minstrel Songs. New York: Garret and Co., 1852.

Woods Minstrel Songs. New York: Dick and Fitzgerald, 1855.

Wood's New Plantation Melodies. New York: Garrett and Co., 1853 and 1855.

The World of New Negro Songs. Philadelphia: Fisher and Brother, 1854.

Wyman, Mary Alice. *Two American Pioneers: Seba Smith and Elizabeth Oates Smith*. New York: Columbia University Press, 1926.

Yizar, Terrye Barron. "Afro-American Music in North America before 1856: A Study of 'The First of August' Celebration in the United States." Ph.D. diss., University of California, 1984.

Young, David. *De Darkies' Comic All-Me-Nig*. Philadelphia: Turner and Fisher, 1846.

Young, William C. *Famous Actors and Actresses of the American Stage*. 2 vols. Documents in American Theater History. New York: Bowker, 1975.

Zillman, Dorf. "Disparagement Humor." In *The Psychology of Humor: Theoretical Perspectives and Empirical Issues*, ed. Jeffrey H. Goldstein and Paul E. McGhee, 85–108. New York: Academic, 1972.

Index

A'Beckett, Gilbert, 387n36
Abrahams, Roger, 252, 258, 259, 401nn69, 70
Academy of Music (New York), 154
Adelphi Theatre, 101, 166
"Adventures of Porte Crayon and His Cousins" (Strother), 265–66
Ahlquist, Karen, 374–75n50, 386n21
Albino Family Troupe, 316
Alboni, [Marietta] (1826–94), 28
Alhambra (New York), 12
American Theater (New York), 379n24
Angelesa Singers, 374n42
"Angelina Baker" (Foster), 35, 36–37
Antebellum songsters (selected), song text frequency in, 367–68
Anti-Slavery Harp (Brown), 196
Anvil Chorus (Verdi), 386n30
Apollo Rooms (New York), 24
Art Union Concert Hall, 377n85
"As I View These Scenes So Charming." *See* "Vi ravviso, o luoghi ameni"
Astor Place Opera House (New York), 5, 24, 29, 118, 209, 388n50
"At Home" (Mathews), 11
Auber, Daniel (1782–1871), 30, 145; *La Bayadere*, 39; *Le Cheval de bronze*, 27, 105, 126, 387n42; *Fra Diavolo: ou L'Hotelière de Terracine*, 20, 102, 384n6; *Masaniello, ou La Muette de Portici*, 340
Audiences, antebellum: attitudes toward opera of, 153, 154, 156; beliefs of, 192, 228, 347, 349; changing nature of, 25, 334; competition for, 18, 26, 269; composition

of, 27, 41, 192; comprehension by, 85, 189, 331; expectations of, 158, 252; general characteristics of, 118, 156, 326, 351; interests of, 166, 168; requirements of, 34, 99
Austin, William A., 411n51
"Away to the Tobacco Fields," 256, 400n61
Ayers, Joe, 215, 307, 406n52, 409n17

Backus's Minstrels, 32, 323, 376n74, 384n2; playbill for, 50
Baker, Benjamin, 91, 312, 318, 325, 407n77
Baker, Houston, 349
Balfe, Michael William (1808–70), 3, 21, 336; *The Bohemian Girl*, 3, 19, 24, 34, 101, 126, 146–53, 340, 388n53; *Enchantress*, 31, 126, 340
Il Barbiere di Siviglia (The Barber of Seville) (Rossini), 118, 386n29
Barnum, P. T. (1810–91), 104, 370n14
Barnum's American Museum, 86, 379n20, 388n56
La Bayadere (Auber), 39
Bayley, Thomas Haines (1797–1839), 408n84
Beecher, Catherine, 324
Beecher, Henry Ward, 78, 82, 83
Bell, Bernard, 329–30, 409n2
"Belle of Baltimore," 269, 271, 402n6
Bellini, Vincenzo (1801–35), 3, 30, 145, 340; *Norma*, 34, 36, 101, 386n29; *La Sonnambula*, 3, 101, 105–9, 125–26, 340, 387n36, 388n50
Benedetti, [Sesto], 28
Bennett, James Gordon, 79

Fowler, Orson, 174
Fox, Charley, 336
Fox, Kate and Margaret, 175–76, 391n41
Fra Diavolo: ou, L'Hotelière de Terracine (Auber), 20, 102, 384n6
Franklin Hall, 371n13
Der Freischütz, 125
"The 'Frinnolygist' at Fault" (Hooper), 72
Fry, William Henry (1813–64), 3, 19, 101, 119, 126, 134, 135–38, 387n40. *See also Leonora*

"Gaily the Nigger Boy," 20
"Gal From the South," 27
Gardioni, 28
Gardner, Dan (1816–80), 95–96, 316, 383n89
Gates, Henry Louis, 377n1
"General Taylor," 196
"Gentle Annie" (Foster), 38, 319
George Christy and Wood's Minstrels, playbill for, 55
George Christy's Minstrels, 323, 396n31; playbill for, 50
Georgia Scenes (Longstreet), 64
Germon, Francis, 22
"Get Off the Track," 68, 196
"Get Out de Wilderness." *See* "Down in Alabama"
Gettin' de Bag to Hold; or, The United States Mail (White), 181, 182
"Gib Us Chaw Tobacco," 400n61
Gilfoyle, Timothy, 203, 318, 403n25, 407n74
"Ginger Blue" (Rice), 125, 198–201, 376n75, 394n8
"Git Along Home Yaller Gals," 23
A Glance at New York (Baker), 91, 312, 318, 325, 407n77
Going for the Cup; or, Old Mrs. Wiliams's Dance (White), 158, 162
"Goin Ober de Mountain" ("Ree, Ro My True Lub"), 16, 17, 372n30
"The Gospel Looking Glass," 380n42
Gould, Julia (1824–93), 106, 325
"Grand Burlesque," 32
"Grand New Burlesque on the Opera of Norma," 144
"Gray Goose and Gander." *See* "The Old Grey Goose"
The Great Phantom Room, 37
Greeley, Horace, 82, 83
Green, Tony, 209
Greenfield, Elizabeth, 410–11n45

Griffin, George, 174, 185, 189, 316, 391n27, 393n66; photo of, in wench costume, 313
Grimke, Angelina and Sarah, 93
Grote, David, 180
"Gumbo Chaff," 20, 88
Guy Mannering (Scott), 31

Hagen, Theodore (1824–71), 386n30
Hall, Neill, 158
Haltunnen, Karen, 165
Hamlet Travestie, 316
Hamm, Charles, 28, 377n80, 394n6, 401n73, 410n23
Hammond, James Henry ("Dandy Jim"), 86, 226–27
Hannibal, Judge Julius, 95
"Happy Are We Darkies [Niggars] So Gay," 39
The Happy Man, 158
Hard Times: A Negro Extravaganza (Emmett), 37, 102, 177, 392n44
"Hard Times Come No More" (Foster), 177
Harmoneon Family, 316
The Harp of a Thousand Strings (Brannan), 381n48
Harrington, George, 22
Havana Opera Company, 24, 34, 104
Hayes, Catherine (1825–61), 376n69
Henry Wood's companies (1852–59), list of, 360
Hérold, Louis-Joseph (1791–1833), 36
Herwig, Leopold (1815?–45), 20
Hill, George "Yankee," 64, 165
Hippotheatron; or, Burlesque Circus (White), 162, 389n9
"De History ob de World," 250
"Hit Him in the Eye Ball, Bim," 34, 145–46, 388n55
Hodges, John. *See* White, Cool
Holland, George (1791–1870), 316
Hooper, Johnson James (1815–62), 71, 72, 82
The Hop of Fashion; or, The Bon-Ton Soiree (White), 5, 157, 174, 390n22, 391n27; as satire of upper classes, 134, 166, 168, 193, 347–48
Horn, Evan "Eph," 92, 374n39, 375nn62, 64
Horncastle, Henry, 118
Howard, Rollin (1840–79), photos of, in wench costume, 313, 315
Howe, Elias, 195
Huggins, Nathan, 330, 343, 349
Humor in minstrelsy: American, 97, 99, 100, 196; characteristic qualities of, 8, 63, 184,

WILLIAM J. MAHAR is a professor of humanities and music and the director of the School of Humanities at Penn State Harrisburg, Capital College. His articles and essays on minstrelsy and other subjects have appeared in *American Quarterly, American Music, Prospects: An Annual Journal of American Culture Studies, Civil War Times Illustrated,* and *The William Carlos Williams Review.*

Music in American Life

"My Song Is My Weapon": People's Songs, American Communism, and the Politics of
   Culture, 1930–50   *Robbie Lieberman*

Chosen Voices: The Story of the American Cantorate   *Mark Slobin*

Theodore Thomas: America's Conductor and Builder of Orchestras, 1835–1905
   Ezra Schabas

"The Whorehouse Bells Were Ringing" and Other Songs Cowboys Sing   *Guy Logsdon*

Crazeology: The Autobiography of a Chicago Jazzman
   Bud Freeman, as Told to Robert Wolf

Discoursing Sweet Music: Brass Bands and Community Life in Turn-of-the-Century
   Pennsylvania   *Kenneth Kreitner*

Mormonism and Music: A History   *Michael Hicks*

Voices of the Jazz Age: Profiles of Eight Vintage Jazzmen   *Chip Deffaa*

Pickin' on Peachtree: A History of Country Music in Atlanta, Georgia   *Wayne W. Daniel*

Bitter Music: Collected Journals, Essays, Introductions, and Librettos
   Harry Partch; edited by Thomas McGeary

Ethnic Music on Records: A Discography of Ethnic Recordings Produced in the United
   States, 1893 to 1942   *Richard K. Spottswood*

Downhome Blues Lyrics: An Anthology from the Post-World War II Era   *Jeff Todd Titon*

Ellington: The Early Years   *Mark Tucker*

Chicago Soul   *Robert Pruter*

That Half-Barbaric Twang: The Banjo in American Popular Culture   *Karen Linn*

Hot Man: The Life of Art Hodes   *Art Hodes and Chadwick Hansen*

The Erotic Muse: American Bawdy Songs (Second Edition)   *Ed Cray*

Barrio Rhythm: Mexican American Music in Los Angeles   *Steven Loza*

The Creation of Jazz: Music, Race, and Culture in Urban America   *Burton W. Peretti*

Charles Martin Loeffler: A Life Apart in Music   *Ellen Knight*

Club Date Musicians: Playing the New York Party Circuit   *Bruce A. MacLeod*

Opera on the Road: Traveling Opera Troupes in the United States, 1825–60
   Katherine K. Preston

The Stonemans: An Appalachian Family and the Music That Shaped Their Lives
   Ivan M. Tribe

Transforming Tradition: Folk Music Revivals Examined   *Edited by Neil V. Rosenberg*

The Crooked Stovepipe: Athapaskan Fiddle Music and Square Dancing in Northeast
   Alaska and Northwest Canada   *Craig Mishler*

Traveling the High Way Home: Ralph Stanley and the World of Traditional Bluegrass
   Music   *John Wright*

Carl Ruggles: Composer, Painter, and Storyteller   *Marilyn Ziffrin*

Never without a Song: The Years and Songs of Jennie Devlin, 1865–1952
   Katharine D. Newman

The Hank Snow Story   *Hank Snow, with Jack Ownbey and Bob Burris*

Milton Brown and the Founding of Western Swing
   Cary Ginell, with special assistance from Roy Lee Brown

Santiago de Murcia's "Códice Saldívar No. 4": A Treasury of Secular Guitar Music from
   Baroque Mexico   *Craig H. Russell*

The Sound of the Dove: Singing in Appalachian Primitive Baptist Churches
   Beverly Bush Patterson

Heartland Excursions: Ethnomusicological Reflections on Schools of Music   *Bruno Nettl*

Doowop: The Chicago Scene   *Robert Pruter*